Marketing AN INTEGRATED APPROACH

Carl McDaniel, Jr.
The University of Texas, Arlington

HARPER & ROW, PUBLISHERS
New York
Hagerstown
Philadelphia
San Francisco
London

To my parents,
Martha and Carl McDaniel

PHOTO CREDITS

Front Cover: (*top*) Burlington Industries; (*center*) Exxon; (*bottom left*) The Port of New York Authority; (*bottom right*) Emily Harste.

Back Cover: (*top*) Taylor, EPA; (*center left*) Census Bureau; (*center*) Emily Harste; (*center right*) Odman, EPA; (*bottom*) Emily Harste.

Text (Part Openings): (*p. 1*) Mazzachi, Stock, Boston; (*p. 36*) Beckwith Studios; (*p. 120*) Ritscher, Stock, Boston; (*p. 200*) Federal Express Corp.; (*p. 284*) Berndt, Stock, Boston; (*p. 344*) Reeberg, DPI; (*p. 460*) Gross, Stock, Boston; (*p. 488*) Sirdofsky, EPA.

Sponsoring Editor: Bonnie K. Binkert/Laurie Caplane
Project Editor: Rhonda Roth
Designer: Emily Harste
Senior Production Manager: Kewal K. Sharma
Photo Researcher: Myra Schachne
Compositor: Ruttle, Shaw & Wetherill, Inc.
Printer: The Murray Printing Company
Binder: The Book Press
Art Studio: J & R Services Inc.

Marketing
AN INTEGRATED
APPROACH

Library of Congress Cataloging in Publication Data

McDaniel, Carl D
    Marketing, an integrated approach.

    Includes bibliographical references and index.
    1. Marketing—United States.   2.   Marketing—United States—Case studies.   I.   Title.
HF5415.1.M3   658.8′00973   78-23830
ISBN 0-06-044355-3

The Marketing Environment

KEY FORCES

Social
Economic
Natural Resource
Shortages
Domestic Competition
Foreign Competition
Legal and Political
Technology
Foreign Governments
Demographics

Source: Adapted from Richard M. Bessom, "New Challenges for Marketing," *Arizona Business, 22* (November 1975): 14.

Contents

Preface xiii
Acknowledgments xv

**I
The Nature
of Marketing
1**

1 THE MARKETING FUNCTION 3

Introduction 3
Implementing the Marketing Concept 4
The Marketing Mix 6
Marketing's Work Functions 7
The Broadened Marketing Concept 8
Social Marketing 10
The Full Scope of Marketing 12
A Preview of the Book 12
The Importance of Marketing 14
Summary 16
Key Terms 17
Questions for Discussion 17
Notes 18

Case 1   Mumford Toasters 20

2 THE MARKETING SYSTEM 21

An Integrated System 21
The Internal Structure of Marketing 23
The Target Market 25
The Role of the Marketing Mix 25
The External Environment 26
Monitoring Change in the Marketing System 27
External Factors That Affect Marketing 28
Summary 33
Key Terms 33
Questions for Discussion 33
Notes 34

Case 2   Shiner Brewery 35

**II
Understanding
the Marketplace
37**

3 MARKET SEGMENTATION 39

The Nature of a Market 39
Market Segmentation 40
Product Differentiation and Market Segmentation 48
The Relationship of Product Positioning to Product Differentiation
    and Market Segmentation 48
Summary 51
Key Terms 52
Questions for Discussion 52
Notes 53

Case 3   North Star Service 55

4 SEGMENTING THE AMERICAN MARKET: DEMOGRAPHIC
AND PSYCHOGRAPHIC DIMENSIONS 56

Trends in the American Population 57
Psychographic/Life Style Segmentation 66
Summary 71
Key Terms 72
Questions for Discussion 72
Notes 73

Case 4   The American Cola Company 75

5 BUYER BEHAVIOR 76

Consumer Behavior 77
The Complexity of Consumer Behavior 77
Major Contributions to the Understanding of Buyer Behavior 78
The Impact of Culture on Buyer Behavior 83
A Model of Human Behavior 83
Industrial Purchasing Behavior 88
Governmental Purchasing Behavior 89
Summary 92
Key Terms 93
Questions for Discussion 93
Notes 94

Case 5   The Creamoline Corporation 96

6 MARKETING INFORMATION SYSTEMS
AND MARKETING RESEARCH 97

What Is Marketing Research? 98
The Development of Marketing Research 98
Marketing Information Systems 99
Who Does Marketing Research? 100
Designing the Marketing Research Project: Preliminary Analysis 103
Designing a Formal Marketing Research Study 104
Summary 114
Key Terms 115
Questions for Discussion 115
Notes 116

Case 6   Cessna Aircraft 119

7 PRODUCT/SERVICE PLANNING AND DEVELOPMENT 123

What Is a Product? 124
The Product Manager Concept 126
Strategic Considerations in New-Product Development 127
The New-Product Development Process 132
Summary 139
Key Terms 139
Questions for Discussion 140
Notes 140

Case 7   General Pet Products, Inc. 142

III

**Product
Concepts
121**

8 A PRODUCT AND SERVICE CLASSIFICATION SYSTEM 144

Consumer Goods 144
Pitfalls of the Product Classification System 148
Industrial Goods 149
Summary 158
Key Terms 160
Questions for Discussion 160
Notes 160

Case 8   The Condor Kite Company 162

9 THE PRODUCT: DEMAND AND SUPPLY 163

An Introduction to the Product Life Cycle 164
Stages of the Product Life Cycle 165
The Product Adoption Process 168
Adopter Categories 171
Product Strategy 172
Service Strategy 174
Summary 176
Key Terms 177
Questions for Discussion 177
Notes 178

Case 9   Great Northwest Amusement Park 180

10 THE NATURE OF PRODUCTS 181

Brands, Trademarks, and Patents 182
Advantages of Branding 184
Types of Brands 184
The Battle of the Brands 187
Stages of Brand Preference 188
Brand Loyalty 189
Product Warranties 189
Product Safety and Product Liability 191
Packaging 193
Labeling 193
Summary 194
Key Terms 196
Questions for Discussion 196
Notes 196

Case 10   California Label Company 199

**IV
Distribution
Structure
201**

11 CHANNEL ROLES AND CHANNEL SYSTEMS 203

Why Are Middlemen Used? 204
How Do Distribution Channels Create Satisfaction? 208
Basic Channel Systems 209
The Behavioral Dimensions of Distribution Channels 212
Selecting a Distribution Channel 214
Factors That Influence Channel Selection 216
Summary 219

Key Terms 220
Questions for Discussion 220
Notes 221

Case 11   Welch Grape Soda 223

12 WHOLESALING 225

The Functions and Roles of Wholesalers 226
Merchant Wholesalers 229
Manufacturers' Sales Branches 234
Agents and Brokers 235
Other Wholesale Institutions 236
Institutions That Facilitate Wholesaling 237
Trends in Wholesaling 238
Summary 239
Key Terms 239
Questions for Discussion 240
Notes 240

Case 12   The Farmer Company 242

13 RETAILING 244

The Importance of Retailing 245
Determinants of Store Patronage 246
A Retail Classification System 248
Major Methods of Retail Operation 249
Franchising 253
Shopping Centers 255
Retail Site Selection Considerations 256
Trends in Retailing 256
Summary 258
Key Terms 258
Questions for Discussion 258
Notes 260

Case 13   Gray Trail Bus Line 263

14 PHYSICAL-DISTRIBUTION STRATEGIES 264

The Costs of Distribution 266
The Objectives of Distribution 267
The Importance of Total Costs 269
The Functions of Physical Distribution 270
Institutions That Facilitate Physical Distribution 277
Legal Carriers 278
Trends in Physical Distribution 279
Summary 280
Key Terms 281
Questions for Discussion 281
Notes 281

Case 14   American Photo Art 283

V

The Nature of Pricing
285

15 DEMAND-ORIENTED PRICING CONCEPTS 287

The Importance of Price 288
Pricing Objectives 289
The Nature of Demand 291
The Four Models of Competition 294
Price Leadership and Price Discrimination 294
Estimating Demand 297
Summary 300
Key Terms 300
Questions for Discussion 300
Notes 301

Case 15   New Mexico Trailmaker Bus Line 302

16 THE ROLE OF COST AND SPECIAL PRICE DETERMINANTS 303

The Importance of Costs 303
The Breakeven Concept 305
Target Return Pricing 309
Other Factors That Affect Price 310
Summary 314
Key Terms 315
Questions for Discussion 315
Notes 316
Appendix: Types of Economic Costs 317

Case 16   Midcontinent Perfume Company 319

17 PRICING STRATEGIES AND CONCEPTS 320

Pricing a New Product 321
Discounts and Allowances 324
Geographic Pricing Policies 325
Special Pricing Policies 330
Product Line Pricing 334
Competitive Bidding 335
Pricing in a Changing Economy 335
Summary 338
Key Terms 340
Questions for Discussion 340
Notes 341

Case 17   Mayfield Chemical Corporation 343

VI

Promotion Concepts
345

18 MARKETING COMMUNICATION: PROMOTION STRATEGIES 347

What Is the Communication Process? 348
The Goals of Promotion 351
Approaches to Promotion 353
The Basic Forms of Promotion 354
Factors That Affect the Promotional Mix 357
Implementation of the Promotional Plan 359
Summary 362
Key Terms 362

Questions for Discussion 363
Notes 363

Case 18   Southern Lubricants 365

19 THE NATURE OF ADVERTISING 366

The Importance of Advertising 366
What Can Advertising Do? 367
The Major Types of Advertising 373
Advertising Media 377
Summary 381
Key Terms 382
Questions for Discussion 383
Notes 383

Case 19   RSVP Restaurants 386

20 ADVERTISING MANAGEMENT 387

The Goals of Advertising 387
The Advertising Budget 389
The Nature of an Advertising Campaign 391
Evaluating Media Alternatives 395
Measuring Advertising Effectiveness and Media Audiences 396
Advertising Agencies 399
The Impact of Advertising Regulation 401
Summary 403
Key Terms 404
Questions for Discussion 404
Notes 405

Case 20   Northeast National Bank 407

21 PERSONAL SELLING 409

The Nature of Selling 410
Should I Choose a Sales Career? 412
The Variety of Sales Positions 413
What Is a Professional Salesperson? 415
Supporting Salespeople 416
Steps in the Selling Process 417
Contributions of the Behavioral Sciences to the Selling Process 421
Summary 422
Key Terms 422
Questions for Discussion 422
Notes 423

Case 21   The First Sales Job 425

22 SALES MANAGEMENT 426

The Objectives of Sales Management 426
Recruiting and Screening Salespeople 427

The Nature of Sales Training 428
Motivating the Sales Force 430
Organizing the Sales Effort 434
Evaluation and Control of the Sales Force 436
Selling in a Changing Economy 438
Summary 439
Key Terms 440
Questions for Discussion 440
Notes 441

Case 22   Iowa American Telephone Company 443

23 SALES PROMOTION AND PUBLIC RELATIONS 445

The Importance of Sales Promotion 445
The Objectives of Sales Promotion 446
Trends in Sales Promotion 448
Problems of Sales Promotion Management 451
Public Relations 453
Summary 455
Key Terms 456
Questions for Discussion 456
Notes 457

Case 23   Northwest Apple Growers 459

24 STRATEGIC MARKETING: PLANNING AND CONTROL 463

Developing Marketing Plans 463
Marketing Organization 470
Marketing Control 474
Summary 483
Key Terms 484
Questions for Discussion 484
Notes 484

Case 24   Savin Business Machines 486

25 CONSUMERISM AND MARKETING'S
SOCIAL RESPONSIBILITY 491

What Is Consumerism? 492
The History of Consumerism 493
The Forces Behind the Consumerist Movement 495
The Response of Business to Consumerism 497
Social Responsibility 498
Organizing for Social Responsibility 502
Summary 503
Key Terms 503
Questions for Discussion 503
Notes 503

Case 25   East–West Manufacturing 506

VII

Marketing
Management
461

VIII

Marketing
in a Changing
World
489

26 INTERNATIONAL MARKETING 507

Why Get Involved? A Macro Perspective 508
The Importance of Trade to the United States 508
The Impact of Multinationals 510
Ways of Entering the International Market 512
The Cultural–Political Environment of International Marketing 515
Developing an International Marketing Mix 517
Organizing for International Marketing 522
Summary 523
Key Terms 524
Questions for Discussion 524
Notes 525

Case 26   The Phelps Company 527

Author Index 529
Subject Index 533

Preface

The world of marketing has undergone tremendous change and has increased in complexity during the 1970s. Yet, most of the leading textbooks, whose first editions appeared more than a decade ago, have not altered sufficiently to reflect these changes. Thus, my goal in developing this text is to present a picture of marketing today—its current environment with a glimpse toward the future.

This book is intended for use in the introductory marketing course. Large business schools will find it comprehensive enough to be used as a foundation for advanced courses. Smaller schools will likewise benefit from its breadth. Both types of institutions will welcome the many options of ancillaries described below, which can provide further depth at the instructor's discretion.

The book has three major features: it is contemporary, managerial, and it uses a systems approach. Its first thrust is contemporary. Hundreds of current and meaningful examples are introduced throughout the book. Issues and topics that are of concern to marketing managers, such as inflation, shortages, the broadened marketing concept, and international competition, are woven into the material.

The book is contemporary in a second important dimension also. Before each chapter was written, current research on the subject was thoroughly reviewed. Traditional concepts have been updated with the latest findings. For those students who want to research a topic further, extensive footnotes to current references are provided at the end of each chapter. Thus, the book is thoroughly researched and documented for the serious student.

The second major thrust of the book is its managerial orientation. Since many students enrolled in their first marketing course may become marketing decision makers, relevant tools, concepts, theories, and cases are covered from the point of view of the marketing manager. Each chapter contains a mini-case that the instructor can use for simulated managerial decision making.

Finally, it is important for students as potential managers to view marketing in a systems context. Marketing is not a hodgepodge of unrelated and autonomous activities. Rather, it consists of a large number of interacting and interdependent relationships. This book explains how the marketing pieces fit together.

Learning will be further enhanced by the student aids that are available with the text. I recorded a series of cassette tapes with top marketing managers that feature both lecture and discussion. Among the taped discussions are: "Marketing and the Energy Crisis," with the vice president of marketing at Continental Oil Corporation; "Women in Marketing," featuring the vice president of marketing at *Ms. Magazine;* and the vice president of marketing research at Lever Brothers speaking on "Pricing Strategies." I know that you will find these tapes interesting and informative. Also available for the instructor is an instructor's manual.

Other student supplements include a marketing simulation game, a readings book, a casebook, and a student study guide. The complete package is designed to enhance the learning experience, whether this will be the student's initial course as a marketing major or the only marketing course he or she will ever take.

A book like this one requires the help of many people. My deepest gratitude is extended to Roger Gates, my colleague, business associate, and friend, who read every page of the manuscript, wrote Chapter 6 of this book, and is an editor of the readings book.

I am also indebted to the other writers and editors of the supplemental materials: Ron Bush and Robert Brobst, who wrote MARKETING SIMULATION: ANALYSIS FOR DECISION MAKING; Howard Thompson who developed the casebook, CASES IN MARKETING: INCLUDING INTERVIEWS WITH KEY EXECUTIVES; and Warren French, William Sekely, and Roger Gates, the editors of the readings book, VIEWS OF MARKETING: A READER. I would also like to thank Spencer Switzer and Eric Pratt, who aided in the preparation of the study guide and instructor's manual, respectively. Thanks must also go to George Prough and Tom Faranda, who worked with me to develop the test banks to accompany the text.

Two other people who have worked hard behind the scenes are my research assistants, Marge Cichon and Jamie Biggers. A special vote of thanks also goes to Irene Koby, who typed the manuscript, and to Debbie Farmer, my secretary. Finally, I must thank Madhav Segal for conceiving the ideas for many of the fine illustrations in the text.

Carl McDaniel, Jr.

Acknowledgments

Special thanks are extended to the following individuals who devoted considerable time to reviewing the manuscript and developing ancillary material:

Robert L. Anderson, University of South Florida
William D. Ash, California State University, Long Beach
Karl Boedecker, University of San Francisco
Robert Brobst, The University of Texas at Arlington
Stephen W. Brown, Arizona State University
Paul Busch, University of Wisconsin at Madison
Ronald F. Bush, Louisiana State University
Ben Butcher, California State University, Long Beach
Pat J. Calabro, The University of Texas at Arlington
Benjamin J. Cutler, Bronx Community College of the City of New York
William A. Dempsey, Temple University
Donald W. Eckrich, Southern Illinois University at Carbondale
Tom Faranda, Inver Hills Community College
Warren A. French, University of Georgia
Roger H. Gates, The University of Texas at Arlington
Joseph F. Hair, Jr., Louisiana State University
Michael G. Harvey, Southern Methodist University
Sanford B. Helman, Middlesex County College, New Jersey
Michael J. Houston, University of Wisconsin at Madison
Thomas I. Kindel, The University of Texas at Arlington
G. E. Kiser, University of Arkansas
Gene R. Laczniak, Marquette University
David H. Lindsay, University of Maryland
Robert D. Miller, Ybor City Campus, Tampa, Florida
Thomas Ness, University of South Florida
Eric Pratt, New Mexico State University
George Prougn, University of Akron
Richard Sandhusen, Kean College of New Jersey
William S. Sargent, University of Houston
William Sekely, University of Dayton
Spencer Switzer, The University of Texas at Arlington
Howard Thompson, Eastern Kentucky University
Noel B. Zabriskie, University of North Florida

The Nature
of Marketing

1

The Marketing Function

OBJECTIVES

■ To define marketing.
■ To understand the basic elements of the philosophy of marketing.
■ To become aware of the variables that make up the marketing mix.
■ To describe the broadened marketing concept of recent years.
■ To understand the importance of studying marketing.
■ To present a preview of the book.

INTRODUCTION

Marketing's responsibilities and functions have changed rapidly in the past 60 years. As values, resources, technology, governments, and other factors change, marketing managers must vary their strategies in order to meet their organizations' changing goals.

What Is Marketing?

A "student-oriented" definition states that "marketing is getting the right goods or services to the right people at the right place at the right time at the right price using the right promotion techniques." This definition tells you that marketing managers control many factors that ultimately determine marketing success. It also emphasizes the need to determine what is "right" for the consumer, that is, what will best satisfy the consumer's needs.

I prefer a very broad definition proposed by Philip Kotler. Kotler claims that the essence of marketing is the transaction, defined as an exchange of values between two parties. Thus marketing is specifically concerned with how transactions are created, stimulated, facilitated, and valued.[1]

I believe this definition is broad enough to withstand the test of time. It implies that marketing involves people (i.e., profit and non-profit organizations) seeking desired responses from other people (i.e., the market). Organizations attempt to obtain the desired response by creating and offering things (goods and services) that the market-place will perceive as having value.

The Marketing Concept

The foundations of the marketing concept are (1) consumer orientation, (2) goal orientation, and (3) a systems approach. In contrast to a production organization, which is internally oriented, the marketing organization is both internally and externally oriented. The production organization examines its resources and capabilities, produces a product, and then turns the product over to the sales department. The focus is internal—let's produce what we think the market wants with the resources available to us. The marketing organization looks not only at itself but also at the wants and needs of the consumer it plans to serve. Indeed, it begins with the consumer.

The marketing concept requires awareness of the wants and needs of the consumer, but not at the expense of company goals. A firm should not serve a market, under most conditions, unless this service adds to its profitability. Satisfying the needs of the consumer must not be viewed as an end in itself.

IMPLEMENTING THE MARKETING CONCEPT

The marketing concept cannot be implemented easily or overnight. It is a philosophy of doing business and must be accepted and believed in by all members of the organization. If top management isn't convinced that the marketing concept is necessary, implementation will surely fail. Simply changing the sales manager's title to marketing manager will be of little or no use. A system must be set up to recognize consumer needs and react to them in a timely fashion. The systems emphasis will be discussed in more detail later in this chapter.

Changing to the marketing concept often requires major revisions in authority and responsibility relationships within the organization. People who have been making "marketing" decisions, such as a production manager who decides what products are produced, may suddenly find that their authority in the product area is virtually nil. By contrast, new personnel in areas such as marketing research may find that they have considerable authority.

One way of gaining acceptance for the marketing concept is to get everyone who will be affected by it to participate in the planning process. One must recognize, however, that some human-relations problems are inevitable during a period of change. Implementing the marketing concept by degree rather than in a revolutionary fashion normally smooths the transition.

Sometimes companies fool themselves into thinking they have the marketing concept when they really don't. Management may concentrate on the "trappings" of marketing, such as:

- declarations of support from top management—speeches, annual reports.
- creation of a marketing organization—appointment of a marketing head and product or market managers, transfer to marketing of the product development and service function, salesmen reassigned around markets, advertising function strengthened.
- adoption of new administrative mechanisms—formal marketing planning approaches, more and better sales information, reporting system restructured around markets.
- increased marketing expenditures—staffing, training and development, advertising, research.[2]

Such "trappings" are no guarantee of success. Successful implementation of the marketing concept requires a basic shift in thinking throughout the organization toward the three basic elements of the concept—consumer orientation, goal orientation, and a systems approach.

Old production-focused ideas and habits aren't easy to change. When a person has been doing something a certain way for many years, change often comes very hard. Consider the following:

> In one capital-goods company, management had historically focused on selling the largest, highest powered, most maintenance-free units possible, with the thought that this approach favored the company's manufacturing economics. However, user needs had shifted toward smaller, less costly units without the rugged engineering characteristics required for maintenance-free operation.
>
> Since this trend was clear, and the company was losing its market leadership position, marketing had recommended a major redesign of the product line. However, the company's manufacturing and engineering executives, who were acknowledged industry experts, argued convincingly that the current product design and cost structure were still superior to any competitor's, and all that was needed was a better selling effort.
>
> Faced with these conflicting points of view, top management decided to stick with the original product concept and put pressure on the marketing group for a more aggressive selling effort. It was not until the company lost substantial market share and its entire profit structure was threatened that the president could bring himself to fly in the face of the expert opinion of his engineering and manufacturing executives and force the redesign through.[3]

THE MARKETING MIX

Establishing the marketing concept is the first step in developing a marketing-oriented organization. Within the marketing department, a marketing mix must be created. The unique blend of pricing, promotion, product offerings, and a distribution system designed to reach a specific group of consumers is called the firm's marketing mix. (See Figure 1.1.) Each factor is important in achieving the firm's marketing objectives. An excellent product with a poor distribution system is often doomed to failure. Many small businesses find this to be all too true. After spending a considerable amount on product development they find themselves unable to establish a successful distribution network for the product.

FIGURE 1.1   **The Marketing Mix**

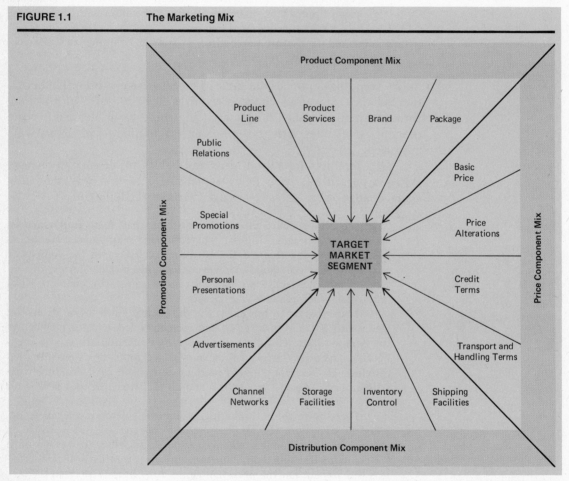

Source: Harry Lipson and Fred Reynolds, "The Concept of the Marketing Mix: Its Development, Uses, and Applications." *MSU Business Topics,* Winter 1970, p. 75. By permission of the publisher, Division of Research, Graduate School of Business Administration, Michigan State University.

Every market requires a unique marketing mix. Kool-Aid is not marketed like Coke, for example, yet both are nonalcoholic beverages. Their promotional themes differ; they appeal to different audiences; Kool-Aid has to be mixed with water while Coke does not; Kool-Aid is rarely, if ever, sold through fountain dispensers; and the list goes on. You can see that each product requires its own distribution system, price strategy, and promotional themes. The marketing mix will be discussed further in Chapter 2.

Even highly similar products require different marketing mixes. Marlboro and Winston are both filter cigarettes that appeal to essentially the same market. Yet their manufacturers spend millions of dollars convincing the consumer that the two brands are different. Is it wrong to create mental distinctions between products? We will delve into this important issue later in the book.

MARKETING'S WORK FUNCTIONS

The marketing mix determines the ultimate success of a product or service and even of a company. So far we have discussed major areas of marketing responsibility—pricing, distribution, promotion, and the product. Let's take a closer look at the specific functions of the marketing department. Figure 1.2 shows the functions for which marketing is normally responsible.

The various work functions have been subdivided into two areas —those concerned with generating demand or sales, and those concerned with servicing the demand after it has been created. Several tasks, such as general marketing administration, financing, and marketing research, support all the other activities necessary to generate and service demand.[4]

Recent research has revealed several things about marketing functions:

1. Actual responsibilities within marketing departments vary widely from company to company.
2. Promotion is the most common marketing function in consumer goods corporations.
3. Sales forecasting and customer relations are the functions most frequently assigned to marketing in industrial goods organizations.
4. Inventory management and warehousing are the areas most likely to be delegated to other departments regardless of the type of organization.[5]

It is clear, thus, that theory and practice often differ. In fact you should keep this in mind whether you are reading this book or any other. The nature of the market (e.g., dispersed vs. concentrated, large customers vs. small customers, sophisticated buyers vs. uninformed purchasers), the availability of qualified personnel, the firm's management philosophy, and tradition can all influence how the mar-

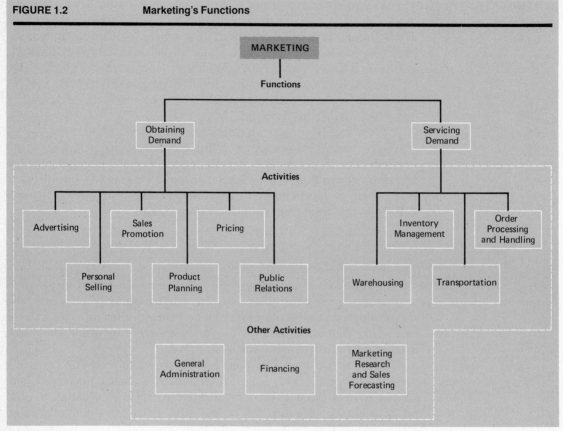

FIGURE 1.2   **Marketing's Functions**

Source: Adapted from Richard Lewis and Leo Erickson, "Marketing Functions and Marketing Systems: A Synthesis," *Journal of Marketing,* 33 (July 1969): 12. By permission of the American Marketing Association.

keting concept is applied and the specific functions carried out by a marketing department.

THE BROADENED MARKETING CONCEPT

The marketing concept has also been subject to change in recent years. Two divergent philosophies of marketing have developed in the 1970s. Professor William Lazer has recommended that extravagant demands for goods and services be recognized as normal to, and justified by, an affluent society.[6] In other words, marketing should be used to justify as well as to stimulate unbounded consumption and self-indulgence.

At the other extreme, the noted marketing scholars Lawrence Feldman, Philip Kotler, and Gerald Zaltman argue that marketing must develop a social consciousness—it should become involved in vital social issues and provide important public services.[7] Kotler and Sidney Levy also recommend that the basic marketing concept be applied to nonbusiness organizations such as hospitals or governmental units.[8] In a hospital, for example, the patient would be the consumer and efficient and effective medical care would be the organization's primary goal. This is known as the broadened marketing concept.

Some hospitals have already embraced this concept. Sunrise Hospital in Las Vegas is encouraging more weekend check-ins in order to better distribute the work level. The hospital has heavily advertised a drawing that is held every week for people checking in on Friday or Saturday. Each week a first-class, all-expense-paid Mediterranean cruise for two is given away. (See Figure 1.3.)

Museums are also applying the broadened marketing concept. They "market" cultural appreciation as their major service. Their customer group is the general public. Even government agencies are utilizing the marketing concept: The Army spent $28 million on advertising in 1976.[9] A few years ago this idea would have been

---

FIGURE 1.3   **Application of the Broadened Marketing Concept**

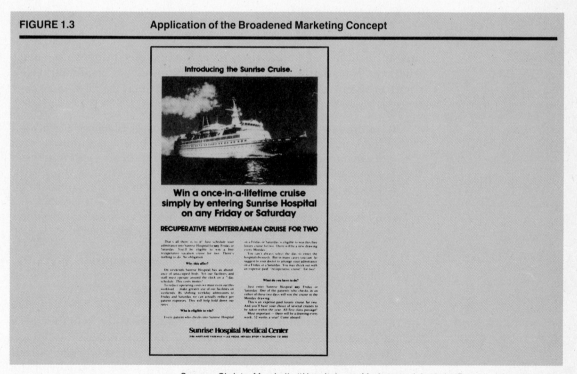

Source: Christy Marshall, "Hospitals as Marketers: Ads Gain Favor," *Advertising Age,* February 21, 1977, p. 30. By permission. Copyright 1977 by Crain Communications, Inc.

TABLE 1.1	Nonbusiness Organizations and Their Customer Groups	
Organization	**Product**	**Customer Group**
Museum	Cultural appreciation	General public
National Safety Council	Safer driving	Driving public
Political candidate	Honest government	Voting public
Family planning foundation	Birth control	Fertile public
Police department	Safety	General public
Church	Religious experience	Church members
University	Education	Students
City	Sight-seeing	Tourists

Source: Philip Kotler, "A Generic Concept of Marketing," *Journal of Marketing,* 36 (April 1972): 47. Reprinted by permission of the American Marketing Association.

laughed at by Army brass. Various organizations and their customer groups are listed in Table 1.1.

The broadened marketing concept seems to be here to stay. One survey of marketing educators found that 95 percent believed that the scope of marketing should include nonbusiness organizations.[10] Scholars also feel that marketing techniques should be used in trying to solve social problems.

SOCIAL MARKETING

The application of marketing theories and techniques to social situations is called social marketing. In essence, social marketing is part of the broadened marketing concept. It may be viewed as consisting of three main elements:

1. *Satisfaction of Human Needs.* The key word is *human* needs—not those that are business or product oriented. An opportunity is seen for marketing techniques to be used to sell clean air, clean water, and adequate housing, for instance.
2. *Expansion to Social Fields.* Marketing is seen as an instrument that can be used to further all the goals of society. It is suggested that marketing techniques can be used to help achieve socially desirable goals such as population control, improved racial tolerance, and increased support of education.
3. *Consideration of Societal Impact.* A new imperative is presented: that business must assess not only the profitability of its actions, but also the overall effect those actions have on society.[11]

Satisfying Human Needs

For the marketing concept to be applied successfully, whether by a private enterprise or in a social context, the consumer's (society's) self-interest must be satisfied. The role of self-interest was recognized as far back as 1776, when the economist Adam Smith conceived the principle of the "invisible hand." This theory states that resources will be allocated efficiently in a free-market system that appeals to individual self-interest.

From a company's viewpoint the marketing manager must identify consumer self-interest and then determine how to react to it. Is this the proper role of the marketing manager? Perhaps not, according to the advocates of social marketing. Consider the following example:

> The tobacco industry has certainly been consumer oriented in postwar years. The industry has adapted skillfully to changing consumer preferences as the major prewar brands have yielded to a proliferation of new shapes and styles. Industry sales and per capita cigarette consumption have gained steadily. Do we conclude that a consumer orientation is enabling this industry to adapt with perfect harmony to environmental change? Hardly. A powerful and growing array of forces are united in an effort to erase the industry altogether. These forces emanate from state and federal government, the medical profession, and concerned citizens at large. They are generated by persons whose most likely common bond is that they are *not* consumers of the product. These individuals have managed to create a steady stream of woe for the tobacco industry.
>
> What had made the future of this industry in the coming decades a question-mark is not its failure to provide consumers with a pleasant, satisfying product but rather the product's vulnerability to society's deepening concern over human well-being.[12]

Changing Social Attitudes and Values

In addition to satisfying human (society's) needs, marketing can be used to achieve social goals. Can marketing change people's attitudes toward such matters as littering, birth control, and law enforcement? Perhaps, but only by ultimately appealing to individual self-interest. The concept of appealing to self-interest is known as the empirical–rational strategy.[13]

Once people become rationally aware of their interests, they will pursue them. An attitude that stems from an individual's basic values (good or bad, right or wrong) and is strongly supported by his or her culture will be difficult to shift in a direction that is incongruent with those values.[14] Marketing strategy cannot change social values. An example is the inability to effectively market birth control information in many parts of the world.

The Problem of Scarce Resources

The third dimension of social marketing is impact. Marketing under conditions of limited resources has added new dimensions to the problem of societal impact. New questions are being raised, such as "Should it be sold?" and "What are the costs to society?" In response Kotler and Levy have coined the term creative demarketing, meaning a strategy designed to discourage consumption in general or to discourage a certain class of customers from consuming a particular product.[15] Oil marketers used this strategy extensively during the 1973–1974 oil crisis.

In addition to managing demand, marketers are examining their product mix and distribution channels more closely in order to identify waste and inefficiency. They are also bracing themselves for more regulation as the government tries to supervise the allocation and usage of scarce resources. Perhaps government involvement is most visible in the automobile industry, where a plethora of laws regulating efficiency of engines, pollution safety, and so on have been passed.

THE FULL SCOPE OF MARKETING

Let's take a moment to put the nature of marketing in perspective. You know that the basic marketing concept has been broadened to include nonprofit institutions and social considerations. Shelby Hunt has conceived the matrix shown in Table 1.2 to explain the scope of marketing, including the broadened concept.[16]

The matrix is divided into eight segments. The first division is between the profit and nonprofit sectors. These sectors are then subdivided along two dimensions: micro versus macro and positive versus normative. *Profit-making institutions* constitute the bulk of the private-sector enterprises. *Nonprofit organizations,* as discussed earlier, include various levels of government, museums, charities, and similar organizations. Micro refers to individual marketing units such as the individual or the firm. Macro implies an aggregate of institutions, such as society as a whole or an entire marketing system. Positive marketing attempts to explain, predict, and understand existing marketing activities and phenomena. Normative marketing is concerned with what ought to be and what people and companies should do.

Thus on a positive, micro basis in the profit sector of marketing we find the study of individual buying and shopping behavior and case studies of how businesses determine their marketing mix and consumer market. In the normative, macro, nonprofit sector of marketing, by contrast, we find the study of how things should be in society from a nonprofit perspective. You should examine the remaining six cells to gain a full appreciation of the scope of the science of marketing.

A PREVIEW OF THE BOOK

As you read this book you will discover that both normative and positive aspects of marketing are covered. You will learn how the marketing manager copes with the ever-changing marketing environment. Problems related to inflation, shortages, changing values, and other contemporary challenges are woven throughout the text. Chapter 2

TABLE 1.2 The Scope of Marketing

		Positive	Normative
PROFIT SECTOR	**Micro**	(1) Individual consumer behavior Case studies of how firms determine factors such as prices, products, promotion, and channels of distribution	(2) Managerial marketing Pricing decisions Product decisions Promotion decisions Packaging decisions Systems approach to marketing Marketing organization Marketing planning Purchasing International marketing Marketing control
	Macro	(3) Institutional approach (wholesalers, retailers) to marketing Work-functional approach to marketing Commodity approach to marketing (tracing the flow of a good or service from producer to consumer) Environmental approach to marketing Legal aspects of marketing Comparative marketing Do the poor pay more? Are marketing systems efficient?	(4) How can marketing systems be made more efficient? Does distribution cost too much? Is advertising desirable? Does marketing have a social responsibility? What role should marketing play in economic development? Is consumer sovereignty desirable? Is stimulating demand desirable?
NONPROFIT SECTOR	**Micro**	(5) Forecasting demand for public goods How do consumers purchase public goods? Case studies of public-goods marketing	(6) Social marketing How nonprofit organizations should manage all elements of the marketing mix How can the demand for public goods be predicted?
	Macro	(7) Does television advertising influence elections? Does public-service advertising (e.g., "Smokey the Bear") influence behavior? Are existing distribution systems for public goods efficient? Recycling as a channels-of-distribution problem	(8) Should society allow politicians to be "sold" like toothpaste? Is "low-informational-content" political advertising desirable? Should the U.S. Army be allowed to advertise for recruits? Should the demand for "public goods" be stimulated?

Source: Adapted from Shelby Hunt, *Marketing Theory: Conceptual Foundations of Research in Marketing* (Columbus, Ohio: Grid, 1976), p. 9. Reprinted by permission of Grid, Inc., Columbus, Ohio 43214.

ties together the many definitions given in Chapter 1. It also presents an overview of the marketing system as a whole.

Part II describes the marketplace. You will learn how and why a market is often subdivided in order to develop a more effective marketing mix. Major segments of the American market are presented and analyzed. After reading Part II you will also have a better understanding of buyer motivations and purchasing patterns. This portion of the book concludes with a description of marketing research and information systems, which provide the information on which marketing managers base their decisions.

In Part III we begin our examination of the marketing mix. After management understands the nature of the marketplace, product and service development can be initiated. Part III also introduces a product classification system and describes product development and product management.

Part IV shows how distribution plays a key role in the marketing mix. Distribution systems are discussed, and the major institutions of wholesaling and retailing are described in detail.

The third variable of the marketing mix, pricing, is the topic of Part V. Key demand and cost strategies and concepts are explained and marketing pricing techniques are discussed.

The last element of the marketing mix, promotion, is the subject of Part VI. Referring back to Kotler's definition of marketing, this section explains how transactions are stimulated. You should be able to tie other aspects of the definition—transaction creation, transaction facilitation, and transaction value—to the other elements of the marketing mix.

Part VII discusses the roles of managers in planning, organizing, and controlling the marketing operation. This section will help you understand how marketing strategies are developed and marketing problems defined and solved.

Part VIII focuses on two topics that are considered very important by many marketing managers. The first topic is consumerism, which affects all of us, not just the business sector. The second is international marketing. As American firms enter the international market they find a vastly different operating environment. You will explore the opportunities and problems of doing business in a world made ever smaller by improvements in transportation and communication.

THE IMPORTANCE OF MARKETING
Delivering a Standard of Living

Why study marketing? There are several reasons.

Think about the number of transactions required every day to feed, clothe, and shelter the people of New York City. What a mind-

FIGURE 1.4   Yearly Food Consumption of an American Family of Four

Source: Richard De Vos, "Human Energy × Tools Equals Material Wealth," *Marketing Times,* Journal of Continuing Education, 14 (May-June 1977): 7. Photo courtesy of the Du Pont Company.

boggling thought! Yet the system works, usually quite well. The distribution function of marketing gets the output of our farms and factories to us in a convenient, economical, and sanitary way.

Look at Figure 1.4. It represents the food consumption of a family of four in just one year — 2½ tons! Marketing makes food available when you want it, in economical quantities, at accessible locations, in sanitary and convenient packages and forms (e.g., instant and frozen foods). Food, of course, is just one of many types of products that are part of our standard of living. The quantity of goods and services relative to a nation's population defines its standard of living.

The Costs of Marketing

Our standard of living is not achieved without significant expense. One study estimates that marketing costs take about fifty cents out of every dollar you spend.[17] This may seem high to you. Look at Figure 1.4 again and think of the costs that would be involved if you had to

TABLE 1.3　　　Business Backgrounds of Key Corporate Officers (N = 640)

Key Positions	Business Background						
	Engi-neering	Finance	Legal	Manu-facturing	Marketing	Research and Develop-ment	General
Board chairman	15%	25%	5%	16%	26%	4%	9%
Vice board chairman	12	22	4	22	23	1	16
Internal board of directors	8	16	3	16	24	1	32
Outside board of directors	5	37	19	7	4	1	27
President	15	16	5	22	31	2	9
Chairman of the executive committee	14	23	5	19	30	3	6
Executive committee	6	19	3	15	23	1	33
Group executive	13	3	1	30	34	2	17
Operating executive	14	5	0	37	30	1	13
Product or brand manager	14	1	0	7	71	2	5

Source: Carlton McNamara, "The Present Status of the Marketing Concept," *Journal of Marketing,* 36 (January 1972): 54. Reprinted by permission of the American Marketing Association.

go to the agricultural producer and pick up those goods yourself. Time and money simply wouldn't allow it. Nevertheless marketing managers are continually striving to find new ways of lowering marketing costs while delivering the same standard of living or an even higher one.

Career Opportunities

Choosing a major field of study can be a hard decision. What are the chances of getting ahead if you major in marketing? Table 1.3 presents the business backgrounds of key officers of major corporations. More board chairpeople and company presidents come from marketing than any other field. The opportunity is there—take advantage of it.

The pay for top marketing executives isn't bad, either. In 1975 the average compensation for 103 marketing executives was $89,938.[18] The highest-paid marketing executive received $258,466.[19] Marketing has not only glamor but opportunities for personal advancement as well.

SUMMARY

The job of the marketing manager is to get the right goods or services to the right people at the right place at the right time at the right price using the right promotion techniques. This definition should give you some idea of what marketing is all about from the firm's point of view. However, in this book we will use a broader definition, which says that marketing is concerned with transactions and how they are created, stimulated, facilitated, and valued. A transaction is an exchange of values between two parties.

The marketing concept consists of consumer orientation, goal orientation, and a systems approach. Implementing the marketing concept is far from easy. Too often firms pay lip service to the concept but actually don't accept the concept in its entirety. Effective implementation of the marketing concept requires that top management believe in it and sell it to the organization from the top down.

The marketing concept can be implemented via the marketing mix: promotion, pricing, distribution, and the product itself. Without a successful marketing mix, the firm is ultimately doomed to failure.

In recent years marketing has expanded beyond the profit-making organization. The basic marketing concept has been successfully applied to many nonbusiness organizations. One aspect of the broadened marketing concept is social marketing. Social marketing entails satisfaction of human needs, expansion into social fields, and consideration of the impact of marketing on society. Social marketing is concerned with the human welfare of all individuals rather than simply with the promotion and selling of goods and services.

KEY TERMS

Marketing	Social marketing
Transaction	Empirical–rational strategy
Marketing concept	Creative demarketing
Consumer orientation	Micro
Goal orientation	Macro
Systems approach	Positive marketing
Marketing mix	Normative marketing
Broadened marketing concept	Standard of living

QUESTIONS FOR DISCUSSION

1. Define and discuss the basic elements of the marketing concept. Do you think most businesses have adopted this concept?
2. What are the problems involved in implementing the marketing concept? Recommend steps by which a firm could make the transition smoothly.
3. What is a firm's marketing mix? Why is it an important determinant of a firm's success?
4. Discuss the two divergent views of marketing that have developed in recent years. Which view do you favor? Give reasons for your answer.
5. How do you think nonprofit organizations can utilize the marketing concept? Give examples to illustrate your answer.
6. What is social marketing? Why is it important?
7. Why is the study of marketing important? Explain the role of marketing in a modern society.
8. Define the following terms:
   a. Marketing
   b. Empirical–rational strategy
   c. Normative marketing
   d. Positive marketing

9. What is meant by creative demarketing? How should this strategy be applied in the context of the energy crisis?

10. Should marketing managers be concerned about social issues? Do you think they have the right or the responsibility to deal with social problems? Give reasons for your answer.

NOTES

1. Philip Kotler, "A Generic Concept of Marketing," *Journal of Marketing,* 36 (April 1972): 49.

2. Charles Ames, "Trapping U.S. Substance in Industrial Marketing," *Harvard Business Review,* July–August 1970, p. 94. Copyright © 1970 by the President and Fellows of Harvard College; all rights reserved. See also "Marketing Concept Under Fire and Other Big Problems for Marketers," *Marketing News,* July 1, 1977, p. 9.

3. Ames, p. 97.

4. Richard Lewis and Leo Erickson, "Marketing Functions and Marketing Systems: A Synthesis," *Journal of Marketing,* 33 (July 1969): 12.

5. Carlton McNamara, "How Marketing Is Practiced in 640 Companies," *Sales Management,* October 15, 1970, p. 60; see also Philip Kotler, "The Major Tasks of Marketing Management," *Journal of Marketing,* 37 (October 1973): 42–49.

6. William Layer, "Marketing's Changing Social Relationships," *Journal of Marketing,* 33 (January 1969): 3–9.

7. Lawrence P. Feldman, "Societal Adaptation: A New Challenge for Marketing," *Journal of Marketing,* 35 (July 1971): 54–60, and Philip Kotler and Gerald Zaltman, "Social Marketing: An Approach to Planned Social Change," *Journal of Marketing,* 35 (July 1971): 3–12.

8. Philip Kotler and Sidney J. Levy, "Broadening the Concept of Marketing," *Journal of Marketing,* 33 (January 1969): 10–15; see also "Kotler Presents Whys, Hows of Marketing Audits for Firms, Nonprofit Organizations," *Marketing News,* March 26, 1976, p. 12; Kelly Shuptrine and Frank Osmarski, "Marketing's Changing Role: Expanding or Contracting?" *Journal of Marketing,* 39 (April 1975): 58–66; Robert Bartels, "The Identity Crises in Marketing," *Journal of Marketing,* October 1974, pp. 73–76; Benson Shappiro, "Marketing for Nonprofit Organizations," *Harvard Business Review,* September–October 1973, pp. 123–132; David Luck, "Broadening the Concept of Marketing—Too Far," *Journal of Marketing,* 33 (July 1969): 53–63; and Philip Kotler and Sidney Levy, "A New Form of Marketing Myopia: Rejoinder to Professor Luck," *Journal of Marketing,* 33 (July 1969): 55–56.

9. "Military Ad Area Under U.S. Study," *Advertising Age,* April 26, 1976, p. 82. For other examples of governmental marketing see Thomas Greer and John Malcolm, "The U.S. Postal Service: A New Marketer?" *MSU Business Topics,* Winter 1973, pp. 47–55, and John Rathmell, "Marketing by the Federal Government," *MSU Business Topics,* Summer 1973, pp. 21–28.

10. Leslie Dawson, "Marketing Science in the Age of Aquarius," *Journal of Marketing,* 35 (July 1971): 71.

11. Andrew Takas, "Societal Marketing: A Businessman's Perspective,"

Journal of Marketing, 38 (October 1974): 2. Other recommended articles on social marketing include E. B. Weiss, "The Coming Change in Marketing," *Advertising Age,* February 3, 1971, pp. 33–34; Philip Kotler, "A Generic Concept of Marketing," *Journal of Marketing,* 36 (April 1972): 46–54; David Luck, "Social Marketing: Confusion Compounded," *Journal of Marketing,* 38 (October 1974): 70–72; and Ben Enis, "Deepening the Concept of Marketing," *Journal of Marketing,* 37 (October 1973): 57–62. Reprinted by permission of the American Marketing Association.

12. Leslie Dawson, "The Human Concept: New Philosophy for Business," *Business Horizons,* December 1969, p. 33.

13. Robert Chin and Kenneth D. Benne, "General Strategies for Effecting Change in Human Systems," in Warren G. Bennis, Kenneth D. Benne, and Robert Chin, *The Planning of Change,* 2d ed. (New York: Holt, Rinehart and Winston, 1969), pp. 32–59.

14. David Krech, Richard S. Crutchfield, and Egerton L. Ballachey, *Individual in Society* (New York: McGraw-Hill, 1962).

15. Philip Kotler and Sidney J. Levy, "Demarketing, Yes, Demarketing," *Harvard Business Review,* December 1971, pp. 74–80; see also Nessim Hanna, A. H. Kizilbach, and Albert Smart, "Marketing Strategy Under Conditions of Economic Scarcity," *Journal of Marketing,* 39 (January 1975): 63–80.

16. Shelby Hunt, *Marketing Theory: Conceptual Foundations of Research in Marketing* (Columbus, Ohio: Grid, 1976), pp. 4–10.

17. Reavis Cox, *Distribution in a High Level Economy* (Englewood Cliffs, N. J.: Prentice-Hall, 1965), p. 149.

18. "Marketing's Finest Hour: Payday," *Sales and Marketing Management,* October 11, 1976, p. 43.

19. Ibid.

CASE 1
Mumford Toasters

In 1955 Ronald Mumford graduated from the University of Wisconsin with a degree in engineering. He went to work for General Electric in the Consumer Products Division. Over the years Ronald had many opportunities to participate in the development of product concepts for a variety of kitchen appliances. As he climbed the corporate ladder he began to feel that he would not be satisfied until he had his own business. Consequently in 1965 he resigned from General Electric and opened Mumford Toaster Products in Racine, Wisconsin.

Ronald took his engineering know-how coupled with years of practical experience and designed an oven–toaster that was basically very simple. The toaster was a square metal box with a heating element in the top that browned the toast. It had a pull-out tray and would hold four regular slices of bread.

At the time no comparable product existed. Sales of the Mumford Toaster rose dramatically from 1,400 units in the first year to 200,000 units in the second year. As the product began to "catch on" and distribution spread from Wisconsin to surrounding states, the giant competitors began to take an interest in it. Yet it was not until the end of the fourth year, when Mumford's sales were slightly over 1 million units, that the competition actually entered the marketplace.

Mumford Toasters has 47 employees. All production and design work is done by Mumford himself when he has time; all of the company's new concepts are based on his ideas. Virtually all the employees are engaged in some form of production, either on the line or in packaging, shipping, or receiving. Other personnel include a sales manager, a bookkeeper, and an accountant. There are no salespeople in the company. The sales manager hires a battery of manufacturer's representatives, who work on a commission basis throughout the United States.

Mumford has examined his operation and decided that in order to effectively meet the competition he will have to adopt the marketing concept. He realizes that he needs someone to help him implement the concept. As a consultant to Mr. Mumford, prepare a detailed memo on how his company might develop and implement the marketing concept. Be sure to explain the benefits that may accrue to the firm from utilizing the concept.

2

The Marketing System

In Chapter 1 we defined marketing and explored the broadened marketing concept. Marketing's functions were described and the marketing mix discussed. Perhaps you are wondering how the various pieces fit together. Specifically, how does marketing function as a system both within the firm and outside the firm?

In this chapter we begin with a discussion of marketing as a system. I then present a model that depicts the basic components of the system — the internal environment of marketing and the external environment faced by marketing managers. The remainder of the chapter is devoted to an exploration of the marketing model.

AN INTEGRATED SYSTEM

A system is an organized whole — or a group of diverse units that form an integrated whole — functioning or operating in unison. They are interdependent and are continually interacting, usually in response

21

to some type of control. The control in marketing is exercised by management, which manipulates the marketing mix (promotion, the product, pricing, and distribution) in order to meet the needs of a target group of customers.

The Marketing Model

The movement or flow of products, ideas, and services is charted in Figure 2.1. This flow diagram (the marketing model) is a visual illustration of the variables that interact, the sequence of their interaction,

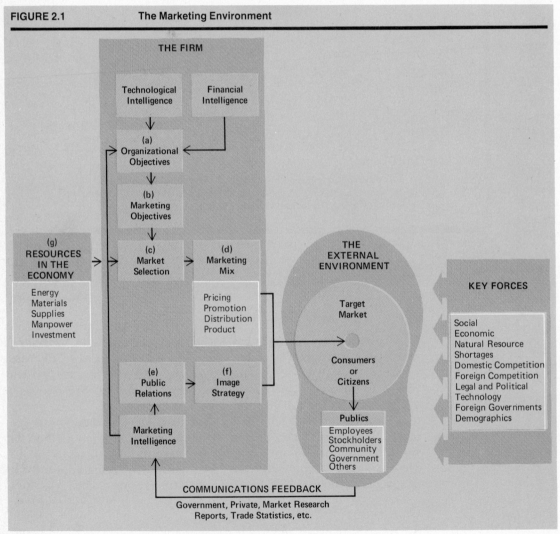

FIGURE 2.1   The Marketing Environment

Source: Adapted from Richard M. Bessom, "New Challenges for Marketing," *Arizona Business,* 22 (November 1975): 14.

and their interdependence. We will focus on this model throughout the chapter.

Marketing's environment may be divided into two major sub-systems—the internal subsystem and the external subsystem. Each major subsystem can limit the success of the enterprise. For example, financial constraints may limit desired inventory levels or the size of the promotional budget. Externally, government regulations can limit package sizes, pricing plans, product names, and a variety of other factors.

Conversely, the subsystems can also present opportunities for increasing the firm's marketing success. Internally, for example, analysis of credit information on existing customers may provide insights for new pricing strategies. Externally, changing social attitudes can offer many growth opportunities such as the movement toward informality that spawned a dynamic increase in denim sales.

Tying the Model to the Definition of Marketing

We have defined marketing as being concerned with how transactions are created, stimulated, facilitated, and valued. A transaction is an exchange of values between two parties. The exchange of value occurs when an effective marketing mix reaches the proper market target and the consumer buys the firm's product or service. If the firm is a nonprofit organization such as a charity, the values exchanged may be cash donations and a sense of well-being and helping others. Values are also exchanged when the firm purchases resources with which to create goods and services.

Transactions are created and stimulated by offering consumers what they want. Marketing information (discussed later in the chapter) helps the firm develop the proper goods and services. Promotion, fair prices, and credit terms help stimulate transactions and determine values (what things are worth). Credit and distribution also facilitate the exchange process. That is, getting the product or service to the consumer and offering terms that enable an individual to acquire the merchandise or service allows exchange to occur. Also, as mentioned earlier, the marketing environment, both internal and external, can either hinder or encourage the exchange process.

THE INTERNAL STRUCTURE OF MARKETING The Importance of Goals

Let's begin our examination of the marketing model by looking at the internal environment of the firm. A firm's goals provide the basis for intelligent organizational planning (Figure 2.1, box *a*). Without well-defined and realistic objectives, a firm is like a ship without a rudder. Control becomes impossible because there are no standards for measuring success or failure.

To be meaningful, goals must never be established in a vacuum. Rather, they must be based on relevant marketing, financial, and technological input. What is our borrowing capacity? What technology do we have available or can we acquire? What are the characteristics of the population we are trying to reach? These and similar questions must be answered before meaningful objectives can be established.

Goals for a Profit-Oriented Organization

Organizational goals are the necessary point of departure for developing a successful marketing mix. An obvious long-run objective for virtually all organizations is survival. In addition to survival, profit maximization is often mentioned as a major goal. But like survival, it offers little direction for marketing planning. Instead, companies strive for a satisfactory level of profits, that is, a return perceived as adequate by the firm's owner/managers or stockholders. An adequate return is normally judged as a return that is commensurate with a perceived level of risk for the industry and for the organization.[1]

Often goals are stated in terms of market share or target return on investment.[2] These goals are measurable and meaningful to management. General Electric, for example, strives for a 20 percent return on investment after taxes. This specific target figure provides management with a planning goal.

In addition to profit goals, many firms are establishing social goals. Examples of social goals include increasing the intrinsic value of the product or service, decreasing the resources needed for production, recycling old products and packages, and reducing pollution. As society has become more aware of pollution, lack of wasteful production processes, product quality (e.g., lack of food value in cereals), and so forth, it has become necessary for the firm to develop a social conscience. If a company or industry does not establish social goals on its own, it may find itself forced to do so by stifling governmental regulations.

Goals for Nonprofit Organizations

Nonprofit institutions such as governmental units, civic organizations, and charities must also develop meaningful organizational goals. A charity may have as a goal the feeding and clothing of 5000 families during the next 6 months. A health organization may strive to provide 200 complete physical examinations per day. The marketing concept is just as applicable to these organizations as it is to profit-oriented companies.[3]

Inputs from Other Departments

Cooperation among all of the organization's departments is necessary for efficient accomplishment of company goals. Indeed, marketing is only one cog in the organizational machine and should not dominate the company. Marketing depends on production for basic information on what can be produced, how many pieces can be produced per unit of time, and so forth. By the same token, there are inherent conflicts between production and marketing goals. Production tends to be pre-occupied with lowering costs. This normally translates into a lack of variety due to long production runs, fewer product features (to avoid production problems), and lengthy intervals between model changes. These desires of the production department are anathema to marketing managers.

Financial management provides critical information on pricing strategies, inventory levels, and product development costs. Again, financial goals may easily conflict with marketing goals. Financial executives may lean toward limited inventories, fewer models, less money for promotion and basic research (owing to the difficulty of measuring returns), and "quick return" pricing policies.

Marketing Objectives

Marketing objectives are a logical extension of corporate objectives (see Figure 2.1, box *b*). The accomplishment of marketing goals should aid in the accomplishment of company goals. For example, if the company's main objective is to obtain a dominant market share in a high-volume market, the main marketing objective should not be to develop a product with exclusive appeal and high price. This would not be a high-volume strategy.

THE TARGET MARKET

After marketing goals have been defined, the company may determine its target market (Figure 2.1, box *c*); that is, it may identify the consumers who are most likely to buy or use its product or service. Only when a clear and precise target has been established can a marketing mix be developed (Figure 2.1, box *d*).

Often setting a target requires breaking down a large market into smaller pieces or segments. For example, segmenting a market by buyer income may reveal more sales opportunities for a given product among middle-income consumers than among high-income consumers. Market segmentation is discussed in detail in Chapter 5.

THE ROLE OF THE MARKETING MIX

The marketing mix is developed in order to achieve marketing and company goals by satisfying a target group of consumers. Yet the mix is constrained by both internal and external trade-offs.

The components of the marketing mix may be viewed as the controllable elements of marketing. These four key variables (price, promotion, distribution, and the product itself) are the "tools" that marketing managers have at their disposal. Public relations (Figure 2.1, box *e*), a component of promotion, plays an especially important part in presenting the corporate image to various publics, for example, stockholders and the community at large.

Different departments are often forced to compromise, and trade-offs must be made between various pricing, product, distribution, and promotion strategies. A typical trade-off is between product quality and price. The ideal situation is a low price and high quality, but this is rarely attainable. Instead, the manager must decide the trade-off values, as perceived by the target market, between raising the quality and also raising the price. Other trade-offs include personal selling versus advertising, intensive product distribution versus lower-quality dealers, and extensive service versus lower prices.

A second set of marketing trade-off decisions has evolved recently. This relates to the broader marketing concept and includes such considerations as the firm versus society and the firm versus the government. Assume, for instance, that a manufacturer can produce a central air-conditioning system for private homes at a relatively low price. Yet because of simplistic design it is an inefficient user of energy. The trade-off is between a low-priced product and high energy consumption.

Many fast-food restaurants do not hesitate to wrap a hamburger in paper and put it in a styrofoam box to retain heat before finally putting the burger in a sack when in fact the patron will eat the burger in the restaurant! The trade-off is a warm hamburger and visual appeal of the package versus potential lower sales without the excess packaging. The packaging also means wasted paper, which uses up natural resources and produces litter. In the long run this becomes a trade-off between the firm and the government. The company must decide whether pleasing the consumer is worth the risk of government legislation against nonreturnable containers. In Oregon, for example, the state government, reacting to the litter problem, has outlawed disposable soft-drink bottles.

THE EXTERNAL ENVIRONMENT

Let's turn now to the external environment and the target market. Remember that trade-off decisions within the marketing mix must ultimately satisfy the target market and society as a whole.

Society: Consumers and Publics

The target market is made up of potential consumers of the product. These consumers also play a role as part of a larger group—the general public. The public comprises not only potential consumers but employees, stockholders, governmental units, and others. As you learned in Chapter 1, marketing managers must consider the needs of the public as well as the target market. The firm, for example, is expected to be a good corporate citizen in the communities in which it conducts business. A company that ignores the public may develop a poor image.

The public that an organization faces is a heterogeneous group including employees, stockholders, the community government, and others. Each of these "publics" has unique needs that must be met to ensure its long-run survival. Stockholders are looking for a certain return on their investments; employers seek security and job satisfaction; the government passes legislation and informal guidelines; and the community requires that the firm be a good neighbor.

All organizations present several distinct images to their various publics and consumers. Part of a company's image may be contrived by a public-relations department (Figure 2.1, box *e*); other aspects of a firm's image include its physical facilities, employee contact with the external environment, and the firm's marketing mix. The firm's image (Figure 2.1, box *f*) is the major determinant of how various publics and consumers interact with it.

Resource Requirements

A second aspect of the external environment is the resources used by the organization (Figure 2.1, box *g*). Resources are acquired by producing a product or service that is desired by society. Without a desirable good or service, the firm will not make sales and thus will not receive the revenues needed to acquire resources. This basic truism is coming under increasing criticism, however. For example, even though consumers have shown that they are willing to pay a premium for disposable bottles and cans, is this an efficient use of resources? Should marketers ask not only "What can we produce at a profit?" but also "Is it good for society?"

MONITORING CHANGE IN THE MARKETING SYSTEM

As noted earlier, the external environment consists of people playing the roles of consumers and of part of the public sector. Figure 2.1 depicts the external environment. The amoeba-like shape is used to denote a state of flux or change. Marketing managers face an external environment that is continually evolving. Moreover, that environment is subject to a number of powerful forces that create and influence changes in consumer demand and in public needs and whims.

These external forces are not under the control of the marketing manager. The manager must understand and forecast how the key forces will affect the external environment and must alter the marketing mix accordingly. The mechanism for monitoring change is the marketing intelligence system.

A marketing intelligence system, as we will see in Chapter 3, is a device for communications feedback. (See Figure 2.1.) Government reports, private research reports, trade statistics, reports from field sales personnel, and market research studies are typical information conduits.

Marketing managers evaluate the information received through the marketing intelligence system and decide what changes, if any, should be made in the marketing mix. For example, increasing government pressure and declining domestic fuel stocks have forced Detroit to produce smaller, more efficient automobiles. General Foods, recognizing the trend toward more women in the work force, decided to bring out more instant, convenience-type foods.

EXTERNAL FACTORS THAT AFFECT MARKETING

Let's examine the key factors that force changes in the external environment. They are social and economic factors, domestic and foreign competition, legal and political factors, technology, foreign governments, and demographic factors.

Social Factors

One of the most important factors in the external environment is social change. People's behavior, their roles, their views, and consumption patterns are all influenced in part by culture. Culture is a group's learned behavior and distinctive life style. Cultural change is the process of adjusting to an environment by questioning traditional standards and values.

Marketing managers have embraced America's changing life styles by offering, among other things, more credit, greater variety, casual clothes, and promotional emphasis on freedom and sexuality. Marketers have also recognized the importance of subcultures such as the southern culture, black culture, and the California life style. Astute managers have developed a marketing mix targeted to specific markets. Coca-Cola, for example, markets its products differently to each of the subcultures just mentioned.

Economic Factors

An excellent strategy may fail miserably if the economy changes dramatically in a short period. Inflation—an increase in an economy's general level of prices—is rapidly becoming an accepted fact of life to consumers throughout the world. As a result people are becoming desensitized to continually rising prices. Marketers who hesitate to raise prices for fear of losing customers often experience a severe loss in their own purchasing capabilities. When they finally do raise prices they often find that demand for the product does not change much.

Inflation is only part of the long-run problem facing marketing managers. For the foreseeable future the growth of real national income will average around 3 percent a year instead of the 3.7 percent achieved during the 1941–1969 period.[4] Slow economic growth will motivate many firms to depend on capturing a large share of the market. They cannot rely on the market to grow. Additional emphasis will be placed on new-product development and improvement, competitive pricing, aggressive promotion, and controlling marketing costs.

Conway Ivy, director of corporate planning at Gould, claims that "in an economic downturn when businesses are forced to go with contingency measures to protect earnings goals, marketing alone among all corporate functions assumes a positive role." During the 1975 recession Gould actually increased its net income by 22 percent through the following measures: (1) Travel and telephone expenses were reduced 69 percent and 55 percent, respectively, by concentrating on specific products and customers; (2) sales and product efforts for the Gelyte battery were accelerated; (3) export sales were emphasized; and (4) special sales promotion was undertaken on finished-goods inventory.[5]

Natural-Resource Shortages

A discussion of inflation and slow economic growth would not be complete without some mention of the scarcity of natural resources. At the time of the 1974 oil embargo Americans relied on imports to meet about one-third of their oil needs.[6] But petroleum is not the only resource that is being used up. Many key metals, natural gas, natural fibers, plastics, and meat routinely experience production shortfalls. Yet energy costs seem to have the greatest impact.

Higher energy costs will push up virtually all prices and will decrease purchasing power. Consumers will try to adjust by seeking lower-priced products, goods that do not become obsolete, and energy-efficient merchandise. The following list summarizes the ways in which marketing managers may react to rising energy costs.[7]

- Prices of all products will rise, especially of those that require a great deal of energy for their manufacture and transport. The same is true of materials. Prices of services also will rise, especially of those that require transportation of the service person.
- To reduce costs, manufacturers will tend to standardize products. They will pay less attention to product differentiation and to catering to the needs and desires of individual market segments.
- New products will be introduced that are more durable, require less service, and require less energy in their manufacture, distribution, and use.
- As the more durable products come into use, production levels will be reduced, because replacements will be needed less frequently. The resulting unemployment may be abated as the trend toward mechanization and computerization is slowed. This slowing may take place as energy-consuming machines become less economical than labor.
- Product R&D will be stepped up initially to develop products that are more durable, require less service, and need less energy. Subsequently, R&D efforts will be reduced to reduce the costs of operation.
- Marketing research aimed at increasing marketing efficiency will be stepped up. Research done in support of proliferation of minute product modifications will be reduced, as a cost reduction measure, as the number of new product introductions is reduced.

- The trend toward lower-cost transportation will be accentuated. Larger and slower shipments will be used. Examples: larger and slower-moving trucks and ships.
- Larger inventories will be maintained to take advantage of the transportation economies noted above.
- In the area of promotion, personal selling will become increasingly costly as the costs of cars, gasoline, transportation services, hotels, and restaurants continue to rise. Less use will be made of personal selling. Substitutes will include promotion through telephone, mail, other forms of communication, and the media. Great emphasis will be placed on increasing the efficiency of whatever personal selling *is* used.
- The amount of industrial advertising will increase somewhat to compensate for the decrease in personal selling.
- The amount of consumer advertising will decrease as marketers seek to cut their costs. The content of the advertising will tend to be more factual as consumers become more interested in tangible benefits of products being advertised.[8]

Domestic Competition

Shortages and inflation tend to intensify levels of competition, as discussed earlier. Increased sophistication of management and information systems also increases intensity of competition. Major companies do not hesitate to spend millions of dollars to introduce new products. Phillip Morris, for example, spent $40 million to introduce Merit cigarettes to the smoking public. It also gave away 1.2 billion of the new cigarettes in key markets.[9] H. J. Heinz became so frustrated in its efforts to penetrate the market for various soup products that it filed a $105 million antitrust complaint against Campbell Soup Company.[10] The basis of Heinz's complaint was Campbell's overly aggressive marketing practices.

Foreign Competition

Domestic firms are not the only ones vying for market share and profits. The automobile, textile, chemical, optical product, and footwear markets, among others, have been deeply penetrated by foreign businesses. But foreign competition is not limited to importation of foreign goods. A number of Japanese and European companies have built plants and marketing facilities in the United States in order to compete more effectively with American companies. International marketing will be explored in detail later in the book.

Legal and Political Factors

The legal environment of marketing defines the parameters within which management must operate. Legislation, like other variables, tends to change over time. New governmental regulations can be a severe blow to a firm's marketing mix. Safety requirements for automobiles meant higher prices for consumers; new packaging regulations required manufacturers to change packaging materials, increase tensile strength, and the like. The removal of cigarette advertising from television was a major crisis for marketing managers in that industry. Consumer concern over the depletion of the ozone layer of the atmosphere and the resultant increase in skin cancer may mean an end to the use of aerosol containers.

Marketing management faces two major sources of regulation—federal and state. Most federal regulation of marketing activities is administered through the Federal Trade Commission (FTC). The FTC, unlike most other regulatory agencies, has broad powers. Its mandate from Congress permits it to regulate almost any industry. Table 2.1 summarizes its major powers.

State legislation that affects marketing varies dramatically from state to state. Oregon, for example, limits utility advertising to 0.5 percent of the company's net income.[11] California has forced industry to improve consumer products and has also enacted legislation to lower the energy consumption of refrigerators, freezers, and air conditioners.[12] Many other examples could be added to these.

TABLE 2.1	The FTC's Growing Powers	
Act	**Purpose**	
FTC	Originally an antitrust law, passed in 1914 and broadened in 1938 to let the agency attack "unfair or deceptive acts or practices in commerce"	
Clayton	The basic antitrust statute, including antimerger provisions and prohibitions on interlocking directorates	
Robinson-Patman	These 1938 amendments to the Clayton Act require that sellers must offer equal deals to all customers	
Truth in Lending	Details the information that must be given to a credit customer	
Fair Credit Reporting	Establishes a customer's rights in disputes with credit bureaus	
Fair Credit Billing	Protects consumers from unfair and inaccurate billing practices	
Equal Credit Opportunity	Bars discrimination by sex, race, religion, or age in loans and credit sales	
Fair Packaging	Outlaws deceptive packaging or labeling	
Fur Products	Requires accurate branding of fur products	
Textile Identification	Requires accurate labeling of fiber content of textile products	
Webb-Pomerene	Provides antitrust immunity for U.S. companies that band together in joint export efforts	
Magnuson-Moss	Extends the agency's reach to local business dealings and confirms its right to regulate by industrywide rules	

Source: "The Escalating Struggle Between the FTC and Business," *Business Week,* December 13, 1976, pp. 52–59. Reprinted by permission.

Technology

Technological changes can either provide tremendous opportunities for marketers who know how to take advantage of them, or they can result in large losses for companies that fail to recognize their impact. Developments in computers, semiconductors, chemicals, and transportation have all had profound effects on the business world. The invention of a dry-paper copier process enabled Xerox to become a giant in American industry. On the other hand, Timex, for many years the dominant firm in the low-priced watch market, suddenly found its market for pin-and-lever watches rapidly eroding as consumers demonstrated a preference for the advanced technology of the digital watch.

The 1980s will present many new opportunities to marketing managers. Communications, for example, is one area in which great changes are expected. The video cassette for home television promises many new marketing opportunities. Mail-order catalog distributors will be able to portray merchandise not only through pictures but also through sound, lighting, and the persuasive words of professional sales representatives. Cable television will also have a major impact, since it will open up two-way communications between sellers and buyers.

Foreign Governments

Foreign governments may be even more important to marketing managers than technology during the 1980s. The actions of foreign governments can have a substantial impact even on businesses that are not engaged in international marketing or facing significant foreign competition. Nowhere is this more evident than in the area of energy supplies.

In 1974, as noted earlier, the oil-exporting nations demanded an artificially high price for their oil and created a worldwide inflation. As domestic oil prices rose, shortages began to develop in petroleum and petroleum-based products such as plastics and synthetic fibers. The actions of the Organization of Petroleum Exporting Countries (OPEC) forced many American firms, even those that were only tangentially related to the petroleum industry, to alter all the variables in their marketing mix. Other nations, noting OPEC's success, have considered forming their own cartels in natural resources such as tin, bauxite, and copper.

Demographic Factors

Demography is the study of vital statistics concerning such things as ages, births, deaths, and locations of groups of people. American's demographic characteristics change slowly, with the result that new markets open up while sales potential evaporates in others. The declining birthrate has forced Gerber's, the baby food manufacturer, to look elsewhere for sustained long-run growth. In 1975, for example, it began testing single-portion dishes that might appeal to the over-55 age group. Demographic changes are discussed in detail in Chapter 4.

SUMMARY

Marketing can be viewed as an integrated system. A system is a set of interacting variables. It is an organized whole with units operating in unison and interacting in an interdependent manner, usually in response to some mechanism of control. The control in marketing is exercised through the marketing mix.

The marketing model consists of two major subsystems—the internal subsystem and the external subsystem. Each subsystem can either limit the firm's success or provide opportunities for increased profitability. The internal system is created on the basis of the firm's marketing goals. Marketing goals, in turn, are derived from corporate objectives.

To achieve its marketing goals the firm develops its marketing mix. The mix is constrained by both internal and external factors. Owing to limited resources, it is normally impossible to allocate unlimited resources to the four components of the marketing mix. Therefore trade-offs typically develop among various departments and various components of the marketing mix.

The external environment consists of two major groups—consumers and publics. Consumers are potential buyers of a company's product or service. The public (which is also a consumer) consists of employees, stockholders, governmental units, and others. Under the broadened marketing concept the firm is expected to satisfy both its target market and the public in general.

The external environment is always changing. Several factors, most of which cannot be controlled by the firm, initiate and influence change. The firm must anticipate changes in these factors and determine what impact these changes will have on the firm. Then, if necessary, it should modify its marketing mix. The firm's long-run survival is predicated upon successful adaptation of the marketing mix to meet the continually changing external environment.

KEY TERMS

System
Internal subsystem
External subsystem
Target market
Public

Marketing intelligence system
Culture
Inflation
Demography

QUESTIONS FOR DISCUSSION

1. Briefly outline the basic components of the marketing system. Relate the marketing model presented in the chapter to the definition of marketing given in Chapter 1.
2. What are the major subsystems of the marketing environment? What roles can these subsystems play?
3. Why are organizational objectives important for the success of any firm? How should goals be established? Give examples of profit goals and social goals.
4. Describe the role of the marketing mix in the marketing system. How does it help a firm implement the marketing concept?

5. Briefly describe the factors that have a bearing on the firm's external marketing environment.
6. Discuss the influence that economic factors can have on a firm's marketing strategy.
7. What is a marketing intelligence system? How does it help marketing managers make decisions?
8. How can the marketing mix be used to fulfill the needs of a firm's external environment (its target market and society as a whole)?
9. What is the impact of governmental regulation on a firm's marketing strategy? Can you name an industry that has been hurt by such regulation?
10. Why do certain actions of foreign governments affect American firms? Give examples to illustrate your answer.
11. Briefly discuss a firm's internal marketing environment. Explain the relationships that can develop between different departments in attempting to achieve company goals. Use examples to illustrate your answer.

NOTES

1. For a detailed discussion of these concepts see William J. Baumal, "On the Theory of Oligopoly," *Economica,* 25 (August 1958): 187–198.
2. See Robert Lanzillotti, "Pricing Objectives in Large Companies," *American Economics Review,* 48 (December 1958): 924–992.
3. See Leo Bogart, "The Marketing of Public Goods," *The Conference Board Record,* November 1975, pp. 20–25, and George Wasem, "Marketing for Profits and Nonprofits," *Bankers Monthly Magazine,* March 15, 1975, pp. 23–27.
4. Neil Jacoby, "Six Big Challenges Business Will Face in the Next Decade," *Nation's Business,* August 1976, p. 37.
5. L. G. Rawl, senior vice president, Exxon, in a speech entitled "Private Enterprise in a Changing Society," presented at an executives' symposium on "Future Shock and the Businessman" at St. Mary's College of California, Moroga, California, February 5, 1976.
6. Ibid.
7. Several good articles on marketing during periods of shortage and inflation are A. B. Blankenship and John Holmes, "Will Shortages Bankrupt the Marketing Concept?" *MSU Business Topics,* Spring 1974, pp. 13–18; David Cravens, "Marketing Management in an Era of Shortages," *Business Horizons,* February 1974, pp. 79–85; and Philip Kotler and V. Balachandran, "Strategic Remarketing: The Preferred Response to Shortages and Inflation," *Sloan Management Review,* Fall 1975, pp. 1–17.
8. Leon Winer and L. S. Schiff, "Rising Energy Costs Will Alter Marketing Patterns," *Marketing News,* May 6, 1977, p. 4. Reprinted by permission of the American Marketing Association.
9. "Phillip Morris: The Hot Hands in Cigarettes," *Business Week,* December 6, 1976, pp. 62–64.
10. Louis Haugh, "Suit vs. Campbell—Admission of Heinz's Marketplace Flops," *Advertising Age,* October 25, 1976, pp. 2, 8.
11. Ralph Friedman, "Oregon Limits Utility Ads to 0.5 Percent of Net Income," *Advertising Age,* July 26, 1976, p. 4.
12. "A Regulatory Shock for Appliance Makers," *Business Week,* July 26, 1976, p. 46.

CASE 2
Shiner Brewery

Shiner is the third-smallest brewery in the United States. It produces less than 75,000 barrels of beer a year. The company has actually doubled its production since 1968, but it isn't planning on getting big. Speedy Beale, the company's sales manager, explains that the brewery just can't manufacture much more and isn't interested in expansion. Most of Shiner's sales are in small towns in south-central Texas, although its beer is available in Dallas and at scattered locations such as Austin, Houston, and San Antonio.

The town of Shiner got its name from the rancher, H. B. Shiner, who donated 250 acres to the town in 1887 provided that it be named after him. The brewery was begun in 1909 and continues to operate much the way it did then. Its sales efforts consist of sending sales people out on the road to spend a week with each beer distributor. Their sales pitch is a smile, a hand-shake, and a bottle of beer.

Shiner doesn't have an advertising agency. Nor does it have a consolidated advertising theme. It uses different approaches in different areas. The most often heard claim about Shiner is that it is a natural beer, brewed pure and simple with loving care that bigger breweries cannot put into their products. The brewery itself looks like a Spanish mission that has been turned into a factory. At one side there's a stand-up bar where visitors and a grateful group of locals can regularly sample the product for which the town is famous. Sometimes as many as 150 people take at least one draught here during an afternoon. The employees mix with the crowd from time to time, standing around with their plastic cups of Shiner like members of the family at a wedding reception.

Originally the beer was brewed darker and heavier than it is now. Then the brewmaster decided that Americans wanted a lighter beer. Today he alone determines the nature of the product produced. Even during the changeover Shiner didn't lose all of the older drinkers who had grown up with its product. The brewmaster believes that they are loyal to the label. Apparently a lot of Texans have more affection for the company than for heavier lager beer.

Shiner is made from artesian well water, barley malt, hops, and corn grits. This is a pretty standard list of ingredients. However, Shiner brews the beer for 30 days in contrast to the major breweries, which take only 7 to 10 days. Also, many larger breweries use substitutes such as fortified corn rather than real grits.

Seventy percent of Shiner's business is in returnable long-necked bottles, the kind that went out with pop-tops and came back in Texas in the 1970s. At Shiner long-necks never really went out.

1. Does Shiner have the marketing concept? If not, what advantages might accrue to the firm from adopting the concept? How might one establish the concept there?
2. Take each of the external variables that might affect the firm and discuss how each might affect Shiner.

3

Market Segmentation

OBJECTIVES

■ To understand what a market is.
■ To understand the concept of market segmentation.
■ To become aware of the strategy of product differentiation.
■ To gain insights into product positioning.

Chapter 2 described the marketing system. You learned the importance of reaching the target consumers with the right marketing mix. This chapter delves into the nature of markets and their various subdivisions. We will discuss the factors involved in segmenting a market, such as population characteristics and life styles, and find out how a market may be subdivided effectively.

THE NATURE OF A MARKET

The heart of any consumer market is people. Similarly, the foundation of an industrial market is the companies that use its products. While people and companies determine the breadth of a given market, they are not the only factors involved. Purchasing power—that is, cash or the ability to borrow—is also a necessary condition for a market to exist. Many people would like a new Rolls Royce, yet few have the financial capacity to buy one.

Another necessary condition is the desire or willingness to buy. There are a multitude of items that you could buy but don't. There are perfumes, toothpastes, shirts, and so forth that you simply don't like. You are not part of the market for those goods. Still another necessary condition for a market to exist is the authority to buy. Individuals in an industrial environment may have a strong desire for certain new equipment yet not have the authority to make the purchase decision. In short, a market is made up of people or companies with the ability and willingness to buy.

The scope of a market depends on many other factors as well. Substitute goods, or the lack of them, will influence a firm's share of a market. Generally speaking, the more substitutes there are for a company's product and the cheaper they are, the smaller the company's market share will be. An item that is unique or can do a job much more efficiently than older products will increase its market share. Complementary goods, such as shoes and socks, beer and pretzels, automobiles and tires, will experience an increase in market share if demand for the complementary product increases. If the demand for stereo sets rises, so should its complement—records.

In the industrial-goods market the demand for machinery depends on the machine's output capability relative to its cost. The greater the equipment's productive capacity compared to its cost, the larger the industrial market. Again, other factors enter the picture, such as demand for the final product, the substitutability of labor for capital, and the number and quality of alternative machines.

MARKET SEGMENTATION

The market for virtually any product is not an amorphous mass of people or firms but a set of subgroups with differing needs and desires. Market segmentation is the process of identifying and evaluating various strata or layers of a market. When Henry Ford began producing the Model T he stated that "they [consumers] can have their car in any color they want as long as it is black." His was an undifferentiated strategy with no segmentation.

Today automobile manufacturers recognize a myriad of segments that, taken as a whole, constitute the market for automobiles. There are segments for hot rodders, mothers with children, young families, status seekers, and even states (for example, California has regulations requiring certain engine modifications).

Forms of Segmentation

There are five basic forms of segmentation: (1) demographic—by age, sex, income, life cycle; (2) geographic—by region, urban or rural; (3) psychographic—by life style or personality; (4) by benefit (e.g., tastes good, feels good); (5) by volume (e.g., heavy user, light user).

FIGURE 3.1   (a) The Concept of Market Segmentation; (b) Market Segmentation
                    Using Two Demographic Bases

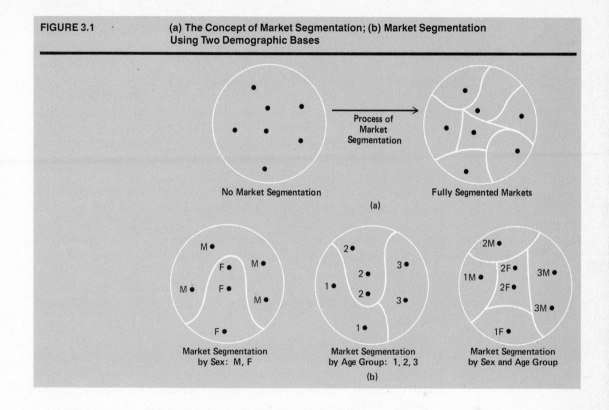

Segmentation is much more than simply "chopping up" a market into one or more of the five basic forms. (See Figure 3.1.) It also requires identifying the level of demand associated with the various segments and designing a marketing mix to meet the unique needs and desires of a specific target segment. Chapter 4 explores the characteristics of various American market segments such as age groups, life styles, and income.

Criteria for Successful Segmentation

For segmentation to be successful four basic criteria must be met:

1. Substantiality — the segments must be large enough to permit a viable market effort directed towards them.
2. Nature of demand — strata must exhibit differences in consumption rates among the segments.
3. Response rates — the segments must exhibit differences in responses to the marketing variables.
4. Accessibility — the segments must permit the firm to direct successfully different marketing effort toward the segments.[1]

We have already discussed the first criterion — substantiality: Demand must be great enough to make the marketing effort worthwhile. The second criterion, nature of demand, refers to the different quantities demanded by the various segments. For example, assume that a company segments by age—under 25, 25 to 50, and over 50. After segmenting it finds that demand in each segment is 10,000 units per month. Segmentation by age would be ineffective, since the age variable does not affect the rate of consumption of the product.

The third segmentation criterion implies that if various segments respond in similar ways to a marketing mix, there is no need to develop a separate marketing mix for each segment. If, for example, all segments respond in identical fashion to price changes, there is no need for different prices for individual segments.

The final criterion requires that segmentation characteristics can be identified and then measured. Most important, the marketer must have access to segmented markets. Assume that a liquor company finds through market research that heavy users of a new brand of Scotch are extraverted female divorcees with a swinging life style. If the company cannot determine which media this group watches, reads, or listens to, or where its members live and shop, segmentation is useless. Of course there may not be a medium that reaches such individuals.

Patterns of Segmentation

Do marketers really believe in segmentation? Definitely. One study has shown that top marketing executives consider it one of their most important tools.[2] If a market can be segmented successfully, several strategic alternatives are available:

1. one product, one mix, all segments—undifferentiated marketing
2. one product, several mixes, relevant segments—particularized marketing
3. one or a few products, one mix, one segment—concentrated marketing
4. several products, several mixes, relevant segments—differentiated marketing (see Figure 3.2)

Undifferentiated Marketing. Undifferentiated marketing goes back to our Model T example, in which one product is produced for everyone who is willing to buy it. No attempt is made to cultivate various strata of the marketplace. Many small businesses and some large ones still follow this strategy. For example, some large bakeries adopt an undifferentiated approach to the selling of bread.

Particularized Marketing. Particularized marketing recognizes that customers may use a product differently. Different promotional

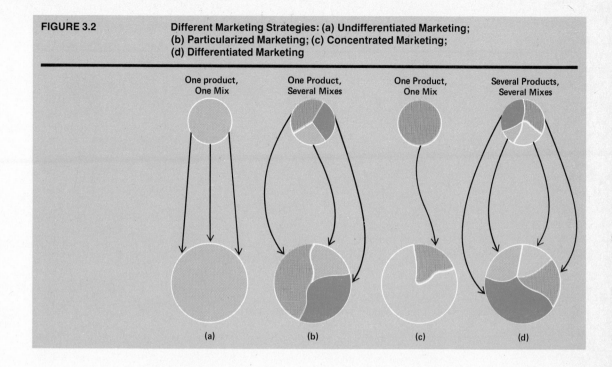

FIGURE 3.2   **Different Marketing Strategies: (a) Undifferentiated Marketing; (b) Particularized Marketing; (c) Concentrated Marketing; (d) Differentiated Marketing**

themes, sales outlets, and prices are used to stimulate greater demand than would be generated under a single mix. (Figure 3.3 illustrates how Bell Telephone segmented its residential long-distance market.[3]) Different promotional strategies can then be developed for different user segments.

Concentrated Marketing. A concentrated strategy is often used by smaller firms entering a market that is already dominated by larger companies. Rather than attempting to meet the bigger competitors head on, they will find a small segment of the market and devote all of their talents and resources to it. Aamco Transmissions has successfully carved out a small segment of the automobile repair market by following a concentration strategy. Featherlite makes duck decoys for duck hunters—a small part of the total hunting market and an even smaller segment of the outdoor-recreation market.

Differentiated Marketing   Differentiated marketing is a common tactic among successful marketers. Most large consumer goods manufacturers (e.g., Gillette, Ralston Purina, General Foods, General Motors, and many others) follow differentiated marketing strategies. An ex-

FIGURE 3.3   Segmentation of the Long-Distance Market by Average Monthly Long-Distance Expenditures in 1972: AID Analysis

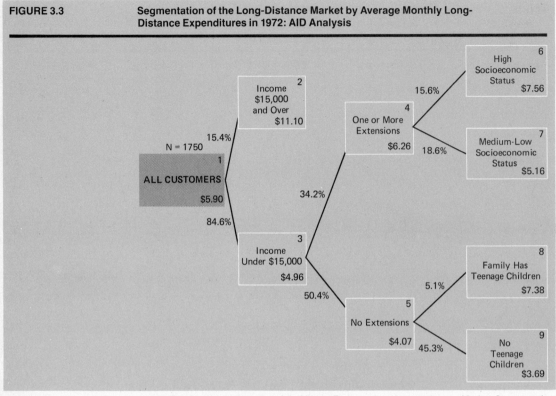

Source: Henry Assael and A. Marvin Roscoe, Jr., "Approaches to Market Segmentation Analysis," *Journal of Marketing,* 40 (October 1976): 75. By permission of the American Marketing Association.

cellent example of the benefits of a differentiated strategy is the following:

> Before its acquisition by Phillip Morris in 1970, Miller could not challenge anyone. While brewing's leaders were growing at 10 percent a year, twice the industry's overall growth rate, Miller's sales remained flat. Then came PM, loaded with excess cash. Because it was making net profits larger than those of the industry leader, Anheuser-Busch, PM's entry into the business caused immediate concern.
>
> The concern was well founded; PM shifted Miller into high gear. The results have been astonishing. Miller's sales leaped from 5 million bbl. in 1972 to 18 million bbl. in 1976. [See Figure 3.4.]
>
> Miller's new managers divided up the U.S. beer market into segments, producing new products and packages specifically for those segments, and then spending with abandon to promote them. Until Miller came along, the brewers operated as if there was a homogeneous market for beer that could be served by one product in one package.
>
> It did not take Miller long to recognize that High Life—the single

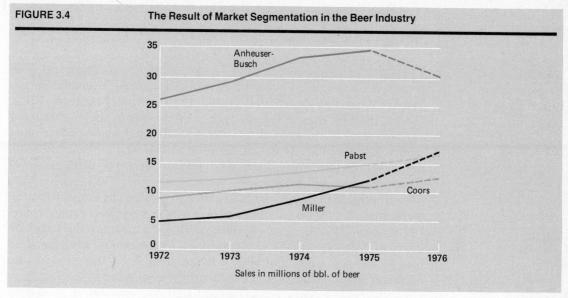

FIGURE 3.4   The Result of Market Segmentation in the Beer Industry

Source: "Miller's Fast Growth Upsets the Beer Industry," *Business Week*, November 8, 1975, p. 58. Reprinted by special permission. All rights reserved.

product the company had when PM took over — was not only not enough but was also aimed at the wrong beer-drinking market. Sold for years as the champagne of beers, High Life was attracting a disproportionate share of women and upper-income consumers who were not big beer drinkers. "A lot of people drank the beer, but none of them in quantity," says a marketing executive. Advertisements for High Life began featuring young people riding in dune buggies and oil drillers sipping on a cool one after squelching an oil blowout.

Then Miller began opening up new market segments, beginning in 1972 with the introduction of a 7-oz. pony bottle, an idea that had failed earlier for several regional brewers. Miller's new product turned out to be a favorite of women and older people, who thought the standard 12-oz. size was simply too much beer to drink.

But the pony's success was only a stage-setter for Miller's big marketing coup, the introduction of lower-calorie Lite beer. First marketed nationally in early 1975, Lite now stands to become the most successful new beer introduced in the U.S. in this century. Like Miller's Lite, both Meister Brau's Lite and Gablinger were low-calorie beers. But they turned out to be disasters largely because they were marketed as diet drinks to diet-conscious consumers who do not drink beer in the first place. By contrast, Miller's heavy advertising program for Lite features sports personalities who offer the message that Lite, with one-third fewer calories, offers the big beer-drinker an opportunity to drink as much beer as before without feeling so filled.

More than a few brewers laughed at what they insisted was

Miller's attempt to enter a market that did not exist. But this year Miller will sell an estimated 5 million bbl. of Lite, equal to its entire beer production four years ago, and the laughter has ceased.[4]

Benefit Segmentation and Perceptual Mapping

The form of segmentation that has received the most attention in recent years is benefit segmentation. A segment is developed on the basis of what a product will do rather than consumer characteristics. One of the first uses of benefit segmentation was in the marketing of toothpaste. The toothpaste market was divided among (1) people who wanted a pleasant flavor, (2) people who wanted to avoid tooth decay, (3) active individuals who wanted brighter teeth, and (4) economy-minded purchasers.[5]

If a marketer knows what benefits are desired by consumers, the marketing mix for an existing product can be modified to reflect market desires. If this isn't possible, perhaps a new product can be developed. It should be easier to develop a promotional program after benefit segmentation has been carried out, since this is how the marketer learns what product features the consumer is seeking.

Perceptual mapping is often used to sharpen a product's perceived-benefits picture. Several brands and product attributes are "mapped" using advanced statistical techniques.[6] The closer together the brands are on the map, the greater the perceived similarity. Also, the closer a particular attribute is to a particular brand, the greater the likelihood that consumers believe that the brand possesses that attribute.

Confusing? Not really. Look at Figure 3.5. This perceptual map shows the relationships among product attributes, brands of sports cars, and typical car owners.[7] For example, "high durability" and "high reliability" are in close proximity to "high resale," indicating that consumers view reliability and durability as important determinants of a high resale value. Also, note that none of the sports cars came close to these benefits—this may indicate a marketing opportunity. Similarly, the Opel was viewed as basically a city car, whereas the Corvette was perceived in terms of speed and racing—yet without the prestige of the Jaguar.

Perceptual mapping helps marketers distinguish among competing brands and find unfilled niches in the marketplace. By examining a brand on a perceptual map the marketing manager can assess the brand's strengths and weaknesses. For example, returning to Figure 3.5, the Ghia is viewed as economical to drive and maintain but hardly beautiful, fast, or prestigious.

Like virtually all other marketing research tools, perceptual mapping is not without problems. If the benefits and brands are closely clustered together, distinctions among brands aren't sharp enough for successful segmentation. Perceived benefits and relative

FIGURE 3.5   **A Perceptual Map of Sports Car Brands, Product Attributes, and Stereotyped Car Owners**

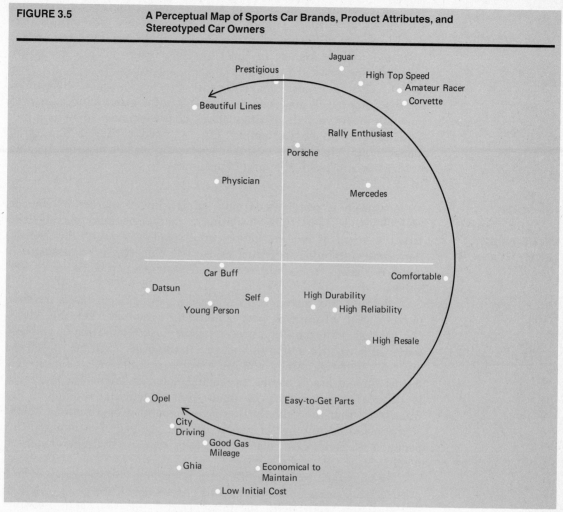

Source: Paul Green, "A Multidimensional Model of Product Features Association," *Journal of Business Research,* 2 (April 1974): 113. By permission.

costs do not always translate into easily predictable buying behavior. Sometimes consumers will tell a researcher how important a benefit is to them but when the time comes to spend their own money it is a different story.[8]

Segmentation Is No Panacea

Segmentation is not a cure-all that should be blindly followed by all companies.[9] In fact some costs may be increased by segmentation. For example, differentiated products mean fewer economies of scale and higher production costs. Greater variety often means greater product complexity and perhaps more "bugs." Different promotional strategies for various segments may mean higher promotional expenditures. If different distribution channels are required, these costs too will be higher. In short, nothing in life is free, including segmentation!

In addition to cost considerations, some markets may be too small to be segmented in an economical way. On the other hand, a market may not have enough distinguishing characteristics (demographic, benefits, etc.) to be segmented. Or, as noted earlier, a marketing manager may discover a basis for segmentation but may not be able to identify and reach the target consumers.[10]

PRODUCT DIFFERENTIATION AND MARKET SEGMENTATION

Segmentation is predicated upon subdividing a market by one or several criteria and then designing a marketing mix to reach the target segment. It is a market-oriented strategy. Product differentiation has a different conceptual basis. The objective is to distinguish one firm's goods from another's. The differences can be either real or superficial.

When Xerox introduced the plain-paper copier it had a number of very real advantages over electrostatic models. Yet the Xerox copiers were differentiated products; they use regular paper and dry toner and produce a sharper image. At the other extreme, bleaches, aspirin, regular gasolines, and some soaps are differentiated by trivial means such as brand names, packaging, color, or smell. The marketer is attempting to convince consumers that a particular product is different and that they should therefore demand it over similar items. If a substantial number of people can be persuaded to demand the product, the seller can usually raise its price above the general market level.

In summary, product differentiation begins with the product and asks, "How can we make this one different from all the rest?" Market segmentation begins with the total market and asks, "What are the characteristics of the overall market and how can it be divided into meaningful segments?"

THE RELATIONSHIP OF PRODUCT POSITIONING TO PRODUCT DIFFERENTIATION AND MARKET SEGMENTATION
Product Positioning and Repositioning

It's hard to find a marketing manager who can discuss new or old products without mentioning product positioning in the same breath. Product positioning is an important part of the marketing manager's vocabulary, yet if we asked a dozen marketers and students of marketing what the term means, we would get a dozen different answers.

Newton Frank, vice president of Data Development, says that positioning is the finding of a niche in the marketplace for a new product.[11] Positioning, for our purposes, refers to the way a consumer views a product or service in relation to all other products or services that the potential buyer perceives as possible substitutes.[12] The posi-

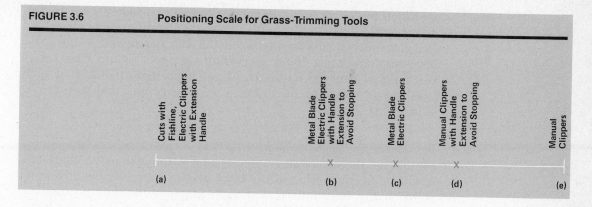

FIGURE 3.6   Positioning Scale for Grass-Trimming Tools

tioning concept may be perceived as a continuum. A simple example is shown in Figure 3.6 using various tools for trimming grass. The data were obtained from an actual research survey.

Given present technology, any "new" product would fall somewhere along the line shown in Figure 3.6. Notice that our example is not concerned with numerous product attributes, such as pricing, packaging, or promotion, that influence a product's image and, therefore, its position. We have simply asked consumers to "position" products on our scale on the basis of their view of the product.

Key characteristics that may have influenced the positioning of the grass-trimming tool are shown in Figure 3.7. Manual or battery

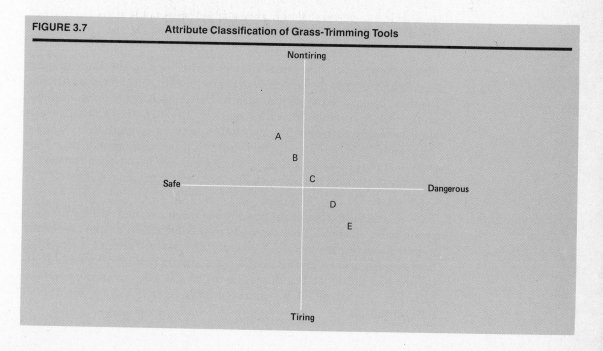

FIGURE 3.7   Attribute Classification of Grass-Trimming Tools

operation per se were not important product considerations; rather, it was convenience or lack of it that made the difference. Safety and fatigue potential are shown to be the key positioning criteria for lawn-trimming tools. Thus marketing managers should view safety and fatigue potential as the two most important attributes of such tools when they are designing a marketing mix and positioning strategy for them.

Positioning for the Same Market. Head-on positioning is becoming a popular marketing strategy after years of unpopularity. When two products are competing in the same perceptual space (i.e., the same point on the continuum), they are engaged in head-on positioning. Tylenol was positioned head-on against Datril, and Gillette put Earth Born shampoo directly against Clairol's Herbal Essence. Armour's Dial deodorant is competing in the same perceptual space as Procter and Gamble's Sure.

It is possible for a manufacturer to influence or change the positioning of a brand by manipulating various factors that affect a person's attitude toward the brand.[13] Through the right promotion the manufacturer can adjust the position of the brand in the mind of the consumer. One success story in this area is the repositioning of Johnson's Baby Shampoo from a product strictly for infants to one "gentle enough to use every day." Johnson's Baby Shampoo is now the world's best-selling shampoo. Similarly, Marlboro was just another lackluster cigarette until it was repositioned with a masculine, outdoor image. In 1976 it moved into the number one position in the filter tip market, a position long held by Winston.

Service Positioning. Services may be positioned in the same manner as products. This is known as service positioning. Avis positioned itself as the aggressive underdog in its battle with Hertz for dominance of the huge automobile rental market. In 1976 the Massachusetts state lottery positioned its new daily numbers game directly against "the mob."[14] The introductory lottery promotion noted that "our system is parimutuel betting, so our payoffs are better than the mob's; the profits go back to your city or town, not to organized crime."

Positioning and Product Differentiation

The relationship between positioning and product differentiation needs to be clarified. Positioning is psychological in nature; it results in certain attitudes toward a product or service. Product differentiation is a strategy to create distinctions among similar products. Positioning can influence the development of attitudes toward a product, and this is what enables a marketing manager to engage in product differentiation.

Cigarettes provide an excellent example of positioning for product differentiation. Eve is viewed as a very feminine cigarette because of its packaging, shape, and promotional themes. It is perceived as being on the other end of the continuum from Marlboro. Few men will smoke Eves, not because an Eve isn't a good smoke but because it is positioned as a feminine cigarette.

Market segmentation is based on differences among consumers. A product or service may be positioned differently to reach several market segments. Tonka Industries, a manufacturer of metal toys, may attempt to reach the parent segment by positioning a toy as durable, educational, and economical. To children the toy may be presented as authentic and fun. Coca-Cola follows a similar strategy. To young, single adults, Coke is presented as an ideal mixer. To teenagers, it is presented as a light beverage that adds life to snacks. These examples illustrate how positioning aids the marketing manager in effectively reaching and penetrating specific market segments.

SUMMARY

One of the major objectives of marketing managers is to identify and serve potential markets. A market consists of people and companies with both purchasing power and the desire or willingness to buy. A market is rarely a homogeneous mass of people. Instead, it typically consists of many subsegments consisting of individuals with different needs and wants. Market segmentation is the process of identifying and evaluating various strata of the market.

There are five basic forms of segmentation—demographic, geographic, psychographic, by benefit, and by volume. In order to effectively carry out one of these forms of segmentation, marketing managers must identify the level of demand associated with the various segments and then design a marketing mix to meet the needs of that segment. Creating a successful marketing mix is not easy. Sometimes segments can be identified yet cannot easily be reached through conventional media and distribution channels.

When a market has been segmented successfully, several strategic approaches are possible. One alternative is to have one product and one marketing mix for all segments. This is referred to as undifferentiated marketing. A second strategy is to have one product with several mixes for the relevant segments; this is called particularized marketing. Concentrated marketing involves one or few products and one mix for one segment. The final strategy, almost always used by large companies, is differentiated marketing. This consists of several products and several mixes aimed toward a number of different market segments.

Segmentation is not a cure-all. Differentiated marketing, for example, can mean fewer economies of scale and higher production costs because of greater product variety. Promotional costs may also rise owing to different promotional strategies for each stratum. Also, some segments may be so small that it is uneconomical to serve them.

Product differentiation has a different conceptual base than market segmentation, yet the two terms are often confused. Product differentiation is a product strategy by which marketing managers attempt to make their goods or services different from all others. Market segmentation begins with the marketplace and is concerned with subdividing the market into meaningful segments and then designing a marketing mix to serve those segments.

Another term that is often misunderstood by both students and businesspeople alike is product positioning. Positioning is a psychological concept that has to do with the way people view a product relative to products that are possible substitutes for it. Product differentiation can be created through product positioning. Since positioning is psychological, creating real or imaginary attributes about a product aids in differentiating that product from other almost identical products.

Market segmentation is based on differences among consumers. A product may be positioned in several different ways to meet the needs of several different market segments. McDonald's, for example, is positioned as a quick, nutritious lunch for working adults. It is also positioned as a fun place to eat, via Ronald McDonald and hamburgers with faces, for children.

KEY TERMS

Consumer market
Industrial market
Substitute goods
Complementary goods
Market segmentation
Undifferentiated marketing
Particularized marketing
Concentrated marketing

Differentiated marketing
Benefit segmentation
Perceptual mapping
Product differentiation
Product positioning
Head-on positioning
Service positioning

QUESTIONS FOR DISCUSSION

1. What is a market? What conditions are necessary for a market to exist?
2. Explain the terms *substitute goods* and *complementary goods*. How do they affect the scope of a market?
3. What is market segmentation? Discuss the basic characteristics by which a market is segmented.
4. How is segmentation useful to marketing managers? Discuss the various strategies used to reach different target markets.
5. What is perceptual mapping? How is it related to benefit segmentation?
6. What is product differentiation? Use examples to show how it differs from market segmentation.
7. Discuss the concept of product positioning and repositioning. Why is it an important element of overall marketing strategy? How is a product positioned?

8. Discuss the relationship between market segmentation, product differentiation, and product positioning. Give examples to illustrate your answer.
9. What criteria are necessary for successful segmentation?
10. What are the problems associated with market segmentation? Can it be used at all times? If not, explain situations in which segmentation may not be desirable or feasible.

NOTES

1. John McCann, "Market Segment Response to the Marketing Decision Variables," *Journal of Marketing Research,* 11 (November 1974): 409. Reprinted by permission of the American Marketing Association.
2. C. Waldo, "What's Bothering Marketing Chaps Most? Segmenting," *Advertising Age,* June 4, 1973, p. 77.
3. Henry Assael and A. Marvin Roscoe, Jr., "Approaches to Market Segmentation Analysis," *Journal of Marketing,* 40 (October 1976): 67–76.
4. "Miller's Growth Upsets the Beer Industry," *Business Week,* November 8, 1976, pp. 58–62. Reprinted by permission.
5. Russel Haley, "Benefit Segmentation: A Decision-Oriented Research Tool," *Journal of Marketing,* 32 (July 1968): 30–35.
6. See Ronald E. Frank, "Market Segmentation Research: Findings and Implications," in Frank M. Bass, Charles W. King, and Edgar A. Pessemier, eds., *Applications of the Sciences in Marketing Management* (New York: Wiley, 1968), pp. 39–68; Donald G. Morrison, "Evaluating Market Segmentation Studies: The Properties of R^2," *Management Science,* 19 (July 1973): 1213–1221; James H. Myers and Mark I. Alpert, "Determining Buying Attitudes: Meaning and Measurement," *Journal of Marketing,* 32 (October 1968): 13–20; David Klahr, "A Study of Consumers' Cognitive Structure for Cigarette Brands," *Journal of Business,* 43 (April 1970): 19–20; Roger N. Shepard, A. Kimball Romney, and Sara Beth Nerlove, eds., *Multi-dimensional Scaling: Theory* (New York: Seminar Press, 1972); Paul E. Green and Frank J. Carmone, *Multidimensional Scaling and Related Techniques in Marketing Analysis* (Boston: Allyn and Bacon, 1970); Paul E. Green and Vithala R. Rao, *Applied Multidimensional Scaling* (New York: Holt, Rinehart and Winston, 1972); Robert Blattberg and Subrata Sen, "Market Segmentation Using Models of Multidimensional Purchasing Behavior," *Journal of Marketing,* 38 (October 1974): 17–28; Ronald E. Frank, William F. Massy, and Yoram Wind, *Market Segmentation* (Englewood Cliffs, N.J.: Prentice-Hall, 1972), pp. 133–134; V. Parker Lessig and John O. Tollefson, "Market Segmentation Through Numerical Taxonomy," *Journal of Marketing Research,* 8 (November 1971): 480–487; Donald E. Sexton, Jr., "A Cluster Analytic Approach to Market Response Functions," *Journal of Marketing Research,* 11 (February 1974): 109–114; and W. Thomas Anderson, Jr., Eli Cox, and David Fulcher, "Bank Selection Decisions and Market Segmentation," *Journal of Marketing,* 40 (January 1976): 40–45.

   To learn how segmentation can be applied to retailing, see A. Coskun Samli, "Use of Segmentation Index to Measure Store Loyalty," *Journal of Retailing,* 51 (Spring 1975): 51–60, and David Appel, "Market Segmentation—A Response to Retail Innovation," *Journal of Marketing,* 34 (April 1970): 64–66.

7. Paul Green, "A Multidimensional Model of Product-Features Association," *Journal of Business Research,* 2 (April 1974): 107–118. See also Robert Krampf and John Daniel Williams, "Multidimensional Scaling as a Research Tool: An Explanation and Application," *Journal of Business Research,* 2 (April 1974): 157–176, and Richard Johnson, "Market Segmentation: A Strategic Management Tool," *Journal of Marketing Research,* 8 (February 1971): 13–19.

8. For an excellent summary of the advantages and disadvantages of perceptual mapping see Nariman Dhalla and Winston Mahatoo, "Expanding the Scope of Segmentation Research," *Journal of Marketing,* 40 (April 1976): 34–41.

9. See "Segmentation Both Good and Bad for Marketers, Prof. Levitt Explains," *Advertising Age,* April 12, 1976, p. 12.

10. Phil Levine, "Locating Your Customers in a Segmented Market," *Journal of Marketing,* 39 (October 1975): 72–73, and B. Stuart Folley, "Identifying Users Through a Segmentation Study," *Journal of Marketing,* 39 (April 1975): 69–71.

11. "Determine Appeal of Concept, Positioning, Use Several Measures," *Marketing News,* April 23, 1976, p. 8.

12. For further reading see John P. Maggard, "Positioning Revisited," *Journal of Marketing,* 40 (January 1976): 63–66; see also John H. Holmes, "Profitable Product Positioning," *MSU Business Topics,* Spring 1973, pp. 27–32.

13. Maggard, p. 64.

14. "Massachusetts Lottery Is Positioned vs. 'The Mob,'" *Advertising Age,* May 3, 1976, p. 3.

CASE 3
North Star Service

Two months ago the president and major stockholder of North State Bank of Bangor, Maine, retired and sold his majority interest to Carl McNutt. The bank is located in the downtown business district and has been in the same location for twenty years. There are four other banks in town; two are in the downtown area. City Bank is the only bank larger than North State, with deposits of $75 million compared to North State's $60 million.

As the new president, McNutt has decided to introduce a special service account called North Star Service in order to attract new accounts and increase bank usage by old customers. This idea has been successfully used in other cities, and McNutt hopes that it will improve the bank's image and establish it as a leader in the community.

For a flat fee of $3.00 per month the following seven services will be available to the customer:

1. Unlimited checking
2. Personalized checks
3. 24-hour banking
4. Master Charge
5. Overdraft protection
6. Safety deposit box
7. No-fee traveler's checks

In conjunction with this new service McNutt wants to introduce a new bank logo.

To supervise the bank's promotional activities McNutt has hired George Hopkins, formerly director of marketing for a New York City bank, as vice president of marketing. In their discussion of the promotion campaign, McNutt expressed concern about what he termed a "conservative New England" attitude on the part of the citizens of the town. After much consideration it was decided that a letter will be mailed along with the Star Service information explaining the bank's new logo and image.

1. Hopkins has been asked to write the letter. What message should he try to communicate? Should the message be different for old accounts than for prospective new accounts? If so, what should the differences be?
2. Suggest several ways in which North State's market can be segmented.

4

Segmenting the American Market: Demographic and Psychographic Dimensions

OBJECTIVES

■ To understand population trends.
■ To learn about other demographic variables that can be used to segment markets.
■ To gain insight into life style segmentation.

Chapter 3 described several different ways of segmenting a market. Historically, segmentation has generally been based on demographic characteristics. Even today most segmentation involves demographic factors such as age or sex. Perhaps the area of segmentation that has received the most attention in the late 1970s is psychographic or life style segmentation. The idea is to market to groups of individuals who do the same things, have the same goals, share common attitudes and problems, or behave in similar ways. A "swinging single" today can be 18 to 40 years old (or older) but may still purchase many of the same products for the "mating game."

This chapter begins with an examination of America's population and how its composition is changing. You will learn about the young and the old, various racial groups, and population migrations. The chapter concludes with a look at contemporary life styles in America.

TABLE 4.1   Population Estimates, 1950–2000

Estimates				Projections			
Population		Percent Change		Population		Percent Change	
1950	152,271	1950–1955	+9.0	1975	213,641	1970–1975	+4.3
1955	165,931	1955–1960	+8.9	1980	225,705	1975–1980	+5.6
1960	180,671	1960–1965	+7.5	1985	211,274	1980–1985	+6.9
1965	194,303	1965–1970	+5.4	1990	257,663	1985–1990	+6.8
1970	204,879			1995	272,685	1990–1995	+5.8
1974	211,909			2000	287,007	1995–2000	+5.3

Source: Population Estimates and Projections (Washington, D.C.: U.S. Bureau of the Census, October 1975), p. 8.

TRENDS IN THE AMERICAN POPULATION
Total Population

The basis for any mass market is people. America's population was approximately 214 million in 1974.[1] By the year 2000 there should be 287 million consumers in our country (see Table 4.1).[2] While this may be heartening to some marketers, it doesn't tell the entire story. Take a close look at Table 4.1. Notice that the percentage increase in population has been falling since 1950. It is expected to rise slightly until 1985 and then to begin falling again.

We are fast moving toward zero population growth (ZPG). This means that the average woman of childbearing age is expected to bear fewer than 2.1 children during her lifetime, and this will not produce the two children required to replace herself and her husband, given the fact that some children die before reaching adolescence.[3]

Population Age Mix

As total population growth slows, some age categories will continue to increase in size. (See Figure 4.1.) In other words, the population age mix will change. A large number of women will reach their prime childbearing years by 1985, causing a dramatic increase in the number of children born. This is good news to marketing managers who cater to the infant segment of the population. Vincent Baraba, former director of the Census Bureau, says that parents spend about $700 to "tool up" for their first child.[4]

Alabe Products has segmented the baby market twelve ways. It has designed twelve different toys for tots between the ages of 3 months and one year. The toys are meant to be used sequentially as a baby grows. The first toy, called Crib Jiminy, is for the stage in which babies begin reaching for things. Next comes Talky Rattle Teether, a toy that infants can grasp. Alabe hopes, of course, that parents will ultimately purchase all twelve toys.[5]

America Grows Up

As the children born during the post-World War II "baby boom" get older, the largest single market will shift from teenagers to people in their late twenties. The average age in 1985 will be 32 years.[6] Unlike

FIGURE 4.1   **A Look-Ahead at the U.S. Population, 1975–1985**

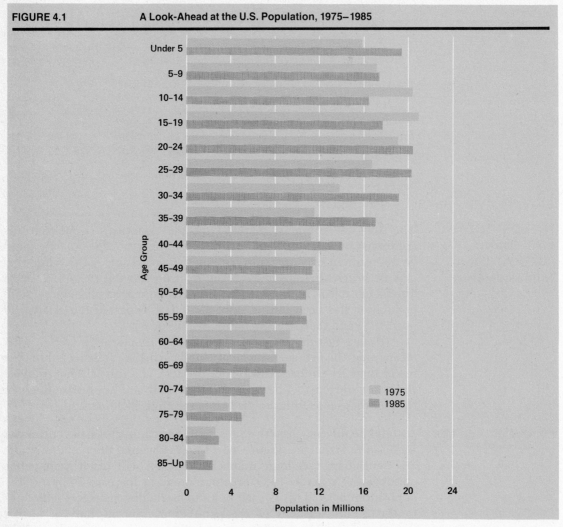

the huge teenage market of the 1960s and early 1970s, the mass market of the 1980s will consist of more mature, self-confident consumers. Phyllis Sewell, vice president of Federated Department Stores, says that her company

> will be going into greater specialization within the store, with more different departments. We will be concentrating more on the fashion business and on utilitarian goods, and deemphasizing hardware and major appliances. Now, we stress the teenager and the young 20s. In 1985 it will be people in their 30s, with different needs.[7]

To the U.S. Forest Service, this older population means a decreasing emphasis on skiing and hunting. Half of all waterfowl hunters are under 25 years old, and two-thirds are under 35.[8] Pepsico believes that soft-drink demand will flatten as the teenage population decreases, but demand for diet drinks and citrus-flavored mixers will increase.[9]

The Elderly Market

A second major population group that continues to grow at a remarkable rate is older people. There are now 42 million people over 55 years old.[10] This figure will continue to grow through the end of this century and the early part of the next century. The general rise in the number of births in the twentieth century largely accounts for the rapid increase in the number of elderly people. Moreover, as medical care continues to improve, the life span of the average American rises.

Elderly consumers are a special market. They require more medical attention and purchase many leisure-related products. The travel, entertainment, and recreation industries will be major beneficiaries of the growth of this market, and the demand for retirement homes should also increase. Many older people have relatively low current incomes but large amounts of acquired assets. Thus buying a home for retirement isn't a problem for many retirees.

Some marketers have recognized the growing demand for goods and services by the elderly and are actively pursuing this market. Discount programs for senior citizens are becoming common throughout the nation. The most widespread plan on a national basis is offered by the American Association of Retired Persons. You must be 55 years old to join, and you pay a $3.00 annual fee. In return the member receives discounts at eight nationwide hotel and motel chains and two rent-a-car companies, Avis and Hertz. The group's other programs include a pharmacy service providing home delivery of prescription drugs and other medical items at low cost.[11]

Population Concentrations in the United States

From the young to the very old, America is a nation on the move. But before we study migration patterns let's examine the current population structure. Table 4.2 lists the top forty-two standard metropolitan statistical areas (SMSAs) in the United States. An SMSA is a city or group of cities with a population of at least 50,000. The SMSA includes the county containing the city or cities and contiguous counties that are economically and socially integrated into the primary county. In 1970 there were 243 SMSAs containing about 69 percent of the nation's population.

SMSAs are essentially integrated trade areas. They were developed in order to more closely approximate the purchasing power and life styles of a geographic area. In an SMSA a central city, such as Chicago, is surrounded by a myriad of bedroom communities that are still part of the greater Chicago market.

TABLE 4.2   The Top Forty-Two SMSAs

| 42 Top Markets are Based on 1975 Census Bureau Figures, and Ranked Accordingly | 000 Omitted | | |
| | Population 1/1/76 | Disposable Personal Income | Total Retail Sales | Per Household Income: 1976 |
Rank Standard Metropolitan Statistical Area				
1. New York, N.Y.	9,670.0	$59,045,129	$23,322,578	$16,389
2. Chicago, Ill.	6,927.8	41,794,081	21,769,920	18,017
3. Los Angeles–Long Beach, Cal.	7,190.5	38,041,515	21,697,191	14,227
4. Philadelphia, Pa.	4,723.1	25,995,327	13,526,290	16,216
5. Detroit, Mich.	4,436.1	24,376,162	12,591,653	17,098
6. Boston–Lowell–Brockton–Lawrence, Mass.	3,912.6	21,530,652	11,459,515	16,595
7. San Francisco–Oakland, Cal.	3,143.3	20,388,254	10,056,313	17,294
8. Washington, D.C., Md., Va.	2,968.6	23,478,895	9,753,700	23,602
9. Nassau–Suffolk, N.Y.	2,699.2	18,748,699	8,602,830	23,542
10. Dallas–Fort Worth, Tex.	2,496.1	13,469,031	7,768,326	15,876
11. St. Louis, Mo.	2,355.8	12,250.087	7,379,382	15,676
12. Pittsburgh, Pa.	2,324.1	12,366,766	6,521,604	15,676
13. Houston, Tex.	2,280.9	12,581,554	8,709,403	16,780
14. Baltimore, Md.	2,135.4	8,549,621	5,839,383	12,334
15. Minneapolis–St. Paul, Minn.	1,959.4	11,337,638	5,914,581	17,841
16. Newark, N.J.	2,034.7	11,555,738	5,579,600	16,979
17. Cleveland, O.	1,970.9	10,380,071	5,646,278	15,668
18. Atlanta, Ga.	1,775.9	8,675,893	5,570,034	14,966
19. Anaheim–Santa Ana–Garden Grove, Cal.	1,711.1	10,275,917	5,383,056	18,301
20. San Diego, Cal.	1,571.2	8,244,262	4,508,566	15,147
21. Miami, Fla.	1,456.0	7,529,614	4,899,329	14,269
22. Milwaukee, Wis.	1,403.2	7,807,420	4,042,470	16,888
23. Seattle–Everett, Wash.	1,377.1	7,694,631	4,921,462	15,665
24. Denver–Boulder, Colo.	1,420.1	7,485,914	4,450,288	15,541
25. Cincinnati, O.	1,362.0	8,089,981	3,804,134	17,800
26. Tampa–St. Petersburg, Fla.	1,416.4	6,533,518	3,952,928	11,613
27. Buffalo, N.Y.	1,323.1	5,850,737	3,300,027	13,285
28. Kansas City, Mo.	1,287.2	6,900,033	3,701,416	15,848
29. Riverside–San Bernardino–Ontario, Cal.	1,231.7	6,177,107	3,434,343	14,593
30. Phoenix, Ariz.	1,239.2	5,776,876	3,692,741	13,867
31. San Jose, Cal.	1,180.7	7,174,594	3,739,593	18,597
32. Indianapolis, Ind.	1,136.8	6,068,194	4,263,002	15,898
33. New Orleans, La.	1,093.9	5,554,237	3,040,779	15,681
34. Portland, Ore.	1,092.2	5,841,590	3,390,386	14,883
35. Columbus, O.	1,055.0	5,801,508	3,179,555	16,440
36. Hartford, Conn.	1,050.3	6,082,739	3,015,522	17,439
37. San Antonio, Tex.	986.7	3,702,699	2,326,855	12,136
38. Rochester, N.Y.	977.3	5,153,347	2,814,033	15,974
39. Louisville, Ky.	882.2	4,091,688	2,429,042	14,017
40. Sacramento, Cal.	893.4	6,465,900	2,759,502	21,096
41. Memphis, Tenn.	819.7	4,009,227	2,454,748	15,600
42. Fort Lauderdale–Hollywood, Fla.	863.4	4,867,238	3,296,863	14,700

Source: Alfred Hony, "Big Sunbelt Markets Lead Growth," Advertising Age, December 13, 1976, p. 1. Copyright 1976 by Crain Communications, Inc. Reprinted by permission.

**America on
the Move**

Some SMSAs are losing large numbers of consumers while others are
growing by leaps and bounds. Since 1970 the population of the booming South and Southwest (the sunbelt) has grown six times as fast as
that of the Great Lakes regions and ten times as fast as that of the
combined Mideast and New England regions.[12] (See Figure 4.2.)

During the 1960s the major movements were of middle-class
whites to the South and low-income blacks to the North.[13] The flows
were approximately equal in each direction, with the South experi-
encing only a small increase. Since 1970, however, dramatic increases
in economic activity have brought the outflow of people from the

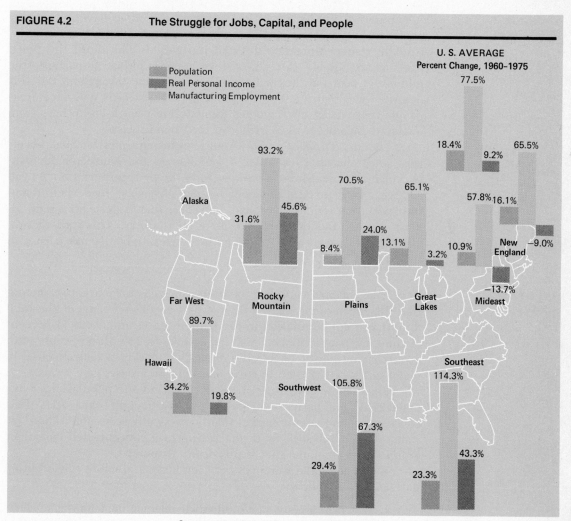

FIGURE 4.2   The Struggle for Jobs, Capital, and People

South and Southwest to a virtual halt and accelerated the flow of people into those regions.

Migration tends to shift income concentrations, and this creates new markets and destroys old ones. As new markets develop, retailers pour in to serve the region. Manufacturing also follows population flows, creating more new jobs and further stimulating immigration. A rapidly expanding tax base (i.e., what is being taxed—incomes, sales, property value) often means that tax rates can be stabilized, making the area even more attractive. The reverse is true in areas that are losing population.

The Role of Money

A population, regardless of its concentration, must have purchasing power to be attractive to the marketer. Americans' incomes are continually rising. More families and individuals can afford the "good life" as disposable (after-tax) incomes rise. Most important, the number of poor families will continue to decline throughout the next decade. (See Figure 4.3.) New consumption patterns will develop as people move from low incomes to moderate wealth and others from moderate incomes to even higher socioeconomic classes.

The largest portion of an American income goes for food, beverages, and tobacco. (See Table 4.3.) Housing and household furnishings claim the next-largest outlays, followed by transportation. As you can see, a large amount of money is spent on basics—food, shelter, and transportation. Did you realize, however, that Americans spend almost as much money on recreation as on clothing? This statistic provides a brief preview of American life styles, to be discussed later in the chapter.

Segmentation by Race

Race, like income, can often be used as a basis for market segmentation. Blacks account for the largest portion (92 percent) of the total minority-group population in the United States and about 11 percent of the total population.[14] This translates into 23 million people with a purchasing power of $33 billion.[15] This market is concentrated in major cities rather than in rural or suburban areas.

Blacks now constitute more than half of the population of five major cities and between 40 and 50 percent in eight other cities. This concentration creates a market that is physically accessible. There are some obvious advantages to marketing to a concentrated consumer group rather than one that is physically dispersed.

A few general differences between black and white consumption patterns are as follows:

- Black families purchase substantially more of the following products than white: cooked cereals, corn meal, cream, rice, spaghetti, frozen vegetables, syrup, vinegar and others.

FIGURE 4.3   Families and Income, by Income Class (Total families, Income, Each Year = 100%; Based on 1974 Dollars)

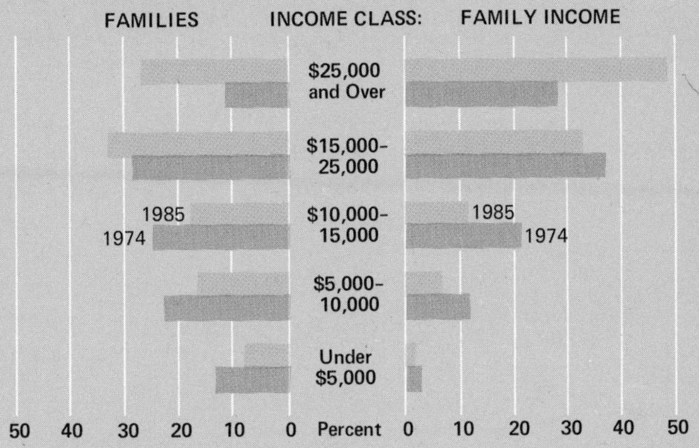

Projections of Families and Income by Income Class
(Percent Distribution, Based on 1974 Dollars)

Income Class	1974	1980	1985
Families (Millions)	55.7	61.3	66.3
Families (Percent)	100.0	100.0	100.0
Under $3,000	5.0	4.0	3.0
$3,000–5,000	7.5	5.5	4.5
5,000–7,000	9.0	7.0	6.0
7,000–10,000	14.0	11.0	10.0
10,000–15,000	24.5	20.00	17.5
15,000–25,000	28.5	32.0	32.5
25,000 and over	11.5	20.5	26.5
Income (Percent)	100.0	100.01	100.0
Under $3,000	.5	.5	.5
$3,000–5,000	2.0	1.0	1.5
5,000–7,000	3.5	2.5	2.0
7,000–10,000	8.0	5.5	4.5
10,000–15,000	21.00	14.0	11.0
15,000–25,000	37.0	35.0	32.5
25,000 and over	28.0	41.5	48.5

Source: A Guide to Consumer Markets 1975/1976 (New York: Conference Board, 1975), p. 117.

- The average black male buys 77 percent more pairs of shoes during his lifetime than the average white male and pays more for them than his white counterpart.
- Depending on the study read, blacks purchase more Scotch than any other market segment with one report stating the figure to be one-half of the total Scotch consumption.

TABLE 4.3

Patterns of Consumer Spending (Billions of Dollars)

Type of Product	1960	1970	1974 Amount	1974 Percent
Total consumption expenditures	324.9	618.8	885.9	100.0
Food, beverages, tobacco	88.0	147.1	203.1	22.9
Food for home consumption	61.6	102.0	141.5	16.0
Purchased meals, beverages	17.2	31.5	44.3	5.0
Food (excl. alcoholic beverages)	70.5	118.6	166.4	18.8
Alcoholic beverages	10.6	17.7	22.9	2.6
Tobacco	6.9	10.8	13.8	1.6
Clothing, accessories, jewelry	32.2	55.6	76.4	8.6
Women's, children's clothing	14.4	25.1	35.8	4.0
Men's, boys' clothing	7.7	13.6	19.2	2.2
Jewelry, watches	1.9	4.1	5.8	.7
Shoes, other footwear	4.5	7.7	10.2	1.1
Clothing services	3.6	4.9	5.3	.6
Personal care	5.2	10.9	13.4	1.5
Toilet articles, preparations	2.9	6.9	9.2	1.0
Personal care services	2.3	4.0	4.2	.5
Housing	48.1	94.0	136.0	15.3
Household operations and furnishings	46.1	87.8	130.5	14.7
Furniture, bedding	4.6	8.2	12.0	1.4
Household appliances	4.2	6.9	10.0	1.1
Other housefurnishings	8.5	18.4	27.9	3.2
Household supplies	3.7	8.6	12.0	1.4
Household utilities, telephone, telegraph	18.0	33.9	53.5	6.0
Medical care	20.0	49.9	75.8	8.6
Drugs, supplies, equipment	4.6	8.4	10.7	1.2
Medical care services	15.4	41.5	65.1	7.4
Personal business	14.2	31.3	44.5	5.0
Transportation	42.4	78.0	115.3	13.0
User-operated transportation	39.1	72.5	108.0	12.2
Automobile purchase	17.2	30.3	41.0	4.6
Gasoline, oil	12.0	22.0	36.4	4.1
Tires, accessories, repairs, etc.	7.6	15.8	24.7	2.8
Public transportation	3.3	5.5	7.4	.8
Recreation	17.9	41.0	60.5	6.8
Radio, TV, records, musical instruments	3.0	8.9	13.3	1.5
Toys, sporting goods	4.5	11.0	16.8	1.9
Books, magazines, newspapers	3.3	6.3	10.1	11.4
Paid admissions, spectator amusements	1.7	3.1	4.0	.5
Private education, research	3.7	9.9	13.5	1.5
Religious, welfare activities	4.9	8.5	11.7	1.3
Foreign travel and other, net	2.1	4.7	5.1	.6

Source: U.S. Bureau of the Census, *Statistical Abstract of the United States, 1976* (Washington, D.C., 1976), p. 396.

- Other products consumed more by blacks than by whites include floor waxes, household insecticides, toilet and laundry soap, and so on.
- Peter Bennett and Harold Kassarjian noted that whites spend more than blacks of similar income for such products as food, housing, medical care, auto transportation and insurance while blacks spend more for such products as clothing and home furnishings, while saving more. The spending for recreation and leisure of blacks and whites of similar incomes is mixed.[16]

You might say that these differences may be due to income variations, since the median black family income is 64 percent of the median white family income. A quick examination of Table 4.4 should dispel this notion, however.[17] Although only a small portion of the study is

TABLE 4.4	Percentage of Negroes and Whites Who Had Recently Purchased or Who Owned Various Household Products		
		$8000 or More	
Products		Whites	Negroes
Food products			
Butter		14.1	45.4
Margarine		69.5	81.8
Frozen vegetables		47.1	54.6
Canned vegetables		40.6	43.2
Dietary soft drinks		25.5	13.6
Nondietary soft drinks		67.1	45.4
Liquor			
All respondents		56.5	54.6
Scotch		19.7	27.3
Bourbon		40.9	40.9
Personal hygiene products			
Shampoo		72.6	50.0
Deodorant		76.6	81.8
Toothpaste		89.1	86.4
Mouthwash		63.5	86.4
Disinfectants		68.6	86.4
Home appliances			
Automatic washing machine		85.5	72.7
Automatic clothes dryer		54.9	27.3
Automatic dishwasher		33.8	—
B&W television		—	—
Color television		—	—
Home ownership			
Own home		81.5	77.3

Source: James Stafford, Keith Cox, and James Higginbotham, "Some Consumption Pattern Differences Between Urban Whites and Negroes," *Social Sciences Quarterly,* 49 (December 1968): 627. Reprinted by permission of the University of Texas Press, Publisher.

reproduced, certain differences are obvious.[18] In addition, it should be noted that there are many subsegments within the black population itself.

PSYCHOGRAPHIC/ LIFE STYLE SEGMENTATION Some Definitions

Race, income, occupation, and other demographic variables are usually helpful in developing segmentation strategies but often do not paint the entire picture. Demographics provide the skeleton, but psychographics add meat to the bones. Psychographics refers to the development of psychological profiles of consumers and psychologically based measures (types) of life styles. Life styles are distinctive modes of living of a whole society or any of its segments.

The Value of Life Style Segmentation

The value of life style segmentation can best be illustrated by the following example. Heavy users of shotgun ammunition tend to be younger, lower in income and education, and concentrated in blue-collar occupations.[19] They are likely to reside in the South and to be from a rural area. Certainly this is helpful to any manufacturer of shotguns and ammunition, but is it enough?

Table 4.5, a psychographic study of the heavy ammunition buyer, reveals many additional facts. Hunting is not an isolated pastime but is associated with other outdoor sports and activities. Thus joint promotion might be possible between camping gear and ammunition manufacturers. Since the heavy ammunition buyer probably enjoys fishing as well, the two products might be stocked close together in a retail store. The ammunition purchasers are likely to be do-it-yourselfers, suggesting that shells might sell where hardware and tools are sold. Since the heavy buyers are not strongly opposed to violence on television, detective stories, westerns, and war programs should reach the "right" market. Finally, this group's heavy newspaper readership may serve as a warning to ammunition manufacturers not to switch from this medium without good reason.

Life Style Dimensions

Several dimensions of life style are shown in Table 4.6. These dimensions can be further subdivided into a number of different styles for each dimension. For example, the recreation dimension can be divided into indoor versus outdoor, participant versus observer, and so forth.

Benefits of Life Style Segmentation

Life style segmentation begins with people and then categorizes them in such a way as to provide a broad, realistic, and lifelike view of the consumer—a user profile. The life style data can be used to position a product on the basis of the user profile that is developed. In other words, the advertiser can show potential buyers how the product "fits" into their lives. An advertiser can learn what "tone of voice" should be used in advertising. Should it be serious or humorous,

Base	Percent Who Spend $11+ per Year on Shotgun Ammunition (141)	Percent Who Don't Buy (395)
I like hunting	88	7
I like fishing	68	26
I like to go camping	57	21
I love the out-of-doors	90	65
A cabin by a quiet lake is a great place to spend the summer	49	34
I like to work outdoors	67	40
I am good at fixing mechanical things	47	27
I often do a lot of repair work on my own car	36	12
I like war stories	50	32
I would do better than average in a fist fight	38	16
I would like to be a professional football player	28	18
I would like to be a policeman	22	8
There is too much violence on television	35	45
There should be a gun in every home	56	10
I like danger	19	8
I would like to own my own airplane	35	13
I like to play poker	50	26
I smoke too much	39	24
I love to eat	49	34
I spend money on myself that I should spend on the family	44	26
If given a chance, most men would cheat on their wives	33	14
I read the newspaper every day	51	72

Source: William Wells, "Psychographics: A Critical Review," *Journal of Marketing Research,* 12 (May 1975): 198. Reprinted by permission of the American Marketing Association.

TABLE 4.6   Life Style Dimensions

Activities	Interests	Opinions
Work	Family	Themselves
Hobbies	Home	Social issues
Social events	Job	Politics
Vacation	Community	Business
Entertainment	Recreation	Economics
Club membership	Fashion	Education
Community	Food	Products
Shopping	Media	Future
Sports	Achievements	Culture

Source: Joseph Plummer, "The Concept and Application of Life Style Segmentation," *Journal of Marketing,* 38 (January 1974): 34. Reprinted by permission of the American Marketing Association.

authoritative or cooperative, upbeat or traditional? Life style segmentation can also help marketers understand what rewards people are seeking in their activities and interests. In turn, this may suggest new-product opportunities.[20]

It should be pointed out, however, that demographic variables are almost always essential to a consumer goods market segmentation program. Assume that a psychographic profile reveals a certain attitude and that a marketer wishes to capitalize on that attitude through promotion. The attitude must be associated with a specific set of demographic statistics to enable the marketing manager to find the right media to reach that particular market segment.

How Life Styles Relate to Social Class

A person's social class is his or her status rank within society. A number of different techniques and criteria have been developed for measuring and defining social class. Some of the more popular rankings are shown in Table 4.7. Depending on whose scheme one is using, the portion of the population in any given rank can vary substantially. For instance, the number of people in the upper class varies from 0.4 percent (Carman) to 10.5 percent (Mathews and Slocum).

Each social class has a number of separate life styles, although individual life styles exhibit greater differences between the social classes than within a given class. The most critical separation between the classes is the one between the middle class and the lower class. It is here that the major shift in life styles appears.

William Wells, a noted marketing scholar, explains the interrelationships of life styles as follows:

> The lower class person typically prefers discipline, structure, order, and directive leadership. He is family-centered with an extended family having many cooperative relationships. He is person-centered;

TABLE 4.7   Social Class Distribution Percentages

Level	Carman[a]	McCann	Warner	Mathews & Slocum	Rich & Jain	Hollings-head[b]
I Upper	0.4%	3.0%	0.9%	10.5%	4.2%	3.0%
II U-Middle	10.8	12.0	7.3	20.6	23.6	8.0
III Middle	30.8	29.5	28.7	27.5	37.2	22.0
IV L-Middle	50.0	34.1	43.4	35.3	13.6	46.0
V Lower	8.0	21.4	19.7	6.1	21.4	18.0

Source: William Wells, *Life Style and Psychographics* (Chicago: American Marketing Association, 1974), p. 241. Reprinted by permission of the American Marketing Association.
[a] Carman's classes are referred to as: Upper; U-Middle; L-Middle; U-Lower; L-Lower.
[b] Hollingshead's distribution allows for 3% unknown.

he sees the locus of cause for events and actions in persons rather than in events and the environment.

A basic characteristic of his life is an orientation toward security. This derives from an occupational requirement that allows little room for anything but following directives of others. The important thing then becomes adopting a "low profile" and building up seniority so as to gain job protection in an industrial society in which he is considered to be an object rather than a person. Obviously, then, this results in "getting by" rather than "getting ahead"—the latter being characteristic of the middle class. Therefore, while interested in a good standard of living, the lower or working class person is not attracted to the middle class life style with concern for status and prestige.

. . .

Manipulating one's life style so as to gain status and prestige is basically a phenomenon of the middle classes. This involves a more outward orientation toward society in general, and one's peers in particular, than is true of the lower classes. It presupposes that a person has some particular goal to attain. This can be likened to a "becoming process," although not perhaps in the healthiest sense of the word. It does seem as if the middle class life style is more dynamic and changing as opposed to the more static life style of the lower class.

Upper social class individuals also seem more likely to think of themselves as "nice looking people" and to be more confident of their own abilities. All of the findings in this paragraph would seem to support the contentions of earlier writers on social class. Apparently, people of upper social class are more confident, outgoing, culturally oriented, and concerned with their own personal vanity than are people of just high income alone. They also seem to be a bit more "permissive" than higher income people, in the sense of being willing to tolerate all the protests that are going on. . . .

It appears that the upper social classes are more likely to try to contribute something to society, in the sense of writing something that has been published, doing volunteer work for charitable organizations, and taking an active part in local civic issues. On the other hand, they seem to have less interest in the home in general, and in children in particular, than do the upper income (and corresponding lower class) individuals.[21]

How Life Styles Are Influenced by the Life Cycle

I said earlier that life styles are distinctive modes of living. The life cycle, on the other hand, describes the ways in which attitudes, and behavioral tendencies, change over time.[22] These changes occur because of developing maturity, experience, income, and status. Everyone must go through the life cycle.

Life styles can be strongly influenced by age-related stages of the life cycle. Teenage life styles are quite different from those of middle-aged people, who, in turn, have life styles that are different from those of the elderly.

TABLE 4.8   An Overview of the Life Cycle

Bachelor Stage; Young Single People Not Living at Home	Newly Married Couples; Young, No Children	Full Nest I, Youngest Child Under Six	Full Nest II; Youngest Child Six or Over Six	Full Nest III; Older Married Couples with Dependent Children
Few financial burdens. Fashion opinion leaders. Recreation-oriented. Buy: Basic kitchen equipment, basic furniture, cars, equipment for the mating game, vacations.	Better off financially than they will be in near future. Highest purchase rate and highest average purchase of durables. Buy: Cars, refrigerators, stoves, sensible and durable furniture, vacations.	Home purchasing at peak. Liquid assets low. Dissatisfied with financial position and amount of money saved. Interested in new products. Like advertised products. Buy: Washers, dryers, TV, baby food, chest rubs and cough medicine, vitamins, dolls, wagons, sleds, skates.	Financial position better. Some wives work. Less influenced by advertising. Buy larger sized packages, multiple-unit deals. Buy: Many foods, cleaning materials, bicycles, music lessons, pianos.	Financial position still better. More wives work. Some children get jobs. Hard to influence with advertising. High average purchase of durables. Buy: New, more tasteful furniture, auto travel, unnecessary appliances, boats, dental services, magazines.

Most people pass through an orderly series of stages in life, as shown in Table 4.8. As you read through the data it should be easy to see how firms can use the life cycle concept as a basis for segmentation.

The general concept of the life cycle is family oriented and, thus, will require modification when applied to single adults. Also, a person may not always move forward through the cycle. Divorce or the death of a spouse can result in life styles quite similar to those of the bachelor stage, while a bachelor who happens to marry a divorcee might skip all the way over to "full nest" II or III.

Many students are in the bachelor stage of the life cycle. Purchases are oriented toward the mating game at this stage in life. Women buy nice-looking clothes, perfumes, and jewelry. Many men purchase "macho" cars, elaborate stereo systems, and other amenities for a bachelor pad. Marriage (stage two) changes all this (as many of you well know). Purchase decisions are often made jointly and are more family oriented. The young family may acquire its first home,

Empty Nest I; Older Married Couples, No Children Living with Them, Head in Labor Force	Empty Nest II; Older Married Couples, No Children Living at Home, Head Retired	Solitary Survivor, in Labor Force	Solitary Survivor, Retired
Home ownership at peak. Most satisfied with financial position and money saved. Interested in travel, recreation, self-education. Make gifts and contributions. Not interested in new products. Buy: Vacations, luxuries, home improvements.	Drastic cut in income. Keep home. Buy: Medical appliances, medical care, products which aid health, sleep, and digestion.	Income still good but likely to sell home.	Same medical and product needs as other retired group; drastic cut in income. Special need for attention, affection, and security.

Source: William Wells and George Gubar, "Life Cycle Concept in Marketing Research," *Journal of Marketing Research,* 3 (November 1966): 362. Reprinted by permission of the American Marketing Association.

which necessitates buying many new durable goods. A refrigerator, lawnmower, and additional furniture become purchase priorities. Children, of course, bring on new consumption needs. Each stage of the life cycle represents a unique market segment.

SUMMARY

America's population of approximately 214 million people is getting older. In 1985 the average age of Americans will be 32 years. This statistic has many ramifications for marketing managers. Basically, it means that many firms will have to revise their marketing mix to cater to a more mature target market. In fact, one of the fastest-growing segments of the American population is the elderly. The medical, travel, entertainment, and recreation industries will be major beneficiaries of this growth.

America is on the move. Many of America's traditional population centers have stopped growing or have begun losing consumers to other areas, while the South and Southwest are booming. Population migration tends to shift income concentrations, thus creating new markets and destroying or modifying old ones.

America is an affluent society. The number of poor families will continue to decline throughout the 1980s. This means more disposable income, thus creating even larger potential rewards for successful marketers.

Markets are often segmented by race. Blacks and other minorities tend to be overconsumers of some products and services and underconsumers of others.

One of the more recent forms of market subdivision is life style segmentation. A life style is a mode of living. There are a wide variety of life styles, but they can be conveniently grouped into three major areas—activities, interests, and opinions. Life style segmentation can often tell more about an individual's consumption pattern than other forms of segmentation. For example, people 25 years of age have many different life styles, each with its own individualistic consumption pattern. Life style segmentation can help marketing managers understand what rewards people are seeking, and this may suggest new opportunities for the firm.

The most commonly used social categories are upper class, upper-middle class, middle class, lower-middle class, and lower class. Consumers in different social classes tend to have different life styles and consumption patterns.

Another factor influencing life styles is the life cycle. The life cycle is an orderly series of stages that all of us go through as we move from adolescence to retirement. The general concept is family oriented.

KEY TERMS

Zero population growth	Life styles
Population age mix	User profile
Standard metropolitan statistical areas	Social class
Disposable income	Life cycle
Psychographics	

QUESTIONS FOR DISCUSSION

1. Briefly describe the various demographic characteristics used to segment the market.
2. Discuss the importance of population trends to marketing management. In what way will zero population growth alter the marketing environment?
3. Examine the effect that migration patterns have on marketing strategy. Give examples of firms that have profited from current migration patterns.
4. Discuss some of the characteristics of blacks as consumers. Using an example, explain how a marketer can meet the needs of this market segment.

5. What is life style segmentation? Describe some of the characteristics that form the basis of such segmentation.

6. Differentiate between the demographic and psychographic factors used for market segmentation. Explain why demographic factors are almost always necessary if a market segmentation program is to succeed.

7. What is meant by social class? How is it related to life styles? Can you give examples of products that are segmented on the basis of social class?

8. How does the life cycle affect a person's life style? What opportunities does it present to marketing managers?

9. What is meant by population age mix? Give an example of a company that has successfully segmented the market on this basis.

10. Why is the elderly market so important to American marketers? What products are likely to be marketed to this segment?

11. As the "baby boom" gets older, how will it affect American life styles? What effect will it have on marketers?

NOTES

1. *Population Estimates and Projections* (Washington, D.C.: U.S. Bureau of the Census, October 1975), p. 8.

2. Ibid.

3. James Foust and Al Southwood, "The Population Fizzle," *Business Horizons,* 16 (February 1973): 5–20.

4. "How the Changing Age Mix Changed Markets," *Business Week,* January 12, 1976, p. 75. Reprinted by permission.

5. "Can the Baby Toy Market Be Segmented 12 Ways?" *Business Week,* February 14, 1977, p. 62.

6. *Population Estimates and Projections,* p. 11.

7. "How the Changing Age Mix Changed Markets," p. 76.

8. Ibid., p. 77.

9. Ibid.

10. *Demographic Aspects of Aging and the Older Population in the United States* (Washington, D.C.: U.S. Bureau of the Census, May 1976), p. 3.

11. "Discounts to Elderly Grow," *The Dallas Morning News,* September 20, 1976.

12. "The Second War Between the States," *Business Week,* May 17, 1976, p. 92.

13. Ibid.

14. Raymond Oladipupo, "The Urban Negro Separate and Distinct," *Media-Scope,* July 1969, p. 75.

15. Thomas Barry and Michael Harvey, "Marketing to Heterogeneous Black Consumers," *California Management Review,* 17 (Winter 1974): 50. Copyright © 1974 by the Regents of the University of California. Reprinted by permission of the Regents.

16. Ibid., p. 51.

17. Ibid., p. 50.

18. James Stafford, Keith Cox, and James Higginbotham, "Some Consumption Pattern Differences Between Urban Whites and Negroes," *Social Sciences Quarterly,* 49 (December 1968): 619–630; see also Donald E. Sexton, Jr., "Black Buyer Behavior," *Journal of Marketing,* 36 (October 1972): 36–39; Charles Van Tassel, "The Negro as a Consumer—What

We Know and What We Don't," *AMA Proceedings,* June 1967, pp. 166–170; Peter D. Bennett and Harold J. Kasserjian, *Consumer Behavior* (Englewood Cliffs: Prentice-Hall, 1972), pp. 125–126; Raymond S. Bauer, Scott M. Cunningham, and Lawrence H. Wortzel, "The Marketing Dilemma of Negroes," *Journal of Marketing,* 29 (July 1965): 1–6; Kelvin A. Wall, "Positioning Your Brand in the Black Market," *Advertising Age,* June 18, 1973, pp. 71ff.; J. P. Majgard, "Negro Market – Fact or Fiction?" *California Management Review,* Fall 1971, pp. 71–80; Dennis H. Gensch and Richard Staelin, "The Appeal of Buying Black," *Journal of Marketing Research,* 9 (May 1972): 141–148; and William Cash and Lucy Oliver, *Black Economic Development: Analyses and Implications* (Ann Arbor: University of Michigan, Graduate School of Business Administration, 1975).

19. William Wells, Psychographics: A Critical Review," *Journal of Marketing Research,* 12 (May 1975): 196–213.

20. Segmentation benefits are taken from Joseph Plummer, "The Concept and Application of Life Style Segmentation," *Journal of Marketing,* 38 (January 1974): 33–37; other books and articles on life style segmentation include James F. Engel, Henry F. Fiorillo, and Murray A. Cayley, eds., *Market Segmentation: Concepts and Applications* (New York: Holt, Rinehart and Winston, 1972); Ronald E. Frank, William F. Massy, and Yoram Wind, *Market Segmentation* (Englewood Cliffs, N.J.: Prentice-Hall, 1972); Michael D. Hutt, William V. Muse, and Robert J. Kegerreis, "Market Segmentation Using Behavioral Variables," *Southern Journal of Business,* 7 (February 1972): 55–64; William H. Peters, "Using MCA to Segment New Car Markets," *Journal of Marketing Research,* 7 (August 1970): 360–363; Douglas J. Tigert, Richard Lathrope, and Michael Bleeg, "The Fast Food Franchise: Psychographic and Demographic Segmentation Analysis," *Journal of Retailing,* 47 (Spring 1971): 81–90; Frederick Wiseman, "A Segmentation Analysis of Automobile Buyers During the New Model Year Transition Period," *Journal of Marketing,* 35 (April 1971): 42–49; Ruth Ziff, "Psychographics for Market Segmentation," *Journal of Advertising Research,* 11 (April 1971): 3–10; Thomas Kinnear and James Taylor, "Psychographics: Some Additional Findings," *Journal of Marketing Research,* 13 (November 1976): 422–425; and Robert Peterson and Louis Sharpe, "Market Segmentation: Product Usage Patterns and Psychographic Configurations," *Journal of Business Research,* 1 (Summer 1973): 11–20.

21. William Wells, *Life Style and Psychographics* (Chicago: American Marketing Association, 1974), pp. 242, 249, 251. Reprinted by permission of the American Marketing Association.

22. Ron Markin, Jr., *Consumer Behavior – A Cognitive Orientation* (New York: Macmillan, 1974), p. 447.

CASE 4
The American Cola Company

Bart Levy, president of American Cola, was quite disturbed by a market research report that crossed his desk recently. The report said that there have been two dramatic changes in the profile of the American population: a sharp increase in the median age and an even sharper rise in the number of people over 65. The so-called aging of America is a result of simultaneous declines in the birth and mortality rates.

Expecting that the trend will continue, the Census Bureau says that by the year 2030 the average age of Americans will be over 37, compared to just under 29 today. Perhaps more important, one in six Americans will be over 65. That's a total of almost 50 million senior citizens, a huge potential market.

Levy forwarded this information to the company's director of long-range planning, asking for comments and a plan. After six months Jim Bell, director of planning, reported the following: The 13–24 age group, which consumes one and one-half times as much cola per capita as the general public, will shrink by 8 percent in the next decade. Accordingly, the planning committee recommends the purchase of a winery and expansion of the company's food division, which manufactures such products as orange juice, coffee, and tea—beverages that are more popular with older consumers.

Levy is not sure whether this would be a wise decision. He believes that there are two approaches to selling to the growing senior-citizen market: (1) creating new products geared specifically to older people or (2) convincing these people that products that are already on the market are appropriate for them. Although the first approach might seem virtually foolproof, several things could go wrong. For one, the new product must satisfy real needs because people will see through a gimmick. But even if older consumers can benefit from a product, they still may not buy it. Items that are intended especially for the elderly seem to carry a certain stigma, and the act of buying them can involve a painful reminder of the greater vulnerability that often accompanies aging. Thus Levy feels that the greatest potential of the growing senior-citizen market may not be in products intended for the elderly but rather in the elderly's willingness to spend more on goods and services that are now being sold mostly to younger customers. He uses blue jeans as an example of a product that was once sold almost exclusively to people under 25 but is now popular with people in their 30s and 40s.

1. Levy has come to you for advice. Which approach would you recommend and why?
2. Are these the only two approaches to the problem? Can you think of others? Is it really critical for the company to tap this market? Does a firm have to be all things to all people?

5

Buyer Behavior

OBJECTIVES

■ To understand consumer behavior.
■ To become aware of the various factors that influence buyer behavior.
■ To study the impact of culture on buyer behavior.
■ To present a model of human behavior.
■ To gain insight into industrial purchasing behavior.
■ To understand the basic elements of governmental purchasing.

Chapter 4 introduced you to several fundamental aspects of consumer behavior. Attitudes, values, social class, and life style strongly influence consumption patterns. This chapter begins with a discussion of the nature of consumer behavior. An example is presented that will illustrate the potential complexity of our buying decisions.

Because of the complexity of human behavior, marketing scholars have borrowed heavily from other disciplines. Contributions from sociology, psychology, and other fields are presented. Next, an integrated model of buyer behavior is illustrated to tie together the individual factors that influence purchase choice.

The chapter concludes with a look at industrial purchasing and government buyer behavior. Industrial behavior differs markedly from the purchasing patterns and motives of individual consumers. Similarly, governmental purchasing behavior is different from industrial and final-consumer buying habits.

CONSUMER BEHAVIOR

The term consumer or buyer behavior is often used rather loosely. You should recognize that consumer behavior is a subset of human behavior. Not all human behavior is consumption oriented. Our work and family activities may have little to do with consumer behavior. Human behavior refers to the total process by which individuals interact with their environment.[1] Every attitude, action, and motivation that people have is part of human behavior.

In the strictest sense consumer behavior is the act of consuming or utilizing a good or service. Buyer behavior accompanies the physical act of engaging in the purchasing process. Buyer decision making includes the thought processes and search activities that lead to acceptance or rejection of product or service alternatives. Actually, three different people may be involved. An infant might be the actual consumer of a vitamin; the parent goes out and buys the vitamin; and the brand or product decision was made by the family physician.

As you can see, even defining terms in this area can be a complex problem. Let us, however, adopt a more informal approach and say that consumer or buyer behavior is the process by which individuals decide whether, what, when, where, how, and from whom to purchase goods and services.[2] It is basically a problem-solving activity. The question of how the problem is attacked and solved is among the topics that will concern us in this chapter.

THE COMPLEXITY OF CONSUMER BEHAVIOR

When you purchase a soft drink, a loaf of bread, small hardware items, and similar goods, the purchase process is uncomplicated. The item may be bought through habit or routine behavior. Buying often becomes more difficult when one is purchasing expensive and infrequently bought items such as new furniture, clothing, or an automobile. A number of factors can influence the buying process. Figure 5.1 reveals some of the more important considerations in consumer purchasing. Note the inputs, such as price, quality, and service, that must be properly evaluated.

Evaluation depends on good information. Consumers obtain information from many sources, some of which may present a rather distorted picture. Will a salesperson always (or ever) present both sides of the product quality issue? Does an advertisement ever criticize the product being advertised? Perhaps you have had family or friends offer "free advice" on product or service attributes about which they know little.

The most important aspect of Figure 5.1 is the buyer's psyche, or

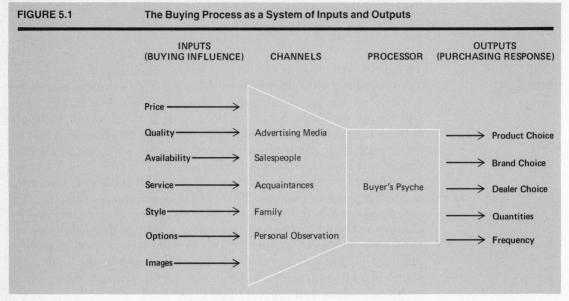

FIGURE 5.1   The Buying Process as a System of Inputs and Outputs

Source: Philip Kotler, "Behavioral Models for Analyzing Buyers," *Journal of Marketing*, 29 (October 1965): 38. By permission of the American Marketing Association.

"black box." This consists of the thought processes, motivations, attitudes, past experiences, and other things that lead to purchase behavior. The buyer's psyche cannot be directly observed but must be inferred from behavior patterns.

Output from the buyer's psyche will include product choice (e.g., a new television set or a vacation), brand choice, dealer choice, quantity, and frequency of repurchase. Later in the chapter we will discuss the buyer's psyche so that you may better understand how purchase behavior is determined.

MAJOR CONTRIBUTIONS TO THE UNDERSTANDING OF BUYER BEHAVIOR
Learning Theory

Many disciplines contribute to the understanding of what goes on in the "black box." These include sociology, psychology, learning theory, and others.

One reason why people buy certain brands is that they have learned to like them. Learning may be defined as response or behavior resulting from practice or experience. Three basic factors are required for learning to occur. First, a relevant stimulus must be encountered. Anything in the environment can be a stimulus—people, trees, buildings, water, a hole in the ground, advertisements, packages, and so forth. A relevant stimulus is one that evokes a response from an individual. At this point one of three things will occur: positive reinforcement, negative reinforcement, or no reinforcement. If you see a package of Doublemint gum (stimulus) in a supermarket, purchase it (response), and find the gum to be quite refreshing, your behavior has been positively reinforced.

On the other hand, assume that you see a new soap product and purchase it. If the soap doesn't do a decent job of cleaning your clothes (negative reinforcement), you won't buy the product again. When there is no reinforcement, positive or negative, there is no strong incentive either to engage in the same behavior pattern again or to avoid it. Thus if a new brand evokes neutral feelings, a price change, an increase in promotion, or some other marketing activity may be required to induce further consumption.

From a marketing perspective learning theory has several important implications. According to Glenn Walters, they are the following:

1. Consumers learn in different ways, and what works on one consumer may not work on another.
2. Marketers, in utilizing promotion, should always associate their product with one or more specific rewards. Consumers respond to benefits, and it is this that marketers must sell rather than physical goods. Consumers tend to be more loyal to brands that satisfy their needs.
3. Habit introduces efficiency into the purchase process. Habit is learned from repetitive promotion or purchase. Habit aids the business by making the customer more loyal, and habit aids the consumer by reducing purchase decisions where problems have been satisfactorily solved.
4. To induce consumers to purchase new products or to change from previously used products may require large amounts of money and energy on the part of marketers. This fact is true because learning new ideas is more difficult than augmenting those already known. However, the cost can be reduced by associating new products with established products.[3]

Psychoanalytic Theory

Psychoanalytic theory developed from the thought of Sigmund Freud. He postulated that the personality has three basic dimensions, the id, the ego, and the superego. The *id* is the mechanism that leads to strong drives and releases large quantities of energy. It is dedicated to finding pleasure and releasing tension. It is not influenced by ethics or morality but compulsively seeks pleasure and satisfaction.

The *ego* is the mechanism that helps an individual cope with reality. It is the equilibrating device that leads to socially acceptable behavior. It imposes rationality on the id. The ego weighs the consequences of an act rather than rushing blindly into pleasurable activity.

Freud defined the *superego* as a person's conscience. It tries to keep behavior in line with what is morally right or wrong. In essence, the id urges an enjoyable act; the superego presents the moral issues involved; and the ego acts as the arbitrator in determining whether to proceed or not.

According to Freud, the mechanism that leads to behavior is largely unconscious. Freud felt that a person's life is centered on sexual gratification. Therefore much of an individual's behavior is triggered by the id, with its strong sexual drive. Over the years psychoanalytic theory has been broadened to include the need for power and personality development as behavior triggers.

Freudian psychology has played an important role in the understanding of consumer behavior. Marketing managers continually ask the question Why? "What caused Mrs. Jones to buy brand X rather than brand Y?" In other words, what were her motivations? Motivation research has uncovered some strange phenomena:

1. People don't eat prunes because the wrinkles make prunes ugly.
2. A woman is very serious when she bakes a cake because unconsciously she is going through the symbolic act of giving birth.
3. Purchasing agents for a large food processor would not buy Corning glass pipe because childhood experiences with breaking a glass often led to a spanking.
4. A person who smokes cigars is engaging in an adult version of thumb sucking.[4]

Certainly these assertions are difficult to prove or validate. Motivation research relies heavily on psychiatrists who use clinical techniques to obtain their findings. Sample sizes are typically very small and not statistically reliable. Yet traditional marketing research techniques would never have uncovered data like those just mentioned.

Holistic Psychology

Holistic or Gestalt psychology is concerned with the development and organization of thought processes. Gestalt psychology claims that we perceive things as organized patterns or wholes rather than individual parts. A good example is shown in Figure 5.2. Most of us would see a dog rather than a group of random ink blots.

Gestalt psychologists argue that human behavior must be viewed as individually patterned totalities. Behavior should be explained in terms of all the factors that are operating the instant the event happens. Thus:

A homemaker may be motivated to buy a bag of potatoes, and be within reach of a bag that has just the right characteristics, selling for an attractive price, but avoid making the purchase because she is too far

FIGURE 5.2   **What Do You See?**

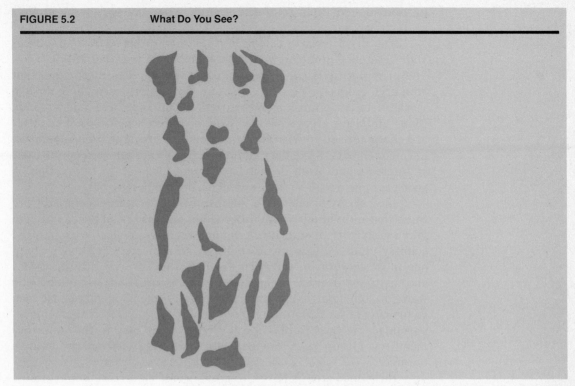

Source: Ron Markin, Jr., *Consumer Behavior: A Cognitive Orientation* (New York: Macmillan, 1974), p. 205. Reprinted by permission of Macmillan Publishing Co., Inc. Copyright © 1974 by Ron J. Markin, Jr.

from home, or because the line at the checkout counter is too long. Had she been expecting company that evening and been planning to serve potatoes, she would have suffered the inconvenience and made the purchase. Part of the marketer's responsibility is to reduce as far as possible all situational barriers to purchase.[5]

Social–Anthropological Theory

So far our theoretical discussions of behavior have centered on the individual, with little mention of external factors. This section explains the roles that groups play in influencing behavior and consumption. Much of the preceding chapter dealt with attitudes, values, and life styles, which are strongly influenced by culture. In this section I will describe culture and how it influences behavior.

Reference Groups. Reference groups are groups that influence our behavior and attitudes. They are the people we rely on in forming our own beliefs and attitudes. In essence, people are psychological participants in their reference groups. They believe in the group's goals, values and activities.

You don't have to belong to a group in order for it to qualify as your reference group. If you are a member, it is called an affiliative group; if not, it is called an aspiratory group. The most important affiliative group for most of us is our family. Others include our co-workers, fellow church members, fellow club members, and so forth. Many affiliative groups are also primary reference groups. The latter are characterized by significant personal interaction and cooperation among members. Secondary reference groups are selected on the basis of interests and often do not have much face-to-face interaction. A good example would be the Republican or Democratic party.

In contrast to affiliative groups, aspiratory reference groups are those that individuals would like to join. You may wish to be invited to join a fraternity or sorority. A young executive might like to join the country club. To gain membership in an aspiratory reference group one must conform to the norms of the group. Norms are the values and attitudes deemed acceptable by the group. Thus a student who wants to join a particular fraternity dresses like its members. He may go to many of the restaurants, clubs, and so on that fraternity members patronize. He tries to play a role that is acceptable to the fraternity members. Group roles are behavior patterns based on the group's norms.

Reference groups have three important marketing implications: (1) They serve as information sources and influencers of quality perceptions; (2) they affect individuals' aspiration levels; and (3) their norms serve as constraints or influences on consumption.

The Importance of the Family.   A discussion of reference groups would not be complete without some exploration of the role of the family. Our parents influence our consumption, behavior patterns, standards, and values from infancy through the teenage years and beyond. Marriage brings forth a new set of roles and purchasing patterns for both partners. A tremendous amount of research has been done on changing family structures, interpersonal influences, and consumption patterns.[6] A summary of the relevant findings follows:

1. The degree of dominance by the husband or wife role can vary with cultural functions, e.g., Oriental vs. United States families.
2. Husband dominance appears to be more likely when the husband is successful in his occupation and has a higher income.
3. The wife's dominance increases if she is employed, and in any event increases with age.
4. The role of the husband as family leader is decreasing in importance over time.
5. There is a lessening of family unity.
6. Husband–wife involvement varies widely by product category.[7]

THE IMPACT OF
CULTURE ON
BUYER BEHAVIOR

Purchase roles within the family are influenced by culture. Culture may be defined as the set of values, ideas, attitudes, and other meaningful symbols created to shape human behavior and the artifacts of that behavior as they are transmitted from one generation to the next.[8] The basic manifestations of American culture are its life styles and values, as discussed in the previous chapter. Culture is environmentally oriented. The nomads of Finland have developed a culture for Arctic survival. Similarly, the natives of the Brazilian jungle have created a culture suitable for jungle living.

The process of learning a culture is called socialization. If a person leaves one society to live in another and learns its culture, the process is referred to as acculturation. In our early years the family is the basic source of socialization. As we enter school other reference groups transmit cultural norms. Culture is a learned response and is often deeply rooted in an individual's value system.

Many cultural norms evolve because of a societal need for solutions to recurring problems. As mentioned earlier, culture helps people adapt to their environment. It also leads to shared habits. For example, eating patterns, home building, dress and bodily adornment habits vary significantly from one culture to another.

Culture is not static. It adapts to changing societal needs and evolving environmental factors. The rapid growth of technological development in this century has accelerated the rate of cultural change. Inventions such as the elevator made possible modern high-rise cities. Television changed entertainment patterns and family communication flows, and heightened public awareness of political and other news events. Automation has increased the amount of leisure time available and largely destroyed the Protestant work ethic.

A MODEL OF
HUMAN BEHAVIOR

Integrating the various concepts discussed so far is a difficult task. Yet by taking the basic learning model and embellishing it with several additional concepts, human behavior can be examined in a broader context. The model is admittedly descriptive. It discusses factors that may impinge on human behavior under varying circumstances. No attempt is made to weigh the variables in terms of their relative importance. Any attempt to do so would go beyond the scope of this book. The objective is simply to give you an appreciation of some of the factors that influence a person's actions. The basic model is shown in Figure 5.3.

Perception

The basic model is quite simple. A stimulus is perceived; meaning is assigned to the stimulus; a response occurs; the response is reinforced in some manner. The heart of the model is the buyer's psyche, in which a stimulus is interpreted.

FIGURE 5.3   A Model of Human Behavior

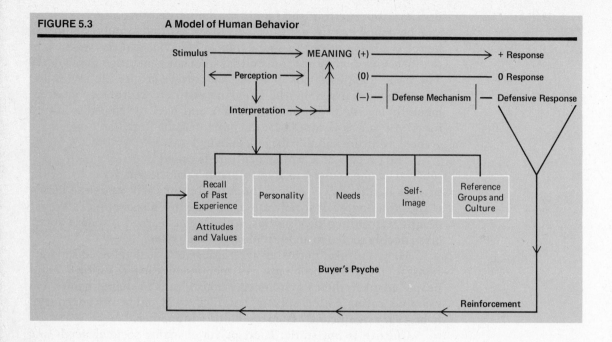

The model begins with the perception of a stimulus. Perception is the way an individual orders, structures, and interprets what is received through the senses. As consumers we mentally interpret or decode all the sensory stimulations that reach our central nervous system. Thus perception is the representation of objects, things, and events that results from organization of stimuli.[9]

A person cannot possibly perceive all the stimuli in his or her environment. Look around you right now and you could probably count several thousand stimuli. Perception is selective. It is a compromise between what we are given to see (the environment), what we are "set" to see (psyche), what we want to see, and even what we want to avoid seeing (psyche).[10]

Recall of Past Experience

After a stimulus has been perceived it must be interpreted. This is the cognitive process, meaning "knowing or understanding." It involves assessing the meaning of that which has been perceived. Thus the psyche affects not only what is seen but also how stimuli are viewed and what they mean.

Past experience is an important part of the perceptual/interpretive process. Generally it can be said that

1. a positive experience is more readily recalled than a negative one. Bad experiences may be repressed.

2. personal involvement heightens stimulus recall.
3. recall is higher and more precise for stimuli encountered recently than for those encountered in the distant past.
4. increasing the frequency of stimuli encountered increases recall.
5. stimuli with little or no meaning are more difficult to recall.

The development of attitudes is part of the cognitive process. It is a mental and neutral state of readiness to respond, organized as a result of experience exerting a directive and/or dynamic influence on behavior.[11] Attitudes are rarely isolated; instead, they are combined with other attitudes. Clusters of attitudes, in turn, are integrated to form an attitudinal system. For example, a person's attitude toward cold cereal is related to his or her attitude toward breakfast, which is in turn related to his or her attitude toward eating habits.

Attitudinal studies of marketing variables abound. In the "product" area researchers have learned that

1. the more favorable the attitude, the higher the incidence of product usage.
2. the less favorable the attitude, the lower the incidence of usage.
3. the more unfavorable people's attitudes are toward a product, the more likely they are to stop using it.
4. the attitudes of people who have never tried a product tend to be distributed around the mean in the shape of a normal distribution.[12]

Needs

A second major component of the human psyche is needs. A need is anything an individual depends on to function efficiently. Needs are said to be at the root of all human behavior. Without needs, there would be no behavior patterns. Life is the only prerequisite for needs.

Categorizing needs has proved to be an arduous task. Perhaps the most popular scheme was conceived by A. H. Maslow. It is presented in Figure 5.4.[13]

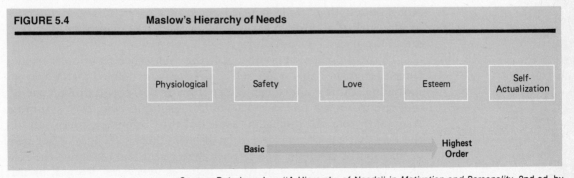

FIGURE 5.4　　　Maslow's Hierarchy of Needs

| Physiological | Safety | Love | Esteem | Self-Actualization |

Basic ————————————→ Highest Order

Source: Data based on "A Hierarchy of Needs" in *Motivation and Personality*, 2nd ed. by Abraham H. Maslow. Copyright © 1970 by Abraham H. Maslow. Reprinted by permission of Harper & Row, Publishers, Inc.

Physiological needs are our most basic requirements and must be satisfied first. Food, water, and shelter are basic to survival. Safety needs include freedom from pain and discomfort. Safety also relates to fear of change. Research has shown that most people prefer an orderly and continuous pattern in their day-to-day activities.

According to Maslow, after our physiological and safety needs have been fulfilled, love becomes the dominant need. Love is defined to include more than sex and romantic love. It also includes acceptance by one's peers. The need for esteem is subdivided into two categories. One form of esteem is self-respect and a feeling of accomplishment. The second category is the esteem of others. Prestige, fame, and recognition for one's accomplishments are manifestations of this form of esteem. Note that love is acceptance without regard to contribution; esteem is acceptance based on contribution to the group.

Self-actualization is our highest need. Many people never reach this level. It refers to self-fulfillment and self-expression—reaching the point in life at which "you are what you feel you should be." Maslow felt that very few people reach this level.

Maslow's hierarchy is not absolute in that one need must be completely fulfilled before another need becomes dominant. As a person obtains increasing fulfillment of one need, a higher-level need becomes more important. Also, some people have stronger needs at one level than at another. For example, safety and the fear of change may be extremely important to one individual and relatively unimportant to another.

The Self-Concept

The third major component of the psyche is the self-concept. We all have several different self-concepts. First there is the real self-image. It refers to how a person really views himself or herself. Next is the ideal self. It represents the way an individual would like to be (e.g., intelligent, popular, witty, charming, and convincing). Generally speaking, we try to raise our real self-concept toward our ideal self (or at least narrow the gap). For example, a consumer doesn't often buy products that would jeopardize his or her self-image. If you consider yourself a contemporary dresser, you will avoid clothing that doesn't project a "with-it" image.

A third form of self-concept is the "reference group self," sometimes called the "real other self." This may be defined as the way an individual thinks other people view him or her. If you think a particular group views you as a leader, for example, you may assume a leadership role. An important aspect of the "reference group self" is the fact that a person's perception of how others view him or her may or may not be realistic. You have probably seen someone play the role of a "big shot" because he or she believes everyone else will be impressed. This is usually not the case, however.

A person's behavior depends largely on his or her self-concept. Consumers tend to see the environment in a way that is compatible with their self-image. Their identity as individuals is something that they want to protect. Thus the products and services we purchase, the stores we patronize, and, to a degree, the credit cards we carry support our self-images.

Marketing managers often try to market their product by appealing to self-image. For example, the Marlboro smoker reinforces a rugged, free-spirit self-image, while the Cadillac driver reinforces a "big shot" self-concept.

Personality

An individual's self-concept is partly reflected in his or her personality. Personality is a broad term; it refers to everything that makes one person different from another. It is a major component of the psyche and is highly interactive with the other components, such as past experience, needs, self-concept, and reference group.

Gordon Allport has defined personality as the dynamic organization within the individual of the psychophysical systems that determine his or her unique adjustments to the environment.[14] Thus personality is a composite of physiological makeup and environmental forces.

An individual's personality is manifested in a consistent pattern of responses to the environment. These consistent behavior patterns or tendencies are called personality traits.

Marketing scholars have used both standard personality tests and customized measures in an attempt to relate personality traits and buyer behavior. Most research has failed to establish a strong relationship between the two. However, low correlations between specific traits and particular products suggest that other factors within the buyer's psyche also influence the purchase decision.

Back to the Model

Now that you have been introduced to the major components of a person's psyche, we can continue our discussion of the model. You will recall that a person has perceived a stimulus and interpreted it within the psyche. If the interpretation is positive, it will lead to positive behavior. A neutral interpretation may lead to no response and only a minimal amount of learning. For example, look around you very carefully. Notice the hundreds of irrelevant stimuli surrounding you. Even concentrating on, say, a dirty mark on the wall may still lead to a neutral, "so what" reaction. You may or may not remember the mark the next time you enter the room.

When negative meaning is assigned to a stimulus we may utilize a defense mechanism before responding. Defense mechanisms help us reduce tension and maintain our self-concept. They are typically a mild retreat from reality. All of us rely on defense mechanisms in our day-to-day living. A typical one is rationalization, which means justifying one's behavior to oneself. You may buy an expensive suit in order to "outclass" your friends. You tell them, of course, that you liked the material and style.

Another defense mechanism is repression, the process of driving thoughts and information from the conscious mind. Assume that you really want a new suit to wear to a dance but can't afford it. You may simply drive the thought of the dance from your mind.

Identification is a third common defense mechanism. It is the tendency to identify with and/or imitate another person. Children often identify with their heroes. Celebrities are used in promotions partly because they will be identified with the sponsor's product. Other advertisers will set up situations (e.g., man buys cigar; beautiful woman arrives to light cigar and begins process of seduction). The hope is that the consumer will identify with the situation—or at least with step one, purchasing the cigar.

There are many other defense mechanisms, but it isn't necessary to list them all. The point is that defensive behavior does not reveal a person's true feelings or motives. It does, however, help preserve the concept of self and reduce tensions.

The last aspect of the model is the feedback function. It serves to reinforce our responses and is stored in our file of past experiences (learned behavior). Negative reinforcement causes us to alter our response patterns. Positive reinforcement generally means that a specific behavior pattern will continue.

INDUSTRIAL PURCHASING BEHAVIOR

So far we have concentrated on the ultimate consumer. Now we turn our attention to the industrial purchaser. Industrial purchasers include manufacturers, farmers, raw-material processors, and others. They will be discussed in detail in Chapter 8. Two of the most important distinctions between final consumers and industrial buyers are (1) multiple influence on purchasing and (2) predominance of rational motives.

Purchase influence can take the form of initiating the decision to buy, actually making the decision, or influencing the decision maker. One study of forty-eight industrial organizations found that top management most often was the "decider" and middle management the "initiator" of purchase decisions (see Table 5.1).[15]

Industrial purchase decisions are motivated by such things as durability, return on investment, tensile strength, continued availability of supply, and stability of a chemical compound. Most buying is deliberate and well planned. Impulse purchasing is rare except in the case of some supply items. Purchasing is based on some predetermined need or expansion plan.

TABLE 5.1	Overlap Between Organizational Positions and Decision Roles		
Organizational Level	**Role**		
	Initiator	**Decider**	**Influencer**
Top	35.4%	50.0%	16.7%
Top + middle	—	27.1	—
Middle	52.1	12.5	18.8
Other	—	—	29.2
No answer	12.5	10.4	35.4[a]
Total	100%	100%	100%
	(48)	(48)	(48)

[a] No other influence 25.8%, no answer 10.4%.

Source: Kjell Gronhaug, "Exploring Environmental Influences in Organizational Buying." *Journal of Marketing Research,* 13 (August 1976): 225–229. Reprinted by permission of The American Marketing Association.

When people are involved, however, emotional factors will always play some role. Purchasing agents, for example, probably like to be thought of as astute, shrewd buyers. They also seek the advancement and monetary rewards that come with doing a good job. If a purchasing committee is making a decision, other members may defer to the individual with the strongest personality. Also, if two companies have products with similar specifications, a buyer will award the contract to the salesperson with whom he or she is most compatible.

GOVERNMENTAL PURCHASING BEHAVIOR

As you learned in Chapter 3, the various branches of government constitute a huge market for sellers of goods and services. The military alone maintains the nation's third-largest food store operation (commissaries) after Safeway and A & P. This is also the third-largest U.S.-owned department/variety store group after Sears and J. C. Penney.[16] Today the U.S. government is the world's biggest buyer.[17]

Our discussion of government purchasing will focus on the federal level. State and local governments generally follow the same procedures but with less formality. Federal procurement is accomplished by two means: formal advertising and negotiation. Formal advertising consists, first, of listing the bid in *Commerce Business Daily,* a publication of the Department of Commerce that enumerates all jobs and procurements going out for bid by federal departments and agencies, and second, of mailing bid invitations to firms listed on specific bidder's lists. (See Figure 5.5.)

Bidder's lists consist of all the firms that have notified an agency that they want to bid on certain items. These firms have also furnished proof that they are capable of supplying the necessary goods and services. Bid invitations usually include a copy of the specifications

FIGURE 5.5   **A Federal Invitation to Bid**

FORM APPROVED O.M.B. NO. 29–R0122

STANDARD FORM 19 JULY 1973 EDITION GENERAL SERVICES ADMINISTRATION FED. PROC. REG. (41 CFR) 1–16.401	INVITATION, BID, AND AWARD (Construction, Alteration or Repair)	REFERENCE *(Include in correspondence)* APPROP. NO. PROJECT NO. CONTRACT NO.
	☐ CHECK IF SMALL BUSINESS SET-ASIDE OR OTHER NEGOTIATED PROCUREMENT *(If checked, "Bid" includes "Proposal")*	

INVITATION FOR BIDS	DATE ISSUED,
ISSUING OFFICE * General Services Administration Public Buildings Service ☐ CONSTRUCTION ☐ REPAIR & IMPROVEMENT	BID RECEIVING OFFICE * General Services Administration Public Buildings Service

Information regarding bidding material may be obtained from the issuing office.

SEALED BIDS in duplicate covering work described in specifications, schedules, drawings and conditions entitled and dated as follows:

will be received at the Bid Receiving Office until _____ local time at the place of bid opening _____
      (Hour)   *(Date)*
and at that time publicly opened.

Sealed envelopes containing bids shall be addressed to the Bid Receiving Office and shall be marked to show: Bidder's Name and Address: * Reference   ; Time and Date of Opening:

BID *(This Section to be completed by Bidder)*	⟶ DATE BID SUBMITTED:

The undersigned agrees, if this bid is accepted within _____ calendar days *(30 days unless a different period is inserted)* after date of opening, to complete all work specified in strict accordance with the above-identified documents and the General Provisions on the reverse hereof, within _____ calendar days after receipt of notice to proceed, for the following amount _____

including all applicable Federal, State, and local taxes. The undersigned further agrees, if any contract award resulting from this bid exceeds $2,000, TO COMPLY with the provisions of Standard Form 19–A, Labor Standards Provisions Applicable to Contracts in Excess of $2,000 and TO FURNISH a performance bond in an amount equal to 100 percent and a payment bond in an amount equal to 50 percent of the contract price with surety or sureties acceptable to the Government, on Government forms within _____ days after forms are furnished.

BID GUARANTEE is required with any bid in excess of $2,000. Bid guarantee shall be in the amount of 20 percent of the amount of the bid, including all add alternates (if any), or $3,000,000, whichever is less.

RECEIPT OF AMENDMENTS. *The undersigned acknowledges receipt of the following amendments of the invitation for bids, drawings, and/or specifications. (Give number and date of each):*

AMENDMENT NO.				
DATE				

The representations and certifications on the accompanying STANDARD FORM 19-B are made a part of this bid.

NAME AND ADDRESS OF BIDDER *(Street, City, State)* * (Type or print.)*	SIGNATURE OF PERSON AUTHORIZED TO SIGN THIS BID ⟶
	SIGNER'S NAME AND TITLE *(Type or print.)*
AREA CODE & PHONE NO.	
AWARD *(This Section for Government only)*	DATE OF AWARD

THE ABOVE BID IS ACCEPTED IN THE AMOUNT OF $

☐ YOU ARE DIRECTED TO PROCEED WITH THE WORK UPON RECEIPT OF THIS AWARD.

☐ NOTICE TO PROCEED WILL BE ISSUED UPON RECEIPT OF ACCEPTABLE PAYMENT AND PERFORMANCE BONDS.

	THE UNITED STATES OF AMERICA
	
	BY _____
	          (Contracting Officer)
	
	_____
	          (Title)

*Include "ZIP CODE" in all mailing addresses.   (GSA OVERPRINT NOV. 1974)

1. CHANGES AND CHANGED CONDITIONS

(a) The Contracting Officer may, in writing, order changes in the drawings and specifications within the general scope of the contract.

(b) The Contractor shall promptly notify the Contracting Officer in writing of subsurface or latent physical conditions differing materially from those indicated in this contract or unknown unusual physical conditions at the site, before proceeding further with the work.

(c) If changes under (a) or conditions under (b) increase or decrease the cost of, or time required for, performing the work, upon assertion of a claim by the Contractor before final payment under the contract, a written equitable adjustment shall be made; except that no adjustment under (b) shall be made unless the notice required therein was given or unless the Contracting Officer waives the requirement therefor. If the adjustment cannot be agreed upon, the dispute shall be decided pursuant to Clause 3.

2. TERMINATION FOR DEFAULT—DAMAGES FOR DELAY—TIME EXTENSIONS

(a) If the Contractor does not prosecute the work so as to insure completion, or fails to complete it, within the time specified, the Government may, by written notice to the Contractor, terminate his right to proceed. Thereafter, the Government may have the work completed and the Contractor shall be liable for any resulting excess cost to the Government. If the Government does not terminate the Contractor's right to proceed, he shall continue the work and shall be liable to the Government for any actual damages occasioned by such delay unless liquidated damages are stipulated.

(b) The Contractor's right to proceed shall not be terminated nor the Contractor charged with actual or liquidated damages under (a) above because of any delays in completion of the work due to causes other than normal weather, beyond his control and without his fault or negligence, including but not restricted to, acts of God, acts of the public enemy, acts of the Government (in either its sovereign or contractual capacity), acts of another contractor in the performance of a contract with the Government, fires, floods, epidemics, quarantine restrictions, strikes, freight embargoes, and unusually severe weather, or delays of subcontractors or suppliers due to causes beyond their control and without their fault or negligence: Provided, That the Contractor shall within 10 days from the beginning of any such delay, unless the Contracting Officer shall grant a further period of time prior to the date of final payment under the contract, notify the Contracting Officer in writing of the causes of delay and the facts relating thereto. The Contracting Officer shall consider the facts and ascertain the extent of the delay, and extend the time for completing the work when in his judgment the facts justify such an extension, and his decision shall be final and conclusive on the parties, subject only to appeal as provided in Clause 3.

(c) As used in paragraph (b) of this clause, the term "subcontractors or suppliers" means subcontractors or suppliers at any tier.

3. DISPUTES

Any dispute concerning a question of fact arising under this contract, not disposed of by agreement, shall be decided by the Contracting Officer, who shall reduce his decision to writing and furnish a signed copy thereof to the Contractor. Such decision shall be final and conclusive unless, within 30 days from the date of receipt thereof, the Contractor mails or otherwise furnishes to the Contracting Officer a written appeal, addressed to the head of the Federal agency. The Contractor shall be afforded an opportunity to be heard and to offer evidence. The decision of the head of the Federal agency or his authorized representative shall be final and conclusive unless fraudulent, or capricious, or arbitrary, or so grossly erroneous as necessarily to imply bad faith, or not supported by substantial evidence. Pending final decision of a dispute hereunder, the Contractor shall proceed diligently with the performance of the contract and in accordance with the Contracting Officer's decision.

4. RESPONSIBILITY OF CONTRACTOR

At his own expense the Contractor shall: (a) obtain any necessary licenses and permits; (b) provide competent superintendence; (c) take precautions necessary to protect persons or property against injury or damage and be responsible for any such injury or damage that occurs as a result of his fault or negligence; (d) perform the work without unnecessarily interfering with other contractors' work or Government activities; (e) be responsible for all damage to work performed and materials delivered (including Government-furnished items), until completion and final acceptance.

5. MATERIAL AND WORKMANSHIP

All material incorporated in the work shall be new and the work shall be performed in a skillful and workmanlike manner. Both materials and workmanship shall be subject to the inspection of the Contracting Officer or his duly authorized representative who may require the Contractor to correct defective workmanship or materials without cost to the Government.

6. PAYMENTS TO CONTRACTOR

Progress payments equal to 90 percent of the value of work performed may be made monthly on estimates approved by the Contracting Officer. Upon payment therefor, title to the property shall vest in the Government. The Contractor will notify the Government when all work is complete. Final payment will be made after final acceptance.

7. OFFICIALS NOT TO BENEFIT

No member of or delegate to Congress, or resident commissioner, shall be admitted to any share or part of this contract, or to any benefit that may arise therefrom; but this provision shall not be construed to extend to this contract if made with a corporation for its general benefit.

8. BUY AMERICAN

The Contractor, subcontractors, material men, and suppliers must comply with the Buy American Act of March 3, 1933 (41 U.S.C. 10a–10d) and Executive Order 10582 of December 17, 1954 (19 Fed. Reg. 8723). (In substance the above require use generally of domestic materials except as otherwise authorized by the Contracting Officer pursuant to the Act and Executive Order.)

9. ASSIGNMENT OF CLAIMS

If this contract provides for payments aggregating $1,000 or more, claims for moneys due or to become due hereunder may be assigned as provided in 31 U.S.C. 203 and 41 U.S.C. 15.

10. CONVICT LABOR

In connection with the performance of work under this contract, the Contractor agrees not to employ any person undergoing sentence of imprisonment at hard labor.

11. COVENANT AGAINST CONTINGENT FEES

The Contractor warrants that no person or selling agency has been employed or retained to solicit or secure this contract upon an agreement or understanding for a commission, percentage, brokerage, or contingent fee, excepting bona fide employees or bona fide established commercial or selling agencies maintained by the Contractor for the purpose of securing business. For breach or violation of this warranty the Government shall have the right to annul this contract without liability or in its discretion to deduct from the contract price or consideration, or otherwise recover, the full amount of such commission, percentage, brokerage, or contingent fee.

12. PAYMENT OF INTEREST ON CONTRACTORS' CLAIMS

(a) If an appeal is filed by the contractor from a final decision of the Contracting Officer under the Disputes clause of this contract, denying a claim arising under the contract, simple interest on the amount of the claim finally determined owed by the Government shall be payable to the Contractor. Such interest shall be at the rate determined by the Secretary of the Treasury pursuant to Public Law 92–41, 85 Stat. 97, from the date the Contractor furnishes to the Contracting Officer his written appeal under the Disputes clause of this contract, to the date of (1) a final judgment by a court of competent jurisdiction, or (2) mailing to the Contractor of a supplemental agreement for execution either confirming completed negotiations between the parties or carrying out a decision of a board of contract appeals.

(b) Notwithstanding (a), above, (1) interest shall be applied only from the date payment was due, if such date is later than the filing of appeal, and (2) interest shall not be paid for any period of time that the Contracting Officer determines the Contractor has unduly delayed in pursuing his remedies before a board of contract appeals or a court of competent jurisdiction.

13. EXAMINATION OF RECORDS BY COMPTROLLER GENERAL

The clause entitled "Examination of Records by Comptroller General" prescribed by 41 CFR Subpart 1–7.1 is applicable if the amount of this contract exceeds $2,500 and was entered into by means of negotiation, including small business restricted advertising, but is not applicable if this contract was entered into by means of formal advertising.

14. UTILIZATION OF SMALL BUSINESS CONCERNS

(The following clause is applicable if this contract exceeds $5,000.)

(a) It is the policy of the Government as declared by the Congress that a fair proportion of the purchases and contracts for supplies and services for the Government be placed with small business concerns.

(b) The Contractor agrees to accomplish the maximum amount of subcontracting to small business concerns that the Contractor finds to be consistent with the efficient performance of this contract.

15. UTILIZATION OF MINORITY BUSINESS ENTERPRISES

(The following clause is applicable if this contract exceeds $5,000.)

(a) It is the policy of the Government that minority business enterprises shall have the maximum practicable opportunity to participate in the performance of Government contracts.

(b) The Contractor agrees to use his best efforts to carry out this policy in the award of his subcontracts to the fullest extent consistent with the efficient performance of this contract. As used in this contract, the term "minority business enterprise" means a business, at least 50 percent of which is owned by minority group members or, in case of publicly owned businesses, at least 51 percent of the stock of which is owned by minority group members. For the purposes of this definition, minority group members are Negroes, Spanish-speaking American persons, American-Orientals, American-Indians, American-Eskimos, and American-Aleuts. Contractors may rely on written representations by subcontractors regarding their status as minority business enterprises in lieu of an independent investigation.

Source: U.S. Government Printing Office.

for the planned purchase, instructions on how to prepare the bid, terms of purchase, and delivery and payment schedules. A contract is awarded to the firm that best meets the bidding specifications.

The role of pricing varies substantially from one contract to another. The selection of a firm to supply janitorial services may be heavily price oriented. On the other hand, a contract to supply complex, high-technology military hardware or strategic consulting services may be based almost solely on the internal capabilities (machinery and competent staff) and technical qualifications of the bidder. We will examine bidding strategy in more detail when we discuss pricing.

When an agency isn't certain how a complex task should be accomplished or is unable to fully describe a specific item, service, or project, it will use negotiated purchasing. The purchasing office still uses the bidder's list to ask for price quotations and/or proposals from selected suppliers, but after reviewing initial proposals the agency may enter extended negotiations with the firms that have submitted successful bids.

SUMMARY

The consumption process may involve three different people: the decision maker, the purchaser who actually acquires the goods, and the user of the product or service. A mother may make a decision to purchase a gym set for her children. The father may buy it, and of course the children will enjoy it.

Consumer behavior is rarely a simple process. The purchase decision can involve many variables, including price, quality, availability, and service. Information regarding these inputs can be obtained from several sources. The advertising media, salespeople, acquaintances, family, and personal observation can provide the data for making purchase decisions. The consumer must then process this information and decide which products and brands to buy, the dealers to patronize, and perhaps the quantity and frequency of purchase.

Several major disciplines, including sociology, psychology, and learning theory, have made major contributions to our understanding of consumer behavior. This chapter develops a stimulus–response model of human behavior in general and purchase behavior in particular. After a stimulus has been perceived, a meaning is assigned to it. The cognitive process is based on a number of factors in the buyer's psyche, such as attitudes and values, recall of past experience, personality, needs, self-image, reference group, and culture. After meaning has been assigned to the stimulus, there will be either a positive, a neutral, or a negative response. A response, in turn, will be reinforced in one of these three ways, thus becoming part of our experience.

The final segment of the chapter is devoted to industrial purchasing behavior. In industrial purchasing there are typically several influences on the purchase decision and rational buying motives predominate. Often industrial purchasing is done by committee or, in the case of major installations, by the board of directors. Middle management may be the initiator of a purchase decision, while the actual decision is made by top management. Industrial purchasers usually consider factors such as durability, return on investment, availability of supply, and technical specifications.

Government purchasing, like industrial-goods buying, is based on rational motives. The government is a huge market for sellers of goods and services. The military, for example, operates the third-largest food store operation in the country, as well as the third-largest department and variety store group. Government buying is accomplished by two means: formal advertising and negotiation. Formal advertising for bids is through the *Commerce Business Daily*. Negotiated purchasing is common when the project is extremely complex or the government is not able to fully describe the task or project envisioned. The purchasing agency still, however, uses the bidder's list to ask for price quotations and proposals from selected suppliers.

KEY TERMS

Consumer or buyer behavior
Buyer's psyche
Learning
Relevant stimulus
Motivation research
Holistic or Gestalt psychology
Reference group
Affiliative group
Aspiratory group
Norms
Culture
Socialization
Acculturation
Perception
Cognitive process
Attitudes
Need
Self-actualization
Self-concept
Personality
Personality trait
Defense mechanism
Feedback
Bidder's list

QUESTIONS FOR DISCUSSION

1. Explain what is meant by consumer behavior.
2. What is the buyer's psyche? Explain its role in the buying process.
3. What is meant by learning theory? What implications does it have for marketing managers?
4. What are the basic concepts of psychoanalytic theory? How do they affect the buying process?
5. Explain the role that groups play in influencing consumer behavior. Do they have any practical value for marketing managers? Give an example to illustrate your views.
6. What is culture? How does it affect a person's buying behavior? Give examples to support your views.
7. Describe the basic elements of the human-behavior model presented in the chapter.

8. Describe the role of needs in determining consumer behavior. Can Maslow's hierarchy of needs be of use to marketing managers? Give specific examples to support your views.
9. What is the self-concept? Give at least three examples to illustrate its role in marketing.
10. What are defense mechanisms? How do they affect the buying process?
11. Differentiate between final consumers and industrial buyers. What factors affect an industrial purchase decision?
12. Why is the government market so important to marketers? What distinguishes the government from other industrial buyers?
13. Briefly describe the governmental buying process.

NOTES

1. Glenn Walters, *Consumer Behavior — Theory and Practice,* rev. ed. (Homewood, Ill.: Irwin, 1974), p. 6.
2. Ibid., p. 7.
3. Ibid., pp. 191–192.
4. These examples are taken from Vance Packard, *The Hidden Persuaders* (New York: Pocket Books, 1975).
5. Joe Kent Kerby, *Consumer Behavior — Conceptual Foundations* (New York: Dun-Donnelley, 1975), p. 77.
6. Perhaps the best source of information on family purchase decision making is Harry Davis, "Decision-Making Within the Household," *Journal of Consumer Research,* 2 (March 1976): 241–260. Other good sources are Robert Ferber and Lucy Chao Lee, "Husband–Wife Influence in Family Purchasing Behavior," *Journal of Consumer Research,* 1 (June 1974): 43–50; Harry Davis and Benny Rigaux, "Perception of Marital Roles in Decision Processes," *Journal of Consumer Research,* 1 (June 1974): 51–62; F. Kelly Shuptrine and G. Samuelson, "Dimensions of Marital Roles in Consumer Decision Making: Revisited," *Journal of Marketing Research,* 8 (February 1976): 87; L. J. Jaffe and H. Senft, "The Roles of Husbands and Wives in Purchasing Decisions," in L. Adler and I. Crespi, eds., *Attitude Research at Sea* (Chicago: American Marketing Association, 1966), pp. 95–110; G. M. Munsinger, J. E. Weber, and R. W. Hansen, "Joint Name Purchasing Decisions by Husbands and Wives," *Journal of Consumer Research,* 1 (March 1975): 60–66; R. A. Scott, "Husband–Wife Interaction in a Household Purchase Decision," *Southern Journal of Business,* 5 (July 1970): 218–225; H. Sharp and P. Mott, "Consumer Decisions in the Metropolitan Family," *Journal of Marketing,* 21 (October 1956): pp. 149–156; E. B. Sheldon, ed., *Family Economic Behavior: Problems and Prospects* (Philadelphia: Lippincott, 1973); J. N. Sheth, "A Theory of Family Buying Decisions," in J. N. Sheth, ed., *Models of Buyer Behavior: Conceptual, Quantitative, and Empirical* (New York: Harper & Row, 1974): pp. 17–33; R. E. Wilkes, "Husband–Wife Influence in Purchase Decisions — A Confirmation and Extension," *Journal of Marketing Research,* 7 (May 1975): 224–227; E. H. Wolgast, "Do Husbands or Wives Make the Purchasing Decisions?" *Journal of Marketing,* 23 (October 1958): 151–158; A. G. Woodside, "Effects of Prior Decision-Making, Demographics, and Psychographics on Marital Roles for Purchasing Durables," in M. J. Schlinger, ed., *Advances in Consumer Research,* vol. 2, *Proceedings of the*

5th Annual Conference of the Association for Consumer Research, 1974 (Chicago: Association for Consumers Research, 1975), pp. 81–91; R. T. Green and I. C. M. Cunningham, "Feminine Role Perception and Family Purchasing Decisions," *Journal of Marketing Research,* 12 (August 1975): 325–332; E. P. Cox, "Family Purchase Decision Making and the Process of Adjustment," *Journal of Marketing Research,* 12 (May 1975): 189–195; I. C. M. Cunningham and R. T. Green, "Purchasing Roles in the U.S. Family, 1955 and 1973," *Journal of Marketing,* 38 (October 1975): 61–64; P. Doyle and P. Hutchinson, "Individual Differences in Family Decision Making," *Journal of the Market Research Society,* 15 (October 1973): 193–206.

7. Human Ostlund, "Role Theory and Group Dynamics," in Scott Ward and Thomas Robertson, eds., *Consumer Behavior — Theoretical Sources* (Englewood Cliffs, N.J.: Prentice-Hall, 1973), pp. 263–267. © 1973. By permission.

8. The definition of culture and much of the discussion that follows is adapted from James Engel, David Kollat, and Roger Blackwell, *Consumer Behavior,* 2d ed. (New York: Holt, Rinehart and Winston, 1973), pp. 72–76.

9. The definition of perception is from Ron Markin, Jr., *Consumer Behavior — A Cognitive Orientation* (New York: Macmillan, 1974), p. 115.

10. The discussion of perceptual principles is taken from Thomas Robertson, *Consumer Behavior* (Glenview, Ill.: Scott, Foresman, 1970), pp. 15–17.

11. George Day, "Theories of Attitude Structure and Change," in Ward and Robertson, p. 306.

12. Markin, p. 204.

13. The discussion of needs is largely adapted from Kerby, pp. 42–64.

14. Gordon Allport, *Personality: A Psychological Interpretation* (New York: Holt, Rinehart and Winston, 1937), p. 48.

15. Kjell Gronhaug, "Exploring Environmental Influences in Organizational Buying," *Journal of Marketing Research,* 13 (August 1976): 225–229.

16. Arthur Weil, "The Military Market — Forgotten Giant of Marketing Opportunities," *Product Management,* October 1976, pp. 19–23.

17. Small Business Administration, *Selling to the U.S. Government* (Washington, D.C., October 1975), p. 1; see also: General Services Administration, *Doing Business with the Federal Government* (Washington, D.C.: Government Printing Office, December 1970).

CASE 5
The Creamoline Corporation

The Creamoline Corporation was founded in 1894 in Philadelphia. Its basic product, a clear, jelly-like petroleum-derivative substance, was the only product manufactured by Creamoline until 1955. Creamoline petroleum jelly can be used for minor cuts and abrasions, preventing diaper rash, soothing chapped lips, and the like.

The company's second product is Creamoline high-care hand lotion. Like the petroleum jelly, it became a huge success. Women use the product to soothe chapped hands and to keep their skin feeling creamy and moist. Buoyed by their success, Creamoline's executives decided to enter the male cosmetics market with an after-shave lotion.

Care was taken to ensure that the new product would succeed. The laboratory spent nine months formulating and testing a number of different compounds designed to quickly soothe burning skin after shaving and to have a pleasant fragrance. At last the lab narrowed the choice to two formulas: A and B. A blind test (no label) was used in six major test markets throughout the United States to compare not only A and B but also the two best-selling brands currently on the market. All the products were in white packages with the label "After-Shave Lotion" followed by the letter A, B, C, or D. Consumers were asked to use each of the four products over an eight-week period, using one product for a week and then switching to another until each of the four brands had been used for a total of two weeks. Strict sampling instructions and usage procedures were set up to assure a reliable test.

When the results were in, the survey showed that test product B was similar in virtually all major attributes with the two leading national brands, C and D. Test product A, however, was viewed as superior in almost all product-attribute categories to both test product B and the two national brands. Thus the company decided to roll out the new product (test brand A) nationally.

The new brand was called Creamoline High-Care After-Shave Lotion. After it had been on the market for four months it became apparent to the firm that it had a real loser. Subsequent interviews with people who had purchased the product revealed a very interesting phenomenon. Almost all claimed that the product was greasy, oily, and seemed to have a petroleum jelly base. These claims had not been made during the blind test, and in fact the product did not contain any greasy or oily ingredients.

Marketing executives could not figure out the cause of this phenomenon. Using the material that you have learned in this chapter, explain why these results may have occurred. How could the company have avoided this costly mistake? If you were called upon as director of marketing research to explain to the marketing manager what happened, what explanation would you offer?

6

Marketing Information Systems and Marketing Research

OBJECTIVES

■ To learn the meaning and importance of marketing research.
■ To present a brief historical outline of marketing research.
■ To understand what is meant by a marketing information system.
■ To gain insight into the marketing research industry—who does what?
■ To learn the steps involved in designing a research project.
■ To gain an understanding of various data collection techniques.
■ To present a brief overview of questionnaire construction, sampling, and data analysis.

The marketing manager's job involves trying to satisfy both the needs of consumers and the goals of the firm. It requires definition of target markets and development of marketing mixes that are attractive to those markets. All this must be accomplished in an environment that may be hostile and is constantly changing. The manager must anticipate changes in this environment—economic, legal/political, social, technological, competitive, demographic—and must foresee the implications of those changes for the firm's marketing programs.

Marketing research is the vehicle by which information is obtained about present and potential customers, their reactions to present and prospective marketing mixes, the changing character of

The author is indebted to Dr. Roger Gates for preparing this chapter.

the external environment, and the degree to which existing marketing programs are achieving their goals.

This chapter begins with an examination of the nature and scope of marketing research. This is followed by a discussion of the marketing information system and the types of firms that do marketing research. The marketing research process is examined in detail as we go step by step through all the decisions that must be made in designing an individual marketing research project. Finally, the role of marketing research in the strategy development process is explored.

WHAT IS MARKETING RESEARCH?

There are as many definitions of marketing research as there are books on the subject.[1] However, most of them have certain characteristics in common. First, most definitions of marketing research describe it as a systematic search for information. Second, nearly all of them suggest that marketing research involves data analysis and interpretation in addition to data collection. The third characteristic that most of these definitions have in common is the recognition that marketing research exists for the purpose of providing decision-making data for management. Marketing research is defined as the collection and analysis of data relevant to marketing decision making and the communication of the results of this analysis to management.

THE DEVELOPMENT OF MARKETING RESEARCH

Marketing research as a separate and distinct business function is of fairly recent origin. An 1879 mail survey of state agricultural officials by the N. W. Ayer & Son advertising agency has been identified as perhaps the earliest marketing research study.[2] There was little real development of the field until the 1920s.[3]

The 1920s saw significant growth in marketing research technology and practice. During this period many new techniques were introduced. However, the Depression and World War II sidetracked the development of marketing research for more than twenty years— 1929–1950. The postwar years of the late 1940s were characterized by such tremendous pent-up demand for goods that had not been available during the war that marketing, and consequently marketing research, continued to take a back seat to production.

During the 1950s this condition gradually changed. Pent-up demand was filled, and emphasis shifted back to production innovation and marketing as it became necessary to appeal to the needs and desires of an increasingly affluent society. During this period there was a corresponding increase in the use of marketing research. It also became more sophisticated. Marketing decisions were becoming more complex, and the consequences of wrong decisions were costly. Thousands of corporate marketing research departments were created, as were many of today's leading marketing research firms. Emphasis was on the development of improved data collection procedures.

The 1960s witnessed a continuation of the trends of growing complexity in marketing and increased use of marketing research. The major development of the 1960s was the application of behavioral-science theory to marketing research. Attitude and personality variables and powerful statistical techniques were introduced.

Marketing research has continued to grow in scope and sophistication in the 1970s. The shortages and unfavorable economic climate of the 1970s appear to have sharpened the need for research. Emphasis has shifted from the problems of data collection to those of data analysis. More powerful statistical methods have been introduced to match the complexity of the data collected. All signs indicate that the need for marketing research will continue to grow in the future.[4]

MARKETING INFORMATION SYSTEMS

Many authors have attempted to make a distinction between the terms marketing information system (MIS) and marketing research or marketing research project.[5] The MIS is "a set of procedures and methods for the regular, planned collection, analysis, and presentation of information for use in making marketing decisions."[6] The distinction between the two terms is that the marketing information system is an ongoing, repetitive process while the marketing research project is an intermittent or irregular activity.[7]

It is usually suggested that the MIS deals with information that is relevant to the monitoring of ongoing marketing activities and that marketing research projects are concerned with information that is relevant to strategic marketing decisions.[8] For example, monthly reports showing sales in each of the firm's sales territories would be considered part of the MIS. A study of several alternate sites for a retail outlet would be viewed as a marketing research project.

It is more realistic to view the MIS concept as a philosophy of information and data management. The marketing information collected by the organization is a valuable resource, and as in the case of the firm's other resources there should be some system for managing it. In this view the MIS is the firm's total system for the collection or assembly of marketing information; its processing, tabulation, and analysis; its dissemination; its cataloging and storage; and its retrieval. It should provide management with the information it needs, when it needs it, in a form that it can understand.

WHO DOES MARKETING RESEARCH?

Two types of organizations actually design and implement marketing research studies—corporate marketing research departments and independent marketing research firms.[9] Corporate marketing research departments include those of manufacturers such as Procter & Gamble, General Foods, and General Mills; retailers such as Sears, K-Mart, and Southland (7-Eleven stores); and service businesses such as McDonald's, Burger King, and Steak & Ale.

An independent marketing research firm is a company whose primary business is the sale of marketing research services. Such firms can be classified in two groups on the basis of the nature of the information they provide—custom or ad hoc research firms and syndicated-service research firms.[10]

Research Firms

Syndicated-service research firms compile a standardized set of data on a continuing basis—every month, every six months, once a year—and distribute it to anyone who subscribes to the service. Examples include the Nielsen and American Research Bureau (ARB) TV audience reports, the ARB radio audience reports, the Simmons and Target Group Index (TGI) magazine audience and readership reports, the Selling Areas Marketing (SAMI) warehouse movement reports, and the Nielsen retail shelf audits.[11] A company subscribes to a syndicated service much the way a consumer subscribes to a magazine. All subscribers to a given service get the same or similar information in the same or similar form.

Data from syndicated services are an important input to the marketing information systems of many firms. These data are usually used for control purposes, that is, to monitor the effectiveness, on an ongoing basis, of the firm's marketing strategies. For example, Nielsen store audit data that show the movement of products off the retail shelf might be used to closely monitor the retail sales of a particular product. Because many subscribers share the costs of collecting and processing the data, the cost to individual subscribers is low. For this reason syndicated services are often good buys on a cost–versus–value-of-information basis.

Custom or ad hoc research firms do one-of-a-kind research projects, usually for the purpose of providing data that are relevant to strategic decision making—where to locate a new store, what creative strategy to use in next year's advertising, and the like. These studies are ordinarily designed and conducted for a single client, with all the data generated by the study becoming the property of that client.

In addition to these two general types of marketing research firms, a number of organizations provide specialized services. Most significant among these is the field service firm.[12] These organizations provide interviewing and other field services to custom research firms, syndicated-service firms, and corporate marketing research departments on a subcontract basis.

The Top Ten

Table 6.1 provides a ranking by actual or estimated 1975 sales volume of the country's ten largest marketing research firms. Other major firms in this industry are Data Development, Decisions Center, Opinion Research (ORC), MPI Marketing Research, Peter deKadt Research, and Oxtoby-Smith.

The top four firms are all syndicated-service firms. Number one, Nielsen, relies heavily on its well-known TV audience reports (which account for 11 percent of its business) and its less well-known retail shelf audit data (65 percent).[13] Number two, IMS, provides a number of services that are similar to Nielsen's except that they specialize in the pharmaceutical–medical area. Half of IMS's sales come from pharmaceutical–medical audits, while the rest come from other syndicated services. Third-ranked Selling Areas–Marketing (SAMI) compiles and sells data on the movement of products, while the American Research Bureau (ARB) provides TV and radio audience data. The next six firms are all custom research firms.

In addition to this group of large marketing research firms, there are a large number of very small firms in the industry. New firms are constantly being formed. Research in Perspective, Research 100, Benson & Benson, Newman-Stein, and Custom Research are examples of successful firms founded in recent years by former officers or employees of other marketing research organizations.

TABLE 6.1	Largest U.S. Marketing Research Companies (Dollars in Millions)					
	Est. $ Volume 1975	Percent Research	Estimated Research Volume	Percent Research Volume in U.S.	Est. U.S. Research Volume	U.S. Rank
1. A. C. Nielsen Co.	$211.0	76	$160.4	50	$ 80.2	1
2. IMS International	53.0	87	46.1	37	17.1	4
3. Selling Areas–Marketing, Inc.	27.0	100	27.0	100	27.0	2
4. American Research Bureau	19.5	100	19.5	100	19.5	3
5. Burke International Research Corp.	15.8	100	15.8	75	11.9	6
6. Market Facts	13.3	100	13.3	98	13.0	5
7. Audits & Surveys	12.0	67	8.0	90	7.2	8
8. Marketing Services Group, Booz, Allen & Hamilton	9.0	100	9.0	100	9.0	7
9. Inmarco Inc.	9.0	100	9.0	75	6.8	9
10. Marketing & Research Counselors	5.7	100	5.7	100	5.7	10
	$375.3		$313.8		$197.4	

Source: Advertising Age, March 15, 1976, p. 1. Copyright 1976 by Crain Communications, Inc. Reprinted by permission.

Corporate Marketing Research Departments

The other type of organization that does marketing research is the corporate marketing research department. A 1973 survey of 3432 corporations by the American Marketing Association (AMA) found that 59 percent of the firms that responded had formal marketing research departments.[14] Another 18 percent of these companies had at least one person responsible for the marketing research function, while 23 percent had no one assigned to this area. The results for various types of firms are shown in Table 6.2. Marketing research departments are most prevalent among consumer products firms and least prevalent, by a narrow margin, among advertising agencies. Surprisingly, 59 percent of the manufacturers of industrial products reported that they had a marketing research department.

The marketing research departments of different companies vary greatly in form and in the jobs they perform. General Foods has a highly developed marketing research group with more than 300 employees that can do all types of marketing research and all phases of a marketing research project in house. Anderson-Clayton Foods, located in Dallas, has fewer than ten people working in marketing research and relies heavily on outside suppliers to design and conduct research studies. However, these two companies have something in common: They both work largely with primary data (i.e., new data). This is in contrast to the marketing research departments of companies like Braniff Airlines that not only are relatively small but deal primarily with secondary data (i.e., data that has already been

TABLE 6.2	Percentages of Different Types of Firms Having Marketing Research Departments		
Type of Firm	Percent Having Formal Marketing Research Departments	Percent Having One Person Assigned to Research	Percent with No One Assigned
Manufacturers of consumer products	70	13	17
Publishing and broadcasting	66	11	23
Manufacturers of industrial products	59	19	22
Retailers and wholesalers	54	11	35
Advertising agencies	53	22	25
Others	53	25	22
All companies	59	18	23

Source: Dik Twedt, *1973 Survey of Marketing Research* (Chicago: American Marketing Association, 1973), p. 6. Reprinted by permission of the American Marketing Association.

gathered from company operations, such as traffic on various routes, and data from library sources such as the *U.S. Census of Population*).[15] It is clear that marketing research departments come in all shapes and sizes and are structured to suit the information needs of the firms they serve.

DESIGNING THE MARKETING RESEARCH PROJECT: PRELIMINARY ANALYSIS

When confronted with a situation that may require marketing research, the researcher has two questions to deal with. First, is formal research really called for in this case? Second, if it is called for, what form should this research take? The answer to the first question is developed in a preliminary analysis, as follows:[16]

1. Reach an agreement on the nature of the problems and the research objectives—this provides focus for the research effort.
2. Perform a background investigation—check existing data for anything relevant to the research problem.
3. Perform an informal investigation—conduct a mini-study.

The first step in the research process must be the development of a problem statement and a statement of research objectives on which the decision maker and the researcher can agree.[17] This is not as easy as it sounds, but it is important because these statements will provide direction for the remainder of the study. Some situations may require only a problem statement; others lend themselves more readily to the specification of research objectives. In some cases identifying and structuring the problem may itself turn out to be the objective of a major research effort.

The background investigation, sometimes referred to as the situation analysis, is particularly important to the outside consultant or to any researcher dealing with a particular type of problem for the first time.[18] The purpose of this step is to permit the researcher to become totally immersed in the problem. It is necessary to become familiar with the company, its products, its markets, its marketing history, the competition, and so forth. On the basis of this background investigation it may become necessary to go back and respecify the problem statement and research objectives developed in the first step.

The informal investigation is the final step in the preliminary analysis.[19] The informal investigation can be looked upon as a mini-research study. In this stage data may be collected from people outside the company—consumers, retailers who handle the product, and others. The purpose is to determine, on the basis of a cursory and relatively inexpensive survey, whether to proceed with a formal study. As in the background investigation, information may be uncovered that suggests a need to respecify the problem. Study of this problem will end here if the solution is clear or if it appears that the cost of obtaining the information required to solve it will outweigh the expected value of the information. If the answer is not clear and if the projected value of the required information exceeds its cost, the next step is to design a formal study.

DESIGNING A FORMAL MARKETING RESEARCH STUDY

The steps involved in designing and conducting a formal study are as follows:

1. Specify the data required to meet the research objectives.
2. Determine the most efficient and accurate means for gathering the required data.
3. Design the data collection forms.
4. Specify the sampling procedures to be used.
5. Specify the data collection procedures.
6. Develop a plan for processing the data.
7. Develop a plan for analyzing the data.
8. Prepare a report to present the results to management.

Specifying Data Needs and Selecting Sources

At this point it is necessary to develop a complete list of all the data required to meet the specified research objective. Then the researcher should determine the sources for each type of data. There are really only two general types of data used in marketing research—primary data and secondary data.

Secondary Data. Secondary data are data that were collected for any purpose other than the one at hand.[20] Major sources of secondary data are outlined in Table 6.3. Most research efforts rely at least in part on secondary data. If a problem can be solved with this type of data, it is desirable to use such data because they can ordinarily be obtained quickly and at relatively low cost. The problem is locating relevant secondary data. There are firms, such as the Information Source in Los Angeles, that specialize in obtaining hard-to-find secondary data for a fee.

Primary Data. Primary data are data that are collected for the first time for the purpose of solving the particular problem under investigation.[21] There are four ways of generating primary data—survey, observation, experiment, and simulation.[22] Survey and observation are basically data assembly procedures in which the researcher takes a passive attitude toward the phenomenon under investigation. This is in contrast to the experiment, which is distinguished by the researcher's manipulation of one or more independent variables (i.e., price, shelf space, advertising expenditures, and package design) for the purpose of measuring the impact of different levels of the inde-

TABLE 6.3	Sources and Descriptions of Secondary Data	

Source	Description
1. Internal information	Any internal company information that may be helpful in solving a particular marketing problem. Examples include sales invoices, other accounting records, data from previous marketing research studies, and historical sales data.
2. Government agencies	The Bureau of the Census and many other federal agencies provide perhaps the largest single source of secondary data for marketing researchers. In particular, the *Censuses of Population, Housing, Business, Agriculture, Manufacturing,* and *Transportation* are widely used.
3. Syndicated research services	Companies such as A. C. Nielsen, Arbition, IMS International, and SAMI, described earlier in this chapter, are major sources of secondary data.
4. Trade associations	Many trade associations, such as the National Industrial Conference Board and the National Retail Merchants Association, collect data that are of interest to their members.
5. Custom research firms	Custom research firms can refer to data from old studies of related problems.
6. Research bureaus, professional associations, foundations	A variety of nonprofit organizations collect and disseminate data that are of interest to marketing researchers.
7. Commercial publications	*Advertising Age, Sales Management, Product Marketing, Merchandising Week,* and many other commercial publications provide useful research data.

pendent variable on the dependent variable (i.e., market share, unit sales, dollar sales, etc.). Simulation in this context typically involves the development of mathematical models of marketing phenomena. The idea is that once this is done various parameters of the model can be adjusted to reflect changes in the firm's marketing program and the impact on sales or profits estimated.

Although no exact figures are available, it is acknowledged that in commercial marketing research the survey is by far the most widely used method of obtaining data. Surveys involve asking people questions, while observation means watching people or phenomena such as traffic flows or the movement of products from a retail shelf. There are good reasons for the dominance of the survey in marketing research. Observation has the advantage of permitting you to see what people actually do rather than what they say they do.[23] However, it has the serious disadvantage of providing no information about who they are or about why they do what they do. In most marketing research the "why" of consumer behavior is important.

Experiments also suffer from this problem. Experiments are

particularly difficult in the marketing field because so many factors (e.g., competitors' advertising, weather, and economic conditions) are encountered in actual market situations that may affect the dependent variable but are beyond the experimenter's control.[24]

Each procedure has its natural place in marketing research. Observation is the natural way to monitor things like the movement of a product off the retail shelf (store audits) or traffic levels (car counters). Experimental designs are widely used in the test marketing of new products and new advertising campaigns and for testing things like the optimal amount of shelf space to devote to a product. Surveys prevail in studies intended to find out what people think or feel or why they like or dislike a particular product, store, price, or the like. The researcher's job is to select the data collection method that will provide the desired data most accurately and efficiently.

Surveys. A number of different survey methods are used in marketing research. The choice of a particular method should be a function of the type of information required and the funds available for the study. The type of information required should be the overriding consideration. Individuals can be interviewed in person, over the telephone, via the mail, or by means of computer terminals.

PERSONAL INTERVIEWS. There are four possible personal-interview situations—door to door, mall intercept, focus group, and executive interview. In the door-to-door interview the respondent is interviewed at home. This is the most costly survey method and is typically regarded as generating the best data.[25] The mall intercept interview involves interviewing people in the common areas of shopping malls. It is the economy version of the door-to-door interview. This approach provides personal contact between the interviewer and the respondent without interviewer travel time and mileage costs. To obtain the right to do this type of interviewing, the research firm may rent office space in the mall or pay so much per day. Mall intercept interviews must be brief, and it is sometimes difficult to obtain a representative sample of the area in question.

The focus group is a third type of personal interview.[26] Seven to ten people with the desired characteristics are recruited by random telephone screening or in some other way. Qualified consumers (i.e., users of the product under investigation) are usually offered an incentive ($10–15 is common) to participate in a group discussion. The place where this discussion is held will probably have a conference table (some are set up like home livingrooms) and audio taping equipment. It is likely to have a viewing room with a one-way mirror so that clients may watch the session, and it may be equipped with video taping equipment. During the session a moderator will lead the group through a discussion of a series of topics. In a study of semimoist dog food, for example, the moderator might lead a group of product users into a discussion concerning their awareness of existing brands, usage rates, words used to describe dog food, and so forth. This technique is used primarily as an exploratory tool—as a prelude to a formal study.

The executive interview is the fourth type of personal interview and can be viewed as the industrial counterpart of the door-to-door interview.[27] Businesspeople are interviewed at their offices concerning their usage, preferences, and perceptions of business products and services—copy machines, computers, telephone services, air travel, financial services, and so forth. These interviews are usually quite expensive because the interviewers must set up appointments, often have to wait to see the appropriate person, and frequently encounter canceled appointments.

TELEPHONE INTERVIEWS. Compared to the personal interview, the telephone interview offers the advantage of lower cost and the potential for the best sample of any of the survey procedures.[28] It is frequently criticized for providing poorer-quality data than the personal interview. However, recent studies have shown that these fears may be exaggerated.[29] There are at least two types of telephone interviewing—from-home interviewing and central-location interviewing. The former, as the term implies, is done from home. Central-location telephone interviewing is done from a "phone room" set up for this purpose. A phone room has a number of phone lines, individual interviewing stations, possibly monitoring equipment, and headsets so that the interviewers can have their hands free.

The principal advantage of the central-location telephone interview lies in the ability to control interview quality and productivity. Its principal disadvantage compared to the from-home interview is the added cost—supervision, facilities, and interviewer travel time and mileage. The use of Wide Area Telephone Service (WATS) lines in conjunction with central-location telephone facilities permits the research firm to interview people across the country from a single location.

MAIL SURVEYS. Mail surveys have a number of apparent benefits—low cost, elimination of interviewers and their biases, elimination of field supervisors, centralized control, actual or promised anonymity for respondents (which may elicit more candid responses), and so forth.[30] Some researchers feel that mail questionnaires give the respondent an opportunity to make more thoughtful replies and to check records, talk to family members, take stock of certain items, and the like.[31] The big problem with mail questionnaires is low response rates.[32] And the problem with low response rates is that certain elements of the population may be more likely to respond than others.[33] This means that the resulting sample will not be representative of the population being surveyed. For example, the sample may have too many retired people and too few working people. In this case answers to a question about attitudes toward social security might indicate a much more favorable view of the system than is actually the case. A second serious problem with mail surveys is that there is no one to prod respondents to clarify or elaborate on their answers.

Mail panels such as those operated by Market Facts, National Family Opinion Research, and NPD Research offer an alternative to the one-shot mail survey. A mail panel consists of a national sample of households recruited to participate for a given period.[34] Panel members often receive gifts in return for their participation. The panel is in essence a sample that is used several times. The panel's composition can be checked to make sure it is a true cross section of the total population. The response rates from mail panels are high compared to those achieved in one-time mail surveys. Rates of 70 percent are not uncommon.[35]

COMPUTER INTERVIEWS. A recent development in marketing research technology is the computer interview, in which interactive computer terminals are used to interview people directly.[36] Questions are printed out on the terminal and the respondent types in replies. At this point questions are limited to the multiple-choice variety. This approach is currently being used in a mall north of Chicago by A. C. Nielsen.[37] Little is known about the pluses and minuses of this type of interviewing, but it may have a very bright future in that it eliminates the interviewer and simplifies data processing.

Observation. Observation in marketing research takes four forms: people watching people, people watching physical phenomena, machines watching people, and machines watching physical phenomena.[38] "People watching people" is illustrated by the use of observers to trace the traffic patterns of customers in order to determine the effects of different merchandise arrangements on those patterns. "People watching physical phenomena" includes the use of human observers to count vehicular traffic flow past a proposed site for a retail store or to keep track of the actual movement of products off a retail shelf. In the two other types of observation, machines—movie cameras, video tape equipment, traffic counters—are substituted for the human observer.

Experiments. In an experiment the researcher manipulates one factor, called the independent variable (e.g., price), and attempts to measure its effect on another factor, called the dependent variable (e.g., sales).[39] For example, management may be divided over how to price a new product. One group feels that it should be priced 20 percent above competing products. The other group feels that its price should be equal to that of competing products. An experiment might be set up in which the product is introduced in two very similar cities on a test basis. Everything would be done exactly the same way in both cities except that the higher price would be charged in one and the lower price in the other. Most experiments are much more complicated than this example, but they follow this general pattern.[40]

Designing the Data-Gathering Forms

Most marketing research projects require some type of data-gathering form. The supermarket auditor needs a form for recording counts; the observer of frozen-food purchasers needs a form for recording observations; the interviewer needs a form from which to read questions and on which to record responses; and experiments may benefit from the use of forms for recording experimental results. Forms ensure that the same observations, questions, or measurements are made in every case. They reach their highest levels of sophistication in the survey questionnaire.

Four basic types of information can be solicited from a respondent—state of mind, state of being, behavior, and intentions information.[41] Examples of the various types of information are provided in Table 6.4. It is generally agreed that it is easier to obtain accurate state-of-being and behavior information than accurate state-of-mind and intentions information. For this reason behavior information is often obtained as a surrogate for preference or intention information. For example, instead of asking people which fast-food restaurant they prefer, ask them which fast-food restaurant they patronize most frequently. Instead of asking a beer drinker which brand of beer he or she intends to purchase next, ask about past purchasing behavior and project it forward. The idea is that the behavior reporting will often provide a better idea of state of mind or intentions than a direct question on the subject. In many cases both the relevant behavior information and state-of-mind or intentions information are sought so

TABLE 6.4	Types of Information Solicited by Marketing Researchers	
Type of Information	**Example**
State of being	Age, income, sex, and other demographic characteristics
State of mind	Attitudes, images, opinions, brand preferences, and the like
Behavior	Actions—brands purchased, frequency of purchase, all facets of consumption behavior
Intentions	Planned actions in regard to consumption behavior—intention to purchase a new car next year

Source: Ben Enis and Keith Cox, *The Marketing Research Process* (Pacific Palisades, Calif.: Goodyear, 1972), pp. 173–174. Copyright © 1972 by Goodyear Publishing Co. By permission.

that they can be compared. One might say that the trick of questionnaire design is to obtain the desired information by asking the respondent a question that he or she can reasonably be expected to answer accurately.

Designing a questionnaire is a tedious and time-consuming process and has been discussed at length by other writers.[42] The first step is the development of a list of topics that must be covered in the questionnaire. This list should be developed with the research objectives in mind. Topics that are not directly related to these objectives should be dropped unless there is some strong reason for including them.

The second step is to write specific questions to deal with each topic. Finally, the preliminary version of the questionnaire should be pretested in a pilot study in order to identify unforeseen problems.

Selecting Sampling Procedures

The selection and development of sampling procedures is an important part of most primary-data collection efforts. Seldom can you take a census of all the possible users of a new product, nor can you interview them all. This being the case, procedures must be developed for selecting or sampling the group to be interviewed. Several questions must be answered before a sampling plan is selected. First, the population or universe of interest must be defined. This is the group from which the sample will be drawn. It should include all the people whose opinions, behavior, preferences, attitudes, and so on are of interest to the marketer. For example, in a study whose purpose is to determine the market for a new canned dog food the universe might be defined to include all current purchasers of canned dog food.

After the universe has been defined, the next question is, Must the sample be representative of the population in all aspects? The answer to this question determines which of the two broad types of sampling procedures—probability or nonprobability—should be used.[43] If the answer to this question is yes, a probability sample is called for. Otherwise, a nonprobability sample might be considered.

Probability Samples. Probability samples have the desirable characteristic of permitting the researcher to estimate how much sampling error is present in a given study. Three types of probability samples are commonly used in marketing research: simple random samples,[44] cluster or area samples,[45] and stratified samples.[46]

The simple random sample must be set up in such a way that every element of the population has an equal chance of being selected as part of the sample.[47] An example would be a situation in which a university is interested in obtaining a cross section of student opinion on a proposed sports complex to be built using student activity fees. If an up-to-date list of all the students enrolled at the university can be obtained, a sample that meets all the requirements of a simple random sample can be drawn by using random numbers from a table (most statistics books have such tables) to select students from the list.

A solution for a number of the problems—lack of up-to-date lists, high costs, the expense of making callbacks—associated with simple random samples can be found in the use of area or cluster samples.[48] In this approach the researcher randomly selects a number of geographic starting points. For example, a grid overlay might be superimposed on a map of the area to be surveyed. Then row and column coordinates can be selected at random. Next, the nearest street intersections to these coordinates are located. Finally, the interviewer is given a route to follow from the starting point. This route will typically consist of a particular city block or blocks. Interviewers are often given additional instructions that include a procedure for selecting respondents.

The third type of probability sample is the stratified sample. A stratified sample is appropriate in cases in which the researcher knows that the population to be investigated is composed of subgroups that are heterogeneous with regard to the variable(s) of interest. For example, assume that previous studies of fast-food restaurant patronage found that adults under 35 eat in fast-food restaurants an average of four times a week while those 35 or over eat in fast-food restaurants only once a week on the average. People under 35 make up 45 percent of the population and people 35 or over make up 55 percent of the population. Age would therefore provide a basis for stratification. This means that when the sample is actually selected (simple random sample or cluster sampling procedures will be used to locate prospective respondents), the people interviewed must be tallied by age group. If the total sample size is 1000, interviewing of people under 35 would cease when 450 had been interviewed. Interviewing of people 35 or over would continue until 550 had been interviewed. More detailed strata might be discovered based on sex, income, occupation, or other factors. The key is that the behavior of people in different strata must be significantly different with regard to the variables that are of interest to the marketer.

Nonprobability Samples.   Nonprobability samples include all samples that cannot be considered probability samples. Specifically, any sample in which there is little or no attempt to ensure that a representative cross section of the population is obtained can be considered a nonprobability sample. Examples of nonprobability samples include the quota sample, the convenience sample, and other, related types of samples.[49] The convenience sample is based on the use of respondents that are "convenient" or readily accessible to the researcher—employees, friends, relatives, and the like. Quota samples are based on the practice of interviewing a certain number of people that meet certain qualifications regardless of how they are located. There is nothing wrong with nonprobability samples as long as the researcher understands the nature of this type of sample. The problem with these types of samples is that there is no way of knowing how much sampling error has been accumulated. Much marketing research is based on nonprobability samples. The main incentive for using this type of sample is its lower cost.

Data Collection Procedures

Whether the study is being administered by a marketing research firm or a corporate marketing research department, the field work or interviewing will most likely be conducted by a subcontractor – a field service firm. Most studies will involve data collection in several cities and require working with a comparable number of field service firms. It is therefore crucial that all of these subcontractors do everything exactly the same way. This requires that detailed field instructions be developed for every job. Nothing should be left to chance. No interpretations of procedures should be left to the subcontractors.

Processing the Data

When the completed data forms or questionnaires have been returned to the local field service firm, the data processing begins. The first step in this process is the editing of the completed questionnaires. This involves checking to see that the respondent is qualified, that all the questions that should have been asked were asked, that questions that should not have been asked were not asked, and that other interviewing standards and procedures were followed.

Next, a certain percentage of each interviewer's work is validated. This involves calling the listed respondents and asking them whether they were interviewed, where they were interviewed, and whether certain questions were asked. The interviews that pass these tests are sent on to the client firm.

When the interviews arrive at the client firm they typically go through the entire process again. Next, codes must be developed for the answers to questions such as "Why do you use brand X?" The many answers to such a question must be placed in a smaller number of categories. After this process has been completed, the data will be converted into some computer-readable medium – computer card, magnetic tape, or disk.

Data Analysis

The next step in the process is analysis of the data. The purpose of this analysis is to interpret and draw conclusions from the mass of data that have been collected. The marketing researcher attempts to impose some order on those data. Three types of analysis are commonly used in marketing research: one-way frequency counts, cross tabula-

TABLE 6.5	A One-Way Frequency Count	
Brand	**Frequency**	**Percent**
Budweiser	38	19
Miller	41	20.5
Schlitz	36	18
Coors	71	35.5
Others	14	7
Total respondents	200	100.0

tions, and statistical analysis.[50] Of these, statistical analysis is the most sophisticated, one-way frequency counts the simplest.

One-way frequency tables provide counts of the various responses to a question. The answers to the question "What brand of beer do you drink most often?" are shown in Table 6.5. One-way frequency tables are nearly always done, at least as a first step, in data analysis. They provide the researcher with a general picture of the results of the study.

Cross tabulations, or "cross tabs," permit the analyst to look at the responses to one question in relation to the responses to one or more other questions. For example, cross tabbing the answers to the questions summarized in Table 6.5 by age of respondent provides the information shown in Table 6.6. This table provides all the information in the previous table; in addition, it shows the relationship between age and brand usage. It indicates that Coors is much more popular among the younger group, while brand preference is much more evenly divided among older beer drinkers. A number of strategy implications for the various brands are suggested.

TABLE 6.6	A Cross Tabulation Based on Table 6.5					
	Age of Respondent					
	Under 35		**Over 35**		**Total**	
Brand	**no.**	**%**	**no.**	**%**	**no.**	**%**
Budweiser	15	15	23	23	38	19
Miller	12	12	29	29	41	20.5
Schlitz	13	13	23	23	36	18
Coors	51	51	20	20	71	35.5
Others	9	9	5	5	14	7
Total respondents	100	100	100	100	200	100

Data analysis involves the use of powerful statistical techniques to analyze the relationships between variables (e.g., income of respondent and brand preferred) and between respondents (e.g., do people over 50 represent a distinct market segment for a particular product?). A discussion of these techniques is beyond the scope of this book, but there are a number of good sources on the topic.[51]

Communicating the Results to Management

The final step in designing and conducting a formal study is to communicate the findings and conclusions of the study to management. This is a key step in the process because if the marketing researcher wants those conclusions acted upon he or she must convince the manager that the results are credible and are justified by the data collected. The researcher will ordinarily be required to present management with both written and oral reports regarding the project. The nature of the audience must be kept in mind when these reports are being prepared and presented. In either case the reports should begin with a clear, concise statement of the research objectives. This should be followed by a complete, but brief and simple, explanation of the research design or methodology employed. A summary of major findings should come next. The report should end with a presentation of conclusions and recommendations for management.

SUMMARY

The fact that marketing research exists to serve the marketing decision maker was stressed in this chapter. If the marketing research function is performed effectively, the batting average of the marketing decision maker should be higher than it would be without marketing research. Moreover, it should be enough higher to justify the cost of the marketing research function. Research has value only to the degree that it helps improve the quality of the decisions made by an organization.

Marketing research is a tool for segmenting markets and identifying target markets. It permits the organization to assess the reactions of target markets to different marketing mixes. Finally, it provides a mechanism for gathering data to project changes in the environment and to evaluate the effects of these changes on the firm's marketing programs.

The structure of the commercial marketing research industry and the types of marketing research firms were presented. Finally, the steps involved in designing and implementing a marketing research project were discussed in some detail.

The quality and quantity of commercial marketing research have grown tremendously since World War II — particularly in the past fifteen years. All signs point to continued rapid growth in the future. The need to appeal to higher human needs and the increasingly competitive nature of the markets for most consumer products assure the future of marketing research.

KEY TERMS

Marketing research
Marketing information system
Marketing research project
Syndicated-service research firm
Custom or ad hoc research firm
Field service firm
Preliminary analysis
Situation analysis
Secondary data
Primary data
Survey
Observation
Experiment

Simulation
Personal interview
Mall intercept interview
Focus group
Executive interview
Telephone interview
Mail survey
Mail panel
Computer interview
Sampling
Probability sample
Nonprobability sample

QUESTIONS FOR DISCUSSION

1. What is marketing research? Why is it so important to marketing management?
2. Define the terms *marketing information system* and *marketing research project*. How do they fit into the overall marketing research function?
3. Distinguish among the different types of firms that sell marketing research services. What functions do each of them perform?
4. Do you think manufacturers of consumer products are more involved in marketing research activities than wholesalers or retailers? Give reasons for your answer.
5. What is the purpose of a preliminary analysis? Describe the basic elements of such a study.
6. Briefly outline the different steps involved in designing a marketing research project.
7. What are secondary data? From what sources could one find the following information?
   a. The population of Ontario, Canada
   b. Average per capita income in Wyoming
   c. The number of new housing units started in California
   d. The number of banks in the Dallas–Fort Worth area
   e. The number of refrigerators imported into the United States in the past year
8. What are primary data? Describe in your own words the different methods used for generating such data.
9. Describe the advantages and disadvantages of the personal interview compared to the mail survey.
10. What are probability samples? Describe the three types of samples that are included in this category. Can you give examples of each type?
11. What is the purpose of data analysis? Explain some of the techniques commonly used in analyzing the data.
12. Do you feel that marketing research will grow in importance in the future? Give reasons for your answer.

NOTES

1. See Donald S. Tull and Del I. Hawkins, *Marketing Research: Meaning Measurement and Method* (New York: Macmillan, 1976), p. 3; Ben Enis and Keith Cox, *The Marketing Research Process* (Pacific Palisades, Calif.: Goodyear, 1972), p. 22; Bertram Schoner and Kenneth Uhl, *Marketing Research*, 2d ed. (New York: Wiley, 1975), p. 20; Harper W. Boyd, Ralph Westfall, and Stanley F. Stasch, *Marketing Research* (Homewood, Ill.: Irwin, 1977), p. 4; Paul E. Green and Donald S. Tull, *Research for Marketing Decisions* (Englewood Cliffs, N.J.: Prentice-Hall, 1975; David J. Luck, Hugh G. Wales, and Donald A. Taylor, *Marketing Research*, 4th ed. (Englewood Cliffs, N.J.: Prentice-Hall, 1974), pp. 8–9.

2. Jack J. Honomichl, "Since First Straw Vote in 1824, Research Grows," *Advertising Age,* April 19, 1975, pp. 106–109.

3. William Lazer, "Marketing Research: Past Accomplishments and Potential Future Developments," *Journal of the Market Research Society,* 16 (July 1974): 186–189; Annette Horne, Judith Morgan, and Joanna Page, "Where Do We Go from Here?" *Journal of the Marketing Research Society,* 16 (July 1974): 158–161.

4. Dik W. Twedt, "Six Trends in Corporate Marketing Research," *Marketing News,* 8 (March 14, 1975): 3.

5. Enis and Cox, pp. 20–21.

6. Keith Cox and Robert E. Good, "How to Build a Marketing Information System," *Harvard Business Review,* May-June 1967, p. 145.

7. Walter B. Wentz, *Marketing Research: Management and Methods* (New York: Harper & Row, 1972), pp. 116–126; Schoner and Uhl, pp. 19–41; Enis and Cox, pp. 18–20, 511–544.

8. Ibid.

9. Wentz, pp. 97–99; Gerald Zaltman and Philip Burger, *Marketing Research: Fundamentals and Dynamics* (New York: Dryden Press, 1975), pp. 13–15.

10. Jack J. Honomichl, "Research Top Ten: Who They Are and What They Do," *Advertising Age,* July 15, 1974, pp. 24, 27.

11. Zaltman and Burger, pp. 13–15; Honomichl, "Research Top Ten," pp. 24–27.

12. Shirley Colby, "The Lonely Field Interviewer," *Advertising Age,* June 30, 1975, pp. 33–38.

13. Jack J. Honomichl, "For Top Ten Researchers, A Good '75," *Advertising Age,* March 15, 1976, pp. 1, 53–54.

14. Dik W. Twedt, *1973 Survey of Marketing Research* (Chicago: American Marketing Association, 1973), pp. 10–11.

15. 1970 Census of Population (Washington, D.C.: U.S. Bureau of the Census, 1970).

16. Boyd, Westfall, and Stasch, pp. 206–211; Tull and Hawkins, pp. 102–107; Zaltman and Burger, pp. 82–92.

17. Tull and Hawkins, pp. 102–107.

18. Robert W. Joselyn, *Designing the Marketing Research Project* (New York: Petrocelli–Charter, 1977), pp. 17–18.

19. William J. Stanton, *Fundamentals of Marketing,* 4th ed. (New York: McGraw-Hill, 1975), pp. 617–618.

20. Tull and Hawkins, p. 116; Schoner and Uhl, pp. 174–192.

21. Danny N. Bellenger and Barnett A. Greenberg, *Marketing Research: A Management Information Approach* (Homewood, Ill.: Irwin, 1978), p. 136; Tull and Hawkins, pp. 106, 116–122.

22. Tull and Hawkins, p. 106; Green and Tull, p. 78.

23. Boyd, Westfall, and Stasch, pp. 132–133.

24. Enis and Cox, p. 298.

25. Boyd, Westfall, and Stasch, pp. 117–122; Enis and Cox, pp. 225–227.

26. Bellenger and Greenberg, pp. 171–184; "Are Focus Groups Useful?" *Marketing News,* August 12, 1977, p. 6; "Approach Focus Group Cautiously," *Advertising Age,* June 13, 1977, p. 23; Myril D. Axelrod, "Marketers Get an Eyeful When Focus Groups Expose Products, Ideas, Images, Ad Copy, etc. to Consumers," *Marketing News,* February 28, 1975, pp. 1, 7; Bobby J. Calder, "Focus Groups and the Nature of Qualitative Marketing Research," *Journal of Marketing Research,* 14 (August 1977): 353–364.

27. G. Birch Ripley, "Confessions of an Industrial Executive Interviewer," *Marketing News,* September 10, 1976, pp. 20–21; Lee Adler, "How to Cut Industrial Marketing Research Costs Without Cutting Quality, Quantity of Studies," *Marketing News,* September 10, 1976, p. 21.

28. Enis and Cox, pp. 225–227; Boyd, Westfall, and Stasch, pp. 122–125; Tull and Hawkins, pp. 377–378; Gilbert A. Churchill, *Marketing Research: Methodological Foundations* (New York: Dryden Press, 1975), pp. 177–183.

29. "Phone vs. Personal Interviews," *Marketing News,* September 10, 1976, pp. 6–7; Theresa Rogers, "Interviews by Telephone and in Person: Quality of Response and Field Performance," *Public Opinion Quarterly,* 50 (Spring 1976): 51–65.

30. Leslie Kanuk and Conrad Berenson, "Mail Surveys and Response Rates: A Literature Review," *Journal of Marketing Research,* 12 (November 1975): 440–453; C. Scott, "Research on Mail Surveys," *Journal of the Royal Statistical Society,* 124, Series A, pt. 2 (1961): 143–191.

31. Ibid.

32. Michael S. Goodstadt, Linda Chung, Reena Kronitz, and Gaynoll Cook, "Mail Survey Response Rates: Their Manipulation and Impact," *Journal of Marketing Research,* 14 (August 1977): 391–395; Herbert Blumberg, C. Fuller, and A. P. Hare, "Response Rates in Postal Surveys," *Public Opinion Quarterly,* 38 (Spring 1974): 113–123; Larry Leslie, "Are High Response Rates Essential to Valid Surveys?" *Social Science Research,* 1 (June 1972): 323–334; J. Scott Armstrong and Terry S. Overton, "Estimating Nonresponse Bias in Mail Surveys," *Journal of Marketing Research,* 14 (August 1977): 396–402.

33. Ibid.

34. Robert C. Nuckols, "Personal Interview Versus Mail Panel Survey," *Journal of Marketing Research,* 1 (February 1964): 11–16; William F. O'Dell, "Personal Interviews or Mail Panels?" *Journal of Marketing,* 26 (October 1962): 34–39; Wentz, pp. 99–112.

35. "Consumer Mail Panels" (Chicago: Market Facts, 1976), pp. 1–17.

36. Robert T. Ritchie, "Which Is Better—A Human- or Computer-Conducted Interview," *Marketing News,* September 10, 1976, pp. 8, 17.

37. Ibid.

38. Enis and Cox, pp. 237–247.

39. Tull and Hawkins, p. 429.
40. Enis and Cox, pp. 306–326; Tull and Hawkins, pp. 436–455.
41. Enis and Cox, pp. 175–184.
42. Churchill, pp. 183–196; Tull and Hawkins, pp. 240–280.
43. Green and Tull, pp. 213–215; Tull and Hawkins, pp. 158–163.
44. Churchill, pp. 268–292.
45. Seymour Sudman, *Applied Sampling* (New York: Academic Press, 1976), p. 69.
46. Ibid., pp. 107–130.
47. Ibid., pp. 49–68.
48. Ibid., pp. 69–84.
49. Churchill, pp. 263–267.
50. Green and Tull, pp. 255–350.
51. For the best general reference on this topic see Green and Tull.

CASE 6
Cessna Aircraft

Cessna Aircraft is one of the largest manufacturers of small, private-business airplanes in the United States. It is always looking for new market opportunities, which may involve cultivating existing segments or developing and exploiting new ones. Recent research by Cessna uncovered that a very small percent of the total adult population enrolls in private pilot-training programs. However, the number of people with pilot's licenses is increasing. About half of the individuals who enter a training program complete it. Eventually about one out of five people with a private pilot's license owns a private airplane. So pilot training is an important part of the total market for Cessna and its competitors.

A small percentage of pilots are women. Similarly, a small percentage of the students in training programs are women. This figure has shown only a slight increase in recent years; moreover, there are very few women instructors in pilot-training programs. A substantial number of women have the necessary skills, time, and income to enroll and complete the basic training program. Cessna would like to know why more women don't enter the program and how the program and/or promotional materials could appeal to and motivate more women to consider or inquire about such programs.

There may be several specific market segments worthy of examination. These include wives of pilots, businesswomen, women who could benefit from the use of business aircraft, women who have the income and desire to travel for pleasure, and young women who seek future employment as corporate aircraft pilots. Cessna realizes that the limiting factor may be low levels of interest or motivation and perhaps attitudes toward the desirability of women pilots. But opportunities for women are increasing in many different fields. Cessna therefore believes that a vital market may exist that is not being fully exploited.

1. Develop a marketing research project that will help Cessna evaluate the importance of the women's market.
2. Suggest research that will determine not only the size of the market segment but also why women are not currently enrolling in training programs.

III Product Concepts

7

Product/Service Planning and Development

OBJECTIVES

- To understand what is meant by a product.
- To discuss the role of a product manager.
- To understand the importance of new-product development and how it is carried out.
- To learn the steps involved in the new-product development process.

When you study marketing you ultimately have to study the product. The planning and development of the marketing mix normally begins with a clear definition of the firm's product or service and proceeds with distribution, promotion, and pricing strategies. For example, King Candy developed a new line of sugarless candy bars with none of the bitter aftertaste that accompanies similar products. The marketing manager was unable to develop his strategy until he knew how the consumer viewed the product. Was it viewed as medicinal, to be consumed by diabetics and others on sugar-free diets, or was it just another candy for weight-conscious consumers?

A product is not just a physical object but what consumers perceive it to be. Many products are symbolic; they help us play our roles in society. A man's tie helps identify him as a white-collar worker. A

123

pin-striped suit is often associated with conservatism. People consume products and services not only for what they do but also for what those products and services mean to other members of society.

This chapter begins with the definition of a product and the role products and services play in our society. The importance and difficulty of developing new products is then discussed. Later, new-product development is explained, and finally, the process of creating new products is examined.

WHAT IS A PRODUCT?

We may define a *product* as any want-satisfying good or service and its perceived tangible and intangible attributes. Packaging, style, color, warranties, options, and size are among the features that a product may have. Just as important are intangibles such as service, the retailer's image, the manufacturer's reputation, and the way you believe others will view the product. (See Figure 7.1.) A Cadillac says "prestige," while a Datsun 280Z tells the public that you are "with it," have a youthful outlook, and are not too conservative.

Many firms offer services rather than physical products. A travel agency's products are convenience and knowledgeable travel planning. A barber sells good grooming; an insurance agent offers security and peace of mind. An impressive 64 percent of our gross national product consists of services.[1]

Societal Implications

Choosing the "right" product to develop an effective marketing mix is critical and cannot be overemphasized. Yet we should also examine the role of products in a broader societal context. Through private property and corporate law, our government has created parameters for the formation and development of private businesses. Society, acting through government, expects something in return for giving sole proprietorships, partnerships, and corporations the right to exist. The expected benefits are want-satisfying products and services. In our mixed capitalist system (in which some resources are owned and controlled by government and the remainder by the private sector), if consumers are dissatisfied with a good or service they refuse to buy it. A lack of sales ultimately forces the firm out of business because it cannot compete in the purchase of resources. Only businesses providing want-satisfying products or services continue to exist. In some cases the process of eliminating marginal firms may be lengthy. Hence legislation has been enacted to protect us against fraudulent practices and harmful products in the long run as well as in the short run.

Want Satisfaction Must Be Interpreted Broadly. Business firms often buy goods and services for resale to other companies or to final con-

FIGURE 7.1   **The Total-Product Concept**

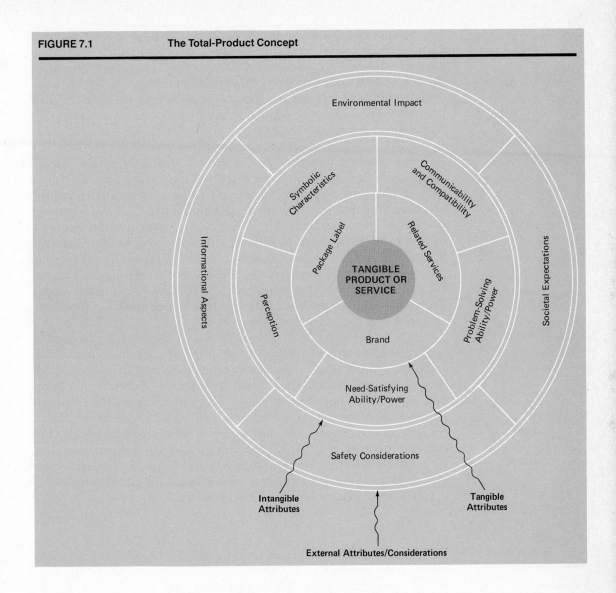

sumers. Wholesalers, for example, buy goods that they hope to sell to retailers, which, in turn, sell to consumers. Want satisfaction is the ultimate motive for buying products for both wholesalers and retailers. They want to earn a profit by purchasing a proper assortment of resale merchandise. Ultimately, the product sold and resold through the distribution channel must satisfy the final consumer. If consumers are not content with a product, no repeat purchases will be made and sales will diminish throughout the channel. Both wholesaling and retailing will be discussed further in Chapters 12 and 13.

Manufacturers often purchase items that become component parts of the producer's finished product, thus losing their individual identity. General Motors doesn't manufacture windshields, nor does Pizza Hut mill flour. Yet both firms must purchase the "right" components in order to meet consumers' expectations of what the final product will be like. The quality of any product is only as good as its weakest component.

**New Products:
A Macro View**

Any new product brought into the market must contain the "right" components in order to survive. Simply adding a new accessory to an item or changing a component doesn't cause people to perceive the item as a new product. It may be new to the firm, but the consumer may view it as a modification of an existing product or an improvement over current market offerings. Procter and Gamble offers a plethora of "new" soaps, toothpastes, and dishwashing powders to the market every few years, yet these could hardly be considered breakthroughs with significant gains in utility. Tide, the laundry detergent, has been modified fifty-five times since 1947, but most consumers never noticed these changes.[2]

As a macro concept, a new product may be defined as a good or service that provides significant increases in consumer satisfaction and has no direct substitutes. Macro refers to society as a whole. Major innovations and technological breakthroughs are necessary attributes of a "new" product. The airplane, transistor, automobile, artificial kidney, and Xerox copier are examples of "new" products in a macro context. Unfortunately, the outpouring of new products seems to be waning. From its 1968 peak, total government and industry spending on research has dropped more than 6 percent in real, or noninflationary, dollars.[3] We will examine the reasons for the slowdown of new-product development in the next section.

**THE PRODUCT
MANAGER
CONCEPT**

When a new product is placed on the market it becomes the responsibility of the product or brand manager or, most commonly, the marketing manager. Larger firms, with their high volume and diverse product lines, typically organize under the product or brand manager concept. This concept focuses managerial attention on specific products or brands that could not be adequately managed by one person. Companies like Kimberly Clark, Quaker Oats, Ralston Purina, Colgate-Palmolive, and Procter and Gamble rely on the product manager concept.

In its original form the product manager's position was to consist of

1. creation and conceptualization of strategies for improving and marketing the assigned product lines or brands.

2. projection and determination of financial and operating plans for such products.
3. monitoring execution and results of plans, with possible adaptation of tactics to evolving conditions.[4]

The product/brand manager was viewed as a "little marketing manager" or "little general manager" with complete profit responsibility.

The product managers of the 1970s often find themselves in a much different position from that of their predecessors. Today the product manager engages in planning product objectives and strategy, monitoring progress, coordinating budget development and control, and working with other departments on product cost and quality.[5] Thus a product manager is now a planner and coordinator rather than an authority over critical functions such as advertising. As the executive vice president of a drugs product company has noted,

> We give much authority to the product manager other than the copy side—sales promotion, for example. But we let him know he is not to be the final authority on advertising. We say the person who knows the most about advertising should make the ultimate decision.[6]

Not only must management obtain decisions from the executives who are most competent to make these decisions, but it must also control the allocation of resources among products. The president of a liquor company comments as follows: "Our brand managers make many decisions but they don't make the key ones. Someone at a higher level must look at the broad allocation of expenditures."[7] The product manager is simply not in a position to see the total picture.

STRATEGIC CONSIDERATIONS IN NEW-PRODUCT DEVELOPMENT
The Importance of New Products

Despite the overall decline in totally "new" product development, the process is given top priority in most successful firms. New food and drug products alone numbered 1023 in 1975—up 10 percent from the figure for the previous year.[8] A company usually cannot grow without new products.

It is commonplace for major companies to obtain 50 percent or more of its current sales from products introduced during the past ten years.[9] Figure 7.2 shows the importance of new products to sales growth in key industries. Generally, a firm must be in a long-run growth market or suffer a declining return on investment in the absence of new products.

Often new products are introduced in response to a consumer need rather than in response to a new scientific or technological discovery.[10] In this case the product manager must fully comprehend the need. For a number of years it has been technically feasible for a computer to read printed characters through pattern recognition. At first glance this seems to be a natural market. Rather than keypunching cards from typewritten documents and then feeding the cards into

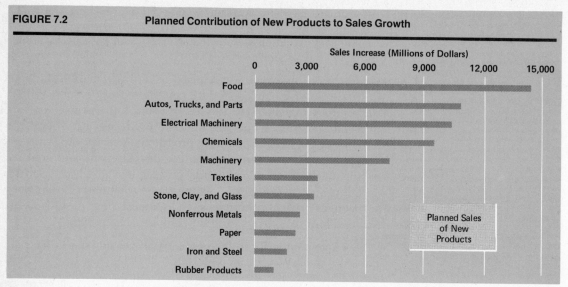

FIGURE 7.2   Planned Contribution of New Products to Sales Growth

Source: Booz, Allen, and Hamilton, *Management of New Products* (Chicago, 1968), p. 2. By permission.

computers, the typewritten documents could be fed directly into computers. Why has this market not developed? Because the real need is for low-cost original data entry. The best way to accomplish this is to create the data and simultaneously enter it into the computer. Even the typewritten document is not necessary![11]

The Risk of Development

Some product managers feel that gambling in Las Vegas has a better chance of success than developing new products. New-product success varies from industry to industry, with success–failure ratios ranging from 6 percent to 84 percent.[12] An overall failure rate would probably fall between 40 and 50 percent.[13] A classic failure was Ford's $50 million loss on the Edsel. A more recent automobile failure was Malcolm Bricklin's Maserati-like sports car, which lasted about one year.

Lists of new-product failures are virtually endless. A few additional examples include Dupont's Corfam leather substitute, Listerol disinfectant (produced by Warner-Lambert, the manufacturer of Listerine), and Post's breakfast cereals with freeze-dried fruits.

The Management of New-Product Development

In order to minimize the possibility of product failure, companies should develop a formal product development procedure. Often a department or committee will be created to manage the development process.

Getting and Managing New Ideas. Sensing new-product ideas may be the responsibility of a single individual—the new-products manager (see Figure 7.3). In several large organizations it is the new-products manager who develops new-product concepts, tests the ideas, and, if a new product results, turns them over to a product manager after they have been introduced into the market. The product manager may have complete authority over a product category or line. For example, a firm may have two product managers—one for consumer products and the other for military hardware. In contrast, the large consumer goods companies may have one individual with authority over a single brand such as Crest toothpaste or Maxwell House coffee.[14] The product or brand manager's role in the organization is changing rapidly, as we will see later in the chapter.

New-Product Committees. Often new-product committees are used rather than having one person make new-product decisions. No one can understand the complexities of new-product development without major input from others. Ideally, information should be obtained from the marketing, engineering, production, and finance areas before making product decisions. Although committees provide more of this information, they may also obscure individual responsibility, take a long time to reach decisions, and include people with interests that are too far removed from company operations to be effective.

New-Product Departments. To overcome the problems that are inherent in committees, some firms have established product development departments that include members from the key functional areas listed earlier. One study revealed that of 2000 large firms in

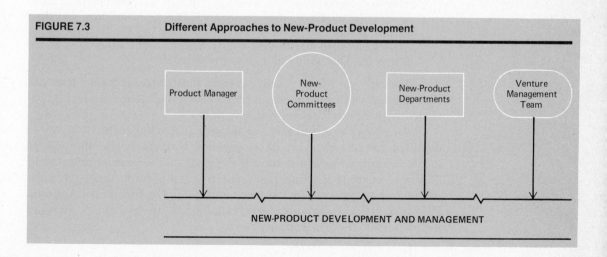

FIGURE 7.3   **Different Approaches to New-Product Development**

Product Manager

New-Product Committees

New-Product Departments

Venture Management Team

NEW-PRODUCT DEVELOPMENT AND MANAGEMENT

several industries, 869 had formal new-product departments.[15] Ideally, people selected for the new department can still communicate effectively with their peers in the operating departments. Also, a formal new-products department means that authority and responsibilities are well defined and given to specific individuals.

Typical of the major responsibilities of a new-products department are recommending new-product objectives and programs, planning explorative studies, evaluating concepts and ideas for new products, coordinating testing, and directing interdepartmental teams.

New-Product Venture Management. A relatively new form of organization for new-product development that is easily adapted to either committee or department organization is venture management. Hanan defines a venture group as an entrepreneurial, market-oriented, multidisciplinary group comprising a small number of representatives for marketing, technology, and finance, focused on a single objective — planning their company's profitable entry into a new business.[16] (See Figure 7.4.)

General Mills, Dupont, Monsanto, 3-M, and Union Carbide have achieved mixed results from venture group experiments.[17] In fact corporate venturing generally has a poor track record.[18] What went wrong? It seems that good product or brand managers, good engineers, or top-notch accountants do not necessarily make good venture managers. What is needed is entrepreneurial talent. As one corporate president says,

> I have an unfailing test for identifying entrepreneurial types. I throw every candidate right in with the alligators. The establishment man complains he can't farm alligators in a swamp. The entrepreneur farms 60% of the alligators, markets another 30% for everything but their squeal, drains their part of the swamp, and leases the land for an amusement park overlooking "Alligatorland." The other 10% of the alligators? That's his delayed compensation.[19]

Not only do many venture groups lack entrepreneurs; they are also saddled with bureaucratic frustrations and generally lack experience with new-product development.

By now you're beginning to wonder just what *is* the best way to organize for new-product development? Unfortunately, there is no magic formula or one best way. It depends on managerial talents and abilities, current organization structure, the importance of new-product development to the firm, and available financial resources. However, several guidelines are available for successful new-product development in organizations.

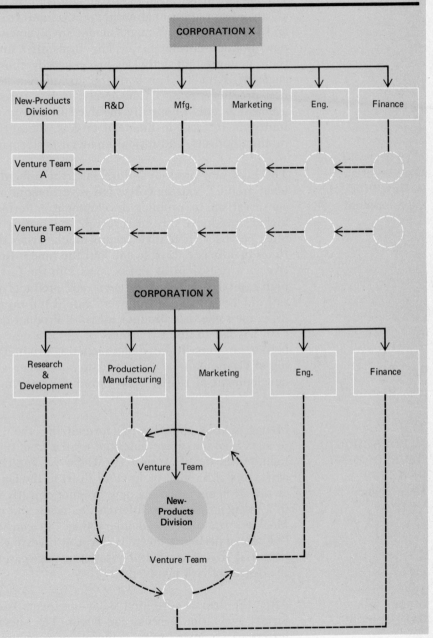

Source: Adapted from Richard M. Hill and James D. Hlavacek, ''The Venture Team: A New Concept in Marketing Organization,'' *Journal of Marketing,* 36 (July 1972): 47. By permission of the American Marketing Association.

New-Product Development Organization. Critical factors for new-product organization are (1) freedom from bureaucratic constraints, (2) an entrepreneurial atmosphere, (3) input from all functional areas, and (4) extensive top-management involvement and commitment to new-product development. The firms that are most successful in their new-product activities are generally those in which top management is involved in both the formulation and implementation of new-product strategy. Conversely, in less successful firms top management is only nominally involved in new-product development or limits its interest to financial targets, the approval of overall new-product budgets, and formal financial performance review.[20]

Conservatism in New-Product Development

The high new-product failure rate, the difficulty of constructing an ideal product, soaring costs, and governmental regulation have led to conservatism in product development.[21] Performance demands are higher; products stay in research and testing longer; and products must pay back their investments much earlier than the 1960s—sometimes in only one-third to one-half the time.[22] Roger R. Robins, executive vice president of Purex, says, "In the last year, on the basis of high capital risk, I turned down new products at least twice as often as I did a year ago. But in every case, I tell my people to go back and bring me some new product ideas."[23] Product development conservatism has led to line extensions (such as a new soup flavor by Campbell) or the repositioning of an existing product (such as the positioning of Grape Nuts as "the back-to-nature cereal") rather than to the development of really "new" products with major societal benefits.

THE NEW-PRODUCT DEVELOPMENT PROCESS
Objectives

Management's objective in formalizing the product development process is to maximize potential return from the total product mix in light of the firm's resources. Table 7.1 indicates the new-product objectives of 35 high-technology firms in the United States. Note that of the 24 firms reporting new-product objectives, 20 expressed them in a financial context. Gillette's chairman and president, Colman M. Mockler, Jr., told stockholders that "in considering new products [we] are applying stringent criteria on investment, profit margins and potential size of market. These factors are carefully weighed against the degree of risk involved."[24]

Stages of Development

After the firm has decided what it expects from new products, the formal evaluation process can begin. The specific stages may be referred to as opportunity exploration; screening; developing a preliminary profit plan; product, strategy, and communications development; test marketing; and market introduction.[25] Figure 7.5 depicts the flow of product development.

TABLE 7.1   New-Product Objectives

Explicit Objectives	Number of Times Specified
Dollar sales volume/growth	6
Profit	4
Profit margin	3
Payback	3
Return on investment	2
Earnings per share growth	1
Market share percentage expansion	2
Product price	2
Value added	1
No explicit objectives	11

Source: Albert V. Bruno, ''New Product Decision Making in High Technology Firms,'' *Research Management,* September 1973, p. 28.

FIGURE 7.5   **Stages of Product Evolution**

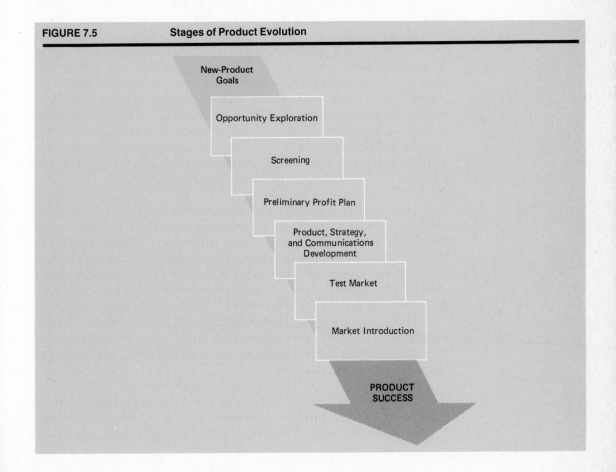

New-Product Goals

Opportunity Exploration

Screening

Preliminary Profit Plan

Product, Strategy, and Communications Development

Test Market

Market Introduction

PRODUCT SUCCESS

Opportunity Exploration.   Product development begins with obtaining new ideas or concepts for products. This is called opportunity exploration. Smaller firms usually depend on employees, customers, investors, and channel members for new ideas. The sporadic nature of informal idea gathering has led most major companies and many of the progressive smaller firms to use brainstorming and focus groups.

Perhaps you have participated in a brainstorming session at one time or another. The goal of brainstorming is to have the group think of as many ways to vary a product or solve a problem as possible.[26] Criticism is avoided, no matter how ridiculous the idea seems at the time. The emphasis is on sheer quantity of ideas, with objective evaluation postponed to later steps of development. Approximately 25 years ago one of the product attributes a brainstorming session conceived for carpet sweepers was "color."[27] Until that time all sweepers had been either black or dull gray. By introducing a line of pastel "decorator" colors, Bissell was able to reverse a declining sales trend.

Focus groups, discussed in Chapter 6, are a widely accepted tool for generating concepts. A manufacturer of small electrical appliances used focus groups composed of homemakers to find out what appliances were most helpful in the kitchen, what functions still had to be done by hand, what tasks they would like to see handled by new appliances, and what existing products were least efficient. Similarly, a baby food manufacturer found that its market was stabilizing and decided to determine the feasibility of producing individual servings of food for the elderly. Focus groups were used to explore the eating habits and food preferences of senior citizens. New product strategies were conceived on the basis of the information supplied by the focus groups.

Screening.   As ideas emerge, they are checked against the firm's new-product goals and long-range strategies, a procedure termed screening. Many product concepts are rejected because of poor product fit (dissimilarity to existing products), unavailable technology, lack of company resources, and low market potential. (There is considerable market potential for a safe, fast-acting weight-reducing product. Much less potential exists for a dog collar with a built-in radio.)

Most ideas are eliminated at this stage as obvious misfits. A judicious job of screening is very important, since concepts that go beyond this stage receive careful scrutiny and a considerable investment of time and company resources.

The Preliminary Profit Plan.   We have noted the importance of financial rewards in new-product development. Now we are ready to make up a preliminary profit plan. The length of payback (time required to recoup the original investment) is often the primary criterion used at this stage to eliminate product concepts. Joseph J. Montesano, director of business development for Norwich Pharmaceutical, says that "the true appeal of a product opportunity should rest in its return on investment. If it doesn't pay out in a reasonable time period, drop the product."[28] Although payback is a quantitative criterion, the input (demand estimate) may be largely subjective, based on estimates by experienced executives.

Product, Strategy, and Communications Development. If the concept passes the preliminary profit plan stage, it is ready for the main part of the development process. Product, strategy, and communications development begin simultaneously, not in sequence. Promotion, for example, doesn't wait until the product is fully developed. An ideal new-product development flow chart is shown in Figure 7.6.

Product testing will vary, depending on how easy it is to manufacture the item. If Seven Seas is testing a new salad dressing flavor, it will go directly into taste tests and perhaps extended home use tests. However, if Seven Seas decided to develop a new line of soft drinks requiring extensive new production facilities, it would most likely engage in extensive product concept testing, examining numerous attributes of the product before actually making the product.

The marketing strategy is being refined as product concept testing and use testing take place. Channels of distribution are selected. Pricing policies are developed and tested. Target market characteristics and demand estimates are determined. Management also continually updates the profit plan as the product moves toward actual introduction.

Communications development feeds into the maturing marketing strategy and product tests. For example, logo and package copy themes can be examined in both product concept tests and home use tests. Communication strategy also entails selection of promotion themes, the media mix, and sales force introduction. The projected cost of the communication strategy is then revised, if necessary, for the profit plan.

Test Marketing. Test marketing, as you have learned, represents the final chance to "tie up the loose ends" before introducing the product nationally or regionally. It gives management an opportunity to evaluate alternate strategies and to see how well the various aspects of the marketing mix fit together. If the test markets are properly selected, they will reflect what will happen in the product's market area. The tests can also provide feedback for improving the entire development process.

FIGURE 7.6   An Idealized View of New-Product Development

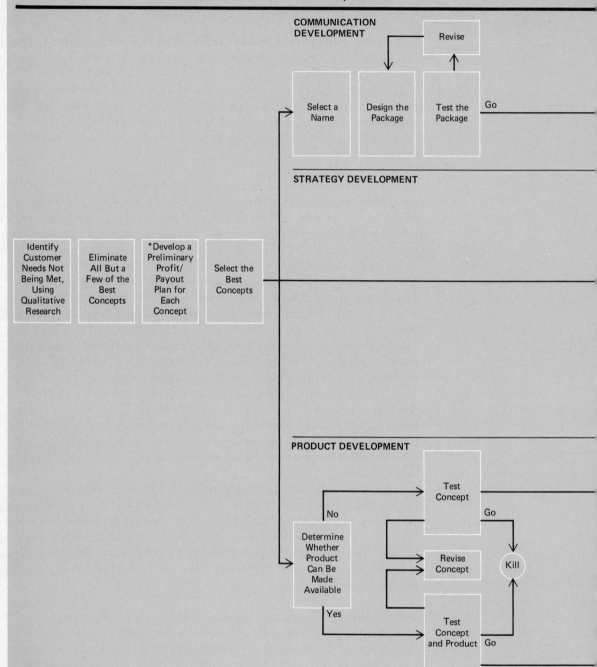

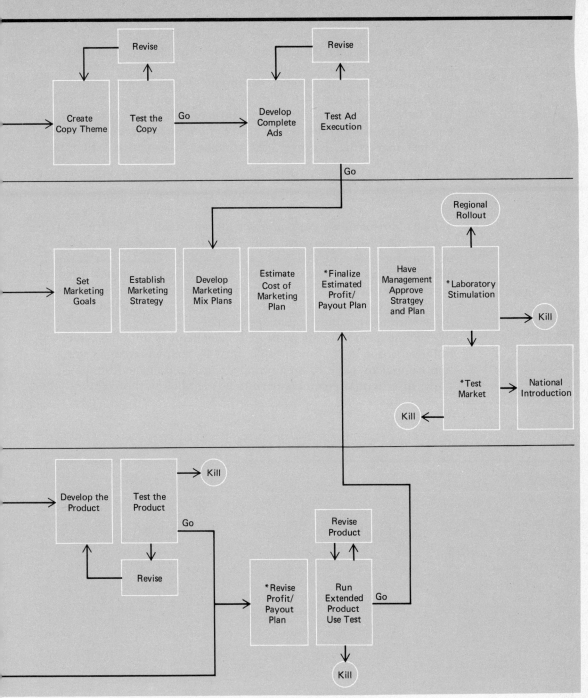

Test marketing isn't cheap. Other problems besides costs include (1) the loss of the surprise element, (2) the difficulty of selecting "representative" test markets, (3) the possibility of having the company name associated with a "dud," (4) the chance that a test market will be sabotaged by competitors through increased promotion or lower prices, and (5) the need to delay production introduction. Without test marketing, however, the company is gambling rather than taking an intelligent risk.

A promising alternative to test marketing is simulation and model building. These techniques were discussed in Chapter 6.

Market Introduction. New-product development is a long, costly process. One study revealed that 58 ideas are required to yield one new product. (See Figure 7.7.)[29] Is it worth it? The answer is yes. It definitely pays to develop a good, sound program for new-product development. Firms with relatively unsophisticated approaches to new-product decision making have lower average profitability than those with more sophisticated approaches.[30]

The expense at this point of development is minimal compared to introduction costs. Salespeople must be trained; complete promotion campaigns have to be developed; production facilities must be built; distribution channels have to be supplied with inventory; and

| FIGURE 7.7 | Mortality of New-Product Ideas (By Stage of Evolution—51 Companies) |

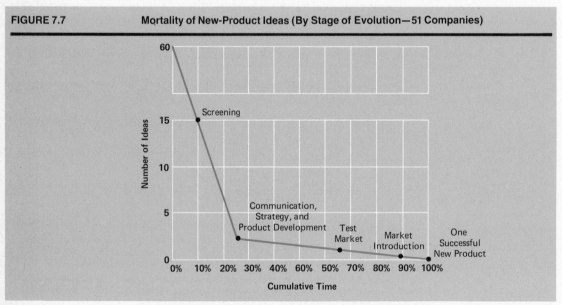

Source: Booz, Allen and Hamilton, Inc., Management Research Department, modified by author. By permission.

sometimes parts must be produced and distributed. Gillette's Good News razor was launched with a $6 million promotion campaign, not counting free samples.[31]

Often products are "rolled out" regionally rather than nationally. Production and inventory requirements are simply beyond the capacity of smaller companies. Logistics and capital requirements occasionally force even the largest firms to follow this strategy.

SUMMARY

A product is much more than a physical object. It is symbolic. It helps consumers play certain roles in society. We consume products and services not only for what they are or for what they do but also for what they mean. A Volkswagen will get you from Point A to Point B, but it is symbolically different from a Cadillac.

Most products that are brought to the marketplace are not new. A truly new product is one that provides significant increases in consumer satisfaction and has no direct substitute. The airplane, the transistor, and the automobile are examples of new products in a macro context. New products are extremely important to the firm. In many industries they provide the impetus for long-run sales growth.

Despite the need for new products, the success rates of such products are quite low. Sometimes product failure can mean bankruptcy or, at the very least, a major disaster for the firm. To minimize the failure of new products many companies have formal new-product development organizations. They, in turn, are responsible for the new-product development process. This includes development of new-product objectives; exploration of new-product opportunities and concepts; screening of concepts and ideas; development of preliminary profit plans; product, strategy, and communications development; test marketing; and market introduction.

After a product has been introduced by a large company, it is usually turned over to a product manager. Originally the product manager was considered a mini-marketing manager. Today, however, the product manager is primarily a coordinator and a planner rather than an operating-line officer. Yet the product manager is still responsible for the sales of particular products.

KEY TERMS

Product	Product development process
Want satisfaction	Opportunity exploration
New product	Brainstorming
Product or brand manager concept	Screening
New-product committee	Preliminary profit plan
Product development department	Product testing
Venture management	Test marketing

QUESTIONS
FOR DISCUSSION

1. Explain what is meant by a product.
2. Define a new product. Which of the following fall into this category?
   a. electronic video games
   b. touch-tone telephones
   c. cable TV system
   d. Concorde flights to Europe
   e. a new church in your locality
3. Why are new products so important to most firms? Give examples to illustrate your answer.
4. What are the functions of a product manager? How have they changed in the past decade?
5. Outline briefly the different stages of the new-product development process.
6. Describe the different types of organization used to manage the new-product development process. Which one do you prefer? Give reasons for your answer.
7. Explain the importance of screening in the new-product development process.
8. What is test marketing? Why do most companies test market their new products? What potential problems are faced at this stage?
9. What product attributes are provided by the following?
   a. a Corvette
   b. a Prudential Life Insurance policy
   c. a Carte Blanche card
   d. a movie theater
   e. a 7-Eleven store.
10. List the chief objectives for new-product development as outlined in this chapter. Do you think companies should consider social objectives while introducing new products?

NOTES

1. Wayer C. Taylor, "Selling the Services Society," *Sales Management,* 108 (March 6, 1972): 23.
2. Edward Harness, *Some Basic Beliefs About Marketing* (Cincinnati: Procter and Gamble, 1977), p. 17.
3. Ibid.
4. David J. Luck, "Interfaces of a Product Manager," *Journal of Marketing,* 33 (October 1969): 32–36. Reprinted by permission of the American Marketing Association. See also David J. Luck, *Product Policy and Strategy* (Englewood Cliffs, N. J.: Prentice-Hall, 1972).
5. Victor P. Buell, "The Changing Role of the Product Management in Consumer Goods Companies," *Journal of Marketing,* 39 (July 1975): 3–11; Richard M. Clewett and Stanley F. Stasch, "Shifting Role of the Product Manager," *Harvard Business Review,* January–February 1975, pp. 65–73; B. Charles Ames, "Dilemma of Product Market Management," *Harvard Business Review,* March-April 1971, pp. 66–74; and Alladi Venkatesh and David Wilemon, "Interpersonal Influence on Product Management," *Journal of Marketing,* 40 (October 1976): 33–40.
6. Buell, p. 7.
7. Ibid., p. 10.

8. "Disastrous Debuts—Despite High Hopes, Many New Products Flop in the Market," *Wall Street Journal,* March 23, 1976.

9. Booz, Allen and Hamilton, *Management of New Products* (Chicago, 1968), p. 2.

10. Theodore J. Gordon, "Changing Technology and the Future of Marketing," *The Conference Board Record,* 11 (December 1974): 22.

11. For a detailed story see William D. Zarecor, "High-Technology Product Planning," *Harvard Business Review,* January–February 1975, 108–115.

12. Booz, Allen and Hamilton, p. 2.

13. "Disastrous Debuts," op. cit.

14. See Luck, pp. 83–94.

15. Booz, Allen and Hamilton, p. 20.

16. Mack Hanan, "Corporate Growth—Through Venture Management," *Harvard Business Review,* January–February 1969, pp. 45–61.

17. Marvin A. Jolson, "New Product Planning in an Age of Future Consciousness," *California Management Review,* 16 (Fall 1973): 25–26.

18. Mack Hanan, "Venturing Corporations—Think Small to Stay Strong," *Harvard Business Review,* May–June 1976, pp. 139–148.

19. Ibid., p. 140. Copyright © 1976 by the President and Fellows of Harvard College; all rights reserved.

20. Philip R. McDonald and Joseph O. Eastlack, Jr., "Top Management Involvement with New Products," *Business Horizons,* 14 (December 1971): 23–31.

21. For further discussion see Thomas A. Staudt, "Higher Management Risks in Product Strategy," *Journal of Marketing,* 37 (January 1973): 49.

22. "The Breakdown of U.S. Innovation," *Business Week,* February 16, 1976, p. 59.

23. Ibid.

24. "Gillette Will Keep Up Its Cost-Conscious Marketing," *Advertising Age,* April 26, 1976, p. 10.

25. The development process is largely adapted from Jay E. Klompmaker, G. David Hughes, and Russell I. Haley, "Test Marketing in New Product Development," *Harvard Business Review,* May–June 1976, pp. 128–138.

26. For a detailed discussion of brainstorming see Alex Osborn, *Applied Imagination: Principles and Producers of Creative Problem Solving* (New York: Scribner, 1963).

27. Dik Warren Twedt, "How to Plan New Products, Improve Old Ones, and Create Better Advertising," *Journal of Marketing,* 33 (January 1969): 53–57. See also Edward M. Tauber, "Discovering New Product Opportunities with Problem Inventory Analysis," *Journal of Marketing,* 39 (January 1975): 67–70.

28. "Launch Product That Fills Real Need, Not Just Parity Product," *Marketing News,* April 23, 1976, p. 6.

29. Booz, Allen and Hamilton, p. 9.

30. Albert V. Bruno, "New Product Decision Making in High Technology Firms," *Research Management,* September 1973, pp. 28–31.

31. "Gillette Will Keep Up Its Cost-Conscious Marketing," p. 10.

CASE 7
General Pet Products, Inc.

A perennial problem of dog and cat owners is ticks and fleas. General Pet Products manufactures a wide array of pet-grooming nonprescription pet drug items. Sargents and Hartz dominate the pet product market with a 58-percent share, followed by General with a 16-percent share.

General's marketing manager, Wayne Lucas, believed that the time was ripe for increased product diversification in the tick and flea collar market. General, Sargents, Hartz, and several other manufacturers offer a clear or black 90-day dog and cat collar designed to fit all breeds, including Great Danes. Excess collar is simply trimmed off and thrown away. Aside from Sargents' flea tag collar, which contains the pesticide in the tag rather than in the collar itself, there is little product differentiation in this market.

Lucas contracted with Qualitative Dimensions, Inc. to explore dog and cat owners' perceptions and needs in the flea and tick collar market, using focus groups in four cities. A summary of the behavior research follows:

1. Approximately 25 percent of all pets have ticks as well as fleas. Most respondents believe that current products are ineffective for controlling ticks, particularly if they have been in use for more than a month.
2. Buckles on the leading brands are cumbersome.
3. Pet owners have little fear that handling the collars is a health hazard. The directions simply remind people to wash their hands after touching the collar.
4. Flea tags are generally viewed in a mixed light. Owners comment that (1) the tag is more permanent than the collar, (2) little children might grab the disk and put it in their mouths, and (3) the dog might chew it off.
5. Most owners feel that $2.00 is a reasonable price to pay for an effective 90-day collar.
6. Owners' design ideas include the following: (1) Make a regular collar with a slit so that the flea protection can be put into it when needed; (2) increase the number of sizes.

Respondents were shown three prototype collars that General is considering. The first is the Dry Thermoset, which releases the chemical slowly as the animal's body temperature increases. This collar will last 120 days and only releases the chemical when the pet is active. Owner comments include the following: (1) It's not gummy, but it's heavy and stiff; (2) if it stayed dry it might work better; (3) it's a very masculine collar; (4) it looks scruffy, not neat and petite.

The second prototype is a leather-lined flea collar. Comments include: (1) It must be expensive; (2) why make it permanent unless it is refillable; (3) it must be stronger than the rest; (4) when leather gets wet it will shrink; (5) the plastic chemical strip looks as if it might come off too easily when children play with the dog.

The final prototype is a perforated tag containing a colored pellet. Comments include: (1) I like seeing the pellet in there; (2) I'm impressed with the idea of replacing it when it melts away; (3) it must have a childproof holder; (4) you can probably save money by buying just pellets rather than the whole collar; (5) flea tags are practical—they should not be overly decorative.

1. Should Lucas introduce any of the prototype products in test markets?
2. Do you feel that General is following a logical sequence for new-product development?

8

A Product
and Service
Classification System

OBJECTIVES

■ To present a classification scheme for consumer goods.
■ To gain insight into the characteristics of industrial markets.
■ To classify industrial goods into six major categories.

Chapter 7 dealt with the ways in which new products are developed and brought to the marketplace. This chapter explores the nature of consumer and industrial goods. As you read the chapter try to picture the various marketing mixes that would be necessary for each product category.

Products can be divided into two general groups—consumer goods and industrial goods. Consumer goods are purchased by the ultimate buyer. Industrial goods are used in making other products. We will look at both types of products in order to better understand why different merchandise requires different market strategies.

CONSUMER GOODS

Consumer goods run the gamut from ice cream and magazines to new homes and expensive cars. Classifying such a diversified array isn't easy, and no classification system is perfect.[1] However, we will

FIGURE 8.1   A Comprehensive Classification for Consumer Goods

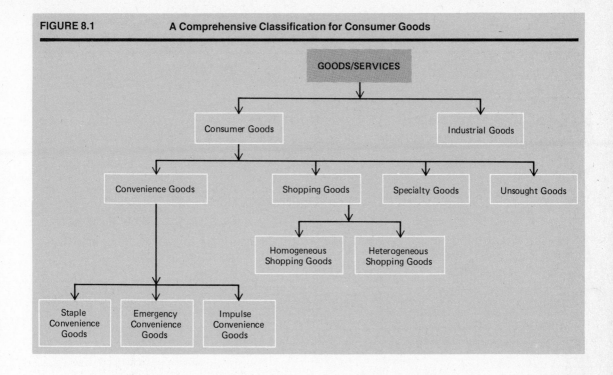

divide consumer products into four categories: convenience, shopping, specialty, and unsought goods. (See Figure 8.1.) This system is based on the way people view and subsequently buy various products. (See Figure 8.2.)

Convenience Goods

Convenience goods are relatively inexpensive items that require little shopping effort. Many food products, candy, soft drinks, combs, aspirin, small hardware items, and countless other things fall into the convenience goods category. They are bought routinely day in and day out, usually without significant planning. This doesn't mean that the consumer is unaware of convenience good brand names. Some, such as Coke, Bayer Aspirin, and Right Guard deodorant, are very well known.

Convenience goods may be further divided into staple, emergency, and impulse items. Any convenience good can suddenly become an emergency good if there is a sudden, strong, compelling desire to buy a product. Assume that you are visiting a distant city and suddenly find yourself caught in a heavy rain. An umbrella may become an emergency good for you. If you wake up in the morning and suddenly find yourself out of coffee, it becomes an emergency good. A woman who wants to wash her hair and discovers that the shampoo has been used up views shampoo as an emergency product. Because

FIGURE 8.2   **The Continuum of Consumer Goods Classification (Based on Degree of Search Effort Expended by the Consumer)**

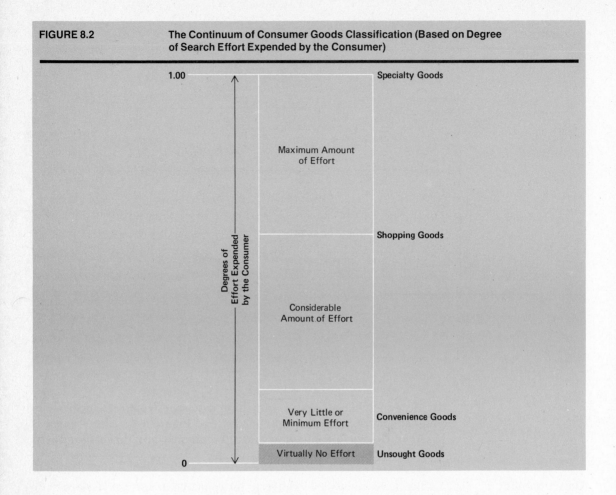

the need is urgent, prices are usually high in a store that specializes in emergency convenience goods, such as 7-Eleven, Circle K, Wag-A-Bag, or U-Totem.

Impulse items are purchased without planning. Often these items are placed near supermarket checkout counters to encourage sales. Razor blades, some magazines, candy, flashlight batteries, pens, and other knickknacks are often impulse items. Some shoppers rarely plan grocery purchases but enter the store and buy on impulse. This raises an important point—the purchaser may be highly aware of general needs, such as meats, drinks, and so on, and yet purchase in specific product categories like ham and beer on impulse. Brand names may also be bought on impulse—Armour Ham and Budweiser beer, for example.

The third category of convenience goods—staples—accounts

for the bulk of convenience purchasing. Items are shopped for routinely, with little planning. Many are perishable, such as bread, milk, and meat, and must be bought frequently. Staples can be bought at supermarkets, hardware stores, drugstores, and variety stores. The important thing to remember is that the consumer is not going to exert much effort to acquire staple products. These items must be close to where the consumer lives, works, or passes by.

Shopping Goods

Shopping goods are usually more expensive than convenience goods and are found in fewer stores. Consumers usually buy these items only after comparing style, suitability, price, and life style compatibility in several stores. People actively seek out shopping good stores for comparison purposes—they are willing to put some effort into this process. Brands are compared as well as stores; service and warranty work are often important considerations as well. Major appliances, automobiles, furniture, and most clothing are typical shopping goods.

A shopping good may not be purchased for a considerable period after the decision to buy the product is made. For example, you may decide to purchase a new home several years before you can save enough money for the down payment. During that period you may actively seek information about the housing options available. Unlike convenience goods, shopping goods may offer substantial monetary savings in return for time expended. Also, since convenience goods are bought very frequently, we have more knowledge about these products than we do about shopping goods, which are purchased less often.

Shopping goods can be further divided into homogeneous and heterogeneous merchandise. Homogeneous products have essentially the same features. Refrigerators, ranges, dishwashers, and television sets are examples of this type of product. Brand names are very important, since consumers view them as assurances of quality. Heavy advertising by firms like Zenith, Whirlpool, and General Electric contributes to heightened brand awareness and consumer preference for the products of these firms over very similar merchandise. This is a classic case of product differentiation, and as a result substantial price decreases may lead to large increases in demand.

Heterogeneous merchandise is nonstandardized and stylistic in nature. Better clothing, most furniture, and some automobiles fall into this category. Retail salespeople often play a role in helping the consumer select heterogeneous shopping goods. They perform an informational function by explaining product features and benefits that are not readily apparent to prospective buyers. Price is usually secondary to life style and self-image compatibility. Single swingers want racy, flashy cars to fit their image. The executive demands a

Cadillac or Continental, and the suburban homemaker wants a station wagon.

Specialty Goods

When consumers will search extensively for an item and are extremely reluctant to accept substitutes for it, it is a specialty good. Fine watches, Rolls Royce automobiles, expensive stereo equipment, very fine clothing, and gourmet food products are generally considered specialty merchandise. Because of the diligent searching effort of specialty goods buyers, only one store in a city or region may carry the item.

In 1976 General Motors produced the last Cadillac convertibles. The final 200 were distinguished by a Bicentennial theme—a white paint job, blue and red striping, and an "official" plaque on the dashboard. Although the cars had a list price of about $13,000, dealers sold them for as much as $50,000. These were indeed very special automobiles.

Specialty goods represent a near-perfect fit between the consumer's physical and/or psychological needs and the product's benefits. Brand names are very important, as well as the quality of service for most specialty products. Selective, ego-oriented advertising is used by a number of specialty good sellers to maintain their products' exclusive image.

Unsought Goods

Products that the consumer doesn't know about or knows about but doesn't actively seek out are referred to as unsought goods. New products fall into this category until advertising and distribution increase consumer awareness of them.

Some goods are perennially marketed as unsought items. Tombstones, insurance, cosmetics and housewares sold door to door, encyclopedias, and similar items necessitate aggressive personal selling and highly persuasive advertising. Leads of potential buyers are aggressively sought by salespeople, using referrals from satisfied buyers. The company must go directly to the consumer through a salesperson, direct mail, or direct-response advertising in magazines, newspapers, and other media, since the consumer usually doesn't seek out the item.

PITFALLS OF THE PRODUCT CLASSIFICATION SYSTEM

Something that is a specialty good to you might be a shopping good or a convenience good to the next person. Ground coffee might be a specialty good to you if you will buy only Yuban. To me it might be a shopping good because I compare flavors and prices. To another person it may be just a convenience good. A candy bar is a convenience good for most adults but may be a specialty or shopping good for children.

What is relevant for the marketing manager is how a majority of the target consumers perceive the product. If most view it as a convenience good, then a convenience good strategy of competitive prices, many retail sellers, and perhaps heavy advertising and promotion are called for. Other types of products, of course, necessitate different strategies.

INDUSTRIAL GOODS

Industrial products are primarily for use in producing other goods. These goods are classified by function performed or by accounting treatment. Functional classification is based on whether the goods become part of the final product or are used to produce other goods. A third functional designation is farm products, which the federal government classifies with industrial goods. The accounting breakdown is on the basis of the tax treatment of the product. Expense items have a relatively short life span and are continually consumed in the company's operations. Capital goods typically last for a number of years and are depreciated over several years. Depreciation is the deduction from accounting income for the possible loss in value of a property due to wear and tear, time, and obsolescence.

Characteristics of Industrial Markets

Before we delve into the industrial-goods classification system you should be aware of some of the unique characteristics of this huge market. The value added to the American economy by the production process was $452,497 million in 1974.[2] There are approximately 321,000 manufacturing establishments in the nation, employing over 20 million people.[3]

The Importance of Large Firms. Despite the large number of producers, a few firms account for most of the manufacturing employment and the value added by manufacturing. (See Table 8.1.) For example, in 1972 approximately 2000 firms (each with over 1000 employees) employed over 5 million people, creating $123 billion in value added. In contrast, slightly more than 200,000 manufacturers (each with fewer than 20 employees) employed 1 million people, for a value added of only $19 billion.

Relocation Trends. Manufacturing employment has gradually shifted since the late 1940s from the northeast and north-central states to the rest of the country. (See Table 8.2.) Although the old manufacturing strongholds continue to provide most of the employment, other regions, such as the southern and Pacific states have growing, vigorous economies.

Many factors enter into the relocation decisions of manufacturers. Lower taxes, progressive local and state governments, abundance

TABLE 8.1	Manufacturers—Summary, by Employee Size-Class: 1954–1972 (Establishments and Employees in Thousands; Money Figures in Millions of Dollars, Except Percents)

		Employee Size-Class of Establishments				
Item and Year	All Estab- lishments	Under 20	20– 99	100– 249	250– 999	1,000 and Over
Establishments:[a]						
1954	287	196	64	16	9	2
1958	299	203	68	17	10	2
1963	307	207	70	18	10	2
1967	306	199	74	20	11	2
1972	313	203	76	21	12	2
Employees:[a]						
1954	15,646	1,196	2,835	2,430	4,082	5,103
1958	15,423	1,202	2,956	2,503	4,055	4,707
1963	16,235	1,175	3,072	2,727	4,312	4,951
1967	18,492	1,042	3,276	3,069	5,042	6,062
1972	18,034	1,114	3,356	3,233	5,156	5,175
Payroll:[a]						
1954	62,963	3,765	10,246	9,171	16,264	23,516
1958	73,875	4,650	12,475	10,963	18,935	26,852
1963[b]	93,289	5,502	15,191	13,926	23,740	34,772
1967	123,481	6,080	19,205	18,172	31,688	48,335
1972	160,433	8,646	25,785	25,362	43,354	57,286
Value added by manufacture:						
1954	116,848	7,207	18,013	17,143	31,286	43,199
1958	141,541	9,214	23,113	21,216	37,502	50,495
1963[b]	192,102	11,310	30,073	28,826	51,054	71,056
1967	261,984	13,271	39,138	38,922	71,036	99,617
1972	353,994	19,128	54,867	56,477	99,932	123,591

Source: U.S. Department of Commerce Statistical Abstract of the United States, 1976 (Washington, D.C., 1976), p. 763.
[a] Excludes administrative offices and auxiliary units.
[b] Individual size-class data do not add to total because they were derived from separate tabulations.

of labor, lower cost of living, the attraction of a more casual life style, and the ability to enjoy more time outdoors are often cited as reasons for migrating to the new growth regions.

Concentration of Industries. Many manufacturing industries are dominated by a small number of companies. This often means similar sales prices, huge organizations with tremendous purchasing power, and similar marketing policies. Some of our more concentrated industries are shown in Table 8.3. In the automotive and telephone industries, two of America's most important industries, four firms account for over 90 percent of all production.

TABLE 8.2 Manufacturing Employment and Value Added (Percent Distribution, by Geographic Division: 1947–1973)

Item	1947	1950	1954	1958	1963	1965	1967	1970	1972	1973
Employment										
New England	10.3	9.8	9.0	8.7	8.4	8.2	8.1	7.6	7.2	7.1
Middle Atlantic	27.7	26.9	26.6	25.7	24.0	23.4	22.6	21.8	20.7	20.2
East North Central	30.2	30.0	28.6	26.6	26.4	27.2	26.7	26.0	25.9	26.2
West North Central	5.5	5.6	6.0	6.0	6.0	6.0	6.2	6.2	6.3	6.4
South Atlantic	10.7	11.1	11.0	11.8	12.5	12.7	12.9	13.6	14.4	14.3
East South Central	4.4	4.4	4.5	4.9	5.2	5.6	5.7	6.1	6.6	6.6
West South Central	3.9	4.0	4.5	5.0	5.1	5.3	5.6	6.1	6.5	6.6
Mountain	1.0	1.1	1.1	1.4	1.7	1.6	1.6	1.8	2.0	2.1
Pacific	6.4	7.0	8.8	10.0	10.6	10.0	10.6	10.3	10.4	10.6
Value Added										
New England	9.2	8.3	7.8	7.4	7.1	7.1	7.2	6.8	6.4	6.2
Middle Atlantic	28.0	26.2	26.0	24.6	22.7	22.5	21.9	21.4	19.9	19.3
East North Central	31.6	33.2	31.2	28.9	29.3	30.2	28.6	27.5	28.2	28.3
West North Central	5.5	5.7	6.1	6.3	6.1	6.2	6.4	6.9	6.7	6.8
South Atlantic	9.3	9.4	9.1	10.1	11.0	11.1	11.2	11.8	12.5	12.4
East South Central	3.9	3.8	4.0	4.5	4.8	5.1	5.2	5.7	6.0	6.1
West South Central	4.1	4.3	4.9	5.5	5.7	5.8	6.3	6.7	7.0	7.0
Mountain	1.1	1.2	1.2	1.6	1.8	1.6	1.7	1.9	2.1	2.1
Pacific	7.5	7.9	9.7	11.1	11.5	10.7	11.3	11.1	11.3	11.7

Source: U.S. Department of Commerce, *Statistical Abstract of the United States, 1976* (Washington, D.C., 1976), p. 763.

TABLE 8.3 Percent of Shipments Accounted for by Large Manufacturing Companies, Selected Industries, 1972

Industry	4 Largest Firms	8 Largest Firms
Motor vehicles	92	98
Aircraft	59	83
Petroleum refining	37	59
Computing equipment	66	83
Telephone and telegraph	92	96
Iron foundries	34	45
Farm machinery and equipment	47	61
Cigarettes	84	100
Organic fibers, noncellulosic	74	91
Soap and other detergents	62	74
Malt beverages	52	70
Aircraft engines and engine parts	77	87
Shipbuilding and repairing	47	63
Metal cans	66	79
Radio and television receiving sets	49	71

Source: U.S. Department of Commerce, *Statistical Abstract of the United States, 1976* (Washington, D.C., 1976), p. 764.

Derived Demand.   Regardless of the degree of economic concentration or the size of the firm, demand in the industrial sector is based on final-consumer desires. That is, demand for industrial goods is derived from demand for consumer goods. The demand for shoe-manufacturing equipment depends on consumer demand for shoes. Demand for cement is based on consumer housing needs, the demand for offices, and so forth.

Sophisticated Purchasing.   As consumer desires create the need for industrial products and services, industrial purchasing agents and buying committees scour the marketplace for the "right" goods.[4] As we learned in our discussion of buying behavior, purchasing of industrial goods is basically rational rather than emotional. Return on investment, durability, and availability of supplies dominate over the emotional factors that sell many consumer products.

Demand Is Relatively Insensitive to Price.   Price is often a secondary factor in the industrial marketplace. If the demand for shoes is surging, relatively large price increases for shoe-manufacturing equipment usually will not halt shoe manufacturers' orders for new machines. Also, durability, quality, and ability to deliver may easily take precedence over price. Often the price of a component, such as a car battery, is an insignificant part of a product's total cost. Yet it is a necessary part of the final product. Thus the manufacturer may be forced to accept large battery price increases.

Large Fluctuations in Demand.   When demand for consumer products rises, it is usually followed by a short spurt of investment in new machinery. For example, machinery demand will begin to rise after the manufacturer decides that increasing shoe demand will be sufficient to justify the new investment. It ends when the desired new level of shoe-manufacturing capacity is reached.

A small change in consumer demand may lead to large increases in industrial demand—the accelerator principle. Table 8.4 presents

TABLE 8.4	The Accelerator Principle			
	XYZ Shoe Demand	Number of Machines	Required	New Machines Purchased
1978	1,000,000	10	10	1
1979	1,200,000	10	12	1
1980	1,200,000	12	12	3

a simple example of the accelerator principle in action. Assume that our shoe manufacturer currently has ten machines with a normal capacity of 100,000 pairs of shoes per year. Also assume that at the end of each year one machine reaches the end of its useful life of ten years. Thus as long as demand remains constant at 1 million pairs of shoes, XYZ Manufacturing will buy one machine a year. In 1979 demand for XYZ shoes rises to 1,200,000 pairs, yet only one machine is bought. Why? If management thinks that the increase in shoe demand is only temporary, an increase in capacity cannot be justified. Part of the 200,000 units may be produced by working overtime and/or adding another work shift. Profit margins per unit will fall, however, because of overutilization of equipment and overtime payments. By 1980 management has decided that the 200,000 additional pairs of shoes is a true long-run change. One machine is needed for replacement, plus two others to meet the new level of demand. Thus a 20 percent increase in consumer demand has caused a 300 percent increase in industrial demand. The principle also works in reverse. A large drop in consumer demand may cut industrial orders to zero.

The Purchasing Environment. Industrial orders are much larger than the average consumer good purchase. Often equipment and new buildings will be bought for many millions of dollars. Because of the complexity of some industrial products, such as giant custom-made production line equipment, sales negotiations and planning can take place over several years. Decisions to buy may be made by committees of top executives and technical experts. Rarely will one person make the procurement decision when complex, expensive capital goods are being bought. Naturally, most industrial products are purchased relatively infrequently because of their durability.

A Classification System

Industrial goods can be broken down into six major categories: installations, accessory items, component parts and materials, raw materials, supplies, and services. (See Figure 8.3.) Our discussion will begin with the capital goods—installations and accessories—and proceed with the remaining industrial goods, which are considered expense items. Expense items are used and paid for within a single accounting period. Because of their relatively short life span, purchases of expense items involve less risk than purchases of capital goods.

Capital goods, such as buildings and plants, represent a major commitment against future earnings and profitability. Their long life span is amortized over a longer period to reflect the gradually declining utility of the capital good. Longer negotiation periods, more exhaustive planning, and the judgments of many individuals may be needed before the decision to purchase a major capital good is made.

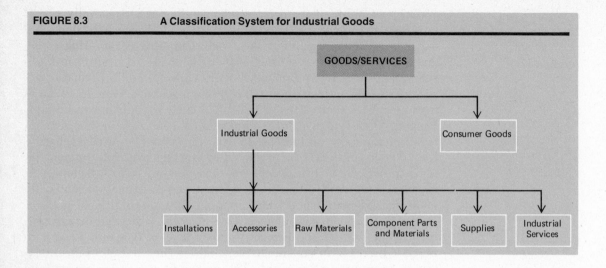

FIGURE 8.3   A Classification System for Industrial Goods

Installations. Installations are large, expensive capital items that determine the nature, scope, and efficiency of a company. Buildings and major production equipment, such as presses, metal stamping equipment, vats, and overhead cranes, are considered installations. Mineral rights and timber holdings, the primary assets of some companies, are also classified as installations. When a company like Anaconda finds and procures a major new source of copper, this changes the scope and capacity of the organization. If General Motors decides to build a new automobile-manufacturing plant, this restructures the firm's productive capabilities.

It may be hard to locate potential buyers of installations because they are purchased so infrequently. Many sellers, such as Butler Buildings, Jay Manufacturing, Piper Aircraft, and IBM, use magazine and trade-newspaper advertising campaigns. The ads not only discuss the merits of the product but suggest that interested parties call collect or fill out a coupon included with the advertisement to obtain more information. These leads are then followed up by salespeople with extensive technical backgrounds.

Accessories. Accessories do not have the same long-run impact on the firm as installations, but they are still capital goods. They are less expensive and more highly standardized than installations. Copy machines, electric typewriters, and smaller machines such as table drills and saws, tractors, and desks are typical accessories. If a company buys one too many desks, this will have almost no impact on profitability. On the other hand, if it builds one too many plants the results could be disastrous.

The smaller impact of accessories on the firm usually means that fewer individuals are involved in the purchase decision. It is quite common for accessories to be bought by a purchasing agent. Since many accessories are standardized rather than custom built, they can be sold through industrial distributors (the supermarkets of industry) and office equipment retailers.

Raw Materials.   In contrast to the first two categories, raw materials do become part of the final product. They can be defined as items that have undergone no more processing than is required for economy or protection before being incorporated in the final product. Raw materials can be further subdivided into natural products and farm products.

Figure 8.4 lists the minerals of which America is a major producer in the world market. Some, such as petroleum, are consumed almost entirely within our own country. Others, such as mica, and molybdenum, are mined in sufficient quantities for export. Many of our timber products are also produced in ample amounts for exportation. (See Table 8.5.)

Because of limited total supplies, raw materials are subject to extensive regulation in many nations. Price fixing and collusion among

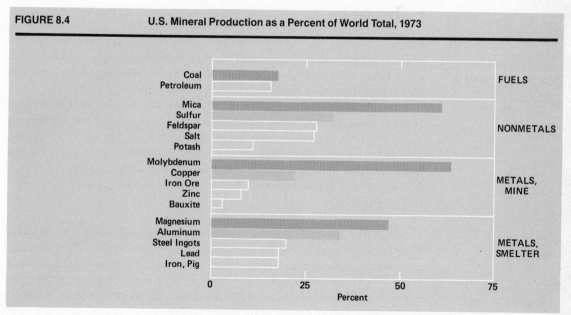

FIGURE 8.4   U.S. Mineral Production as a Percent of World Total, 1973

Source: U.S. Department of Commerce, *Statistical Abstract of the United States,* 1975 (Washington, D.C., 1976), p. 672.

TABLE 8.5	Log Exports and Imports, by Major Species: 1960–1975 (In Millions of Board Feet, Log Scale)							
Item	1960	1965	1970	1971	1972	1973	1974	1975
Exports	266.3	1,192.8	2,753.0	2,292.4	3,143.3	3,221.6	2,642.4	2,626.5
Softwoods	210.3	1,111.4	2,684.1	2,233.4	3,049.4	3,107.2	2,523.7	2,600.6
Douglas fir	27.5	111.3	487.7	448.1	662.2	899.2	752.7	820.4
Port Orford cedar	37.2	39.1	54.1	40.2	45.1	29.7	35.6	38.7
Other	145.6	961.0	2,142.3	1,745.1	2,342.0	2,178.3	1,735.4	1,741.5
Hardwoods	56.0	81.4	68.9	59.0	93.9	114.4	118.7	26.0
Walnut	10.2	23.6	17.4	12.9	15.2	16.1	7.8	8.5
Other	45.9	57.9	51.5	46.2	78.7	98.2	110.8	17.5
Imports	112.5	68.1	144.4	84.0	39.3	33.5	76.6	85.5
Softwoods	32.3	13.5	106.5	55.7	11.3	8.5	45.6	68.5
Hardwoods	80.2	54.6	37.9	28.3	28.0	25.0	31.0	17.0
Mahogany	25.2	12.8	6.8	3.3	3.6	2.1	3.4	1.6
Other	55.1	41.8	31.1	25.0	24.4	23.0	27.6	15.3

Source: U.S. Department of Commerce, *Statistical Abstract of the United States, 1976* (Washington, D.C., 1976), p. 686.

exporting countries have resulted in artificially high prices for petroleum, bauxite, and other natural products. America's raw-materials industries tend to be dominated by a small number of large firms. Over the year this oligopolistic structure has also resulted in price fixing and high prices.

The second category of raw materials—farm products—has a much different industry structure. There are approximately 2½ million farms employing a total of over 8 million people.[5] (See Figure 8.5.) Price and crop production is strongly influenced by governmental policy rather than by free-market actions.

Virtually all farm products are grown seasonally, so that storage plays a large part in total price. Also, most crops lend themselves to more efficient growth in certain regions, such as apples in Michigan and Washington, citrus fruits in California and Florida, and cotton in the South. Specialization by region often requires extensive transportation to distant markets. Long hauls typically mean higher distribution costs.

Component Parts and Materials.   Like raw materials, component parts and materials are incorporated into the end product. They may be custom-made items such as a drive shaft for an automobile, a cabinet for a computer, or a special pigment for paint. In other situations component parts may be standardized for sale to numerous industrial users. Integrated circuits for mini-computers, cement for the construction trade, and steel for various applications are common examples of standardized component parts and materials.

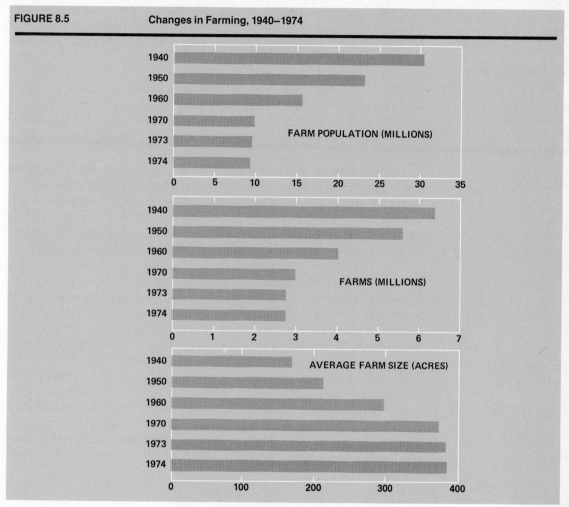

FIGURE 8.5   **Changes in Farming, 1940–1974**

Source: U.S. Department of Commerce, *Statistical Abstract of the United States,* 1975 (Washington, D.C., 1976), p. 608.

Availability of supply and consistency of quality are two critical considerations in component-parts and materials purchases. Lack of parts can shut down an entire assembly line. Lack of uniform quality can result in product failures, which cause bad will and costly warranty repairs.

In some cases extensive replacement markets develop. Tires and batteries for cars and trucks, paper for a computer printer, and batteries for electric watches are excellent examples of part-replacement markets. Sometimes companies make more money from component parts in the long run than they make from the primary product. Inexpensive "instant cameras" vastly stimulated the demand for costly instant color film. Mr. Coffee II's are designed to appeal to the cost-conscious consumer, yet they create additional demand for Mr. Coffee filters. Brand names become very important in these and similar replacement markets.

Supplies.   The fifth category of industrial goods is supplies, which are purchased routinely and in fairly large quantities by lower-echelon personnel. Supplies are expense items and do not become part of the final product. Thus they have less impact on the firm's long-run profits.

Supply items run the gamut from pencils and paper to paint and machine oil. Usually these items are purchased from office supply stores or industrial distributors. Distribution of such items is extensive, since industrial buyers will rarely search for supply items. Competition, however, may be intense. Bic and Paper Mate, for example, compete heavily in the inexpensive ball point pen market.

Services.   The last category of industrial products is services. Companies employ service organizations to plan, facilitate, or support their operations. The selling of a service, whether it is a janitorial cleaning service or management consulting, is usually done on a personal basis. Service purchasers must be convinced of their need for the special skills of outside firms and/or the cost effectiveness of hiring them. Although a company can usually afford to hire its own maintenance personnel, it may find it less expensive to enter a maintenance contract with repair personnel who agree to be "on call." Sometimes consultants in fields such as marketing, engineering, and production can bring unique talents to bear on a specific problem that does not occur frequently enough to warrant the hiring of full-time professionals.

SUMMARY

Products and services can be divided into two broad groups: consumer goods and industrial goods. Consumer goods, in turn, may be divided into four major categories: convenience, shopping, specialty, and unsought goods. The criteria for categorizing consumer goods is based on the way people view products and subsequently purchase them.

Convenience goods are items that are relatively inexpensive and require little shopping effort. They are bought routinely, day in and day out, without significant planning. Shopping goods are usually more expensive than convenience goods and are found in fewer locations. They are usually bought only after the consumer has compared quality, style, suitability, price, and life style compatibility in several different stores.

A specialty good is one that is so desirable to consumers that they are willing to search extensively for it. Fine watches, expensive stereo equipment, and fine clothing are often considered specialty merchandise. Usually brand names are very important in the purchase of specialty goods, and advertising of such items is ego oriented.

The fourth category of consumer goods is unsought merchandise. These are goods that the consumer either is unaware of or does not actively seek out. Some products are typically marketed as unsought items. These include insurance, cosmetics and housewares sold door to door, and encyclopedias.

No classification system is perfect. Something that is a convenience good for one person might be a shopping good for another. It is important, however, for marketing managers to determine how the majority of the target market views their products. This will have a significant impact on the marketing mix.

The industrial-goods market has several unique characteristics: (1) a few firms account for most of the manufacturing employment; (2) sophisticated purchasing is done by trained purchasing agents and buying committees; (3) there are large fluctuations in demand; and (4) the market is relatively insensitive to price changes.

Industrial goods can be broken down into six major categories — installations, accessory items, component parts and materials, raw materials, supplies, and services. Installations are large, expensive capital items that determine the nature, scope, and efficiency of a company. These include things like buildings and major pieces of equipment.

Accessories do not have the same long-run impact on the firm, but they are still capital goods. They are less expensive and more highly standardized. It is quite common for accessories to be bought by a purchasing agent; installations, by contrast, usually require a committee decision.

Raw materials, in contrast to the first two categories, become part of the final product. They are typically divided into natural products (e.g., oil, bauxite, and timber) and agricultural products.

Component parts and materials also become part of the final product. Often these are custom-made items such as a carburetor for an automobile or special pigment for a paint. Availability of supply and consistent product quality are two critical considerations in component-parts and materials purchases. Often extensive replacement markets develop for component parts.

Supplies are routinely purchased in relatively large quantities. They typically do not have a significant impact on the long-run operation and profitability of the firm. Supplies include paper, pens, paper clips, and similar items.

Services are used to plan, facilitate, or support a company's operations. They include everything from janitorial services to highly skilled consulting. Services are purchased when special skills are needed that are unavailable within a company or when it is more cost-effective to hire an outside company to perform those services.

KEY TERMS

Consumer goods

Industrial goods

Convenience goods

Shopping goods

Specialty goods

Unsought goods

Accelerator principle

Capital goods

Expense items

Installations

Accessories

Raw materials

Component parts and materials

Supplies

Services

QUESTIONS FOR DISCUSSION

1. What are consumer goods? How are they classified? Are these classifications rigid? Give examples to support your views.
2. What is a specialty good? Using a hypothetical example, describe how you would market such a good.
3. What are unsought goods? Give at least three examples. How does the marketing mix for an unsought good differ from the mix for a convenience good?
4. What factors must be considered in classifying industrial goods?
5. Explain some of the important characteristics of industrial markets.
6. Differentiate between the terms *derived demand* and *replacement demand*. Can you give examples of each?
7. How does the purchasing environment for industrial goods differ from the environment for consumer goods? What does this mean to marketing managers?
8. Briefly outline the classification system for industrial goods. Are these classifications rigid? Give examples to support your answer.
9. Determine whether each of the products in the following list is a consumer good, industrial good, or both. Also classify it into the appropriate subclass.
   a. the *Wall Street Journal*
   b. milk
   c. a typewriter
   d. a paper mill
   e. Funk and Wagnall's encyclopedia
10. What do the following mean to marketing managers?
   a. concentration of industrial power
   b. derived demand
   c. large fluctuations in industrial demand

NOTES

1. The original classification system was suggested by Melvin T. Copeland in "Relation of Consumer's Buying Habits to Marketing Methods," *Harvard Business Review* (April, 1923):282–289.
2. U.S. Bureau of the Census, *1974 Annual Survey of Manufacturers* (Washington, D.C., 1975), Table 1A.

3. U.S. Department of Commerce, *Statistical Abstract of the United States, 1976* (Washington, D.C., 1976), p. 757.
4. See Donald Lehmann and John O'Shaughnessy, "Difference in Attribute Importance for Different Industrial Products," *Journal of Marketing,* 38 (April 1974): 36–42. See also Thomas Semon, "A Cautionary Note on Difference in Attribute Importance for Different Industrial Products," *Journal of Marketing,* 39 (January 1975): 79.
5. U.S. Department of Commerce, *Statistical Abstract of the United States, 1976* (Washington, D.C., 1976), p. 632.

CASE 8
The Condor Kite Company

Since the dawn of humanity people have wanted to fly like the birds. They have tried to launch themselves from any available precipice using all imaginable contraptions. Leonardo da Vinci designed a hang glider but never flew it. The first true hang gliders emerged in the late nineteenth century. In fact the Wright brothers' first effort was a hang glider. Their aircraft was simply a hang glider with an engine.

In the 1950s a NASA scientist designed a glider for possible space capsule reentry, but funds for the project were cut from the budget. In the late 1960s sports enthusiasts in California picked up his design and used it to glide from the sand dunes to the beach. Since then the sport has mushroomed in the United States. There are approximately 45,000 fliers and 30,000 hang gliders active today. Hang gliding has been declared the fastest-growing sport in America.

Eight to ten manufacturers account for 75 to 80 percent of all hang glider sales. Fifteen smaller companies account for the remaining market share. Hang gliders come in many designs and range in price from $400 to $2500. Most of the companies are in California.

Condor Kite Company was founded in August 1973 in Missouri. During its first year sales were quite low, since few people in that part of the country knew what a hang glider was and those who did thought that anyone who would engage in the sport was insane. Gradually, however, sales increased and dealers were acquired across the state and the nation. Condor now has twelve dealers in the United States and Brazil. The product is as good as or better than those of the industry leaders. Performance is way above the industry norm, but the price of Condor gliders is 15 percent below that of the industry leaders.

Condor has regular promotional tours of its facilities and sends out literature to all of its dealers. It enters meets throughout the country and often wins. Condor advertises only during the seasonal months and in major hang-gliding publications. Little is actually known about the individuals who buy hang gliders, why they buy them, or what types of gliders they prefer. Identifying potential customers is extremely difficult. Also, the company's sporadic advertising has not kept the name "Condor" in the minds of many potential buyers. There are not enough Condors flying to create the word-of-mouth advertising needed to sell them.

1. How would you classify the Condor product?
2. Given the classification you have selected, outline a marketing mix for the product.

9

The Product: Demand and Supply

OBJECTIVES

■ To understand the product life cycle.
■ To describe the product adoption process.
■ To become aware of the different product mix strategies available to marketing managers.
■ To note some of the unique aspects of service marketing.

In Chapter 7 you learned how new products should be developed. You also learned how marketing managers view the "product" as much more than a physical object. In Chapter 8 you learned how products can be classified. Now you are ready to observe the life cycle of the product after it has been developed and introduced. You will examine how strategies must be altered as the product goes through its life cycle so that the firm can compete effectively in the marketplace.

After studying the life cycle you will discover how people select new products. Not everyone is equally likely to "adopt" a new product when it reaches the market. Also, individuals who are most willing to try new products and services have characteristics that tend to differ from those of other groups, such as "late tryers."

Next we will take a look at the management of a product during its life cycle. You will find out what criteria are important in determining whether a product should be added, modified, or dropped from a product line. Finally, we will focus on how the management of services differs from the management of products. You will learn what factors make service marketing quite different from the marketing of tangible products.

AN INTRODUCTION TO THE PRODUCT LIFE CYCLE

Once the product or service reaches the market, it enters the product life cycle. Like people, goods and services grow, mature, and eventually pass from the scene. This is their life cycle. The product life cycle is a theoretical concept, just as pure competition is a theoretical concept in microeconomics. It can serve as a conceptual base for examining product growth and development. Rarely will you find a product that exactly fits every detail of the product life cycle. (See Figure 9.1.)

Characteristics of Life Cycles

The life cycle is nothing more than the pattern of demand for a product over time. A basic product life cycle consists of four stages: (1) introduction, (2) growth, (3) maturity, and (4) decline. Before examining these stages, several additional points need to be made. First, not every product goes through every stage. In fact many goods never get past the introduction stage. Second, the length of time a product spends in any one stage may vary dramatically. Third, some products, such as fad items, move through the entire cycle in weeks. Others, such as Scotch whisky and filter cigarettes, have been in the maturity stage of the cycle for years.

Repositioning a product can lead to a new growth cycle. Repo-

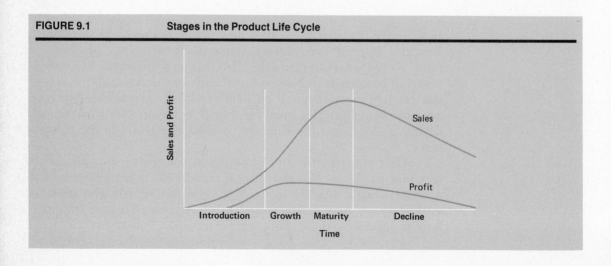

FIGURE 9.1   **Stages in the Product Life Cycle**

sitioning is basically changing the image or perceived uses of the product. Arm and Hammer repositioned its 130-year-old baking soda in 1970 as a multipurpose product useful for everything from brushing your teeth to eliminating refrigerator odors.

The Life Cycle as a Managerial Tool

In addition to providing a theoretical framework, the product life cycle concept may be used as a managerial planning tool. Marketing strategies must change as the product goes through the life cycle. If managers understand the cycle concept, they are in a better position to forecast future sales activities and plan marketing strategies.

STAGES OF THE PRODUCT LIFE CYCLE
Introduction

Animal contraceptives, huge television sets (measuring 84 inches diagonally), and hand-held CB radios recently entered the product life cycle. They face many obstacles.

A high product failure rate, little competition, frequent product modification, and limited distribution typify the introduction stage of the life cycle. Demand comes from the core market, in which there is an almost perfect match between the product offering and consumer needs. The consumers in the core market are most likely to buy the product.

Both production and marketing costs are high because of the lack of mass production economics. Often this leads to high retail sales prices in an attempt to recover costs quickly. High dealer margins, often necessary to obtain adequate distribution, may also necessitate a strategy of high prices. Sony's huge-screen television set is priced at about $4000.

Promotion strategy is centered on developing product awareness and informing consumers about how the product or service can benefit them. Intensive personal selling is required to gain acceptance for the product among wholesalers and retailers. Promotion of convenience goods often requires heavy consumer sampling and couponing. Shopping and specialty goods demand educational advertising and personal selling to the final consumer.

Growth

If a product survives the introductory stage, it moves into the growth stage of the life cycle. Sales are now growing at an increasing rate; many competitors are entering the market; large companies are beginning to acquire the small pioneering firms; and profits are healthy. Emphasis begins to switch from promotion of a product category (e.g., home video tape recorders) to aggressive brand advertising (e.g., Sony vs. Panasonic and RCA).

Distribution becomes a major key to success during the growth stage, and in later stages as well. Manufacturers scramble to acquire dealers and distributors. Without adequate distribution it is impossible to establish a strong market position.

Toward the end of the growth phase prices normally fall and profits begin to peak out (reach maximum levels). Price reductions result from increasing economies of scale and increased direct competition. Also, development costs have been recovered. Demand is no longer limited to high-income consumers as the product reaches the vast middle-income market.

Products currently in the growth stage include men's hair color products, food processors, home smoke and fire detectors, and minicomputers. Nonaerosol spray products have reentered the growth stage because of the possible ozone depletion caused by aerosol propellants.

Maturity

A period during which sales continue to increase, but at a decreasing rate, signals the beginning of the maturity stage of the life cycle. Most products are in the maturity stage of the life cycle, and therefore most marketing strategies are for mature products. Normally this is the longest stage of the cycle.

During the maturity stage annual models begin to appear for shopping goods and many specialty goods. Product lines are widened to appeal to many market segments, and service and repair take on a more important role as manufacturers strive to distinguish their products from others. Product design tends to become stylistic (how can the product be made different?) rather than functional (how can the product be made better?). Powdered drink mixes, slow-cook pots, and high-meat-content dog foods are good examples of products that are in the maturity stage of the life cycle.

As prices and profits continue to fall, marginal competitors begin dropping out of the market. Dealer margins also shrink, resulting in less shelf space for the mature product, lower dealer inventories, and a general reluctance to push the product.

Promotion to the dealer is often intensified during this stage in order to retain their loyalty. Heavy consumer promotion by the manufacturer is also required if market share is to be maintained. Long product usage and intensive promotion lead to strong brand loyalties. Coca-Cola, Winston, Smucker Jellies, Visine, and Ford Motor all have millions of loyal customers who will search extensively for these brands and accept few or no substitutes.

Decline

A permanent drop in sales signals the beginning of the decline stage. The rate of decline is governed by how rapidly consumers' tastes change and/or substitute products are adopted. Many convenience goods and fad items lose their markets overnight, leaving large inventories of items such as pet rocks and hoola hoops that cannot be sold. Others die more slowly, like the convertible, black-and-white console television sets, and nonelectric watches. In 1976 and 1977 more than 16,000 skilled Swiss watchmakers lost their jobs because of the shift in demand to digital watches.

Falling demand forces many, if not all, competitors from the market. Often a small specialty firm will buy manufacturing rights for a product and sell it to the original core market. Ipana toothpaste was acquired by two Minnesota businessmen after being dropped by a major packaged-goods company in 1968. By 1973 the new firm had over 1,500,000 loyal Ipana users.[1]

Promotion becomes very selective as the market continues to shrink. Exposure of the product to the consumer declines in importance. Mass retailers may drop the product, thereby requiring the manufacturer to distribute through specialty outlets.

Not all products face an inevitable death as they move through the life cycle. Sometimes they can be given new life through repositioning. Johnson and Johnson's success with baby-shampoo repositioning has given management the confidence to try the same tactic again. Recent ads tout Johnson's baby lotion as being not only for the baby but also for cheek protection, leg shaving, face washing, all-over body massaging, and after-sun moisturizing.[2]

Repositioning can result in a product's reentering the growth stage of the life cycle. Figure 9.2 makes this point and illustrates several ways in which product repositioning can occur. Recycles A, B, C, and D result from marketing actions 1, 2, 3, and 4, as follows:

1. Promoting more frequent use of the product by current consumers.

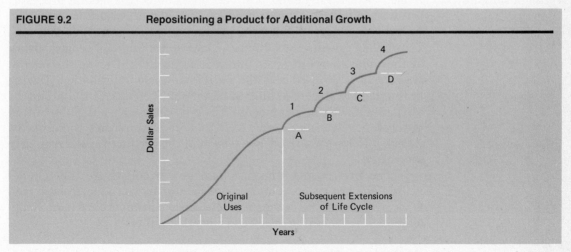

FIGURE 9.2   Repositioning a Product for Additional Growth

Source: Adapted from Theodore Levitt, "Exploit the Product Life Cycle," *Harvard Business Review,* November-December 1965, pp. 81–94, with the permission of the publisher.

2. Developing more varied use of the product by current consumers.
3. Creating new consumers for the product by expanding the market.
4. Finding new uses for the product.

The Proper Use of the Life Cycle

A brief summary of strategic considerations at various stages of the product life cycle is presented in Table 9.1. Care must be taken to make certain that a product has moved from one stage to the next before altering the marketing strategy. A temporary sales decline could be misinterpreted as a sign that the product is going "down the tubes" and stimulate a pull-back of marketing support. This amounts to a self-fulfilling prophecy.

THE PRODUCT ADOPTION PROCESS

A marketing manager should understand the product adoption process in order to increase the chances that a new product will move beyond the introduction stage of the product life cycle. This involves, first of all, knowing what is meant by *innovation* and *diffusion*. An innovation is any product or service that we perceive as new (e.g., a once-a-day pill that would take the place of eating). Note that a product may have been around for a long time yet still be seen as new. The diffusion process is the sales rate of a new product through an economic system over time. The adoption process consists of the decision-making steps that consumers go through before buying a good or service.

Product Adoption Stages

Armed with these definitions, we can examine the mental processes involved in adopting a new product. The pioneer of diffusion theory, Everett M. Rogers, defined the product adoption process as shown in Figure 9.3.[3] During the *awareness* stage an individual becomes aware of the innovation but lacks information about it. During the *interest* stage need is aroused and the individual seeks information. During the *evaluation* stage the individual mentally compares the product's attributes to his or her needs. The *trial* stage consists of an initial purchase to determine how well the product satisfies those needs. *Adoption* follows a satisfactory trial, and the product is used regularly thereafter.

The first people who purchase new products are called innovators. The last group of individuals to buy a new product are referred to as laggards. As you will see below, some consumers are more likely to adopt a new good or service earlier than others.

Awareness, Interest, and Evaluation.   By understanding the adoption process a new-product manager can speed the acceptance of a product or service. To create awareness and stimulate interest, the right media

TABLE 9.1　　　　Strategic Considerations in the Product Life Cycle

Effects and Responses	Stages of the Product Life Cycle			
	Introduction	**Growth**	**Maturity**	**Decline**
Competition	None of importance	Some emulators	Many rivals competing for a small piece of the pie	Few in number with a rapid shakeout of weak members
Overall strategy	Market establishment; persuade early adopters to try the product	Market penetration; persuade mass market to prefer the brand	Defense of brand position; check the inroads of competition	Preparations for removal; milk the brand dry of all possible benefits
Profits	Negligible because of high production and marketing costs	Reach peak levels as a result of high prices and growing demand	Increasing competition cuts into profit margins and ultimately into total profits	Declining volume pushes costs up to levels that eliminate profits entirely
Retail prices	High, to recover some of the excessive costs of launching	High, to take advantage of heavy consumer demand	What the traffic will bear; need to avoid price wars	Low enough to permit quick liquidation of inventory
Distribution	Selective, as distribution is slowly built up	Intensive, employ small trade discounts since dealers are eager to store	Intensive; heavy trade allowances to retain shelf space	Selective; unprofitable outlets slowly phased out
Advertising strategy	Aim at the needs of early adopters	Make the mass market aware of brand benefits	Use advertising as a vehicle for differentiation among otherwise similar brands	Emphasize low price to reduce stock
Advertising emphasis	High, to generate awareness and interest among early adopters and persuade dealers to stock the brand	Moderate, to let sales rise on the sheer momentum of word-of-mouth recommendations	Moderate, since most buyers are aware of brand characteristics	Minimum expenditures required to phase out the product
Consumer sales and promotion expenditures	Heavy, to entice target groups with samples, coupons, and other inducements to try the brand	Moderate, to create brand preference (advertising is better suited to do this job)	Heavy, to encourage brand switching, hoping to convert some buyers into loyal users	Minimal, to let the brand coast by itself

Source: Nariman K. Dhalla and Sonia Yuspeh, "Forget the Product Life Cycle Concept," *Harvard Business Review,* January–February 1976, p. 104. Copyright © 1975 by the President and Fellows of Harvard College; all rights reserved.

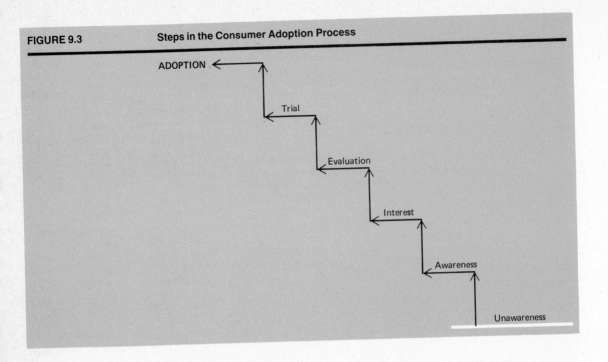

FIGURE 9.3   **Steps in the Consumer Adoption Process**

mix must be chosen. Distribution channels must be chosen so that consumers are reached at locations where they expect and want to buy the product.

Trial and Adoption.   The fourth stage of the adoption process (trial) is basically an exercise in attempted risk reduction by the consumer. One obvious way to lower perceived risk is to offer the new product in small quantities.[4] This isn't much consolation to a manufacturer of microwave ovens. Its only strategic move may be to offer a "free home trial," an effective guarantee, or something of a similar nature. Many producers of consumer goods, however, can market trial sizes to gain consumer acceptance. Hidden Valley Salad Dressings offers ten-cent miniature bottles of its new flavors to induce trial.

Several other determinants of trial are relative advantage, communicability, and complexity.[5] Relative advantage is the degree to which an innovation is perceived as being better than any possible substitute. The microwave oven has a strong relative advantage over a conventional oven for rapid cooking. Communicability is the ability to verbalize product attributes. Much more can be said about a new car than about a new salt shaker. If a product is complex, extra promotional effort on the part of the marketing manager may be required.

ADOPTER CATEGORIES

Everett Rogers has classified product adopters into five groups, as shown in Figure 9.4. Before we discuss these categories, however, it should be noted that they were forced into a normal statistical distribution quite arbitrarily. A product with a high relative advantage will tend to display a positively skewed distribution.[6] In other words, more than 16 percent of the market will be innovators and early adopters and a smaller percentage will be in the late majority of adopters and laggards. The reverse is true of a new product with a relatively low comparative advantage. For example, microwave ovens had many early purchasers because of the advantages of microwave cooking over conventional cooking.

Innovators and Early Adopters

For many products, early adopters are relatively young, have more disposable income than their peers, and are better educated. Studies show that early users read more magazines, particularly ones that relate to potential purchases. These consumers belong to more organizations and are more mobile than other consumers. They also exhibit strong needs for achievement, change, and exploration. While they do not actively seek risk, early users are more likely to take risks than other consumers. Also, different groups of individuals may be early adopters for different products.[7] An early purchaser of new soaps may not be an early purchaser of new appliances.

Early Majority

Early-majority buyers (34 percent) are much more cautious and thoughtful in making purchase decisions. They do not consider buy-

FIGURE 9.4   Adopter Categorization on the Basis of Relative Time of Adoption of Innovations

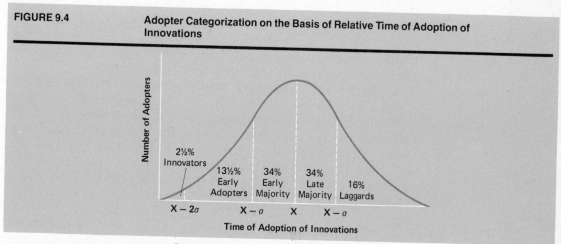

Source: Everett M. Rogers, *Diffusion of Innovations* (New York: Free Press, 1962), p. 162. By permission.

ing a good or service until they have communicated with early triers. Most early-majority buyers are of above-average socioeconomic status.[8] This group is generally willing to assume some risks but will not engage in extensive risk taking.

Late Majority

The next 34 percent of consumers are referred to as the late majority. They are below average in socioeconomic status and tend to have a higher average age than the other groups. These consumers are strongly oriented toward their reference groups and do not depend on advertising or personal selling for information. In this category production adoption normally results from economic need rather than from the influence of an opinion leader.

Laggards

Laggards represent the bottom rung of the social and economic ladder. By the time this group adopts a product the early adopters have switched to something new. This group strongly resists change. Its members cling to the past and tend to associate with people who hold viewpoints similar to their own. Advertising to this group is virtually a waste of time and money.

PRODUCT STRATEGY Product Mix Strategy

Product Depth and Width.   The marketing or product/brand manager must determine the product mix that will most effectively reach his or her target market—early adopters, the majority, or even laggards. Three important variables must be examined in developing a product strategy. First, management must decide the proper depth of each product line. Product depth is the average number of goods or services offered by a company within each product line. General Foods, for example, offers a large number of different types and flavors of cereals, thereby creating a deep product line. (See Figure 9.5.) Xerox offers twenty-two copiers, also creating a deep product line.

Polaroid and Xerox have deep product lines but little product width. The width of a product mix may be defined as the number of different product lines found within the company. It is the second variable that must be examined in developing a product strategy. Allegheny Ludlum Industries utilizes a very wide product mix, including Allegheny Steel, Special Metals, Jacobsen mowers, True Temper tools and sporting goods, Carmet and IPM audio products, and Arnold magnetic tapes.

Product Line Consistency.   Product lines that are closely related in end use, production requirements, or distribution channels are characterized by product line consistency—the third element of the product mix. Allegheny Ludlum obviously lacks consistency in its product

FIGURE 9.5   **The Concepts of Product Mix and Product Line as Applied to Selected General Food Products**

← ——————————————— WIDTH OF PRODUCT MIX ——————————————— →

Coffees	Desserts	Cereals	Household Products	Pet Foods	Other Grocery Products
· Maxim Freeze-Dried Coffee · Maxwell House Coffee (Regular) · Instant Maxwell House Coffee · Instant Sanka Coffee · Sanka Coffee—97% Caffein Free	· Jell-O Gelatin Desert · Jell-O Pudding and Pie Filling · Jell-O Instant Pudding · Dream Whip · Dream Whip Whipped Topping Mix	· Grape-Nuts, 40% Bran Flakes · Raisin Bran, Sugar Crisp · Corn Flakes, Fruit Cereal · Honeycomb, Oat Flakes	· SOS Soap Pads · Satina Ironing Aid · Tuffy Plastic Mesh Ball (Dishwashing Aid)	· Gaines Meal · Gaines Biscuits · Gaines Bits · Gaines Variety	· Kool-Aid Soft Drink Mix · Log Cabin Syrup · Tang Instant Breakfast Drink · Baker's Cocoa · Baker's Instant Chocolate Flavor Mix · Good Seasons Salad Dressing Mixes · Good Seasons Open-Pit Barbecue Sauce · Good Seasons Shake 'n Bake Seasoned Coating Mixes for Chicken and Fish

↕ DEPTH OF PRODUCT MIX

lines. General Foods, on the other hand, has a very wide product mix with a high level of consistency.

A firm with a wide product line attempts to reach many, if not all, segments of its present market. It is relying on a well-defined image in the marketplace to help sell its products. If a company develops an inconsistent product line mix, it tacitly implies that the firm's best profit opportunities lie in widely diverse markets. An organization with a highly consistent product mix attempts to reap greater economies of scale from current production lines, channels of distribution, media mix, and so forth. A depth strategy is an attempt to reach virtually all consumers by giving them a plethora of product choices.

Product Modification

Even if a company has only one product, it will sooner or later have to decide whether to alter the product or drop it. Product modification is often less drastic than dropping an item and usually has less impact on long-run profits. Many times the change may be a subtle modification in quality or style that may not even be perceived by consumers. For example, in 1976 many liquor distillers dropped the proof of their whiskeys from 86 to 80 with scarcely a gurgle from the drinkers.

Sometimes modifications consist of nothing more than redesigning a logo or package. Morton Salt has changed the hair style and skirt length of its "when it rains, it pours" girl several times in the past seventy-five years in order to give the product a contemporary image. Another common practice is to modify components—plastic radiator fans on automobiles instead of metal ones, for example.

Product Deletion

Why Products Are Dropped.   The decision to drop a product—product deletion—is usually a critical one and is far more serious than product recall.[9] Yet most companies don't have formal policies or procedures for systematically reviewing their product lines.[10] Most products are eliminated because of low profits, low sales, and/or poor future prospects.

Ramifications of Dropping a Product.   Dropping a product affects not only the company but its customers as well. Retailers may lose large profits if the dropped item sold well in their stores. Consumers who used the product may have to make major changes in their consumption patterns and/or life styles. Discontinuation of the Studebaker drastically changed the purchase patterns of loyal Studebaker owners.

SERVICE STRATEGY

Our discussion throughout this chapter has focused on products, yet in most cases the word *services* could easily have been interchanged with the word *products*. There are important distinctions between them, however.

The Importance of Services

Today more than half of our personal consumption expenditures go for services. One study claims that services account for 68 percent of all the jobs in America.[11]

Rising affluence, fulfillment of basic needs (food, clothing, shelter), the complexity of society (your income tax), more leisure time, the dying protestant work ethic, and the complexity of products have led to ever-increasing demand for services.

Services generally fall into two categories: personal and business. Personal services include financial services, transportation, health and beauty, lodging, advising and counseling, amusements, maintenance and repair, real estate, and insurance. Of course this is not an exhaustive list, nor are all of these services intended strictly for the final consumer. Business firms, for example, utilize all of the services just mentioned plus others that are strictly business oriented, such as advertising agencies, market research firms, and economic counselors.

Many large manufacturers have recognized the movement toward services and have jumped onto the bandwagon. Coca-Cola has developed a multimedia learning system for schools. G. D. Searle, a pharmaceuticals manufacturer, has a new service entitled Project Health that will sell preventive-medicine programs to industry. Singer is moving into preschool education. Upjohn, another pharmaceuticals maker, has a subsidiary that performs paramedical and housekeeping chores for newly discharged hospital patients. Gerber Products is moving into nursery schools and insurance.[12]

How Service Strategies Differ

A good image is even more important to a service firm than to a company that sells tangible products. There are very few objective standards for measuring service quality. Products can be examined on the basis of ingredients, tensile strength, weight, size, and so on, but services are judged subjectively. Another reason for the importance of image to service firms is that many people utilize certain services, such as plumbing, carpentry, and television repair, rather infrequently and therefore choose a company on the basis of perceived reputation.

Price competition such as that found in car rental companies, figure studios, and the airlines is quite severe, since each company offers essentially the same thing. Another reason for price cutting is the difficulty of demonstrating dependability, skill, and creativity. Some firms have attempted to overcome this problem by offering low introductory rates to new customers. Not only is a service usually complete before a buyer can evaluate its quality but defective services cannot be returned!

Another unique aspect of service marketing is the difficulty of standardizing the output. One ball game is very exciting; the next one is an exercise in boredom. Similarly, flying Delta today won't guarantee on-time arrival even though you flew Delta last week and arrived fifteen minutes early. It is therefore incumbent on marketing managers to pay particular attention to quality control in an attempt to achieve a satisfactory level of service.

Services can't be saved. Once the game is over, that's it! This is particularly important for promoters of amusements, transportation services, hotels, and the like. An empty room or seat brings in no revenue. Sometimes a variable pricing strategy (i.e., charging different prices to different purchasers for the same service) may induce the low-price buyer into the market even though the incremental revenue is below total cost.

Another unique problem of service is the difficulty of increasing productivity. In some cases capital intensification simply is not possible. How, for example, does one increase the productivity of a marriage counselor? The small scale of most service establishments also acts as a hindrance to increased productivity.

The Marketing Concept in Service Organizations

Because of the unique problems facing service firms, many have been slow to adopt the marketing concept. Where the concept has been utilized, the company is less likely to have all of its marketing mix activities carried out in the marketing department. Responsibility for new service offerings and evaluation of present offerings are often handled by other departments.[13] Such fragmentation of the marketing function makes control more difficult and probably reduces the effectiveness of the marketing strategy.

Service firms also tend to spend less on marketing activities than product manufacturers.[14] The lack of financial support for marketing may also partially explain why service companies do more of their advertising development "in house" and use marketing research and consulting firms less frequently. It is extremely difficult to develop an effective marketing program without a strong financial, as well as philosophical, commitment to the function. Perhaps as the service industries continue to mature there will be a shift in their commitment to marketing.

SUMMARY

All products move through a life cycle. The life cycle is a measurement of sales and profits over time. The four stages of the life cycle are introduction, growth, maturity, and decline. Changing consumer attitudes, competition, the number of dealers carrying a product, and other factors normally necessitate a different marketing mix for each stage of the product life cycle. Most products never get through all four phases. Indeed, the majority never leave the introduction stage. Sometimes products can be repositioned to enter a new growth stage.

A sequence of events must occur before consumers will utilize a new product. Individuals must become aware of a product; their needs must be aroused; the product's attributes must match their needs; and this may lead to trial purchase. If the trial is satisfactory, then product adoption may follow.

Not everyone is equally likely to adopt a new product. Individuals who purchase a good or service before most others are referred to as early adopters. These people are relatively young, have more disposable income than their peers, and are better educated. The next group of consumers that adopt a product is called the early majority. This group, which is above average in social and economic terms, is willing to assume some purchase risk but does not actively engage in risk taking.

The late majority is the third category of adopters. These consumers are below average in economic status and tend to be older than members of the first two groups. The final category of adopters is the laggards. These individuals strongly resist change and are of low socioeconomic status.

10

The Nature of Products

OBJECTIVES

■ To understand the role of branding in developing a total product.
■ To gain insight into the "battle of the brands."
■ To become aware of the different stages of brand preference.
■ To achieve a better understanding of issues concerning product safety and product liability.
■ To appreciate the role of packaging and labeling in product marketing.

No study of "products" would be complete without an examination of important product attributes besides those of the physical unit itself. This chapter begins by examining the role and importance of branding. Several different types of brands compete for market share.

Next you will learn how warranties and guarantees add a further dimension to perceived product quality and may aid in developing brand loyalty. Even when express warranties are not issued with a product, companies face growing responsibility for product liability.

Finally, the roles of packaging and labeling in developing a total product will be investigated. These two important product attributes are closely monitored by marketing managers. The government has recently stepped into the packaging and labeling area, further complicating marketing decision making.

BRANDS,
TRADEMARKS,
AND PATENTS
Some Definitions

Brand is a very broad term used to describe product identification by word, name, symbol, or device, or a combination of these. Manufacturers and middlemen use brands to identify their goods and distinguish them from others. Trademark is a legal term that includes only words, names, or symbols (logotypes) that the law designates as trademarks. A brand name is the part of the brand that can be vocalized, such as "McDonald's"; the golden arches symbol, as well as the name, are McDonald's trademarks.

Service marks are used to identify services — an example is "H&R Block." Certification marks are used to identify goods and services as having met certain qualifications. The Good Housekeeping seal and the "UL" mark of Underwriters Laboratories signify that a product has met the testing standards of those organizations.

Two other useful terms are *copyrights* and *patents*.[1] Copyrights concern literary and artistic expression. An original song or a new dress design can be copyrighted. Patents, on the other hand, concern inventions that have to do with function or design. A new device for making milk (i.e., a replacement for a cow) could be patented. Specifically, how the machine works (its function) or the design of the machine would be patented. Figure 10.1 illustrates the major differences among copyrights, patents and designs.

Legal Aspects
of Branding

One of the most important aspects of trademark law is that the mark need not be registered to be protected. According to common law, trademark rights can be acquired only by using the mark in marketing

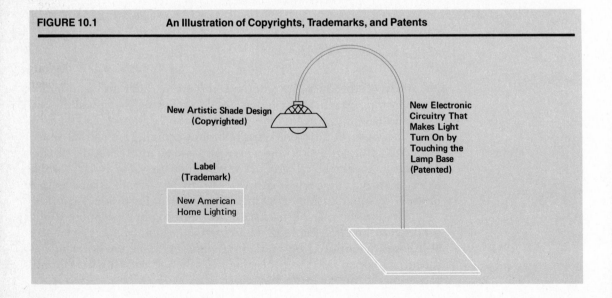

FIGURE 10.1   **An Illustration of Copyrights, Trademarks, and Patents**

New Artistic Shade Design
(Copyrighted)

New Electronic
Circuitry That
Makes Light
Turn On by
Touching the
Lamp Base
(Patented)

Label
(Trademark)

New American
Home Lighting

a good or service. The Lanham Act of 1946 provides for the registration of marks with the U.S. Patent Office but doesn't require such registration. (Perhaps one reason that people confuse trademarks and patents is that both operations are handled by the Patent Office.) In addition to providing a way of registering trademarks, the Lanham Act specifies what types of marks can be protected and the various remedies available for trademark violations.

Advantages of Mark Registration. Any good or service shipped in interstate commerce can have its mark registered as a trademark. The process of registration takes about one year after the application is filed. Once a person or corporation has received federal registration, it has the following advantages:

1. It is constructive notice of the registrant's claim of ownership, applicable nationwide to everyone subsequently adopting marks (a trademark search report should always be obtained before adopting a new mark).
2. It will be listed on search reports obtained by others.
3. It is evidence, although rebuttable, of the registrant's exclusive ownership rights, shifting the burden of proof to anyone challenging those rights, and in some circumstances it can be conclusive evidence of those rights.
4. It gives federal courts jurisdiction to hear infringement and related claims of unfair competition under state law.
5. It can be used as a basis for registration in some foreign countries.
6. It can be recorded with the U.S. Customs Service to prevent importation of infringing foreign goods.[2]

Also, registration allows the use of "Registered U.S. Patent Office," "Reg. U.S. Pat. Off.," or ® as notification to others that the trademark is registered.

The Life Span of Trademarks. Rights to trademarks continue as long as the mark is used. Normally the mark is considered to have been abandoned if the firm does not use it for two years. If a new user picks up the mark after owner abandonment, the new user can claim exclusive ownership of the mark.

Infringement Remedies. If two firms happen to be using the same trademark, the first user is considered the rightful owner. This holds true even if the second company registered the mark first. When an organization is convicted of trademark infringement, it faces severe penalties. For example, the injured party can sue for (1) triple the amount of damages actually suffered and (2) any profits the offending firm made from the mark. Federal law also allows for the destruction of all materials bearing the infringing mark. This could be very costly if a company has a warehouse full of merchandise bearing the illegal mark.

ADVANTAGES OF BRANDING
Advantages to the Firm

Ownership of a brand has no value unless the brand has a positive image among consumers. Certainly names like "Coke," "Xerox," "IBM," "Scotch Tape," "Fritos," and "Kleenex" are worth millions of dollars. The goal of marketing managers is to build a large consumer franchise for their brand through the development of an effective marketing mix. Once a good brand image is established, the company must continue to closely monitor its mix in order to maintain its brand image in an ever-changing marketplace.

Advantages to the Consumer

The names just mentioned are valuable not only to the manufacturer but also to the consumer. People know what the corn chips are going to taste like when they purchase a bag of Fritos. Similarly, people have expectations, based on past experiences or product promotions, regarding how well their car will run on Exxon gasoline and the quality of service they will receive if their car is rented from Hertz. Branding simplifies product identification for the consumer. As such, it simplifies the shopping task. After a person has eaten a box of Post's Grape-Nuts he or she decides whether or not to purchase the item again. If the consumption experience was satisfactory, the consumer can select another box and expect the same product quality. This newly developed confidence becomes an additional dimension of the total product.

TYPES OF BRANDS
Family Brands

When several different products have the same brand name, it is referred to as a family brand. Nabisco markets a number of different cookies and crackers using the familiar Nabisco name and shield. Sony puts its family brand on radios, television sets, stereos, and other electronic products. Marketing managers must decide whether or not a new product may be covered by an existing family brand.

It is usually to the manufacturer's advantage to use a family brand name when possible because it facilitates the introduction of new products. You would probably be more likely to buy a new frozen dessert with the "Sara Lee" family brand name on it rather than one with "Joe's Frozen Desserts" on it. Since consumers are already familiar with the "Sara Lee" name, less money is required to promote the new product.

Manufacturers' Brands and Dealer Brands

The brand of a manufacturer, such as "Kodak," "La-Z-Boy," "Fruit-of-the-Loom," and "Harley Davidson," is called a national brand or a manufacturer's brand. The term *national brand* obviously is not always accurate, since many manufacturers serve only a regional market. I use the term *manufacturer's brand* because it more precisely defines the brand's owner.

Historically, the brands of wholesalers and retailers have been labeled *private brands*. Again, this term is not always an accurate description. The connotation of the word *private* is that items bearing this brand are distributed only in the retailer's or wholesaler's own stores, whereas most manufacturers' brands are marketed through a variety of middlemen. (See Figure 10.2.) A definitional problem arises here, because some manufacturers restrict their retail distribution to a particular geographic area. "Oldsmobile," "Magnavox," "Hart Shaffner and Marx," and "Rolex" products are just as privately distributed as most middleman brands. To avoid this problem we will use the term dealer brand for all brands of wholesalers or retailers.

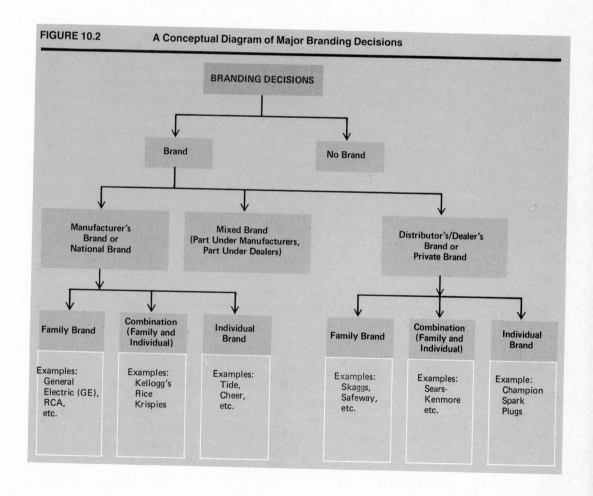

FIGURE 10.2   A Conceptual Diagram of Major Branding Decisions

"Penncrest" (a J. C. Penney's brand), "Craftsman" and "Kenmore" (Sears brands), "Signature" and "Airline" (Montgomery Ward brands), and "IGA" (Independent Grocers' Association) are all dealer brands. Sears' own brands now account for over 90 percent of the company's volume.[3]

Advantages and Disadvantages of Manufacturers' Brands

Advantages of Manufacturers' Brands to Dealers. Most middlemen are too small to develop their own brands and rely instead on manufacturers' brands. As retailers and wholesalers grow, they ultimately have to decide whether to establish their own dealer brands or continue to sell only manufacturers' brands.

There are several good reasons for staying with the manufacturers' brands and not developing dealer brands.[4] Heavy advertising to the consumer helps "presell" the buyer and develop strong consumer loyalties. All the dealer has to do is store the merchandise and display it, since the consumer already has a strong desire to buy it. It is not uncommon for Procter and Gamble, Colgate-Palmolive, or Gillette to spend over $10 million a year promoting a single product.

Well-known manufacturers' brands can help bring in new customers and enhance the dealer's prestige. For example, a small lawn mower and bicycle repair shop in a midwestern college town was fortunate enough to acquire the right to distribute Lawnboy lawn mowers. Sales grew rapidly; the shop was remodeled for a higher-quality clientele; and the entire operation acquired a more professional and businesslike image.

Intensive promotion by the manufacturer also encourages rapid turnover, which aids in lowering the dealer's selling costs. Most manufacturers offer rapid delivery to dealers, thus enabling the middlemen to carry less inventory. Lower inventory requirements mean that less working capital is required.

A final factor that is quite important to many retailers and wholesalers is varying product quality. If, for example, a retailer sells a manufacturer's brand that happens to be of poor quality, the customer may simply switch manufacturer's brands but continue to trade with the retailer. If it had been the retailer's own brand, it might have lost a customer.

Disadvantages of Manufacturers' Brands to Dealers. You may be wondering at this point, Why even have dealer brands? Again, there are several good reasons. Manufacturers' brands typically offer a lower gross margin than the dealer can earn on its own brand. Moreover, the manufacturer retains control over the brand and may decide to drop the product or remove the dealer as a distributor. Dealers that spend substantial sums of money developing a consumer franchise dislike the uncertainty of future supply associated with some manufacturers' brands.

Advantages and Disadvantages of Dealer Brands

Advantages of Dealer Brands.   Dealer brands offer higher gross margins and tie the customer to the dealer. If a person likes Lucerne cottage cheese, he or she may purchase it only at Safeway. Since dealer brands do not identify the manufacturer, the retailer or wholesaler can switch producers without the consumer ever knowing it. A dealer might find it advantageous to convert to a new manufacturer if the firm can produce the dealer brand cheaper, offer faster and more dependable delivery, or offer higher quality at the same cost.

Disadvantages of Dealer Brands.   Dealer brands have several drawbacks that can cut deeply into their larger gross margin. For example, the dealer must promote its own brands; no one else will do it. Promotion can be very expensive. Sears spent $83 million and Penney's $16 million on major media promotion in 1975.[5]

In order to sell merchandise at a competitive price, dealers must buy their brands in fairly large quantities. Not only do large inventories tie up working capital; they also entail risks such as fire, theft, obsolescence, deterioration, and the like. As you can see, a high gross margin may result in a lower net margin when the disadvantages of dealer brands are enumerated. Even though a dealer can change sources of supply without the consumer knowing it, it still has to find the right suppliers. It is often a headache to continually locate good, reliable manufacturers to produce dealer brands. Some manufacturers refuse to produce dealer-branded goods because they believe that they're cutting into their own market.

A final disadvantage of dealer brands is that if the product is not good, the consumer has only the dealer to blame. Poor-quality dealer brands can result in loss of customers and the creation of a negative image for the dealer. If you buy an Airline color television from Montgomery Ward that proves to be unsatisfactory, you may decide that the television set is indicative of the quality of all Ward's products and may simply stop shopping at Ward's.

THE BATTLE OF THE BRANDS

As dealer brands continue to grow in sales, distribution, and promotion, consumer brand awareness also increases. The fight for distribution and shelf space between manufacturers' and dealer brands has been called "the battle of the brands."

The Growth of Dealer Brands

Dealer brands currently account for 40 percent of the auto tire volume and 30 percent of all grocery volume.[6] The thrust of dealer brand growth has been the giant retailers. Most of these organizations hope to have at least one-third of their sales in their own brands.[7] In one emerging technique for stimulating wider distribution, retailers' brands are placed in noncompetitive outlets such as service stations.

Giant retailers, because of their extensive retail distribution systems and close contact with the ultimate consumer, are finding that they can supply product services more efficiently than the manufacturer. Ultimately this will result in further erosion of manufacturer's brands and perhaps lower prices for the consumer.

The Future of Manufacturers' Brands

The battle of the brands does not imply the ultimate demise of manufacturers' brands. It simply means that the competition between dealer brands and manufacturers' brands for shelf space will continue to intensify. Dealers are not without problems. Severe supply problems, shrinking shelf price differentials between manufacturers' and dealer brands, and consumer dissatisfaction with the quality of some dealer brands assure the long-run viability of manufacturers' brands.

STAGES OF BRAND PREFERENCE

Consumers acquire degrees of brand preference for products over time. The four stages of brand preference are nonrecognition, brand recognition, brand preference, and brand loyalty.

Nonrecognition

The plethora of brands on the market makes it impossible for us to "know" each one or even a large fraction of all the brands available. Most brands are meaningless to consumers. Can you name two brands of desk calendars, fly swatters, plastic eating utensils, or garden hoses? Many convenience goods (such as those mentioned in the previous sentence) are perceived as homogeneous by most people. Middlemen and manufacturers continue to brand these items for purposes of inventory control and promotional strategy. When the target market does not recognize a brand name, it is in stage one—nonrecognition.[8]

Brand Recognition

A brand name is in stage two, brand recognition, when a person remembers having seen or heard of the brand. Most marketing managers are elated if their brand reaches this degree of brand preference in the marketplace. Consumption of the brand will naturally depend on the degree of brand availability and consumer needs.

Brand Preference

The third stage, brand preference, is reached when customers buy the product out of habit or past experience. We buy products routinely because we have had satisfactory consumption experiences with them in the past and it simplifies the purchasing process.

Brand Insistence

Rarely does a product reach the fourth stage for a majority of its target customers. If consumers insist on a brand and will accept no substitutes and will search extensively for it, the good or service has reached the fourth stage, brand insistence. A select group of fine clothing, jewelry, and automobiles has reached this stage. You probably know someone who buys only Ford cars and swears by their quality and durability. For that person Ford has reached brand insistence. Unfortunately for Ford, this doesn't hold true for the entire target market. The marketing manager must determine the degree of brand preference for a product. The marketing strategy should be based on this knowledge.

BRAND LOYALTY

When customers reach brand preference or brand insistence for a product, they have acquired a degree of brand loyalty. Brand loyalty is consistent repeat purchasing of a brand over time.[9] Achieving consumer loyalty for a specific brand is very important for marketing managers. Loyalty ensures future sales and usually gives the brand good word-of-mouth advertising.

Brand Loyalty and Risk Reduction

The importance of reducing consumer risk is an important dimension of brand loyalty. As consumers develop more information and experience about a brand or product group, these help reduce risks for future purchases. The correctness of our decision to buy brand A is continually reinforced as we keep using brand A and finding the results satisfactory. As long as a product meets preconceived expectations, actual performance is often ignored. In a recent study of purchases of women's clothing, one respondent said, "I am satisfied because it did not rip, shrink, or fade." Overt research for a new brand would have begun only if one of the negatives had occurred.[10]

PRODUCT WARRANTIES
Definition of Warranty

When many people try a different product and find it defective, they often switch brands rather than complain to the manufacturer.[11] Manufacturers may try to discourage brand switching through the offer of an expressed product warranty. A warranty is intended to be a confirmation of the quality or performance of a good or service. An express warranty is made in writing, while an implied warranty is an unwritten guarantee that the good or service is fit for the purpose for which it was sold. All sales have an implied warranty under the Uniform Commercial Code.

The Complexity of Warranties

Express warranties range from simple statements such as "100 percent cotton" (a guarantee of quality) and "complete satisfaction guaranteed" (a statement of performance) to extensive documents written in obscure language. Warranties are important marketing tools because the consumer views them as a dimension of product quality.[12] Yet, as shown in Table 10.1, far more than a college education is required to comprehend warranties on products priced above $120.00.[13]

According to a study by Kelly Shuptrine, the more expensive the product, the greater the difficulty of understanding the warranty.[14] Ultimately this means that many customers are at the mercy of the dealer or perhaps the manufacturer for a proper interpretation of the

TABLE 10.1	Difficulty Calculations for Product Warranties and Guarantees			
Product	Approximate Price	Average Sentence Length (Words)	Hard Words (per Hundred)	Educational Requirement Index
Cross pen	$ 5.00	13.0	4.0	6.8
Sunbeam alarm clock	6.00	19.5	9.4	11.6
Ronson lighter	10.00	18.3	11.0	11.7
Coleman camp stove	17.00	25.3	9.5	13.9
Schick hair dryer	20.00	23.3	9.0	12.9
Midas muffler	22.00	20.5	1.0	8.6
Elgin watch	30.00	30.1	5.9	14.4
Panasonic tape recorder	70.00	22.2	9.9	12.8
Realistic stereo speaker	120.00	23.0	9.0	12.8
Wickes water heater	150.00	43.4	20.0	25.4
Frigidaire washer	350.00	34.4	15.5	20.0
Gibson food freezer	400.00	42.3	17.3	23.8
Frigidaire refrigerator	450.00	40.9	23.1	25.6
RCA television	550.00	61.9	16.2	31.2

Source: F. Kelley Shuptrine, "How Understandable Are Warranties by the Average Consumer?" in Henry W. Nash and Donald P. Robin, eds., *Proceedings, The Southern Marketing Association 1975 Conference.*

warranty. Shuptrine also noted that 40 percent of the American people in 1973 did not have the educational background to properly interpret the average warranty on products priced under $100.00.[15]

New Warranty Legislation

Congress passed the Magnuson–Moss Warranty–Federal Trade Commission Improvement Act on January 4, 1975 to aid consumers in understanding warranties and to eliminate lethargic action by manufacturers and dealers. If a manufacturer promises a full warranty, it must meet certain minimum standards, including repair "within a reasonable time and without charge" of any defects and replacement of the merchandise or a full refund if the product does not work "after a reasonable number of attempts" at repair. And the new law demands that any warranty that does not live up to this tough prescription must be "conspicuously" promoted as a limited warranty.[16]

General Motors, Goodyear, Zenith, and Bulova have all switched to limited warranties as a result of the new law. Wright and McGill, the manufacturer of Eagle Claw hooks, rods, and reels, dropped the "lifetime guarantee" from their products. Others have shed their warranties altogether, including Fisher-Price toys, Kroehler furniture, and Levi Strauss. "They [warranties] don't sell pants anyway," explains Levi Strauss' lawyer, Willard Ellis.[17] Thus in several cases the new law has resulted in less protection (at least explicit protection) in the consumer goods market than there was before it was passed.

PRODUCT SAFETY AND PRODUCT LIABILITY
The Product Safety Record

In 1970 the National Commission on Product Safety reported to Congress that each year 30,000 Americans are killed in accidents involving products, 110,000 are permanently disabled, and 20 million are injured.[18] On the basis of these data 2 Americans will be killed, 7 permanently disabled, and 114,000 injured by products in approximately the time it will take you to read this chapter. The major offenders are listed in Table 10.2.

The Consumer Product Safety Act

The poor product safety record led Congress to pass the Consumer Product Safety Act in 1972. Briefly, this Act

1. established a 5-member Consumer Product Safety Commission (CPSC) whose purpose is to reduce the risks faced by consumers in their use of consumer products.
2. gives the Commission a variety of remedies for dealing with hazardous products, depending on the severity of the hazard. Ban and seizure are appropriate for "imminently hazardous" products.

TABLE 10.2	The Twenty Most Dangerous Products	
Rank	**Item**	**Frequency–Severity Index**
1	Bicycles and bicycle equipment	863,490
2	Stairs, ramps, and landings	833,120
3	Nonglass doors	389,950
4	Cleaning, caustic compounds	386,310
5	Nonglass tables	369,990
6	Beds	304,890
7	Football	296,700
8	Playground apparatus	287,260
9	Liquid fuels	267,150
10	Architectural glass	267,100
11	Power lawn mowers	264,410
12	Baseball	262,310
13	Nails, tacks, and screws	257,650
14	Bathtubs and showers	187,800
15	Space heaters and heating stoves	182,720
16	Swimming pools	178,770
17	Cooking ranges and ovens	161,180
18	Basketball	158,770
19	Nonupholstered chairs	151,380
20	Storage furniture	143,610

Source: Paul Weaver, "The Hazards of Trying to Make Consumer Products Safer," *Fortune,* July 1975, p. 135. Reprinted by permission.

Note: Twenty products were identified by the CPSC's National Electronic Injury Surveillance System as those most often involved in accidents. The index numbers represent the number of injuries associated with each product, multiplied by the average severity of those injuries measured on a geometric scale. Injuries sustained by persons 10 or under, an accident-prone group, are given double weight.

3. provides for rather severe civil and criminal penalties for violation of the law or Commission rules.[19]

The Growing Number of Product Liability Suits

If you are injured by a product, you can sue the manufacturer or the dealer. Specifically, the purchaser of the product can sue regardless of whether or not he or she bought the product from the manufacturer. The nonpurchasing user or consumer can sue, and finally, the bystander can sue. A bystander, for example, would be an individual who is hit by an automobile that goes out of control because of a defect in the steering mechanism.[20] Awards of $250,000 to $500,000 are not uncommon in product liability cases, with claims now occurring at a rate of over 1 million per year.[21]

Manufacturer Defenses

A manufacturer or dealer has three basic defenses against a product liability lawsuit. First, if the user discovers a product defect and continues to use the item, knowing the risks that he or she is taking, the manufacturer is relieved of responsibility. Second, the manufacturer or dealer is absolved of liability if the consumer misuses the product. If, for example, a person falls off a chair while standing on one of its arms and trying to reach an object on a high shelf, the chair manufacturer would not be held liable in a product lawsuit. The last defense is that the product isn't defective. For example, a man trying to reach his car keys through a side vent window inadvertently hit his eye on the point of the window and put it out. The jury held that the window was not defective and that its design was adequate for normal use.[22]

Product Recall

Consumerism, the growing importance of the Consumer Product Safety Commission, recognition by manufacturers of their social responsibility, and attempts to avoid lawsuits and maintain customer good will have resulted in an ever-increasing number of product recalls. The CPSC was involved in recalls of over 15 million product units during its first 20 months of operation.[23] Approximately 25 percent of all consumer goods firms listed in *Fortune's 500* were involved in such recalls in 1974, and the Conference Board estimates that more than 25 million product units will be recalled every year.[24] In 1975, for example, Matsushita Electric Corporation recalled 300,000 color television sets because of radiation emission and General Motors recalled 234,000 Cadillacs after a faulty hood latch was discovered.[25]

Product recall can be very costly for the company. General Motors spent $3.5 million on postage alone when a problem with motor mounts was detected in 6.5 million of its cars.[26] Bon Vivant, a soup manufacturer, went bankrupt when botulism was discovered in its canned vichyssoise. Its failure was due partly to the enormous expense of the product recall. As a result some companies are purchasing product recall insurance, although it is expensive, restrictive in its provisions, and offered by very few firms.

PACKAGING
The Functions of Packaging

Traditionally, packages have been viewed in a very utilitarian fashion, that is, as a means of holding contents together (e.g., a box of salt) or as a way of protecting the product as it moves through the distribution channel. Today, however, the package plays a much greater role in marketing-oriented firms. The package should have the following characteristics:

1. Visual appeal—it should stand out on the shelf.
2. Information—the label should reflect the package contents and proper use of the product.
3. Emotional appeal—some packages should have an expensive look, others an old-fashioned look, and so forth.
4. Ease of handling—it should be easy to open and reclose and able to maintain freshness.

Packaging Responsibility

As top management has become aware of the importance of packaging in the marketing mix, responsibility for the function has been escalated up the corporate hierarchy. George Weissman, president of Philip Morris, has stated that

> if there is a single concept underlying the success of Philip Morris packaging, it is that we don't regard packaging as a disjointed or low-echelon endeavor. To us, excellence in our packaging is virtually indistinguishable from excellence of product. Both are absolutely top priority items.
>
> And so our packaging operations involve executives representing production, quality control, sales, marketing, advertising, purchasing, and accounting—all the way to senior management: our chairman, our president, and others. All regularly review every contemplated innovation or change in packaging. For many years, Philip Morris has been most keenly aware of its vital importance, and that's an understatement.[27]

Some companies, such as the National Biscuit Company and General Foods, have vice presidents in charge of packaging. In other organizations packaging is a key responsibility of the marketing manager.

LABELING
Legislation

An integral part of any package is its label. The Food and Drug Act of 1906 signaled the beginning of congressional concern with labeling information. This Act prohibited false labeling of foods and drugs. As the economy continued to grow and develop, Congress realized that the 1906 legislation was too vague and general to provide adequate consumer protection.

In 1967 the Fair Packaging and Labeling Act was passed. It sought regulations "requiring labels and packages to disclose sufficient information regarding product ingredients and composition as will establish or preserve fair competition between competitive products by enabling consumers to make rational comparisons with respect to price and other factors or to prevent consumer deception."[28]

Seals and Certifications

Seals and certifications such as the "Good Housekeeping Seal," "Parents Magazine Seal," and "Underwriters' Laboratory Seal" are granted to manufacturers of goods and services that meet the requirements of the seal-granting institutions. These seals are intended to add an implicit quality guarantee to the product. Research by Thomas Parkinson has shown that consumers view products with seals and certifications as being of higher quality than those without such seals.[29] His study also showed that the symbols were broadly recognized and well known, a feature that adds to their utility for the manufacturer.

Metric Conversion

A final dimension of labeling that we should examine is the process of metric conversion. Our new system of weights and measures is the decimal-based method known as SI (meaning Système International d'Unités), which is a modernized version of the metric system used by all advanced industrial nations. More than half of our canned goods are already labeled in both metric and customary units.[30] Soft-drink bottlers such as 7-Up are coming out with new liter bottles utilizing the slogan "A quart and a liter bit more." The firm has also sponsored a "Miss Liter" contest in order to draw further attention to the new container size. The conversion is occurring slowly and at great expense to many firms. In the long run, however, it will facilitate international marketing and make weight and length calculations much easier. As a new button suggests, "Take me to your liter!"

SUMMARY

A brand is a word, name, symbol, or device, or a combination of these, used by a manufacturer or middleman to identify its goods and services and distinguish them from others. *Trademark* is a legal term that includes only the words, names, or symbols that the law designates as trademarks. Copyrights concern literary and artistic expression; patents concern inventions related to function and design.

The Lanham Act of 1946 provided for the registration of trademarks with the U.S. Patent Office. Although a mark does not have to be registered, many advantages accrue to firms that register their marks. If a firm is judged guilty of trademark infringement, the injured party can sue for triple damages, profits made from the mark, and destruction of all materials bearing the infringing mark.

Brands and trademarks help consumers identify products and services that they wish to purchase and those that they wish to avoid. The manufacturer's brand is sometimes referred to as a national brand. Dealer brands, those of a wholesaler or retailer, have historically been labeled "private brands." Both types of brands offer unique advantages and disadvantages to the dealer. This has led to a "battle of the brands." In recent years the battle has resulted in significant dealer brand growth.

There are four stages of brand preference for the consumer. The first is nonrecognition. The second, brand recognition, is reached when a consumer remembers having seen or heard of a brand. The third stage is brand preference. This stage is reached when consumers buy a product out of habit or past experience. Stage four, brand insistence, is a utopian one for most marketing managers. If consumers insist on a particular brand and will accept no substitutes, and will search extensively for it, the product has reached the level of brand insistence.

A person who has reached brand preference or brand insistence is said to be brand loyal. Brand loyalty may be defined as consistent purchase of a given brand over time.

One factor that induces brand loyalty is a strong product warranty. An express warranty is made in writing; an implied warranty is an unwritten guarantee. The Magnuson–Moss Warranty–Federal Trade Commission Improvement Act was designed to aid consumers in understanding warranties and to eliminate slow warranty action by manufacturers and dealers.

Congress passed the Consumer Product Safety Act in 1972 to reduce the number of product accidents that kill or injure many consumers each year. Growing rates of product-related injuries and deaths have led to an increasing number of product liability suits. The possibility of incurring a product liability suit coupled with the impact of the new Product Safety Act has led to a growing number of product recalls.

An aspect of product marketing that is often overlooked in marketing textbooks is packaging. Packaging has become an increasingly important element of the product mix in major corporations. It represents the manufacturer's last chance to "sell" the product before the consumer makes the purchase/no purchase decision. Thus many package labels contain information that is not only informative but also highly persuasive.

KEY TERMS

Brand
Trademark
Brand name
Service mark
Certification mark
Copyright
Patent
Family brand
Manufacturer's brand
Dealer brand

Nonrecognition
Brand recognition
Brand preference
Brand insistence
Brand loyalty
Warranty
Full warranty
Limited warranty
Product liability
Product recall

QUESTIONS
FOR DISCUSSION

1. What is a trademark? What are the advantages of registering a trademark?
2. Discuss the remedies available to the injured party in a trademark infringement case.
3. What is a brand? List the different types of brands described in this chapter. Give examples of each.
4. How does a consumer benefit from branding? What about the manufacturer?
5. What is meant by a family brand? Under what circumstances would it be advantageous for a manufacturer to use this type of branding?
6. What is "the battle of the brands"? What strategies should manufacturers use to promote their brands?
7. Explain the different stages of brand preference.
8. What is a product warranty? Do you agree with the view that warranties are too complex? What can be done about this problem?
9. Explain the terms *full warranty* and *limited warranty*. How have they affected the marketplace?
10. Explain the defenses available to a manufacturer in a product liability suit.
11. Why is packaging so important to marketing managers? What functions should a package perform?
12. What is a label? How does it differ from a certification mark?

NOTES

1. This section is largely adapted from William M. Borchard, "A Trademark Is Not a Copyright or a Patent," *Executive Newsletter,* no. 25 (New York: U.S. Trademark Association, July 1977), pp. 1–2. © 1974, 1977 by the United States Trademark Association. Reprinted by permission.
2. Ibid.
3. E. B. Weiss, "Private Label? No, It's Now Presold—Wave of Future," *Advertising Age,* September 30, 1974, p. 27.
4. Much of this section is adapted from E. Jerome McCarthy, *Basic Marketing: A Managerial Approach,* 5th ed. (Homewood, Ill.: Irwin, 1974), pp. 257–259.
5. "Top 100 Put $3.8 Billion into 75 Ads," *Advertising Age,* May 24, 1976, p. 34.
6. Weiss, op. cit.; Herbert Zeltner, "Big Stores, Non-Foods, and Private

Brands Wane in Supermarket Field," *Advertising Age,* January 5, 1976, p. 32.

7. Weiss, p. 66.

8. Stages of brand preference have been fully developed by McCarthy, pp. 253–254.

9. For a detailed theoretical view of brand loyalty, see Jacob Jacoby and David Hyner, "Brand Loyalty vs. Repeat Purchasing Behavior," *Journal of Marketing Research,* 10 (February 1973): 1–9; for rebuttal, see Lawrence X. Tarpey, Sr., "A Brand Loyalty Concept—A Comment," *Journal of Marketing Research,* 11 (May 1974): 214–217.

10. John E. Swan and Linda Jones Combs, "Product Performance and Consumer Satisfaction: A New Concept," *Journal of Marketing,* 40 (April 1976): 25–33.

11. C. L. Kendall and Frederick A. Russ, "Warranty and Complaint Policies: An Opportunity for Marketing Management," *Journal of Marketing,* 39 (April 1975): 42.

12. Carl McDaniel, "The Relevance of Price–Warranty Interaction on the Perception of Product Quality," paper presented to the Southern Marketing Association, Atlanta, 1974.

13. F. Kelly Shuptrine, "How Understandable Are Warranties by the Average Consumer?" in Henry W. Nash and Donald P. Robin, eds., *Proceedings: Southern Marketing Association 1975 Conference,* pp. 139–141.

14. Ibid.

15. Ibid.

16. "The Guesswork on Warranties," *Business Week,* July 14, 1975, p. 51.

17. Ibid. See also "Ads Not Part of Final Warranty Rules," *Advertising Age,* January 5, 1976, p. 2; "New Warranty Law Under Attack by Business," *Advertising Age,* July 7, 1975, p. 1; and "Initial FTC Guides for Warranty Law Out; Ad Rules Still Coming," *Advertising Age,* July 21, 1975, pp. 2ff.

18. Arnold A. Bennigson, "Product Liability—Producers and Manufacturers Beware," *Research Management,* 18 (March 1975): 16.

19. Lawrence Kushner, "Consumer Product Safety Commission: What It Is and What It's Doing," *Research Management,* 18 (March 1975): 12. Reprinted by permission.

20. Bennigson, p. 8.

21. Howard C. Sorenson, "Products Liability: The Consumer's Revolt," *Best's Review,* 75 (September 1974): 48; see also Conrad Berenson, "The Product Liability Revolution," *Business Horizons,* 15 (October 1972): 71–80.

22. Bennigson, p. 19; see also Eugene G. Combs, Jr., "Products Liability—The User's Role," *The National Underwriter,* Property Edition, 79 (December 26, 1975): 11ff.

23. George Fish and Rajan Chandran, "How to Trace and Recall Products," *Harvard Business Review,* 53 (November–December 1975): 90–96.

24. E. P. McGuire, "Product Recall and the Facts of Business Life," *The Conference Board Record,* February 1975, pp. 13–15; see also "Managing the Product Recall," *Business Week,* January 1975, pp. 46–48.

25. Roger A. Kerin and Michael Harvey, "Contingency Planning for Product

Recall," *MSU Business Topics*, Summer 1975, pp. 5–12. The section on product recall is largely adapted from this article.

26. Kerin, p. 10.
27. Dale Brubaker, "Five Reasons Why Brand Managers Should Get Out of Packaging," *Marketing News*, July 1, 1974, p. 5. Reprinted by permission of the American Marketing Association.
28. U.S. Congress, Senate, Committee on Commerce, *Fair Packaging and Labeling*, 89th Cong. 1st sess. on S .985 (Washington, D.C.: Government Printing Office, 1965), p. 471.
29. Thomas L. Parkinson, "The Effect of Seals and Certifications of Approval on Consumers' Perceptions of Products," in Robert L. King, ed., *Proceedings of the Southern Marketing Association 1973 Annual Conference*, pp. 244–249.
30. "Think Metric," *Time*, June 9, 1975, p. 48.

CASE 10
California Label Company

The growth of the labeling industry has been slow but steady—held back to some extent by rapid adoption of direct printing methods on some types of containers. About 1½ billion paper labels worth $450 million are used in this country at present. Pressure-sensitive labels are the fastest-growing segment of this industry.

It is difficult to determine the cost of producing labels, since they come in such a variety of types and sizes. A typical artist's sketch for a new label may cost $75. Converting this to a black-and-white mechanical drawing suitable for reproduction will cost another $50. The cost of printing plates will vary according to the process used, ranging from $25 for offset plates to $1500 for a gravure cylinder. Printing expense for a small label will be about $4 per 1000 for two colors printed offset.

The California Label Company was established in 1923. Its primary function was to manufacture and distribute pharmacists' prescription labels, packaging, and record-keeping items used in filling and dispensing prescriptions. Since 1923 the firm has expanded so much that it now has a sales force of eleven full-time salespeople serving eight states.

Federal and state laws required that a prescription filled by a pharmacist bear a prescription label with certain pertinent information typed on it by the pharmacist. This means that the pharmacist must type a prescription label for each prescription filled and dispensed. Also, the pharmacist must assign a number to the prescription, and this number must be written on the prescription blank that the doctor gives to the patient as well as on the prescription label.

Pharmacists must perform certain other record-keeping procedures. They must record the prescription number along with the name of the patient, the doctor, the date, and the ingredients of the prescription. They must also see that the customer gets a receipt that can be used for tax or insurance purposes. If the customer wishes to charge the drug, the pharmacist must make a record of this so that it will appear on the customer's monthly statement.

California Label, recognizing the problems faced by the pharmacist, is in the process of developing a new label-and-form combination to be called the "professional form." It is simply a form with several copies by means of which a prescription label may be fed into the typewriter. The pharmacist's paper work is facilitated by the carbon copies that result. One problem faced by the company in designing this form is that of ascertaining exactly what types of information should be recorded. For example, should a pharmacist develop a family prescription record that would record medications dispensed and drug sensitivity?

1. What kinds of information should be included in the professional forms? How should California Label determine the answer to this question?
2. Is California Label ignoring the promotional role of labeling?

IV Distribution Structure

11

Channel Roles
and Channel Systems

OBJECTIVES

■ To appreciate the importance of middlemen in the distribution function.
■ To become aware of how distribution channels help create consumer satisfaction.
■ To understand some of the basic channel systems.
■ To learn about the behavioral dimensions that affect distribution channels.
■ To become aware of different factors that influence channel selection.

A channel of distribution is the mechanism by which goods flow from the producer to the consumer. The channel consists of the institutions (e.g., wholesalers and retailers) that move goods from producer to ultimate user. The success of any channel depends on how well it meets the shopping needs and habits of the target consumers and the costs constraints of the seller.

Channels have several important functions besides the movement of merchandise. A channel consists of a series of institutions, such as wholesalers and retailers, that facilitate the flow of goods. Wholesalers sell to other middlemen or to manufacturers. Retailers sell to the final consumer. Since channel institutions tend to form buying and selling relations among themselves, they may be viewed as a system. The nature of channel systems and their behavioral dimensions, such as power, control, and institutional conflict, will also be described in this chapter. We will conclude with a discussion of the factors influencing channel selection.

WHY ARE MIDDLEMEN USED?
Facilitating the Flow of Goods

We will begin our study of channels of distribution by examining why they exist and what their functions are. The fundamental task of any channel is to move merchandise in an efficient manner. Efficiency is enhanced by (1) reducing the number of individual transactions, (2) removing discrepancies of quantity, and (3) reducing discrepancies of assortment.

Reducing the Number of Transactions.   Assume for a moment that there are 20 students in your class. Also assume that your professor requires 5 textbooks, each from a different publisher. If there were no bookstore (or middleman), 100 transactions would be necessary for each student to obtain the necessary books. (See Figure 11.1.) If a middleman is inserted between the publishers and the students, the number of transactions is reduced to 25. Each publisher sells to one bookstore rather than to 20 students. Each student buys from one bookstore instead of from 5 publishers.

Eliminating Discrepancies of Quantity.   Perhaps the easiest way to understand the idea of a discrepancy of quantity is to relate it to our mass production economy. Economies of scale are achieved in industry through the use of efficient equipment capable of creating tremendous outputs of homogeneous products. Economies of scale, specialization of labor, and the use of professional management normally result in a lower average cost of production per unit.

To illustrate, assume that a record manufacturer has acquired the production rights to the latest Barry Manilow songs. The company has equipment capable of pressing 200,000 disks a day. Even the most fanatical Manilow fan couldn't possibly use a single day's output, much less one week's production. The quantity produced is too big for the individual target consumer. It is also too big for any single record shop. Mass production has created a discrepancy of quantity.

A channel can alleviate a discrepancy of quantity by breaking bulk, that is, taking a large quantity of homogeneous products and dividing it into smaller, more manageable quantities. Our record producer can do this by selling to several wholesalers, which, in turn, sell even smaller quantities to individual retailers. (See Figure 11.2.)

Eliminating Discrepancies of Assortment.   Our devoted Barry Manilow fan goes to the neighborhood record shop and purchases one new

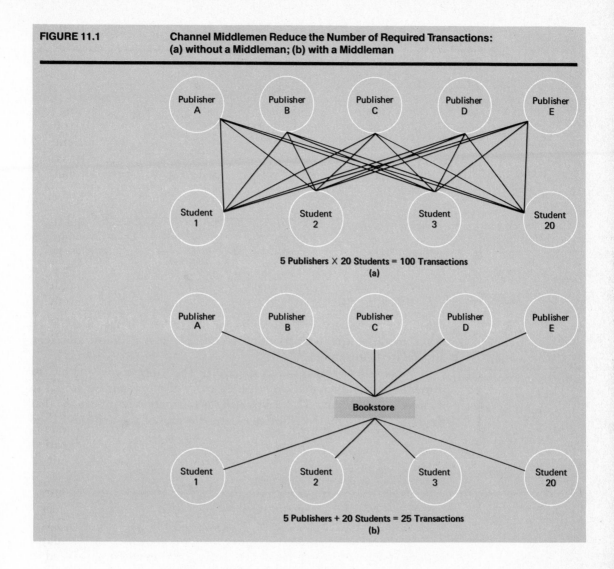

FIGURE 11.1

Channel Middlemen Reduce the Number of Required Transactions: (a) without a Middleman; (b) with a Middleman

5 Publishers X 20 Students = 100 Transactions
(a)

5 Publishers + 20 Students = 25 Transactions
(b)

album (maybe two). Upon returning to the apartment he finds that his roommate has abruptly moved out and taken all of the stereo equipment. The new record has suddenly dropped in utility (satisfaction). Without a stereo system, the new record may have to be converted into a frisbee.

Mass production creates not only discrepancies of quantity but also discrepancies of assortment. Firms achieve economies of scale by producing either a homogeneous product or a base product with minor variations. Our record producer manufactures a base product—rec-

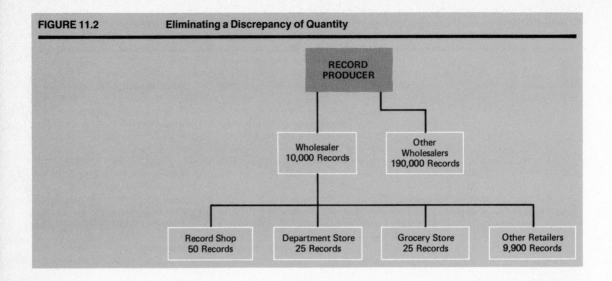

FIGURE 11.2   Eliminating a Discrepancy of Quantity

ords. The variations are the different artists and songs. It relies on other manufacturers to produce record players, needles, speakers, and related equipment.

Wholesalers and retailers engage in the process of assorting, or providing the target market with an array of merchandise suited to its needs. (See Figure 11.3.) Assorting is a synergistic process in that the total utility created is greater than the sum of the utilities of the

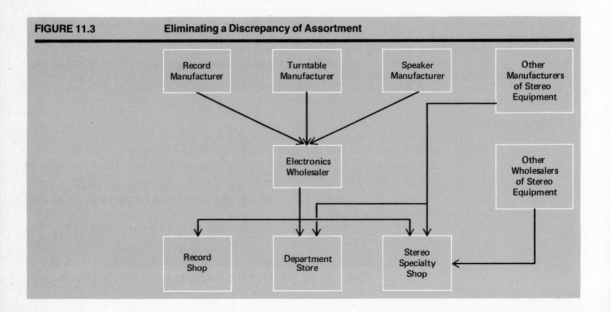

FIGURE 11.3   Eliminating a Discrepancy of Assortment

individual products. In other words, the satisfaction derived from a stereo system *plus* a record is greater than the satisfaction derived from these two items *separately*.

Returning for a moment to our dejected Barry Manilow fan: He has decided to take his Master Charge card and head for the nearest Radio Shack. Radio Shack, a chain of consumer electronic-products stores, has eliminated the discrepancy of assortment by providing a wide array of turntables, speakers, and amplifiers, as well as records. Our fan can purchase the equipment necessary to enjoy his record by going to one store.

Other Channel Functions

Communications. In addition to the primary channel functions of reducing the number of transactions, breaking bulk, and assorting, channels provide several auxiliary functions. Channels are a communications conduit. Promotional information flows from the manufacturer through the middleman and, in some cases, to the ultimate consumer. Information, such as product price, begins at the manufacturing level and is passed down to the final consumer. Manufacturers promote their products to wholesalers, which, in turn, promote them to retailers. Retailers must convince consumers to buy their merchandise; otherwise they will be burdened with worthless inventory. Communication also flows upward in the channel. Retailers receive comments, ideas, and complaints about products. This information is either passed directly to the manufacturer or relayed to the wholesaler, which then tells the manufacturer what consumers are thinking.

Financing. Channels also have a financial function. First, a channel of distribution consists of middlemen that get the manufacturer's product to the market. It saves the manufacturer the cost of providing the distribution network (e.g., buildings, equipment, and parking space). Coke is sold in hundreds of thousands of locations throughout the world. Can you imagine the expense that would be involved if Coca-Cola had to set up a distribution network that was entirely company owned?

A second aspect of the channel's financing function is the credit provided to channel intermediaries. Inventories are financed as products flow through or are held in the channel. In most channels manufacturers provide credit to wholesalers and to retailers that buy directly from the manufacturer. Many wholesalers also grant credit terms to retailers. Thus a channel may provide a source of financing for its middlemen.

Locating Buyers. Channel members must locate buyers for their merchandise. A wholesaler seeks "the right" retailers in order to sell a profitable volume of merchandise. A sporting-goods wholesaler, for example, must find the retailers that are most likely to reach sporting-goods consumers. Retailers have to understand the buying habits of the final consumer and locate stores where the consumer wants and expects to find the merchandise. Every member of a channel of distribution must locate buyers for the products it is attempting to sell. This process is discussed in more detail later in the book.

Storage.   Merchandise must be stored within the channel in order for goods to be available when the consumer wants to purchase them. The high cost of retail space often means that storage is done by the wholesaler or the manufacturer.

Manufacturers serve wide markets covering large geographic areas. Many times prompt delivery at reasonable cost can best be provided by strategically located warehouses close to the manufacturer's major markets. Thus wholesalers are usually responsible for finished-goods storage. It should be noted, however, that some manufacturers and retailers establish their own wholesaling operations.

HOW DO DISTRIBUTION CHANNELS CREATE SATISFACTION?

By storing a product until consumers are ready to buy it, channels create time utility or time satisfaction. Satisfaction, in turn, enhances the value of the product. Winter clothing, for example, is produced beginning in early summer. It begins to enter distribution channels many months before consumers will purchase the items.

Channels create place utility by physically moving a product close to where consumers want to purchase it. A can of Maryland Club coffee would not be worth much to you sitting on a dock in Brazil — it has no place utility. Transportation creates place utility.

Channels also facilitate possession utility — acquisition of a good or service — by locating stores close to where a shopper wishes to buy a product. Promotion also helps create possession utility by telling consumers where a product can be bought. Possession utility is also facilitated by the flow of title from the manufacturer to the retailer. Title is passed to the consumer upon purchase or fulfillment of credit obligations.

Breaking bulk, a channel function discussed earlier, creates a fourth type of utility — form utility. Form utility is produced when a product or raw material is changed into a more usable form. Processing trees into lumber or paper creates form utility. Form utility is generally associated with production processes such as creating pots and pans from aluminum. Although the channel usually doesn't engage in production per se, it does reduce large homogeneous outputs to a manageable form or size by packaging goods in convenient sizes.

Sometimes channel members may create form utility as a secondary function. Soft-drink bottlers, for example, are wholesalers; the manufacturer is the syrup producer.

BASIC CHANNEL SYSTEMS

Figure 11.4 depicts common channels of distribution. Some of the members of those channels are described in the following list.

- *Agents and Brokers.* Agents and brokers do not take title to the merchandise and rarely handle the merchandise itself. A broker brings the buyer and seller together. Brokers are common in markets where it is hard to find potential buyers and sellers. An agent is a representative of a manufacturer or wholesaler. Agents do not take title and have little, if any, authority over the terms of a sale.
- *Industrial Distributors.* These are independent wholesaler organizations that purchase related product lines from many manufacturers and sell to industrial users. An industrial distributor often maintains a sales force to call on account executives, make deliveries, extend credit, and provide information.
- *Industrial Users.* Industrial users buy products for internal use or for further processing as part of the production process. They include manufacturers, utilities, airlines, railroads, and service institutions such as hotels, hospitals, and schools.

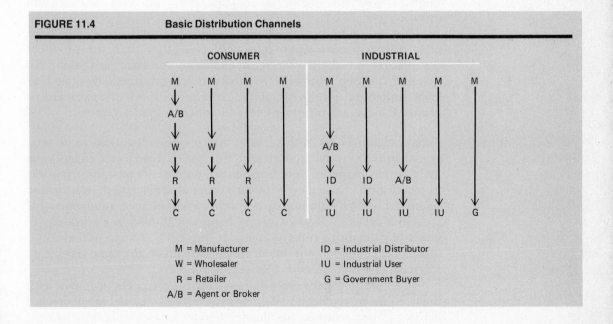

FIGURE 11.4   **Basic Distribution Channels**

M = Manufacturer   ID = Industrial Distributor
W = Wholesaler   IU = Industrial User
R = Retailer   G = Government Buyer
A/B = Agent or Broker

- *Government Buyers.*   State, local, and federal government purchasing agents buy virtually every good and service imaginable. Because of the quantities and specifications involved, these transactions are usually between the government and the manufacturer. Manufacturers are invited to submit proposals and prices for specific goods and services.

The number and types of middlemen in a channel depend on a variety of factors, to be discussed later in the chapter. First, however, three important channel concepts need to be understood. These are (1) the inability to eliminate channel functions, (2) service channels, and (3) the systems concept of distribution.

The Inability to Eliminate Channel Functions

Regardless of whether or not middlemen are present in the channel, the channel functions discussed earlier must still be performed. If there is no wholesaler, someone must physically store and move the merchandise, locate suitable retailers, promote the product, and so forth. Similarly, if a manufacturer decides to be its own retailer, it must decide on the number of stores, their locations, their layout, promotions and displays, and all the other retail and wholesale functions.

Service Channels

Our discussion so far has centered on the distribution of goods rather than services. Most services have a very short channel: from the producer (the provider of the service) to the consumer.[1] Unlike goods, services can't be stockpiled, transported, or inventoried. They must be created and distributed simultaneously. Examples include barber shops, physicians, bankers, lawyers, hotel accommodations, and movies.

Yet in a narrow sense longer service channels can evolve. This phenomenon occurs when intermediaries other than the producer are utilized to make the service available and/or more convenient. An example is group insurance written through intermediaries, such as labor unions or employers. Retailers who accept Bankamericard or Master Charge are intermediaries for a bank's credit services.

Vertical Channel Systems

Today, channels for both services and merchandise tend to be integrated into a system. Historically, this wasn't the case. Conventional distribution channels were fragmented, potentially unstable networks in which firms bargained with each other at arm's length, terminated relationships with impunity, and otherwise behaved autonomously.[2]

In a vertical channel system firms are aligned in a hierarchy of levels (e.g., manufacturer–wholesaler–retailer). A horizontal channel system, in contrast, contains firms that are all on the same level (e.g., a system of wholesalers or a system of retailers).

Competition between different vertical channels, together with the need for more effective control by dominant channel members, has led to a closer relationship among channel participants. Efficient accomplishment of channel functions requires coordination among the various intermediaries and fulfillment of certain role expectations. A manufacturer, for example, expects wholesalers in the channel to promote its products to retailers and to perform several other functions as well.

Allocation of functions, operation of the system, and control are achieved through centrally positioned firms that manage the entire vertical system. Sometimes the managing institution is referred to as the "channel captain" or "system leader." Not all channels are coordinated, nor do they always have a leader. In fact they tend to resemble the old-fashioned conventional system described earlier. These should gradually phase out because experience is proving that centralized coordination considerably improves the efficiency of distribution.[3]

All channels have members that rely on each other. This has led to the evolution of three basic types of vertically coordinated systems: corporate, administered, and contractual.

Corporate Systems. A corporate distribution system represents the ultimate in channel control. When a single firm owns the entire channel, there is no need to worry about the cooperation of middlemen. Sherwin Williams, for example, operates over 2000 paint stores; Hart Schaffner and Marx, a long-established manufacturer in the men's-wear field, owns over 100 clothing outlets; Sears has an ownership equity in production facilities that supply over 30 percent of the company's inventory requirements; and large food chains obtain almost 10 percent of their requirements from captive manufacturing facilities, many of which were acquired in the 1950s.[4]

Corporate systems are no panacea. When a corporation assumes the entire channel responsibility the need to perform channel functions is not eliminated. Singer has learned this the hard way. Lack of marketing know-how at the retail level is partially responsible for its poor financial performance in the 1970s.

Administrative Systems. An administrative system is established when a strong organization assumes a leadership position. The strength and power of the firm may consist of sheer economic domination of other channel members. On the other hand, it can stem from a well-known brand name. Companies like Gillette, Hanes, Campbell, and Westinghouse are administrative-system leaders. An administrative leader can often influence or control the policies of other channel members without the costs and expertise required in a corporate system. This may be accomplished by threatening to withdraw well-known brand names, advertising rebates, or planning aids. Yet the vertically aligned companies can work as an integrated unit to achieve information, transportation, warehousing, promotion, and other economies. The net result, compared to a conventional system, is usually lower overall cost, a better assortment of merchandise, faster turnover, and the ability to adjust to changing consumer preferences.

Contractual Systems.   The third form of vertical marketing system is the contractual system, which may be defined as a system of independent firms at different levels (manufacturer, wholesaler, retailer) coordinating their distribution activities by contractual agreement. The objectives of a contractual system are essentially the same as those of an administrative system.

Franchise organizations are a common form of contractual system. Their operations and characteristics will be discussed in more detail in the chapter on retailing (Chapter 13).

Horizontal Marketing Systems

Lee Adler describes a recent tendency for two or more companies to develop a joint marketing strategy to exploit new opportunities as symbiotic marketing.[5] One company, for example, may have developed a new product but may lack the proper channel of distribution to effectively reach the target market. Dr. Pepper found that the easiest way to break into many new market areas was to license existing Coca-Cola bottlers to bottle Dr. Pepper.

Magnavox found that Xerox had an excellent marketing organization to handle the telecopier Magnavox makes, and quickly entered into a marketing agreement with Xerox to handle its products. When A&P launched its massive modernization program, hundreds of stores were closed in marginal market areas. Southland recognized that A&P's "8 O'Clock" brand of coffee had a strong consumer franchise. Southland entered into an agreement to sell the coffee at its 7-Eleven stores in trade areas vacated by A&P. Thus symbiotic marketing can result from changing distribution patterns, lack of capital, lack of marketing knowledge, or a desire on the part of two organizations to use their resources more efficiently.

THE BEHAVIORAL DIMENSIONS OF DISTRIBUTION CHANNELS

A channel of distribution is more than a series of institutions linked by economic ties. Social relationships also play an important part in developing cohesiveness among the channel members. The basic social dimensions of channels are member roles, power, and conflict. An understanding of how these concepts affect channel intermediaries will provide you with a better appreciation of channel systems.

Member Roles

Each channel member has a certain role to play if the distribution system is to function smoothly. Henry Tosi has said that

> when channels of distribution are viewed as social systems, individual channel members are recognized as occupying distinct positions in the

channel structure. A position pertains to the tendency for persons or organizations occupying a particular location in a system of social relationship to behave alike. One position becomes differentiated from other positions by virtue of the fact that the member exhibits predictable patterns of performance which elicit predictable responses from the other members.[6]

Every marketing channel must meet certain minimum role expectations in order to exist. For example, without some indication of what the wholesaler will do, the manufacturer would face a chaotic distribution system.

Each channel member tends to develop policies regarding services rendered, market served, and product offered. Each member must accept other members' "functional domain" or conflict will result. As new marketing institutions evolve, they often force old intermediaries into new, different roles—or out of business. The supermarket, for instance, developed entirely outside of the traditional channel for food. In fact the old channel members actively fought against the supermarket concept.[7]

Channel Leadership, Power, and Control

As channel members jockey for power, control, and leadership roles within the system, conflict often results. Channel power may be defined as a firm's ability to achieve its goals in a state of conflict or potential conflict. Control occurs when one organization intentionally affects the behavior of another person, group, or organization.[8] Leadership is the exercise of authority and power in order to achieve control.[9]

Channel power tends to emanate from the following: financial strength, brand ownership, contractual agreements, and the channel member's role within the channel.[10]

Financial Strength and Dependence.   Generally, the more one member of a channel is financially dependent on another member of the channel, the more power the wealthier member has. Administrative-system leaders often draw much of their power from their financial strength. When one firm obtains a majority of its sales revenue from one customer, significant power is often exercised by the buyer. For example, Kellwood had sales of $283 million in 1971. Sears accounted for $226 million of that amount.[11]

Brand Ownership.   Ownership of a popular brand name may lead to channel power primarily because of the ultimate financial impact of the brand. Gillette's Right Guard deodorant has such strong consumer acceptance that it offers virtually "guaranteed sale" to middlemen. Intermediaries are attracted to companies with popular brand names because of the potential for solid financial gains and low risk. If, during the product's life, competitive pressures result in loss of popularity for a brand, the brand owner may experience an erosion of its power base.

Contractual Power. Franchise agreements provide a legal base for the exercise of contractual power. A franchisee may agree to provide timely financial reports, pay royalty and promotion fees, maintain certain service standards, and so forth. A similar form of contractual power is the relationship between shopping center tenants and the developer. The developer often restricts small tenants in terms of types of merchandise carried, store hours, advertising, and similar factors. The ultimate source of the franchisor's or developer's power, however, is the financial reward anticipated by the franchisee or tenant.

Channel Position Power. A channel participant may "earn influence" because of its initial position or expertise. A broker, for example, may be selected for his or her knowledge of certain geographic markets. In another case a retailer such as Neiman-Marcus or Saks Fifth Avenue may be chosen because of its prestige. The key to position power is access to desirable markets.

Channel Conflict

When channel members perceive that their goals are not being met or that they can achieve a stronger financial position, they may elect to exercise additional channel power. An attempt to exert power—for example, by changing required inventory levels or price policies or bypassing a middleman—can lead to conflict. In a broad context conflict may not be bad but may even be beneficial. Often it arises because staid, traditional channel members refuse to keep pace with the times. The removal of an outmoded intermediary may result in a reduction of costs for the entire distribution system.

It is often difficult to resolve a conflict. In fact it may not be resolved until one member is eliminated or completely dominated by another, as when a manufacturer establishes its own retail outlets. Sometimes conflicts can be resolved through bargaining or negotiation.

SELECTING A DISTRIBUTION CHANNEL

Now that you are aware of the behavioral aspects of distribution channels as well as their economic functions, you should have a better appreciation of the task of channel selection. This is a critical decision for the marketing manager.

The Channel Selection Process

Key steps in the channel selection process are shown in Figure 11.5. We will describe this process from two viewpoints—that of a very large manufacturer (Westinghouse) and that of an extremely small

FIGURE 11.5   A Channel Selection Process

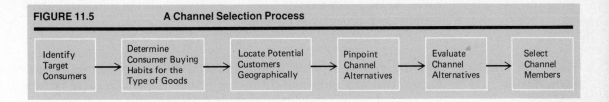

company (Falcon Hang Gliders).[12] Regardless of the size of the firm, the basic selection process involves the same steps.

First, potential users of a good or service must be identified and examined. Are they clustered geographically? Where do they expect to buy the product? Next, the manufacturer must determine whether a channel or channels already exist that will reach target customers. If so, what functions, such as storage and promotion, will they perform? If no channel is available, can the manufacturer economically establish a new system?

If the manufacturer can isolate a desirable channel that contains several possible middlemen, it must select the one that best meets its needs. The potential member is scrutinized carefully to determine its capabilities (i.e., storage, promotion, informational feedback, and the cost of these services).

The manufacturer also must ascertain whether it can fulfill the expectations of the middleman. Can the manufacturer provide the intermediary with adequate product flow? Can it offer adequate financial terms? Can it provide timely deliveries? Channel relationships must be based on the perceived benefits for each member, and those benefits should exceed the costs of joining the channel.

**The Ability
to Choose**

A huge organization like Westinghouse, with an established reputation, tremendous financial resources, many existing distribution channels, and quality products, is usually in a position to select its channel members.

On the other hand, Falcon Hang Gliders (whose average output is two per month) is in an ill-defined market with virtually no financial resources. Assuming that a reasonable channel can be defined, it may be very difficult to enter the channel. The heart of the problem of small entrepreneurial manufacturers is often credibility—even for those that are well financed. How does a dealer know, for example, that the manufacturer will be able to supply quality merchandise whenever needed over the long run?

If the middleman is already handling a competing line, it usually makes it much harder for the entrepreneurial firm to gain acceptance. The problem of selecting the "best" channel may be a moot point. The question is, Will anyone handle the product? Many small manufacturers with good products have fallen into bankruptcy because they couldn't reach potential buyers.

FACTORS THAT
INFLUENCE
CHANNEL
SELECTION
Product-Related
Factors

The differences between Westinghouse and Falcon illustrate several factors that can influence channel selection. Generally, these factors are related to the product, market, or company.

The nature of the product is a major determinant of its distribution channels. For example, except for supply items, industrial merchandise tends to be more expensive and technically complex than consumer goods. Usually, the higher the product's unit value, the shorter the channel (fewer middlemen), and vice versa. Also, the more technically complex the product, the greater the need for the producer to work directly with the end user and, thus, the shorter the channel. Similarly, custom-made products usually flow through a very short channel. Westinghouse's nuclear-power plants are sold by the firm's highly specialized field salespeople to a relatively small number of easily identifiable customers—electric utilities.

Bulky items, such as lumber, coal, and gravel, tend to move through shorter channels. Costs of storage and lack of storage facilities render lengthy channels unsuitable. With some products it is cheaper to move bulk quantities to central markets and either package or reformulate the product there. For example, milk is gathered in bulk from the countryside and brought to large cities for final processing and packaging. Soft-drink manufacturers ship syrup in bulk to bottlers throughout the country rather than producing finished drinks at one plant. Similarly, some inexpensive wines are bottled by local distributors after being shipped in tank cars from the vineyards.

Another important product aspect of distribution channels is the extent of the product line. If a firm has an extensive product line, even if it consists of low-priced products, total sales to individual retailers may be high enough to justify direct distribution. Oscar Meyer sells a complete line of packaged meat products directly to supermarkets through company salespeople. This might not be economically feasible if the company sold only hot dogs. Generally speaking, the wider the product line, the shorter the channel—as long as the quantities justify such an approach.

Returning to the hang glider manufacturer, its product is a consumer specialty good, or perhaps a shopping good, and by definition usually requires only a few dealers per area. Interested parties will search for the product until it is found and evaluated. But most hang glider enthusiasts live in California, and Falcon is located in Texas. Hang glider retailers have sprung up in larger West Coast cities to serve the growing market. Elsewhere in the country hang glider retailers are virtually nonexistent. As you can see, geographic customer concentration is a key market consideration for Falcon. They have a limited number of potential buyers near their manufacturing facilities.

Buyers, particularly in industrial markets, often have widely varying needs even when they are purchasing the same product. Such a situation may call for multiple channels of distribution. The following statement by a Westinghouse executive illustrates the multiple-channel strategy:

> Small motors are sold to original equipment manufacturers (OEM's), motor repair shops, industrial plants, and consumers. To reach all of these, we must use several different distribution channels.
>
> For example, we sell and service very large OEM's directly. This is mainly because of the large number of motors involved, which leads to extreme competition — often to the point where we are negotiating for pennies. In addition, large OEM accounts need the technical expertise that specialized factory salesmen can best provide (the salesman in this case is, in effect, an application engineer). Various types of distributors, as well as chain stores, are used to sell small motors to other types of users.
>
> The small motor division continuously analyzes the rationale used in selecting each distribution channel or combination of channels. They want the most effective way for getting the division's motors to the various market segments. Among the factors considered: required technical application assistance, inventory practices, advertising and sales promotion, and packaging.[13]

Consumer goods also flow through multiple channels because of differing needs of buyers. For example, Remington sells its shotguns through discount stores, sporting-goods stores, and gun shops, to name a few of its many outlets.

Customer order size is another important channel determinant. In industrial markets operating supplies are commonly sold through industrial distributors because orders typically are not large enough to make direct sales economically feasible. Small hardware stores must rely on hardware wholesalers for similar reasons. Large orders make it possible to use shorter channels.

Company-Related Factors

In addition to market and product factors, organizational considerations strongly influence channel strategies. Probably the most important of these considerations is financial strength or the lack of it. In the case of Falcon Hang Gliders, for example, the company was founded by two young men just out of college with a $5000 loan from one partner's father. Direct sales leads proved too costly, so in desperation Falcon turned to sporting-goods retailers and motorcycle shops. The company's poor financial condition meant that it could not supply inventory or even a single demonstration model to the eight retailers who agreed to sell the product. Instead, pictures and brochures were used as sales aids. After using the new channel for three months Falcon closed its doors. It had an unusual product, it's true; but it faced the distribution problems that have forced countless small entrepreneurial firms out of business.

Returning to our giant manufacturer, Westinghouse, the focus is on the other end of the financial spectrum. Well-financed companies may be able to set up corporate systems that completely remove the outside middleman from the picture. Or, as in the case of Westinghouse, they may establish their own wholesale operations yet sell to independent retailers (e.g., electrical distributors).

Intensity of Market Coverage

Product, market, and organizational factors will influence the intensity of distribution as well as the channel selected. There are three basic coverage strategies: intensive, selective, and exclusive distribution.

Intensive Distribution. Intensive distribution is maximum market coverage. The manufacturer tries to offer the product in every outlet where the potential customer might want to buy it. If a buyer is unwilling to search extensively for a product (as is true of convenience goods and operating supplies), the product must be taken closer to the buyer. Assuming that the product is of low value and frequently purchased, a lengthy channel may be required. Candy, for example, is found in just about every type of retail store imaginable. It is typically sold in small quantities to retailers by a food or candy wholesaler. The cost of selling Wrigley gum directly to every service station, drugstore, supermarket, and discount store that sells gum would be enormous.

Most manufacturers pursuing an intensive distribution strategy sell to a large percentage of the wholesalers that are willing to stock the product. Retailers' willingness—or lack of it—to handle the item tends to control the manufacturer's ability to reach intensive distribution at the retail level. For example, if a retailer is already carrying ten brands of gum it may show little enthusiasm for another one.

Selective Distribution. Selective distribution involves screening dealers to eliminate all but a few in any single geographic area. Since only a few retailers are selected, the consumer must be willing to seek out the product. Shopping goods and some specialty products are distributed selectively. Accessory-equipment manufacturers in the industrial-goods market usually follow a selective distribution strategy.

Several screening criteria are used to find the "right" dealers. An accessory-equipment manufacturer may seek firms that are able to properly service its product. A television set manufacturer may look for service ability and a quality dealer image. On the negative side, poor credit risks and chronic complainers are quickly removed from consideration. If the manufacturer expects to move a large volume of merchandise through each dealer, it will select only those that seem capable of handling such volume. This may remove many smaller retailers from consideration.

Exclusive Distribution. The most restrictive form of market coverage is exclusive distribution. This normally entails establishing one or perhaps two dealers within a given geographic area. Since buyers may have to search or travel extensively to acquire the product, exclusive distribution is usually limited to consumer specialty goods, a few shopping goods, industrial installations, and accessory products at the retail level. Wholesale exclusive distributorships may cover a much wider array of products.

SUMMARY

A channel of distribution is a series of institutions through which goods flow from the producer to the consumer. Middlemen are used within the channel to facilitate the flow of goods and services, reduce the number of transactions, and eliminate discrepancies of quantity and assortment. Distribution channels also provide a means of communication between their various members, intrachannel financing, ways of locating buyers, and storage of merchandise.

Elimination of any channel member does not eliminate the function it performs. Thus the question is which member can perform the channel function most efficiently and economically. Services, unlike products, cannot be stockpiled, transported, or inventoried. They must be created and distributed simultaneously.

Historically, channels of distribution have been unstable networks in which relationships were terminated with impunity and channel members behaved autonomously. In recent years closer relationships have developed among vertical channel participants. As these relationships have developed, certain role expectations have evolved. There are three basic types of vertically coordinated systems: corporate, administrative, and contractual.

As channels develop, social dimensions begin to evolve. Channel members develop roles, communication links, and power structures, and sometimes engage in conflict.

Choosing a channel is not always easy. Target consumers have to be identified and their buying habits examined; customers must be located geographically and channel alternatives developed. Channel members are selected from available alternatives or new channels are created.

Often a small firm has little choice in the channels it uses. In fact it may be lucky to obtain distribution at all. If channel alternatives do exist, the nature of the product, the type of market to be served, and company resources become important criteria for selection.

The intensity of distribution depends on consumer consumption patterns, the product, and the organization. Intensive distribution is maximum market coverage. Selective distribution is typified by a screening process to eliminate all but the most desirable dealers in a given geographic area. Exclusive distribution is highly restrictive and is used only for specialty goods and a few shopping goods. In industrial markets it is used for installations and accessory products.

KEY TERMS

Channel of distribution   Horizontal channel system
Discrepancy of quantity   Corporate distribution system
Breaking bulk   Administrative system
Discrepancy of assortment   Contractual system
Assorting   Symbiotic marketing
Time utility   Channel power
Place utility   Intensive distribution
Possession utility   Selective distribution
Form utility   Exclusive distribution
Vertical channel system

QUESTIONS FOR DISCUSSION

1. Explain the different functions performed by distribution channels.
2. How do distribution channels add to consumer satisfaction? Give examples to illustrate your answer.
3. What characteristics distinguish the distribution of services from the distribution of goods? How do the respective distribution channels differ?
4. What is a vertical channel system?
5. What is a "system leader"? Discuss the role of the system leader in different vertical channel systems.
6. Explain the concept of symbiotic marketing. Why is it being used? Can you give a few examples?
7. What are the sources of channel power? Give several examples.
8. Explain some of the factors that influence channel selection.
9. Why is it often very difficult for a small entrepreneurial firm to establish a sound distribution network? What can be done to overcome this problem?
10. Differentiate between intensive, selective, and exclusive distribution strategies. How would the following products be distributed normally?
    a. offshore oil-drilling equipment
    b. Rolls Royce cars
    c. Pierre Cardin men's accessories
    d. Wilkinson blades
    e. Kodak film

11. What role do social relationships play in the working of a distribution channel? Can you give examples to clarify your answer?

NOTES

1. This section is largely taken from James H. Donnelly, Jr., "Marketing Intermediaries in Channels of Distribution for Services," *Journal of Marketing,* 40 (January 1976): 50–70.

2. Bert C. McCammon, Jr., "The Emergence and Growth of Contractually Integrated Channels in the American Economy," in Louis E. Boone and James C. Johnson, eds., *Marketing Channels* (Morristown, N.J.: General Learning Press, 1973), p. 214.

3. Michael Etgar, "Effects of Administrative Control on Efficiency of Vertical Marketing Systems," *Journal of Marketing Research,* 13 (February 1975): 12–24.

4. McCammon, p. 215.

5. Lee Adler, "Symbiotic Marketing," *Harvard Business Review,* November–December 1966, pp. 59–71.

6. Henry L. Tosi, "The Effects of Expectation Levels and Role Consensus on the Buyer–Seller Dyad," *Journal of Business,* 39 (October 1966): 516–529. Reprinted by permission of The University of Chicago Press.

7. Lynn Gill and Louis Stern, "Roles and Role Theory in Distribution Channel Systems," in Louis Stern, ed., *Distribution Channels: Behavioral Dimensions* (Boston: Houghton Mifflin, 1969), pp. 36–37.

8. Lawrence Richard, "A Framework for the Measurement of Control in Distribution Channels," in Barnett Greenberg, ed., *Proceedings Southern Marketing Association 1974 Conference,* pp. 87–88.

9. Adel I. El-Ansary and Robert Robicheaux, "A Theory of Channel Control: Revisited," *Journal of Marketing,* 38 (January 1974): 2–7.

10. Some excellent articles on channel power are Michael Etgar, "Channel Domination and Countervailing Power in Distribution Channels," *Journal of Marketing Research,* 13 (August 1976): 254–262; Joseph Barry Mason, "Power and Channel Conflicts in Shopping Center Development," *Journal of Marketing,* 39 (April 1975): 28–35; Conway Rucks, "Power Analysis in Distribution Channels," in Henry Nash and Donald Robin, eds., *Southern Marketing Association 1975 Proceedings,* pp. 189–191; Kenneth Roering, "A Laboratory Study of Bargaining in Distribution Channels," in ibid., pp. 178–180; Adel El-Ansary, "Determinants of Power-Dependence in the Distribution Channel," *Journal of Retailing,* 51 (Summer 1975): 59–74; Louis P. Bucklin, "A Theory of Channel Control," *Journal of Marketing,* 37 (January 1973): 30–47; Adel I. El-Ansary and Louis W. Stern, "Power Measurement in the Distribution Channel," *Journal of Marketing Research,* 9 (February 1972): 47–52; James L. Heskett, Louis W. Stern, and Frederick J. Beier, "Bases and Uses of Power in Interorganization Relations," in Louis P. Bucklin, ed., *Vertical Marketing Systems* (Glenview, Ill.: Scott, Foresman, 1970), pp. 75–93; Shelby D. Hunt and John R. Nevin, "Power in a Channel Distribution: Sources and Consequences," *Journal of Marketing Research,* 11 (May 1974): 186–193; Robert W. Little, "The Marketing Channel: Who Should Lead This Extra-Corporate Organization?" *Journal of Marketing,* 34 (January 1970): 31–38;

Louis W. Stern and J. L. Heskett, "Conflict Management in Interorganizational Relations: A Conceptual Framework," in Louis W. Stern, ed., *Distribution Channels: Behavioral Dimensions* (Boston: Houghton Mifflin, 1969), pp. 92–116; Louis W. Stern, "A Concept of Channel Control," *Journal of Retailing*, 43 (Summer 1967): 14–20; and Louis W. Stern, "The Interorganizational Management of Distribution Channels: Prerequisites and Prescriptions," in George Fish, ed., *New Essays in Marketing Theory* (Boston: Allyn & Bacon, 1971), pp. 301–314.

11. Louis E. Boone and James C. Johnson, *Marketing Channels* (Morristown, N. J.: General Learning Press, 1973), p. 234.

12. The Westinghouse examples are taken from S. C. Mulle, "Distribution Channel Strategies," in Earl L. Bailey, ed., *Marketing Strategies: A Symposium* (New York: Conference Board, 1974), pp. 77–80.

13. Ibid., p. 78.

CASE 11
Welch Grape Soda

Welch has been producing grape products since 1869, when founder Thomas B. Welch first developed pasteurized "unfermented wine" for his church's communion service. This grape juice is still used in many Protestant churches today.

Welch's Foods has grown into an agricultural cooperative owned by 2000 grape growers. Between 1962 and 1976 the company introduced some 36 new products. One of them, carbonated grape soda, seemed to have great market potential as a soft drink.

The soft-drink industry's annual case volume totals about 4.6 billion cases. Grape soda's share of that market is about 3 percent. That's about $460 million for grape soda alone. However, there is no major national brand of grape soda. Perhaps this is because there is no nationally advertised brand.

Welch had several big advantages over other grape soda distributors. First, Welch was synonymous with grape products. Second, throughout its grape processing more than 25 separate inspections and analyses are made at plant laboratories for control over taste, purity, and uniform quality.

Welch tested the product and modified the formula continually over a five-year period before deciding that it was ready for introduction. At that point market tests showed that the product was strongly preferred over any of the existing competitive brands.

Welch had expected to tie into its own food store broker network, which used a warehouse delivery system. An alternative would have been to franchise an independent soft-drink bottler that could distribute the product via store delivery. Welch selected the first alternative because it believed that it would generate higher profits on a per-case basis. The wholesale cost was about $5 for 24 twelve-ounce bottles. At that price Welch was earning about a $2 margin. The product was put into a test market in Buffalo, New York. The results were very poor.

After examining the situation Welch found that its problem was trying to crack a strong bottler delivery system. Bottlers control their shelf locations and shelf inventory. The bottler salespeople put the product on the shelf, thereby freeing store personnel for other tasks. The food broker salespeople were unable to get into retail outlets more than once a month. So they couldn't hold or check on the shelf space they needed. By means of frequent delivery soft-drink bottlers could obtain better shelf space. Primary shelf space was reserved for Coke, Pepsi, and 7-Up.

Franchising presented other problems. One was loss of control over product quality and distribution. A second problem was a much smaller return per case. However, bottlers dominate the shelf space and can produce a full line of package sizes. They also have huge inventories of merchandising hardware, including coolers, racks, vending machines, and the like, which could be used to support Welch's product outside the supermarket.

What should Welch do at this point to obtain distribution for its product? How should it go about making the distribution channel decision? Why wasn't the Buffalo failure foreseen? How can these mistakes be avoided in the future?

12

Wholesaling

OBJECTIVES

■ To define the term *wholesaler.*
■ To learn the different functions performed by wholesalers.
■ To become aware of the different types of wholesalers.
■ To gain insight into present and future trends in wholesaling.

Chapter 12 introduces you to the enigmatic world of wholesaling. Wholesaling is a study in contrasts—the firm involved may be progressive or staid, small or complex, private or public.

There are, however, three major categories of wholesalers (merchant wholesalers, agents and brokers, and manufacturers' sales branches). These will be defined and discussed so that you can put wholesaling into proper perspective. Next you should learn about a group of institutions that facilitate wholesaling operations but aren't really wholesalers. The chapter concludes with a discussion of trends in wholesaling.

225

THE FUNCTIONS AND ROLES OF WHOLESALERS
Defining Wholesaling

As the preceding paragraph suggests, it is hard to develop an all-encompassing definition of wholesaling. We know that a wholesaler is an institution located somewhere within the channel system yet not at either end of the system (i.e., it is not a consumer or a manufacturer). Using this notion as a starting point, a wholesaler may be defined as an institution that

1. sells finished goods to other institutions (primarily retailers) that will, in turn, resell it to the final user.
2. sells to other institutions (hospitals, schools, manufacturers) that utilize the product in performing their basic function. A hospital, for example, may purchase cleaning supplies from a wholesaler as part of its function of providing a relatively germ-free environment. A different example is the manufacturer that purchases grinding tools to be used in the product fabrication process.
3. sells to institutions (mostly manufacturers) that will incorporate the item into the manufacturer's product. A small manufacturer of trailers may purchase tires from a tire wholesaler. The tires, of course, form an integral part of the trailer.

In a general sense the distinction among wholesalers, manufacturers, and retailers may become blurred. A retailer may have its own warehouse facility and perhaps even sell some of the merchandise to other retailers. Its primary function, however, is to sell to final consumers.

A manufacturer may sell merchandise to another manufacturer, thereby assuming the role of a wholesaler. In order to categorize an organization properly, we must determine its primary function. Is it basically a wholesaler that engages in limited manufacturing or a manufacturer that sometimes "wholesales" part of its output?

What Do Wholesalers Do?

Figure 12.1 illustrates the basic functions of wholesalers. As you might imagine, very few wholesalers perform all of these functions. Most, in fact, perform only a limited number of them. Moreover, retailers and manufacturers perform some of the same activities.

Anticipating Customers' Needs, Buying, Assorting, and Communicating. Wholesalers buy goods to resell to others. Firms that assume ownership (acquire title) to the merchandise are called merchant wholesalers. Agents, by contrast, may sell products for a manufacturer, but they never acquire title.

Buying the "right mix" of merchandise implies that the wholesaler has properly anticipated the needs of its customers. A wholesaler must understand industry trends, be informed about new product offerings, and even monitor changing use patterns and atti-

FIGURE 12.1   **Wholesaler Functions**

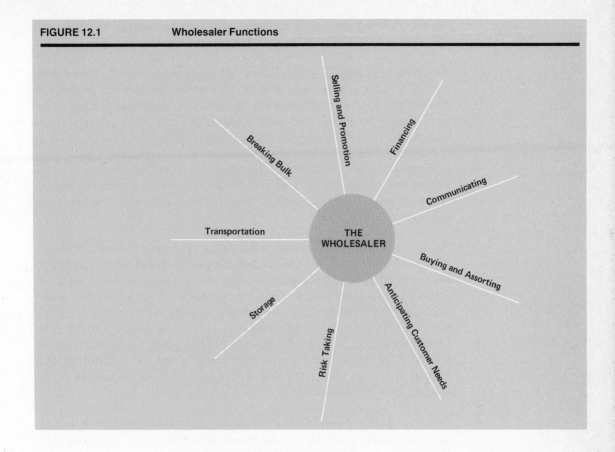

tudes of final consumers in order to purchase an appropriate assortment of goods at the wholesale level.

Selling and Promotion. Perhaps the only function that *all* wholesalers perform is selling. In very small operations the owner/agent may be the only salesperson. Other widespread corporate wholesale operations sometimes employ several hundred salespeople.

Traditionally, most of the wholesaler's sales effort has focused on personal selling. More progressive wholesalers such as wholesale druggists are utilizing in-house telephone sales techniques to supplement the activities of the field sales force. Some drug wholesalers are taking 80 percent of their orders over the telephone.[1] Personal salespeople limit their calls to key accounts, special customers, and prospects that show high potential.

Wholesalers also supplement their sales efforts by mailing out fliers, catalogs, and brochures. The rapidly rising prices of the mid-1970s forced many firms to print catalogs without printing a price next to the picture and description of the merchandise. Monthly and sometimes weekly price list updates were mailed to catalog recipients.

Financing. While all wholesalers sell to their customers, fewer than half offer financing to their clients. In some industries the practice of providing credit or granting cash discounts is traditional. Other channels feature both cash-and-carry wholesalers and wholesalers that are willing to provide financing. An unusual form of financing that is sometimes found in seasonal items such as toys and beach play equipment consists of delivering the merchandise several months before the season begins and not billing the retailer until the season is under way. The wholesaler often must acquire and finance large inventories of its own.

Storage. When a wholesaler develops an assortment of merchandise, it usually must store the goods until they are ordered by the customer. Storage and inventory control are an integral part of financial management. Most wholesalers attempt to reduce lengthy storage times and increase product flow. Five basic reasons why storage is necessary are (1) seasonal production, (2) erratic demand requirements, (3) conditioning (such as the ripening of bananas), (4) speculation (in the hope of an increase in product value), and (5) realization of a special discount (for accepting delivery during an off season or reduced price on closeouts).[2]

Breaking Bulk. Purchase of closeouts or large quantities often results in rail carload or truckload shipments of merchandise. Not only does the wholesaler receive quantity and other special discounts for purchasing large amounts, but it also obtains a lower freight ratio for full-car or truckload shipments. Usually the wholesaler will store the goods and fill orders, one or several cases at a time, from inventory. As you learned in the preceding chapter, this process is referred to as breaking bulk. Manufacturers and small retailers cannot afford the high cost of shipments of "less than carload" to individual retailers. It is more economical to sell in bulk to wholesalers, which, in turn, offer smaller quantities to local merchants. (See Figure 12.2.)

Transportation. Since the wholesaler tends to serve a limited geographic area, it is usually closer to the retailer than to the manufacturer. Consequently the retailer gets quicker delivery and perhaps a lower total cost of goods. The lower prices result from not having to buy goods in lots of less than a carload from the manufacturer. If the retailer can depend on the wholesaler for fast delivery, the retailer can reduce its inventory. Lower inventories mean lower working-

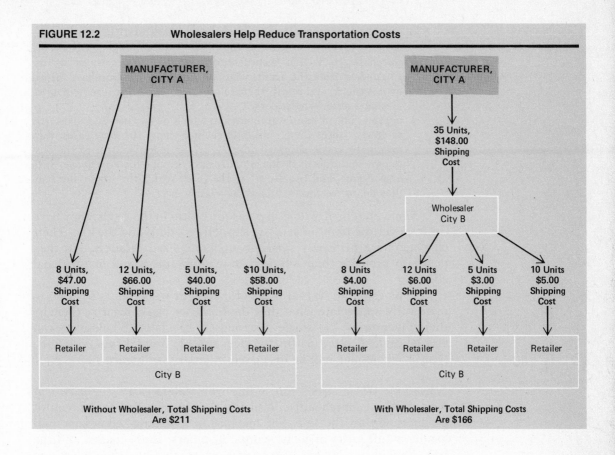

FIGURE 12.2   **Wholesalers Help Reduce Transportation Costs**

capital requirements and reduced risks of fire, theft, deterioration, and obsolescence to the retailer.

Risk Taking. Carrying inventory involves some risk that the goods will not be sold. In addition, inventory requires the assumption of the other types of risk just mentioned. As the wholesaler increases inventory to avoid stock-outs (i.e., when all inventory has been sold), it increases the risk of not selling all the goods that are stored. Ultimately a trade-off must be reached between not having some items in stock (and perhaps losing a sale) and the risk of a large inventory.

**MERCHANT
WHOLESALERS**

Of the 369,792 wholesalers in existence in 1974, 249,390 were merchant wholesalers.[3] These organizations accounted for $321 billion of the $684 billion total of wholesale sales in 1972.[4]

A merchant wholesaler can be defined as an institution that

1. purchases goods from manufacturers for their own account (as distinguished from the agent, who typically does not purchase for his own account) and resells them to other businesses, government agencies, and other wholesalers.
2. operates one or more warehouses in which he receives and takes title to goods, stores them, and later reships them. (In some cases, they may have goods shipped directly by the manufacturer to the customer, so the goods do not actually pass through his warehouse. Still, a good part, and usually all, of the goods which the wholesaler handles do, in fact, pass through his warehouse.[5]

Since merchant wholesalers acquire title to the goods, they have control over the items of sale — price, delivery date, and the like. Their customers are primarily small or moderate-sized retailers, but they may also promote their offerings to manufacturers and institutional clients.

Let's examine several types of merchant wholesalers in order to more fully appreciate what they do. First, we can categorize them by their inventories: (1) single line, and (2) specialty. Wholesalers can also be divided into: (1) full service, and (2) limited function. Each type of wholesaler will be discussed in order (see Figure 12.3).

Single-Line Wholesalers. Single-line wholesalers carry one or two, at most, lines of merchandise. Usually, they stock a full assortment of products within the line. For instance, a hardware wholesaler will handle a full array of tools, paints, fasteners, rope, chains, and the like. In addition to hardware markets, single-line wholesalers are common in the drug, grocery, and clothing markets.

The target market of this type of wholesaler is the single-line retailer, such as supermarkets, drugstores, clothing stores, and hardware stores. As retail chains continue to grow in size and market

FIGURE 12.3   The Family Tree of Merchant Wholesalers

share, the single-line wholesaler tends to gradually lose market position. The retailers establish their own wholesale operations or purchase directly from the manufacturer.

Specialty Wholesalers.   Specialty wholesalers offer part of a line to target customers. An example would be a meat wholesaler or a fish and seafood wholesaler, as opposed to a single-line grocery wholesaler. The specialty wholesaler usually offers much greater depth within the scope of the product line than a single-line wholesaler. Customers, for example, are more likely to find unusual seafood at a seafood wholesaler rather than a grocery wholesaler.

Specialty wholesalers offer their customers several advantages in addition to greater variety. They usually have excellent product knowledge, which can be very important, for example, to a sausage packaging house when purchasing spices from a specialty spice wholesaler. There are literally hundreds of spices and combinations to choose from. A specialty industrial-goods wholesaler may handle only ball bearings. Another may specialize in drilling bits. Each offers a complete product line and information to aid potential buyers.

Specialty wholesalers that carry perishables turn over their merchandise quite rapidly, thus offering fresher merchandise. A specialty meat company sells only fine cuts of meat, such as rib eyes, sirloins, and filets to better hotels and chain restaurants. A steak that you are eating on a Friday night at a Steak and Ale restaurant may have completed the curing process at a Standard Meat facility earlier that morning.

Full-Service Wholesalers.   A second means of categorizing merchant wholesalers is by the number of services they perform. It is basically a different way to look at the same wholesaler. A single-line wholesaler can be either full service or limited function. A full-service merchant wholesaler usually carries stock, has a sales force to call on customers, offers credit, makes deliveries, gives advice to clients, and services the merchandise it sells. Of course not all full-service merchant wholesalers engage in each of these activities, but most offer a majority of these services.

The philosophy of good service pervades the entire full-service merchant wholesaler organization. It is manifested in many ways, such as granting credit, setting up promotional displays, and explaining new product offerings, and not just in maintaining a sales force.

Industrial Distributors.   Most, but not all, industrial distributors can be described as merchant wholesalers. Typically, they sell to manufacturers rather than to retailers. Full-service distributors usually have internal and external sales forces, offer credit, stock merchandise, provide delivery, and keep a full product assortment.[6]

The products stocked by industrial distributors include maintenance, repair, and operating supplies (MRO items); original equipment (OEM) supplies, such as fasteners, power transmission components, hydraulic equipment, and small rubber parts, which become part of the manufacturer's finished product; equipment used in the operation of the business, such as hand tools, power tools, and conveyors; and machinery used in making raw materials and semifinished goods into finished products.[7]

It is estimated that there are slightly under 12,000 industrial distributors in the United States.[8] In 1974 their total sales volume was approximately $23.5 billion.[9] Most distributors are relatively small, yet their average size is growing each year. Distributors that carry a smorgasbord of industrial products (i.e., a general line) are referred to as "mill supply houses" or "the supermarkets of industry."

Rack Merchandisers. The rack merchandiser, or rack jobber, performs the functions of the merchant wholesaler and even some that are usually carried out by the retailer. Rack merchandisers serve drug and grocery retailers, in contrast to the industrial distributor, whose customers are manufacturers.

In addition to the normal full-service functions, rack merchandisers stock nonfood merchandise on racks or shelves for their retail clients. The toy racks and occasional clothing displays that you've seen in a supermarket were probably placed there by a rack merchandiser.

The rack merchandiser sells on consignment in most cases, meaning that the jobber retains title to the goods and the retailer doesn't pay for the merchandise until it is sold. The delivery person employed by the jobber maintains inventory records, prices the goods, keeps the merchandise fresh, restocks the racks or shelves, and assembles any promotional display material that is used at the point of sale.

Limited-Function Merchant Wholesalers. As the name implies, limited-function merchant wholesalers perform only a few of the activities of merchant wholesalers. Several important types of limited-function wholesalers are cash-and-carry wholesalers, truck jobbers, drop shippers, and retail cooperatives. It should be pointed out that limited-function wholesalers represent only a small portion of the merchant wholesaling industry.

Cash-and-Carry Wholesalers. The cash-and-carry wholesaler sells for cash and usually carries a limited line of fast-moving merchandise.

Customers (mostly small retail grocers) must go to the cash-and-carry wholesaler's warehouse and transport the goods to their retail outlets. Although the selling prices of cash-and-carry wholesalers are usually lower than those of full-service wholesalers, the total cost to the retailer may be higher.

As mentioned earlier, you can eliminate a middleman but you cannot eliminate the functions performed by middlemen. The retailer that patronizes a cash-and-carry wholesaler must provide its own credit, transportation, and personnel to move the merchandise. Because of higher total distribution costs, this form of wholesaling shows little promise of growth. The cash-and-carry wholesaler's market is limited to small retailers.

Truck Jobbers. Truck jobbers also usually sell for cash. They combine the functions of salesperson and delivery person. Normally they carry a very limited line of semiperishable merchandise. Typical products handled by truck jobbers are milk, bread, snack foods, beer, and candy. Naturally, their major customers are supermarkets, but truck jobbers also serve hospitals, restaurants, factory refreshments shops, and hotels.

Drop Shippers. Drop shippers do not inventory or physically handle the products they sell. Instead, orders are placed with the manufacturer and shipped directly to the customer. Drop shippers are usually found in the bulk industries, such as coal, lumber, bauxite, heavy equipment, and some agricultural products.

Like cash-and-carry wholesalers, drop shippers can offer lower prices because they perform relatively few wholesale functions. In this case warehousing and storage are eliminated.

The drop shipper is still a merchant middleman even though it may never see the goods. It takes title to the merchandise and therefore sets the terms of the sale. Also, drop shippers arrange shipping terms and take the risks of ownership during the shipment; in addition, they locate suppliers and sometimes offer credit.

Producers' Cooperatives. Producers' cooperatives are nonprofit institutions established and operated for the benefit of their members. If any surplus revenues accrue, they are normally dispersed to the members at the end of the year. Farmland Industries, a huge supply cooperative, distributed $44 million to its members in 1975.[10] If a member dies or retires, his or her share must be sold back to the cooperative.

Marketing co-ops are usually dedicated toward improving product quality and promoting a co-op brand name. Sun Maid raisins, Diamond walnuts, Ocean Spray cranberries, and Sunkist oranges and lemons are examples of how a co-op can use promotion to differentiate a very homogeneous product.

Mail-Order Wholesalers.   Mail-order wholesalers generally offer a wide array of merchandise to their customers at relatively low prices. Goods are sold by catalog and shipped by mail, truck, or other suitable mode of transportation. Mail-order wholesalers generally cater to small retailers, often in rural areas. They are most common in dry goods, hardware, and sporting goods.

MANUFACTURERS' SALES BRANCHES

As manufacturers grow in size, they often establish wholesale operations similar to full-service merchant wholesalers. Yet these wholesale institutions, called manufacturers' sales branches, are managed, controlled, and owned by the manufacturer. Table 12.1 reveals their sales relative to merchant wholesalers and agents and brokers. Although manufacturers' sales branches and offices account for only about 13 percent of all wholesale institutions, they represent almost 37 percent of all wholesale sales.[11]

Since 1967 manufacturers' sales offices and branches have been the most rapidly growing type of wholesaling as manufacturers seek tighter control over their channels of distribution. Table 12.1 shows that manufacturers' sales branches (which carry inventory) and offices (which don't stock merchandise) are much larger in average dollar volume than merchant wholesalers, agents, or brokers.

The growth of manufacturers sales branches is due partly to a general increase in the importance of inventory control at the wholesale level. This is particularly true in the automotive, transportation equipment, and lumber, millwork, and plywood industries.[12] In cases in which inventory is not carried by the wholesaler, manufacturers'

TABLE 12.1   Sales of Various Categories of Wholesalers

Category	Number	Percent of Total	1972 Sales in Millions	Percent of Total
Merchant wholesalers	289,980	78.4	$353.3	50.8
Manufacturers' sales branches and offices	47,191	12.8	255.5	36.7
Agents and brokers	32,621	8.8	86.9	12.5
Totals	369,792	100.0	$695.7	100.0

Source: U.S. Bureau of the Census, *Census of Wholesale Trade, 1972, Summary Statistics* (Washington, D.C., 1973).

sales offices have grown at the expense of agents and brokers. This phenomenon is most noticeable in the drygoods and notions industries.

A third trend has been for manufacturers' sales branches to grow by forcing out merchant wholesalers. Lack of wholesaler promotion, high costs, the need for better control, and wholesalers' unwillingness to carry adequate inventories have prompted many manufacturers to create sales branches. This trend has been most noticeable in the drug, hardware, and commercial-equipment industries.

AGENTS AND BROKERS

Agents and brokers represent retailers, wholesalers, or manufacturers and do not take title to the merchandise. Title reflects ownership, and ownership usually implies control. A wholesaler that owns the merchandise can establish the terms of sale. It is then up to the buyer to decide whether the terms are acceptable. An agent or broker generally has little input into the terms of sale (except in the case of commission merchants, to be discussed later). As you will see, they facilitate sales but usually do not determine the conditions of the sale. Agents and brokers receive a fee or commission based on sales volume. Many perform fewer functions than limited-function merchant wholesalers. Agents and brokers account for less than 13 percent of all wholesale sales.

Brokers

The broker's function is to bring buyers and sellers together. Brokers exist in markets where two parties would otherwise have difficulty locating one another. Brokers do not usually handle the goods involved in the sale or finance either the buyer or the seller. Their basic function is to represent the buyer or seller in finding another party to complete the sales transaction. Typically, a broker locates a potential buyer/seller and then lets the two parties work out matters such as price, quantity, delivery date, specifications.

The broker performs only the locating function and therefore operates on a very low margin. The fee is paid by the principal who engaged the broker, never by both parties.

Manufacturers' Agents

Like brokers, manufacturers' agents, sometimes called manufacturers' representatives, rarely have much voice in the terms of a sales contract.[13] They represent either one manufacturer or several manufacturers of complementary lines and follow the terms established by the manufacturer. Agents work on a commission basis and therefore must be good salespeople if they want to earn an adequate living. They generally have excellent product knowledge and extensive knowledge of customer preferences within their territory.

Small producers that cannot afford to maintain a field sales force often employ manufacturers' agents. Larger firms use agents to open new territories and then substitute company salespeople when volume justifies such action. If a territory doesn't have the long-run potential to support a salesperson, the manufacturer will develop a continuing relationship with the manufacturer's agent.

Commission Merchants

Commission merchants (or houses) differ from manufacturers' agents and brokers in that they take possession of the merchandise. Usually they are not employed on a long-term basis but instead are used to sell specific lots of goods. They are given wide discretionary powers over price, delivery dates, and other terms of sale. In fact merchants even collect the bills, deduct their fees, and remit the balance to the principal.

Commission merchants are most common in agriculture where farmers cannot or don't want to sell their products locally. The merchant is located in central market cities and engages in many market transactions daily. The farmer rarely sets the specific price of the sale but instead empowers the commission merchant to obtain the best price possible. Withholding produce or fruits from the market in order to obtain a higher price is often very risky because of the high perishability of such items. The merchant is expected to do the best it can under the circumstances. It may even grant credit to the potential buyer.

OTHER WHOLESALE INSTITUTIONS

The wholesalers that we have discussed account for a significant portion of sales by merchant wholesalers, agents, and brokers, and manufacturers' sales branches and offices. Yet there are several minor wholesale institutions that deserve mention.

Agricultural Assemblers

The agricultural assembler is actually a merchant wholesaler that buys grain for farmers and assembles it into large quantities and sells it to governments, bakers, and other food processors.

The Census Bureau also lists petroleum bulk plants as a separate type of assembler–wholesaler because of their unique storage and distribution facilities. Actually they are either merchant wholesalers or manufacturers' sales branches, depending on their ownership. Petroleum bulk plants are engaged in the collection, storage, distribution, and sale of oil, gasoline, and similar petroleum derivatives.

Auction Companies

A unique form of brokerage is performed by auction companies. Like agricultural assemblers and bulk plants, they account for a small portion of total wholesale volume but are very important in several industries. Whenever it is necessary for goods to be seen and inspected prior to purchase, auction houses provide a unique advantage. Buyers come together and bid against one another until only one bidder remains. Unless the bid is below a predetermined minimum, the products are sold to the highest bidder. Auctions are common in certain areas of agriculture, such as tobacco and livestock, and in industrial bankruptcies.

Selling Agents

A final type of agent/broker that is often overemphasized is the selling agent. Actually the term *selling agent* is somewhat misleading, since the agent usually takes over the entire marketing operation of a company. In some industries, such as textiles, selling agents may even offer financial assistance to their clients. They normally work on a commission basis and contract to sell the entire output of the manufacturer. Selling agents are used mostly by small firms. For example, some electronics firms, founded and managed by engineers who have little interest in marketing, depend on selling agents.

INSTITUTIONS THAT FACILITATE WHOLESALING
Resident Buyers

Two institutions that facilitate the wholesale function are resident buyers and merchandise marts. Resident buyers perform the purchasing function for small retailers. If a low-volume retailer is located hundreds of miles from a major market, it is difficult to keep abreast of rapidly changing styles and trends as new merchandise reaches the market.

More important, it would be uneconomical to go to market and purchase in small quantities. This is where resident buyers come in. Since resident buyers are located in New York, Chicago, and other major market cities, they can easily monitor new trends and purchase for the retailer accordingly. Also, because resident buyers represent many retailers, they can purchase in large quantities and pass the savings on to the retailer.

When retailers "go to market" once or twice a year, their resident buyer generally acts as host, guiding them to the "right" manufacturers and arranging for the retailer to see sellers that might otherwise ignore a very small retailer. A resident buyer typically specializes in a single line such as a certain type of wearing apparel, toys, or furniture.

Merchandise Marts

Many times a retailer "goes to market" at a merchandise mart. Most merchandise marts are huge buildings containing hundreds of individual exhibition spaces that are leased by manufacturers. An entire mart may be devoted to one type of product, such as furniture or apparel. Merchandise marts are permanent showrooms that remain open throughout the year.

Fairs or shows are held several times a year in the market cities. Christmas gift and jewelry shows, for example, are usually held in July in such cities as New York, Los Angeles, Dallas, and Chicago. In addition to the permanent exhibitors at the merchandise marts, hundreds of temporary exhibitors set up booths at convention centers, auditoriums, or exhibition halls during the major shows.

Wholesaling today resembles an awakening giant. For years wholesalers have been considered traditional, staid, and unwilling to accept change. This image has been valid in some cases, and many such wholesalers have passed from the scene.

Progressive wholesalers view themselves as more than "bulk breakers" or "warehousers." Instead, they believe that wholesaling plays a vital role in effective distribution and requires full application of the marketing concept to their businesses. Modern wholesalers examine the needs of their markets and determine how those needs can be fulfilled using contemporary marketing concepts. For example, grocery wholesalers have added a sales effort geared to growing institutional markets, including hotels, airport restaurants, hospitals, and schools.[14] As they analyze their market segments these wholesalers are sensitive to inventory requirements and new product lines.

Some wholesalers have found their markets so drastically changed that they have either set up their own chains (voluntary chains) or franchised retail operations. Super Value, Ace Hardware, Butler Brothers (Ben Franklin Stores), and Western Auto are all examples of this trend. Other wholesalers have moved back up the channel and entered manufacturing. Midas International, originally an automotive wholesaler, not only franchises retail outlets but manufactures mufflers as well.

Progressive wholesalers are using new techniques to build sales volume. One is promoting to the final consumer. Naturally, this increases the retailers' sales, and they, in turn, order more merchandise from the wholesaler. Constantino Brokerage, a St. Louis grocery wholesaler, regularly uses multibrand coupons in newspaper inserts.[15] Sometimes wholesalers will bear the entire cost of the promotion campaign, but usually part of the expense is carried by the manufacturer. A few wholesalers have carried promotion a step further by setting up their own in-house advertising agencies.

Wholesalers are also fostering sales growth through the establishment of outlets in new territories. Strong wholesaler networks have begun to develop where the distributor is selling relatively undifferentiated products coupled with excellent product line knowledge and familiarity with the local market. This has led to increased market power and channel control for the multibranch wholesalers. Naturally, many manufacturers are disturbed by the aggregation of wholesalers into fewer and larger companies. One manufacturer recently examined its distribution network and found that its wholesalers operate in 290 locations, that those locations belong to 60 wholesalers, and that 5 of those wholesalers operate half of the locations.[16]

SUMMARY

Wholesalers sell finished goods to retailers and institutions. They do not sell directly to the final consumer. Wholesalers anticipate customers' needs and purchase accordingly for their target market. They are also expected to communicate with manufacturers and retailers regarding changing market trends. Many wholesalers also provide financing for their clients and store merchandise until the goods are ordered. They typically buy in very large quantities and ship in smaller units to retailers and other institutions.

Merchant wholesalers are the largest category of wholesalers. They purchase goods for their own account, operate one or more warehouses, take title to the goods, store them, and later reship the merchandise. Merchant wholesalers can be subdivided according to their inventories (general line, single line, or specialty wholesalers) or according to the services they offer their customers (full service or limited service).

Large manufacturers often establish wholesale operations similar to that of a merchant wholesaler. These are referred to as manufacturer sales branches and offices. They account for almost 37 percent of all wholesale sales. Their growth has been due primarily to an increase in the need for better inventory control and sales efforts at the wholesale level.

Agents and brokers do not take title to merchandise. They generally perform fewer functions than merchant wholesalers. Other wholesale institutions include agricultural assemblers, auction companies, and selling agents. Resident buyers and merchandise marts are not actually wholesalers, but they facilitate the wholesaling process.

For many years wholesaling has not been as progressive as other marketing institutions. Yet many wholesalers are awakening to the belief that their function plays a vital role in effective distribution and requires full application of the marketing concept. Some wholesalers are setting up their own chains and franchised retail operations. Others are using new techniques, such as promoting directly to the final consumer, to build sales volume.

KEY TERMS

Wholesaler

Merchant wholesaler

Full-service merchant wholesaler

Industrial distributor

Rack merchandiser

Limited-function merchant wholesaler

Cash-and-carry wholesaler

Truck jobber

Drop shipper

Producers' cooperative

Mail-order wholesaler

Manufacturers' sales branches

Agent

Broker

Manufacturers' agents

Commission merchant

Agricultural assembler

Auction company

Selling agent

Resident buyer

Merchandise mart

1. What is a wholesaler? Can you name some wholesalers that are located in your area?
2. Explain briefly the various functions performed by a wholesaler. Do all wholesalers perform those functions?
3. Explain what is meant by the term *merchant wholesaler*. What are some of the characteristics of this category of wholesalers?
4. Differentiate between an industrial distributor, a mail order wholesaler, and a producer's cooperative. Give an example of each.
5. What are the characteristics of a manufacturer's sales branch? Why has this institution been growing rapidly in importance?
6. Describe the role that agents and brokers play in the distribution process. How do they differ from commission merchants?
7. What is meant by the terms *resident buyer* and *merchandise mart*? Explain their importance to the wholesale function.
8. Comment on the statement "Wholesaling today resembles an awakening giant."
9. Can you describe the services provided by each of the following?
   a. selling agent
   b. rack merchandiser
   c. auction company
10. Explain why wholesalers are so important to marketing managers.
11. Express your views on the statement "Costs can be cut by eliminating the wholesaler." Give reasons to justify your answer.

NOTES

1. Richard S. Lopata, "Faster Pace in Wholesaling," *Harvard Business Review*, July-August 1969, pp. 130–143. Copyright © 1969 by the President and Fellows of Harvard College; all rights reserved.
2. Donald Bowersox, *Logistical Management* (New York: Macmillan, 1974), pp. 230–231.
3. U.S. Bureau of the Census, *Census of Wholesale Trade, 1972, Summary Statistics* (Washington, D.C., 1973).
4. Ibid.
5. Lopata, p. 133.
6. Frederick Webster, Jr., "The Role of the Industrial Distributor in Marketing Strategy," *Journal of Marketing*, 40 (July 1976): 10–16.
7. Ibid.
8. Ibid.
9. Ibid.
10. "Speaking of Bigness . . . ," *Forbes*, 114 (October 15, 1974): 57–60.
11. U.S. Bureau of the Census, op. cit.
12. Much of this section is taken from James C. McKeon, "Conflicting Patterns of Structural Change in Wholesaling," in Louis Boone and James Johnson, eds., *Marketing Channels* (Morristown, N.J.: General Learning Press, 1973), pp. 95–114.
13. Several good articles on the manufacturer–manufacturer's agent relationship are "Manufacturers' Reps vs. Factory Salesmen," *Air Conditioning, Heating and Refrigeration News*, November 29, 1971, p. 32; Al Lincoln, "Manufacturers' Representatives: Two Points of View," *Air

Conditioning, Heating and Refrigeration News, July 12, 1971, pp. 27–28; and T. H. Ford, "Evaluating the Rep Leads to Even Closer Involvement," *Air Conditioning, Heating and Refrigeration News,* July 19, 1971, pp. 8–9.

14. Lopata, p. 133.

15. David Berkus, "How Food Brokers Build Merchandising Muscle with Multi-Brand Coupon Ads," *Advertising Age,* September 27, 1976, p. 54.

16. "All Manufacturers Are Not Pleased with the Growth of Wholesaling Chains," *Air Conditioning, Heating and Refrigeration News,* September 23, 1974, pp. 1, 20.

CASE 12
The Farmer Company

For many years the Farmer Company was a wholesaler of plumbing equipment and supplies throughout the state of Virginia. It handled all types of plumbing equipment and fixtures, heating and air-conditioning equipment, and hot water heaters. The Farmer Company had sales of approximately $21 million last year and was the largest plumbing wholesaler in the state.

Service to customers was a primary company objective and seemed to be one of the key factors in its long-run growth. In fact service was offered without a great deal of attention to cost and growth.

Dan Smith, president of the Farmer Company, noticed several subtle changes during the past few years in manufacturer–wholesaler relationships. These began to worry him. In a few instances, for example, manufacturers had begun selling directly to large plumbing contractors. This was not considered a major problem, since the market was dominated by a large number of relatively small contractors.

There were other problems, however, that needed attention. First and foremost were sudden and substantial price increases. Many plumbing contractors use a bid basis for procuring new jobs. Bids, of course, are predicated on existing price levels. When unexpected large price increases come through, it may make existing construction and recently procured jobs unprofitable for the contractor. This creates ill will between the wholesaler and the contractor.

A second problem is unannounced and abrupt model changes. Often manufacturers discontinue models without warning, again creating ill will. Sometimes model changes are made without notice. Since most plumbing jobs are made to specific specifications, model changes may make it hard to find the right fixture. It also creates a problem with existing inventories, since once the new models come out, contractors no longer want to install the old models. It also means carrying additional parts for the discontinued items.

A third problem is defective or damaged merchandise received from manufacturers. At present over 15 percent of the porcelain-enameled fixtures received by Farmer are damaged to some degree. Often it takes many months to obtain price rebates and adjustments from the manufacturer. However, the products are sold to the plumbing contractors within a short time at substantially reduced prices, a policy that creates cash flow problems for Farmer.

Still another problem is dissemination of new-product information and training materials to the plumbing contractors. Many plumbers shun new items because they are unfamiliar with installation techniques or with the advantages of the new products over existing models. Thus the company's sales efforts often suffer.

1. It appears that the wholesaler is "caught in the middle." Do you believe that this is a typical situation? What can be done to overcome this dilemma?
2. How would you suggest that the company solve its problems? Suggest a strategy that the wholesaler can follow to avoid similar situations in the future.

13
Retailing

OBJECTIVES

- To understand the importance of retailing in the American economy.
- To present a classification system for retail stores.
- To become aware of the different types of retail operations.
- To define franchising.
- To gain insight into present and future trends in retailing.

This chapter begins with a discussion of the importance of retailing to the American economy. We will then examine some of the reasons that people choose one store over another. Naturally, this is a matter of critical importance to individual merchants, since patronage is a major factor in the long-run success or failure of the firm.

After learning why people shop in certain stores we will examine a system for classifying retail outlets. Next I will describe some important characteristics of major types of stores, such as department stores and discounters. Special attention is given to two major retailing phenomena: franchising and shopping centers. Both have had profound effects on American retailing.

It is sometimes said that three things determine the success of a retail operation—location, location, and location. That being the case, we will investigate factors to consider when choosing a site. The chapter concludes with a look at future trends.

THE IMPORTANCE OF RETAILING
Employment

American retailing is ubiquitous. It affects all of us directly and indirectly every day. Retailing includes all activities directly related to the sale of goods and services to the ultimate consumer for personal, nonbusiness use. Over 28 million Americans are engaged in some form of retail activity.[1] It is a major source of income and employment. Almost 16 million individuals work in services such as barbershops, repair shops, and car washes.[2] Medical services account for the largest percentage of service employment, followed by nonprofit organizations and educational institutions.

Sales

Figure 13.1 shows retail sales by store type in 1974. Several interesting things emerge from the data. Nondurable-goods sales account for 66 percent of all nonservice retail sales. Food and grocery stores are responsible for the bulk of these sales. The largest durable goods retailer category is automotive dealers, representing 56 percent of durable-goods sales.

The Giant Retailers

Most retailers are quite small. However, 8½ percent of all retail establishments accounted for 52½ percent of total retail sales in 1972 and employed 39½ percent of all retail workers. Thus the industry is actually dominated by giant organizations.

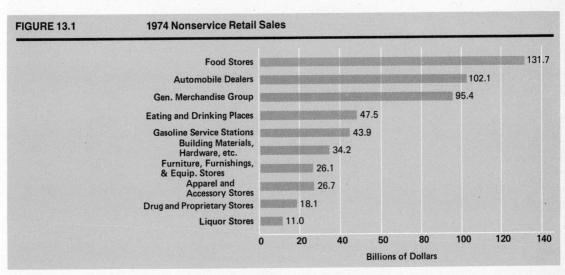

FIGURE 13.1   **1974 Nonservice Retail Sales**

Store Type	Billions of Dollars
Food Stores	131.7
Automobile Dealers	102.1
Gen. Merchandise Group	95.4
Eating and Drinking Places	47.5
Gasoline Service Stations	43.9
Building Materials, Hardware, etc.	34.2
Furniture, Furnishings, & Equip. Stores	26.1
Apparel and Accessory Stores	26.7
Drug and Proprietary Stores	18.1
Liquor Stores	11.0

Source: U.S. Department of Commerce, *Statistical Abstract of the United States, 1976* (Washington, D.C., 1976), p. 773.

Who are the giant retailers? Table 13.1 lists America's twenty-five largest retailers as of 1975. It probably comes as no surprise to find that Sears heads the list with sales of over $13 billion. Sears is also the largest retail employer, with 30,700 employees.

Safeway stores had the second-largest volume—almost $10 billion. These sales required far fewer employees per dollar of sales than Sears' because supermarkets are less labor intensive than department stores. Also, supermarket inventory turnover is faster.

DETERMINANTS OF STORE PATRONAGE

People shop at certain stores for a variety of reasons. Two of the most important determinants of store patronage are store image and perceived shopping risk.

Store Image

The image of a store can be a critical determinant of store sales. Studies have shown that a person's behavior toward a given store is influenced greatly by his or her perceptions of various retail outlets.[3]

TABLE 13.1	The Twenty-Five Largest Retailing Companies Ranked by Sales		
Rank, 1976	Company	Sales ($000)	Employees Number
1	Sears, Roebuck (Chicago)	14,950,208	30,700
2	Safeway Stores (Oakland)	10,442,531	28,598
3	S.S. Kresge (Troy, Mich.)	8,483,603	33,593
4	J.C. Penney (New York)	8,353,800	3,400
5	Great Atlantic & Pacific Tea (Montvale, N.J.)	6,537,897	23,800
6	Kroger (Cincinnati)	6,091,149	19,715
7	Marcor (Chicago)	5,280,280	1,831
8	F.W. Woolworth (New York)	5,152,200	23,200
9	Federated Department Stores (Cincinnati)	4,446,624	1,900
10	Lucky Stores (Dublin, Calif.)	3,483,174	21,135
11	Winn-Dixie Stores (Jacksonville)	3,265,916	25,800
12	American Stores (Wilmington)	3,207,248	8,660
13	Jewel Companies (Chicago)	2,981,429	23,500
14	City Products (Des Plaines, Ill.)	2,521,400	1,250
15	Food Fair Stores (Philadelphia)	2,507,040	37,500
16	Rapid-American (New York)	2,346,125	4,958
17	May Department Stores (St. Louis)	2,133,235	10,000
18	Southland (Dallas)	2,115,768	1,036
19	Dayton Hudson (Minneapolis)	1,898,544	8,900
20	Allied Stores (New York)	1,813,846	8,325
21	Supermarkets General (Woodbridge, N.J.)	1,612,692	8,449
22	Grand Union (Elmwood Park, N.J.)	1,611,195	14,000
23	Gamble-Skogmo (Minneapolis)	1,590,372	943
24	Associated Dry Goods (New York)	1,538,849	1,060
25	Albertson's (Boise)	1,490,839	3,710

Source: Fortune, July 1977, pp. 168–169. Reprinted by permission.

In some cases consumers may buy from store A because they don't like stores B and C. This is not a case of loyalty to a particular store but one of disloyalty to other stores. The managers of store A are in a precarious situation if this is generally true among its customers.

If a retailer has a positive image, it creates a "halo effect" that extends to many facets of the firm's marketing mix (e.g., lower prices, courteous personnel, better-quality goods, and good services). One savings and loan association with a very positive image was perceived by potential depositors as paying a higher interest rate than its four major competitors. In fact, all such associations in the city paid the same rate of interest.[4]

The Importance of Risk

Another important aspect of store patronage is perceived risk. Risk can be divided into two major categories—social and economic. If a product has high social risk, a person's purchase decision will strongly affect other people's opinions of that person. If a product has high economic risk, the purchase decision will affect the consumer's ability to make other purchases.

One study categorized products by risk characteristics, as shown in Figure 13.2.[5] If a product is thought to have low social risk, it does not tend to affect patronage attitudes toward discount and department stores.[6] On the other hand, products associated with high social risk create less favorable shopping attitudes toward discount stores among consumers in upper socioeconomic strata. Members of higher

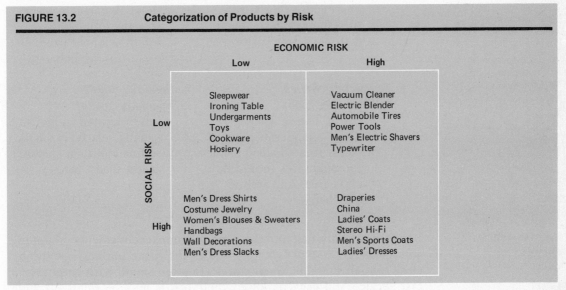

FIGURE 13.2   Categorization of Products by Risk

ECONOMIC RISK

	Low	High
SOCIAL RISK — Low	Sleepwear Ironing Table Undergarments Toys Cookware Hosiery	Vacuum Cleaner Electric Blender Automobile Tires Power Tools Men's Electric Shavers Typewriter
SOCIAL RISK — High	Men's Dress Shirts Costume Jewelry Women's Blouses & Sweaters Handbags Wall Decorations Men's Dress Slacks	Draperies China Ladies' Coats Stereo Hi-Fi Men's Sports Coats Ladies' Dresses

Source: V. Kanti Prasad, "Socioeconomic Risk and Patronage Preferences of Retail Shoppers," *Journal of Marketing,* 39 (July 1975): 44. By permission of the American Marketing Association.

social classes prefer department and specialty stores for products with high social risk.

A RETAIL CLASSIFICATION SYSTEM

As we have seen, people shop for a variety of reasons. Now that you know why people patronize certain stores, let's examine the types of stores available to the consumer. The following list combines categories of goods and major types of stores.[7] Unsought goods were omitted from the classification system because they are generally sold over the telephone, door to door, or through a referral system.

1. *Convenience Stores*
   Convenience goods
      (7-Eleven, Circle K, etc.)

2. *Convenience Stores*
   Shopping goods
      (branch of department store in large neighborhood shopping center, furniture store in a neighborhood center)

3. *Convenience Stores*
   Specialty goods
      (specialty restaurant in upper-class neighborhood)

4. *Shopping Stores*
   Convenience goods
      (large, integrated food store with clothing, drugs, hardware, etc.)

5. *Shopping Stores*
   Shopping goods
      (warehouse-type furniture showroom, regional mall department store)

6. *Shopping Stores*
   Specialty goods
      (large department-type store handling only infant-oriented products, e.g., cribs, highchairs, etc.)

7. *Specialty Stores*
   Shopping goods
      (e.g., "The Bedroom Shop"—moderate-sized stores located along major thoroughfares in middle-class areas and selling only beds)

8. *Specialty Stores*
   Specialty goods
      (often located in malls, usually relatively small, selling clothing, sporting goods, foods, etc.)

Convenience Stores

Stores may be divided into three major groups: convenience, shopping, and specialty. Convenience stores, as the name implies, are located close to their markets. Such stores are often small, with emphasis on fast service and easy parking. Their prices may be relatively high, thereby forcing the consumer to pay dearly for convenience.

Shopping Stores

Shopping stores usually carry a wide assortment of merchandise with significant product line depth (i.e., many items to choose from in a product line). These stores offer enough variety to permit the consumer to price and compare a number of products. Comparisons may be based on quality, style, suitability, and other factors. The range and quality of services offered by shopping stores (credit, returns, etc.) is normally greater than the range offered by convenience stores. Shopping stores are also more sensitive to price competition than convenience stores. Shopping stores are often clustered along major thoroughfares or located in shopping centers.

Specialty Stores

The merchandise lines of specialty stores may be narrower but are typically deeper than those of shopping or convenience stores. Product quality is stressed in most specialty stores, and fashionability is emphasized where appropriate. The prices of specialty stores are either comparable to or higher than those of shopping stores.

Many specialty stores place special emphasis on service. This may range from attentive and knowledgeable clerks to free delivery and home decorating consultations. Because of the nature of the product line and clientele served, location is less important to specialty stores than to convenience stores and most shopping stores. Many specialty stores, however, are found in large shopping centers and malls because some of their target customers may view the retailer as a shopping store.

MAJOR METHODS OF RETAIL OPERATION

In this section we will examine major retail operations from the standpoint of what they do. We will discuss department stores first and then focus on discounters, mail order houses, and supermarkets.

Department Stores

A department store sells a variety of merchandise. By housing many departments under one roof it achieves economies in promotion, buying, service, and control. Each department is headed by a buyer. In effect, each buyer's department is treated as a separate profit center and thus has a modicum of autonomy. A buyer not only selects the merchandise mix for his or her department but may also be responsible for promotion within the department and for its personnel. Central management establishes broad policies regarding types of merchandise and price ranges in order to build and maintain a consistent, homogeneous store image. The central administration is also responsible for the overall advertising program, credit policies, store expansion, customer service, and so forth.

Because of their size and buying power, most department stores buy directly from manufacturers. In fact it is not unusual for a manufacturer to produce merchandise under the department store's brand name. Some department stores have so much buying strength that they literally dominate small manufacturers. The manufacturer's profit margins, delivery dates, merchandise specifications, and transportation methods used are virtually dictated by the department store in some instances.

The Importance of Department Store Chains. It's difficult to find a large independent department store today. Most are owned by large national chains. The five largest department store chains are shown in Table 13.2. As you can see, each had 1975 sales of over $1 billion. Federated is huge: It operates 262 stores in 18 states.[8] Some of its better-known department stores are Bloomingdale's and Abraham & Straus on the East Coast, I. Magnin and Bullock's on the West Coast, Filene's in New England, Burdine's in Florida, Foley's and Sanger Harris in Texas, Shillito's in the Midwest, and Goldsmith's in Memphis. Many consumers are unaware of the dominance of department store chains because the parent company's name is not actively promoted.

Problems, Old and New. Department stores have begun to experience some new problems since the mid-1970s as well as having to contend with some nagging old ones. For years they attempted to be all things to all people. They carried wide ranges of both soft goods (clothing) and hard goods (appliances, sporting goods, hardware). Discounters have cut severely into the hard-goods market, so that many department stores are cutting back on low-margin hard goods.

A second problem is personnel. Finding and retaining good sales clerks is an endless battle. But the problem doesn't stop there. Department store chains have a hard time attracting college graduates because of their low starting pay, poor training programs, and long, irregular working hours.

TABLE 13.2	The Five Largest Department Store Chains (In Millions)		
	Sales	**Cost of Goods Sold**	**Net Income**
Federated Department Stores	$3,713.0	$2,669.0	$157.4
May Department Stores	2,004.0	1,412.0	66.7
Allied Stores	1,755.0	1,192.0	55.5
Dayton Hudson	1,693.0	1,230.0	51.3
Associated Dry Goods	1,391.0	1,008.0	43.1

Source: "Federated: The Most Happy Retailer Grows Faster and Better," *Business Week,* October 18, 1976, pp. 76–77. Reprinted by special permission. All rights reserved.

Mass Merchandising Shopping Chains

Mass merchandising shopping chains such as Sears, Penney's, and Montgomery Ward are similar to department store chains in many respects. Yet their sheer size in terms of sales volume, promotional budgets, dealer brands, and number of stores sets them apart from regular department store chains. Sears, as noted earlier, had sales of $13 billion in 1975.[9] In fact Sears is so large that it accounts for approximately 1 percent of America's GNP.[10] The company has 900 stores, 1700 catalog stores, 13 huge distribution centers, and 124 warehouses.[11] These organizations are vertically integrated, owning either all or part of many manufacturers that supply their merchandise. Sears also depends on 12,000 independent suppliers in addition to those that they control.

The mass merchandising shopping chains are high-volume operations that almost always purchase directly from manufacturers. They do not need to utilize wholesalers, since they are larger than any independent wholesaler and can purchase in larger volume. Most of their buying is highly centralized, but local managers are given limited purchasing authority.

Since Sears and Penney's cover most of the U.S. market network, television advertising is both feasible and economical for them. Heavy national television exposure also contributes to name identification and a strong company image. Network promotion usually centers on high-margin dealer-branded items such as the Diehard battery or Sears' steel-belted radial tires.

Specialty Stores

The term specialty stores is used not only to refer to a type of store but also to identify a method of retail operation. That is, such stores specialize in a given type of merchandise—children's clothing, men's clothing, candy, baked goods, sporting goods, pet supplies. A typical specialty store carries a deeper assortment of merchandise in its specialty than a department store would carry. In addition, it often offers more attentive customer service and more knowledgeable sales clerks.

Specialty stores face many of the opportunities and challenges that confront department stores. For example, specialty chains have become very powerful in apparel and other areas. A typical specialty chain is The Gap, a 192-unit chain that caters to the "jeans generation" in a 26-state market.[12] Bonwit Teller, a 13-unit women's specialty retailer, caters to the affluent young professional woman with a blend of youth-oriented goods and designer merchandise.[13]

Price is usually of secondary importance in fashion specialty outlets. Instead, the distinctiveness of the merchandise, the physical appearance of the store, and the caliber of the personnel determine shopping preferences.[14]

There are many types of specialty chains that aren't clothing oriented. Examples include McDonald's, Hickory Farms, Pier One, Singer Sewing Outlets, Kinney Shoes, Hallmark Cards and Gifts, and Zales Jewelers.

Discount Stores

Today's discount stores still stress high volume and low prices. Chain discounters usually carry a complete line of well-known, nationally branded hard goods, such as RCA, GE, and Hamilton-Beach appliances, and an extensive selection of soft goods. They generally price manufacturers' and dealer brands well below the suggested retail price. The difference is easily recognized by most customers.

Like department stores, national chains dominate the discount industry. The largest, Kresge (K-Mart), had sales of $4.6 billion in 1974.[15] Kresge operates over 750 K-Marts and plans to have over 1300 by 1980. Other major discount chains include Treasury (J. C. Penney's), Target (Dayton Hudson), Gold Circle (Federated), Venture (May), Almart-T. B. Hunter (Allied), and Woolco (Woolworth's).

The early success of the discount chains led to rapid expansion and oversaturation in many markets. Management controls broke down as the chains attempted to cope with a large number of stores in a wide variety of markets. "High-priced artificial flowers don't move in a college town," grumbled one store manager.[16]

Perhaps the dilemma of the discounter was best exemplified in early 1976 when W. T. Grant's, with assets of $512 million and liabilities at $1.2 billion, declared bankruptcy.[17] Many factors led to Grant's downfall, including most of those mentioned in the preceding paragraph as well as a blurred image ("What is W. T. Grant's?"), an overly liberal credit policy, poor store locations, and a strained expansion plan.[18]

Direct Retailing

If the 1950s and 1960s were the era of the discounter, the 1970s and 1980s may be the era of the direct marketer. The direct marketer sells either by telephone, by mail, or through personal visits to customers. In 1975 approximately $7.5 billion was spent on direct marketing, of which $3.9 billion went for direct mail.[19] The primary advantage offered by direct marketing is the convenience of ordering merchandise without leaving home.

The success of mail order retailing depends on the quality of the mailing list. Lists are available based on virtually any demographic characteristic. A typical mailing-list house sells names at $35 per thousand. Some of the more exclusive lists may sell for up to $60 per thousand.

Mail order retailers often develop warehouse-type operations for the sake of low overhead. Many specialty mail order retailers offer products that can't be found in most communities. For some companies direct mail has been the most effective way to achieve adequate distribution.

Newspaper and magazine advertisements that ask the consumer to "call in" or send in a coupon are another popular form of direct marketing. Similarly, the use of preprinted newspaper inserts and magazine bind-in cards has become increasingly popular.

Door-to-door retailing is a third form of direct marketing. Usually the target consumers are in the middle and lower socioeconomic groups. Companies such as Avon, Fuller Brush, Amway, and World Book Encyclopedia depend entirely on this technique. The trend seems to be away from cold door-to-door canvassing, however, with direct marketers relying instead on "party plans" in which one person acts as a "host" and gathers together as many prospective buyers as possible. Most parties are a combination social affair and sales demonstration. The underlying strategy is that the host will invite only people who are likely to buy something.

Telephone selling is becoming increasingly common in today's energy-short society. Department stores have used the practice for years, but numerous other retailers have recently discovered the value of this form of retailing. Land developers, repair services, appliance marketers, and others rely heavily on telephone selling. Many consumers resent telephone selling as an invasion of their privacy. "Canned" presentations and high-pressure appeals are also repugnant to many people. Nevertheless the effectiveness of telephone solicitation cannot be denied, and it will probably continue to grow in popularity unless restrictive legislation is passed.

FRANCHISING

Franchise sales of goods and services totaled approximately $195 billion in 1976. The older types of franchises, such as automobile dealerships, service stations, and soft-drink bottlers, account for the bulk of the business, but newer types are gaining ground.

Franchising is nothing new. Singer has used this approach since 1863, General Motors since 1898, and Rexall since 1901.

The Nature of Franchising

A franchise is a continuing relationship in which the franchisor grants operating rights to a franchisee. The franchisor is the one with the trade name, product, methods of operation, and so forth. The franchisee pays an initial fee to the franchisor plus a monthly royalty fee based on sales.

Some franchises, such as McDonald's, offer a turnkey (i.e., ready to operate) operation for $150,000 or more. The McDonald's franchisee is also required to spend up to three weeks at Hamburger University in Des Plaines, Illinois. Other franchises offer little more than a name or a product; the franchisee is responsible for the success of the operation.

Why Get a Franchise?

Franchising is supposed to offer the following advantages:

1. It gives the individual an opportunity to become an independent businessperson.
2. Franchises have lower failure rates than other businesses.

There is no doubt that franchising offers many opportunities in many different areas (see Table 13.3). Freedom, however, is a different matter. Most good franchises have a number of specific operating policies and financial guidelines that franchisees are expected to follow.

Many restrictive franchisor policies have come under close scrutiny by the Federal Trade Commission.[20] Before 1970 most franchisors required franchisees to buy only from the franchisor. At one

TABLE 13.3   Number of Franchisees and Franchisors, 1974

Kinds of Franchised Business	Franchisors	Franchisees
Total — all franchising	82,985	398,924
Automobile and truck dealers	301	32,652
Automobile products and services	5,259	43,918
Business aids and services		
Accounting, credit, collection, and general business systems	97	2,402
Employment services	803	2,641
Printing and copying services	105	1,300
Tax preparation services	3,506	3,966
Miscellaneous business services	69	5,345
Construction, home improvement		
Maintenance and cleaning services	280	13,216
Convenience stores	8,620	5,177
Educational products and services	409	1,262
Fast-food restaurants (all types)	8,919	31,488
Gasoline service stations	42,200	168,800
Hotels and motels	1,278	4,714
Campgrounds	56	1,495
Laundry and drycleaning services	139	3,822
Recreation, entertainment, and travel	63	4,412
Rental services (auto–truck–aircraft–boats)	1,706	7,460
Rental services (equipment)	185	1,126
Retailing (non-food)	7,446	46,593
Retailing (food other than convenience stores)	1,316	12,042
Soft drink bottlers	100	2,520
Miscellaneous	128	2,573

Source: U.S. Department of Commerce, *Franchising in the Economy 1972–1974* (Washington, D.C.: Government Printing Office, 1975), p. 47.

point more than half of Kentucky Fried Chicken's profits came from such sales.[21] A federal court ruling required companies to strike such clauses from their franchise contracts. Today franchisors usually offer to sell merchandise but allow franchisees to buy elsewhere as long as they meet strict quality standards.

Do franchises have lower failure rates than other kinds of businesses? Research data are inconclusive on this question. Individually, of course, the success of the franchise depends on the franchisee. Some, like McDonald's, One-Hour Martinizing, and United Rent Alls, have an extremely low failure rate. On the other hand, Roy Rogers Roast Beef, Minnie Pearl's Fried Chicken, and Joe Namath's Girls (an employment agency) have been less successful. In 1975, 55 franchisors failed and 48 others stopped franchising.[22]

SHOPPING CENTERS

The tremendous growth of shopping centers began after World War II as the U.S. population started its migration to the suburbs. The first shopping centers were strip centers, typically located along a busy street and including a supermarket, a variety store, and perhaps a few specialty stores.

Next came the larger community shopping centers with one or two small department store branches, more specialty shops, a restaurant or two, and several apparel stores. These centers offer a wider variety of shopping, specialty, and convenience goods, have large off-street parking lots, and usually range in size from 75,000 to 300,000 square feet.[23]

The Mall Era

Finally, along came the huge regional malls. Randall Park Mall in suburban Cleveland, Ohio, is the largest shopping mall in America. It sprawls over 143 acres and has room for five major chain or department stores and about 250 smaller shops. Regional malls are either entirely enclosed or roofed to allow easy shopping in any weather. Many offer benches, trees, fountains, sculptures, and similar items to enhance the shopping environment. Acres of free parking are characteristic of malls. The "anchor stores" or "generator stores" (Penney's, Sears, or a major department store) are usually located at opposite ends of the mall. This arrangement usually creates a heavy pedestrian traffic flow.

Reaching Saturation

In 1970 retail sales in shopping centers amounted to $118 billion and accounted for one-third of all retail sales.[24] Retail shopping center sales are projected to reach $200 billion by 1980.[25]

Mall and shopping center development seems to be reaching a saturation point, however. Sales per square foot are dropping, vacancy rates are climbing, and some centers and malls have declared bankruptcy.[26] As major markets become saturated, new construction will be highly selective and concentrated in fast-growing areas like the Southwest. Future malls will be smaller, probably in the 400,000-square-foot range, as developers concentrate on medium-sized and smaller cities. A spokesman for Arlen Realty and Development, a major shopping center developer, says, "We don't build in Cleveland, Ohio, but we will in Cleveland, Tennessee."[27]

RETAIL SITE SELECTION CONSIDERATIONS

The retailer's product/service offering must be compatible with the store's potential trade area. A trade area is the geographic area within which most of the store's customers are contained. Most regional shopping malls have trade areas of at least fifty square miles.[28]

Rarely is a trade area a perfect circle around a given site. Instead, its boundaries depend on the location of the store, the store's image, population concentrations, the number and quality of major traffic arteries, ease of entry and exit from the site, compatibility of nearby businesses, availability of public transportation, and incomes of customers.

TRENDS IN RETAILING

Clearly retailing institutions are in a continual state of evolution. What does the future hold for retailing? One trend is increased reliance on computers.

The Computer Enters in a Big Way

The biggest increase in computer usage in retailing is occurring at the point of sale. Computers are often used in conjunction with optical scanning equipment. One system, called Ultraphase and manufactured by Bergen Brunswig, utilizes an optical scanner to read the universal product code. The universal product code is a standardized bar code stamped on packages, which can be read by scanners at checkout counters. The code identifies the size and brand of the product. The terminal, which resembles a small electronic calculator, connects with a transmitter that relays product counts and orders to suppliers' computers over regular telephone lines.[29]

Improved inventory control will mean the stocking of far fewer brands, varieties, sizes, and types in supermarkets.[30] Unprofitable items will be quickly eliminated and emphasis will be placed on rapid turnover of products for which demand is heavy. In a typical supermarket 8000 items are carried and only 6000 are profitable.[31] As younger, better-educated retail managers enter the picture, the demand for accurate inventory and financial data will increase even more.[32]

Another phenomenon that will have a major impact on retailing is electronic funds transfer systems (EFTS). Basically, EFTS enables a retailer to transfer payments from a customer's bank account to its own. One problem facing EFTS is that in-store terminals may be considered branch banks.[33] If so, they will fall under heavy regulation by state and federal banking authorities.

Computers will also be used to aid decision making in such matters as store layout, product mix, store construction, pricing, promotion, and personnel and service levels.[34] Advanced mathematical applications in retailing are still in an early stage of development. It is apparent, however, that the retail managers of the future will have to understand these tools.

The Growth of Specialty Retailing

Another important retailing trend is the growth of specialty retailing. Specialty stores will segment and resegment their markets, often catering to a very narrow market target. Examples include The Limited (junior apparel), Mervyn's (family apparel), Aaron Brothers (artists' supplies), and Hickory Farms (specialty foods).[35] Many specialty stores will concentrate not only on fashion merchandise but on "life style goods" as well. Items such as recreational equipment, cameras, gourmet cooking equipment, and arts and crafts materials will provide the bases for numerous specialty outlets.[36]

The Importance of Positioning

As retailers zero in on precise market segments, "positioning" becomes extremely important. The product mix and image must exactly fit the needs of the target market. Pier I, for example, concentrates on the under-35 market. Pottery Plus attempts to reach the upper-middle-class china buyer. The Limited aims directly at the 18- to 35-year-old woman who is style and fashion conscious and willing to pay moderately high prices to satisfy her desire for tasteful apparel.[37] Its entire marketing effort is geared toward this market segment. It carries primarily junior sizes and emphasizes coordinated outfits; its displays are casual and youth oriented; and its employees are in the same age category and project the same life style as the target customers. Effective positioning will enhance store loyalty and perhaps shield retailers from direct competition.

Even window displays in specialty stores and some department stores are becoming "happenings" that attempt to project the store's image. Perhaps the ultimate in urbane displays occurred in downtown Washington, D.C., when live female models posed in the sixteen-foot-high windows of a unisex boutique and occasionally changed their outer clothes in full view of passers-by.[38]

Warehouse Retailing

Perhaps less glamorous, but no less important, is the growth of warehouse retailing. The key to the success of this form of retailing is its ability to undercut prices of conventional retailers by from 10 to 30 percent.[39] Firms like Levitz and Best Products will continue to be a major force in this form of retailing.

One warehouse retailer, Grocery Warehouse of Detroit, leaves food in its original packing cases and lets shoppers bag their purchases themselves.[40] Cashiers periodically check to make sure that the price on the outside matches the goods inside. This is essentially an honor system designed to cut costs. The long-run viability of the concept is yet to be determined.

Other Trends

Here are some other important trends:

1. The use of temporary-help firms, such as Manpower, to permanently staff convenience stores.[41]
2. An increase in consignment selling, particularly in nonfood sales to supermarkets.
3. The continued growth of dealer brands.
4. The rapid growth of in-home shopping.

SUMMARY

Retailing permeates our lives. It's one of America's largest industries, employing over 28 million people. The industry is dominated by giant organizations—a very small percentage of retail establishments accounts for a majority of retail sales.

One factor that determines where people shop is store image. A retailer with a good positive image tends to benefit from a halo effect that extends to its entire marketing mix. Some consumers patronize stores that minimize either social or economic risk. Social risk refers to how an individual's purchase decision will affect other people's opinions of that individual. Economic risk refers to the ability to purchase other goods and services.

Department stores constitute one of the most important forms of retail operation. They are dominated by large national chains. Department stores have historically experienced problems in choosing an appropriate merchandise mix and hiring capable personnel.

The mass merchandising shopping chains include Sears, Penney's, and Montgomery Ward. Their huge size, promotional budgets, dealer brands, and numerous stores set them apart from regular department store chains. Mass merchandising shopping chains have extensive market coverage. This makes network television advertising an economical way of promoting their own brands.

Specialty stores, like department stores, are becoming dominated by chains. They usually specialize in a given type of merchandise such as men's clothing, candy, or sporting goods. Specialty stores face many of the same opportunities and challenges that confront department stores.

Discounters first entered the market after World War II. Chain discounters usually carry a complete line of well-known nationally branded hard goods. They are dominated by national chains such as K-Mart, Target, and The Treasury.

Franchising grew rapidly during the late 1960s and early 1970s. The franchisor grants operating rights to the franchisee for an initial fee plus a monthly royalty. Franchising increases the opportunities for independent businesspeople, and franchises typically have lower failure rates than other businesses.

The movement to the suburbs has resulted in the growth of shopping centers, often at the expense of downtown areas. The 1970s has been the era of huge regional malls. Many malls contain over 200 retail specialty stores and several major department store chains. Their rapid growth seems to have brought them close to the saturation point. Today they account for approximately one-third of all retail sales.

Selecting a retail site is a difficult task. Many people believe that it is the most important aspect of retail marketing. Often it is necessary to choose between locating in a mall or building a free-standing facility.

One of the most important trends in retailing is increased use of the computer. A second major trend is the increased use of positioning as retailers zero in on specific market targets. Warehouse retailing is also becoming more common as consumers seek lower prices with fewer frills.

KEY TERMS

Retailing	Discount store
Store image	Direct marketer
Perceived risk	Franchise
Social risk	Franchisor
Economic risk	Franchisee
Convenience store	Strip center
Shopping store	Community shopping center
Specialty store (1)	Regional mall
Department store	Trade area
Buyer	Universal product code
Mass merchandising shopping chain	Electronic funds transfer systems
Specialty store (2)	Warehouse retailing

QUESTIONS FOR DISCUSSION

1. Discuss the importance of retailing to the American economy.
2. What is meant by store image? Are there any stores in your area that have a bad image? Why do you think so?
3. How does social risk affect store patronage patterns? Can you give examples to illustrate your answer?
4. Differentiate between shopping stores and specialty stores. Give examples of each in your locality. Are these distinctions rigid?

5. List the different categories of retailers discussed in this chapter. Describe the activities of any two.

6. What is direct marketing? Why is it growing so important? Can you name a few direct marketers?

7. Explain the nature of franchising. What are the advantages commonly associated with a franchise?

8. Into what general categories do the following retail operators fall?
   a. Pizza Hut
   b. Franklin Mint
   c. Fotomat stores
   d. Kroger

9. What are some of the factors to be considered in selecting a retail location?

10. How has the shopping center changed over the past three decades? What are its future prospects?

11. List some of the important trends that are occurring in the retailing sector. Describe the role that computers will play in future retail operations.

12. What is warehouse retailing? Why is it growing so rapidly? Do you think this growth will continue? Give reasons for your answer.

NOTES

1. U.S. Department of Commerce, *Statistical Abstract of the United States, 1975* (Washington, D.C., 1976), p. 772.

2. Ibid.

3. V. Parker Lessig, "Consumer Store Images and Store Loyalties," *Journal of Marketing,* 37 (October 1975): 72–74; Leonard L. Berry, "The Components of Department Store Image: A Theoretical and Empirical Analysis," *Journal of Retailing,* 45 (Spring 1969): 3–20; Robert H. Myers, "Sharpening Your Store Image," *Journal of Retailing,* 36 (Fall 1960): 129–137; Stuart Rich and Bernard D. Portis, "The Imageries of Department Stores," *Journal of Marketing,* 28 (April 1964): 10–15; W. B. Weale, "Measuring the Consumer's Image of a Department Store," *Journal of Retailing,* 37 (Spring 1961): 40–48; Robert F. Kelly and Ronald Stephenson, "The Semantic Differential: An Information Source for Designing Retail Patronage Appeals," *Journal of Marketing,* 31 (October 1967): 43–47; Pierre Martineau, "The Personality of the Retail Store," *Harvard Business Review,* January-February 1958, pp. 47–55; Bruce J. Weale, "Measuring the Customer's Image of a Department Store," *Journal of Retailing,* 37 (Summer 1961): 40–48; Stephen A. Greyser, "Making Image Research Work for You," speech delivered at National Retail Merchants Association Conference, January 1973; Peter J. McClure and John K. Ryan, "Difference Between Retailers and Consumers' Perceptions," *Journal of Marketing Research,* 5 (February 1968): 35–40; Eleanor G. May, *Department Stores' Images: Basic Findings* (Cambridge, Mass.: Marketing Science Institute, March 1972), pp. 23–37; and Dev Pathak, William Crissy, and Robert Sweitzer, "Customer Image Versus the Retailer's Anticipated Image," *Journal of Retailing,* 50 (Winter 1974–1975): 21–29.

4. Carl McDaniel, Jr., *Methods of Image Measurement: A Case Study of Savings and Loan Associations,* unpublished doctoral dissertation, Arizona State University, 1970.

5. V. Kanti Prasad, "Socioeconomic Product Risk and Patronage Preferences of Retail Shoppers," *Journal of Marketing,* 39 (July 1975): 42–47.

6. Ibid.

7. The original store classification system was Louis P. Bucklin, "Retail Strategy and the Classification of Consumer Goods," *Journal of Marketing,* 27 (January 1963): 50–55. For a recent refinement see Michael J. Houston, "The Classification of Goods Theory: A Basis for Identifying Market Positions and Short-Run Marketing Goals," in Ronald C. Curhan, ed., *1974 Combined Proceedings* (Chicago: American Marketing Association, 1975), pp. 444–449. See also Helmut Soldner, "Conceptual Models for Retail Strategy Formulation," *Journal of Retailing,* 52 (Fall 1976): 47–56.

8. "Federated: The Most Happy Retailer Grows Faster and Better," *Business Week,* October 18, 1976, pp. 74–80.

9. "Sears' Identity Crisis," *Business Week,* December 8, 1975, p. 52.

10. Ibid.

11. Ibid.

12. "The Gap Shapes Expansion Aimed at Second Generation," *Advertising Age,* November 15, 1976, p. 38.

13. "Bonwit's Turns Up the Heat," *Business Week,* October 11, 1976, pp. 120–122.

14. Joseph Barry Mason and Morris Mayer, "Insights into the Image Determinants of Fashion Specialty Outlets," *Journal of Business Research,* 1 (Summer 1973): 73–80.

15. "Keeping Up with Kresge," *Business Week,* October 19, 1974, pp. 70–76.

16. Ibid., p. 74.

17. "Dividing What's Left of Grant's," *Business Week,* March 1, 1976, p. 21.

18. "Retailer on the Rocks," *The Wall Street Journal,* October 3, 1975; see also: "How W. T. Grant Lost $175 Million Last Year," *Business Week,* February 24, 1975, pp. 74–76.

19. Robert J. Coen, "Ad Dollar Gain in 1976 Biggest Ever," *Advertising Age,* July 5, 1976, p. 32.

20. Ronald Stephenson and Robert House, "A Perspective on Franchising," *Business Horizons,* 14 (August 1971): 35–42; see also Donald Dixon, "The Impact of Recent Antitrust Decisions upon Franchise Marketing," *MSU Business Topics,* Spring 1969, pp. 68–79.

21. "Cramping the Business Style of Franchisers," *Business Week,* June 16, 1975, p. 82.

22. "Franchising Future is Favorable" Says a Government Forecast, *The Wall Street Journal,* April 15, 1976, p. 1.

23. Raymond Marquardt, James Makens, and Robert Roe, *Retail Management: Satisfaction of Consumer Needs* (Hinsdale, Ill.: Dryden Press, 1975), p. 118.

24. Ibid.

25. Ibid.

26. David Elsner, "Shopping Center Boom Appears to Be Fading Due to Overbuilding," *The Wall Street Journal,* September 7, 1976.

27. Ibid.

28. Carl Larson, Robert Weigard, and John Wright, *Basic Retailing* (Englewood Cliffs, N.J.: Prentice-Hall, 1975), p. 110.

29. "Marketing Observer," *Business Week,* May 24, 1976, p. 97.
30. Herbert Zeltner, "Big Stores, Non-Foods, Private Brands Wane in Supermarket Fields," *Advertising Age,* January 5, 1976, p. 32.
31. "Consumer of the 80's Will Be Volatile: Harper," *Advertising Age,* September 6, 1976, p. 4.
32. Robert Stevens, "Retail Managers: Information Availability and Usage," *Journal of Retailing,* 51 (Summer 1975): 53–57.
33. "Electronic Funds Transfers: You Can Bank on Them," *Sales and Marketing Management,* October 11, 1976, p. 90.
34. See M. S. Moyer, "Management Science in Retailing," *Journal of Marketing,* 36 (January 1972): 3–9.
35. See James Kenderdine and Bert McCammon, "Structure and Strategy in Retailing," in Henry Nash and Donald Robin, eds., *1975 Proceedings: Southern Marketing Association,* pp. 117–119.
36. Walter Neppl, "New Directions in Retailing," *The Conference Board Record,* 11 (September 1974): 62–64.
37. Albert Bates, "The Troubled Future of Retailing," *Business Horizons,* 19 (August 1976): 28.
38. Deborah Sue Yaeger, "Chic Shops' Displays No Longer Are Just Window Dressing," *The Wall Street Journal,* September 9, 1976; see also Leah Rozen, "Window Shoppers Getting an Eyeful These Days," *Advertising Age,* August 16, 1976, pp. 37–38.
39. Kenderdine and McCammon, p. 119.
40. "Marketing Observer," *Business Week,* June 28, 1976, p. 51; see also: William Nickels, "Central Distribution Facilities Challenge Traditional Retailers," *Journal of Retailing,* 49 (Spring 1973): 45–51.
41. "Now Manpower, Inc., Goes in for Steady Jobs," *Business Week,* August 23, 1976, p. 41.

CASE 13
Gray Trail Bus Line

Gray Trail serves the New England area with an aggressive management and a modern fleet of interstate buses. Recently it conducted a market study in order to develop a strategy for the company during the 1980s. The results of the study are as follows.

The bus traveler market includes both young and older individuals, typically with relatively low income and below-average education. Many don't drive or own cars. A number of people travel frequently for rather common reasons. They go by bus because they don't like to drive, don't own a car, or find it less expensive than other modes of transportation.

Gray Trail's market position results from size, points served, schedules, and the fact that the company is well known in New England. It seems that one of the most important opportunities to compete for additional market share will be in a total program that delivers better service. Better routes and schedules and more terminals and points served are other important long-range needs. The lack of service to certain points is a major complaint of people who currently travel on competing carriers.

The market is a challenging mix of occasional and frequent bus travelers. Some of the frequent travelers have no strong preference for which carrier they patronize. Most bus travelers also utilize other modes of transportation, particularly car and airline.

Real growth in the bus travel market is probably limited by three factors. First, the increasing affluence of young people means less travel by bus. Second, older people reach a point at which they can no longer travel. Third, people do not have a strong desire to travel by bus and often prefer other modes of transportation.

Yet there may be new opportunities in the bus travel market. For example, the younger and older segments of the market are constantly changing, so that new target markets are developing.

The economical nature of bus travel is very important, yet only a few people say that they would travel by bus more frequently if the fares were lower. Thus lower fares probably wouldn't increase traffic.

There is a well-defined, though minimal, opportunity to "switch" frequent air and car travelers to Gray Trail. These travelers know some of the advantages of bus travel. However, in their opinion, those advantages are more than balanced by the disadvantages. Market opportunities also seem to exist in the characteristic that experienced travelers like most about bus travel: There is no need to drive, so you can rest and relax.

1. Armed with this market study, develop a marketing strategy for the 1980s.
2. Do you feel that the market research information just presented is complete? What additional data might be utilized? Is it necessary to conduct a research study like this one in order to develop long-range plans? Remember that research studies are often based on current phenomena, but the company is planning for the 1980s.

14

Physical-Distribution Strategies

OBJECTIVES

■ To understand the meaning of physical distribution.
■ To learn the objectives of physical distribution.
■ To become aware of the functions of physical distribution.
■ To learn about the institutions that facilitate physical distribution.
■ To gain insight into present and future distribution trends.

Physical distribution consists of all business activities that are concerned with transporting finished inventory and/or raw-material assortments so that they arrive at the designated place when needed and in usable condition.[1] It can be divided into three broad areas of managerial responsibility: physical distribution management, logistical coordination, and material management.[2] The key functions of physical distribution are shown in Figure 14.1.

Physical-distribution managers are responsible for getting the finished product to the consumer or user. This is an integral part of the total marketing mix. You don't sell products that you can't deliver, and salespeople don't (or shouldn't) promise deliveries that they can't make. Of course there are exceptions, but they usually mean the loss of a customer. The physical product is inseparable from accurate order filling, billing, timely delivery, and arrival in good condition. It is also part of the price of the product.

FIGURE 14.1   Physical Distribution Activities and Their Interrelationships

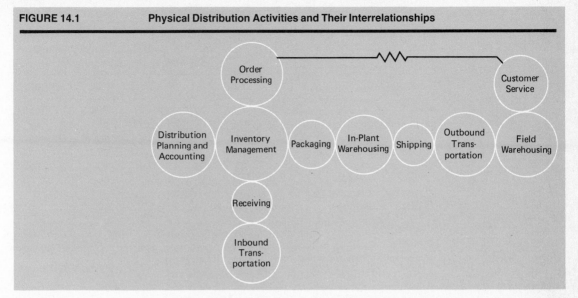

Source: Wendell Stewart, "Physical Distribution: A Key to Improved Volume and Profits," *Journal of Marketing* (January 1965) 66. By permission of the American Marketing Association.

An example will illustrate the importance of distribution. Polaroid's first serious direct competition came in the summer of 1976, when Kodak announced a new line of instant cameras and film. Introductory promotion was splashy, dramatic, and heavy. A five-page spread in *TV Guide* dramatically announced, "It's Here! The Kodak Instant." Yet a key marketing element had hit a snag—physical distribution. Most dealers had only a few cameras, and many had none. One buyer for a major department store chain noted that "people aren't inclined to wait—they will switch to Polaroid instead. So, the situation seems to be that Kodak is advertising for Polaroid." In fact, the buyer added, "We've been urged by Polaroid to stock up on their material in anticipation of nondelivery of the Kodak item."[3]

Logistical coordination is a critical element of effective physical distribution management. It is the synchronization of physical distribution and materials management. The coordination effort depends heavily on forecasting to develop plans for incoming items, production scheduling (in-plant holding and moving), and the monitoring of materials and finished-goods inventories.

Materials management, the third area of physical-distribution responsibility, is concerned with finding sources of supply, acquiring raw materials to keep the production line running smoothly, and getting them at a reasonable cost.

Physical distribution managers are responsible for three flows: (1) the flow of materials to the factory, (2) the flow of semifinished

TABLE 14.1	Responsibilities of the Physical-Distribution Department			
	Percent of Firms Indicating Responsibility for Activity by Date of Study			
Activity	1962	1966	1968	1971
Transportation	90%	89%	100%	100%
Warehousing	66	70	98	98
Inventory management	72	55	85	90
Customer service	NA	36	93	93
Order processing	12	43	89	88
Protective packaging	40	9	85	73
Production planning	36	38	61	60
Market forecasting	NA	25	43	40
Number of firms interviewed	50	47	87	NA

Source: Daniel DeHayes, Jr., and Robert Taylor, "Moving Beyond the Physical Distribution Organization," *Transportation Journal,* Spring 1974, p. 34.

products within the plant and between plants, and (3) the flow of finished goods to the consumer. These three flows overlap and are interdependent. A materials shortage, for example, ultimately means a slowdown in finished-goods delivery.

Physical distribution has only recently been recognized as an integrated activity totally responsible for the three flows just listed. In general, the core functions of physical distribution (transportation, warehousing, inventory management, and customer service) have been integrated into physical-distribution departments since the early 1960s.[4] Production planning and forecasting—two key coordinating areas of physical distribution—are not yet fully meshed into the logistical network. (See Table 14.1.) As you can see, however, the trend is definitely toward an integrated department.

THE COSTS OF DISTRIBUTION

As distribution departments have evolved, their emphasis has changed from obtaining the lowest transportation rates to minimizing total distribution costs, both explicit and implicit, relative to a predetermined level of service (we will discuss this in more detail in the next section). In fact the ability to achieve significant cost savings has been one of the primary reasons for the establishment of physical-distribution departments. Also, distribution costs can act as a constraint on territory covered and, therefore, on the firm's market potential, as the following example shows.

Olympia Brewing was the biggest beer producer in the West but could not penetrate the profitable Midwest and East Coast markets owing to high distribution costs.[5] Efficient mass advertising in the beer industry requires national market coverage, and heavy promotion is usually the only way to maintain market share. Lack of promotional funds has ultimately spelled the demise of most regional brewers. Olympia's strategy was to acquire Lone Star Brewing in Texas and Theodore Hamm in Minnesota in order to open up new distribution routes. Thus physical distribution, or the lack of it, will play a major role in Olympia's long-run ability to survive.

Distribution costs are of extreme importance to executives at Olympia Brewery. In some industries, such as machinery, total distribution costs average about 10 percent of total sales. At the other extreme, food distribution costs are equivalent to approximately 30 percent of total sales.[6] Overall, the costs of distribution average almost 22 percent of sales, according to one study.[7] The largest single component of distribution costs is the cost of transportation. If a firm can control its distribution costs, it may have an important competitive advantage.

THE OBJECTIVES OF DISTRIBUTION

At this point the following caveat is necessary: Cost minimization per se can have disastrous results. Marketing managers must consider the impact of any cost saving on the quality of the distribution system. The objective of physical distribution is to provide good service at low cost. Good service increases the probability of repeat sales, a high customer retention rate, and the addition of new customers.

Perhaps the best measure of distribution service is order cycle time. This is the elapsed time between the initial effort to place an order and the customer's receipt of the order in good condition.

A buyer may feel that the availability of timely and reliable order status information is an important part of the "total product." Consistent delivery schedules enable companies to lower the level of stock they need to keep on hand to guard against the possibility of out-of-stock situations. This means lower inventory carrying costs and a reduction in the amount of capital tied up in inventory.

How important is physical-distribution service? Although measures are lacking in the consumer market, a survey of 400 purchasing agents for large manufacturers revealed that distribution service is second only to product quality.[8] In fact it is more important than price! The same study indicated that 25 percent of the purchasing agents surveyed canceled back orders more than 35 percent of the time. Thus inability to make on-time deliveries often translates into lost revenue for the seller.

One may quickly jump to the conclusion that a company should never be out of stock, but this is not the case. Each unit of increased customer service required greater incremental expenditure. For example, a firm that strives to support a service standard of overnight delivery at 95 percent consistency may confront costs that are nearly double the total cost of implementing a program of second-morning delivery with 90 percent consistency.[9] Thus the shortest order cycle time (one day in Figure 14.2) is not always the most profitable policy.

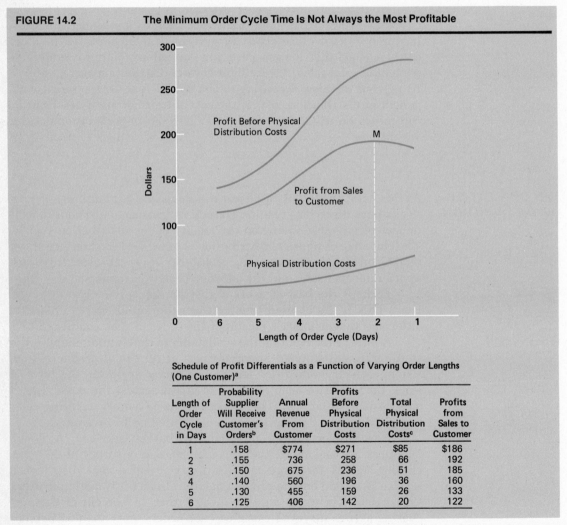

FIGURE 14.2   **The Minimum Order Cycle Time Is Not Always the Most Profitable**

Schedule of Profit Differentials as a Function of Varying Order Lengths (One Customer)[a]

Length of Order Cycle in Days	Probability Supplier Will Receive Customer's Orders[b]	Annual Revenue From Customer	Profits Before Physical Distribution Costs	Total Physical Distribution Costs[c]	Profits from Sales to Customer
1	.158	$774	$271	$85	$186
2	.155	736	258	66	192
3	.150	675	236	51	185
4	.140	560	196	36	160
5	.130	455	159	26	133
6	.125	406	142	20	122

Source: Ronald Stephenson and Ronald Willett, "Selling with Physical Distribution Service," *Business Horizons,* December 1968, pp. 78–79. By permission.
[a] Based on hypothetical data.
[b] Assumes a single acceptable level of consistency in order cycle lengths.
[c] Includes placement costs (where covered), processing costs, transportation costs, and control costs.

THE IMPORTANCE OF TOTAL COSTS

Let's look again at the concept of total distribution costs. Physical-distribution managers should examine the interrelationship of such factors as number of warehouses, finished-goods inventory, and transportation expenses. Each component of distribution expense should be examined in light of the other cost centers in the distribution system. Finally, the cost of any single distribution system should be analyzed relative to its quality of customer service (order cycle time).

One classic study justified the high cost of air transportation when viewed in a systems context.[10] The rapid delivery capabilities of air freight have drastically reduced the number of warehouses required at distant locations as well as outlying inventory requirements. Thus the cost increase of using air freight was more than justified by the savings in inventory and warehouse expenses.

Figure 14.3 illustrates the interrelationship among transportation, inventory carrying cost, and number of warehouses. The WW curve declines as the number of warehouses increases. The more warehouses a firm has, the lower the transportation cost from ware-

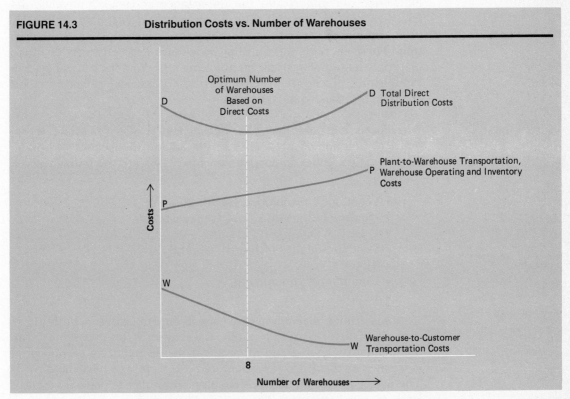

FIGURE 14.3   Distribution Costs vs. Number of Warehouses

Source: Adapted from Wendell Stewart, "Physical Distribution: A Key to Improved Volume and Profits," *Journal of Marketing,* 29 (January 1965): 65–70.

house to customer. If Jones Manufacturing, our theoretical company, serves fifty markets and has a warehouse in each one, the warehouse-to-customer transportation costs are going to be low. In contrast, if the company has only one warehouse the transportation expenses will be much higher.

The PP curve represents plant-to-warehouse transportation and warehouse operating and inventory costs. Plant-to-warehouse costs will rise as the number of warehouses increases because the plant will be forced to make small shipments to numerous points (small shipments generally cost more than carload or truckload shipments via a common carrier). Warehousing and inventory costs rise because of the duplications in overhead at each location.

As you can see, the decline in WW is ultimately offset by the increase in PP such that total distribution costs (DD) begin to rise. The lowest point of DD corresponds to eight warehouses, yielding the lowest total distribution cost.

THE FUNCTIONS OF PHYSICAL DISTRIBUTION

Now that you understand the importance of viewing physical distribution as a system and the role of costs and customer service has been explained, we will examine the functions of physical distribution. These include determining warehouse locations, establishing a materials-handling system, maintaining an inventory control system, establishing procedures for processing orders, and selecting modes of transportation. (See Figure 14.4.)

Warehouse Locations

Warehouse location, like distribution center site selection, is primarily a function of markets to be served and the location of production facilities. Other important considerations are the following:

- Markets to be served
- Location of production facilities
- Quality and versatility of transportation
- Quantity and quality of labor
- Cost and quality of industrial land
- Taxes
- Community government
- Utilities

Sometimes a manufacturer must choose between building its own warehouse or using a public warehouse. Public warehouses are independently owned and often specialize in handling certain products, such as furniture or refrigerated products, and household goods. The use of public warehouses enables a producer to place inventories close to key customers. This means quick delivery without the cost of building a private facility. Other reasons for using public warehouses include (1) avoiding investment in new capital structures,

FIGURE 14.4   Physical Distribution as a Part of the Marketing Mix

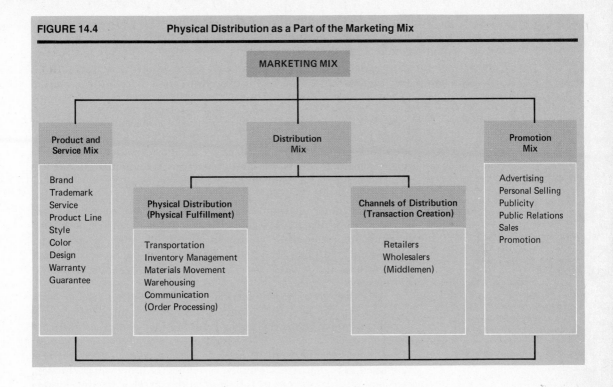

(2) reducing distribution risks and increasing flexibility when entering new markets, and (3) meeting seasonal demand.

Distribution centers are a special form of warehouse. Public warehousemen and many private firms are turning to distribution centers rather than constructing traditional warehouses. The emphasis of such centers is either on making bulk (consolidating shipments) or breaking bulk, and not on storage. Conceptually, a distribution center strives for rapid inventory turnover as opposed to serving as a long-term merchandise depository.

A distribution center can be distinguished from a warehouse in a number of ways. It is a centralized warehousing operation that

- serves a regional market.
- consolidates large shipments from different production points.
- processes and regroups products into customized orders.
- maintains a full line of products for customer distribution.
- is primarily established for movement of goods, rather than for storage.
- provides services for shippers and consignees of goods.
- usually employs a computer and various materials-handling equipment, and may be highly automated rather than labor intensive.
- is large and single-storied rather than multi-storied.[11]

The role of the computer in maintaining an efficient flow of merchandise into and out of the distribution center cannot be overemphasized. In fact the computer is often cited as the key to the success of the distribution center concept. Let's examine how one large company incorporates the computer into its distribution center network.

Norwich Pharmaceutical Company is the pharmaceutical division of Morton-Norwich Products, Inc., a diversified, consumer-product oriented corporation marketing pharmaceuticals, cosmetics, food service and household products, specialty chemicals, and industrial and ice-control salt through a number of marketing divisions.

The new teleprocessing system puts the company's five distribution centers across the country as close as a keyboard to central headquarters. Sales, distribution and invoicing are handled "on location," communicating constantly with centralized inventory, accounts receivable and credit files. Major files are linked; on-line processing keeps them always up to date. The result is a dynamic new operating environment.

As orders are received, operators at the distribution center enter them through the keyboard terminals and inquire into headquarters files on inventory status, customer credit ratings and other customer data.

Responses appear on the local terminal screen. Problems, if any, are flagged in headquarters. Finally, assuming the order can go through, the complete order document is flashed on the screen at the distribution center for the operator's inspection. Once OK'd, it is printed out, along with shipping papers, on the printer next to the terminal. From there, it goes directly to the warehouse for picking.

They can now pull, pack and ship each order much faster than before. All bill-of-lading and delivery information is in the shipping papers, so the man at the warehouse need only enter data in the correct boxes on the bill-of-lading. And the invoices, which used to be prepared and mailed in Norwich, are now ready and can either go directly with the shipment or directly into the mail.

If an order should be flagged for credit reasons, a printout in the credit department gives the name of the customer, distribution point where the order was entered, and a code indicating a past due bill, a credit limit overage or an account that requires special handling—a rush order, for example.

This printed information goes to the credit director or one of his six credit managers. Based on a detailed display of the customer's account, which they call out on a nearby 3270 visual display terminal, they can decide whether the order should be shipped or held.[12]

Establishing a Materials-Handling System

A computerized distribution information system still requires an efficient materials-handling system to rapidly move the inventory. In 1976 American businesses spent over $300 million for materials-handling equipment.[13] The breakdown is shown in Table 14.2.

TABLE 14.2	Breakdown of Materials-Handling Equipment Purchases, 1976

Equipment	Percent
Power lift trucks	35
Automated high rise storage	18
Racks, shelving	13
Building expansion	7
Conveyor equipment	4
Packaging, weighing, marking equipment	23
Total	100

Source: "Material Handling for Distribution," Handling and Shipping, January 1976, p. 39.

A discussion of materials handling would not be complete without a mention of containerization. Containerization means putting the goods in a box for protection and ease of handling. This form of distribution has become extremely popular in international shipping. Approximately 60 percent of all international shipments move this way.[14] A container, often a special form of truck trailer body, can be loaded and locked in Yuma, Arizona. A truck tractor then hauls the load to Phoenix, where the container is placed on a special railroad flatcar ("piggyback freight"). The train arrives at the port of embarkation, say, San Diego, where giant cranes lift the container onto special container ships ("fishyback"). The reverse process occurs at the port of destination.

Maintaining an Inventory Control System

The third function of physical distribution is the establishment of an inventory control system. Inventory levels are subject to many internal pressures, depending on the goals of the operating department. The following passage illustrates those pressures:

> The field salesman will try to convince you to maintain large stocks so that none of his customers will have to wait. Purchasing agents will tend to buy in large quantities in order to take advantage of quantity discounts and price speculations, and to hedge against a cut-off in supply, perhaps caused by labor problems. The traffic specialist will also opt for large shipment quantities to take advantage of lower freight rates. All these are forces at work in a firm which tends to increase the amount of inventory on hand, as well as the quantity ordered.
>
> Then there are opposing forces pushing for low inventory levels. The firm's financial officers, for example, will pressure for reduced inventory levels. Less inventory not only means less capital tied up, but also lower warehousing costs.[15]

Who's right? In a general sense, everyone is. All objectives should be considered in designing an inventory control policy.

Three basic elements are at the heart of an inventory control system: ordering costs, inventory carrying costs, and the costs of lost

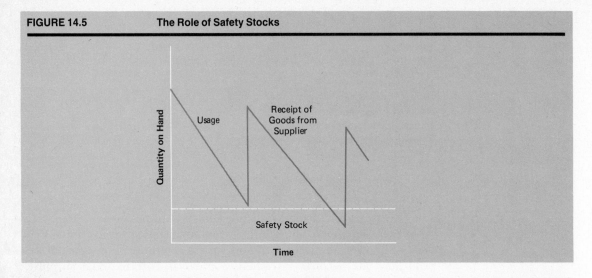

FIGURE 14.5   **The Role of Safety Stocks**

FIGURE 14.6   **Determining the Economic Order Quantity**

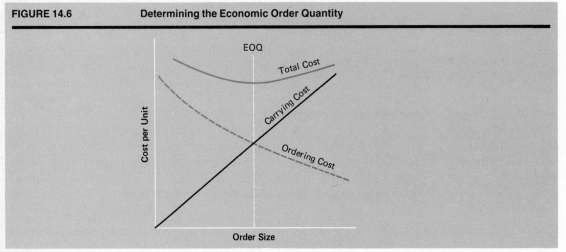

sales or stockouts. The last element may necessitate safety stocks. Unpredictability of usage or unreliability of supplier delivery times may cause lost sales if safety stocks are inadequate. (See Figure 14.5.)

The level of inventory that should be ordered at any one time is aided by the economic order quantity (EOQ). EOQ minimizes the sum of the ordering cost and the inventory carrying costs. (See Figure 14.6.)

Ordering Cost. Ordering cost is the total of operating expenses for the ordering or purchasing department, the follow-up required, the operating expenses for the receiving department, the expenses incurred in paying invoices, and, in many cases, an allocation of the data-processing costs related to purchasing and acquisition of inventory. The cost is then divided by the number of orders placed per year to arrive at an ordering cost per order.

Carrying Cost.   Carrying cost is the total of all the expenses involved in maintaining inventory. Such expenses include the cost of capital tied up in idle merchandise, the cost of obsolescence, space charges, handling charges, insurance costs, property taxes, losses due to depreciation, losses stemming from deterioration, and losses resulting from the inability to use the capital involved in other ways. In the examples that follow we will use 24 percent per year (2 percent per month) of the unit cost per year—a fairly typical figure for most businesses.

You can figure out the EOQ using this formula:[16]

$$EOQ = \sqrt{\frac{2 \times \text{average usage} \times \text{ordering cost}}{\text{unit cost} \times \text{carrying cost } (\%)}}$$

Average usage (units sold)—600 per year*
Ordering cost—$48 per order
Unit cost (not selling price)—$24
Carrying cost—24% per year*

$$EOQ = \sqrt{\frac{2 \times 600 \times 48}{24 \times 0.24}} = 100 \text{ (or two months' usage)}$$

* Must be in same time units.

EOQ should be used carefully. The basic assumptions of the economic lot size or economic order quantity model are as follows: (1) Usage is at a constant rate throughout the year; (2) the price of inventory items is constant, that is, no quantity discounts are available; and (3) carrying costs are linear, based on the average inventory.[17]

Establishing Procedures for Processing Orders

An efficient inventory control system goes a long way toward reducing order cycle time. Another important activity is the establishment of an effective order-processing system (the fourth physical distribution function).

The starting point of an order-processing system is the placement of an order by a customer. A salesperson transmits the order to the office (this is the order-transmittal time), usually on a standardized order form. As the order enters the system, management must monitor two flows: the flow of goods and the flow of information. (See Figure 14.7.)

The importance of proper order processing cannot be overemphasized. Slow shipment, incorrect merchandise, or partially

FIGURE 14.7   **The Path of a Customer's Order**

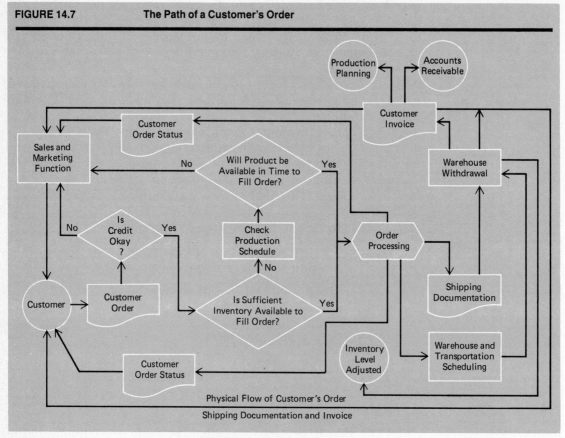

Source: Bernard LaLonde and John Grashof, "The Role of Information Systems in Physical Distribution Management," in Donald Bowersox, Bernard LaLonde, and Edward Smykay, Readings in *Physical Distribution Management* (New York: Macmillan, 1969), p. 197.
Note: All of the connecting lines in the figure are flows of information except the "Physical Flow of Customer's Order."

filled orders can create just as much dissatisfaction as stockouts or slow delivery. The flows of goods and information must be continually monitored so that mistakes can be corrected before the bill is submitted to the customer and the merchandise shipped.

Selecting Modes of Transportation

Shipping brings up the question of which mode of transportation should be used (the fifth function of physical distribution). The usage rates of the five major modes of freight transportation are shown in Table 14.3.

The modes of transportation actually selected by the firm will depend on the unique needs of the shipper. Table 14.4 ranks each mode of transportation relative to important service characteristics.

TABLE 14.3	1975 Revenue Ton Miles (Millions)	
		Percent
Rail	752,816	33.0
Air	4,000	0.2
Water (domestic)	568,755	25.0
Pipeline	488,000	21.0
Truck	488,000	21.0
Total	2,301,571	

Source: U.S. Department of Transportation, Office of Public Affairs, *Transportation USA* (Washington, D.C., Fall 1976), p. 3.

TABLE 14.4	Service Rankings of the Basic Modes of Transportation				
Speed	**Frequency**	**Dependability**	**Payload Flexibility**	**Points Served**
Air	Pipeline	Pipeline	Water	Highway
Highway	Highway	Highway	Rail	Rail
Rail	Air	Rail	Highway	Air
Water	Rail	Water	Air	Water
Pipeline	Water	Air	Pipeline	Pipeline

Source: Adapted from J. L. Heskett, Robert M. Ivie, and Nicholas A. Glaskowsky, Jr., *Business Logistics* (New York: Ronald Press, 1964), p. 71.

INSTITUTIONS THAT FACILITATE PHYSICAL DISTRIBUTION
Small-Shipment Carriers

The most innovative and progressive small freight shipper is Federal Express. Started by a young Vietnam War veteran in the early 1970s, Federal has mushroomed in popularity among shippers. Its rates have generally been lower than those of other small-shipment carriers, and its customer service has been superb. The key to Federal's success was the acquisition of its own private fleet of small jets that fan out from Memphis, Tennessee, every evening.

All freight is returned to Memphis late at night, resorted, and flown to its new destination before the beginning of working hours on the next day. Thus a Federal truck will pick up merchandise in, say, El Paso at 5:00 P.M. and it will be sitting on the client's desk in New York early the next morning. Federal handled about 19,000 packages a night in 1976 and served 31,000 shippers with 41 Falcon jets.[18]

Freight Forwarders

Freight forwarders collect less-than-carload shipments from a number of shippers and consolidate them into carload lots. Their rates are equivalent to less-than-carload rates, but the forwarder pays carload rates; thus their profit comes from the difference between the two rates. Unlike Federal Express, forwarders do not own their long-haul equipment. Instead, they use available modes of transportation. Most offer pickup and delivery service along with the speed and efficiency of handling carload merchandise. Historically, ground freight forwarders have handled consumer durable goods such as clothing, sporting equipment, and appliances.[19]

LEGAL CARRIERS
Private Carriers

Some shippers may decide to provide their own transportation— private carriers—rather than using other carriers. Private carriers (company-owned transportation equipment) normally cannot haul goods for other firms, since they're not in the transportation business. When customized operations are necessary or special equipment is required, private ownership may be the only feasible solution to a company's problem. Generally, however, an economical operation requires that shipment be limited to a relatively few destinations and that volume be sufficient to justify the costs of private carriage. Better control, reliability of delivery, and rate increases by public carriers have stimulated greater utilization of private ownership.

Common Carriers

At the other extreme is the common carrier. Common carriers offer to transport goods for hire without discrimination among shippers. Rates are published and are identical for the same quantities and types of freight among all shippers. Common carriers are highly regulated, resulting in a complex array of regulations, operating routes, and time schedules.

The number of common carriers—there are over 14,500 motor carriers, for example—means that the flexibility and availability of service are very high.[20] This is often a powerful incentive for many shippers to use common carriers rather than establishing their own fleets. Partially loaded trucks, empty backhauls, and uneconomical routing have long been the nemesis of private carriers.

Contract Carriers

Contract carriers, a third type of legal carrier, limit their service to one or a few shippers. Contract times may range from a few months to several years. If goods are moved across state lines, the contract carrier is subject to many of the same regulations that govern common carriers. Some shippers prefer contract carriers because they gain most of the advantages of private carriage without the costs of equipment ownership.

Exempt Carriers

Exempt carriers need only conform to the licensing and safety laws of the states in which they operate. Exempt carriage had its origin in agriculture, in which unprocessed farm products could be hauled to major processing centers under certain exemptions. Today such exemptions cover many product categories as well as certain geographic regions (usually around metropolitan areas). For example, it would be almost impossible to "keep up" administratively with all local delivery trucks in a big city.

TRENDS IN
PHYSICAL
DISTRIBUTION
Better Organization

One important trend is the broadening of the scope, functions, and power of distribution/logistics managers.[21] The need for better service and cost control in most companies will continue to amplify the importance of distribution.

More Red Tape

On the regulatory front, transportation will probably continue to be bogged down in bureaucratic red tape. Although the Department of Transportation has paid lip service to greater flexibility in rate setting and fewer restrictions on carriers, little has been done in the way of follow-up.[22] The bankruptcy of the Penn Central Railroad, among others, coupled with the precarious financial situation of many railroads, may ultimately mean nationalization of the rail system. Conrail, a quasi-public system created from the ruins of Penn Central, is a step in that direction.

Shared Services

A third trend is toward greater use of shared services. Increased use of freight forwarders, shippers' associations, and other freight consolidators exemplifies this trend. Also, the growth of public warehousing and the establishment of national chains of public warehouses testify to the economies that may stem from the sharing of facilities and carriers. Tight money (loans difficult to obtain at reasonable interest rates) in this capital-intensive function is a further inducement to logistics managers to share services. Such sharing will occur in the areas of data processing, pallet exchanges, and freight bill payment systems.[23]

The Energy Crisis

America's energy crisis will continue to have an important long-run impact on distribution. Continually increasing energy costs will force distribution/logistics managers to push for greater productivity. The railroads may emerge as our primary carrier because of their energy efficiency relative to other modes of transportation.

New Technology

New materials-handling technology will be developed as labor costs continue their upward climb. Energy-efficient conveyor systems, lifts, and protective packaging will further reduce the need for human cargo handling.

The Role of
Consumerism

Consumerism will create a demand for better handling to reduce the quantity of damaged merchandise. The importance of sanitation in distribution will also expand. Already several major food chains have been placed under criminal indictment as a result of unsanitary conditions in their warehouses.[24]

Some manufacturers are constructing systems for tracing and recalling everything that they produce. This will present even greater challenges to logistics managers. Model numbers will no longer suffice—now it is often necessary to know the package number, the city where the item was sold, and to whom it was sold.

SUMMARY

Physical distribution consists of all business activities that are concerned with transporting finished inventory and/or raw-material assortments so that they arrive at the designated place when needed and in usable condition. The goal of physical distribution is to minimize total distribution costs relative to a predetermined level of service. Cost minimization per se can lead to disastrous results unless the impact on the quality of service is considered. The best measure of good distribution service is order cycle time. This is the elapsed time between the initial effort to place an order and the customer's receipt of the order in good condition.

In order to lower distribution costs one must consider the interrelationships among many factors, such as finished-goods inventory, number of warehouses, fixed warehouse expenses, and transportation costs. Sometimes, for example, the high cost of air transportation is offset by the reduction in the number of warehouses needed and in inventory requirements.

Specific physical-distribution functions include determining warehouse locations, establishing a materials-handling system, maintaining an inventory control system, establishing procedures for processing orders, and selecting modes of transportation.

An inventory control system has three basic elements: ordering costs, inventory carrying costs, and the cost of lost sales or stockouts. Stockouts can be avoided by maintaining safety stocks. However, large safety stocks increase the cost of inventory.

One of the most demanding tasks of physical distribution is selecting the proper mode of transportation. Railroads have long been the backbone of U.S. freight transportation. Trucks are America's most flexible mode of transportation, yet their rates are often higher than those of other modes for the long haul. Air freight is the most expensive but also the fastest form of freight transportation.

Several types of legal carriers exist to serve shippers. There are private carriers that do not haul goods for other firms; common carriers that offer to transport goods for hire without discriminating among shippers; contract carriers that limit their service to one or a few shippers; and exempt carriers that conform only to the laws of the states in which they operate. The many types of carriers and the vast array of products carried have led to an extremely complex set of freight rates.

Marketing managers can expect to see more red tape in the area of physical distribution. However, this problem is being partially offset by better physical-distribution organization and management.

For example, many physical-distribution managers are turning to shared services such as freight forwarders and shipping associations in order to lower distribution costs.

KEY TERMS

Physical distribution
Logistical coordination
Materials management
Order cycle time
Public warehouse
Distribution center
Containerization
Economic order quantity (EOQ)

Ordering cost
Carrying cost
Freight forwarder
Private carrier
Common carrier
Contract carrier
Exempt carrier

QUESTIONS FOR DISCUSSION

1. Explain the terms *logistical coordination* and *materials management* in the context of the physical-distribution function.
2. What are the objectives of a good physical-distribution system? How important is the cost factor?
3. What factors must be considered in locating a warehouse?
4. What is a distribution center? How does it differ from a warehouse?
5. Define the terms *ordering cost* and *carrying cost*. How do they affect the firm's inventory control system?
6. What is meant by economic order quantity? What assumptions underlie this concept? Do you think this concept can be used successfully by all firms?
7. Explain the role that freight forwarders play in the physical-distribution process. How do they differ from small-shipment carriers?
8. Briefly outline some of the applications of the computer in the physical-distribution area.
9. What are some of the factors that are expected to influence distribution trends in the future?
10. What is meant by order cycle time? Why is it such an important element of the total marketing mix?
11. Explain the importance of physical distribution to marketing managers.

NOTES

1. Donald Bowersox, "Physical Distribution Development, Current Status, and Potential," *Journal of Marketing,* 33 (January 1969): 63–70.
2. This material is taken from Donald Bowersox, *Logistical Management* (New York: Macmillan, 1974), pp. 14–15.
3. "Slow Deliveries Dog the Kodak Instants," *Business Week,* July 26, 1976, p. 43.
4. Daniel DeHayes, Jr., and Robert Taylor, "Moving Beyond the Physical Distribution Organization," *Transportation Journal,* Spring 1974, pp. 30–41; see also Peter Lynagh, "Physical Distribution Seventies Style," *Business Perspectives,* 4 (Summer 1973): 28–31.
5. "Olympia Brewing Aims to Go National," *Business Week,* September 20, 1976, pp. 32–33.
6. Richard E. Snyder, "Physical Distribution Costs," *Distribution Age,* 62 (December 1963): 35–42.

7. Wendell Stewart, "Physical Distribution: Key to Improved Volume and Profits," *Journal of Marketing*, 29 (January 1965): 65–70.

8. The terms in this paragraph are taken from William Perreault and Frederick Russ, "Physical Distribution Service in Industrial Purchase Decisions," *Journal of Marketing*, 38 (April 1976): 3–10; see also their "Physical Distribution Service: A Neglected Aspect of Marketing Management," *MSU Business Topics*, Summer 1974, pp. 37–45.

9. Ibid.

10. Bowersox, "Physical Distribution Development," p. 66.

11. Marjorie Person and Diane Mitchell, "Distribution Centers: The Fort Wayne Experience," *Business Horizons*, 18 (August 1975): 89–95. Copyright, 1975, by the Foundation for the School of Business at Indiana University. Reprinted by permission.

12. Vincent Gallagher, "Distributing Line," *Transportation and Distribution Management*, May-June 1974, pp. 50–51; see also Arthur M. Geoffrion, "Better Distribution Planning with Computer Models," *Harvard Business Review*, July-August 1976, pp. 92–99.

13. "Material Handling for Distribution," *Handling and Shipping*, January 1976, p. 39.

14. Jacob Merriwether, Gunnar Sletmo, and Orville Goodin, "Distribution Efficiency and Worldwide Productivity," *Columbia Journal of World Business*, Winter 1974, p. 90.

15. C. G. Chentnik, "Inventory: Controlling Its Costs," *Transportation and Distribution Management*, May-June 1976, p. 23. Reprinted by permission.

16. D. B. Moritz, "Cut Costs by Controlling Inventory Level," *Supervisory Management*, September 1975, p. 19.

17. James Don Edwards and Roger Roemunich, "Scientific Inventory Management," *MSU Business Topics*, Autumn 1975, p. 42.

18. "Why Airlines Fear the Federal Express Bill," *Business Week*, September 13, 1976, p. 116.

19. For an excellent article on the future of freight forwarders, see Jim Dixon, "Which Way for Forwarders?" *Distribution Worldwide*, June 1975, pp. 39–42.

20. Bowersox, *Logistical Management*, p. 152.

21. Bernard LaLonde and Douglas Lambert, "Research: The PD Manager 1972–1975," *Transportation and Distribution Management*, March-April 1976, pp. 33–36; see also Bernard LaLonde and Douglas Lambert, "Survey: The PD Executive Profile," *Transportation and Distribution Management*, May-June 1976, pp. 37–40.

22. U.S. Department of Transportation, *A Statement of National Transportation Policy* (Washington, D.C., 1975), pp. 1–22; see also "Will Politics Change Transportation?" *Traffic Management*, January 1976, pp. 29–44.

23. Walter Friedman, "Physical Distribution: The Concept of Shared Services," *Harvard Business Review*, March-April 1975, pp. 24–36.

24. Kenneth Ackerman, "Physical Distribution—A New Business Revolution," *Business Horizons*, 17 (October 1974): 63–66.

CASE 14
American Photo Art

Ed Gerloff, an avid amateur photographer and inventor, spent many long nights and weekends in his garage perfecting a unique way of displaying photographs. Essentially, the process involved floating the image emulsions off the photograph and onto an artist's canvas and then bonding the materials under pressure and heat. The final product is a photograph impregnated in artist's canvas.

Gerloff was elated that he had in fact developed a new product. It was neither an art print nor a photograph but a combination of both. The product was impressive enough to attract the financial backing of four acquaintances, who helped Gerloff form American Photo Art. Equipment constraints meant that sizes must be limited to 24 by 30 inches and 30 by 40 inches; all pictures were framed in one-inch brushed aluminum with a choice of silver or bronze colors. It was decided that the first offering would be entitled "America the Beautiful" and consist of ten pictures, each submitted by a recognized outdoor photographer. The wholesale prices were $40 for the smaller pictures and $55 for the larger ones. It was believed that most retailers would simply double the wholesale price.

After consulting his backers, Gerloff decided that wholesaling offered the greatest opportunity for success, given their limited budget and manpower. The full-time organization consisted of one full-time production worker, one of the financial backers, Pat Calabro, and of course, Gerloff. The other backers held full-time jobs and agreed to help "whenever they could."

Calabro, who had been a furniture manufacturer's representative before joining Photo Art, suggested that interior decorators would be ideal prospects for a direct-mail campaign using all the photographs and an explanation of the process in brochures. She argued that this approach, coupled with a trade ad in *Interior Design* and *Modern Interiors,* should be very successful. Costs were estimated at $14,000 for 25,000 mail pieces and two quarter-page, four-color ads.

Gerloff wasn't against promoting to interior decorators but felt that the market was broader than that. Indeed, he recognized the importance of prospective buyers actually seeing the new product. He believed that obtaining space at decorative-accessory trade shows would be much more beneficial. These shows are attended by buyers for major department stores and specialty shops as well as interior decorators. They are held in major U.S. cities two to four times a year. Temporary exhibition space is relatively inexpensive ($150–225 for approximately 120 square feet). The only major costs would be travel expenses for each six-day show and a one-time $5000 fee for display facilities that could easily be transported from city to city.

1. What are the advantages and disadvantages of each of the suggested alternatives?
2. Are there any critical factors that Gerloff may have overlooked?
3. What channel would you recommend for American Photo Art?
4. Are there other distribution alternatives that may have been overlooked?

V The Nature of Pricing

15

Demand-Oriented Pricing Concepts

OBJECTIVES

■ To understand the importance of pricing to the American economy.
■ To become aware of different pricing objectives.
■ To learn the nature and elasticity of demand.
■ To discuss price leadership and price discrimination.
■ To understand the concept of demand estimation.

This chapter introduces you to pricing objectives, price theory, and the nature of demand. The chapter begins with a discussion of pricing's role in our economic system. Next, the importance of price to marketing managers and pricing objectives are discussed. We then turn to elasticity theory, price leadership, and price discrimination. The chapter concludes with a look at demand estimation in theory and practice.

We live in a mixed capitalist free-enterprise society that depends primarily on a complex system of prices to allocate goods and services among consumers, governments, and businesses. A mixed economy is one in which both the government and the private sector exercise economic control. Free enterprise refers to the right to engage in virtually any economic enterprise. You can be a doctor or a salesperson or almost anything else provided that you have the necessary qualifications. The American government plays a minor role in guiding business endeavors compared to the governments of most countries.

Since the government plays a minor role in resource allocation, something else must fulfill the role of allocator in our society. Consumers play this role quite nicely through the exercise of "dollar votes." If people believe that a merchant has established a fair price for a good or service, they vote for (purchase) that product. Business firms that do a good job in satisfying the needs of the consumer receive more dollar votes (sales). The earned revenue may then be used by the firm to purchase additional resources to produce more goods and services. Companies that don't satisfy the consumer (and thus lack dollar votes) cannot effectively compete for resources and eventually switch their production to another product or go out of business.

THE IMPORTANCE OF PRICE
Price and the Marketing Mix

It is evident that prices play a major role in determining which firms survive and which ones don't. Marketing executives have begun to notice the importance of pricing in the marketing mix. This has not always been the case, as Table 15.1 shows. The survey represented in the table crossed many industrial lines and included manufacturers of industrial and consumer goods, transportation companies, and utilities.

TABLE 15.1   Comparison of 1964 and 1975 Rankings of Marketing Activities

Marketing Activity	1975 Rank Order of Importance	1964 Rank Order of Importance
Pricing	1	6
Customer services	2	5
Sales personnel management	3	3
Product research and development	4	1
Marketing cost budgeting and control	5	9
Physical distribution	6	11
Market research	7	2
Marketing organization structure	8	7
Advertising and sales promotion planning	9	4
Distribution channel control	10	8
Extending customer credit	11	10
Public relations	12	12

Source: Robert A. Robicheaux, "How Important Is Pricing in Competitive Strategy?" in Henry W. Nash and Donald P. Robin, eds., *Proceedings, The Southern Marketing Association 1975 Conference.*

Why Pricing Is So Important

Pricing increased in strategic importance (from the sixth position to the first) during the late 1960s and early 1970s primarily because of changes in the external environment. In the early 1960s supply exceeded market demand in many industries. The downward pressure on prices resulted in many firms either meeting competition or tacitly colluding with other firms in their industry.[1] Also, the rapidly rising affluence of American consumers during the early 1960s pushed prices into the background.

Today, shortages of critical raw materials, inflation, recessions, high unemployment, threats of governmental regulation, the costs of pollution controls, rising consumerism, and skyrocketing energy costs have forced marketing managers to become more price conscious. While pricing is considered the most crucial marketing activity by manufacturers of consumer and industrial goods, it is ranked only third among transportation and utility companies. (See Table 15.2.) Perhaps the price insensitivity of the latter group is due to heavy governmental regulation and a general lack of competition.

PRICING OBJECTIVES
Realistic Pricing Objectives

Companies need objectives that are concrete, attainable, and measurable. Realistic pricing goals require periodic monitoring in order to determine the effectiveness of the company's pricing strategy. Although profit maximization is often advocated by economists, it doesn't provide managers with criteria for evaluating performance. Many firms do not have adequate accounting data for maximizing profits in a normative sense (i.e., so that marginal costs equal marginal

TABLE 15.2	Rankings of Marketing Activities by Different Types of Companies[a]	
Manufacturers of Industrial Goods	**Manufacturers of Consumer Goods**	**Transportation and Utility Companies**
1. Pricing	1. Pricing	1. Customer service
2. Customer service	2. Product research and development[b]	2. Public relations
3. Sales personnel management	3. Sales personnel management	3. Pricing
4. Product research	4. Customer services	4. Sales personnel management
5. Physical distribution	5. Marketing cost budgeting and control	5. Marketing cost budgeting and control

Source: Robert A. Robicheaux, "How Important Is Pricing in Competitive Strategy?" in Henry W. Nash and Donald P. Robin, eds., *Proceedings, The Southern Marketing Association 1975 Conference.*

[a] Ranked by mean rating on a seven-point scale from unimportant (1) to extremely important (7).

[b] Product research and development and sales personnel management were tied for second.

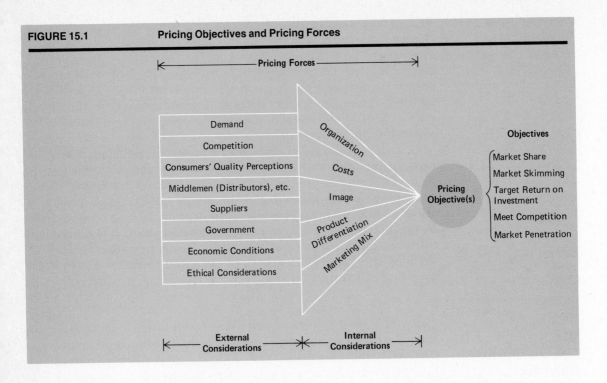

FIGURE 15.1   **Pricing Objectives and Pricing Forces**

profits). Realistic and measurable pricing goals include target return on investment, market share, and several others to be discussed in the following paragraphs. (See Figure 15.1.)

Target Return on Investment

Alcoa, DuPont, General Electric, General Motors, International Harvester, Union Carbide, and Johns-Manville have a target return on investment as their principal pricing goal.[2] In the large corporations studied by the economist John Lanzillotti, the average target return was about 14 percent of invested capital after taxes.

A target return enables a company to establish the level of profits that it feels will yield a satisfactory return. The marketing executive can use the standard to determine whether a particular price–and–marketing-mix combination is feasible. Any given mix and price either will attain the target return or will not do so. In addition, the manager must weigh the risk of a given strategy even if the return is in the acceptable range.

Market Share

Many companies believe that maintaining or increasing their market share is a key to the effectiveness of their marketing mix. Research organizations such as A. C. Nielson and Ehrhart-Babic provide excellent market share reports for many different industries. Thus many firms can determine their market share. Most important, market share and return on investment are strongly related, as is shown in Figure 15.2. On the average, a difference of ten percentage points in market share is accompanied by a difference of about five points in pretax return on investment (ROI). A larger market share probably increases profitability because of greater economies of scale, market power, and ability to adequately compensate top-quality management.[3] American Can, Kroger, Sears, Swift, and Exxon have all made maintaining or increasing market share their primary pricing objective.[4]

Meeting Competition

A less aggressive pricing strategy, followed by many companies such as Goodyear, Gulf, and National Steel, is to meet competition.[5] Usually this goal is easier to accomplish than those just mentioned and requires relatively little planning. Often firms competing in an industry in which there is an established price leader (e.g., steel) follow the passive policy of meeting the competition. As a result these industries typically have fewer price wars than those in which firms engage in direct price competition.

THE NATURE OF DEMAND

When pricing goals are primarily sales oriented, as is true of market share, cost considerations are usually subordinated to demand considerations. Demand refers to the quantity of a company's product that will be purchased during a specific period and at various prices.

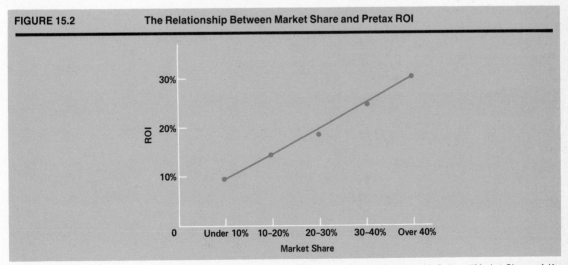

FIGURE 15.2   **The Relationship Between Market Share and Pretax ROI**

Source: Robert D. Buzell, Bradley T. Gale, and Ralph G. M. Sultan, "Market Share—A Key to Profitability," *Harvard Business Review*, 53 (January-February 1975): 98. Copyright © 1974 by the President and Fellows of Harvard College; all rights reserved.

Elasticity of Demand

To fully appreciate demand analysis you should understand the concept of elasticity.[6] Elasticity of demand refers to the responsiveness or the sensitivity of consumers to changes in price. If they are sensitive, demand is elastic; if they are insensitive, demand is inelastic. Elasticity over a range of a demand curve can be measured by the following formula or by observing changes in total revenue:

$$\text{Elasticity} = \frac{\text{percentage change in quantity of good A}}{\text{percentage change in price of good A}}$$

If Σ is greater than 1, demand is elastic.
If Σ is less than 1, demand is inelastic.
If Σ is equal to 1, demand is unitary.

Assume that demand for American Product's goods are as shown in Figure 15.3. Demand for AP's product is found to be elastic from $5.00 through $1.00 because as the price decreases, total revenue rises. When the price falls to $.75, demand becomes inelastic. We can just as easily use the formula to measure elasticity. For example, if the price drops from $2.00 to $1.00, elasticity of demand is as follows:

$$\Sigma = \frac{\%\ \Delta Q^*}{\%\ \Delta P}$$

$$\Sigma = \frac{\dfrac{|\Delta Q|}{aoQ}}{\dfrac{|\Delta P|}{aoP}}$$

$$\Sigma = \frac{\dfrac{4785 - 2130}{2130 + 4785}}{\dfrac{2 - 1}{2}}$$

$$\Sigma = \frac{\dfrac{2655.0}{3457.5}}{\dfrac{1.00}{1.50}}$$

$$\Sigma = \frac{.767}{.666}$$

$$\Sigma = 1.15 \qquad \text{Demand is elastic.}$$

* Our illustrations utilize only arc elasticity. Point elasticity may be found by using the following formula:

$$\Sigma = \frac{\lim}{\Delta P \to 0} \frac{\Delta 0}{\Delta P} \times \frac{P}{Q}$$

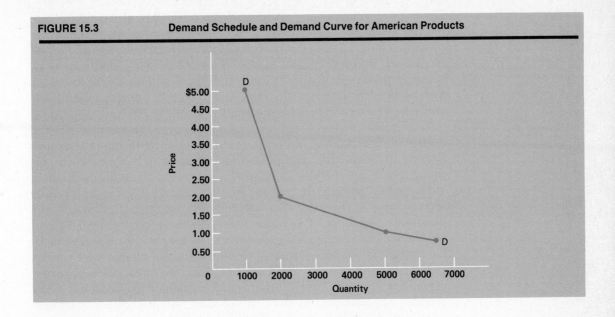

FIGURE 15.3   Demand Schedule and Demand Curve for American Products

Understanding Elasticity

Let's look at why demand was inelastic when the price fell from $1.00 to $.75. Remember, of course, that AP's demand schedule does not allow it to sell 4785 units for $1.00 and then sell an additional 6375 units at $.75 — instead, it's an "either–or" proposition. Therefore in order to sell 6375 we are sacrificing $.25 on 4785 units that could have been sold at $1.00 instead of the new price of $.75. The total sacrifice when the price is dropped from $1.00 to $.75 is $1196.25 (4785 × $.25). Demand must be sensitive enough to the price change to cover the sacrificed revenue or total revenue will fall (i.e., demand will be inelastic). Note that AP sold an additional 1590 units when it dropped the price to $.75. Thus the gross revenue gain from the price cut was $1192.50 ($.75 × 1590). AP's gain of $1192.50 was not enough to offset the $.25-per-unit loss ($1196.25) on the 4785 units that could have been sold for $1.00. Demand was inelastic because not enough additional sales were made when the price fell to $.75.

Elastic		Inelastic	
$P\uparrow$	$TR\downarrow$	$P\uparrow$	$TR\uparrow$
$P\downarrow$	$TR\uparrow$	$P\downarrow$	$TR\downarrow$

Factors That Affect Elasticity

Elasticity of demand is affected by a number of factors such as (1) the availability of substitute goods and services, (2) the price relative to a consumer's purchasing power, (3) the durability of a product, and (4) the other uses of a product. When a large number of substitute products are available, the consumer can easily switch from one brand to another, making demand elastic. If a price is so low that it is an inconsequential part of a firm's budget, demand will tend to be inelastic. For example, if the price of salt doubles, you will not stop putting salt and pepper on your eggs because salt is so cheap anyway.

Durable products such as automobiles often give consumers the option of repairing the old product rather than replacing it, thus prolonging its useful life. If a person had planned to buy a new car and the prices of automobiles suddenly began to rise, he or she might elect to fix the old one and drive it for another year. In other words, people are sensitive to the price increase and demand is elastic. Finally, the greater the number of product uses, the more elastic demand will tend to be. If a product has only one use, as may be true of a new medicine, there is not much chance that quantity purchased will vary as price varies. A person will consume only the prescribed quantity, regardless of price. On the other hand, a product like steel has many possible applications. As the price of steel falls it becomes more economically feasible to use it in a wide variety of applications, thus making demand relatively elastic.

THE FOUR MODELS OF COMPETITION

Demand-oriented pricing theory may be based on four different models: pure competition, monopolistic competition, oligopoly, or monopoly. Each of these models rests on a series of assumptions that may or may not exist in the "real world." Every firm, however, must operate either with or without direct competition, and its situation may approximate one of the four competitive models. Understanding the models will help you understand marketing price strategies and policies. They are discussed in any introductory economics textbook.

PRICE LEADERSHIP AND PRICE DISCRIMINATION
Price Leadership

Two common pricing phenomena encountered by marketing managers are price leadership and price discrimination. Let's examine each of these situations in turn.

The rigors of price competition have often caused one firm in an industry to assume the role of price leader. U.S. Steel, American Tobacco, Alcoa, International Harvester, DuPont, American Can, and General Motors have all served as price leaders in their respective industries.[7] Researchers have observed that a price leader is often the low-cost firm in the industry, as Figure 15.4 illustrates.

Theory of Leadership Pricing. The "typical firm" faces demand curve

FIGURE 15.4   **Price Leadership by a Low-Cost Firm**

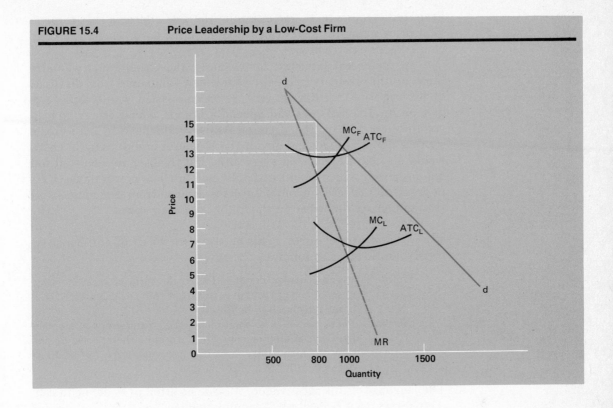

dd in the industry with a price leader. Our price leader is shown as having the lower set of cost curves (ATC_L and MC_L); the other firms in the industry have the higher set of cost curves (ATC_F and MC_F). As a result the low-cost leader establishes its price at $13.00 with an output of 1000 units. In contrast, the typical high-cost firm would like to charge $15.00 and sell 800 units.

Theoretically, the high-cost firms will follow the price leadership of the low-cost leader and sell their products at around $13.00. There may be a slight difference in price because the products are not homogeneous. Market power rests with the low-cost firm, since it can charge a price of, say, $8.00 and earn a profit. The $8.00 price is below the average total cost of the follower firms; thus it would drive them from the market in the long run. We should note, however, that extinction pricing by a low-cost firm is rare in practice.

Pricing Legislation Related to Market Structure. The possibility of action by the antitrust division of the Justice Department and the Federal Trade Commission (FTC) for monopolistic practices has led to high-cost firms setting the market price and dominant low-cost firms following suit. If, for example, the FTC decides that there is tacit price fixing through price leadership, the government often recommends drastic remedies.

In the cereal industry, for example, the Commission wants to break up the oligopoly by creating three new companies from divisions of Kellogg, the industry leader.[8] The Commission wants Kellogg to give up its Rice Krispies and Special K brands, among others, to help get the new firms going. General Mills would have to help create another new company and give it the Wheaties brand. General Foods would also have to develop a new firm, but the Commission staff has not suggested which brand it should give up. The power of the FTC to break up the cereal manufacturers is derived from three important acts, which are described in the following paragraphs.

The Sherman Act of 1890.   This act is at the heart of antimonopoly legislation. It reads as follows:

> Section 1. Every contract, combination in the form of trust or otherwise, or conspiracy, in restraint of trade or commerce . . . is hereby declared to be illegal. . . .
>
> Section 2. Every person who shall monopolize, or attempt to monopolize, or combine or conspire with any other person or persons, to monopolize . . . trade or commerce . . . shall be deemed guilty of a misdemeanor.

The language of this act is vague; it made no attempt to define in concrete terms what is meant by "combination" or "restraint" or "trade" or "monopolize." It thus left the way open for court rulings that made the law ineffective. Yet it did declare in forthright language the two main targets of antitrust action: (1) "restraint of trade"—restraining others from competing, and (2) "monopolizing"—eliminating, or trying to eliminate, competitors.

The Clayton Act of 1914.   In this law Congress tried to remedy the weaknesses of the Sherman Act by prohibiting four specific kinds of monopolizing behavior:

1. Discrimination in the prices charged to different buyers. (This prohibition was aimed both at local price cutting and at the granting of favored treatment to particular buyers, which gave them an unfair advantage over their rivals.)
2. Leasing or selling goods under "tying contracts." (A tying contract requires the lessee or buyer to refrain from using or dealing in the goods of any competitor.)
3. Combining two or more competing corporations by acquiring or pooling ownership of their stock. (This was aimed at the merger movement.)

4. Being a director of two or more competing corporations. (This was intended to prevent the suppression of competition by means of interlocking directorates.)

Since the purpose of the act was to preserve competition, the first three practices were forbidden only "where the effect . . . may be to substantially lessen competition or tend to create a monopoly." This qualifying clause seems fair and reasonable, yet it has made the job of prosecuting violators more difficult. In each individual case the government's lawyers must convince the judges that competition has been or might be adversely affected.

The Federal Trade Commission Act of 1914. Enacted at the same time as the Clayton Act, this law did two things. First, it established a new, independent agency, the Federal Trade Commission, to deal with antitrust matters. Second, it outlawed "unfair methods of competition." What methods were to be regarded as unfair? The law did not say. It left that decision to the new Commission.[9]

Price Discrimination

The Robinson–Patman Act. The Robinson–Patman Act of 1936 explicitly prohibits a seller from giving quantity discounts or charging different prices to different buyers, except to the extent that lower prices can be justified by lower costs. A firm can, however, lower a price to meet an equally low price of a competitor.[10]

Secret Deals. Price discrimination may take the form of a secret "special deal" in which a merchant gives a buyer a secret discount off list price. This will be profitable to the merchant as long as the revenue received is greater than the marginal cost. Also, as long as the deal is kept secret the discriminator's competitors won't lower their prices to meet this "new competition." Another advantage to the discriminator is that it can charge all of its other customers the higher list price and make a larger total profit.

ESTIMATING DEMAND
Demand Estimation in Practice

Demand-oriented pricing policies, and even price discrimination, are difficult or impossible to implement unless the firm has a reasonable estimate of demand. The use of demand estimation is not as widespread as the theoretical treatment of price might lead one to believe. A study found that slightly more than 50 percent of the responding companies engaged in some form of demand estimation.[11] Often the estimation is limited to choosing among two or three potential prices.

Two reasons why many firms don't attempt to estimate demand are (1) the sheer difficulty of the process and (2) the fact that the potential cost may be greater than the payout. Economists know that the law of demand — as prices fall, demand increases, and vice versa — holds in general. For example, from January 1975 to January 1976 retail coffee prices rose almost 19 percent and consumption declined 5 percent, to 31.6 gallons per capita.[12] Yet empirical research indicates that many demand curves are not smooth and negatively shaped. Studies by Pessemier and Tull show many unusual demand functions with positive slopes, kinks, and sudden backward bends.[13]

Actual Demand Curves

Bennett and Wilkinson systematically raised or lowered the prices of several products sold in a discount store.[14] The resulting demand curves are shown in Figure 15.5. Any number of factors might account for the unusual shape of the curves. Perhaps the kink in the Quaker State Oil at $.38 was due to previous stockpiling as the price fell below normal levels. In contrast, the M&M candy prices were gradually raised over a six-week period, resulting in a very elastic demand curve up to $.51. Buyer behavior is difficult to explain as the price rose to $.60.

The highly unusual demand curve for Bayer aspirin probably reflects strong brand loyalty and general price insensitivity. Janitor in a Drum's price started at $.95 and was lowered 10 percent a week until it reached $.56. Again, the backward kink at $.62 may reflect previous stockpiling.

Studies of durable goods conducted for longer periods have found the price elasticity of demand to be 0.5 for housing, -1.07 to -2.06 for refrigerators, and -0.6 to -1.1 for automobiles.[15] Since automobiles are generally marked up 13.5 percent and jewelry and gifts 43 percent, this would imply that demand for the latter items is less elastic. Thus knowing traditional markups and using good judgment will result in demand estimates based on experience.

Statistical Estimation of Demand

Experience can be carried a step further by using statistical analysis to examine past sales and prices. Simple least-squares regression analysis may show that for every $1.00 increase in price, sales will decline by 412 units.* If the variation in quantity sold may be largely "explained" by price variations (a high coefficient of determination), then merchants may use the information as a reliable basis for building a demand curve.

Simple regression can be further extended by using multiple regression to examine a number of factors besides sales price that might influence demand. Factors such as inflation sales, competitors' prices, advertising volume, and retail stores selling the product may

---

* The idea of least-squares regression analysis is to fit a straight line to the points of a two-variable scatter diagram so as to minimize the sum of the squared vertical deviations between the points and the line, thus giving a "best fit."

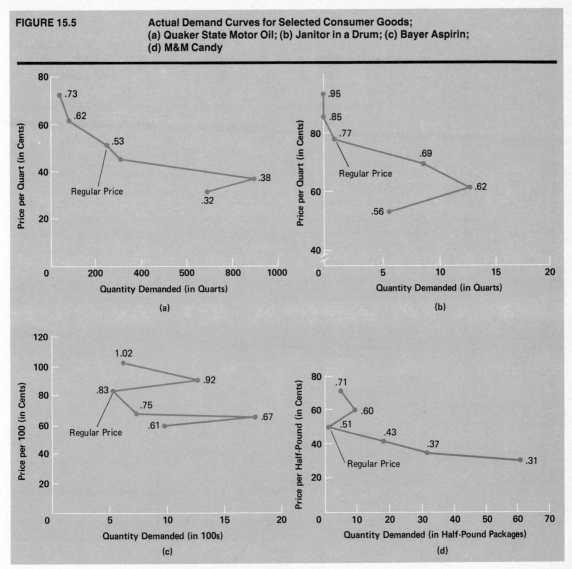

FIGURE 15.5   Actual Demand Curves for Selected Consumer Goods;
(a) Quaker State Motor Oil; (b) Janitor in a Drum; (c) Bayer Aspirin;
(d) M&M Candy

Source: From Sidney Bennett and J. B. Wilkinson, "Price-Quantity Relationships and Price Elasticity Under In-Store Experimentation," *Journal of Business Research*, 2 (January 1974): 30–34. By permission.

be included in the analysis to further refine the determinants of demand.

Laboratory experiments in which consumers pretend they are purchasing products were pioneered by Pessemier. Often, however, they are just that—pretending. Although the methodology of laboratory experimentation seems to be sound, unrealistic purchase conditions taint the usefulness of this technique.

SUMMARY

Price serves as an allocator of goods and services in our economic system. According to a recent survey, it is considered the most important marketing activity. In order to develop an effective price strategy, realistic objectives must be established. Objectives such as target return on investment, market share, and meeting competition are used by many large companies.

A sound pricing strategy requires accurate estimates of demand. One of the most important concepts in demand estimation is elasticity of demand. Elasticity refers to the responsiveness of consumers to changes in price. Elasticity is affected by the availability of substitute goods and services, the price of the product, durability, and other uses of the product.

Sometimes prices are established on the basis of price leadership. In other situations firms may attempt to increase profits by charging different prices to different purchasers. This practice is prohibited under the Robinson–Patman Act. The Sherman Act of 1890 and the Clayton Act also prohibit price discrimination.

It is difficult to establish a demand-oriented pricing strategy without a reasonable estimate of demand. Many firms do not attempt to estimate the demand curve because of the difficulty and cost involved. Actual demand curves often have very unusual shapes and rarely conform to traditional demand curves.

KEY TERMS

Price	Meeting competition
Mixed economy	Demand
Free enterprise	Elasticity of demand
Profit maximization	Price leadership
Target return on investment	Price discrimination
Market share	Demand curve

QUESTIONS FOR DISCUSSION

1. Explain the role of prices in resource allocation.
2. What is profit maximization? Is it feasible in practice? Justify your answer.
3. What are some of the pricing goals of large corporations?
4. Explain the concept of elasticity of demand. How does it affect pricing policy?
5. Outline some of the factors that affect elasticity of demand. Can you give examples to support your answer?
6. What is price leadership? Under what conditions is this type of pricing policy successful?
7. Explain the concept of price discrimination. How does the Robinson–Patman Act affect this practice?
8. Give some examples of products for which demand is elastic and some for which demand is inelastic.
9. What are some of the difficulties marketing managers face in making accurate estimates of future demand?
10. Discuss the role of governmental regulation in the pricing sphere.

NOTES

1. Robert A. Robicheaux, "How Important Is Pricing in Competitive Strategy?" in Henry W. Nash and Donald P. Robin, eds., *Proceedings, The Southern Marketing Association 1975 Conference;* see also Jon G. Udell, "How Important Is Pricing in Competitive Strategy?" *Journal of Marketing,* 28 (January 1964): 44–48.
2. Robert F. Lanzillotti, "Pricing Objectives in Large Companies," *American Economic Review,* December 1958, pp. 921–940.
3. Robert D. Buzzell, Bradley T. Gale, and Ralph G. M. Sultan, "Market Share — A Key to Profitability," *Harvard Business Review,* January–February 1975, pp. 97–106.
4. Lanzillotti, p. 928.
5. Ibid.
6. For an interesting discussion of profits and elasticity, see John F. Nask, "A Note on Cost–Volume–Profit Analysis and Price Elasticity," *The Accounting Review,* 50 (April 1975): 384–490; for research on the relationships between price and quantity and between price and elasticity, see Arch G. Woodside and J. Taylor Sims, "Retail Experiment in Pricing a New Product," *Journal of Retailing,* 50 (Fall 1974): 56–65.
7. F. M. Sherer, *Industrial Pricing: Theory and Evidence* (Chicago: Rand McNally, 1970), pp. 38–47.
8. "FTC Tells Cereal Plan: Break Up Three Leaders, Take Away Some Brands," *Advertising Age,* March 22, 1976, pp. 1f.
9. Lawrence Abbott, *Economics and the Modern World,* 2d ed. (New York: Harcourt Brace Jovanovich, 1967), pp. 564–565.
10. For an excellent discussion of the cost defense of the Robinson–Patman Act, see B. J. Linder and Allan H. Savage, "Price Discrimination and Cost Defense — Change Ahead?" *MSU Business Topics,* Summer 1971, pp. 22–26.
11. Mark Alpert, *Pricing Decisions* (Glenview, Ill.: Scott, Foresman, 1971), p. 78.
12. John C. Maxwell, "Price Boosts Hurt Coffee Consumption, Maxwell Says," *Advertising Age,* April 12, 1976, p. 8.
13. Edgar A. Pessemier, "An Experimental Method for Estimating Demand," *Journal of Business,* 33 (October 1960): 373–383, *Experimental Methods of Analyzing Demand for Branded Consumer Goods with Applications to Problems in Marketing Strategy* (Pullman: Washington State University, 1963), "Forecasting Brand Performance Through Simulation Experiments," *Journal of Marketing,* 28 (April 1964): 41–46, and "A New Way to Determine Buying Decisions," *Journal of Marketing,* 23 (October 1959): 41–46; also, Tull, Boring, and Gonsior, pp. 186–191. See also J. Douglas McConnell, "The Price–Quantity Relationship in an Experimental Setting," *Journal of Marketing Research,* 5 (August 1968): 300–303, and "Price Sensitivity of the Consumer," *Journal of Advertising Research,* 4 (December 1964): 40–44.
14. Sidney Bennett and J. B. Wilkinson, "Price–Quantity Relationships and Price Elasticity Under In-Store Experimentation," *Journal of Business Research,* 2 (January 1974): 30–34.
15. Arnold C. Harberger, *The Demand for Durable Goods* (Chicago: University of Chicago Press, 1960), pp. 3–14.

CASE 15
New Mexico Trailmaker Bus Line

New Mexico Trailmaker is a relatively small intrastate bus line headquartered in Albuquerque, New Mexico. The company was founded in 1949 by Al Goode. Goode received his basic training in Arizona during World War II and subsequently decided to move from his native state of Pennsylvania to the sunny Southwest. One driver was hired in 1949 to share the driving load with Goode on the line's only route, Albuquerque to Santa Fe. Over the years the line has prospered under good management; it now employs 187 people, who drive and maintain 41 buses.

John Zigler, vice president for accounting, came to Goode in July 1974 with a proposal that he felt would partially offset the decline in revenue–passenger miles experienced by trailmaker during the past twelve months. Zigler suggested that Trailmaker take advantage of the natural growth in tourist traffic that occurred every summer. Specifically, he recommended that an excursion fare be offered between Albuquerque and four major tourist destinations. Goode, a rather cautious man, reluctantly agreed to the rate decreases. He believed that this was an odd thing to do when total revenues were already declining, but he had trusted Zigler's advice for many years. The results of the excursion fare experiment are shown in Table 15.6.

In February 1975 Zigler proposed to Goode that Trailmaker petition the New Mexico Transportation Authority for permanent excursion fares between Albuquerque and Gallup, Santa Fe, and Carlsbad. El Paso was excluded because Trailmaker could not use the main bus terminal, since that would require crossing the Texas border and would put the firm in interstate competition. Instead, Trailmaker used a satellite station in suburban El Paso that was located just inside the New Mexico border. Zigler believed that the company's El Paso market consisted of people living or visiting in areas near the satellite station. These consumers liked the convenience of the suburban terminal and were less price sensitive than those in the other markets.

1. Should Goode go along with Zigler's recommendation?
2. Did the study reveal elastic or inelastic demand for bus service?
3. Does additional research need to be done? If so, what kind?

TABLE 15.6   Results of Trailmaker's Excursion Fare Experiment

			Number of Passengers		
Destination	One-Way Fare from Albuquerque	Special Excursion Fare June 1– August 30, 1974	Average Weekday, Month Before June 1, 1974	Average Weekday, June 1– August 30, 1974	Average Weekday, 3 Months After August 30, 1974
Gallup	$10.00	$ 8.00	312	401	341
Santa Fe	8.00	6.50	390	560	385
El Paso	14.00	10.00	30	75	70
Carlsbad	18.00	12.00	114	502	161

16

The Role of Cost
and Special Price
Determinants

OBJECTIVES

■ To appreciate the role of costs in determining prices.
■ To understand the meaning and applications of breakeven analysis.
■ To become aware of various other factors that affect pricing.

THE IMPORTANCE OF COSTS

Sometimes companies minimize or ignore the importance of demand and price their products laregly or solely on the basis of costs. Prices that are determined strictly on the basis of costs may be too high for the target market, thereby reducing or eliminating sales. On the other hand, cost-based prices might be too low, causing the firm to earn a lower return than it should.

This chapter begins with an examination of the types of costs encountered by businesses. We then discuss the relationships among costs, stock turnover, and profits. Next we turn to the concepts of breakeven and target return pricing, and the chapter concludes with an analysis of other factors that affect price.

Types of Costs

Economists use a variety of cost concepts in determining profitability and optimal output levels. The appendix on pages 317–318 depicts the cost schedules commonly used in price theory.

303

Markup Pricing

Markup pricing is the most popular method used by wholesalers and retailers in establishing a sales price. When the merchandise is received, the retailer adds a certain percentage to the figure to arrive at the retail price. An item that costs $1.80 and is sold for $2.20 carries a markup of $.40, or 18 percent. The initial markup is also referred to as the "mark-on." If the retailer had to cut the price to $2.00 before the product could be sold, the difference between the cost and the selling price would be only $.20, or 10 percent. The latter figure is called gross margin or maintained markup. You can easily see that the maintained markup reflects actual demand and is much more important than the mark-on.

Assume that a retailer determines from past records that operating costs are 32 percent of sales and profit is 7 percent. It can mark up its merchandise by 39 percent and both cover costs and earn a profit. However, if 7 percent is considered an unsatisfactory profit, the merchant will have to add more than 39 percent to the merchandise costs. There will be some markdowns, pilferage, and employee discounts. If these three factors amount to an additional 5 percent, the retailer will have to use a mark-on of 41.90 percent to earn a 7-percent profit. The formula is

$$\text{Mark-on} = \frac{\text{gross margin (39\%)} + \text{retail reduction (5\%)}}{100\% + \text{retail reductions (5\%)}}$$

$$= \frac{44\%}{105\%}$$

$$= 41.90\%$$

Thus to achieve a maintained margin of 39 percent we must use an initial markup of 41.90 percent.

Sometimes retailers must establish a retail price based on a predetermined maintained margin and the unit cost. Suppose a merchant wants a gross margin of 42 percent (on retail) and an item costs $3.46. The formula for determining the retail price is

$$\text{Retail price} = \frac{\text{cost (3.46)}}{100 - \text{mark-on (42\%)}} \times 100$$

$$= \frac{3.46}{58} \times 100$$

$$= \$5.97$$

A selling price of $5.97 will provide the merchant with the desired gross margin on retail.

Markups are often based on experience, yet this doesn't necessarily mean that they are established without forethought. Among the factors that often influence markups are the appeal of the merchandise to the customer, past response to the markup (an implicit demand consideration), the promotional value of the item, the seasonality of the goods, fashion appeal, the traditional selling price of the product, and competition. The majority of retailers find it important to deviate widely from any set markup because of considerations like those just mentioned.

Costs, Stock Turnover, and Profits

Stock turnover refers to the number of times during a given period (usually a year) that the average amount of goods on hand are sold. Following are two common techniques for calculating inventory turnover:

1. Opening inventory at retail $18,000
   Closing inventory at retail   4,200

        2) 22,200

   Average inventory at retail $11,100
   Net sales $48,200

   $$\frac{\$48,200}{\$11,100} = 4.34 = \text{stock turnover}$$

2. Opening inventory at cost $ 9,000
   Closing inventory at cost   2,100

        2) 11,100

   Average inventory at cost $ 5,550
   Cost of goods sold $24,087

   $$\frac{\$24,087}{\$ 5,550} = 4.34 = \text{stock turnover}$$

Rapid stock turnover may mean limited investment in inventory, less need for storage space, fresher merchandise, or fewer markdowns. Generally speaking, high stock turnovers lead to higher profits, as is shown in Table 16.1. There are exceptions to this rule, however. Assume, for example, that a dealer reduces its stock and holds sales constant (an increase in turnover). Purchasing in small quantities may mean the loss of quantity discounts; higher expenditures for receiving, checking, and marking merchandise; and greater correspondence and clerical costs.

THE BREAKEVEN CONCEPT

If the general relationship between higher markup and higher profits holds true, it will have a profound effect on the breakeven point, since costs per unit are assumed to be constant. Therefore total variable costs will increase in proportion to volume and total profits will become higher and higher the further sales go beyond the breakeven point. Breakeven theory determines what sales volume must be

TABLE 16.1	Rate of Stockturn and Profits in Selected Types of Retail Trade, 1975		
Line of Business (and Number of Concerns Reporting)	Net Profits on Net Sales (Percent)	Net Sales to Inventory (Times)	
Auto & home supply stores (47)	1.54	5.7	
Children's & infants' wear stores (37)	1.68	5.4	
Clothing & furnishings, men's & boys' (202)	1.72	4.5	
Department stores (280)	1.61	5.7	
Discount stores (180)	1.42	5.3	
Furniture stores (149)	2.00	4.5	
Gasoline service stations (70)	4.97	10.9	
Grocery stores (114)	0.94	16.1	
Household appliance stores (78)	1.20	4.7	
Jewelry stores (78)	3.79	3.0	
Motor vehicle dealers (69)	1.02	6.6	
Radio & television stores (45)	1.48	4.8	
Shoe stores (89)	1.34	3.7	
Women's ready-to-wear stores (175)	1.82	7.1	

Source: Dun's Review, 107 (September 1976): 91. Reprinted by permission of Dun's Review. Copyright, 1976, Dun & Bradstreet Publications Corporation.

reached for a product before the company "breaks even" (i.e., total costs equals total revenue).

The typical breakeven model assumes a given fixed cost and a constant average variable cost (variable cost per product). American Products has fixed costs of $2000, and the cost of labor and materials for each unit produced is $.50. Assume that it can sell up to 7000 units of its product at $1.00 without having to lower its price. Table 16.2 and Figure 16.1 illustrate AP's breakeven point.

Average variable costs increase by $.50 every time a new unit is produced, and total fixed costs remain constant at $2000 regardless of the level of output. Therefore 4000 units of output give AP $2000 in fixed costs and $2000 in total variable costs (4000 units × $.50), or $4000 in total costs. Revenue is also $4000 at 4000 units (4000 units × $1.00), giving a net profit of zero dollars at "breakeven." Notice that once the firm gets past the breakeven point the gap between TR and TC gets wider and wider, since both functions are assumed to be linear.

A simple formula for calculating breakeven quantities is as follows:

$$\text{Fixed-cost contribution (FCC)} = \text{price} - \text{AVC}$$
$$= \$1.50$$
$$= \$\ .50$$

TABLE 16.2   Costs and Revenue for American Products

Output	Total Fixed Costs	Average Variable Costs	Total Variable Costs	Average Revenue (Sales)	Total Revenue	Total Costs	Profit or Loss
500	$2000	$.50	$ 250	$1.00	$ 500	$2250	($1750)
1000	2000	.50	500	1.00	1000	2500	($1500)
1500	2000	.50	750	1.00	1500	2750	($1250)
2000	2000	.50	1000	1.00	2000	3000	($1000)
2500	2000	.50	1250	1.00	2500	3250	($ 750)
3000	2000	.50	1500	1.00	3000	3500	($ 500)
3500	2000	.50	1750	1.00	3500	3750	($ 250)
4000	2000	.50	2000	1.00	4000	4000	(0)[a]
4500	2000	.50	2250	1.00	4500	4250	$ 250
5000	2000	.50	2500	1.00	5000	4500	$ 500
5500	2000	.50	2750	1.00	5500	4750	$ 750
6000	2000	.50	3000	1.00	6000	5000	$1000

[a] Breakeven point.

$$\text{Breakeven quantity} = \frac{\text{total fixed costs (TFC)}}{\text{fixed-cost contribution (FCC)}}$$

$$= \frac{\$2000}{\$.50}$$

$$= 4000 \text{ units}$$

FIGURE 16.1   Breakeven Chart for American Products

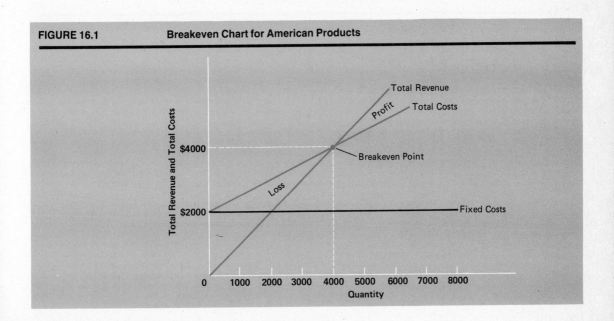

Advantages and Disadvantages of Breakeven Theory

The advantage of breakeven theory is that it provides a quick glance at how much the firm must sell to break even and how much profit can be earned if higher sales volume is obtained. If a firm is operating close to the breakeven point, it may want to see what can be done to reduce costs or find out whether any reasonable measures can be taken to increase sales. A final advantage is the fact that it is not necessary to compute marginal costs and marginal revenues. Often this is very important owing to the lack of "marginality" accounting data.

Breakeven theory is not without several important limitations. Sometimes it is very difficult to ascertain whether a cost is fixed or variable. For example, if labor wins a tough guaranteed-employment contract, are the resulting expenses a fixed cost? What about middle-echelon executives—are their costs fixed? More important than cost determination is the fact that simple breakeven theory ignores demand. How does American Products know that it can sell 4000 units at $1.00? Could it sell the same 4000 units at $2.00 or even $5.00? Obviously this would have profound effects on the firm's breakeven point.

The Modified Breakeven Concept

The usefulness of breakeven analysis can be increased with the addition of demand considerations. Figure 16.2 shows various revenue functions for American Products at different sales prices. Letters A through D represent the "best estimates" of actual demand (a demand

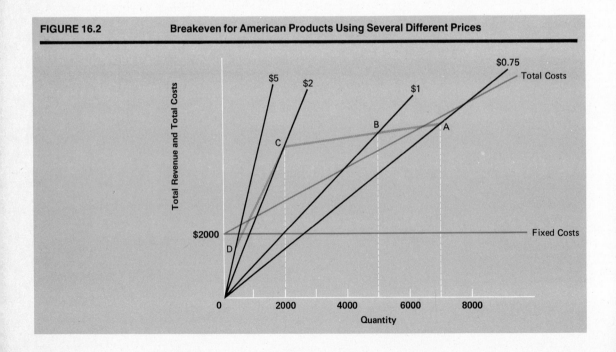

FIGURE 16.2   Breakeven for American Products Using Several Different Prices

curve) at various prices. If AP charges a price of $5.00, sales are estimated at 400 units and $2000 total revenue. Total costs will be $2000 fixed costs plus $200 variable costs (400 × $.50), or $2200. Thus if AP charges $5.00 a unit it will end up losing $200. Using the same procedure you can see that a price of $2.00 will be the most profitable for the company ($1050 total profit). Point C also represents the point farthest from the TC line, indicating the largest total profit.

TARGET RETURN PRICING

Target return pricing is the most popular method of choosing a selling price.[1] Merchants can easily figure a target return price by treating the desired profit as an addition to fixed cost. Desired profit, of course, is established by managerial judgment. If American Products has a desired profit of $900, it can be plugged into the basic formula as follows:

$$FCC = \$2.00 - \$.50 = \$1.50$$

$$Breakeven\ point = \frac{total\ fixed\ cost + total\ desired\ profit}{fixed\text{-}cost\ contribution\ per\ unit}$$

$$= \frac{\$2000 + \$900}{\$1.50}$$

$$= 1933.33\ units$$

American Products can easily achieve its target return on investment, assuming that its expected-value-of-output forecast is correct. Since AP requires only 1933 units to achieve its target return and expects to sell 2130 units at $2.00, the firm will exceed its target return.

Large firms that use target return pricing usually come quite close to their goals. (See Table 16.3.) Our example of target return pricing is simplified owing to space considerations. Many companies use much more sophisticated and detailed approaches to the calculation of target return.

TABLE 16.3				Comparison of Target Returns with Actual Returns for a Fifteen-Year Period			
Rate of Return	General Motors	Steel	Alcoa	Exxon (Standard Oil of New Jersey)	Dupont	Weighted Average	Un-weighted Average
Target	20.0%	8.0%	10.0%	12.0%	20.0%	14.6%	14.0%
Actual	20.2%	8.4%	9.5%	12.6%	22.2%	15.1%	15.1%
Deviation	0.2	0.4	−0.5	0.6	2.2	0.5	1.1

Source: David R. Kamerchen, "The Return of Target Pricing?" Journal of Business, 48 (April 1975): 244. Reprinted by permission of The University of Chicago Press. Copyright © 1975.

OTHER FACTORS THAT AFFECT PRICE

Many other factors besides demand and costs affect price. The stage of the product's life cycle, the competition, product distribution, promotion strategy, and perceived product quality can have an important impact on pricing strategy.

The Stage of the Product's Life Cycle

As a product moves through its life cycle, its demand and competitive conditions tend to change. Phillip W. Goodell, director of corporate market research for Bell and Howell, states that price strategy must always consider the product life cycle.[2] Prices are usually high during the introduction stage (but not always, as we will see in the next chapter) because demand originates in the core of the market and management hopes to cover developmental production costs. Prices generally begin to stabilize as the product enters the growth stage. Competitors enter the market, increasing the available supply. The product begins to appeal to broader, and often lower, income groups. Finally, economies of scale enable lower costs to be passed on to the consumer in the form of lower prices.

Maturity usually brings further price declines as competition increases and inefficient, high-cost firms are eliminated. Distribution channels are very complex and are a significant cost factor owing to wide product lines for highly segmented markets, extensive service requirements, and the sheer number of dealers necessary for high-volume production. The firms that remain in the market toward the end of the maturity stage typically offer similar prices. Only the most efficient remain, and they have comparable costs. The final stage of the life cycle, product decline, brings on further price declines as the few remaining competitors attempt to salvage the last vestiges of demand. When only one firm is left in the market, prices begin to stabilize, in fact they may eventually rise as the product moves into the specialty good category.[3]

The Competition

Competition, of course, varies during the product life cycle and at times may strongly influence pricing decisions. For example, although a firm may not have any competition, high prices can eventually influence another firm to enter the market. Tylenol, the nonaspirin pain reliever, had a stranglehold on its $60-million market for ten years. Johnson and Johnson's profit margin on this product was approximately 40 percent of sales. This plum looked so appealing to Bristol Myers that it jumped into the market with an almost identical product, Datril, in 1974.

Bristol Myers' marketing managers decided that the best way to obtain a significant market share quickly was through intensive price competition. Datril entered the market promoting its 100-tablet bottle at $1.85, claiming that this price averaged $1.00 lower than that of a comparable bottle of Tylenol.[4]

Competitors' actions can lead to spiraling inflation and, at times, deflation. When demand is strong one firm's price increase leads to a competitor's raising prices even further; this process feeds on itself. When the economy enters a period of decline the situation may reverse itself. Dayton Malleable Iron is a good example of the downward spiral. Dayton uses an escalation pricing formula based on scrap prices in Chicago, Cleveland, and Pittsburgh. In 1975 the scrap market began spiraling downward as one company tried to better the prices of its competitors. The average price eventually fell below Dayton's base and produced a negative surcharge.[5]

Distribution Strategy

Adequate distribution for a new product can often be attained by offering a larger-than-customary margin on the item. A variation on this strategy is to give dealers a large promotional allowance to help offset the costs of promotion and further stimulate demand at the retail level. An effective distribution network can often overcome other minor flaws in a marketing mix. Perhaps a price is perceived by consumers as being slightly higher than normal, but if the good is located in a convenient retail outlet they may go ahead and purchase it anyway.

Promotion Strategy

Price is often used as a promotional tool in order to increase consumer interest. Pick up your Thursday newspaper and turn to the grocery section. You will see ads for a number of products with special low prices designed to induce consumers to shop in a particular store. Manufacturers also place discount coupons in this section in the hope of influencing consumers to purchase their brand.

Manufacturers typically promote introductory price offers in order to help a product get through the introductory stage of the product life cycle. Salespeople will discount list prices in order to close deals that might otherwise go to competitors. Manufacturers may also bring out a "fighting brand" at a low price in the hope of reaching a lower-income market segment.

Perceived Quality

A "fighting brand" is often viewed as a relatively low-quality product in the absence of additional product information. Conversely, consumers tend to rely heavily on a high price as a predictor of good quality when there is a substantial degree of uncertainty involved in the purchase decision. A number of studies have proved this relationship for products such as coffee, stockings, aspirin, salt, floor wax, shampoo, clothing, furniture, perfume, and whiskey.[6] Reliance on price seems to exist for all products, but it manifests itself more strongly for some items than for others.[7] The assumption people make is that prices are higher because the products contain better-grade materials and more careful skilled workmanship. That is, "you get what you pay for."

A recent study, however, has shown that dealer brands (usually priced lower than manufacturers' brands) are usually a better buy.[8] It follows that marketing managers can utilize high prices to enhance the image of their product. The Cadillac Seville is a moderate-sized car, yet it carries a $16,000-plus average price tag. Joy perfume breathlessly claims to be the most expensive in the world. This tactic is sometimes used for rather mundane products, as is illustrated by the Fuji bicycle ad shown in Figure 16.3. Marketing managers who

FIGURE 16.3   Using Price to Enhance a Quality Image

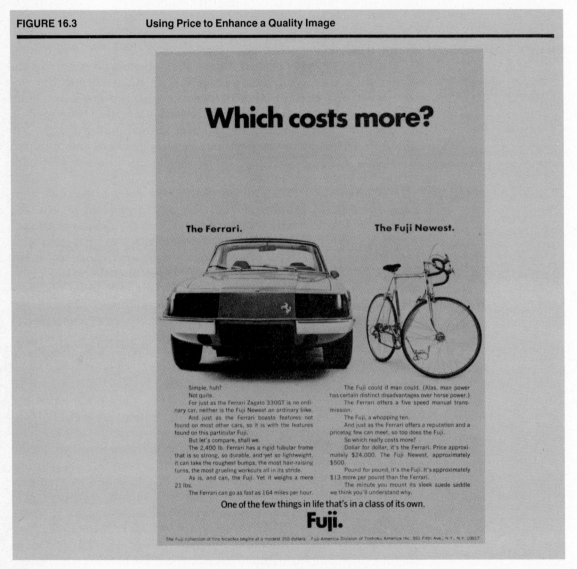

Source: Photo courtesy of Masco Inter-Marketing, Inc.

TABLE 16.4   Attitudes Toward Repair Costs

Product	Percent of Respondents Regarding Repair Cost as Too High	
	1972	1975
Automobile	61	25
Television	58	21
Stereo	57	16
Refrigerator	43	28
Vacuum cleaner	42	13
Stove	39	19
Toaster	33	13
Electric can opener	NA	13
Typewriter	NA	8
Pocket calculator	NA	0

Source: Lee Adler and James D. Hlavacek, "The Relationship Between Price and Repair Service for Consumer Durables," *Journal of Marketing*, 40 (April 1976): 80–82. Reprinted by permission of the American Marketing Association.

attempt to raise the quality image of their product by selling at relatively high prices are following a prestige pricing strategy.

A General Electric marketing executive has noted that "consumers don't seem to be afraid of more expensive models [of small electrical appliances such as radios and irons] . . . our battery operated Home Sentry smoke alarm, which is the highest priced model, is our best seller."[9] Naturally, this strategy won't work for all products; therefore managers must determine whether the price–quality relationship for their product is strong or weak.

When Quality Is Important. Quality generally is more important when the risk of expensive repairs is high. Table 16.4 lists several product categories in which consumers feel that repair costs are too high. These products may be good candidates for prestige pricing if such a strategy will blend properly with the remainder of the marketing mix. Clearly, a dealer can't charge a premium price for a product that is obviously of poor quality.

Prestige Pricing. Prestige pricing theoretically means that more merchandise and services will be bought at higher prices than at lower prices. This unusual condition violates the law of demand and results in a backward-bending demand curve, as shown in Figure 16.4.[10]

Price Consciousness

While we may be very aware of the prices of shopping goods and specialty goods, we are often oblivious to those of convenience goods. For example, a study by *Progressive Grocer* revealed that many shoppers do not know the prices of items that they buy regularly. In the survey,

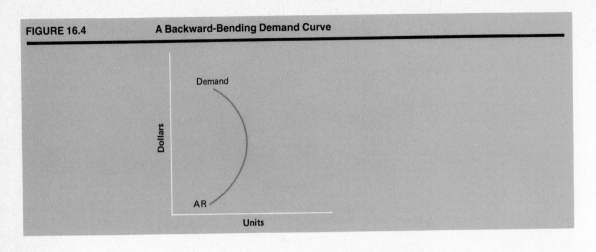

FIGURE 16.4   A Backward-Bending Demand Curve

which covered thirteen fast-selling product brands and about 200 New York City shoppers, fully 40 percent of the people who said that they bought Coca-Cola missed the price by more than 5 percent. Fewer than four out of ten users came within 5 percent on Del Monte fruit cocktail. On a $1.19 package of Kraft Miracle Whip, users estimated the price at anywhere from $.62 to $1.89; and the list continued with similar statistics. "You can only begin to guess how these misconceptions affect buying intentions and the composition of shopping lists," says Edgar B. Walzer, *Progressive Grocer's* president and editor in chief.[11]

A similar study of drug purchase patterns in rural areas indicates that most consumers did not know which pharmacies had the lowest prices.[12] Further research on gasoline price awareness has also indicated a general lack of knowledge.[13] The lack of price sensitivity for convenience goods means that the marketing manager must look to other elements of the marketing mix, such as effective promotion, eye-catching packaging, good product distribution, and desirable shelf locations, to sell the product. Price insensitivity may also allow the marketer to raise prices and thus increase total revenue.

SUMMARY

Prices based strictly on costs, ignoring demand, may cause the firm to lose potential profit. Markup pricing is the most popular method used by wholesalers and retailers to establish selling prices. Markup pricing is a cost-plus technique. The difference between the cost and the selling price is the maintained markup. Markups can be figured on the basis of either cost or retail price.

Markup and stock turnover determine gross profits. Generally speaking, higher stock turnovers will lead to higher profits.

Breakeven analysis determines the sales volume that must be obtained before total cost equals total revenue. A simple breakeven model assumes a given fixed cost and a constant average variable cost. Breakeven analysis provides a quick look at how many units the firm must sell before it starts earning a profit. The technique also reveals how much profit can be earned if higher sales volumes are obtained. A more advanced form of breakeven analysis considers estimated demand at various prices.

Target return pricing is the most popular pricing strategy in American business. It involves establishing a price that will earn the firm a predetermined level of profits. Many large firms that use target return pricing come very close to their profit goals.

Many other factors besides costs and demand can affect prices. These include the stage of the product life cycle, competition, distribution and promotional strategy, perceived quality, and price consciousness.

KEY TERMS

Markup pricing
Maintained markup
Stock turnover

Breakeven theory
Target return pricing
Prestige pricing

QUESTIONS FOR DISCUSSION

1. What is markup pricing? What are some of the factors that influence a markup?
2. Spices of the Indies incurs average operating costs of 29 percent of sales and further incurs pilferage and markdowns running to 6 percent of sales. What mark-on should it put on its products to earn a profit of 8 percent?
3. What is stock turnover? How is it related to overall profits?
4. Explain briefly the concept of the breakeven point. What are some of the limitations of this theory?
5. Explain the modified breakeven concept. How does it improve on traditional breakeven theory?
6. Referring to Table 16.2, find the breakeven point in each of the following cases:
   a. Labor costs increase by $.05 per unit.
   b. Owing to increased demand, American Products increases its prices by 5 percent even though costs remain constant.
7. Briefly explain the basic elements of target return pricing. Use an example to illustrate your answer.
8. How does the product life cycle affect pricing strategy?
9. Explain the use of prices as a promotional tool. Give some diverse examples to make your point.
10. What is prestige pricing? Which of the following products are generally priced in this manner?
    a. perfumes
    b. automobile parts
    c. cigarettes
    d. TV sets

11. Several studies have shown that consumers are not very price conscious with regard to convenience goods. What implications does this have for the marketing manager of a large consumer goods company?

NOTES

1. For a good approach to target return pricing see Douglas G. Brooks, "Cost-Oriented Pricing: A Realistic Solution to a Complicated Problem," *Journal of Marketing,* 39 (April 1975): 72–74, and for an excellent theoretical discussion see David R. Kamerschen, "The Return of Target Pricing," *Journal of Business,* 48 (April 1975): 242–252.
2. Earl L. Bailey, *Marketing Strategies: A Symposium* (New York: Conference Board Record, 1974), p. 32.
3. See William Crissy and Robert Boewadt, "Pricing in Perspective," *Sales Management,* 106 (June 15, 1971): 43–44.
4. "Punching Is Furious in Tylenol–Datril Fight for Non-Aspirin Users," *The Wall Street Journal,* May 24, 1976.
5. "Seller's Market Puts Pressure on Prices," *Purchasing,* 78 (April 1, 1975): 10–11. For other examples of competitive pricing see Leonard J. Parsons and W. Bailey Price, "Adaptive Pricing by a Retailer," *Journal of Marketing Research,* 9 (May 1972): 127–133, and Theodore D. Frey, "Forecasting Prices for Industrial Commodity Markets," *Journal of Marketing,* 34 (April 1970): 28–32.
6. A number of excellent studies have been conducted on the price–quality relationship. See, for example, Arthur G. Bedeian, "Consumer Perception of Price as an Indicator of Product Quality," *MSU Business Topics,* Summer 1971, pp. 59–65; Alfred R. Oxenfeldt, "Developing a Favorable Price–Quality Image," *Journal of Retailing,* 50 (Winter 1974-1975): 8–17; Benson P. Shapiro, "Price Reliance: Existence and Sources," *Journal of Marketing Research,* 10 (August 1973): 286–294; David M. Gardner, "Is There a Generalized Price–Quality Relationship?" *Journal of Marketing Research,* 7 (May 1971): 241–243; Harold J. Leavitt, "A Note on Some Experimental Findings About the Meaning of Price," *Journal of Business,* 41 (October 1968): 205–210; J. Douglas McConnell, "An Experimental Examination of the Price Perceived Quality Relationship," *Journal of Business,* 41 (October 1968), pp. 439–444; James E. Stafford and Ben M. Enis, "The Price–Quality Relationship: An Extension," *Journal of Marketing Research,* 6 (November 1969): 456–458; D. S. Tull, R. A. Boring, and M. H. Gonsior, "A Note on the Relationship of Price and Imputed Quality," *Journal of Business,* 37 (April 1964): 186–191; Jon G. Udell and Evan E. Anderson, "The Product Warranty as an Element of Competitive Strategy," *Journal of Marketing,* 32 (October 1968): 1–8; and Harry Neptrom, Hans Tamsons, and Robert Thams, "An Experiment in Price Generalization and Discrimination," *Journal of Marketing Research,* 12 (May 1975): 177–181.
7. Shapiro, p. 294.
8. John E. Swan, "Price–Product Performance Competition Between Retailer and Manufacturer Brands," *Journal of Marketing,* 38 (July 1974): 52–59.
9. Louis J. Haugh, "G.E. Keying Marketing Strategy to Upturn in Buyer Confidence," *Advertising Age,* May 31, 1976, p. 2.

10. Myron H. Ross and Donald Stiles, "An Exception to the Law of Demand," *Journal of Consumer Affairs*, 7 (Winter 1973): 128–144.
11. "Marketing Observer," *Business Week*, April 26, 1976, p. 109.
12. Richard A. Jackson, Michael R. Ryan, and Charles E. Treas, "A Study of Pharmacy Patronage Motives and Price Awareness," in Robert L. King, ed., *Proceedings, 1973 Conference of the Southern Marketing Association*, pp. 181–186.
13. Gordon L. Wise and Alan L. King, "Price Awareness in the Gasoline Market," *Journal of Retailing*, 49 (Fall 1973): 64–77. For further research on consumer awareness of retail food prices see J. N. Uhl and Harold L. Brown, "Consumer Perception of Experimental Retail Food Price Changes," *Journal of Consumer Affairs*, 5 (Winter 1971): 174–185. Research on children's price awareness is available in Lowndes F. Stephens and Roy L. Moore, "Price Accuracy as a Consumer Skill," *Journal of Advertising Research*, 15 (August 1975): 27–34.

APPENDIX: TYPES OF ECONOMIC COSTS

A variable cost is one that varies with changes in the level of output; an example is materials costs. Fixed costs do not vary or change as output is increased or decreased; examples are rent and executive salaries.

In order to compare the cost of production to the sales price of the goods or services, it is helpful to calculate costs per unit or average costs. Average variable cost (AVC) equals total variable costs divided by output. Average total cost (ATC) equals total costs divided by output. You will note in Table 16.5 that AVC and ATC are basically U-shaped. Average fixed costs decline continually as output increases because total fixed costs are constant. Marginal cost (MC) is the

TABLE 16.5   Basic Cost Schedules

Output	Total Fixed Costs	Total Variable Costs	Total Costs	Average Variable Costs	Average Fixed Costs	Average Total Costs	Marginal Costs
0	$15	0	$ 15	0	—	—	—
2	15	$ 10	25	$5.00	$7.50	$12.50	$ 5.00
6	15	20	35	3.33	2.50	5.83	2.50
12	15	30	45	2.50	1.25	3.75	1.66
19	15	40	55	2.11	0.79	2.89	1.43
25	15	50	65	2.00	0.60	2.60	1.66
30	15	60	75	2.00	0.50	2.50	2.00
34	15	70	85	2.06	0.44	2.50	2.50
37	15	80	95	2.16	0.41	2.57	3.33
39	15	90	105	2.31	0.38	2.69	5.00
40	15	100	115	2.50	0.38	2.88	10.00
40.5	15	110	125	2.72	0.37	3.09	20.00

FIGURE 16.5   Basic Cost Curves

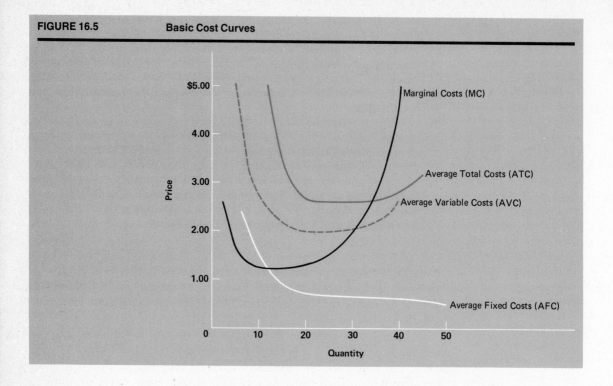

change in total costs associated with a one-unit change in output. For example, when production rises from 37 to 39 units, the change in total cost is $10. This figure, however, is for two units; therefore marginal cost is $5.00.

All of the curves illustrated in Figure 16.5 have a definite relationship. For example, AVC plus AFC equals ATC. Also, MC falls for a while and then turns upward with the twenty-fifth unit. This means that diminishing returns have set in, causing less output to be produced for every additional dollar spent on variable input. MC intersects both AVC and ATC at their lowest possible points. When MC is less than AVC or ATC, the incremental cost will continue to pull the averages down. Conversely, when MC is greater than AVC or ATC, it pulls the average up and ATC and AVC begin to rise. The minimum point on the ATC curve is the least-cost point for a fixed-capacity firm; it is not necessarily the most profitable point.

CASE 16
Midcontinent Perfume Company

Midcontinent Perfume of Milwaukee, Wisconsin, distributes a wide line of quality women's perfumes to intermediate and high-priced department and specialty stores. It has recently decided to add a new, lower-priced line to its product mix in order to capture a slightly different segment of the market. The new product is called "Passion Flower."

A recent market test revealed the following estimated total demand for the product at the quoted prices.

Price	Quantity
$15.00	25,000 units
$20.00	20,000 units
$22.50	19,000 units
$25.00	11,000 units
$27.50	10,000 units

The accounting department figured that the average variable cost for the new perfume would be $13.00 per unit. Fixed costs are estimated at $40,000.

1. Assuming that the market research studies are accurate, what price should be charged for the perfume?
2. What kind of market research study could have been done to determine the demand schedule for the perfume? Assume that fixed costs are $140,000 rather than $40,000. Should the company have produced in the short run? in the long run?
3. Discuss the advantages and disadvantages of breakeven analysis.
4. What is the breakeven point for this perfume? Of what significance is that point?

17

Pricing Strategies and Concepts

OBJECTIVES

■ To learn about new-product pricing strategies.
■ To become aware of the role of discounts and allowances in pricing a product.
■ To understand various geographic and special pricing policies.
■ To understand product line pricing.
■ To gain insight into recent pricing trends.

In Chapter 15 you learned about pricing objectives. You have also discovered the roles of costs and demand in determining prices. Chapter 17 examines the "real world" of pricing. The concepts and theories of the previous chapters will help you appreciate the pricing techniques to be discussed here.

First, basic strategies for pricing new products are described. Then you will learn how pricing strategies can be "fine-tuned" through discounts and allowances and special pricing policies. Next, pricing for an entire product line rather than an individual item is examined. The chapter concludes with a discussion of bidding strategy (which is very important in industrial and governmental pricing) and pricing considerations in a changing economy.

PRICING A NEW PRODUCT

The degree of freedom a company has in pricing a new product or service depends on the nature of the market. If, for example, a firm brings out a new item that is very similar to a number of other goods already on the market, its pricing freedom will be highly restricted. The company will probably have to charge a price that is relatively close to the average market price if it is to be successful. On the other hand, a firm that is introducing a totally new product with no close substitutes will have considerable pricing freedom.

Price Skimming

A firm with pricing freedom can select either a penetration pricing strategy or a skimming pricing strategy for its new offering. Price skimming means charging a high introductory price, often coupled with heavy promotion.[1] As the product moves through the product life cycle the firm lowers its price so as to reach successively larger market segments. Price skimming has been described by some economists as "sliding down the demand curve." Examples of a "skim-the-cream" strategy include the pricing of pocket calculators, citizens'-band radios, digital watches, shower massagers, Concorde tickets, and microwave ovens.

When Is Skimming Successful? Price skimming is successful when demand is relatively inelastic. If, for example, people will pay $350 for a microwave oven, some individuals will probably pay $450 for one with a digital timer. When a product is well protected legally or represents a technological breakthrough or has in some other way blocked entry to competitors, price skimming can be utilized effectively. A third situation in which managers may follow a skimming strategy occurs when production cannot be expanded rapidly because of technological difficulties, shortages, or the time demands of skilled craftsmen. An artist can hand paint only so many pieces of fine china per hour!

The Advantages of Skimming. A successful skimming strategy enables management to quickly recover its product development costs or educational costs. Often we must be "taught" the advantages of a radically new item such as home video tape recorders. Even if an introductory price is perceived as "too high" by the market, managers can easily correct the problem by lowering the price. Thus firms often feel that it is better to "test the market" at a high price and then lower it if sales are not forthcoming. They are tacitly saying, "If there are any premium price buyers in the market, let's reach them first and maximize our revenue per unit." Naturally, a skimming strategy will encourage potential competition, as the following example shows:

> Wella Corporation introduced its Wella Balsam hair conditioner at a hefty $1.98, compared with $1.19 for standard cream rinses. So Alberto-

Culver Company came in with Alberto-Balsam at $1.49, socked $621,000 into a big advertising sendoff (versus $62,000 for Wella), and claims it surpassed Wella in only ten months. Today, Alberto claims 55% to 60% of the hair conditioner market. "We would have liked the profit margins that Wella had with its higher price," says Randy Irion, Alberto-Balsam's senior brand manager. "But we just couldn't get enough market penetration at $1.98."[2]

Penetration Pricing   Penetration pricing represents the other end of the continuum from skimming strategy. Penetration, for example, tends to discourage competition. When a firm introduces a new product at a relatively low price, hoping to reach the mass market in the early stages of the product life cycle, it is following a penetration pricing strategy.

Planning Requirements.   Penetration pricing requires more accurate planning and forecasting than skimming because the firm must "gear up" for mass production and mass marketing. If the product does not reach its sales goals, the firm may experience heavy losses. Thus penetration is usually a much riskier strategy than skimming.

Effects of Penetration Pricing.   Penetration pricing is predicated upon an elastic demand curve and the low unit costs resulting from economies of mass production. A successful penetration strategy can effectively block entry into the industry, as is shown in Figure 17.1.

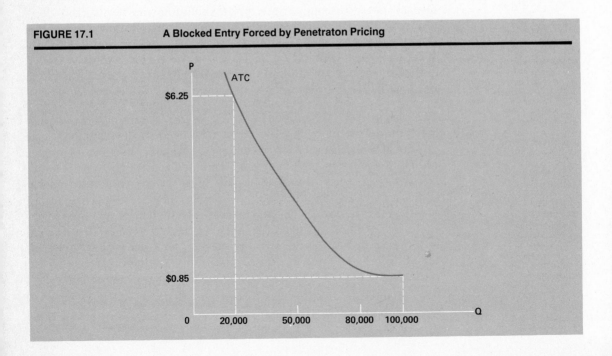

| FIGURE 17.1 | A Blocked Entry Forced by Penetraton Pricing |

Assume that Dynamic Dynamo has as its company goal a 12-percent return on investment. The firm (DD) will reach this goal at a sales level of 80,000 units. Also assume that total market demand for the product is only 100,000 units and that any firm that entered the industry would have a cost structure similar to DD's. Thus when DD achieves its maximization goal by selling 80,000 units at $3.00 each, only 20,000 units of demand remain for any potential competitor. If a competitor entered and sold 20,000 units at $3.00 each, its average cost would be $6.25 for a total loss of $65,000. The lack of economies of mass production makes profitable entry impossible for almost any new competitor. A well-financed organization would have to be willing to sustain substantial short-run losses to obtain penetration.

Sometimes competitors in an oligopoly situation will be following a skimming policy only to find a new firm entering with a penetration price. In 1975, for example, digital-watch manufacturers were slowly and profitably sliding down the demand curve. Texas Instruments pricked their pricing balloon by announcing a $20 watch in January 1976. As Robert J. Holtcamp, vice president of Litronix, a California digital watch producer, put it, "Our buyers stopped buying."[3] Just fifteen months earlier the lowest-priced digital watch had been selling for $125.

The only way Texas Instruments could profitably initiate a $20 penetration price was through huge economies of mass production. The firm shipped 4 million watches during 1976—more than the total of digital watches shipped by all the world's digital-watch manufacturers in 1975.[4]

Another firm using penetration pricing is BSR, a British manufacturer of record changers. BSR sells record changers for virtually all the well-known phonograph brands except Magnavox. It produced and marketed 70 percent of the changers used on the 5.1 million phonographs sold in the United States in 1975.[5] BSR's management believes that penetration pricing is the key to the firm's success.

Still another example is Liggett and Myers, which used penetration pricing to introduce Eagle 20s. Eagle 20s were priced at $.05 less per pack and $.50 less per carton than such brands as Marlboro, Winston, and Viceroy.[6]

Extinction Pricing.   Penetration pricing may be viewed as a long-run strategy. Extinction pricing, a derivative of that strategy, is basically short run in nature and is used as a way of eliminating competition. It involves pricing the product way below cost (often below variable costs) in order to drive independent or underfinanced competitors from the market. After the marginal competitors have been driven from the market, the firm raises its prices back to normal levels. Several national chains were guilty of extinction pricing during their early years. More recently, independent retail petroleum marketeers have claimed that the multinational firms are using extinction pricing to force small independents from the market.

DISCOUNTS AND ALLOWANCES

A penetration price or a skimming price may be altered (i.e., lowered) through the use of discounts and allowances. Discounts take a variety of forms and have several different objectives.

Quantity Discounts

Probably the most common form of discount is the quantity discount. When a purchaser receives a lower price for purchasing in multiple units or above a specified dollar amount, he or she is receiving a quantity discount. In theory, the discount is based on the savings in transportation, administrative, and other costs realized by the seller.

A noncumulative quantity discount is intended to increase the size of the order. In contrast, the cumulative quantity discount is calculated on the basis of total orders placed over time. This form of discount does not necessarily increase the average order size but will tie the buyer to the seller. The development of customer loyalty may lead to more stable long-run purchasing patterns. As a result sales forecasting is easier and the scheduling of production runs is less risky.

Quantity discounts can be placed on slow-moving items in order to increase their sales potential. Temporary quantity discounts may be established to help bolster sales during off periods. Also, these discounts can be used by wholesalers to discourage retailers from attempting to purchase directly from the manufacturer. If the discount is comparable to what the retailer might receive by going directly to the manufacturer, it may continue to utilize the wholesaler.

Functional Discounts

A second common form of discount is the functional discount. When a middleman performs a service or function within a channel of distribution, it must be compensated. This compensation is typically a percentage discount from the base price and is called a functional or trade discount. The amounts of functional discounts vary substantially from channel to channel, depending on the tasks performed by the middlemen.

A typical discount schedule results when a manufacturer quotes a retail list price of $500 and discounts of 45 and 8 percent. The retailer's cost will be $275 ($500 minus 45 percent). The wholesaler will pay $253 ($275 minus 8 percent). You will note that the total discount is not 53 percent off list price. Instead, discounts are figured on a chain basis from one level of the distribution channel to the next.

The complicated nature of today's physical-distribution networks sometimes results in institutions receiving discounts that do not accurately reflect the services performed. Although the Robinson–Patman Act specifies that functional discounts must be justified on a service/cost basis, the FTC has shown little enthusiasm for delving into the functional-discount question.

Cash Discounts

All of us have had opportunities to receive cash discounts. An invoice billed 3/15 n/30 means that you have 15 days from the invoice date in which to pay your bill and receive a 3 percent discount. If you don't take advantage of the discount, the whole bill is due within 30 days from the date of the invoice. In other words, if the purchaser does not exercise the discount option, he or she is borrowing funds for 15 days (in this example) at an interest rate of 3 percent of the invoice price. Firms usually choose to take cash discounts because of the savings involved. In our example the interest rate for not taking the discount is 73 percent per year (there are 24.3 fifteen-day periods in a year; 24.3 × 3% = 73% annual rate).

Seasonal Discounts

A seasonal discount is a price reduction for buying merchandise out of season. It shifts the storage function forward to the purchaser. Seasonal discounts also enable manufacturers to maintain a steady production schedule year round. For example, a bathing suit manufacturer offers seasonal discounts in the fall and winter in order to keep its sewing crew employed full time. One of the most familiar examples of a seasonal discount is the half-price sales on Christmas decorations that begin December 26. Other examples are off-season rates at motels and resorts and discount air fares during off seasons.

Promotional Allowances

A promotional allowance serves a dual role: as a pricing tool and as a promotional device. As a pricing tool, a promotional allowance is similar to a functional discount. If, for example, a retailer runs an ad for a manufacturer's product, the manufacturer may pay half of the cost. If a retailer sets up a special display, the manufacturer may include a certain quantity of "free goods" in the retailer's next order. Promotional allowances, like other forms of discount, must be made available to all purchasers on essentially the same terms. The Robinson–Patman Act prohibits differences in advertising allowances to similar purchasers.

GEOGRAPHIC PRICING POLICIES

Since many sellers ship their wares to a nationwide or even a worldwide market, the cost of freight can have a significant impact on the total cost of a product. Several different geographic pricing policies may be utilized to moderate the impact of freight costs on distant customers.

FOB Origin

If a product is priced "FOB origin," the buyer pays the cost of transportation from the selling point. The term FOB origin means that the goods are placed free on board a carrier and that at that point title passes to the buyer and transportation charges are paid by the buyer. Any damage claim beyond the point of origin must be filed by the purchaser against the common carrier.

Effects of FOB Pricing

FOB pricing treats all purchasers alike (there is no geographic price discrimination—the farther a buyer is from a seller, the more he or she pays). As a result of FOB origin pricing natural market monopolies tend to develop, such as the one shown in Figure 17.2. American Products, located in Los Angeles, is selling FOB origin at a price of AM. As potential buyers are located farther from Los Angeles, we find delivered prices (origin plus freight) rising along path MO. Boston Bananas (BB), marketing a similar product to American Products, sells FOB origin at a price of BN, with total cost rising along path NP.

American Products has a freight advantage territory extending from slightly east of Oklahoma City back to the West Coast (market segment AX). Boston Bananas' freight advantage territory is segment BX. Assuming that both firms follow the FOB pricing policy strictly, each will be blocked from the other's market. The only way BB can increase its geographic market (assuming that it is unwilling to alter

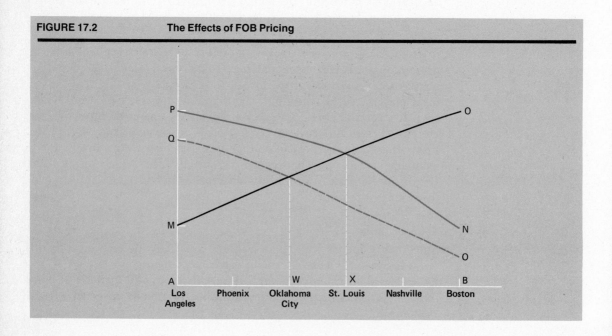

FIGURE 17.2   The Effects of FOB Pricing

its pricing policy) is to cut the selling price at the origin. If BB follows this strategy, its new market segment would be BW at a price of OB.

Uniform Delivered Pricing

The opposite of FOB pricing is uniform delivered pricing or "postage stamp pricing." Under this policy the seller pays the actual freight charges and bills every purchaser an identical flat freight charge. This policy equalizes the total cost for all buyers, regardless of where they are located. Naturally, uniform delivered pricing discriminates in favor of purchasers that are located far away from the seller, but price competition among buyers is eliminated. All buyers pay the same total price for the product.

This policy may be used when a firm is trying to maintain a nationally advertised price. Postage stamp pricing is also common when transportation charges are a minor part of total costs. The uniform delivered pricing policy is relatively easy to administer and, according to the FTC, is not illegal.

Zone Pricing

Zone pricing is a modification of uniform delivered pricing. Rather than placing the entire United States (or its total market) under a uniform freight rate, the firm divides it into segments or zones. (See Figure 17.3.) A flat freight rate is charged to all customers in a given zone. For example, customers of Boston Bananas located in zone one might pay $5.00 per unit freight; those in zone two, $10.00; and those in zone three, $20.00.

Zone pricing eliminates price advantage among purchasers within large geographic areas. The zone pricing policy discriminates against the buyers that are located closest to the seller within any given zone. A buyer located in Indianapolis pays the same rate as a

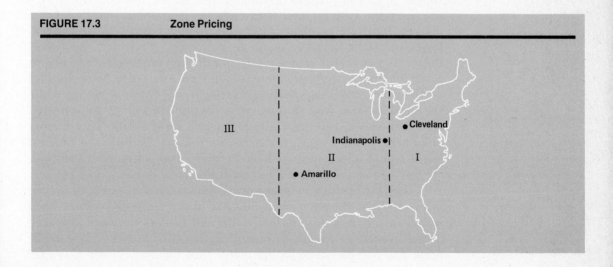

FIGURE 17.3   Zone Pricing

purchaser in Amarillo, yet the Amarillo buyer is over 900 miles farther from Boston than the Indianapolis purchaser. Thus the Indianapolis buyer may seek another seller. Another problem of zone pricing is determining where to place the zone boundaries. A Cleveland buyer pays $5.00 freight, whereas the Indianapolis purchaser must pay $10.00 — a 100 percent increase. The U.S. Postal Service's parcel post rate structure is probably the best-known pricing system in the country.

Basing-Point Pricing

Basing-point pricing is not as popular as it once was as a result of a number of adverse court rulings. A single-basing-point price policy requires the seller to designate a location (say, Louisville) as a basing point and charge all purchasers the freight cost from Louisville regardless of the city from which the goods are shipped. If Boston Bananas used Louisville as its basing point and sold merchandise to another firm located in Boston, the buyer would pay freight charges from Louisville. This would be true even though the merchandise was shipped from BB's Boston warehouse. Freight fees charged when none were actually incurred are called "phantom freight."

The Popularity of Basing-Point Pricing. Basing-point pricing has been prevalent in the steel, cement, lead, corn oil, linseed oil, wood pulp, automobile, sugar, gypsum board, and plywood industries, as well as many others.[7] The basing-point system is used most often by firms that sell relatively homogeneous products and for which transportation costs are an important component of total costs.

Effects of Basing-Point Pricing. A basing-point system eliminates freight price competition (assuming that all the firms in an industry use the same system), and it extends the geographic boundaries of a market. By charging phantom freight to some buyers the firm covers losses on transportation to other customers. Consider our friend Boston Bananas. BB makes a sale to a Boston customer. (See Figure 17.4.) That buyer pays phantom freight from Louisville. Now consider a BB customer in Chicago who pays freight only from Louisville, while the merchandise was shipped from Boston. In effect, BB's Boston customer subsidizes the Chicago buyer's freight bill. This basing-point scheme works in favor of Boston Bananas because the Chicago buyer would have purchased goods from a competitor if it had been charged the actual freight fee from Boston.

If all the firms in an industry use the same basing point, delivered prices will be the same. If a Phoenix buyer requested quotes from sellers in Chicago, Boston, Louisville, and El Paso for wood pulp, the quotes would be identical, assuming that all have the same retail price and use the same basing point. (See Figure 17.4.) In this case

FIGURE 17.4   A Basing-Point System

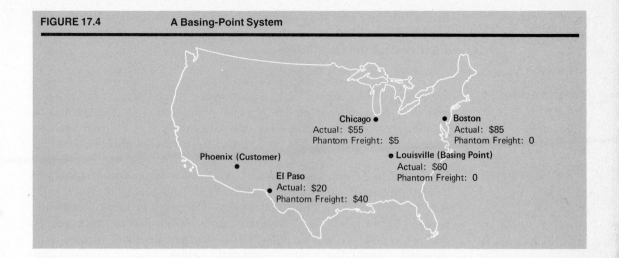

Chicago ●
Actual: $55
Phantom Freight: $5

● Boston
Actual: $85
Phantom Freight: 0

Phoenix (Customer)
●

El Paso
● Actual: $20
Phantom Freight: $40

● Louisville (Basing Point)
Actual: $60
Phantom Freight: 0

the Chicago seller and the El Paso seller both charge phantom freight while the Boston dealer actually loses money on freight charges. In another example, manufacturers were all able to quote a price of $3.286854 per barrel in response to a government request for bids on cement delivered to Tucumcari, New Mexico, by following the basing-point rules.[8]

Multiple Basing Points.   A variation on the single-basing-point system is the multiple-basing-point technique. There is no essential difference between the two except that several basing points are used rather than one. Thus prices are established from several cities rather than just one. U.S. Steel went to a multiple-basing-point system in 1948 after a twenty-year court battle with the FTC. Basing-point pricing is not illegal per se, but most single and multiple basing-point systems were outlawed during the 1940s in a series of Supreme Court decisions.

When a basing-point scheme involves price discrimination or collusion, the firms involved may be held in violation of both the Sherman Act and the Clayton Act. Price discrimination is, of course, illegal under the Robinson–Patman Act. Finally, Section Five of the Federal Trade Commission Act specifically outlaws any basing-point pricing system if it results in "unfair competition."

Freight Absorption Pricing

In freight absorption pricing the seller absorbs all or part of the actual freight charges. This policy may be used in areas where competition is extremely intense, or it can be used to break into new market areas. A seller may follow this policy to achieve greater economies of scale. If the economies of scale are greater than the absorbed freight costs, the firm's total profits will increase. Sometimes a seller will offer all buyers the same price (uniform delivered pricing), but it will absorb all or part of the freight fee.

SPECIAL PRICING POLICIES

Special pricing policies, unlike geographic price policies, are unique and defy neat categorization. Special policies may be established to promote certain types of merchandise, to increase store patronage, to offer the consumer greater choice, and for a variety of other reasons.

Price Variability

In the United States most prices are fixed without negotiation between purchaser and seller. Indeed, the foundation of mass self-service policies is a one-price policy. Can you imagine going into Kroger, Safeway, or A&P and bargaining for all of your groceries? A one-price policy is easier on sellers because it does not require personnel to spend their time negotiating prices. Also, it provides the dealer with a consistent profit margin. Many consumers feel more comfortable with a one-price policy because they do not enjoy haggling over prices. Similarly, the merchant will not incur the ill will of customers who find out that they have paid a higher price than someone else because they are not as good at bargaining.

The Advantages of Flexible Pricing. Flexible pricing or variable pricing is sometimes found in the sale of shopping goods and specialty merchandise as well as many industrial goods. Under such a policy different customers pay different prices for essentially the same merchandise bought in equal quantities. Automobile dealers and many appliance retailers commonly follow this practice. It allows the retailer to adjust for competition by meeting another dealer's price. Also, flexible pricing enables the seller to "close a sale" with price conscious consumers. If a buyer shows promise of becoming a large-volume shopper, variable pricing can be used to procure his or her business.

The Disadvantages of Flexible Pricing. The obvious disadvantages of variable pricing are (1) the lack of consistent profit margins, (2) the potential ill will of high-price purchasers, (3) the tendency for salespeople to "automatically" lower the price in order to make a sale, and (4) the possibility of a price war among sellers.

Single-Price Policy

A single-price policy is as much a promotional tool as a variable-price policy. A merchant using this strategy offers all goods and services at the same price (or perhaps two or three prices). Thus a retailer specializing in men's ties sells every tie for $3.00. The retailer also carries belts for $5.00, but that is the extent of its product line.

Single-price selling removes price comparisons from the buyer's decision-making process. The consumer simply looks for suitability and for the highest perceived quality. The retailer enjoys the benefits of a simplified pricing system and the minimization of clerical error. Continually rising costs are a constant headache for retailers following this strategy, often leading to frequent upward revisions of the selling price.

Multiple-Unit Package Pricing

Multiple-unit package pricing attempts to increase the quantity sold in each individual transaction. A familiar example is the six-pack of soft drinks, beer, or even outboard-motor oil. Sometimes discounts are given for purchasing more than one item at a time. Recently, however, many retailers have moved toward not reducing the per-unit prices of multiple-unit packages. In fact some retailers charge a premium for the convenience of buying a number of items in one package!

Price Lining

When a merchant establishes a series of prices for a type of merchandise, it has created a price line. For example, a dress shop may offer women's dresses at $40, $70, and $100 with no merchandise marked at prices between those figures. Thus instead of a normal demand curve running from $40 to $100, the retailer has three demand points (prices) — the "curve" exists in a theoretical sense because people would buy goods at the in-between prices if it were possible to do so. For example, a number of dresses could be sold at $60, but no sales will take place at that price because it is not part of the price line.

The Advantages of Price Lining. Price lines reduce confusion for both the sales clerk and the consumer. The consumer may be offered a wider variety of merchandise at each established price. Thus for consumers the question of price may be quite simple: All they have to do is find a suitable product at the predetermined price. The retailer may be able to carry a smaller total inventory than it could without price lines. This may mean fewer markdowns, simplified purchasing, and lower inventory carrying charges.

The Disadvantages of Price Lining. Price lines are not without disadvantages. If costs are continually rising, the retailer must begin placing lower-quality merchandise in stock at each established price or change the prices. Frequent price line changes create consumer confusion. A third alternative to rising costs is to accept lower profit margins and hold quality and prices constant. While this is admirable in the short run, in the long run it may put the retailer out of business.

Another major problem is attempting to determine where to place the prices within a line. If the prices are too close together, the consumer may wonder why the price of one article is higher than that of another. If the price lines are too far apart, the dealer may lose a customer who is looking for a price (and quality) somewhere between the existing prices. Also, a salesperson will find it difficult to "trade up" customers (persuade them to buy higher-priced merchandise) if the price lines are too far apart.

Leader Pricing

Leader pricing is a legitimate attempt by a seller to induce store patronage through pricing. It involves selling a product near cost or even below cost to attract customers. You see this type of pricing every week in the newspaper advertising of supermarkets, specialty stores, and department stores. Leader pricing is normally used on well-known items that consumers can easily recognize as bargains at the special price.

Cents-Off Promotion

Cents-off promotion is a common pricing tactic that is similar to leader pricing. However, rather than being initiated by the retailer, cents-off promotions are used by the manufacturer to increase the sale of a specific brand. With the exception of trade deals (discounts to wholesalers and retailers) and advertising, cents-off advertising is the most heavily used form of convenience goods promotion.[9]

Occasionally a retailer promotes a cents-off item yet does not actually lower retail prices. One study of 3357 cents-off promotions showed that 19 percent of the retailers never passed the savings along to the consumer.[10] These stores were generally small, independent retailers rather than large chains.

Bait Pricing

In contrast to cents-off campaigns and leader pricing, which are genuine attempts to give the consumer a reduced price, bait pricing is deceptive. The idea is to get the consumer into a store through false or misleading advertising and then use high-pressure selling to persuade the consumer to buy more expensive merchandise.

You may have seen this ad or a similar one:

> REPOSSESSED . . . Singer slant-needle sewing machine . . . take over 8 payments of $5.10 per month . . . ABC Sewing Center.

This is "bait." When a customer goes in to see the machine it has "just been sold," or else a salesperson shows the prospective buyer a piece of junk that no one would buy. Then the salesperson says, "But I've got a really good deal on this fine, new model." This is the "switch" that may cause a susceptible consumer to walk out with a $400 machine.

Bait-and-switch advertising is illegal under the Wheeler–Lea Amendment to the Federal Trade Commission Act. In 1974 the FTC charged America's largest retailer, Sears, with bait-and-switch advertising on its sewing machines and appliances.[11] Sears has strongly denied the charge and the matter is still pending. Bait-and-switch techniques are generally limited to shopping goods and a few specialty items.

Psychological Pricing

Psychological pricing means pricing at odd prices to denote bargains and even pricing to imply quality. For years many retailers have priced their products at odd prices ($99.95, $49.95, etc.) to make consumers feel that they are paying a "lower" price for the product. Does it work? Research has shown that such pricing has mixed results.[12] If odd pricing is effective, it will have a curious effect on demand, as may be seen in Figure 17.5. Since people will buy more at odd prices, demand will be relatively elastic and then inelastic for even prices as you move down the demand curve. Such a situation will create a "sawtoothed" demand curve. Odd prices will stimulate demand and even prices will curtail demand.

Even pricing is sometimes used to denote quality, as in the case of a fine perfume at $100 per bottle, a good watch at $250, or a mink coat for $3000. It is assumed in these cases that more will be sold at even prices than at odd prices. The demand curve for such items would also be "sawtoothed," except that the outside edges (the points farthest from the Y axis) would represent even prices (and, hence, elastic demand).

Unit Pricing

Unit pricing is designed—at least theoretically—to aid the economy-minded purchaser in getting the most product per unit without regard to quality. For example, if two jars of peanut butter weigh 14 ounces and 18 ounces and their respective prices are $1.82 and $2.25, their costs per ounce are 13¢ and 12½¢. The numerous manufacturers' and

FIGURE 17.5   A Demand Curve Where Odd-Even Pricing Is Effective

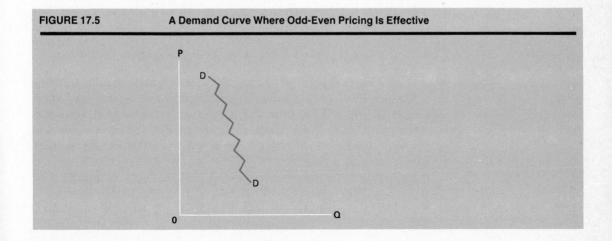

dealers' brands are easier to compare where unit pricing is available. This policy seems to be most applicable to grocery pricing.

Do consumers switch brands to lower-cost alternatives? It depends on whose research you trust. For example, a study by Kroger revealed no tendency to switch brands.[13] Yet studies by Stop and Shop, Safeway, and King Soopers indicated that consumers were switching brands and purchasing different package sizes.[14] Academic research has also shown mixed results.[15]

PRODUCT LINE PRICING

Product line pricing differs from unit pricing because the marketing manager attempts to achieve maximum profits (or other goals) for the entire line. The emphasis is on the entire line rather than on any single component of the line.

Relationships Among Products

The manager must first determine the type of relationship that exists among the various products in the line. Items may, for example, be complementary, meaning that an increase in the sale of one good causes an increase in demand for the complementary product, and vice versa. The sale of Xerox paper and Xerox toner is predicated upon the demand for Xerox machines; thus the items are complementary.

A second possibility is for two products in a line to be substitutes for each other. If a buyer purchases one item in the line, he or she is less likely to purchase a second item in the line. If you go to an automotive supply store and buy a certain type of car wax for your car, it is very unlikely that you will buy another car wax made by the same manufacturer (or by any other manufacturer) in the near future.

The third possible relationship among two products is a neutral one; that is, demand for one of the products is not related to demand for the others. Ralston Purina sells chicken feed and Wheat Chex, but the sale of one of these products has no impact on demand for the other.

Joint Costs

Joint costs — costs that are shared in the manufacturing and marketing of a product line — pose a unique problem when it comes to product pricing.[16] In oil refining, for example, fuel oil, gasoline, kerosene, naphtha, paraffin, and lubricating oils are all derived from a common production process. Any assignment of joint costs must of necessity be somewhat subjective.

Suppose that a company produces two products, X and Y, with joint costs where costs are allocated on a weight basis; product X weighs 1000 pounds and product Y weighs 500 pounds based on a common production process. Gross margins (sales less cost of goods sold) might be as follows:

	Product X	Product Y	Total
Sales	$20,000	$6,000	$26,000
Less: cost of goods sold	15,000	7,500	22,500
Gross margin	$ 5,000	($1,500)	$ 3,500

This statement reveals a loss of $1,500 on product Y. Is that important? Yes, any loss is important. However, the firm must realize that on an overall basis a $3,500 profit was earned on the two items in the line. Also, weight may not be the "right" way to allocate the joint costs. Other bases that might have been used include market value or quantity sold.

COMPETITIVE BIDDING

Selling in the industrial-goods market or to various levels of government may require pricing on a bid basis. Bid pricing is unique in that the quantity demanded is specified in the bidding prospectus or specifications. The bid price therefore becomes a function of (1) cost and (2) competitors' actions. The bid price is usually the most important determinant of the winning bid, but other factors may enter into consideration. For example, governmental agencies may also evaluate the bidder's past experience (particularly in the area of research and development) and the technical competence of its employees.

PRICING IN A CHANGING ECONOMY
Long-Term Inflation

Rising consumer demand, demands for higher wages and unemployments benefits, governmental actions, policies of cartels, shortages, and archaic pricing policies have stimulated relatively high rates of inflation in the 1970s. To meet the continuing challenge of inflation, marketing managers are adopting new pricing policies. These policies can be conveniently categorized as based on either cost or demand.[17]

Cost-Oriented Strategies

Elimination of Low-Margin Products. One popular cost-oriented strategy is culling low-margin products from the product line. This strategy may backfire because of (1) the high volume and, thus, high profitability of a low-margin item or (2) a loss of economies of scale as certain products are eliminated, which lowers the margins on other items. Also, the entire price/quality image of the line may be affected. An example is Ducommun, Inc., a $190-million metals and electronics distributor located in Los Angeles.

"Two years ago," says Executive Vice President Charles K. Preston, "we decided that since we couldn't raise our prices (because of controls), we'd concentrate on those items that would make us the best profit." So Ducommun boosted its salesmen's commissions five percent to ten percent on its higher margin products, such as cutting tools and coated abrasives.[18]

Adoption of Delayed-Quotation Pricing.   Delayed-quotation bidding is very popular for industrial installations and many accessory items. Price is not set on the product until the item is either finished or delivered. Long production lead times and continual inflation have forced this policy on many firms. When Bechtel began building a new electrolytic copper refinery for ASARCO in Amarillo, Texas, in early 1973, the total price tag was estimated at $111 million. By the summer of 1974, with the plant 85 percent finished, the cost had moved up to $190 million.[19]

Use of Escalator Clauses.   Escalator pricing is similar to delayed-quotation pricing in that the final selling price will reflect cost increases incurred between the times when the order is placed and delivery is made. An escalator clause allows for price increases (usually across the board) based on the cost-of-living index or some other formula. As with any price increase, the ability to successfully implement such a policy is based on an inelastic demand curve for the purchase involved. About one-third of all industrial-products manufacturers now use escalator clauses.[20] However, many companies do not apply the clause in every sale. Often it is utilized only for extremely complex projects of long duration and/or with new customers.

Any cost-oriented pricing policy that attempts to maintain a fixed gross margin under all conditions can lead to a vicious circle. For example, a price increase will result in decreased demand, which, in turn, increases production costs (due to lost economies of scale). Increased production costs require a further price increase leading to further diminished demand, and so forth.

Demand-Oriented Strategies

Demand-oriented pricing policies concentrate on using price to reflect changing patterns of demand caused by inflation. Naturally, cost changes are considered, but primarily in the context of how increased prices will affect demand.

Elimination of Price Shading.   Price shading involves the use of discounts by salespeople to increase demand for one or more products in a line. Often shading has become habitual and is done routinely without much forethought. Ducommun and Fairchild are among the major companies that have succeeded in eliminating the practice:

> Ducommun sales managers have given salesmen the rule, "that we want no deviation from book price," unless authorized by management.

Within its largest division, Ducommun has even created a price "czar" who consults with salesmen on any price changes. "We monitor the price on every order before the sale closes."

At Fairchild, semiconductor salesmen have begun operating on price lists established by individual product marketing managers who must approve any special deals. "In the past," says Corrigan, "Fairchild salesmen were able to commit the company to pricing decisions. Today, the selling function no longer even reports to the division general managers who carry profit responsibility."[21]

Shipment Pricing Without Notification. When a firm determines that demand for its product is highly inelastic, it can increase prices after the merchandise is shipped with prior purchaser notification. Obviously, this is not a very popular practice among buyers:

"You get the stuff," grumbles one maker of logging equipment, "and you find the price is higher than was quoted." Adds a leading gear manufacturer, "Everybody we see is breaking every rule in the book. The price quoted to you when you place the order no longer means a thing. You won't take anybody to court over this. The courts would be jammed for years. So, you sit down with your important suppliers and work it out."[22]

Unbundling of Services. One technique for controlling price increases is to provide "extra" services only if they are demanded. Repair services, peripheral equipment, and replacement parts are now priced separately rather than being included in a total package. Although it is not a new concept, unbundling has become increasingly popular in the industrial-goods market, where there is considerable pressure to hold down price increases.

Reducing Cash and Quantity Discounts. A natural tendency during inflationary periods is to reduce both cash and quantity discounts. The more progressive firms are maintaining their discounts on high-margin items and reducing or eliminating discounts on low-profit merchandise. Thus discounting is used to positively alter demand rather than being arbitrarily eliminated.

Shortage Pricing

The recession of 1974–1975 brought the specter of goods shortages to the forefront of the marketing pictures. Many marketing managers didn't know how to deal with this new phenomenon and had to hurriedly develop shortage marketing strategies. Several new shortage price policies evolved from this situation.

Buyers' reactions to the shortage environment varied from hoarding and stockpiling to long-range purchase contract demands and increased price awareness. Competition for market share also tended to decline. Several new competitive trends began to emerge: (1) less reliance on price competition, (2) some sharing of marketing resources, (3) increased efforts to integrate vertically to ensure a larger share of supplies, (4) a search for new ways to reduce marketing costs, (5) a reactivation of bartering arrangements, and (6) less reliance on demand stimulation activities.[23]

Some marketers raised prices on low-margin items during shortage periods in order to (1) kill off demand and (2) still keep the products available for consumers who simply must have them, even at a higher price.[24] Also, many firms forgo penetration pricing during times of shortage, since they are unable to produce and deliver the volume of merchandise required to make such a strategy feasible.

Demand may also become more inelastic as firms struggle for existing supply. As a result sellers are in a position to raise prices even further. The ever-present threat of governmental price controls during periods of shortage may damp enthusiasm for significant increases.

Other shortage-related price strategies include (1) tightening credit to minimize risk, (2) less reliance on discounts as a means of generating sales, (3) instituting more flexible price policies, (4) frequent price increments to maintain or improve margins, (5) reduction of freight absorption and delivered-price practices, (6) greater use of flexible sales contracts to incorporate frequent price increases, and (7) more centralized management of price adjustments.[25]

SUMMARY

When pricing a new product a firm normally uses either a skimming policy or a penetration policy. Skimming means charging a high introductory price, often coupled with heavy promotion. As a product moves through its life cycle its price is lowered to reach the mass market. Skimming is usually more successful when demand is relatively inelastic, the product is well protected legally, and production cannot be rapid.

Penetration pricing is a mass market strategy. The product is introduced at a relatively low price. This strategy involves more risk than a skimming policy because the firm must gear up for mass production and mass marketing. The objective of penetration pricing is to obtain a large volume of sales, thus achieving economies of mass production. Low cost and low prices will often preclude entry by other competitors. Extinction pricing, while somewhat similar to penetration pricing, is designed to eliminate competition rather than block entry and achieve economies of scale.

A skimming or penetration pricing policy may be altered through the use of discounts and allowances. Common types are quantity, functional, cash, and seasonal discounts.

Many companies use geographic pricing policies to account for the cost of freight. In FOB pricing title passes to the buyer and transportation charges are paid by the seller at the selling point. The effect of FOB pricing is higher total cost to purchasers located farther from the seller.

Uniform delivered pricing equates freight charges to all buyers by charging a flat rate. Zone pricing equates freight rates within large geographic areas. The effect of this strategy is to equate purchase advantages among buyers in large geographic regions.

Basing-point pricing requires the seller to designate a location as a basing point and charge all buyers as if the product were shipped from the basing point. If a firm charges freight fees when none were actually incurred, the fee is referred to as phantom freight. The effect of basing-point pricing is to eliminate freight price competition and extend the geographic boundaries of a market.

Freight absorption pricing is used by sellers in areas where competition is extremely intense or to break into new market areas. The seller absorbs either all or part of the freight cost. Sometimes the additional economies of scale will more than offset the expense to the seller of paying the freight, thus increasing total profit.

Marketing managers use a number of special pricing policies to meet specific competitive situations. Flexible pricing is often used in the sale of shopping and specialty goods. Under this policy different customers pay different prices for essentially the same merchandise. A single-price policy offers all goods and services at the same price within a given store. It removes price comparisons from the buyer's decision-making process and simplifies shopping.

When a merchant establishes a series of prices for a category of merchandise, it has created a price line. Price lines usually minimize confusion for the consumer and the sales clerk. The seller may offer a wider variety of merchandise at each established price and still carry a smaller total inventory. One problem merchants face when using price lines is that of where to establish the various prices. If prices are too far apart, the sales clerk may have difficulty trading up customers.

Leader pricing is designed to increase consumer patronage of a particular store. A product is sold at cost or even below cost to attract customers. Cents-off promotions are often used in the same fashion. In contrast to these two strategies or tactics, bait pricing is not a genuine attempt to give the consumer a bargain. The dealer hopes to get the customer into the store with the false price (the bait) and then use high-pressure selling to persuade the consumer to buy more expensive merchandise.

Odd–even pricing is an attempt to use consumer psychology. Rather than pricing a product at $100, the price may be established at $99.95, thus giving consumers the feeling that they are paying a lower price for the product. Even prices are sometimes used to denote quality. For example, a fine watch may be offered at $400.

Unit pricing is designed to help the economy-minded purchaser get the most product per unit without regard to quality. It is typically used in grocery stores.

Joint costs are an unusual situation in product pricing. They occur when products are derived from a common production process, so that any allocation of costs is somewhat arbitrary. Joint costs can, however, affect the stated profitability of a product, depending on the allocation technique used.

Inflation poses a unique problem for marketing managers. Some companies have eliminated low-margin products. Others have adopted delayed-quotation pricing and escalator clauses. Still other firms have increased prices without notifying the purchaser. One common technique is unbundling of services. This involves charging extra for services when they are demanded and not providing them otherwise.

KEY TERMS

Price skimming	Flexible pricing
Penetration pricing	Price line
Extinction pricing	Leader pricing
Quantity discount	Cents-off promotion
Functional or trade discount	Bait pricing
Cash discount	Psychological pricing
Seasonal discount	Unit pricing
Promotional allowance	Product line pricing
FOB origin	Joint costs
Uniform delivered pricing	Bid pricing
Zone pricing	Delayed-quotation pricing
Basing-point pricing	Escalator clause
Multiple-basing-point pricing	Price shading
Freight absorption pricing	

QUESTIONS FOR DISCUSSION

1. Describe the strategy of price skimming. When is it most effective? What are the advantages of using this strategy?
2. What is penetration pricing? When do firms use this strategy? How does it differ from extinction pricing?
3. Explain the difference between a quantity discount and a functional discount. What purpose does each of them serve?
4. What is FOB pricing? Discuss it from the viewpoint of the firm and from that of the consumer.
5. What are some of the advantages of using flexible prices? Why is this type of pricing not used by most retailers?
6. Define the term *leader pricing*. How does it differ from cents-off promotions?
7. Outline some of the factors that affect product line pricing. When is this strategy used?

8. What effect do shortages have on pricing policies? What price strategies are appropriate in such an environment?

9. Differentiate between price shading and delayed-quotation pricing. Can you give an example of each?

10. What pricing strategies should be used for the following hypothetical new products? Give reasons to justify your answer.
   a. a proved remedy for baldness
   b. a minicomputer for home use
   c. an improved version of an electric car
   d. a new digital watch
   e. a new video-recording system

NOTES

1. For an example of skimming in monopolies see Alan Reynolds, "A Kind Word for Cream Skimming," *Harvard Business Review,* November 1974, pp. 113–120.

2. "Pricing Strategy in an Inflation Economy," *Business Week,* April 6, 1974, p. 47.

3. "How TI Beat the Clock on Its $20 Digital Watch," *Business Week,* May 31, 1976, pp. 62–64.

4. Ibid.

5. "Why BSR Dominates the Record-Changer Market," *Business Week,* June 7, 1976, pp. 84–85.

6. "L&M Expands Eagle 20s, Says Trade Likes Low Price," *Advertising Age,* May 31, 1976, p. 8.

7. F. M. Sherer, *Industrial Pricing Theory and Evidence* (New York: Rand McNally, 1970), p. 137.

8. Ibid., p. 139.

9. Alfred Gross, "Cents-Off: A Critical Promotion Tactic," *MSU Business Topics,* Spring 1971, pp. 13–20.

10. F. Robert Shoaf and Edward L. Melnick, "Retail Grocer Pricing Responses to Manufacturer-Initiated Cents-Off Package Promotions," *Journal of Consumer Affairs,* 8 (Summer 1974): 76–85; see also Craig L. Thrasher, "Price Leader Error Manipulation: Some Preliminary Views," *Journal of Consumer Affairs,* 7 (Summer 1973): 77–83.

11. "Sears Denies FTC Charge of Using Bait and Switch Ad," *Advertising Age,* July 15, 1974, p. 7.

12. Kent B. Monroe, "Buyers' Subjective Perceptions of Price," *Journal of Marketing Research,* 10 (February 1973): 70–80; Jan Stapel, " 'Fair' or 'Psychological' Pricing?" *Journal of Marketing Research,* 9 (February 1972): 109–110; Peter Cooper, "Subjective Economics: Factors in a Psychology of Spending," in Bernard Taylor and Gordon Wills, eds., *Pricing Strategy* (Princeton, N.J.: Brandon Systems Press, 1970), pp. 112–121: Lawrence Friedman, "Psychological Pricing in the Food Industry," in Almarin Phillips and Oliver Williamson, eds., *Prices: Issues in Theory, Practice and Public Policy* (Philadelphia: University of Pennsylvania Press, 1967), pp. 187–201; André Gabor and Clive Granger, "On the Price Consciousness of Consumers," *Applied Statistics,* 10 (November 1961): 170–188, and "Price Sensitivity of the Consumer," *Journal of Advertising Research,* 4 (December 1964): 40–44; Eli Ginzberg, "Customary Prices,"

American Economic Review, 26 (June 1936): 296; "How Much Do Customers Know About Retail Prices?" *Progressive Grocer,* 43 (February 1964): C104–C106; Jacob Jacoby, Jerry Olson, and Rafael Haddock, "Price, Brand Name, and Product Composition Characteristics as Determinants of Perceived Quality," *Journal of Applied Psychology,* 55 (December 1971): 470–479; and Joseph Kamen and Robert Toman, "Psychophysics of Prices," *Journal of Marketing Research,* 7 (February 1970): 27–35.

13. T. David McCullough and Daniel I. Padberg, "Unit Pricing in Supermarkets: Alternatives, Costs and Consumer Reaction," *Search, Agriculture,* 1 (January 1971): 1–25.

14. Martin Cohen, "Report #1-203: Unit Pricing Study," Internal Report to Stop and Shop, Inc., June 29, 1970; Monroe Friedman, *Dual-Price Labels: Usage Patterns and Potential Benefits for Shoppers in Inner-City and Suburban Supermarkets* (Ypsilanti, Mich.: Eastern Michigan University, Center for the Study of Contemporary Issues, 1971); Lawrence M. Lamont and James T. Rothe, "The Impact of Unit Pricing on Channel Systems," in Fred C. Auvine, ed., *Combined Proceedings 1971 Spring and Fall Conferences* (Chicago: American Marketing Association, 1972), pp. 653–658.

15. William E. Kilbourne, "A Factorial Experiment on the Impact of Unit Pricing on Low Income Consumers," *Journal of Marketing Research,* 11 (November 1971): 453–455.

16. See Arthur V. Corr, "The Role of Cost in Pricing," *Management Accounting,* 56 (November 1974): 15–32; Alfred R. Oxenfeldt, "Product Line Pricing," *Harvard Business Review,* July-August 1966, pp. 137–144; for an interesting study on internal transfer pricing, see David Granick, "National Differences in the Use of Internal Transfer Prices," *California Management Review,* 17 (Summer 1975): 28–40.

17. Much of this section is taken from Joseph P. Guiltinan, "Risk-Aversive Pricing Policies: Problems and Alternatives," *Journal of Marketing,* 40 (January 1976): 10–15.

18. "Pricing Strategy in an Inflation Economy," p. 45.

19. Edmund Faltermayers, "The Hyperinflation in Plant Construction," *Fortune,* November 1975, p. 102.

20. Judith Bauer, "Coping with Inflationary Costs—By Hiking Product Prices," *The Conference Board Record,* 11 (September 1974): 53.

21. "Pricing Strategy in an Inflation Economy," p. 45.

22. Ibid., p. 48.

23. Nessim Hanna, A. H. Kizilbash, and Albert Smart, "Marketing Strategy Under Conditions of Economic Scarcity," *Journal of Marketing,* 39 (January 1975): 63–80.

24. Paul Blackwell, "Shortages: The Pain We All Feel and What to Do About It," *Sales Management,* 112 (July 22, 1974): 26.

25. Hanna et al., p. 65; see also E. Patrick McGuire, "Living with Scarcity—Poses Problems for Marketers," *Conference Board Record,* 11 (March 1974): 5–9.

CASE 17
Mayfield Chemical Corporation

Mayfield Chemical has held the largest share of the suntan products market for the past sixteen years. Brown Body, Mayfield's suntan product brand, comes as a lotion, cream, or oil. It is packaged in both spray and squeeze bottle containers and is available in virtually every major drugstore in the United States.

Monroe Helm, director of new-product development, has been experimenting with an extract of the prickly-pear cactus referred to in the lab as MC-5. This substance has proved to be an extremely effective sunscreen — it blocks ultraviolet rays yet does not prevent tanning. Tests on paid volunteers revealed that when MC-5 was formulated into a cream-based product it was 50 percent more effective than any comparable product now on the market. That is, a person could stay in the sun approximately twice as long without getting sunburned or blistered. By the same token, it took much longer to get a tan with the new product.

A six-ounce container of Brown Body Cream costs Mayfield $.68 to manufacture and distribute. This figure includes a fixed-cost allocation based on sales volume for the past year. The product has a suggested retail price of $1.40, and most retailers adhere to this price.

Brown Body Sunscreen has been selected as the name for the new product containing MC-5. Ken Price, the marketing manager, has received first-year demand estimates from the marketing research department as follows: retail price $1.10 — 1,400,000; retail price $1.40 — 1,000,000; retail price $1.80 — 800,000. Total unit costs will be approximately $.73 for 1,000,000 to 2,000,000 units and $.77 for 800,000 to 1,000,000 units.

Mayfield's pricing strategy for new products has always been to start with a relatively high price and then gradually lower it as production capacity increases or when it meets with significant sales resistance at the high prices. Several factors have caused Price to question whether this strategy should be followed in introducing Brown Body Sunscreen. First, the new Jacksonville, Florida, production facility has approximately 200,000 units per month of unused production capacity. Second, Goldtone, Mayfield's leading competitor, has developed a habit of emulating Mayfield's new products and then offering the merchandise at a price approximately 15 percent below Mayfield's. Third, Mayfield's excellent physical-distribution system allows it to obtain intensive distribution of any new product within a short period. Finally, Brown Body Sunscreen has obvious and easily demonstrable advantages that will require little educational effort.

1. Should Mayfield change its pricing strategy?
2. How might the factors listed by Price affect the pricing strategy?

VI Promotion Concepts

18

Marketing Communication: Promotion Strategies

OBJECTIVES

■ To understand the basic elements of the communication process.
■ To learn about the different goals of promotion.
■ To become aware of the basic forms of promotion.
■ To learn about the various factors that affect the promotional blend.
■ To understand the steps involved in developing a sound promotional plan.

When a company develops a new product, changes an old one, or simply wants to increase sales of an existing product or service, it must transmit its selling messages to potential customers. This chapter begins by examining the basic process of communication and its relationship to promotion. Next we will discuss the goals of promotion and the types of promotion that can be utilized to achieve those goals. After that we will study the factors that influence the selection of a specific medium or blend of media. The chapter concludes with a strategy for integrating the promotional plan and an investigation of the impact of promotion on society.

WHAT IS THE COMMUNICATION PROCESS?
Defining Communication

Communication may be divided into two major categories. Explicit communication involves the use of language to establish common understandings among people. The second form of communication, implicit communication, involves "intuitive interpretation" of the "relatively unconscious symbolisms of gesture and the unconscious assimilation of the ideas and behavior of one's own culture."[1] This nonverbal communication is expressed in dress, driving habits, facial expressions, and so forth. People communicate symbolically by transmitting meaningful symbols (such as a raised eyebrow) to others.

Communication requires a common understanding, which, in turn, requires overlapping frames of reference. If you said, "Let's go eat at the golden arches" to a person from the Soviet Union, it is doubtful that meaning would be shared. Since McDonald's is unknown in the Soviet Union, the visitor would not understand your frame of reference. The act of communication would be even more difficult if our foreign friend could not speak English. We sometimes miscommunicate because of subtleties of meaning. Differences in age, social class, or ethnicity also often lead to lack of understanding.

The Communications Flow

Communication consists of five components. These are (1) the source, (2) encoding, (3) the transmission channel, (4) reception, and (5) decoding. (See Figure 18.1.) Note that the overlapping circles imply a common frame of reference—the necessary ingredient for understanding.

The source is the originator of the message. It may be a person or an organization. Encoding requires the conversion of the source's ideas and thoughts into message form. As I write this material I am encoding my thoughts just as I would if we were engaged in a two-way conversation. If the source happened to be a business trying to sell a good or service, the firm might rely on an advertising agency to act as an encoder.

Transmission of a message requires a channel such as a voice, radio, newspaper, or any other communication medium. A changed facial expression can also serve as a channel. Reception occurs when the message is detected by the receiver and enters his or her frame of reference. Reception is normally high in a two-way conversation. The message of mass communication may or may not be detected by the desired receivers. It is a shotgun approach. For example, some mem-

FIGURE 18.1   **The Basic Communication Process**

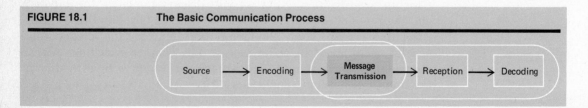

bers of the desired audience will be watching a certain TV program and others will not.

Decoding involves interpretation of the language and symbols sent by the source through a channel. Again, without common understanding and overlapping frames of reference the message will not be understood. Just because a message is received does not mean that it will be properly decoded. If you see an advertisement written in Chinese, you can't decode it (unless, of course, you read Chinese).

Face-to-face communication also involves feedback. Feedback to the source may be verbal, as in "I agree," or nonverbal, as in a nod, a smile or a frown, or many other gestures. A mass communicator is cut off from direct feedback and must rely on market research or sales trends for indirect feedback.

The application of behavioral-science techniques to the study of communication has enabled scholars to better understand the total information transfer process. Perception, learning, persuasion, and cognitive dissonance all relate to communication.

Communication and Perception

Perception theory provides important insights into the nature of communication. People tend to organize their conscious perception of the environment in terms of the highest available level of organization.[2] For example, when a person looks at a refrigerator, he or she does not view it as a combination of sheet metal, insulation, tubing, and a motor, but as a refrigerator. Organized perception has led to advertising campaigns such as this one for Salem cigarettes: "You can take Salem out of the country . . . but you can't take the country out of Salem." This jingle was played 1½ times; on the second round, the silence after "You can take Salem out of the country, but . . ." invited the listener to complete the message mentally.[3]

Perception is also selective. People cannot possibly perceive every stimulus in their environment. One study showed that of all the promotions to which consumers are subjected every day, only between 70 and 80 are perceived.[4]

Perception depends on the stimulus. The color of an advertisement, the familiarity of a brand, the contrast in a picture, movement, intensity (e.g., increased volume), and of course the message itself influence perception. A recent study in which individuals were told that a drink would taste sweet found that these people were more likely to perceive the drink to be sweet than people who were not exposed to the test.[5] The next step for a beverage bottler would be to determine the importance of sweetness to the target market.

Communication and Learning

Learning, like perception, is an integral part of communication theory. We may subdivide learning into two types: intentional learning and incidental learning.[6] A person who intends to learn is more perceptive of message content than a person who happens to learn while engaged in another activity. Promotional learning is almost always incidental to entertainment. Yet a person searching for a good or service may actively utilize various media for intentional learning.

After learning takes place we begin to forget almost immediately. Losses from memory are very great at first and then slowly level out.[7] The greater the complexity and length of the message communicated, the greater the amount of repetition necessary to produce retention.[8] Also, "noise" or interference may increase forgetting. For example, competing messages may increase the time necessary to produce retention.[9]

As we all know, promotional repetition can sometimes be carried to an extreme. Eventually the message may become boring and thus reduce perception and learning. Unfortunately, research has not produced a magic number that, if exceeded, will hinder the learning process.

Communication and Persuasion

In order to be persuaded by a given message, consumers must first receive the message and then comprehend it. After that they must yield to it; that is, change their attitudes accordingly. If marketers are interested in changing long-run behavior patterns, the receiver must also retain the information. Finally and (usually) most important, the receiver must act or take a position based on the new attitude. This is persuasion. For example, the March of Dimes may have convinced us that birth defects are bad, yet the organization has not achieved its goals until young people take positive action to prevent birth defects.

Research on persuasive communication has taught us several things. Carl Hovland found that overemphasis on yielding (getting someone to give in to your position) can be a serious error.[10] Persuadability tends to increase with intelligence and education. Although more intelligent people are more resistant to persuasion, their increased attention to and comprehension of the message make them more vulnerable.[11]

Cognitive Dissonance

The ability of a source to persuade a receiver is also at least partly a function of cognitive dissonance. When people are aware of a lack of consistency among their attitudes, values, and opinions, they tend to feel an inner tension. This phenomenon is called cognitive dissonance. If a student decides to cut class in order to visit a friend, he or she may feel somewhat apprehensive about this action. The student's behavior is inconsistent with his or her beliefs about attending class.

The theory of cognitive dissonance holds that

> when a person chooses between two or more alternatives, discomfort or dissonance will almost inevitably arise because of the person's knowl-

edge that while the decision he has made has certain advantages, it also has some disadvantages. That dissonance arises after almost every decision, and further, that the individual will invariably take steps to reduce this dissonance.[12]

The magnitude of dissonance is a function of the following factors:

1. The more attractive the rejected alternative, the greater will be the magnitude of the dissonance.
2. The more important the decision, the stronger will be the dissonance.
3. The intensity of dissonance becomes greater as the number of negative characteristics increase.
4. As the number of rejected alternatives increases, the greater will be the dissonance.
5. The greater the perceived similarity of alternatives (cognitive overlap), the greater the dissonance.
6. The more recent the decision between alternatives, the greater will be the magnitude of dissonance because of the phenomenon of forgetting.
7. A decision that violates a strongly held attitude produces greater dissonance than a decision that rebuts a weaker belief.[13]

Consumers can reduce dissonance in several different ways. Obtaining new information through communication can help reduce dissonance. Naturally, the new data should be consistent with previous decisions. Also, information can be avoided that would contradict those decisions. It has been shown, for example, that new-car owners read significantly more advertisements for the car they have just purchased than for other cars.[14] Another study found that after a specific phonograph record had been selected, the unchosen alternative was downgraded.[15] In some instances people will deliberately seek out discrepant facts in order to refute them and reduce dissonance.[16] If a decision maker can find weak arguments against a particular decision, they will build the decision maker's confidence.

Marketing managers can aid in reducing dissonance by communicating effectively with purchasers. A note inside the package congratulating the purchaser on making a wise decision may aid in dissonance reduction. Research has shown that postpurchase letters sent by manufacturers and dissonance-reducing statements in instruction booklets result in fewer product returns and future-order cancellations.[17]

THE GOALS OF PROMOTION
Behavior Modification

People communicate for many reasons. They seek amusement, ask help, give help or instructions, provide information, and express ideas and thoughts. Promotion, on the other hand, seeks to (1) modify behavior and thoughts (e.g., get you to drink Pepsi rather than Coke)

FIGURE 18.2   **Promotional Objectives**

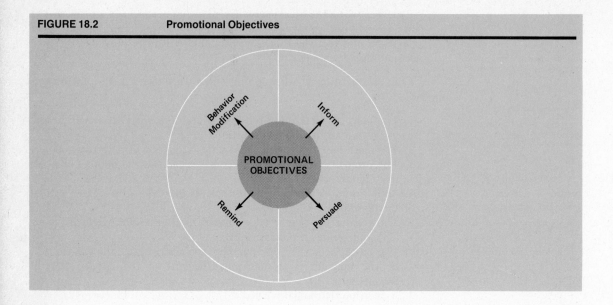

or (2) reinforce existing behavior (e.g., get you to continue to drink Pepsi once you have converted). (See Figure 18.2.) The source (the seller) hopes to create a favorable image for itself (institutional promotion) or to motivate purchases of the company's goods and services.

Informing

All promotions are designed to inform, persuade, or remind the target market about the firm's offerings. Often a company will attempt to accomplish several of these objectives simultaneously. Informative promotion is generally more prevalent during the early stages of the product life cycle. It is a necessary ingredient for increasing primary demand. People typically won't purchase a good or service until they know what it will do and how it may benefit them. Consumerists and social critics generally applaud the informative function of promotion, since it aids the consumer in making more intelligent purchase decisions.

Persuading

Persuasive promotion is not viewed in a favorable light by many consumerists. Yet most promotions attempt to persuade. Persuasive promotion is designed to stimulate purchase. Often the firm is not attempting to obtain an immediate response but to create a positive image in order to influence long-term buyer behavior. Persuasion normally becomes the primary promotion goal when the product enters the growth stage of the product life cycle.

Reminder Promotion

Reminder promotion is used to keep the product brand name in the public's mind and is prevalent during the maturity stage of the life cycle. Coca-Cola, Pepsi-Cola, Bell Telephone, and the FTD florist association use large amounts of reminder promotion. This form of promotion tacitly assumes that the target audience has already been persuaded of the merits of the good or service. It simply serves as a "memory jogger."

Specific Objectives

The objectives of informing, persuading, or reminding serve as general guidelines for promotional campaigns and strategies. However, they are not sufficient for measuring the results of promotion. Russel Colley has developed a technique known as DAGMAR—Defining Advertising Goals, Measuring Advertising Results—that is predicated upon lucid advertising (or promotion) objectives. Colley writes,

> Advertising's job purely and simply is to communicate, to a defined audience, information and a frame-of-mind that stimulates action. Advertising succeeds or fails, depending on how well it communicates the desired information and attitudes to the right people at the right time and at the right cost.[18]

Thus, in order to be measurable, goals should be defined in the following manner:

1. To increase brand awareness among 21–30-year-old males with two or more years of college by 10 percent between November 15 and April 1.
2. To obtain a 5-percent increase in retail distribution in all southwestern communities with populations over 5000 by June 15.

These objectives are precise, quantified, and measurable, and have a specific time frame. Marketing research can be used to determine whether or not the first goal was achieved. A syndicated audit service such as the National Retail Tracking Index or Neilsen reports may be purchased to evaluate the second objective. Firms like General Motors, Shell Oil, Exxon, and Rockwell-Standard all use the DAGMAR approach in setting and measuring their promotional goals.

**APPROACHES
TO PROMOTION
The AIDA Concept
and the Hierarchy
of Effects**

The objectives of promotion require the target consumer to pass through a series of stages that lead to purchase behavior. (See Figure 18.3.) The first stage is cognitive — this is when a message is received and interpreted. The second stage is affective and requires the formulation of a positive product image. The final, conative stage consists of motivation and purchase.

E. K. Strong developed the AIDA (Attention–Interest–Desire–Action) concept in 1925. First, the marketing manager obtains a person's attention by means of a greeting and approach (personal selling) or loud volume, unusual contrasts, bold headlines, movement, bright colors and so forth (mass media). Next, a good sales presentation or

FIGURE 18.3	Stages Leading to Purchase		
THE AIDA CONCEPT	1. Attention	2. Interest 3. Desire	4. Action
HIERARCHY OF EFFECTS	1. Awareness 2. Knowledge	3. Liking 4. Preference	5. Conviction 6. Purchase
STAGES	Cognitive Stage	Affective Stage	Conative Stage

promotional copy creates interest in the product. Illustrating how the product's features will satisfy the consumer's needs creates desire. Finally, a special offer or simply a strong closing sales pitch may be used to obtain purchase action. The hierarchy-of-effects theory is basically an updated version of the AIDA concept.

Sequencing of Stages

The three-stage approach to purchase behavior suggests that promotional effectiveness can be measured in terms of people moving from one stage to the next. Certainly there cannot be conviction without knowledge or knowledge without awareness. Also, measuring the effectiveness of promotion at various stages avoids the problem of directly relating promotion and sales.

Testing the Stages

An early study failed to confirm that movement from one stage to another increases the probability of purchase.[19] However, more recent studies have proved more promising. A Sears, Roebuck project found positive relationships between advertising recall and purchase intention. Sears also found a positive relationship between purchase intention and actual purchase.[20] Another study found that awareness exists before attitude change and that intention to purchase exists before purchase.[21]

THE BASIC FORMS OF PROMOTION

Rarely will a single communication resource be the most effective means of accomplishing the firm's promotional objectives. Instead, a blend of various factors must be used to reach the target market. That blend is referred to as a company's promotional mix. The four major tools that make up a promotional mix are

- *Advertising*—any paid form of nonpersonal presentation and promotion of ideas, goods, or services by an identified sponsor.

FIGURE 18.4   Promotion as a Substrategy of a Master Marketing Strategy

- *Personal Selling*—oral face-to-face presentation in a conversation with one or more prospective purchasers for the purpose of making sales.
- *Sales Promotion*—those marketing activities, other than personal selling, advertising, and publicity, that stimulate consumer purchasing and dealer effectiveness, such as displays, shows and exhibitions, demonstrations, and various nonrecurrent selling efforts not in the ordinary routine.
- *Publicity*—nonpersonal stimulation of demand for a product, service, or business unit by planting commercially significant news about it in a published medium or obtaining favorable presentation of it upon radio, television, or stage that is not paid for by the sponsor.[22]

The role of promotion in the total marketing mix is shown in Figure 18.4. (Some scholars include packaging, since it can serve as a means of communication.)

Advertising

Advertising is a form of impersonal one-way mass communication. It may be transmitted by many different media, including television, radio, newspapers, magazines, books, direct mail, billboards, transit cards, and so forth. Since advertising lacks a direct feedback mechanism, it cannot adapt as easily as personal selling to the changing preferences, individual differences, and personal goals of the consumers.

Advertising has two main decision areas: (1) determining the message to be transmitted to the target market and (2) selecting the media. Neither choice is easy, and both involve a number of different dimensions. We will examine these in detail in Chapter 19.

Personal Selling

Advertising dollars are spent primarily on the promotion of consumer goods, whereas personal selling is more prevalent in the industrial-goods field. Industrial products are less homogeneous and often do not lend themselves to mass promotions. Instead, many products must be tailored to the needs and financial status of the buyer. In order to effectively design and sell a custom-made product, rapid buyer feedback is necessary. Thus personal selling must be used rather than advertising. The role of advertising may be to create general buyer awareness and interest through advertisements in trade media. Print media advertising often includes coupons soliciting the potential customer to "fill this out for more detailed information." In this manner advertising can be used to locate potential customers for the sales force. Effective sales presentations aren't cheap. The cost of face-to-face selling of industrial goods climbed to an average of $71.27 per sale in 1975. The costs of a sales call ranged from $83.48 for companies with fewer than 10 salespeople to $54.84 for those with a sales force of more than 50. Sales costs have doubled since 1965.[23]

Sales Promotion

Sales promotion is a "catchall" category that consists of all promotions other than personal selling and advertising. The following list includes many of the tools used in sales promotion:

Trial-size bottles and cans	Tours
Free samples	Point-of-purchase displays
Coupons	Contests
Trading stamps	Free use of products in movies
Catalogs	Cents-off packages
Directories	Cash refund offers
Badges	Gifts for secretaries and
Decals	executives
Premiums and giveaways	Calendars
Demonstrations	Packages with secondary uses
Trade shows	(e.g., cigar boxes)
Free films	Toll-free numbers

A major promotion campaign may involve the use of several sales promotion tools as well as advertising and personal selling. Sales promotion is generally a short-run tool used to stimulate immediate increases in demand. Research shows that sales promotion complements advertising by yielding faster responses in terms of sales. Promotions appeal to the consumer looking for a deal, who often sees all products as equal or is willing to sacrifice quality for price.[24]

Publicity

Corporations are concerned about their public images and often spend large sums of money to build a positive consumer image. This is publicity. Too many firms have found that a negative industry and/or company image often leads to new and restrictive governmental legislation. Automobiles, toys, and cereals are three prime examples.

While good publicity is expensive, bad publicity is often free. When a firm pollutes a stream, produces a defective product, has executives who are engaged in payoffs or bribes, or becomes involved in other undesirable acts, the world hears about it through the mass media. Bad publicity can often be avoided by conducting a social-responsibility audit. The audit examines company activities that are socially desirable and those that have potential for negative publicity. Management can take the offensive and eliminate sources of potential trouble before they occur.

FACTORS THAT AFFECT THE PROMOTIONAL MIX
Introduction

Promotional mixes vary significantly from one product and industry to the next. Normally, advertising and personal selling are the primary product and service promotional tools and are, in turn, supported and supplemented by sales promotion. Publicity aids in developing a positive image for the organization and the product line.

The Nature of the Product

A study by Jon Udell identified the relative importance of several facets of the promotional mix.[25] (See Table 18.1.) Personal selling was most important in industrial goods and least important in consumer

TABLE 18.1 Relative Importance of the Elements of Marketing Communications[a]

	Producers of:		
Sales Effort Activity	Industrial Goods	Consumer Durables	Consumer Nondurables
Sales management and personal selling	69.2	47.6	38.1
Broadcast media advertising	0.9	10.7	20.9
Printed media advertising	12.5	16.1	14.8
Special promotional activities	9.6	15.5	15.5
Branding and promotional packaging	4.5	9.5	9.8
Other	3.3	0.6	0.9
Total	100.0	100.0	100.0

Source: Jon Udell, "The Perceived Importance of the Elements of Strategy," Journal of Marketing, 32 (January 1968): 38. Reprinted by permission of the American Marketing Association.
[a] The data are the average point allocations of 336 industrial, 52 consumer durable, and 88 consumer nondurable goods producers. Nine responses are excluded because of point allocations that did not equal 100.

nondurables (mostly convenience goods). Broadcast advertising was used heavily in consumer goods promotion, particularly for nondurables. Print media, on the other hand, were employed for all three product categories. Industrial goods were advertised primarily through special trade magazines. Consumer goods, in contrast, were advertised through newspapers and various consumer-oriented magazines. Sales promotion, branding, and packaging were approximately twice as important for consumer goods as for industrial goods.

Industrial goods, with the exception of supply items, tend to rely more heavily on personal selling than on advertising. Consumer goods, on the other hand, are promoted primarily through advertising. Persuasive personal selling is also important at the retail level for shopping goods such as automobiles and appliances. Informative personal selling is common in better furniture stores and with specialty goods as well as industrial installations, accessories, and component parts and materials.

Market Characteristics

Widely scattered potential customers, highly informed buyers, and a large number of brand-loyal repeat purchasers generally require a blend of more advertising and sales promotion and less personal selling. Sometimes personal selling is required even when buyers are well informed and geographically dispersed. Industrial installations and component parts may be sold to extremely competent individuals with extensive education and work experience. Yet the salesperson must still be present to explain the product and work out the details of any purchase agreement. Often firms sell goods and services in markets where potential customers are difficult to locate. Advertising is used to locate potential customers by inviting the reader to "call collect" for more information or "fill out the coupon" for a detailed brochure. Salespeople are sent to the potential customers as the calls or coupons are received.

Another market characteristic that may dictate the use of salespeople depends on whether physical stocking of merchandise (detailing) is traditional for a product class. Milk, bread, and other convenience goods, for example, are generally stocked by the person who makes the delivery. This practice is becoming increasingly common in the convenience good field as sellers strive to ensure attractive display and adequate shelf space for their wares.

Available Funds

Money, or the lack of it, may easily be the most important factor in determining the promotional blend. A small, undercapitalized manufacturer may rely heavily on free publicity if its product is of a unique nature. If the situation warrants a sales force, the financially strained firm may turn to manufacturers' agents who work strictly on a commission basis with no advances or expense accounts. Even smaller, well-capitalized organizations may not be able to afford the advertising rates of publications such as *Better Homes and Gardens, Reader's Digest,* or *The Wall Street Journal.* The price of a single advertisement in these media could often support a salesperson for a year.

Stage of the Product Life Cycle

The stage of the product life cycle can also be an important determinant of a product's promotional blend. If the product reaches the growth stage of the life cycle and obtains adequate distribution, the promotional blend may shift. Often a change is necessary because different types of individuals enter the target market. The promotion blend in the later stages of the life cycle might shift toward personal selling to maintain adequate distribution. Various promotion techniques can be used to stimulate repeat purchases and top-of-the-mind awareness among potential late buyers (see Chapter 19).

IMPLEMENTATION OF THE PROMOTIONAL PLAN

A promotional plan involves several distinct steps: (1) setting objectives, (2) identifying the target market, (3) developing a budget, (4) choosing a message, (5) determining the promotional mix, (6) selecting the media mix, (7) managing the promotion, (8) measuring effectiveness, and (9) following up and modifying the promotion campaign. (See Figure 18.5.) Each step follows in a logical sequence, resulting in a promotion campaign that is geared to specific objectives. Several steps require the completion of an earlier task before they can be undertaken—for example, the setting of objectives should come before budget development. Others can occur simultaneously and, in fact, may occur in reverse order. This is particularly true of message selection, choice of promotional mix, and media selection.

Setting Objectives

The need for specific, realistic objectives has already been discussed and needs little elaboration. It is the starting point for any promotional

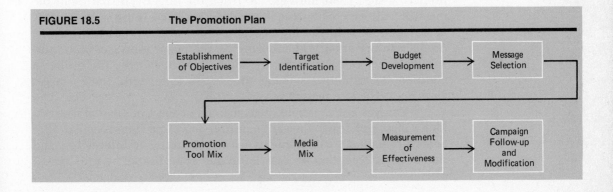

FIGURE 18.5   **The Promotion Plan**

campaign. Indeed, it is impossible to plan a promotional program unless the marketing manager knows what goals he or she is trying to achieve!

A corollary to the establishment of specific objectives such as level of message awareness or number of sales completed as a percentage of sales calls made is the development of positioning goals. All four promotional tools must be developed and utilized in terms of a specific "positioning" goal for the good or service in question. Each tool, whether it is publicity, personal selling, advertising, or sales promotion, should aid in placing the good or service at a specific point on the positioning continuum for a specific target market. A woman's handbag premium offer would hardly aid in positioning Marlboro cigarettes.

Identifying the Target Market

The market segment that the firm wants to reach in a given promotional campaign should be explicitly defined both demographically and, perhaps, psychographically through market research. Naturally, the target market should consist primarily of the individuals who are most likely to purchase the product within a relevant period. For a new product, in-home use tests, test marketing, and focus groups provide valuable insights into characteristics of potential buyers.

Developing a Budget

After a marketing manager has specified the promotional goals and identified the relevant market segments, a concrete promotional budget can be developed. This is no simple task, nor is there a "cookbook approach" that will lead to an optimal promotional budget. Top-management decision making is usually required to define the role of promotion in the marketing mix. The importance of promotion is determined largely by things such as competitors' actions and type of product (discussed earlier in the chapter).

Choosing a Message

After promotional objectives have been created, target markets identified, and promotional budgets established, management can begin preparing the "right message" to reach the target. The nature of the message will vary, of course, depending on the goals of the promotion. If the product is in the introductory phase of the product life cycle, product information will probably be the major message. More persuasive promotional themes are addressed later in the life cycle; in addition, an attempt is made to communicate with "new" target audiences (the late majority).

Messages are channeled to consumers from a number of sources. Many messages leave a negative impression or no impression at all.[26] Some promotional communications are boring or uninteresting, and the message reception process is further complicated by the "noise" problem.

Determining the Promotional Mix

Often different message themes are developed for each promotional tool. For example, public relations may be charged with creating a positive corporate image among target customers. Advertising will focus on developing corporate and product awareness to complement personal selling. The function of personal selling will be to interact with the customer by amplifying and explaining the advertising messages and designing the right product or service to meet the specific needs of the customer. Sales promotion may come into the picture by communicating a "special discount" to prospective buyers if they purchase now. Thus public relations, advertising, and sales promotion are all aimed toward increasing sales effectiveness.

John Morrill studied the promotion of 129 brands of 23 products in the utility, commodity, electronic, metalworking, and chemical industries.[27] His research revealed that advertising exposure increased positive buyer attitudes and sales response. He found that dollar sales per sales call were much higher for customers who had been exposed to advertising before the sales call than for those who had not. Other research has shown that a positive company image increases the effectiveness of industrial salespeople.[28]

Selecting the Media Mix

The advertising media mix to be used in conjunction with the other three promotional tools will be discussed fully in Chapter 20. At this point you should know that different types of media tend to appeal to different audiences. Also, different specific media, such as country-and-western radio stations, will have different audiences than other specific media, such as stations playing only classical music.

Measuring Effectiveness

It is incumbent on promotion managers to measure the effectiveness of their promotional campaigns. Since the effectiveness of various tools is measured quite differently, this concept will be discussed in detail in Chapters 20 and 21. Without some measurement of the outcome of promotional campaigns, there would be no way of determining whether their objectives are being met.

Following Up and Modifying the Promotion Campaign

After measuring the outcome of a promotional endeavor, it may be necessary to change the promotion plan. Change often occurs in the promotional blend, the media mix, the message, the total promotional budget, or the way the budget is allocated.

Follow-up must also ask the question, What do we know now that we didn't know before we began the promotional campaign? The firm should learn from its mistakes and ensure that policies are established so that the same mistake can be avoided in the future. Unfortunately, many firms ignore this phase of the promotion plan.[29]

SUMMARY

Communication can be either explicit or implicit. Implicit communication involves intuitive interpretation of symbols such as gestures and the unconscious assimilation of the ideas and behavior of one's own culture. The communication process requires a common understanding, which necessitates overlapping frames of reference. It consists of five components: a source, encoding, a transmission channel, reception, and decoding.

Learning is an integral part of communication theory. Promotional learning is almost always incidental to entertainment. After learning something, we begin to forget almost immediately. Retention increases with repetition, meaningful material, and the order in which the material is presented.

Cognitive dissonance refers to the awareness of a lack of consistency among a person's attitudes, values, and opinions, and the inner tension that results from that inconsistency. Obtaining new information through communication can help reduce dissonance. Research has shown that consumers actively seek out data that will help them reduce their dissonance.

The goal of promotion is to modify behavior or to reinforce existing behavior. Specifically, promotion hopes to inform, persuade, or remind. To accomplish promotion objectives an advertisement must first procure the attention of the consumer. Second, it must increase or generate consumer interest. Third, it should create a desire for the good or service. Fourth, a purchase should result.

A blend of several forms of promotion is usually necessary. The four basic forms are advertising, personal selling, sales promotion, and publicity. The nature of the product, market characteristics, the funds available for promotion, and the stage of the product life cycle all affect the promotional blend.

A promotional blend begins with the establishment of objectives and the identification of target consumers. Next a budget is developed, a message chosen, and a promotional mix established. A media mix is determined; promotional management is established; and effectiveness measures are set and monitored. The process concludes with campaign follow-up and modifications where necessary.

KEY TERMS

Communication
Explicit communication
Implicit communication
Source
Encoding
Transmission
Reception
Decoding
Feedback
Perception
Intentional learning

Incidental learning
Persuasion
Cognitive dissonance
Cognitive stage
Affective stage
Conative stage
Advertising
Personal selling
Sales promotion
Publicity

**QUESTIONS
FOR DISCUSSION**

1. Explain the communication process as it relates to the marketing of a product.
2. Explain the role of perception and learning in communication theory.
3. What is cognitive dissonance? What steps must a marketing manager take to reduce dissonance?
4. Briefly outline the major goals of promotion. Give examples of each.
5. What is the AIDA concept? What techniques could be used to gain the attention of a prospective customer?
6. What is meant by the promotional mix? Explain any two components of the mix.
7. Differentiate between advertising and personal selling. How could they be used as complementary tools?
8. Explain the effect that the product life cycle has on the promotional mix for a product.
9. What is the first step in formulating a promotional plan? What are positioning goals? Give at least one example to clarify your views.
10. Into what general categories would you place the following promotional activities?
    a. Direct mailing of coupons for household products.
    b. TV commercials for agencies such as HUD and CPSC.
    c. A newspaper ad announcing a special sale at a local supermarket.
    d. AMF's TV commercial with the theme "We make weekends."

NOTES

1. Edward Sapir, "Communication," *Encyclopedia of the Social Sciences* (New York: Macmillan, 1933), IV, 79.
2. Thomas G. Bever, "Language and Perception," in George A. Miller, ed., *Communication, Language and Meaning* (New York: Basic Books, 1973), p. 149.
3. Stewart H. Britt, "Applying Learning Principles to Marketing," *MSU Business Topics*, Spring 1975, p. 10.
4. See Raymond A. Bauer and Stephen A. Greyser, *Advertising in America: The Consumer View* (Boston: Harvard University, Graduate School of Business Administration, Division of Research, 1968).
5. Beverlee B. Anderson and J. P. Culea, "The Influence of Information Cues on Expectations and Taste Perceptions," Robert L. King, ed., *Proceedings: Southern Marketing Association, 1973 Conference,* pp. 98–101.
6. Britt, p. 5.
7. James J. Jenkins, "Language and Memory," in Miller, p. 160.
8. Leo Bogart, *Strategy in Advertising* (New York: Harcourt Brace Jovanovich, 1967).
9. Benton J. Underwood, "Interference and Forgetting," *Psychological Review,* 64 (January 1957): 49–60.
10. William J. McGuire, "Persuasion," in Miller, pp. 243–255.
11. Ibid.
12. Leon Festinger and Dana Bramel, "The Reactions of Humans to Cognitive Dissonance," in Arthur J. Bachrach, ed., *Experimental Foundations of Clinical Psychology* (New York: Basic Books, 1962), pp. 251–262.
13. Rom J. Markin, Jr., *Consumer Behavior: A Cognitive Orientation* (New York: Macmillan, 1974), pp. 145–147. Copyright © 1974, Rom J. Markin, Jr. Reprinted by permission of Macmillan Publishing Co., Inc.

14. D. Ehrlich, S. Guttman, P. Schonbach, and J. Milles, "Post-Decision Exposure to Relevant Information," *Journal of Abnormal and Social Psychology,* 54 (May 1957): 98–102.

15. L. A. LoScuito and R. Perloff, "Influence of Product Preference on Dissonance Reduction," *Journal of Marketing Research,* 4 (August 1967): 286–290.

16. J. L. Freedman, "Preference for Dissonant Information," *Journal of Personality and Social Psychology,* 8 (August 1968): 172–179.

17. J. H. Donnelly, Jr., and J. M. Ivancevich, "Post-Purchase Reinforcement and Back-Out Behavior," *Journal of Marketing Research,* 7 (May 1970): 399–400; see also S. B. Hunt, "Post-Transaction Communications and Dissonance Reduction," *Journal of Marketing,* 34 (July 1970): 46–51.

18. Russell H. Colley, *Defining Advertising Goals* (New York: Association of National Advertisers, 1961), p. 21.

19. Kristian S. Palda, "The Hypothesis of a Hierarchy of Effects, A Partial Evaluation," *Journal of Marketing Research,* 3 (February 1966): 13–24.

20. "G & R Research Links Recall, Buying Intent," *Advertising Age,* August 16, 1971, p. 3.

21. Terrence O'Brien, "Stages of Consumer Decision Making," *Journal of Marketing Research,* 8 (August 1971): 283–289.

22. *Marketing Definitions: A Glossary of Marketing Terms* (Chicago: American Marketing Association, Committee on Definitions, 1960).

23. "Adbeat," *Advertising Age,* June 28, 1976, p. 59.

24. Robert George Brown, "Sales Response to Promotions and Advertising," *Journal of Advertising Research,* 14 (August 1974): 33–38.

25. Jon G. Udell, "The Perceived Importance of the Elements of Strategy," *Journal of Marketing,* 32 (January 1968): 34–40.

26. Leo Bogart, "Where Does Advertising Go from Here?" *Journal of Advertising Research,* 9 (March 1969): 6.

27. John E. Morrill, "Industrial Advertising Pays Off," *Harvard Business Review,* March-April 1970, pp. 4–14.

28. Theodore Levitt, *Industrial Purchasing Behavior: A Study of Communications Effects* (Boston: Harvard University, Graduate School of Business Administration, Division of Research, 1965).

29. James F. Engle, Hugh G. Wells, and Martin R. Warshaw, *Promotional Strategy,* 3d ed. (Homewood, Ill.: Irwin, 1975), p. 545.

CASE 18
Southern Lubricants

Southern Lubricants is a new company organized to distribute a complete line of new synthetic lubricants in the Atlanta area. Its lubricants represent a new concept with numerous advantages over petroleum-based lubricants. The most important advantage is the increase in the life of the oil, which increases the interval between lubricant changes by a factor of 10 to 15. In terms of cost, the initial expense is about 5–7 times that of premium petroleum lubricants; however, the decreased change interval normally results in savings of approximately 50 percent.

Fred Selby is vice president of marketing and has been called upon to present his promotion plan to the company's executive committee. Selby claims that the company faces two major promotional problems: (1) the fact that it is marketing a new concept in lubricants and (2) the fact that on a per-quart basis its selling price is extremely high compared to that of petroleum-based lubricants. However, the long-range cost savings of over 50 percent is an advantageous selling point.

The manufacturer is capable of supplying large enough quantities to satisfy both the commercial and retail markets. The product has not yet received extensive promotion or advertising in either market. Southern is currently undertaking a limited national advertising campaign and intends to leave local promotion up to the individual distributors.

Selby made the following statement to the management committee: "Owing to the limitations of our promotional budget, I feel that trying to establish Southern in the commercial and retail areas at the same time would be spreading ourselves too thin. The advantage of a larger profit margin in retail sales is offset by the smaller average sales at the retail level. Sales to larger-volume commercial buyers are countered by smaller profit margins. On the basis of the available information, I believe our promotion plan and our area of concentration should be as follows . . ."

1. Should the company concentrate in the commercial area or the retail area? Why?
2. What promotion tools should it use? Why?

19

The Nature
of Advertising

OBJECTIVES

■ To present a brief overview of advertising.
■ To understand the impact of advertising on both the macro and micro levels.
■ To become aware of the different types of advertising
■ To learn some of the factors to be considered in selecting media.
■ To understand the characteristics of different media.

This chapter begins with a discussion of the magnitude of advertising spending in the United States. Next, a brief history of advertising is presented in order to show you how advertising has reached its current level of influence. Questions often arise as to just what advertising can do. These questions are answered in both a macro and a micro context, and the types of advertising used by today's businesses are introduced. The chapter ends with an examination of major media and their characteristics.

THE IMPORTANCE OF ADVERTISING
Total Advertising Expenditures

Advertising, which many people consider the most glamorous function of marketing, grows in dollar volume each year. U.S. advertising expenditures were estimated at $30.7 billion in 1976.[1] But while advertising expenditures may seem large, the industry itself employs only approximately 500,000 people. This figure includes not only people who work in the advertising departments of manufacturers, wholesalers, and retailers but also the employees of America's 5000 advertising agencies as well as the media (radio and television, magazines and newspapers, and direct-mail firms).[2]

Company Advertising Budgets

Students are often amazed at the magnitude of the advertising budgets of American firms (see Table 19.1). Procter and Gamble, for example, spent over $370 million on advertising during 1977.[3] It is even more astounding when one realizes that this figure doesn't include the costs of sales promotion, personal selling, or public relations. This figure is larger than the budgets of all but a handful of U.S. cities. Newspaper advertising attracts the largest single share of the advertising dollar, followed by television and direct mail (see Table 19.2).

WHAT CAN ADVERTISING DO?

Even though advertising has shown a tendency to grow steadily, in the long run it is not a panacea. Its impact on America's socioeconomic system has been subject to extensive debate by economists, marketers, sociologists, psychologists, politicians, professors, homemakers, consumerists, bureaucrats, and other assorted groups. With something like 1700 newspapers, 3000 magazines, 6000 AM–FM radio stations, 600 television stations, billions of pieces of direct mail, and thousands of billboards, advertising and promotion must have an impact on us. The question is, What is that impact? Perhaps the best approach to answering this question is to divide the answer into macro and micro components.

The Macro Impact

Attitudes and Values. Vance Packard, a popular writer on socioeconomic phenomena, claims that "there are large-scale efforts being made through advertising, often with impressive success, to channel our unthinking habits, our purchasing decisions, and our thought processes by the use of insights gleaned from psychiatry and the social sciences."[4] Although this claim sounds impressive, it is more fiction than fact.

An attitude that stems from an individual's basic value pattern (good or bad, right or wrong) and is strongly supported by his or her culture will be almost impossible to change through advertising.[5] Advertising cannot change strongly held values and therefore cannot manipulate society against its will. All of the advertising in the world is not going to convince Moslems to eat pork or Americans to eat horse meat or to let elderly citizens starve to death.

Advertising can influence product and brand selection when a neutral or favorable frame of reference already exists.[6] For example,

TABLE 19.1   The Top 50 National Advertisers, 1977 Six Media Total.
Expenditures in Thousands of Dollars.

Rank	Company	Total	Mag-azines	Supple-ments	Network TV	Spot TV	Network Radio	Outdoor
1.	Procter & Gamble Co.	$372,085.9	$21,442.3	$ 766.6	$235,251.3	$114,625.7	$ ——	$ ——
2.	General Foods Corp.	247,020.6	29,026.8	1,655.8	143,312.8	71,987.7	833.8	203.7
3.	General Motors Corp.	174,586.7	44,029.4	4,417.2	90,699.5	26,748.3	2,915.1	5,777.2
4.	Bristol-Myers Co.	157,424.6	23,316.2	726.3	114,414.7	18,952.7	——	14.7
5.	American Home Products Corp.	152,794.9	5,928.6	421.3	108,428.7	35,250.5	2,765.8	——
6.	Sears, Roebuck & Co.	148,924.7	41,344.7	50.6	80,226.9	22,072.2	5,143.4	86.9
7.	General Mills Inc.	144,497.1	15,764.0	1,000.2	82,535.0	44,253.8	876.3	67.8
8.	R. J. Reynolds Industries Inc.	126,713.5	59,558.9	23,611.1	5,148.4	4,842.8	——	33,552.3
9.	Philip Morris Inc.	123,565.6	48,232.8	10,712.3	31,756.1	10,375.9	——	22,488.5
10.	Ford Motor Co.	121,460.6	24,788.8	429.5	66,085.4	28,033.7	1,007.1	1,116.1
11.	Lever Bros. Co.	111,956.5	7,160.8	450.8	68,418.3	35,926.6	——	——
12.	McDonald's Corp.	97,720.4	328.3	——	37,353.6	58,334.9	——	1,703.6
13.	Colgate-Palmolive Co.	93,030.2	6,283.5	592.6	51,146.3	34,800.0	170.5	37.3
14.	Warner-Lambert Co.	88,176.4	785.9	271.4	62,098.3	20,158.6	4,191.6	670.6
15.	Chrysler Corp.	81,715.2	18,883.4	23.2	31,901.6	29,790.7	635.3	481.0
16.	Nabisco Inc.	81,003.1	4,372.6	1,494.6	63,024.6	12,080.5	——	30.8
17.	PepsiCo Inc.	77,851.8	1,510.6	201.0	35,141.1	40,305.1	——	694.0
18.	Ralston Purina Co.	73,244.6	10,132.4	600.9	50,136.4	11,529.9	61.2	783.8
19.	American Telephone & Telegraph Co.	68,476.1	10,459.1	22.4	28,963.1	28,276.7	14.1	740.7
20.	Kraft Inc.	68,424.8	14,783.4	1,142.9	21,153.8	28,330.4	2,368.1	646.2
21.	Sterling Drug Inc.	67,532.8	6,270.3	192.6	49,252.3	8,767.0	2,926.8	123.8
22.	B.A.T. Industries Ltd.	66,723.7	32,269.2	14,850.0	713.9	5,547.1	——	13,343.5
23.	Gillette Co.	64,025.2	5,603.5	120.1	46,401.9	11,898.7	——	1.0
24.	Johnson & Johnson	63,655.5	10,592.2	136.6	48,549.8	4,376.9	——	——
25.	Kellogg Co.	62,933.6	3,081.5	943.0	41,650.4	17,250.4	——	8.3

Revlon can influence women to buy "Charlie" perfume through advertising because society perceives a pleasant body odor as a desirable trait. On the other hand, Revlon would find it difficult indeed to convince American women to purchase "the new Revlon nose ring" because our society does not view nose rings as acceptable jewelry.

Economic Consequences. Although advertising cannot reverse strongly held attitudes, economist John Kenneth Galbraith and others believe that advertisers "manage demand" and that this has negative economic consequences. The chain of logic leading to this conclusion is shown on the left-hand side of Table 19.3. That is, advertising ultimately blocks other firms from entering an industry (barriers to entry), leading to market power for the firm and ultimately to higher prices.

Rank	Company	Total	Mag-azines	Supple-ments	Network TV	Spot TV	Network Radio	Outdoor
26.	Heublein Inc.	62,863.3	14,818.2	367.8	20,498.7	20,409.0	262.4	6,507.2
27.	Nestle Enterprises Inc.	60,098.6	2,103.3	561.1	35,684.7	21,714.1	—	35.4
28.	Pillsbury Co.	60,060.6	3,920.9	456.1	39,881.3	15,501.8	—	300.5
29.	Norton Simon Inc.	59,927.1	14,872.7	539.8	29,440.7	12,506.4	196.7	2,370.8
30.	Coca-Cola Co.	52,385.8	3,426.7	1,125.0	18,094.8	27,264.2	444.3	2,030.8
31.	Eastman Kodak Co.	51,876.6	17,562.2	518.7	30,444.5	2,633.2	389.1	328.9
32.	Int'l Telephone & Telegraph Corp.	50,062.9	5,655.2	173.6	15,640.3	27,090.7	1,059.3	443.8
33.	General Electric Co.	48,475.3	10,518.7	581.5	24,248.8	11,641.7	1,321.4	163.2
34.	Anheuser-Busch Inc.	48,286.8	2,964.4	199.1	32,165.4	10,236.8	1,842.0	879.1
35.	Esmark Inc.	47,569.0	2,518.8	697.9	34,208.4	10,090.3	—	53.6
36.	General Motors Corp. Local Dealers	47,311.0	44.5	—	—	44,141.5	—	3,125.0
37.	Schering-Plough Corp.	46,379.5	9,222.7	—	26,176.4	6,631.2	2,723.7	1,625.5
38.	Richardson-Merrell Inc.	46,303.6	3,654.2	10.2	34,275.5	7,981.0	382.7	—
39.	RCA Corp.	45,191.7	16,747.3	775.1	16,142.1	11,133.8	66.6	326.8
40.	American Brands Inc.	45,028.2	29,011.6	38.4	5,227.7	2,984.5	144.7	7,621.3
41.	Quaker Oats Co.	44,854.7	8,870.4	945.2	18,057.8	16,977.3	—	4.0
42.	Mobil Corp.	42,593.7	4,024.3	3,156.6	7,334.9	27,834.9	168.0	75.0
43.	CBS Inc.	41,245.5	23,404.3	6,524.7	—	10,346.4	398.0	572.1
44.	Volkswagenwerk A. G.	41,005.4	12,832.5	205.9	18,249.7	9,588.5	—	128.8
45.	Jos. Schlitz Brewing Co.	40,832.3	731.1	—	33,847.1	6,196.5	—	57.6
46.	Time Inc.	40,292.4	18,955.7	591.7	1,390.4	18,225.0	1,119.8	9.8
47.	Clorox Co.	39,925.7	6,102.7	278.0	28,423.9	5,119.9	—	1.2
48.	Revlon Inc.	39,689.7	8,411.7	126.6	18,093.5	12,464.1	591.7	2.1
49.	Liggett Group Inc.	39,473.4	18,596.8	1,789.3	6,552.4	6,308.2	—	6,226.7
50.	Chesebrough-Pond's Inc.	38,955.6	3,787.1	447.0	27,350.7	7,368.4	—	2.4

Source: "Ad Spending Among Leaders Jumped 14 Percent," Advertising Age, May 1, 1978, p. 80. Reprinted by permission. Copyright 1978 by Crain Communications, Inc.

Jean-Jacques Lambin's research, also outlined in Table 19.3, generally refutes this contention.[7]

Quality Implications. Firms advertise to accomplish a variety of goals, as we will see in the next section. Generally, large-scale advertising makes sense only if the advertiser can expect repeat purchases.[8] Heavy advertising normally implies that the seller is counting on acceptance and repeat business.

Naturally, consumers will buy a product again only if it meets their standards. Thus it is apparent that the advertiser has built some quality into the product. If it were of poor quality the advertiser would not expect repeat purchases. This is one reason why the words *nationally advertised* are prominently shown on many displays and

TABLE 19.2   Advertising Volume, 1974–1975

Medium	1974[a] Millions	1974[a] Percent of Total	1975 Millions	1975 Percent of Total	% Change, '75 vs. '74
Newspapers					
Total	8,001	29.9	8,442	29.9	+ 5.5
National	1,194	4.5	1,221	4.3	+ 2.3
Local	6,807	25.4	7,221	25.6	+ 6.1
Magazines					
Total	1,504	5.6	1,465	5.2	− 2.6
Weeklies	630	2.3	612	2.2	− 2.9
Women's	372	1.4	368	1.3	− 1.0
Monthlies	502	1.9	485	1.7	− 3.4
Farm publications	72	0.3	74	0.3	+ 3.0
Television					
Total	4,851	18.1	5,272	18.6	+ 8.7
Network	2,145	8.0	2,310	8.2	+ 7.7
Spot	1,495	5.6	1,630	5.7	+ 9.0
Local	1,211	4.5	1,332	4.7	+10.0
Radio					
Total	1,837	6.9	2,025	7.2	+10.2
Network	69	0.3	85	0.3	+22.5
Spot	405	1.5	440	1.6	+ 9.0
Local	1,363	5.1	1,500	5.3	+10.0
Direct mail	3,986	14.9	4,155	14.7	+ 4.2
Business publications	900	3.4	919	3.2	+ 2.1
Outdoor					
Total	309	1.2	335	1.2	+ 8.3
National	203	0.8	220	0.8	+ 8.3
Local	106	0.4	115	0.4	+ 8.3
Miscellaneous					
Total	5,270	19.7	5,583	19.7	+ 5.9
National	2,752	10.3	2,881	10.2	+ 4.7
Local	2,518	9.4	2,702	9.5	+ 7.3
Total					
National	14,725	55.1	15,400	54.5	+ 4.6
Local	12,005	44.9	12,870	45.5	+ 7.2
Grand total	26,730	100.0	28,270	100.0	+ 5.8

Source: Robert J. Coen, "Ad Dollar Gain in 1976 Biggest Ever," *Advertising Age,* July 5, 1976, p. 32. Reprinted by permission. Copyright 1976 by Crain Communications, Inc.
[a] Revised.

packages. In a sense the seller is assuring the purchaser of product quality.

Elasticity of Demand.   Advertising transmits information both directly and indirectly. One study showed, however, that consumers feel that very few ads (5.8 percent) contain much information about the product itself.[9] Yet how does the information that does get through affect consumer demand? It probably makes demand more elastic. This con-

TABLE 19.3   The Advertising Controversy

Steps in the Advertising Controversy	Assumed Roles or Effects of Advertising	Observed Roles or Effects of Advertising
1 Advertising	Large companies advertise in order to create a preference for their brands	**Yes, but . . .** they also use advertising to perform communication tasks required by the market situation; large-scale advertising has no built-in advantage for the large companies, although a threshold level exists that may privilege the deep purse
2 Consumer buying behavior	Consumers perceive real or apparent differences among brands and develop preferences	**Yes, but . . .** the advertising effect is modest in both absolute and relative value; consumers are less responsive to noninformational advertising
3 Barriers to entry	Preferences lead to brand loyalty, or consumer inertia, that constitutes a barrier to entry of new brands into the market	**Yes, but . . .** many other factors explain consumer inertia or loyalty; where consumer inertia is high, advertising intensity is not necessarily also high
4 Market power	Protected brand positions reduce active rivalry and give the company more discretionary power	**No . . .** we observed no basic incompatibility between the presence of intensive advertising in a market and the degree to which that market exhibits active rivalry **but . . .** advertising escalation does not benefit the consumer as does a price war or a technological race
5 Market conduct	Discretionary power allows the company to ignore more tangible forms of competition (price and product quality) and lets it charge higher prices	**No . . .** consumer responsiveness to price and product quality remains high in advertising-intensive markets; a company may react to rival advertising by advertising, price, or even quality adjustments
6 Market performance	Higher prices result in high profits that furnish incentive to continue advertising	**Yes . . .** advertising increases the capacity of the company to charge higher prices to the consumer **but . . .** no continuous association is observed between market concentration and advertising intensity; sales maximization under profit constraints seems to be the company's objective, although long-term profitability is likely for several brands

Source: Jean-Jacques Lambin, ''What Is the Real Impact of Advertising?'' *Harvard Business Review,* May-June 1975, p. 145. Copyright © 1975 by the President and Fellows of Harvard College; all rights reserved.

tention is contrary to that of most textbooks, but the facts seem to bear it out.[10]

Lack of information makes for more inelastic demand. If consumers do not know what substitute brands are available, it is harder to switch brands as the price of a given brand rises. Lack of advertising thus complicates the shopping process. Advertising information allows individuals to confine their brand selections to the products that are most closely related to their own tastes and to buy comparable products at the lowest price.

Influence on Preferences.   Since advertising does inform and persuade, it is safe to say that it does influence consumer preferences. We cannot say that those preferences are any better or worse because of advertising.[11] More important, although preferences are influenced by advertising, research has shown that it does not increase monopoly power. In fact the evidence indicates that advertising tends to reduce monopoly power.[12] Also, research has shown that advertising does not have any detectable effect on the choice between spending and saving.[13] Thus advertising doesn't siphon off investment funds from capital formation and economic growth.

Micro Effects

So far we have examined how advertising affects society as a whole and economic activity in general. Now our attention will turn to the firm.

What can advertising do? In one case a German electric-shaver manufacturer tripled its advertising budget and doubled its market share while maintaining good product quality and keeping prices stable.[14] In Belgium, Italy, and Denmark major gasoline marketers overspent on advertising with little improvement of market share.[15] These and other examples often lead to quick conclusions regarding a firm's advertising. In the first example it seems that advertising had a strong positive effect on sales; the second example appears to have had the opposite effect.

Advertising's Effect on Sales.   Studies have found that additional increments of advertising do yield increasing sales returns, up to a point, in most situations.[16] Advertising influences not only sales of the advertised brand but also sales of other brands.[17] It may, for example, force competing firms to raise their promotion budgets in order to maintain market share.

Although advertising is a powerful determinant of demand, it usually has less impact than environmental factors such as population and income.[18] On repeat purchases advertising is usually less important than product quality, distribution, and price.[19] In other words, long-run sales are predicated upon a sound total marketing mix, not just advertising.

Advertising's Impact on Market Share.   Brands with a small market share tend to spend proportionately more for advertising than those with a larger market share.[20] This is probably due to two factors: (1) Beyond a certain volume of advertising expenditure diminishing returns set in, causing firms with large market shares to hold back on advertising. (2) There is a minimum level of exposure needed for advertising to have a measurable effect on purchase habits.[21] But that threshold varies from one product to another.

Other Micro Effects.   As mentioned in the preceding chapter, advertising helps increase the effectiveness of the sales force. Advertising builds brand, product line, and company familiarity and thus makes the sales job easier. It also may lower a buyer's price resistance, thereby enabling the salesperson to close a sale that might otherwise not have been made.[22]

THE MAJOR TYPES OF ADVERTISING

Advertising goals are the major determinant of the type of advertising used by the firm. (See Figure 19.1.) If the goal is to build up the image of a product, service, company, or industry, the advertiser will use

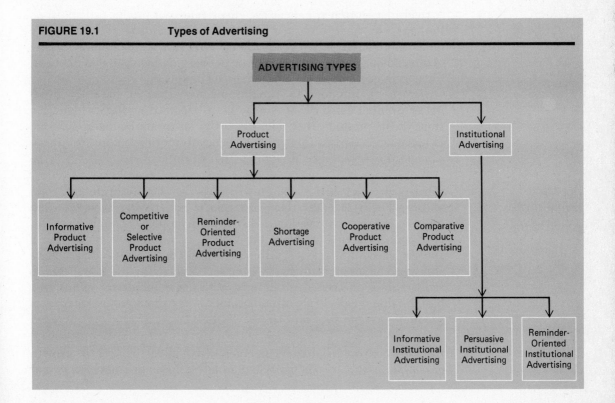

FIGURE 19.1   Types of Advertising

institutional advertising. When the objective is to sell a specific product, service, or cooperative mark (e.g., Sunkist oranges), an advertiser will utilize product or institutional advertising.

Institutional Advertising

Institutional advertising, in contrast to product advertising, is not always directed only to consumers of the company's products and services. Instead, it may be aimed at any of the various publics (stockholders, consumerists, legislators, etc.) that may have an impact on the firm. It is not product oriented; rather, it is designed to enhance the image of the company.

Alcoa devotes a significant portion of its advertising budget to institutional advertising. The goal of its program is to focus on issues and attitudes that can have a significant influence on the company.[23] Alcoa's institutional objectives are to

1. establish and reinforce in the minds of America's most influential publics the fact that aluminum products are vital to our economy and way of life.
2. develop a sharp sense of awareness among those publics that these uses of aluminum also contribute to the conservation of energy.

Product Advertising

A good image often enhances the effectiveness of product advertising Perhaps you have observed that some product advertisements are much more informative than others. This is a normal characteristic of advertising that is used to create primary demand, that is, demand for a product category rather than for a specific brand. Pioneering advertising is intended to stimulate primary demand for a new product or product category. It is heavily utilized during the introduction stage of the product life cycle. Recently, for example, manufacturers of home video tape equipment have been attempting to educate Americans on the advantages of owning such equipment.

Selective Competitive Advertising

When a product enters the growth phase of the life cycle and competitors begin to enter the marketplace, advertising becomes competitive or selective. No longer is the main emphasis on building general primary demand. Now the goal is to influence demand for a specific product or service. Often promotion becomes less informative and more emotional during this phase. Advertisements may begin to stress subtle differences in brands, with heavy emphasis on building brand name recall. Price often becomes a key promotional weapon as products become very similar.

Comparative Advertising

A highly controversial trend in competitive advertising is the growth of comparative advertising. When an advertisement compares two or more specific brands in terms of product/service attributes it may be defined as comparative advertising. This isn't really new; 1931 Plymouth ads suggested that the consumer "Look at All Three" before buying.[24] The Avis–Hertz battle of the 1960s also involved comparative advertising. As recently as 1973–1974, only 1 out of 30 commercials on prime-time television was of this type. By the end of 1975, however, the number was 1 out of 12 and growing.[25] A major reason for this growth is the Federal Trade Commission's fostering of comparative advertising. Joan Bernstein, assistant director of the FTC, has stated that comparative advertising "delivers information not previously available to consumers" and also that "advertisers and agencies are more skillful than the government in communicating information."[26]

Even though comparative advertising has received the FTC's blessing, not everyone is for it. Andrew G. Kershaw, chairman of Ogilvy and Mather, one of the world's largest advertising agencies, says, "If the FTC told us it was permissible to jump out of the window, I for one would not jump."[27] Why the controversy? There is general disagreement on the effects of comparative advertising. Perhaps the recent flurry of comparative advertising can be traced to Shick's naming of its competitors in ads for the Fleximatic electric shaver. Its market share rose from 8 percent to 24 percent, with a net sales gain of $28 million.[28]

Not everyone has been satisfied with the results of comparative advertising, however. A study by the Gallup and Robinson media research firm of 97 comparative TV commercials found that three out of ten were ineffective.[29] As in any other kind of advertising, some comparative ads are better than others.

The only academic research on the subject was conducted by V. K. Prasad. He found that

1. the message recall effectiveness of the comparison advertisement was higher than that of its "brand X" counterpart.
2. brand recall effectiveness was equal.
3. claim recall effectiveness was considerably higher for the comparative advertiser.[30]

Shortage Advertising

Comparative advertising reveals the intensity of competitive advertising. When shortages occur, advertising often disappears into the background. When the oil crisis hit in 1974, petroleum advertising virtually disappeared. Yet enlightened marketers have found that advertising is still a viable marketing tool during times of shortage. This is referred to as shortage advertising. Instead of decreasing the advertising budget, they change their promotional objectives. Their new goals might include (1) educating the user on more efficient means of utilizing the product, thus reducing demand, (2) explaining the firm's situation, thereby helping reduce customer pressure on the sales force, (3) improving good will, and (4) informing the market about how the firm's products will save resources.

Many companies were quick to position themselves around the energy crisis. General Electric introduced a new product as "the first fluorescent lamp specially designed for the energy crisis." The Bell System has taken advantage of the fuel shortage by promoting long-distance phone calls as an alternative to travel. Textron pushes solar power for such things as offshore drilling platforms. Bechtel promotes the environmental advantages of nuclear power, and investor-owned electric light and power companies advertise the impressive safety records of nuclear power plants.

Corporate—rather than product—advertising is still another approach to shortage situations. For example, Allegheny Ludlum's ad goes, "Allegheny Ludlum Industries: A group of our companies makes light work of supplying energy." St. Joe Minerals says, "We're growing with three kinds of energy. Energy is a growing business. We're in on the ground floor."[31]

Cooperative Advertising

Cooperative advertising involves payments by manufacturers to retailers (and sometimes to wholesalers) for advertising products through local advertising media. For example, the local television retailer receives a check for $200 as partial compensation for an ad placed in a local newspaper advertising the availability of the manufacturer's sets at the local store.

Use of co-op advertising by manufacturers is almost universal. One recent study revealed that over 90 percent of all manufacturers engage in cooperative advertising.[32] Moreover, the research found that 65 percent of the manufacturers planned to expand their co-op budgets by an average of 48 percent during the next five years.

Often cooperative advertising budgets are quite large. Expenditures on cooperative advertising in 1976 were estimated at $4 billion.[33] Normally the manufacturer gives the dealer a rebate based on the number of units or dollar amount purchased. In either case it is traditional for the dealer to pay half of the actual cost of the ad. Most co-op advertising is confined to the print media. Only a few firms, such as True Value Hardware and International Harvester, have used co-op dollars in television advertising.[34]

One reason that manufacturers use cooperative advertising is the impracticality of listing all their dealers in national advertising. Also, co-op advertising encourages the dealer to devote more effort to the manufacturer's lines. If a new product is involved, it helps the dealer develop demand and thus encourages adequate stocking of the new item.

Sometimes co-op advertising ties the dealer closer to the manufacturer and aids in developing good will. Most important, the manufacturer obtains more total promotion, since the dealer is sharing part of the expense. Usually local advertisers (dealers) actually place the advertisements. Since local advertising rates are normally less expensive than national rates, the manufacturer effectively receives a discount.

ADVERTISING MEDIA
Selecting Media

Promotional objectives and the type of advertising a company plans to use will have a strong impact on the selection of media channels. A number of factors enter into media selection. Basically, management must determine what it wants to say and how (by what media) it wants the message delivered.

Two of the most important criteria of media selection are costs and audience. If marketing managers are trying to reach female teenagers, they would not select *Barron's* financial paper but might select *Teen* magazine. Even when audience profiles match media profiles, other factors, such as circulation and image, must be considered. For example, *Teen* magazine might reach the "right" market, but this might be only a small fraction of the firm's market. Also, how do teenagers perceive *Teen* magazine? Is it viewed as a lot of "hype" and, therefore, low in credibility? Perhaps it is a "how to" magazine and is used as a reference guide by many teenagers. If this is true, it should strengthen advertiser credibility.

No two media are the same, yet all can be evaluated by certain selection criteria. Table 19.4 combines a number of important factors used in media selection. Cost per contact is the cost of reaching one

TABLE 19.4			Key Media Characteristics (0 = nonapplicable; L = low; M = moderate; H = high)							
	Cost per Contact	Total Cost	Market Selectivity	Geographic Selectivity	Source Credibility	Visual Quality	Noise Level	Life Span	Pass-Along Rate	Timing Flexibility
Television	L	H	M[a]	M–H	L–M	H	M–H	0	0	L–M
Radio	L	L	M[b]	H	L–M	0	M–H	0	0	H
Newspaper	L	L	L	M[c]	L	L–M	H	L	L	H
Magazines	M–H[d]	M–H	M–H	M–H[e]	M–H	M–H	M	M–H	M–H	L
Direct mail	L–H[f]	M–H	H	H	L–M	M–H	L	L–M	L	M–H
Billboard	L	L	L	M	L	M	H	L	0	M
Catalog	M–H	M–H	H	H	M	M–H	L–M	M–H	M–H	L

[a] Market selectivity by correlating program audience profiles with target markets.
[b] Selective for broad groups: black, teen, adult.
[c] Some geographic selectivity, but not for a small area such as a particular suburb.
[d] Higher cost per contact than newspaper, but lower cost per potential customer.
[e] Some magazines such as *Time*, have over 50 regional breakdowns.
[f] Cost depends on quality of mailing list.

member of the audience. Naturally, as the size of the audience increases so does the total cost. We will discuss cost evaluations in more detail in the next chapter.

Market selectivity is another important media characteristic. Some media, such as general newspapers, appeal to a wide cross-section of the population. Others, such as *Flying,* the *Journal of Marketing,* and *Architectural Record,* appeal to very specific groups. Geographic selectivity refers to coverage of a specific area. Local radio, newspapers, and television all cover limited geographic areas. Network television and many magazines offer nationwide coverage. Other magazines, such as *New West, Sunset, Southern Living, Texas Monthly,* and *Chicago,* offer good coverage in limited areas.

Although a lot of work still needs to be done, some generalizations can be made regarding source credibility (trust). Radio, for example, tends to have lower credibility than major retail catalogs. Trade and professional magazines generally offer the highest level of reader trust and believability.

The reproduction capabilities of some media are higher than those of others. How often have you seen a blurred four-color newspaper advertisement? Unless the color ad is printed separately and inserted into the newspaper, its quality may be quite poor. Slick magazines, on the other hand, can usually provide excellent color reproduction.

Because of printing timetables, paste-up requirements, engraving, and so forth, some magazines require final ad copy several months before publication. The advertiser thus loses flexibility and is unable to adapt to changing market conditions. Radio, on the other hand, provides maximum flexibility, usually enabling the advertiser to change the ad on the same day.

Another important media characteristic is "noise level." Television, for example, often requires both audio and visual attention for the promotional message to be fully understood. It is often viewed in the presence of other individuals, who may contribute to the "noise" factor. In contrast, direct mail is a private medium. There are no other advertising or news stories to compete for the reader's attention. Generally, direct mail offers a very low "noise" level.

Some media have relatively long life spans, whereas those of other media are quite short. When a radio commercial is over, it's over. You can't repeat it unless you've tape recorded the program—a rare event. Advertisers overcome this problem by repeating their ads often.

A trade magazine, in contrast, has a relatively long life span. A person may read several articles, put it down, and pick it up a week later to continue reading. Some families naturally save back issues of *Playboy, Gourmet, National Geographic,* and similar magazines. Similarly, magazines and catalogs often have a high "pass-along rate." One person will read the publication and then give it to someone else.

Table 19.4 offers a good overall view of the major media. Now we will take a brief look at some current media trends.

Newspapers. Newspaper advertising volume totaled $8.6 billion in 1975. From 1974 through 1975 newspaper advertising grew 40 percent compared to television's 35 percent.[35] Automobiles, transportation, tobacco, and food are the largest advertising categories. These large-volume advertisers continue to consider newspapers, the largest medium in terms of circulation, most attractive. Final consumers also make a significant contribution to newspaper advertising via the classified section. In 1975 classifieds accounted for $215 billion of newspaper advertising.[36] Cards and color inserts are also becoming a significant form of newspaper promotion. It is estimated that over 15 billion advertising pieces are inserted into newspapers each year.[37]

Magazines. Although magazines' cost per contact is usually higher than that of other media, their cost per potential customer may be much lower. This difference is due to the specialized nature of magazine audiences. Magazines fall into two general categories: (1) consumer and (2) trade and professional. Among the fastest-growing publication areas are in-flight, mechanical and science, and home and apartment magazines.

Magazine advertising was estimated at $1.6 billion dollars in 1976,[38] and the long-run prognosis for magazines is good. A rising level of education coupled with an ever-increasing number of special-interest areas provides ample opportunities for magazine growth.

Radio. In major metropolitan markets radio provides a station for just about every taste. Denver, for example, has 12 stations, and Phoenix is licensed for 49.[39] There is no area of the country that can't be reached by one of America's 7000 radio stations.[40] Like television, radio offers network (though limited), spot, or local advertising. The major networks are CBS, NBC, Mutual, and the four ABC networks devoted to contemporary living, information, entertainment, and FM.[41] Spot advertising means that the advertisers "spot" or select certain stations for their campaigns. Local advertising refers to local radio advertisements by retailers and other groups. Radio stations often develop loyal followings and "radio personalities." Some advertisers can overcome credibility problems or simply increase their effectiveness by using radio personalities in their spot and local radio advertisements.

Television.   From its takeoff period in the late 1940s through the mid-1970s, television advertising has grown continuously. In 1975, 513 companies poured $2.4 billion into network television.[42] General Motors alone spent over $54 million on network television in 1975.[43] Why this popularity? Mass audiences, low costs per contact, and most of the advantages of personal selling (sight, sound, and demonstration). Also, television reaches just about all of us. One 1975 study showed that television is viewed by 95 percent of all adults and children.[44]

Spot and local television expenditures together total slightly more than network advertising. Spot advertising is highly popular with regional advertisers and with national advertisers attempting to reach selected markets. Local television is dominated by companies that serve a single city or county.

Television seems to be entering another growth market through cable television. It is estimated that cable TV revenues will grow by 14 to 18 percent from the mid-1970s through 1980.[45] By the end of 1980 sales should reach $1.5 to $1.8 billion, with 4 million subscribers. Cable television will continue to grow until virtually all rural markets are served, along with special programing (first-run movies, sporting events, education courses) for all metropolitan markets.

Television is not without problems. The cost of advertising time has been rising by 15 to 30 percent per year, forcing many advertisers to turn to other media.[46] The ever-increasing pace of new-show introduction and cancellation makes it difficult to evaluate audiences and build brand loyalty among viewers. As an executive with Norton Simon Communications has put it, "Magazine rates have been holding relatively well over the years, and this continues to make print more and more desirable."

Other advertisers are concerned about the quality of network programs. Borden, for example, has shifted its emphasis to fully sponsored network specials. One of its marketing managers says, "We want our brands to be associated with wholesome, family entertainment."[47]

Direct Mail.   Direct mail can be either the most efficient medium an advertiser uses or the least efficient, depending on the quality of the mailing list and the effectiveness of the mailing piece. Good mailing lists are available from list brokers for about $35 per 1000 names. Prestigious lists or lists of people who have bought merchandise through the mail in the past few months normally cost $50 per 1000 names.

Many of America's largest firms are just beginning to experiment with mail order promotions. General Foods, General Mills, and Avon have recently begun to utilize direct mail. Other companies have long been committed to direct mail and spend huge sums of money on this medium each year. In 1976 the Franklin Mint announced that it would spend over $500 million on promotion during the next five years.[48] The bulk of those expenditures were for direct mail. Direct mail is not limited to consumer goods and inexpensive industrial-goods marketing. General Automation, a minicomputer manufacturer, traced the sale of a $100,000 computer system to a direct-mail piece.

Outdoor Advertising. Outdoor advertising is a flexible, low-cost medium. Often advertisers make large purchases on an area basis (e.g., city, county, or SMSA). Large outdoor buys are referred to as "showings." A showing of 100, the maximum, is defined as reaching 90 percent of all adults in a given market in 30 days.[49]

Outdoor advertising reaches a broad and diverse market, and therefore it is normally limited to convenience goods and select shopping goods. Advertisers usually base their billboard use on census tract data. They assume that the people who are most likely to see a certain billboard will have demographic characteristics similar to those of the tract in which the billboard is located. For example, products such as luxury cars and expensive liqueurs are advertised in high-income census tracts. Traffic count data are supplied by the Traffic Audit Bureau (TAB) – they enable the advertiser to determine the total number of potential exposures per site. Recently TAB has come under increasing criticism for providing questionable data.[50] For example, TAB audits traffic flows once every three years. Major changes in traffic patterns can occur during such a long period.

Catalogs. Catalogs offer the opportunity to pinpoint specific audiences (e.g., existing store customers or extensive users of certain types of products such as electronics, fishing equipment, or office supplies). The readership rate is usually high, and so is the pass-along rate. Spiraling costs (usually over $5.00 each for major seasonal catalogs) have forced retailers to maintain careful control over catalog distribution. Cards are sent to customers informing them they can now pick up their copy of the catalog in the store. Mailing lists are carefully pruned in order to remove the names of people who do not order a specified volume of merchandise. Montgomery Ward has even opened its catalog to noncompetitive outside advertisers.[51] Time-Life books, Encyclopedia Britannica, and Columbia Records have experimented with this medium.

SUMMARY

American industry spends over $30 billion a year on advertising. Yet the advertising industry itself employs only a half-million people.

Advertising can reinforce positive attitudes and influence neutral attitudes. However, it cannot change basic value patterns.

Advertising also does not manage demand or block market entry. Heavy advertising implies that a seller is counting on product acceptance and repeat business; it is an implicit degree of quality.

Since advertising transmits information about available products, it tends to make demand more elastic. It also influences consumer preferences, however, so in some circumstances it can create a more inelastic demand situation. Advertising may or may not increase a firm's sales and market share, depending on its quality.

Institutional advertising is not oriented toward a product or service but, instead, is designed to create good will for a company. A good image often enhances the effectiveness of product advertising.

Product advertising often begins with pioneering promotions. The emphasis is on building primary demand for a product type rather than for a specific brand name. As the item enters the growth stage of the life cycle, advertising becomes more competitive. Competitive promotion is designed to increase sales of a specific brand rather than a general category of products.

An important trend is the growth of comparative advertising. When a promotion compares two or more specific brands on the basis of their product and service attributes, it is comparative advertising. This trend is not new. Its recent growth is due partly to its effectiveness in selling merchandise and to its endorsement by the FTC. Comparative advertising is no panacea, however. It must be of high quality to stimulate sales.

The 1974 oil crisis precipitated shortage advertising. Competitive advertising gave way to telling the user how to use the product more efficiently, explaining the firm's shortage situation, and trying to improve good will. Some firms have engaged in shortage advertising in which they describe how their products will save resources. Bell Telephone suggests dialing long distance rather than driving.

In cooperative advertising manufacturers pay retailers and wholesalers for advertising the manufacturer's products through local advertising media. Cooperative advertising is almost universal and expenditures in this area total an estimated $4 billion.

Media selection can be a difficult task. The criteria used for media selection include cost per contract, total cost, market selectivity, geographic selectivity, source credibility, visual quality, noise level, life span, pass-along rate, and timing flexibility.

KEY TERMS

Advertising
Institutional advertising
Product advertising
Pioneering advertising
Competitive or selective advertising
Comparative advertising
Shortage advertising

Cooperative advertising
Cost per contact
Market selectivity
Network advertising
Spot advertising
Local advertising

QUESTIONS FOR DISCUSSION

1. What are your views on the statement, "Advertising manipulates demand"? Do you think competition will increase in the absence of advertising? Give reasons to support your views.
2. Discuss the effects of advertising on a micro level.
3. What is institutional advertising? What purpose does it serve? Give a few examples.
4. What is meant by comparative advertising? Why is it so controversial? Give a few examples.
5. Define cooperative advertising and shortage advertising. Give an example of each.
6. Explain some of the factors that affect media selection.
7. Briefly discuss the advantages and disadvantages of television advertising compared to direct-mail advertising.
8. List the major types of advertising discussed in this chapter. Then classify the following advertisements into one of those categories.
   a. A recent TV commercial for the Ford Granada that compares it with the Mercedes-Benz.
   b. A TV commercial sponsored by the American Bankers Association outlining the role of banks in the American economy.
   c. TV commercials by the U.S. Army that emphasize the theme, "Join the people who join the army."
   d. An ad placed in the Dallas Times Herald by Homer Bros. promoting General Electric appliances.
   e. TV spots by Coors Beer emphasizing the company's devotion to a clean environment.
9. What are some of the advantages of outdoor advertising? Which of the following products could be promoted in this manner?
   a. a motel
   b. household goods
   c. airline routes and fares
   d. minicomputers
10. Discuss some of the features of magazine advertising. In what types of magazines should the following products be advertised?
    a. a new textbook on linear programing
    b. a watch for underwater divers
    c. a new word processor from Datapoint
    d. household cleaners and disinfectants
    e. rare coins

NOTES

1. "Advertising Spending Is Stepped Up as the Economy Gains," *Advertising Age,* April 29, 1976, p. 1.
2. "Showing Ad Agencies How to Grow," *Business Week,* June 1, 1974, pp. 50–56.
3. "Biggest Hike Ever for Top 100 Advertisers," *Advertising Age,* August 29, 1977, p. 1.
4. Vance Packard, *The Hidden Persuaders* (New York: McKay, 1957).
5. David Krech, Richard S. Crutchfield, and Egerton L. Bauachey, *Individual in Society* (New York: McGraw-Hill, 1962).
6. Paul F. Lazerfield and Robert K. Merton, "Mass Communications, Popu-

lar Taste and Organized Social Action," in Wilbur Schramm, ed., *Mass Communications* (Urbana: University of Illinois Press, 1949), pp. 459–480.

7. Jean-Jacques Lambin, "What Is the Real Impact of Advertising?" *Harvard Business Review*, May–June 1975, pp. 139–147.

8. Richard Schmalensee, "Advertising and Economic Welfare," in S. F. Divita, ed., *Advertising and the Public Interest* (Chicago: American Marketing Association, 1973), p. 85.

9. Raymond A. Bauer and Stephen A. Greyser, *Advertising in America: The Consumer View* (Cambridge, Mass.: Harvard University Press, 1968).

10. Phillip Nelson, "The Economic Consequences of Advertising," *Journal of Business*, 48 (April 1975): 213–241.

11. See William S. Comanor and Thomas A. Wilson, "Advertising and the Distribution of Consumer Demand," in Divita, p. 71.

12. Nelson, p. 213–241.

13. Comanor and Wilson, p. 59.

14. Lambin, p. 139.

15. Ibid.

16. Robert S. Weinberg, *An Analytical Approach to Advertising Expenditure Strategy* (New York: National Association of Advertisers, 1960); see also Gary L. Lilien, Alvin J. Silk, Jean-Marie Choffray, and Murlidhar Rao, "Industrial Advertising Effects and Budgeting Practices," *Journal of Marketing*, 40 (January 1976): 16–24, and Peter Doyle and Ian Fenwich, "Planning and Estimation in Advertising," *Journal of Marketing Research*, 12 (February 1975): 1–6.

17. Darrol G. Clarke, "Sales–Advertising Cross-Elasticities and Advertising Competition," *Journal of Marketing Research*, 10 (August 1973): 250–261.

18. Lambin, p. 142.

19. Ibid.

20. Ibid., p. 144.

21. Lilien et al., pp. 18–22.

22. Lambin, p. 146.

23. "Alcoa: Focusing on the Issues," *Public Relations Journal*, 30 (November 1974): 33–34.

24. King Harris, "How Stirling Getschell Chased Walter Chrysler—and Hired a Mail Boy," *Advertising Age*, July 31, 1967, pp. 59–62.

25. Stanley I. Tannenbaum, "For Comparative Advertising," *Advertising Age*, July 5, 1976, pp. 26–27.

26. William L. Wilkie and Paul W. Farris, "Comparison Advertising: Problems and Potential," *Journal of Marketing*, 39 (October 1975): 7–15.

27. Andrew G. Kershaw, "Against Comparison Advertising," *Advertising Age*, July 5, 1976, pp. 25–26.

28. "Schick, Inc., Teeters on the Razor's Edge," *Business Week*, May 5, 1975, p. 38.

29. Tannenbaum, p. 36.

30. V. Kanti Prasad, "Communications-Effectiveness of Comparative Advertising: A Laboratory Analysis," *Journal of Marketing Research*, 13 (May 1976): 128–137.

31. Examples are taken from Al Ries, "Today's Crises—New Opportunity for Advertisers?" *Management Review*, 63 (September 1974): 29–33.

32. "Marketing Briefs," *Marketing News,* June 18, 1976, p. 2.
33. Martin Everett, "Co-op at the Crossroads," *Sales and Marketing Management,* December 13, 1976, p. 41.
34. Alfred Masini, "Searching for the Lost Kingdom of Retail Co-op Funds," *Broadcasting,* 88 (June 23, 1975): 10; see also Edward Zimmerman, "Make Your Co-op Advertising Pay Off," *Product Marketing,* February 1977, pp. 17–21.
35. "Newspapers See Healthy Category Gains for 1975," *Advertising Age,* June 23, 1975, pp. 3f.
36. Ibid.
37. Ibid.
38. "Magazine Ad Growth Continues in Second Quarter," *Advertising Age,* July 19, 1976, p. 1.
39. "Here Are Six Things Wrong with National Spot Radio," *Advertising Age,* December 6, 1974, p. 49.
40. Ibid.
41. Gay Mayer, "It's That Extra Thought and Planning That Make a Winning Radio Campaign," *Broadcasting,* 87 (July 29, 1974): 12; see also Robert Danielenko, "The New Golden Age of Radio," *Product Management,* December 1976, pp. 33–37.
42. "Net TV Outlays for 1975 Up $100 Million: TOB," *Advertising Age,* March 22, 1976, p. 32.
43. Ibid.
44. *BBDO Audience Coverage and Cost Guide,* 14th ed. New York (1975), p. 8.
45. "Marketing Briefs," *Marketing News,* July 2, 1976, p. 2.
46. "Frustrated TV Advertisers Study Shifts to Other Media," *Advertising Age,* April 19, 1976, pp. 1f.
47. Ibid.
48. "Big Companies Moving into Direct Response, DMMA Finds," *Advertising Age,* July 8, 1974, p. 16; see also "In the News," *Advertising Age,* May 24, 1976, p. 8.
49. "Outdoor Made Miss America More Than Just a Pretty Face," *Advertising Age,* May 19, 1975, p. 65.
50. "Need Outdoor Numbers, TAB Told," *Advertising Age,* February 3, 1975, p. 4.
51. "Wards Opens Catalog to Outside Advertisers," *Advertising Age,* March 15, 1976, p. 1.

CASE 19
RSVP Restaurants

RSVP Restaurants is opening two new restaurants, one in Kansas City and the other in St. Louis. The theme of the restaurants is "the total concept of dining." This encompasses the entire dining experience—atmosphere, food, and service. The European atmosphere emphasizes intimacy. The menu is oriented toward the expanding interest in gourmet foods. A typical dinner begins with a tureen of hot or cold soup (depending on the season) complemented by hot bread. A green salad follows, topped by one of the restaurant's three specially prepared dressings. An assortment of entrees is offered, such as veal cordon bleu, beef stroganoff, breast of chicken bordeaux, and shrimp barsac, accompanied by freshly cooked vegetables served in typical European style. A dessert cart comes to the table after the meal, offering such choices as strawberries quorum, rum cream pie, and zqetch-genknodel (Bavarian plum dumplings) for an additional charge.

RSVP Restaurants' target market is the middle- to upper-income individual. Research reveals that the average customer spends between $15.00 and $20.00 on a meal, including cocktails, dinner, and wine. After an introductory period of six months, RSVP Restaurants in Denver, Colorado Springs, and Phoenix had built up enough business to seat customers by reservations only.

Irene Colby, director of marketing, is responsible for deciding which media to use in the advertising campaign.

1. What media would she choose for the introductory period?
2. What media would she choose for a continuing advertising campaign? Explain your selections.

20

Advertising Management

OBJECTIVES

■ To become aware of the various goals of advertising.
■ To learn about the different techniques used for setting advertising budgets.
■ To understand the steps involved in creating a successful advertising campaign.
■ To learn some of the techniques used to measure advertising effectiveness.
■ To learn about the role of advertising agencies.
■ To understand the regulatory aspects of advertising.

This chapter focuses on the management of advertising. Now that you are acquainted with the basic attributes of advertising, we will explore the ways in which it is managed and controlled. The chapter begins with a discussion of advertising goals and how goals provide the foundation for an advertising campaign. Next, I'll describe media budgets, evaluation, and the measurement of advertising effectiveness. A discussion of advertising agencies and their function reveals how marketing managers use this valuable institution. The chapter ends with an analysis of how changing federal regulations are affecting advertising management.

THE GOALS OF ADVERTISING

Effective advertising management requires the establishment of goals as a first step. These goals will provide a basis for planning and evaluating advertising efforts. Like promotional goals (discussed in

Chapter 15), advertising objectives usually involve behavior modification or reinforcement of existing behavior.

Communications and Sales Goals

Effective advertising planning cannot take place without very specific objectives. These objectives can be either communication goals or sales goals. A communication goal would be to convey information or to maintain top-of-the-mind awareness. For example, research conducted by the Potato Board in 1973 found that people viewed potatoes as fattening and not very nutritious.[1] One-third of all potato consumers felt that potatoes were too high in calories. Specific communication goals were established to reeducate the potato eater. By 1975 only one-fourth of the potato consumers believed that potatoes had too many calories.

When one sets communication goals one assumes that achieving those goals will ultimately lead to higher sales, a better image, or both. Rather than attempting to set specific communication goals, such as increasing brand awareness 5 percent in Evansville, Indiana, some marketing executives attempt to measure the end result—changes in sales. Total sales volume and market share are widely used sales indexes. (See Chapter 6.)

Specific Goals

The variety of advertising objectives can be bewildering. Some of the general areas in which specific objectives might be set are shown in Table 20.1. Again, these objectives must ultimately be geared to increased sales and profits.

TABLE 20.1   Advertising Goals

Inform	Persuade	Remind
(1) New-product introduction	(1) Persuade to purchase now	(1) Maintain top-of-the-mind awareness
(2) Build company image	(2) Aid the sales force	(2) Maintain product and company image when salesperson isn't available
(3) Reduce consumer's fears of risk involved in purchase	(3) Change relative importance of product attributes	(3) Maintain image during off seasons
(4) Suggest new uses of the product	(4) Persuade to let salesperson make presentation or demonstration	(4) Remind users where to buy product
(5) Inform of change in marketing mix, e.g., price	(5) Build brand preference	(5) Remind consumers that the product will be needed in the near future
(6) Tell consumers who is using the product now	(6) Increase switching to advertiser's brand	
(7) Explain how the product works	(7) Attempt to offset competitors' advertising	
(8) Explain various uses of the product or service	(8) Build employee morale	
(9) Correct false impressions		

THE ADVERTISING BUDGET

After objectives have been established, an advertising budget must be developed. (See Figure 20.1.) Common techniques for setting budgets may be termed arbitrary allocation, percent of sales, market share, and objective and task. These traditional techniques of budget setting, while they are practical, rarely lead to an optimal dollar quantity or an optimal blend. In fact an optimal technique has yet to be developed.

Arbitrary Allocation

The easiest way to set an advertising budget is simply to pick a number. This is called arbitrary allocation. An offshoot of a recent study by the author among seven moderate-sized commercial banks found that in all cases but one the advertising budget was set arbitrarily. One bank had allocated a constant dollar amount to advertising for eight years. Discussions with a number of bank officers did not reveal why that specific amount had been chosen. No one knew! Another bank simply followed the recommendation of its advertising agency. If the amount seemed too high, the board of directors would "lop off" a certain amount. Perhaps the reason for this illogical approach to budget setting is the difficulty of measuring the effectiveness of advertising.

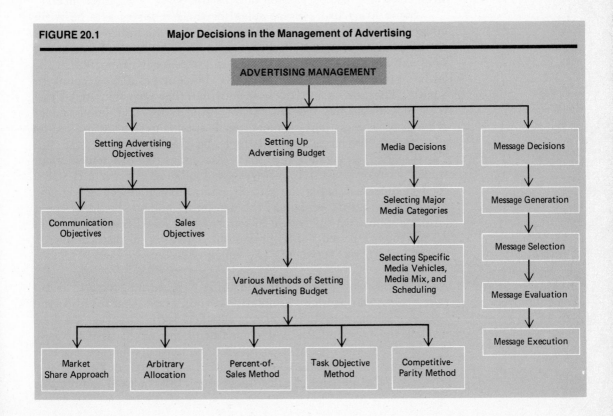

FIGURE 20.1　　　**Major Decisions in the Management of Advertising**

Percent of Sales

A second method of establishing a promotional budget is to use a certain percentage of total sales. In other words, promotion dollars = $n\% \times$ total sales. The percent-of-sales approach is not limited to total sales; it can also be based on sales by product, territory, customer group, and so forth. The inherent weakness of this approach is that the budget becomes a consequence of sales rather than a determinant of sales. As sales go down, the promotion budget falls proportionately. Yet research has shown that industrial advertisers that maintain their promotional budgets during recessionary periods have better sales than those that do not.[2]

The appeal of the percent-of-sales technique is its simplicity. Even large firms like Beatrice Foods base their promotional budgets on sales.[3] It is obvious that many others follow this practice, since advertising expenditures tend to rise and fall with the business cycle.[4] The technique is easy to use and easy for managers to relate to, since they often view costs in percentage terms. It also gives the illusion of definiteness.

Selected advertising-to-sales ratios by product category are shown in Table 20.2. One study showed that many firms that use this approach use the same percentage year after year.[5] Variable ratios often come into use only when new products are being introduced.

Some firms use average sales for their industry as a basis for budgeting. There are certain fallacies in following industry averages, however.[6] The fact that one firm's promotion budget is 5 percent of sales and another's is 10 percent doesn't necessarily indicate that the latter's promotion is twice as effective. Percentages don't account for quality. They also ignore the base on which they are calculated. Procter and Gamble has the lowest percent-of-sales ratio among major producers of soaps and cleaners, yet it spends over $400 million on advertising — the largest advertising budget in the world.

Finally, an average is just that — an average. When a nonswimmer wades across a river that averages one foot in depth, there is still a good chance that he or she will drown! One student of advertising determined that 20 percent of the marketing budget should be spent on promotion[7] and that until 20 percent is reached the firm has not reaped the full benefits of its promotion. This is a simplistic approach and at best should serve only as a rough guideline.

The Market Share Approach

Another frequent approach to budgeting is based on trying to maintain a given market share or obtain a certain target share. This is the market share approach. If a firm is satisfied with its market share, it may decide to spend the dollar amount or percentage that it spent previously. If the organization plans to increase its market share, it can increase its promotional expenditures accordingly.

Like the percent-of-sales technique, this method completely

ignores quality and creativity. Who is to say that spending $5 million this year will be more or less effective than last year's expenditures? Also, the firm is letting its competition set the parameters of its promotion budget.

The market share approach also ignores potential new-product offerings. Generally, a new product requires a heavier promotional budget to educate the target market and build product awareness. Aside from recognizing the importance of competition for market share, this approach does not improve much on the methods already discussed.

Borden uses a market share approach coupled with a formal working relationship between its top management and its advertising agency. The agency is answerable for every dollar of ad spending and the achievement of specific market share objectives. In 1977 Borden spent $1.7 million on Cracker Jack advertising compared to $1.5 million in 1976. Its goal was to increase market share from 59 percent to 63 percent. It calculated the cost of four additional percentage points of market share at $200,000 worth of advertising.[8]

Objective and Task The most popular approach to setting an advertising budget is the objective-and-task approach. (See Table 20.3.)

The objective-and-task approach offers management a sound technique for setting a promotion budget. First, objectives are established. Second, the communication tools required to achieve those objectives are delineated. Then a budget is built by summing the costs of the promotional activities and programs required.

This approach implies managerial understanding of the effectiveness of various promotional tools in eliciting the desired audience response. It also assumes that achieving the objectives will be worth the costs.

Missouri Valley Petroleum used the objective-and-task approach to test promotion effectiveness. It found that approximately doubling its promotion budget had a profound effect on demand. Tripling the budget led to only minimal further increases.[9] Anheuser-Busch also used the objective-and-task approach. It showed that it could often reduce promotion expenditures and still increase sales. Promotion dollars were utilized more effectively, and this accounted for the sales increases.[10]

THE NATURE OF AN ADVERTISING CAMPAIGN After promotional objectives have been established and an advertising budget has been determined, the advertising campaign can be planned. A campaign is a carefully planned sequence of advertisements designed around a common theme. The goals of a specific program will vary, depending on whether it is a product/service campaign

TABLE 20.2   Advertising as a Percentage of Sales

Ad Rank	Company	Advertising	Sales	Advertising as % of Sales
	Cars			
2	General Motors Corp.	$287,000,000	$47,181,000,000	0.6%
7	Ford Motor Co.	162,000,000	28,839,661,000	0.5
19	Chrysler Corp.	110,000,000	15,537,800,000	0.7
48	Volkswagen of America	60,500,000	8,900,000,000	0.7
67	Toyota Motor Sales, U.S.A.	42,418,000	7,173,911,000	0.6
72	Nissan Motor Corp., U.S.A.	40,000,000	7,362,200,000	0.5
74	American Motors Corp.	38,535,400	2,315,470,000	1.6
99	American Honda Motor Co.	19,928,300	2,927,600,000	0.7
100	British Leyland Motors Corp.	18,349,000	385,000,000	4.8
	Food			
3	General Foods Corp.	275,000,000	3,641,600,000	7.6
13	General Mills	131,600,000	2,908,404,000	4.5
20	McDonald's Corp.	105,000,000	3,063,000,000	3.4
25	Norton Simon Inc.	91,634,000	1,342,491,000	6.8
27	Nabisco Inc.	90,100,000	2,027,300,000	4.4
31	Ralston Purina Co.	87,780,000	3,393,800,000	2.6
	Gum and Candy			
71	Mars Inc.	40,850,000	735,000,000	5.6
82	Wm. Wrigley Jr. Co.	32,529,000	370,198,000	8.8
	Liquor			
14	Heublein Inc.	129,143,000	1,550,902,000	8.3
45	Seagram Co. Ltd.	66,000,000	2,048,970,000	3.2
92	Hiram Walker-Gooderham & Worts Ltd.	26,000,000	875,000,000	3.0
	Soaps, Cleansers (and Allied)			
1	Procter & Gamble Co.	445,000,000	5,300,000,000	8.4
12	Unilever	135,000,000	1,226,504,000	10.7
15	Colgate-Palmolive Co.	118,000,000	3,511,492,000	3.4
68	S. C. Johnson & Son	42,000,000	315,000,000	13.3
69	Clorox Co.	42,000,000	822,101,000	5.1
	Tobacco			
9	Philip Morris Inc.	149,000,000	4,293,782,000	3.5
11	R. J. Reynolds Ind. Inc.	140,276,400	5,753,568,000	2.4
32	American Brands	87,000,000	4,125,800,000	2.1
55	Liggett Group Inc.	53,209,000	851,877,100	6.2
	Drugs and Cosmetics			
5	Warner-Lambert Co.	199,000,000	1,300,000,000	15.3
6	Bristol-Myers Co.	189,000,000	1,986,370,000	9.5
8	American Home Prod. Corp.	158,000,000	1,800,000,000	8.8
16	Richardson-Merrell	115,507,000	745,877,000	15.5
24	Gillette Co.	94,000,000	1,491,506,000	6.3

Ad Rank	Company	Advertising	Sales	Advertising as % of Sales
41	Sterling Drug Inc.	70,000,000	638,938,000	11.0
43	Johnson & Johnson	68,900,000	1,493,172,000	4.6
47	Revlon Inc.	61,000,000	600,000,000	10.2
49	Chesebrough-Ponds, Inc.	60,000,000	746,986,000	8.0
50	Schering-Plough Corp.	60,000,000	871,537,000	6.9
	Beer			
57	Jos. Schlitz Brew. Co.	50,950,000	1,214,662,000	4.2
59	Anheuser-Busch Inc.	49,021,000	1,752,998,000	2.7
	Oil			
10	Mobil Corp.	146,500,000	28,046,467,000	0.5
83	Exxon Corp.	32,000,000	52,626,000,000	0.1
98	Shell Oil Co.	21,000,000	9,309,000,000	0.2
	Airlines			
85	Trans World Airlines	28,400,000	2,970,453,000	1.0
88	Eastern Airlines	27,800,000	1,825,475,000	1.5
89	UAL Inc.	27,199,000	2,929,637,000	0.9
91	American Airlines	26,250,000	2,007,883,000	1.3
97	Delta Air Lines	21,735,800	1,616,089,000	1.3
	Soft Drinks			
23	PepsiCo Inc.	95,000,000	2,727,455,000	3.5
26	Coca Cola Co.	91,334,540	1,698,000,000	5.3
87	Royal Crown Cola Co.	28,000,000	281,995,000	9.9
	Appliances, TV, Radio			
21	RCA Corp.	100,000,000	5,363,600,000	1.9
28	General Electric Co.	90,000,000	15,697,000,000	0.6
	Retail Chains			
4	Sears, Roebuck & Co.	245,000,000	12,535,000,000	2.0
35	J. C. Penney Co.	81,600,000	8,353,800,000	1.0
	Chemicals			
22	American Cyanamid Co.	95,880,300	732,835,250	13.0
66	Union Carbide Corp.	42,458,000	6,342,700,000	0.7
	Photographic Equipment			
37	Eastman Kodak Co.	74,332,000	4,000,000,000	1.9
77	Polaroid Corp.	35,316,300	950,032,000	3.7
	Telephone Service, Equipment			
18	American Telephone & Telegraph Co.	112,762,700	32,815,000,000	0.3
30	International Telephone & Telegraph Co.	87,842,000	11,764,106,000	0.7

Source: "100 Leaders' Advertising as Percent of Sales, *Advertising Age*, August 29, 1977, p. 30. Reprinted by permission. Copyright 1977 by Crain Communications, Inc.

TABLE 20.3	Techniques for Setting Promotion Budgets Among 557 Firms
Percentage of sales	24.8%
Arbitrary	27.7
Other	11.9
Task	35.6
Total	100.0%

Source: Murray Harding, "Project Future: More Advertisers Mad Than Glad About Budget Policy," *Industrial Marketing,* 53 (August 1968): 58.

or an institutional campaign. Every campaign requires the determination of a theme or message, the selection of a media mix, media scheduling, and measurement of the campaign's effectiveness. Research has shown that an effectively designed campaign will have a significant impact on sales.[11]

The Message

Messages are developed in three stages: (1) message generation, (2) message evaluation, and (3) message execution.[12] Message generation is the creative development of things to say about the good or service. Message generation is undertaken in light of promotional objectives, the product's current image, and the desired positioning of the product. As the marketing environment changes, so must the basic campaign theme. Coke, for example, began phasing out the "It's the real thing" theme in 1976 and switched to a more upbeat "Coke adds life to . . ."

Message evaluation normally involves market research to determine the best theme among those that have been developed. Evaluation criteria include desirability, exclusiveness, and believability. The message must first make a positive impression on the target audience. It must also be unique in that consumers can easily differentiate the advertiser's message from those of competitors. Most important, it should be believable. A theme that makes extravagant claims not only wastes promotional dollars but also creates ill will for the advertiser.

Message execution means developing the copy and illustrations for the campaign. Copy is the written or spoken material. Illustrations (drawings, photographs, etc.) are used to complement and reinforce the advertising copy. Finally, the advertising format must be developed for print media and television. Copy and illustrations must be balanced on the page or screen, headline sizes determined, and colors chosen.

Media Mix and Scheduling

We will reserve our discussion of the media mix for the next section of this chapter. Media scheduling is based on the frequency with which an advertiser wants to reach its audience. When a message is to be heard or seen only once, the advertiser attempts to maximize its reach. Reach is the number of different consumers exposed to an advertisement in a given period (usually four weeks). The goal of the single-frequency advertiser would be to reach as many different people as possible with the single message. This often occurs for special sales, year-end model deals, close-outs, and the like.

EVALUATING MEDIA ALTERNATIVES
The Qualitative Aspect

Media selection may require a kind of managerial judgment that defies quantification. Perhaps management feels that an endorsement is important; this requires the use of *Parents' Magazine* or *Good Housekeeping* seals. If quality is important, management should shy away from cheap magazines and some independent low-budget television stations.

Media Costs

Cost per thousand (CPM) is the standard criterion for comparing media. The formula is

$$CPM = \frac{\text{price of a single ad}}{\text{audience size (in thousands)}}$$

If the cost of an ad is $50,000 and the audience is 24 million people, CPM is $2.08. The costs of all media have been rising rapidly since 1970. Sunday magazines (e.g., *Parade*), newspaper advertising, and spot radio have shown the greatest CPM increases. Naturally, this improves the cost attractiveness of competing media.

There are several problems with CPM comparisons. First is the question of audience measurement. Does the figure include the pass-along rate or is it base circulation? A large pass-along rate can drop CPM substantially. CPM data also make the tacit assumption that everyone in the audience is part of the target market. Rarely is this the case.[13] Finally, media are so different in form, content, reputation, editorial content, display quality, audio capabilities, and so forth that cross-media comparisons based only on CPM become meaningless.

Duplication

Another factor that complicates the media selection process is audience duplication. Assume that *Newsweek* has a circulation of 3,400,000 and *Time* has a circulation of 4,500,000. If 800,000 people subscribe to both publications, the nonduplicated circulations are 2,600,000 and 3,800,000 for *Newsweek* and *Time,* respectively. (See Figure 20.2.)

Usually, the greater the number of media selected, the greater the problem of duplication. If an advertising campaign does not have dual exposure among its goals, duplicated circulation results in wasted advertising dollars.

FIGURE 20.2   The Duplication Problem

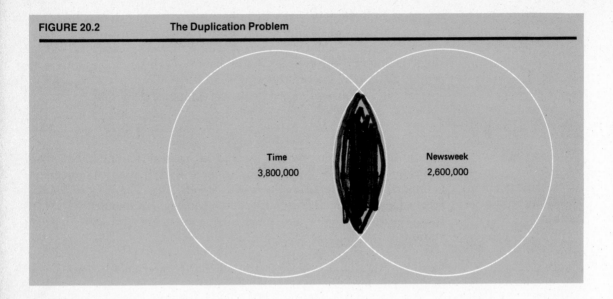

Time
3,800,000

Newsweek
2,600,000

MEASURING ADVERTISING EFFECTIVENESS AND MEDIA AUDIENCES

Arthur W. Schultz, chairman of the board of Foote, Cone and Belding, says, "The biggest waste in advertising is in the advertising itself—because advertising doesn't do what it is supposed to do."[14] Obtaining the proper media mix is only half the battle; the "right" message must reach the target market. Any message that aids in accomplishing the advertising goal is the "right" message.

Communication goals can be measured before the advertisement is placed in the media (pretest) or afterwards (posttest). Of course, actual sales effectiveness must be measured after the advertisement has been run. Sales effects may be forecast, however, by using simulation models. To date most advertising simulation models have been of minimal use in measuring advertising effectiveness. Simulation models are not of much value to creative personnel because they don't explain why an ad or a campaign was successful or unsuccessful. As one advertising executive has said, "I know that fifty percent of my advertising is ineffective; the problem is that I don't know which fifty percent."

Tests of Communication Effectiveness

Recall Tests.   Recall tests can be either pretests that compare several ads or posttests that determine the amount of information learned by the target consumer. A pretest can take place in the home, in a shopping center, or in a laboratory situation. One form of recall testing in which the author was involved centered on measuring recall for two convenience grocery commercials. Participants were shown a thirty-minute television program interspersed with the normal array of commercials, including the test commercials.

First, unaided recall was measured by asking the respondents to write down all of the commercials they remembered. Next, they were asked to write down whatever details of the commercials they recalled. Answer papers were collected and a series of aided-recall papers were distributed sequentially. Aided recall provides certain cues to jog the interviewee's memory, for example, "What do you remember about the grocery shopping commercials?" "What did the man say to the clerk?" "What was the theme of the customer–clerk grocery commercial?"

Recognition Tests. Hooper-Starch, a market research company, conducts posttest magazine research that also requires recall but is referred to by Starch as a recognition test. Each interviewer carries a portfolio of sample pages and advertisements of up to sixteen magazines. The researcher goes to the respondent's home and asks whether he or she has read a particular periodical. If the answer is yes, the interviewer will show the respondent an ad and ask, "Did you see or read any part of this advertisement?" Starch reports three basic findings:

1. *Noted*—the percentage of respondents who remember seeing the ad.
2. *Seen Associated*—the percentage of respondents who recall seeing or reading part of the ad.
3. *Read Most*—the percentage of respondents who reported reading at least half of the ad.

One problem with Hooper-Starch data is that the respondent may not tell the truth about remembering the advertisement. More important, heavy readers are taken through a large number of portfolios. As a result the interview may last 2½ to 3 hours, resulting in interviewee fatigue and poor responses.

Attitude Measures. Often attitude measures are incorporated into recall and recognition tests. Interviewers may ask interviewees to tell them whether an ad is believable, convincing, dull, imaginative, informative, phony, realistic, silly, and so forth. They may also ask, "How did the ad affect your desire for the product: (1) increased very much, (2) increased somewhat, (3) unaffected, (4) decreased somewhat, (5) decreased very much"

Physiological Tests. In order to avoid the bias that is sometimes encountered in the tests just described, some advertisers have turned to physiological testing. Galvanic skin tests, eye movement experiments, pupil dilation measurement, and so forth are used as measures of advertising awareness and interest. Most advertisers have failed to prove satisfactorily that there is a strong relationship between the findings of physiological tests and actual purchase behavior.

Cable TV Panel Tests.   A major advance in coupling experimental design methodology and cable television has been accomplished by AdTel. The technique uses a dual-cable CATV system and two consumer purchase diary panels. The system results in a highly controlled but realistic testing environment. By using different ads on the dual-cable system AdTel can measure sales response. The more detailed information recorded in the diary provides additional insight into why a test succeeded or failed.

Audience Measurement

Magazines.   Audience measures are generally made by the same research organizations that gauge advertising effectiveness. In addition to Starch, TGI and Simmons specialize in periodic magazine audience studies. Another organization, the Audit Bureau of Circulation (ABC), audits the paid-circulation figures of both magazines and newspapers.

Radio.   Arbitron is the largest research firm specializing in radio audience measurement. Information is gathered by consumer diaries sent to randomly selected households. In 1978, no other researcher provided a nationwide radio audience survey.

Newspapers.   Newspaper audience measurement is not dominated by any single firm. Beldon Associates and Markets In Focus probably conduct more newspaper research than any other company. Newspaper audience data are usually gathered through telephone or in-home interviews. Consumption patterns and demographic profiles are also obtained for promotional purposes. A trade ad may then read, "Ninety-three percent of all Detroit scotch drinkers read the Detroit Daily News."

Television.   Television audience data are usually gathered by means of consumer diaries. A. C. Nielsen and the American Research Bureau (Arbitron) dominate the syndicated measurement studies. An example of a Nielsen television report is shown in Figure 20.3. When quick audience results are needed, telephone interviews are taken by A. C. Nielsen and several other research companies. In addition to diaries and telephone surveys, Nielsen also uses an audiometer that measures the number of sets that are tuned in to a particular station.

Nielsen's national television sample consists of only 1170 out of a total of 68.5 million TV-owning households in the country.[15] Each set in the sample has an audiometer that feeds channel selection information into Nielsen's computers over special telephone lines. Audiometer data are "reinforced" by the 100,000 families a year who

FIGURE 20.3   Nielsen Television Ratings

FAST WEEKLY PROGRAM AUDIENCE ESTIMATES   SEPT. 26–OCT. 2, 1977

Program Name	Time	Dur	Day	Ntwk	Households (000)	%	Share %	No. Prog.	Sta. Covg.
EVENING									
ABC EVENING NEWS	6:30	30	SAT.	A	3,500	4.8	11	117	67
ABC FRIDAY NIGHT MOVIE	9:00	120	FRI.	A	12,900	17.7	33	192	99
ABC NEWS-REASONER/WALTERS	6:30	30	M-F	A	5,980	8.2	18	191	99
ABC SUNDAY NIGHT MOVIE	9:00	120	SUN.	A	12,830	17.6	29	193	99
ABC WEEKEND NEWS-SATURDAY	11:00	15	SAT.	A	6,270	8.6	18	163	95
ABC WEEKEND NEWS-SUNDAY	11:00	15	SUN.	A	4,160	5.7	13	156	97
ALICE	9:30	30	SUN.	C	17,060	23.4	38	187	99
ALL IN THE FAMILY	8:30	30	SUN.	C	18,810	25.8	41	183	99
BARETTA-11:30PM	11:30	60	TUE.	A	4,300	5.9	18	158	93
BARETTA	10:00	60	WED.	A	16,550	22.7	41	202	99
BARNABY JONES	10:00	60	THU.	C	11,740	16.1	25	191	99
BARNEY MILLER	9:00	30	THU.	A	14,290	19.6	31	189	99
BETTY WHITE SHOW	9:00	30	MON.	C	13,050	17.9	27	194	99
BIG EVENT	9:00	120	SUN.	N	14,870	20.4	33	207	99
BIG HAWAII	10:00	60	WED.	N	9,400	12.9	23	198	99
BIONIC WOMAN	8:00	60	SAT.	N	12,100	16.6	32	216	99
BOB NEWHART SHOW	8:00	30	SAT.	C	10,860	14.9	30	191	99
BUSTING LOOSE	8:30	30	WED.	C	9,620	13.2	22	180	97
CAROL BURNETT SHOW	10:00	60	SAT.	C	8,890	12.2	23	203	99
CARTER COUNTRY	9:30	30	THU.	A	12,540	17.2	26	186	99
CBS EVENING NEWS-CRONKITE	6:30	30	M-F	C	9,910	13.6	30	201	99
CBS SAT. NEWS-SCHIEFFER	6:30	30	SAT.	C	6,420	8.8	21	159	89
CBS SUNDAY NEWS-BRADLEY	11:00	15	SUN.	C	6,560	9.0	20	138	80
CBS WEDNESDAY NIGHT MOVIE	9:00	101	WED.	C	12,030	16.5	28	183	95
CHARLIE'S ANGELS	9:00	60	WED.	A	19,320	26.5	43	203	99
CHICO AND THE MAN	8:30	30	FRI.	N	9,840	13.5	26	197	99
CHIPS	8:00	60	THU.	N	11,960	16.4	27	182	95
DONNY AND MARIE	8:00	60	FRI.	A	14,430	19.8	38	200	99
EIGHT IS ENOUGH	8:00	60	WED.	A	14,290	19.6	34	195	99
FAMILY	10:00	60	TUE.	A	15,310	21.0	36	191	99
FISH	8:00	30	SAT.	A	9,910	13.6	27	191	99
FITZPATRICKS, THE	8:00	60	TUE.	C	7,800	10.7	18	182	97
GOOD TIMES	8:00	30	WED.	C	12,680	17.4	30	189	99
HAPPY DAYS	8:00	30	TUE.	A	22,450	30.8	53	208	99
HARDY BOYS/NANCY DREW	7:00	60	SUN.	A	11,300	15.5	28	184	99
HAWAII FIVE-O	9:00	60	THU.	C	11,370	15.6	24	194	97
→ HEAVYWEIGHT BOXING CHPSHP(S)	9:00	150	THU.	N	27,190	37.3	57	208	99
JEFFERSONS, THE	9:30	30	SAT.	C	12,100	16.6	30	195	99
KOJAK	10:00	60	SUN.	C	13,630	18.7	32	186	98
LATE MOVIE I	11:30	VAR	M-F	A	4,520	6.2	24	167	91
LATE MOVIE II	VAR	VAR	TUWF	A	3,060	4.2	23	167	91
LAVERNE AND SHIRLEY	8:30	30	TUE.	A	23,550	32.3	53	207	99
LIFE-TIMES-GRIZZLY ADAMS	8:00	60	WED.	N	13,190	18.1	31	208	99
LITTLE HOUSE-PRAIRIE	8:00	60	MON.	N	15,600	21.4	35	211	97
LOGAN'S RUN	9:00	60	FRI.	A	10,060	13.8	25	194	99
LOU GRANT	10:00	60	TUE.	C	12,170	16.7	29	201	99
LOVE BOAT	10:00	60	SAT.	A	15,240	20.9	39	183	98
M*A*S*H	9:00	30	TUE.	C	15,600	21.4	33	205	99
MAUDE	9:30	30	M-F	C	12,540	17.2	26	188	99
MIDNIGHT SPECIAL	1:30	90	FRI.	N	2,620	3.6	34	190	98
→ MOVIE OF THE WEEK(S)	9:00	120	TUE.	N	12,320	16.9	28	200	99
NBC LATE NIGHT MOVIE	11:30	60	SUN.	N	4,080	5.6	23	117	74
NBC MONDAY NIGHT MOVIES	9:00	120	MON.	N	16,550	22.7	36	199	99
NBC NEWS UPDATE-M-F	8:58	01	M-F	N	11,960	16.4	27	183	95
NBC NEWS UPDATE-SAT.	8:58	01	SAT.	N	11,300	15.5	29	191	97
NBC NEWS UPDATE-SUN.	8:58	01	SUN.	N	11,960	16.4	26	198	97
NBC NIGHTLY NEWS-SAT.	6:30	30	SAT.	N	6,490	8.9	21	153	84
NBC NIGHTLY NEWS-SUN.	6:30	30	SUN.	N	3,060	4.2	9	92	49
NBC NIGHTLY NEWS	6:30	30	M-F	N	8,160	11.2	25	203	98
NBC SATURDAY NIGHT MOVIES	9:00	135	SAT.	N	12,390	17.0	32	202	99
NEWSBREAK-M-F	VAR	01	M-F	C	9,910	13.6	23	177	93
NEWSBREAK-SAT.	8:58	01	SAT.	C	10,790	14.8	28	178	92
NEWSBREAK-SUN.	9:28	01	SUN.	C	17,930	24.6	39	175	94
NEWSBRIEF-M-F	VAR	01	M-F	A	13,780	18.9	31	180	96
NEWSBRIEF-SAT.	9:58	01	SAT.	A	14,510	19.9	36	184	97
NEWSBRIEF-SUN.	8:58	01	SUN.	A	12,470	17.1	27	190	98
NFL MONDAY NIGHT FOOTBALL	9:00	209	MON.	A	15,750	21.6	39	195	98
ONE DAY AT A TIME	9:30	30	TUE.	C	15,160	20.8	32	200	99
OPERATION PETTICOAT	8:30	30	SAT.	A	11,590	15.9	30	192	99
OREGON TRAIL	9:00	60	WED.	N	10,790	14.8	24	198	99
POLICE STORY	11:30	65	THU.	A	4,160	5.7	20	166	96
QUINCY, M.E.	10:00	60	FRI.	N	13,630	18.7	36	204	99
RAFFERTY	10:00	60	MON.	C	10,860	14.9	25	190	99
REDD FOXX SHOW	10:00	60	THU.	A	6,930	9.5	15	186	99
RHODA	8:00	30	SUN.	C	15,380	21.1	35	189	99
RICHARD PRYOR	8:00	60	TUE.	N	9,110	12.5	21	191	99
ROCKFORD FILES	9:00	60	FRI.	N	13,560	18.6	34	206	99
SAN PEDRO BEACH BUMS	8:00	60	MON.	N	12,680	17.4	29	186	98
SANFORD ARMS	8:00	30	FRI.	N	9,480	13.0	26	190	97
SIX MILLION DOLLAR MAN	8:00	60	SUN.	A	14,430	19.8	32	194	99
60 MINUTES	7:00	60	SUN.	C	15,970	21.9	40	202	99
SOAP	9:30	30	TUE.	A	15,820	21.7	34	175	97
STARSKY AND HUTCH	9:00	60	SAT.	A	14,360	19.7	35	198	99
STARSKY AND HUTCH-11.30	11:30	63	WED.	A	5,320	7.3	29	166	96
SWITCH	10:00	60	FRI.	C	8,460	11.6	22	188	99
THREE'S COMPANY	9:00	30	TUE.	A	18,740	25.7	40	166	98
THURSDAY NIGHT SPECIAL	12:35	57	THU.	A	2,040	2.8	19	161	95
TOMORROW SHOW	VAR	45	M-TH	N	1,530	2.1	21	172	97
TONIGHT SHOW	VAR	VAR	M-F	N	6,490	8.9	35	210	99
TONY RANDALL SHOW	9:30	30	SAT.	C	10,210	14.0	25	197	99

△ Partial time interruption within program. → Delays which occurred after the week of telecast but during the current National TV Ratings Report two-week interval are excluded from the audience estimates in this preliminary report; they will be included in the final ratings for this program, in the next National TV Ratings Report. (S) Special or Preempting Program (B) Breakout due to coverage or change in telecast day. (See NTI/NAC Reference Supplement.)

U.S. TV Households: 72,900,000   1

Source: Nielsen Television Index, "Fast Weekly Household Audiences Report, Week of Sept. 26–Oct. 2, 1977. Copyright 1977 A.C. Nielsen Company.

fill out television diaries on a weekly basis. According to Nielsen's management, "the diary and meter results are consistently almost identical."[16] Accuracy is of extreme importance to television advertisers, since a percent rating change (a Nielsen point) will be worth an average of $17 million or more during the winter of 1976–1977.[17]

ADVERTISING AGENCIES

Advertising agencies occupy a unique position in the business environment. No other function of business is delegated to outside organizations to the extent that advertising is.

TABLE 20.4   America's Largest Full-Service Agencies

Rank	Agency	1976	1975
1	Young & Rubicam	$85.8[a]	$71.5[a]
2	J. Walter Thompson Co.	77.3	64.8
3	Leo Burnett Co.	74.3	58.4
4	BBDO International	63.3	53.8
5	Ogilvy & Mather Int'l.	51.4	39.9
6	Grey Advertising	51.0	43.2
7	Foote, Cone & Belding	46.8	41.3
8	Doyle Dane Bernbach	46.2	34.7
9	Ted Bates & Co.	44.4	37.5
10	McCann-Erickson	44.3	34.7

Source: James O'Gara, "First Time: Gross Income for 626 Agencies," *Advertising Age,* March 14, 1977, p. 1. Reprinted by permission. Copyright 1977 by Crain Communications, Inc.
[a] Gross income in millions.

Agency Functions

Full-service advertising agencies generally perform five functions: creative services, media services, research, merchandising counsel, and advertising planning.[18] America's largest full-service agencies are listed in Table 20.4.

Creative personnel conceive promotional themes and messages, write copy, design layouts, and draw illustrations. Media service departments aid in selecting the media mix, scheduling, and controlling the media program. Several major agencies are now subcontracting television buying to media purchasing boutiques because of the complexity of television advertising.[19]

Larger advertising agencies also aid in the formulation and analysis of market research studies. Often the agency goes far beyond media research by aiding in new-product development research, positioning research, and the like. In virtually every case the actual research and most of the design work are done by a marketing research subcontractor.

Some agencies also develop contests, premium offers, point-of-purchase displays, and other forms of sales promotion for their clients. They also prepare brochures for the sales force and aid in package design.

Almost all full-service agencies work with their clients in campaign design and planning. Promotional goals are established, positioning strategies defined, promotional alternatives examined, and campaigns created. The agency also aids in developing control procedures to measure the campaign's effectiveness.

The responsibility for maintaining a channel of communication between the agency and the advertiser rests with the account executive. Account executives transmit plans, objectives, and concepts to the agency's creative personnel and present proposed campaigns to the advertiser. Usually, account executives are also the agency's sales force and are expected to make presentations to potential new accounts.

Agency Compensation

Historically, advertising agencies have been paid a standard 15-percent commission on the cost of media time and space. In the late 1960s the industry began to realize that some advertisers were not getting their money's worth whereas others received far more than a 15-percent commission would justify. Today the fee system is rapidly replacing the standard commission. Advertisers are charged a fee for services actually rendered rather than a fixed percentage. Many large advertisers have substantial in-house capabilities and need help only in special areas. To meet this need, "creative boutiques" have sprung up, specializing in creative planning.

Agency Switching

Perhaps because of the difficulty of measuring advertising effectiveness and/or advertiser demand for creative freshness, advertisers often switch agencies. Sometimes a change of agencies is justified because promotional goals have not been achieved. In other cases advertisers with internal capabilities are dropping full-service firms in favor of boutiques. All too often, however, advertisers change for emotional rather than rational reasons. Such shifts are not limited to small advertisers. In 1974, 221 large accounts (over $500,000) changed agencies.[20]

THE IMPACT OF ADVERTISING REGULATION

In addition to rapid account changes, advertising agencies have to cope with the growing role and scope of advertising regulation. The 1914 Federal Trade Commission Act gave the FTC authority under Section 5(a) to prevent unfair methods of competition in interstate commerce. The role of advertising regulation was clarified in 1938 with the passage of the Wheeler–Lea Amendment to the FTC Act. The amendment extended the Commission's authority to the elimination of unfair or deceptive acts or practices in commerce.

Deceptive Advertising

Until 1972 most of the Commission's efforts were directed toward deceptive advertising.[21] In the landmark case of *Federal Trade Commission* v. *Sperry & Hutchinson Co.,* the Supreme Court ruled that the FTC didn't have to prove that a practice was "deceptive," only that it was "unfair" to consumers.[22]

Deceptive advertising is not limited to manufacturers but applies equally to wholesalers and retailers. Pricing and "sales that aren't" seem to draw most of the FTC's attention at the retail level. Items marked "reduced" must have actually been sold at the old price, not just offered for sale. Retailers must show the old price and the sale price—they cannot simply mark an item "reduced to $10."[23] The following is an example of recent FTC action against a large retailer:

> The Federal Trade Commission has obtained a consent settlement from Levitz Furniture Corp., Miami, which bars the big furniture chain from a variety of advertising practices related to price and quality claims.
>
> Under the settlement, Levitz must disclose in dollars or percentages the amount of price reduction on a sale item, and it must stop advertising reduced prices on items which have been advertised at substantially the same price during the preceding 30 days (unless it discloses that the item is being offered at a repeat sale price).
>
> Other sections of the settlement relate to charges that Levitz ads misrepresented the construction and material composition of furniture, and failed to disclose that certain "as-is" furniture was used. FTC also charged that Levitz used advertising phrases which falsely implied that it was a wholesaler or distributor.
>
> FTC said Levitz sales through 60 outlets in 27 states in 1974 totaled $350,000,000. The settlement will be subject to the public comment until Aug. 19. Then, the FTC will decide whether to make it final.
>
> Levitz said the FTC charges referred to actions of the former management.[24]

Unfair Advertising

Unfair advertising is much more difficult to pin down than deceptive advertising. The question arises, Unfair to whom? A person with a college degree is less likely to be misled than a grade school dropout. The commission has concentrated on advertisers who make claims without adequate proof. Also, advertising to special audiences such as children, the ghetto dweller, and the elderly is being closely watched.

Corrective Advertising

Since 1970 the FTC has begun requiring corrective advertising in certain cases. The basis for corrective advertising is that a deceptive ad might continue to influence consumers even if it is removed from the media. As a result "corrective" product information in future advertisements would protect the public interest. So far, corrective advertising has been very limited. ITT Continental and Ocean Spray have run corrective ads for Profile bread and Ocean Spray cranberry juice cocktail at a rate of 25 percent of their advertising budgets for one year.[25] The effects of corrective advertising are still being researched.[26]

Self-Regulation

To avoid increasing governmental regulation (and distasteful settlements like those just mentioned), the advertising industry has set up procedures for regulating itself. The National Advertising Division of the Council of Better Business Bureaus (NAD) is intended to serve as a consumer complaint bureau, while the National Advertising Review Board (NARB) serves as an appeals board should NAD rule in favor of the complainant. The NARB is a five-judge panel (three representing advertisers, one representing agencies, and one representing consumer groups).

NAD receives about twenty complaints a month and is effective in screening for deceptive ads. The NARB uses adverse publicity to enforce its rulings. Thus it can often change advertising campaigns before they come before the FTC.

State and Local Regulation

The complex web of state and local advertising regulations make it difficult to generalize in this area. It seems fair to say, however, that most state and local governments have not been effective in regulating advertising. But there are several notable exceptions to this rule. For example, strong state laws enabled a Seattle judge to sentence a stereo equipment retailer to ninety days in jail for false advertising. The only other case of a person's being sent to jail for deceptive advertising occurred in the District of Columbia, where a retailer was convicted of using "bait-and-switch" tactics in the advertising of sewing machines.[27]

California has been active in pursuing false and misleading advertising. It has filed claims against such giants as Montgomery Ward and Sears. Ward's issued coupons to customers for specific discounts on certain items, then raised the prices of those products, thereby making the coupons worthless. The state claims that Sears' ads were structured so that all the items on a page appeared to be on sale when many were not.[28] Another suit filed in California claims that Arm and Hammer's baking soda ads encouraging consumers to put a pound of baking soda in each 10,000 gallons of swimming pool water to control Ph balance are misleading. It asked that the company be enjoined from using the ads and fined $2500 per proved misrepresentation.[29]

SUMMARY

Advertising management begins with the establishment of meaningful goals. These goals can take the form of either communication or sales objectives. Regardless of the type selected, they should be specific and measurable.

After objectives have been established, an advertising budget can be developed. There are several techniques for setting budgets: arbitrary allocation, percent of sales, market share, and objective and task. Arbitrary allocation, the easiest to use, is also the least scientific. The percent-of-sales approach makes advertising a consequence rather than a determinant of sales.

The market share technique is predicated upon the desired level of market penetration. This approach may ignore quality and creativity. It also does not account for potential new-product offerings. The objective-and-task approach is the most popular. Objectives are stated and tasks delineated. Promotional dollars are then allocated to accomplish the necessary tasks.

After objectives have been established and an advertising budget determined, the campaign can be planned. Every campaign requires a theme or message, selection of a media mix, media scheduling, and measurement of campaign effectiveness.

Media selection is often a difficult task. For example, duplication may complicate the process. Advertising recall tests, recognition tests, physiological tests, and attitude measures are common ways of examining the effectiveness of advertising.

No function of business is delegated to outside organizations more than advertising. This is due to the creative aspects of the process and the large number of specialized personnel required. A full-service advertising agency provides creative services, media services, research, merchandising counsel, and advertising planning. Historically, advertising agencies have been paid a standard 15-percent commission on media placements. Today a fee system is rapidly replacing the standard commission.

Advertisers and their agencies must continually adapt to changes in the role and scope of advertising regulation. The Federal Trade Commission Act gave the FTC authority to prevent unfair methods of competition, including advertising. The Wheeler–Lea Amendment to the FTC Act provided further authority for the elimination of unfair and deceptive acts or practices in interstate commerce. Since 1970 the FTC has begun requiring corrective advertising in certain cases to remedy unfair promotions. As a hedge against further regulation, the industry has set up two groups for self-regulation.

KEY TERMS

Communication goals	Reach
Sales goals	Cost per thousand (CPM)
Arbitrary allocation	Audience duplication
Percent-of-sales approach	Recall tests
Market share approach	Recognition tests
Objective-and-task approach	Attitude measures
Message generation	Physiological testing
Message evaluation	Deceptive advertising
Message execution	Unfair advertising
Advertising copy	Corrective advertising
Media scheduling	

QUESTIONS FOR DISCUSSION

1. What are advertising goals? Can you name three specific goals and give an example of each?
2. List the different methods used to set advertising budgets. Which one do you feel is most effective? Why?
3. Explain the percent-of-sales method of establishing an advertising budget. What is the basic defect of this technique?

4. Explain the objective-and-task approach to setting advertising budgets. What kinds of objectives can be used?
5. What are some of the factors that influence media selection?
6. Differentiate between recall tests and physiological tests. Which type is more effective?
7. What is meant by the term *audience measurement?* How can this be achieved for each of the following media?
   a. radio
   b. magazines
   c. TV
8. What are some of the functions of an advertising agency? Why do most companies use advertising agencies?
9. Explain the differences between a full-service advertising agency and a "creative boutique." Which type of organization is used more?
10. Differentiate between the terms *deceptive advertising* and *unfair advertising.* Explain the purpose of corrective advertising.
11. Comment on the statement, "Advertising increases sales."

NOTES

1. "Marketing Briefs," *Marketing News,* July 2, 1976, p. 2.
2. *Advertising in Recession Periods 1949, 1954, 1958, 1961 – A New Yardstick Revisited* (Chicago: Buchen Advertising, 1970).
3. "Advertisers' Spending Is Stepped Up as the Economy Gains," *Advertising Age,* April 29, 1976, p. 1.
4. Ibid.
5. David L. Harwood, "How Companies Set Advertising Budgets," *The Conference Board Record,* 5 (March 1968): 34–41.
6. For a good discussion of the problems of using the percent-of-sales approach for promotion budgeting, see John M. Trytten, "How Advertising Helps Sales," *Sales Management,* 113 (December 9, 1974): 46.
7. John W. DeWolf, "A New Tool for Setting and Selling Advertising Budgets," paper presented at the Eastern Regional Meeting of the American Association of Advertising Agencies, New York, November 7, 1973, p. 21.
8. "Measuring How Well Ads Sell," *Business Week,* September 13, 1976, pp. 104–106.
9. James F. Engle, Hugh G. Wells, and Martin R. Warshaw, *Promotional Strategy,* 3d ed. (Homewood, Ill.: Irwin, 1975), p. 205.
10. Ibid.
11. Peter Doyle and Jan Fenwick, "Planning and Estimation in Advertising," *Journal of Marketing Research,* 12 (February 1975): 1–6.
12. See Philip Kotler, *Marketing Management Analysis, Planning and Control,* 3d ed. (Englewood Cliffs, N.J.: Prentice-Hall, 1976), pp. 357–360.
13. See Arch Woodside and David Reid, "Is CPM Related to the Advertising Effectiveness of Magazines?" *Journal of Business Research,* 3 (October 1975): 323–334.
14. Arthur W. Schultz, "Stretching the Advertising Dollar," *Marketing Strategies, a Symposium* (New York: Conference Board Record, 1975), p. 38.

15. David M. Elsner, "A. C. Nielsen Co. Does a Lot More Than Just Rate Television Shows," *Wall Street Journal,* August 2, 1976.
16. Ibid.
17. Ibid.
18. David W. Nylen, *Advertising: Planning, Implementation and Control* (Cincinnati: Southwestern, 1975), pp. 80–83.
19. Ibid.
20. "Account Shifts Grew in 1974; $500 Million Billings Moved," *Advertising Age,* January 20, 1975, p. 2.
21. Dorothy Cohen, "The Concept of Unfairness as It Relates to Advertising Legislation," *Journal of Marketing,* 38 (July 1974): 8–13.
22. *Federal Trade Commission* v. *Sperry and Hutchinson Co.,* 405 U.S. 233, 1972.
23. "The Price Had Better Be Right," *Sales Management,* 113 (July 22, 1974): 12; see also: James R. Krum and Stephen K. Keiser, "Regulation of Retail Newspaper Advertising," *Journal of Marketing,* 40 (July 1976): 29–34.
24. "FTC Settles with Levitz; Sets Ad Rules," *Advertising Age,* June 28, 1976, p. 67. Reprinted by permission. Copyright 1976 by Crain Communications, Inc.
25. William L. Wilkie, "Research on Counter and Corrective Advertising," *Advertising and the Public Interest,* ed. S. F. Divita (Chicago: The American Marketing Association, 1973), p. 191.
26. See Michael B. Mazis and Janice E. Adkinson, "An Experimental Evaluation of a Proposed Corrective Advertising Remedy," *Journal of Marketing Research,* 13 (May 1976): 178–183; Robert E. Wilcox, "Recent FTC Actions: Implications for the Advertising Strategist," *Journal of Marketing,* 38 (January 1974): 55–61; and Robert F. Dyer and Philip G. Duehl, "The Corrective Advertising Remedy of the FTC: An Experimental Evaluation," *Journal of Marketing,* 38 (January 1974): 48–54.
27. "Seattle Suit Results in First Jail Sentence for False Ads," *Advertising Age,* July 14, 1975, p. 109.
28. "Wards, Sears to Defend Ads in California Action," *Advertising Age,* August 11, 1975, p. 46.
29. "Baking Soda Ads Mislead, California Suit Says," *Advertising Age,* August 18, 1975, p. 2.

CASE 20
Northeast National Bank

Northeast National Bank is a progressive Buffalo, New York, bank with $180 million in deposits. John Nash, vice president for marketing, came up through the commercial loan department and, at 41 years of age, had hopes of becoming president of the firm by the age of 45. One area that he had trouble "tying down" was advertising effectiveness. With a budget of slightly over $100,000 per year, he wondered just what the bank was getting for its money. He decided that the only way to really understand the situation was to delve into it himself.

As a first step, Nash reviewed the minutes of the advertising committee for the past six months. Although he was a member of the group, he normally took a passive role and let Erma Fine, the promotion manager, set the tone of the discussion. The minutes were skimpy at best and dwelled basically on future advertising themes brought up by committee members. Most of the meetings were dominated by George Yob, the account executive for Cranston-Yost, the bank's advertising agency. Fine opened the meetings; Yob told the committee what the agency was doing and what it planned to do for the next two months; Fine then asked several questions, and then the campaign was routinely approved. Table 20.5 shows the media mix and themes approved for the months of June and July.

TABLE 20.5   Schedule of Media Mix and Message

Media	Percent	Description
Billboards	33⅓	24 locations in southwest quarter of metropolitan Buffalo in points of high traffic flow
Radio	33⅓	30-second commercial on two different stations—station choice based on listener characteristics
Newspapers	33⅓	Ads in three newspapers in area of from 300 to 600 agate lines; two separate ads on same theme

Advertising Message During Test
1. Loans for home improvements
2. Loans for new automobiles
3. High interest on savings deposits
4. General bank image—"Home of the Free"

Nash decided that some information would be better than none, so he designed a short questionnaire for new accounts covering media, theme recall, and bank services used. The services that the respondents mentioned are listed in Table 20.6; the media selected are shown in Table 20.7. A final question proved to be the real shocker. Each person was asked why he or she had chosen Northeast National. These results are presented in Table 20.8.

TABLE 20.6   Services Used

Type	Percentage
Checking accounts	48
Savings accounts	23
Safe deposit box	5
Installment loan	24

TABLE 20.7   Media Chosen

Medium	Percentage
Radio	55
Billboards	10
Newspapers	35

TABLE 20.8   Why Northeast Was Chosen

Reason	Percentage
Personal recommendation	26
Special services	14
Location of the bank	48
Bank employee was known or a friend	6
Advertising	3
Other reasons	3

Nash, who tends to be impulsive, fired off a copy of his results to Fine along with a curt note stating that Northeast should immediately begin a search for a new advertising agency. Fine, who is rather bullheaded, decided that changing agencies would not solve the problem.

1. Prepare Erma Fine's reply to John Nash.
2. How could the advertising study be improved?
3. Was George Yob performing his job properly?
4. Should the media mix be changed? How?
5. Has Nash analyzed his study thoroughly?

21
Personal Selling

OBJECTIVES

■ To understand the nature and importance of selling.
■ To become aware of the opportunities offered by sales careers.
■ To describe different sales positions.
■ To understand the basic elements of the selling process.

Selling is one of the more important functions of marketing. I. K. Dealey, Jr., national sales manager for Veeco Instruments, notes that

> the order that I must get tomorrow will be responsible for our purchasing agent ordering more material; our engineering department producing new designs; our manufacturing department producing more merchandise; our personnel department hiring more people; and for me and my family and all the other Veeco employees and their families, enjoying the better life that all begins with professional salesmanship![1]

The old maxim "Nothing happens until a sale is made" is often true.

This chapter discusses the essence of the selling function from both a practical and a theoretical viewpoint. You will learn what

409

attracts people to this growing field and the variety of opportunities and positions it offers. Next, we will examine the selling process and analyze each step. After you have become familiar with the selling process, we will investigate the contributions of other behavioral sciences to understanding the sales function.

THE NATURE OF SELLING
Everyone Is a Salesperson

In a sense all of us are salespeople. It really isn't a matter of choice. When you leave school you may become a plant manager, a chemist, an engineer, or a member of any of a multitude of professions, yet you will still have to sell. To reach the top in most organizations you will have to sell your ideas and concepts to peers, superiors, and subordinates. You will be expected to "sell" the company to stockholders, customers, and other public groups. Most important, you must sell yourself and your ideas to just about everyone with whom you develop a continuing relationship and to many other people whom you will see only once or twice in your life.

Selling as a Communication Process

It is easy to understand that selling is a form of communication. (See Figure 21.1.) The source is the salesperson, who encodes the presentation on the basis of the perceived needs of the consumer. The message is usually transmitted to the potential buyer through the spoken word. Sales representatives will often reinforce the message through visual aids such as a brochure or product demonstration. The salesperson's facial expressions, gestures, voice inflections, dress, and mannerisms serve as nonverbal forms of communication.

    If the salesperson has properly ascertained the needs of the prospective buyer and has effectively communicated those needs in

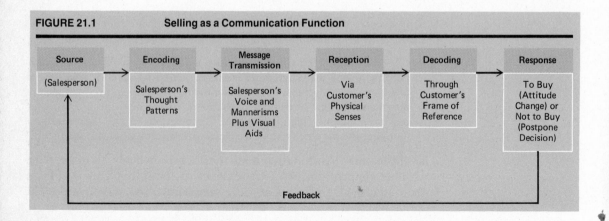

FIGURE 21.1   **Selling as a Communication Function**

Source	Encoding	Message Transmission	Reception	Decoding	Response
(Salesperson)	Salesperson's Thought Patterns	Salesperson's Voice and Mannerisms Plus Visual Aids	Via Customer's Physical Senses	Through Customer's Frame of Reference	To Buy (Attitude Change) or Not to Buy (Postpone Decision)

Feedback

the sales message, the response may be a sale. Perhaps the response will be a request for more information or an objection to some aspects of the sales message. In either case the sales representative usually receives rapid feedback because of the face-to-face nature of the situation. The message can then be altered in a further attempt to make the sale.

Unlike advertising, personal selling often involves a reversal of communication roles as the salesperson becomes a receiver and the prospect becomes the source—the feedback process. The better the sales representative understands the product or service and the needs and personality of the potential customer, the more effective the sales message will be. Naturally, this doesn't guarantee a sale. Other salespeople may make a better presentation, offer a superior product, or offer a comparable product at a lower price.

Sales Functions

Effective communication requires a lot of advance preparation. The salesperson must locate companies that need their product or service, identify the buying decision maker, make the sales presentation, process the order (if it is obtained), and follow up to make sure the product functions as promised. In addition to performing sales functions, the sales representative may be required to educate the buyer's employees on how to use the product properly; service the product or see that it is adequately serviced; collect financial information about buyers; fill out marketing intelligence reports; and perhaps engage in public-relations work as well. Of course not all sales representatives perform all or even a majority of these tasks. It depends on the nature of the industry, the company, and the sales manager. But regardless of the ancillary tasks, selling is always the fundamental job of the salesperson.

The Importance of Selling

Generally speaking, as the number of potential customers decreases, the complexity of the product increases, and as the value of the product grows, the role of personal selling becomes more important. (See Figure 21.2.) About 5½ million people are engaged in personal selling in the United States; over 3 million of them are male.[2]

This large figure reflects all sorts of sales occupations, from the sales clerks who take your orders at fast-food restaurants to engineers with MBA's who custom-design large and complex production line systems for major manufacturers. Nevertheless the sheer size of the group of people who earn a living from sales is tremendous compared, for example, with the advertising industry, which employs only a half-million workers. Chances are that if you are a marketing major you may start your professional career in sales.

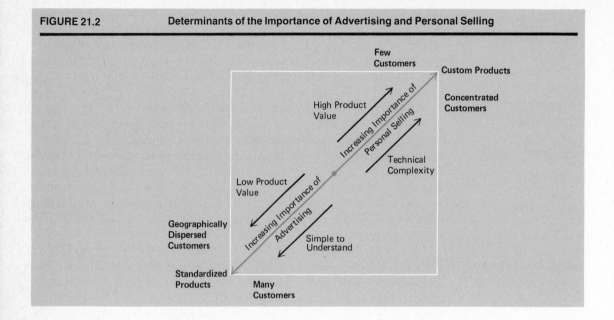

FIGURE 21.2   Determinants of the Importance of Advertising and Personal Selling

SHOULD I CHOOSE A SALES CAREER?

Students often view sales occupations in terms of the "traveling-salesperson" stereotype, with its negative personal attributes. In a free-association study some 3000 college students were asked to write down the first five words that came to mind in connection with the word *salesman*. The ten most common replies, in rank order, were *travel, money, personality, sales, fast talker, commission, appearance, products, high pressure,* and *aggressive*.[3]

High-Caliber Personnel

Sales opportunities for college graduates are a far cry from the work of a traveling salesperson. Instead, firms are seeking high-caliber individuals who can effectively and creatively communicate product or service characteristics to prospective buyers. Most of the firms that recruit college graduates for sales careers demand high-caliber individuals. Management realizes that the person they hire often represents the company to the customer.

Personal Freedom

Not only does the salesperson represent the company to the customer, but he or she interacts with the buyer in an environment of personal freedom. The college-trained salesperson may serve a territory covering several hundred square miles and be visited only once a month by his or her superior. No one is looking over the salesperson's shoulder. Route planning, callback frequency, specific product recommendations, and new-account development are often left to the discretion of the salesperson. The salesperson's decisions are tempered only by general policy guidelines.

Monetary Rewards

If time is used wisely, enticing monetary rewards tend to follow. Good salespeople frequently advance in terms of both pay and position early in their careers. In fact progressive firms are adopting "fast-track" advancement programs to accelerate the promotion of capable sales personnel.[4] Rather than waiting 10 or 15 years before being promoted, qualified individuals may become supervisors in as little as 15 months after being hired.

THE VARIETY OF SALES POSITIONS
Selling to Wholesalers and Retailers

Serving as a manufacturer's salesperson (selling to wholesalers and retailers) or as a wholesaler's salesperson (selling to retailers) may not be very hard for a college graduate. Although the purchasing motives of wholesale and retail buyers are rational rather than emotional, and some creative selling may be involved, the job often involves little more than taking orders. When a firm buys products for resale, its main concern is usually purchasing the "right" product mix, making sure it has an adequate supply, and reordering merchandise promptly when necessary. Often the retailer expects the manufacturer's salesperson to stock the merchandise on the store's shelves and set up promotional materials approved by the store. Sometimes these sales jobs are entry level training positions that can lead to more challenging and demanding sales opportunities.

Selling to Purchasing Agents

A purchasing agent is in charge of procurement for all or part of his or her organization. Purchasing agents are found in government, manufacturing, and the institutional market (e.g., hospitals and schools). They are sophisticated buyers who know their needs and the capabilities and limitations of many products that can fill those needs. Thus selling to a purchasing agent often amounts to disseminating information. That is, it involves telling the agent how the product or service can benefit the agent's firm. The purchasing agent looks for credibility (can the salesperson deliver the merchandise of the proper quality when needed?), service after the sale, and a reasonable price. The message that the salesperson must get across is one of dependability and reliability.

Often purchasing agents rely on hidden buyers such as engineers, general managers, secretaries, or other "experts" who may actually specify characteristics of the product or service that the purchasing agent buys. Sales representatives must be aware of "hidden buyers" and attempt to "read" them as well as the purchasing agent.

Selling to Committees

Perhaps the most demanding form of selling in terms of professionalism and creativity is selling to a committee. When a purchase decision is so important that it will have a substantial impact on the buyer's long-run profitability and success, it is usually made by a committee. The committee may be the board of directors, a group of top executives, or the top executives and subordinates who will be most closely involved in the use of the proposed product or service. Purchases of new plant locations, buildings, major capital equipment, long-term supply contracts, and so forth often require a committee decision.

Usually a committee sales presentation is based on extensive analysis of the potential buyer's needs. An elaborate audiovisual presentation is common. Sometimes prospects are chauffeured to existing installations of the product so that its major characteristics and advantages over competing products can be demonstrated. Question-and-answer sessions follow the formal presentation. After the buyer has heard several presentations from competing potential suppliers, each alternative is carefully weighed before the purchase decision is made.

Committee selling is often very time-consuming and demanding. The stakes are high, and sales may be spaced far apart owing to the limited size of the market. When a sale is made, however, the salesperson often receives a generous award. Kim Kelly, a Honeywell computer salesman, spent three years closing an $8-million sale.[5] His commission was $80,000.

Selling to Professionals

Another form of informational selling is selling to professionals. Individuals who sell to the medical profession are called detail men. Their job is to build good will among physicians and to explain the new products offered by pharmaceutical houses. College graduates in fields related to medicine are typically preferred by the manufacturers for this type of selling because they can discuss the medicines intelligently and establish rapport with the physician. Detail men also call on select drugstores for promotional support and to sell nonprescription items.

Selling Directly to Final Consumers

Direct selling to consumers may be done in retail stores, over the phone, or door to door. Retail selling is rarely attractive to college graduates and typically offers low pay, few advancement opportunities, and little job satisfaction. There are exceptions, such as the management training positions offered by J. C. Penney's and Sears, as well as some real-estate sales positions.

Door-to-door selling is probably the most grueling form of selling. Yet it is a very big business. For example, Avon products has 800,000 salespeople worldwide and over 50 million customers.[6] Fuller Brush, another large door-to-door retailer, has recently increased the size of its sales force and reverted to its original marketing strategy. According to a spokesman for the brush manufacturers, "We are selling high-quality merchandise at moderate prices without fancy gimmicks."[7]

Door-to-door selling is often characterized by high-pressure tactics, deceptive entrance plays, and shoddy merchandise.[8] Despite these problems, door-to-door selling offers several advantages to the consumer: the entire family can be consulted; some firms allow trial before purchase; and there is the convenience and comfort of in-home buying.[9]

Another form of direct selling is by telephone. Sears has used phone sales for two decades to remind people to use its catalogs. As the costs of personal selling and direct mail continue to rise, more firms are turning to direct phone selling. Such different organizations as *Women's Wear Daily,* the U.S. Post Office, and the Center for the Study of Democratic Institutions utilize phone selling.[10] It is the least expensive form of personal selling. A major tire company has forty people continually phoning customers who are too small or isolated to be visited by a sales representative more than once or twice a year. It has reportedly added millions of dollars to its annual sales total.[11]

WHAT IS A PROFESSIONAL SALESPERSON?

Not everyone who sells is a professional salesperson. It's hard to define the term *professional sales representative*. Being a college graduate or earning a large income does not necessarily indicate professionalism. Instead, a professional sales representative should have two dominant characteristics: complete product knowledge and creativity.

The professional salesperson knows the product line from A to Z and understands each item's capabilities and limitations. He or she also understands how to creatively apply the product or service mix to customers' needs. For example, a sales representative may devise a new way of installing the firm's conveyor equipment that would lower the cost of a prospect's intracompany product movement. As a sales representative for IBM puts it,

> I get inside the business of my key accounts. I uncover their key problems. I prescribe solutions for them, using my company's systems and even, at times, components from other suppliers. I prove beforehand that my systems will save money or make money for my accounts. Then I work with the account to install the system and make it prove out. Every success I have sells my next system for me. I may never have to "sell" again.[12]

Other factors naturally come into the definition of a "professional salesperson"—being well organized, having a pleasant personality, being able to converse intelligently about many topics, having an optimistic attitude and a strong desire to sell. The professional sells ideas and concepts and the buyer purchases satisfaction. It is an old adage that a good sales representative "sells the sizzle, not the steak."

SUPPORTING SALESPEOPLE

Professional sales representatives and even some order takers receive support from missionary salespeople and technical representatives. Both types can be vital to the sales effort, yet neither takes the sales order itself. Almost all supporting sales representatives are employed by manufacturers.

Missionary Salespeople

Missionary salespeople are common in consumer packaged-goods industries such as food and drug products. Their job is to stimulate good will within the channel of distribution and to support their company's sales efforts. A missionary sales representative may travel with a wholesaler's sales representative for a while to reinforce the promotional effort for the product. Sometimes a missionary salesperson will work with the manufacturer's new sales personnel to help them learn the territory and the accounts.

At the retail level, missionary sales representatives may set up displays, check the stock and shelf space, and explain new-product offerings to retailers. Usually they are "old hands" who know the territory and product well. In the area of industrial goods, they usually perform a communication function between the manufacturer and key accounts. Any problems that arise are relayed back to the manufacturer via the missionary representative, and new products or product applications are passed forward to the customer.

Technical Specialists

Technical specialists have backgrounds in chemistry, engineering, physics, or the like. They work out the details of custom-made products and communicate directly with the technical staff of the potential buyer. The sales representative may make an initial presentation to a purchasing committee, with the technical specialist's presence required only for the question-and-answer phase.

If interest in the seller's product develops, the specialist plays a larger role in planning the exact product specifications and installation procedures and overseeing the actual installation. After the sale has been made, the sales representative usually relies on feedback from the technical specialist pertaining to installation dates, debugging time, and similar information.

Smaller firms may not be able to afford sales representatives and technical specialists. In fact some large firms may feel that the job is best handled by one person. In this case the company may look for a person with the appropriate undergraduate degree plus an MBA. To date research has not shown conclusively that one approach is better than the other.

FIGURE 21.3   **Personal Selling and the AIDA Concept**

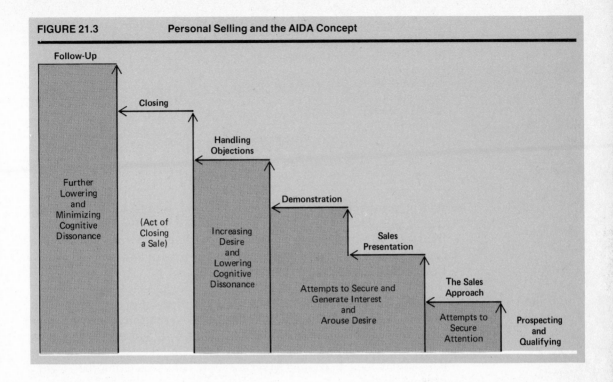

STEPS IN THE SELLING PROCESS
The Relationship of Selling to the AIDA Concept

If a person enters the field of industrial selling, he or she will generally follow the same basic selling process. The steps in selling are (1) prospecting and qualifying, (2) the sales approach, (3) the sales presentation, (4) demonstration, (5) handling objections, (6) the closing, and (7) follow-up. (See Figure 21.3.) Like other forms of promotion, selling basically follows the AIDA concept. Once a salesperson has located a prospect with the authority to buy, an attempt is made to secure attention. Interest is generated by means of effective presentation and demonstration.

When initial desire is generated (preferably during the presentation and demonstration), proper handling of objections should increase desire and lower cognitive dissonance. The salesperson seeks action in the closing by attempting to obtain an agreement to purchase. Follow-up, the final step in selling, not only lowers cognitive dissonance but may also open up new opportunities to discuss further sales.

Prospecting

Before the communication process between the potential buyer and the seller begins, groundwork must be done. This is called prospecting. Not everyone, of course, is a prospect for a firm's good or service. Nor are all prospects equally likely to purchase. Identifica-

TABLE 21.1	Salespeople's Opinions on the Most Effective Way of Acquiring New Accounts	
	Recommendations from customers	38%
	Recommendations from business associates	22
	Observation of new business construction	12
	Trade shows	11
	Advertising leads	10
	Conventions	4
	Listing in local, state, and national directories	3

Source: "Two Views of Those Vital 30 Seconds," *Sales and Marketing Management,* 109 (October 30, 1972): 29. Reprinted by permission. Copyright 1972.

tion of prospects requires several different sources of information. (See Table 21.1.) Other sales representatives selling noncompeting lines are often good sources of potential buyers. Other sources are company records of past purchases, newspapers and trade publications, referrals, and cold canvassing.

The Sales Approach

Once a prospective buyer has been located, the communication process begins. If prospecting has not uncovered the name or names of the decision makers, they must be identified. Sometimes this is as simple as asking the switchboard operator. On other occasions a salesperson may have to contact several people before reaching the "right" prospect.

It is critical that the decision maker be properly identified. Otherwise significant time and effort may be wasted. For example, a sales representative for a materials-handling system spent three months with the director of western warehouse operations of a large New York–based manufacturing company. This person continually assured the sales representative that he made all the decisions for his area. Unfortunately, the competition got the business for the four regional warehouses because it won over the vice president of operations in New York, who was in charge of budget approval for all new warehouse systems.[13]

Some companies use screening committees or individuals who filter out salespeople offering products that are not compatible with the firm's needs. This is done in order to save the time of the decision maker. As mentioned earlier, the salesperson may find a decision maker with the authority to buy who relies almost exclusively on other individuals to select which product is bought. For example, a secretary may recommend a brand of typewriter or a foreman may offer advice on a new stamping machine. Perhaps the most successful approach letter of all time is illustrated by the following story:

> When the Boeing Co. caught wind that China might be interested in joining the jet set, it sent clandestine emissaries to neutral consulates

and supposedly "well-placed private sources." All met with a great wall of silence. As a last resort, Byron H. Miller, Boeing's international sales director, sent an air mail letter in English to the Chinese government's Machinery Import & Export Corp. in Peking. Synopsis: Boeing makes jet aircraft and would the People's Republic of China be interested in its wares? In three weeks, Miller got a reply: Come to Peking and we'll talk about it.

As proof that opening the sale isn't tantamount to a red carpet, Miller and two colleagues spent three of the next five months in the Chinese capital in what he described as "the most arduous sales negotiations I've ever been involved in." He lost 10 pounds, but flew home with a contract for 10 Boeing 707's and the first cash-only deal ($125 million, to be paid off by 1974) ever involved with a foreign government. In Seattle, the news bolstered corporate morale, still sagging from cancellation of the SST.[14]

The Sales Presentation and Demonstration

After the sales representative has reached the proper person, the sales presentation takes place. If the salesperson understands the key variables that will determine the sale, such as dependable delivery, cost, compatibility with other components or machines, and so forth, he or she is much more likely to succeed. The following is a list of the key elements in a good sales presentation. As you will note, the presentation generally flows from action to analysis to implementation.

- *Management Summary* — ties the presentation to the individuals involved in the sale, reflects mutual agreement already reached with the top decision makers, and makes note of the customer's criteria for selection.
- *Scope* — states the objectives and nature of the problems being solved or challenges being addressed.
- *Advantages* — spells out the advantages in such a way that the presenting company's products or services are made exclusive (i.e., so that they cannot be duplicated by competition).
- *Recommended Solutions* — tailors the specific products, services and/or programs to the prospect's requirement, environment and management objectives.
- *Financial Analysis and Cost Justification (reached through mutual agreement)* — shows the economic justification to favor the seller company's method over the prospect's current means of performing the function and over possible proposals from competition.
- *Implementation Schedule* — describes the seller's and the prospect's responsibilities, the people to be involved and dates of completion for the main tasks.
- *Contact* — spells out the terms and conditions of the sale, which have already been discussed with the prospect.[15]

Sales presentations are augmented with visual aids and audiovisual equipment. Movies, brochures, manuals, maps, samples, and slides are commonly used sales aids. Fairchild and Kodak manufacture a simple, briefcase-sized sound projector and screen for "at the desk" audiovisual presentations. Actual demonstrations are excellent supplements to presentations. When a prospect can participate in the presentation by manipulating a product, he or she becomes better acquainted with the product's features and remembers them longer.

Handling Objections

Rarely does a prospect say, "I'll buy it," right after a presentation. Often there are objections or perhaps questions about the presentation and product. The potential buyer may complain that the price is too high, the delivery date is too far away, and the like.

The best way to prepare for objections is to anticipate them and have a reply in mind. A good sales representative handles objections in a relaxed manner and considers them a legitimate part of the purchase decision. They should be viewed as requests for information, not as setting the stage for a confrontation. If the salesperson takes the latter attitude, he or she may lose a sale.

Closing the Sale

If the prospect's objections are handled properly, the salesperson can attempt to close the sale. It might be pointed out that whenever the customer makes a commitment to buy, the close and order processing should begin. But if this doesn't occur, a number of techniques can be used in an attempt to close the sale.[16] One popular approach is the "assumption close." The salesperson assumes that the prospect is going to buy and says something like, "Which do you want delivered, product A or product B?" or "When do you want the merchandise shipped?"

A second closing technique is to summarize the benefits of the product and ask for the sale. Sometimes a salesperson will withhold a special concession until the end of the selling process and use it in closing the sale. Examples are price cuts, free installation, free service, and trial orders.

In today's economy salespeople can use the "sense" or "urgency" close in many industries. They may say, "Prices will be going up in six weeks" or "We don't anticipate being able to deliver new models for six months owing to component shortages, but we have three of this year's models left."

Follow-Up

A salesperson's responsibilities do not end with making the sale and placing the order. One of the most important aspects of the sales job is follow-up. The salesperson must make sure delivery schedules are met, that the product or service performs as promised, and that the buyer's employees are properly trained in the use of the product.

Most businesses depend on repeat sales, and repeat sales depend on thorough follow-up. When customers feel that they have been abandoned, cognitive dissonance arises and repeat sales decline. One survey revealed that three out of four sales managers feel that customer service is an increasingly important determinant of long-run sales performance.[17]

**CONTRIBUTIONS
OF THE
BEHAVIORAL
SCIENCES TO THE
SELLING PROCESS**
Customer
Interaction

The selling process is not only a communication interaction but a social situation as well.

The probability of successfully closing a sale is partially dependent on social power. Social power is the ability of the salesperson to evoke the behavior desired by the seller. Usually the goal is to obtain an agreement to buy from the prospect. Two important aspects of social power are expert power and referent power.

A sales representative's expert power is derived from knowledge, information, and skills related to the product or service. Referent power is based on the perceived attraction between the salesperson and prospective purchasers. Similar social backgrounds, convergent personalities, comparable sports interests, and pleasing physical appearance can enhance referent power. For example, in Phoenix, Arizona, the mode of dress in most business establishments is casual (e.g., no tie). This is probably due to the extreme heat and the influence of western styles of dress. An eastern salesperson who flies into Phoenix and begins calling on customers in a suit complete with tie will probably lose referent power. A tie is the symbol of an outsider— someone who doesn't understand or relate to the environment of the Southwest. There is less shared identity.

The most extensive research on the impact of social power on the selling process has been conducted by Paul Busch and David Wilson.[18] Their major findings are as follows:

1. The stronger the expert and referent power bases, the more trustworthy the sales representative is perceived to be by the customer.
2. Expert power is more important than referent power in building trust.
3. Sales representatives with a large amount of referent power have a wider range of influence than those with lower amounts of referent power. In other words, greater referent power enables the salesperson to exert influence in a variety of situations.

These findings have many implications. The importance of product knowledge and, therefore, training of salespeople is obvious. If a salesperson doesn't understand the product or service and its applications, he or she has little expert power. Since referent power is particularly important when a sales representative must sell a wide variety of goods and services in a variety of markets, sales recruitment and screening techniques should be highly refined. Progressive firms recognize the importance of social power in the selling process and have designed recruitment and training programs based on behavioral findings.[19]

SUMMARY

We are all salespeople to some extent. We all have to sell ourselves as individuals. Selling is a form of communication, a personalized form with direct feedback.

As the number of potential customers decreases, the complexity of the product increases, and the value of the product grows, the role of personal selling tends to increase. There are about 5½ million people engaged in personal selling in the United States. A sales career offers personal freedom, monetary rewards, and opportunities to associate with middle and top managers.

The sales positions open to college graduates include some retail and wholesale positions and some that involve selling to purchasing agents, committee sales, sales to professionals, and, on a limited basis, selling directly to the final consumer.

Sales support positions are also available. Missionary salespeople stimulate good will within the channel of distribution. Technical specialists have backgrounds in technical fields. They work out the details of custom-made product orders and communicate directly with the customer's technical staff.

The steps in the selling process are (1) prospecting and qualifying, (2) the sales approach, (3) the sales presentation, (4) demonstration, (5) handling objections, (6) the closing, and (7) follow-up. This process is not cut and dried, however. In fact any time a sale can be closed at an earlier point in the process it should be closed as quickly as possible.

The selling process is a social situation as well as a personal interaction. Sales success is partially dependent on social power. Social power is the ability of the salesperson to evoke the desired action. It depends on expert and referent powers. Referent powers are based on perceived attraction between a salesperson and the prospective purchaser. Expert power is derived from knowledge, information, and skills related to the product or service.

KEY TERMS

Purchasing agent	Prospecting
Hidden buyers	Screening committees
Detail men	Social power
Missionary salespeople	Expert power
Technical specialists	Referent power

QUESTIONS FOR DISCUSSION

1. Describe the various functions that a salesperson may be required to perform.
2. Define the term *professional salesperson.* Contrast this role with those of supporting sales personnel.

3. Describe in detail the steps involved in the selling process. Do sales-people go through all of these steps when selling a product to a customer? Why or why not?

4. Why is follow-up such an important aspect of the selling process?

5. Differentiate between the terms *expert power* and *referent power*. How do they relate to the selling process?

6. List the different types of sales positions available. Discuss the mechanics of committee selling as opposed to direct selling.

7. Define the following terms:
   a. hidden buyer
   b. detail man
   c. missionary salesperson
   d. screening committee

8. Describe the factors that would lead a person to choose a career in sales.

9. Why is it that college students often have a negative view of sales occupations? Do you think this view is justified?

10. Explain the statement "Nothing happens until a sale is made" with special emphasis on the importance of selling in economic terms.

NOTES

1. Leonard F. Saxton, "What the Hell Am I Doing in This Business, Anyway?" *Sales and Marketing Management,* 114 (January 20, 1975): 19. Reprinted by permission. Copyright 1975.

2. U.S. Department of Commerce, *Statistical Abstract of the United States, 1975* (Washington, D.C.: Government Printing Office, 1975), p. 359.

3. Donald L. Thompson, "Stereotype of the Salesman," *Harvard Business Review,* January–February 1972, pp. 20–30.

4. Andrall E. Pearson, "Sales Power Through Planned Careers," *Harvard Business Review,* January–February 1966, pp. 105–116; see also Marvin A. Jolson, "The Salesman's Career Cycle," *Journal of Marketing,* 38 (July 1974): 39–46.

5. "To Computer Salesmen, the 'Big-Ticker' Deal Is the One to Look For," *Wall Street Journal,* January 22, 1974.

6. "Door-to-Door Selling Is Still the Big Thing for Some Companies," *Wall Street Journal,* June 3, 1976.

7. Ibid.

8. For consumer and direct-salesman impressions of door-to-door selling, see Marvin A. Jolson, "Direct Selling: Consumer vs. Salesman," *Business Horizons,* 15 (October 1972): 87–95.

9. Ibid.

10. "Selling by Phone Is Ringing the Bell," *Business Week,* November 11, 1972, pp. 162–164.

11. Ibid.

12. Mack Hanan, "Join the Systems Sell and You Can't Be Beat," *Sales and Marketing Management,* 109 (August 21, 1972): 44. Reprinted by permission. Copyright 1972.

13. Example taken from Benson P. Shapiro and Ronald S. Posner, "Making the Major Sale," *Harvard Business Review,* March–April 1976, pp. 68–78.

14. "The $125 Million Sales Letter," *Sales and Marketing Management,* 109 (October 30, 1972): 51–52. Reprinted by permission. Copyright 1972.

15. Benson P. Shapiro and Ronald S. Posner, "Making the Major Sale," *Har-*

vard Business Review, March-April 1976, p. 77. Copyright © 1976 by the President and Fellows of Harvard College; all rights reserved.

16. For a number of sales-closing techniques see C. A. Kirkpatrick and F. A. Russ, *Salesmanship,* 6th ed. (Cincinnati: Southwestern, 1976), pp. 381–389.

17. David S. Hopkins and Earl L. Bailey, *Customer Service — A Progress Report* (New York: Conference Board, 1970), p. 1.

18. Paul Busch and David T. Wilson, "An Experimental Analysis of a Salesman's Expert and Referent Bases of Social Power in the Buyer–Seller Dyad," *Journal of Marketing Research,* 13 (February 1976): 3–11. For other research efforts see Harold J. Leavitt, "Selling and the Social Scientist," *Journal of Business,* 27 (April 1954): 41–43; R. B. Evans, "Selling as a Dyadic Relationship — A New Approach," *American Behavior Scientist,* 6 (May 1963): 76–79; and Arch Woodside and J. William Davenport, Jr., "The Effect of Salesman Similarity and Expertise on Consumer Purchasing Behavior," *Journal of Marketing Research,* 11 (May 1974): 198–202.

19. Joseph W. Thompson and William W. Evans, "Behavioral Approach to Industrial Selling," *Harvard Business Review,* March–April 1969, pp. 137–151.

CASE 21
The First Sales Job

Steve Canon will receive his MBA degree at the end of this semester. His area of concentration is marketing. Three years ago he completed his BS in biology; he has been working as a lab technician for a large medical research laboratory while continuing his education. Last week Canon's department manager called him in to discuss his future plans. He informed him that the job of group manager would be open in four months. The manager wanted to know whether Canon would accept the promotion.

During the same week a local pharmaceutical manufacturer offered Canon a job as a salesman. The company is a nationally recognized firm listed on the New York Stock Exchange. It would be classified as a medium-sized company within the industry. Canon would be hired as a detail salesman.

Canon feels that he knows the duties and opportunities involved in the job of group manager but does not believe he knows enough to properly evaluate the sales opportunity. He has decided to make up a list of questions about the sales job.

1. Make a list of the questions that you would ask in such a situation.
2. What sources would you use to answer those questions?

22

Sales Management

OBJECTIVES

■ To learn about various techniques used in recruiting and training salespeople.
■ To understand some of the factors that affect the motivation of a sales force.
■ To understand the different ways of organizing the sales force.
■ To become aware of various methods used to evaluate the performance of the sales force.
■ To gain insight into the changing role of the salesperson.

Now that you have gained an appreciation of the nature of personal selling, we can explore the role of the sales manager. This chapter begins by defining the objectives of sales management. Sales recruiting and training are then discussed. Next, sales motivation techniques and organization structures are presented. An examination of sales evaluation and control procedures follows, and the chapter concludes with a discussion of the changing role of the sales manager.

THE OBJECTIVES OF SALES MANAGEMENT

The policies established by the sales manager must be directed toward the accomplishment of sales force goals. The following list presents the major areas in which such goals must be determined.

426

A. Sales targets
  1. Level of volume
  2. Product mix
  3. Customer mix
  4. New accounts

B. Service goals
  1. Displays installed
  2. Complaints handled
  3. Special orders
  4. New-product information

C. Training goals
  1. New-product training
  2. Refresher training
  3. Increase the effectiveness of the training program

D. Motivation
  1. Increase productivity
  2. Revise incentive mix and emphasis

E. Evaluation control
  1. Establish new evaluation tools
  2. Provide faster feedback

F. Recruiting
  1. More accurate job descriptions
  2. Revise screening techniques
  3. Establish new personnel sources

RECRUITING AND SCREENING SALESPEOPLE

Sales force recruitment should be based on an accurate, detailed description of the sales task as defined by the company. The job description, in turn, is developed in light of the sales force objectives. An accurate job description will tell the sales manager whether he or she should attempt to hire an order taker or an aggressive professional salesman. Perhaps the job description will indicate a need for a technical specialist, a missionary salesperson, or a detail person.

There Is No Ideal Test

No single group of demographic or personality characteristics is typical of a successful salesperson. It depends on the unique needs of the firm. The vice president of marketing for Remington Rand looks for "an above average student but not an egg-head, a college graduate who worked part-time in school, a person with at least one child."[1] Remington, of course, makes many exceptions to this general profile.

The Interview

A variety of tools are used to screen sales candidates. The interview is by far the most helpful tool for selecting new salespeople.[2] (See Table 22.1.) It is also the most costly screening tool.[3] Rapiston, a manufacturer of materials-handling equipment, attempts to interview applicants in a communication situation similar to the company's selling situation (i.e., a committee or group); the interview is conducted as a group meeting.[4] Rapiston believes that shy people are auto-

TABLE 22.1   Rating of Selection Tools on the Basis of Helpfulness

	Percent of Respondents Checking				
Selection Tool	Very Helpful	Quite Helpful	Somewhat Helpful	Slightly Helpful	Not Used or Other Answer
Interviews	98%	2%	0%	0%	0%
Application blanks	54	33	10	3	0
Physical exams	35	20	20	14	11
References	19	24	26	28	3
Intelligence tests	16	33	30	8	13
Aptitude tests	13	31	27	10	19
Personality tests	12	13	34	12	29

Source: Thomas R. Wotruba, "An Analysis of the Salesman Selection Process," *Southern Journal of Business*, 5 (January 1970): 45. By permission.

matically eliminated—some individuals drop out as soon as they see that it is a group interview.

Sources of Sales Candidates

Sales recruits can be solicited from a number of sources: colleges, other salespeople, trade journal and newspaper ads, employment agencies, and even competitors. Sometimes companies find that their nonselling employees are attracted to sales. The advantages that we have already discussed are offered as reasons for entering the sales field. Company benefits such as a car, incentive pay, and similar features complete the recruitment pitch.

THE NATURE OF SALES TRAINING
Topics Covered

After the sales recruit has been hired and given a brief orientation, sales training begins. A new salesperson generally receives instruction in five major areas: company policies and practices, selling technique, product knowledge, industry and customer characteristics, and nonselling duties such as account servicing and filling out market information reports.

Training Objectives

A good training program will build job confidence, improve morale, increase sales, and build better customer relations. Classroom instruction may last several days for company policies and several weeks to a month for actual sales techniques. Trainees are taught everything from how to prospect through servicing the account after the sale. Generally speaking, industrial-goods firms offer more extensive training programs than consumer goods organizations. Median total training times are shown in Table 22.2.

| TABLE 22.2 | Length of Training Period for New Salespeople | | | | | |
</br>

	Type of Company					
	Industrial Products		Consumer Products		Services[a]	
Time Period	1974	1973	1974	1973	1974	1973
0 to 6 weeks	17%	20%	55%	34%	44%	51%
Over 6 weeks to 3 months	28	24	20	38	19	9
Over 3 months to 6 months	—	13	15	14	19	15
Over 6 months to 12 months	33	33	10	14	3	21
Over 12 months	22	10	—	—	15	4
Total	100%	100%	100%	100%	100%	100%
Median Training Period (wks.)	28	24	4	10	12	6

Source: "Double-Digit Hikes in 1974 Sales Training Costs," *Sales and Marketing Management*, January 6, 1975, p. 54. Reprinted by permission. Copyright 1975.
[a] Includes insurance, financial, utilities, transportation, retail stores, etc.

Trends in Training

Progressive organizations emphasize human interaction in the sales process. For example, transactional analysis (TA) is often used to improve sales effectiveness.[5] If you speak to a friend, it is referred to as a transactional stimulus. Your friend's response is a transactional response. If the response is complimentary (parallel lines in Figure 22.1), communication continues. If an uncomplimentary transaction occurs, communication stops, is impeded, or is unproductive. Salespeople can act out the customer–salesperson relationship to sharpen their transactional abilities. Closed-circuit television is often used to teach sales recruits how to use TA in lifelike situations.

Building Product Knowledge

Lectures, demonstrations, films, and other visual aids are used in the next phase of training—building product knowledge. Depending on the firm and the nature of its product line, the salesperson may learn the characteristics and applications of the simpler items first and then be periodically brought in from the field for additional product training.

Obtaining Sales Experience

The fourth phase of training often incorporates lectures and on-site visits by the trainee with other salespeople. The final step, nonselling activities, is handled either as the last step before field training or as an adjunct to the selling process. After classroom education has ended, on-the-job training continues for many months. A sales representative may start by working with another sales representative, a missionary salesperson, or a district sales manager. As salespeople gain experience and confidence, they are gradually left on their own. Other companies start sales representatives alone with simple, low-volume accounts and then slowly build up their accounts and territories.

FIGURE 22.1   **Transactional Analysis in a Sales Environment**

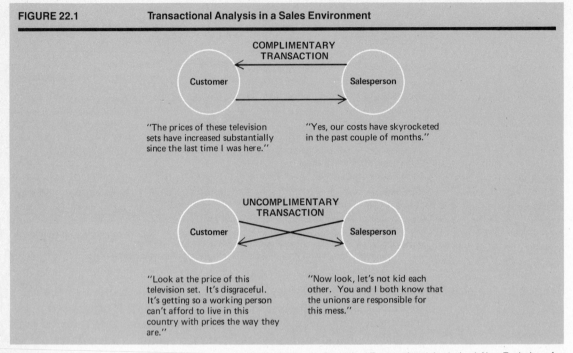

Source: Adapted from William L. Shanklin, "Transactional Analysis: A New Technique for Sales Training," in *Proceedings Southern Marketing Association 1974*, pp. 232–235.

The Costs of Sales Training

Sales training is expensive. Companies recognize, however, that a properly trained and motivated sales force will pay dividends for years to come. Training costs vary significantly from one type of company to another. The training programs of industrial firms selling complicated equipment and systems are not only the longest but also the most elaborate and expensive.[6] Consumer products sales training is more fundamental and is relatively short and inexpensive.[7]

MOTIVATING THE SALES FORCE

Training equips the salesperson with the necessary tools for selling. Once an individual has acquired sales skills, he or she must be motivated to properly use them. Research has shown that pay, promotion, working conditions, security, and intrinsic aspects of the job are of primary concern to the average employee.[8] Frederick Herzberg has determined that some job characteristics (achievement, recognition, advancement, growth, and responsibility) lead to job satisfaction. Other factors (salary, working conditions, company policy, and job security) are job maintenance factors. When maintenance factors are inadequate, job dissatisfaction will result.

Expectancy Theory   Victory Varoom, a management theorist, suggests that motivational force (a salesperson's effort) depends on the expectation that one's behavior will produce certain outcomes and on the attractiveness of those outcomes. For example, a sales representative may expect that selling more than his or her quota will produce a promotion or a salary increase. The degree of motivation will depend on how important a promotion or salary increase is to the sales representative.

Figure 22.2 depicts expectancy theory as it applies to the sales force. A salesperson may study the job description and determine its behavioral demands (loyalty, positive work attitude, and so forth) and subjectively evaluate his or her chances of successfully accomplishing the tasks (expectancy). Next, he or she must subjectively evaluate the probability of being promoted or rewarded. If a tangible reward is received (a maintenance factor), it may enhance intrinsic motivators such as desire for self-actualization.

In summary, the strength of one's motivation to perform effectively represents a belief that one's efforts can be converted into performance and the net attractiveness of the rewards that are believed to come from good performance.

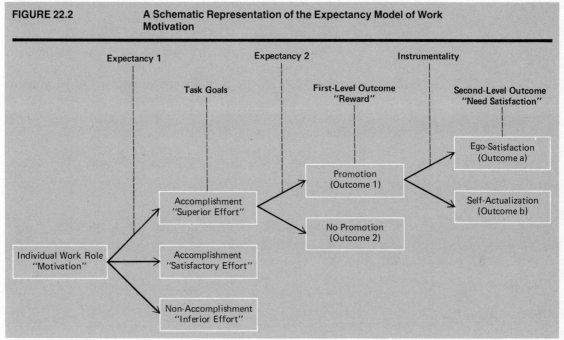

FIGURE 22.2   **A Schematic Representation of the Expectancy Model of Work Motivation**

Source: David A. Gray, Harvey Kaholas, and Wayne E. Leininger, "An Integration of Managerial Motivation and Micro-Manpower Modeling," *Journal of Business Research,* 2 (July 1974): 282. By permission.

**Nonfinancial
Motivation**

Research has shown that salespeople's performance is dependent on expectancy perceptions.[9] Other studies have shown that the role of the sales manager is very important in developing a salesperson's expectations. Also, the sales manager and company policy are the two most significant factors that determine sales job satisfaction.[10] Income is important, but it ranks only third as determinant of satisfaction.

Robert Sweitzer and Dev Pathak have demonstrated that salespeople's performance is based on perceived and expected fulfillment.[11] They found that self-actualization was the most significant factor in the satisfaction of high performers. Thus salespeople who believe that they are realizing their own potential and doing something intrinsically worthwhile are not only current high performers but are more likely to perform well in the future.

One technique for building intrinsic satisfaction is to program management functions, such as planning and quota development, into the activities of the sales force. Other techniques include increasing the amount of interaction between the sales force and the sales manager, increasing the status and rank of the sales job, and providing public acknowledgments (e.g., sales awards) of the value management places on the individual.[12]

**Financial
Incentives**

The Role of Money.   The amount that a sales representative is paid is an important factor in job turnover (i.e., money is a maintenance factor). The method of payment may be a motivator.[13] Behavior modification theory can best explain why the role of money is unclear. Simply stated, behavior modification theory involves systematic reinforcement of desirable behavior and nonreinforcement or punishment of unwanted behavior.[14] If the salesperson perceives only an overall "flow of pay" in return for a "flow of work" in a specified period, neither money nor method of compensation will act as a motivator.[15] The stimulus (pay) is too far removed from the response (work) to appreciably affect the salesperson's behavior. The money fails to reinforce the particular responses for which it was intended.

The Commission System.   Although a commission system is consistent with basic behavior modification theory, the commission must be received within a reasonably short period after the sale in order to be a motivator. A typical commission plan provides salespeople with a specified percentage of their sales revenue. If it is a straight commission plan, the salesperson receives no revenue until a sale is made. Salespeople must also pay their expenses from the commission.

A book publisher, Holt, Rinehart and Winston, has successfully applied the straight commission plan to achieve behavior modification.[16] Before the commission system was introduced, salaries and commission were equal to 8.3 percent of sales. The new commission plan called for 8 percent on a salesperson's total sales, but the sales-people must pay their own expenses. Expense accountability proved to be a special problem for some salespeople because they were used to giving dozens of free books to professors without knowing whether they would lead to sales. The new plan resulted in a 30 percent de-cline in sample book costs during the first year.

Sales commission systems require good planning. Some firms that switch from a salary plan to a commission system experience no increase in company profits.[17] Although the new system may seem to motivate some of the sales force, the remainder may tend to slack off after they reach a perceived acceptable level of income. If the sales-person ceases to be motivated, he or she may not make follow-up calls on good customers.

Salary and Control.   The above illustrates an important point: Com-mission systems increase the difficulty of controlling the sales force. In effect, the salespeople may view themselves as their own bosses.

Filling out information reports, servicing accounts, calling on smaller customers, and performing any other nonselling task becomes very unpalatable to the commission salesperson. In contrast, a straight salary plan offers maximum control but little incentive to produce. Therefore most firms have opted for a combination plan involving a salary plus a commission or bonus. (See Table 22.3.)

TABLE 22.3	Various Sales Compensation and Incentive Plans, 1975				
	Percent of Companies Using the Plan				
	All Industries		**Consumer Products**	**Industrial Products**	**Other Commerce/ Industry**
Method	**1975**	**1974**			
Straight salary	25.5%	23.4%	14.1%	25.3%	52.4%
Straight commission	0.9	1.4	2.1	0.7	—
Draw against commission	5.3	4.6	9.9	3.9	4.8
Salary plus commission	25.6	23.6	23.3	27.7	15.8
Salary plus individual bonus	28.4	25.3	34.5	28.5	14.3
Salary plus group bonus	3.8	6.7	6.3	3.3	1.6
Salary plus commission plus individual or group bonus	7.2	6.9	4.9	7.8	7.9
More than one method of payment	3.3	8.1	4.9	2.8	3.2
Total	100.0%	100.0%	100.0%	100.0%	100.0%

Source: "1976 Survey of Selling Costs." Reprinted with permission of American Manage-ment Associations from 1976 *Executive Compensation Sales Personnel Report.*

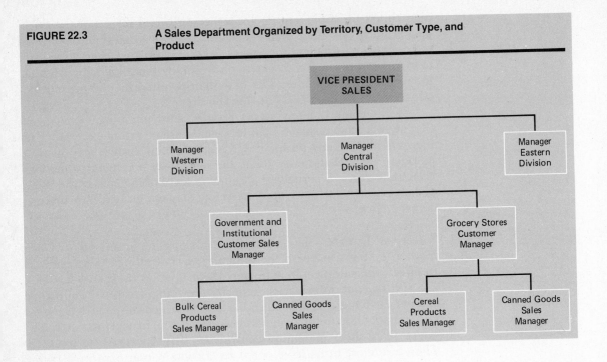

FIGURE 22.3   A Sales Department Organized by Territory, Customer Type, and Product

ORGANIZING THE SALES EFFORT
Organization Structure

Since personal selling is so costly, a sales department cannot afford to be poorly organized. The sales department is generally organized along customer, product, or territorial lines or some combination of the three. Figure 22.3 shows a combination organization.

A firm may organize on a customer basis when groups of purchasers have distinctly different needs and buying habits. Sometimes a customer organization form is used when several key accounts represent a major percentage of a company's sales revenue.

A product organization is used when the company has a large product line with distinctly different end uses or buyers. Territorial divisions are established when the span of managerial control becomes too large to be responsive to customer or employee needs.

Territorial organization forces the salesperson to become knowledgeable in the firm's entire product mix. Salespeople must also familiarize themselves with the multitude of needs of all types of potential buyers. Conversely, a product sales force allows for concentration of product knowledge. Customer-oriented sales organizations enable the salesperson to devote close attention to the unique needs of groups of customers. The largest drawback of a product sales organization is having two or more salespeople calling on the same account. Not only will this increase sales expense, but it may also create confusion in the mind of the customer ("Was it John Smith or Mary Doe who told me about that new product?").

Size of Sales Force   Another important aspect of sales organization is sales force size.[18] A commonly used approach is the workload technique. The formula for using the workload procedure is

$$\text{Number of salespeople} = \frac{\left[\begin{array}{cc}\text{number of} & \text{number of}\\ \text{existing} & + \text{potential}\\ \text{customers} & \text{customers}\end{array}\right] \times \begin{array}{c}\text{ideal}\\ \text{frequency}\\ \text{of calls}\end{array} \times \begin{array}{c}\text{length}\\ \text{of calls}\end{array}}{\text{selling time available from one salesperson}}$$

Assume, for example, that a firm has 3,000 customers and marketing research has estimated that there are 1,000 potential customers. Sales analysis has revealed that sales calls average 1.5 hours and that each customer should be seen 7 times a year. Further examination of records has revealed that each salesperson has 2,000 hours of selling time available per year. Thus

$$\text{Number of salespeople} = \frac{[3,000 + 1,000] \times 7 \times 1.5}{2,000} = \frac{42,000}{2,000} = 21$$

If the company now has 18 people in its sales force, 3 new people should be hired.

The major advantage of the workload approach is its simplicity. Successful application of the technique depends on the sales manager's ability to estimate the ideal frequency of calls and the number of potential customers. Also, the workload approach fails to consider either the cost of increasing the work force or the costs and profits associated with each sales call.

A second method of ascertaining the size of the sales force is marginal analysis. In theory, salespeople are added until the profits generated by the last individual hired equal the costs associated with hiring that person. Companies with good records know the cost of training a salesperson. This cost, plus actual field expenses and the salary of a new person, can be compared with the revenue generated by sales activities. Two drawbacks of marginal analysis are (1) the assumption that a new salesperson will not increase in efficiency as he or she becomes more experienced and (2) the fact that the territorial assignment of the last person hired may have a significant effect on the revenue generated by that person.

Developing Sales Territories   Sales territories can also be designated on the basis of marginal analysis. This is done by creating territories so that the marginal profit to sales effort in each territory is equal. If this procedure is followed, all territories will have equal potential.[19]

In contrast, the workload approach can be used by first estimating the ideal frequency of calls and then determining the average length of the sales call. Next, average available sales hours per salesperson are determined. The last step is to locate customers geographically until that amount of time has been used up for one person.

Referring back to our previous example, it was estimated that each account should be called upon seven times a year and that each call lasted approximately 1.5 hours. Every salesperson has 2,000 hours of selling time available per year. Every customer or potential customer will require 10.5 sales hours per year (7×1.5). Therefore each salesperson can handle approximately 190 present and potential customers ($10.5 \div 2,000$).

While the workload technique balances sales calls among territories, it doesn't necessarily equate sales potential between territories. One study has shown that territorial potential is a more important determinant of territorial sales than a sales representative's workload. Assuming that this finding may be generalized, it implies that marginal analysis rather than the workload technique should be used in designating sales territories.

Devising Sales Quotas

After a sales representative's territory has been delineated, most companies establish a sales quota. It has been estimated that about 75 percent of all sales managers set quotas for their sales force.[20] The quota is usually based on sales volume alone, but approximately 20 percent of the sales managers also use some measure of profitability.[21]

The foundation of a quota is the sales forecast. Most firms accept input from the sales force before setting quotas.[22] Participation by the sales staff increases the acceptability of the quota to the salesperson and provides the satisfaction of interacting with management. Two other important considerations in setting quotas are the physical nature of the territory and the experience of the sales representative. Obviously, a territory of two square blocks in the heart of Chicago will be easier to cover than one that encompasses all of New Mexico and Nevada. Yet both territories may have the same potential. An old hand can usually cover a territory more efficiently and in less time than a new salesperson. A sales manager may want to ease the pressure on a new sales representative by setting a lower-than-normal quota for that person.

Quotas can be motivators. If a quota is easy to obtain, motivation tends to decline.[23] In fact it may decline so much that an easier quota is less likely to be attained than a more difficult one. Sales managers should set product quotas at challenging levels and attach a great deal of significance to the quota. If the sales force doesn't perceive quota attainment as being particularly important, motivation will be lacking.

EVALUATION AND CONTROL OF THE SALES FORCE
Quota Attainment

The final major tasks of the sales manager are evaluating and controlling the sales force. Quota attainment, or the lack of it, is an important tool for evaluation and control. The fact that a salesperson is below quota doesn't necessarily mean that he or she isn't doing a good job. Often uncontrollable factors such as the closing of a plant, a major sales effort by the competition on key accounts, and the like can affect sales performance. On the other hand, greatly exceeding a quota doesn't always indicate superior effort. Perhaps a new client moved into a territory and gave the salesperson a large windfall sale.

Quota attainment, or the lack of it, is the tip of the iceberg. Large deviations on either side of the quota should be thoroughly investigated by the sales manager. A comprehensive list of factors that determine sales performance is presented in Figure 22.4. Usually, the most important single factor is the number of accounts assigned to the salesperson.[24]

FIGURE 22.4   Factors Accounting for Sales Territory Performance

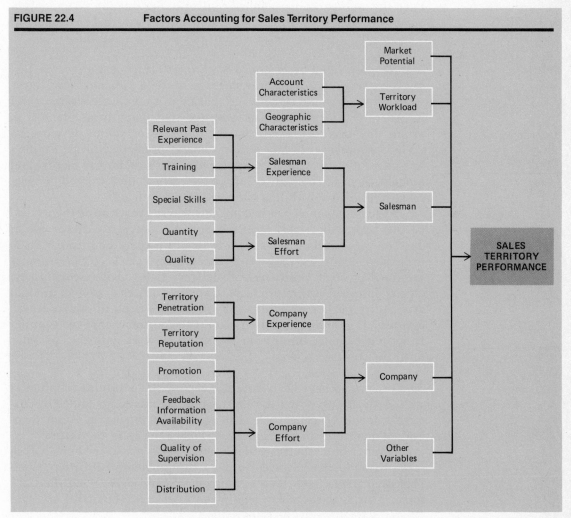

Source: David W. Cravens, Robert B. Woodruff, and Joe C. Stamper, "An Analytical Approach for Evaluating Sales Territory Performance," *Journal of Marketing,* 36 (January 1972): 32. By permission of the American Marketing Association.

**Call Record
Reports**

The quota usually serves as a tool for periodic evaluation and control. The call record report, by contrast, is a daily control device. Although call record reports vary from one firm to another, they generally contain information on the number of sales calls and the quality of those calls. Quality is measured by such yardsticks as calls per order, sales or profits per call, or the percentage of calls that achieve specific objectives. The latter may include sales of products that the firm is emphasizing. Improvement in call quality can increase total volume, change the product mix, or decrease sales costs.[25]

**SELLING IN A
CHANGING
ECONOMY**

Even the most carefully planned control and evaluation systems often must be revised because of major changes in the external environment. Two recent causes of such revisions are shortages and inflation.

Shortages

A study conducted by *Sales and Marketing Management* magazine during the energy and materials shortage of 1974 indicated that fewer sales meetings would be held and that there would be less sales travel in general.[26] The survey also indicated that many firms planned to prune slow-moving items from their lines. Companies developed a variety of measures to cope with the energy problem. Georgia-Pacific's fine-paper division took its salespeople off the road for two months and brought them to company headquarters, where they worked on long-range allotment scheduling and new-product ideas.[27]

Other companies are seeking new ways of motivating their salespeople during shortages. Diamond Shamrock involves salespeople in deciding what actions the company should take in the future.[28] Some firms have counseled their sales representatives to keep the customer informed of stock positions and delivery dates, avoid seeking new clients, offer substitute products, take early orders to protect product availability for key accounts, and use the "we're all in this together" approach.[29] The latter position assures the customer that the supplier is not out to gouge him or her but wants to work with the customer until the shortage is over.

Inflation

Sales managers have been forced to cope with continuing inflation as well as shortages. Often the shortage problem is compounded by customers trying to cope with rising prices by buying in larger-than-normal quantities in anticipation of higher prices in the future.[30]

Even where shortages don't exist, sales managers have had to make major policy changes to meet the problem of inflation. Compensation plans have been revamped to avoid overpaying the sales force. This is particularly true when sales representatives are paid a fixed percentage of the sales dollar.

Salespeople must bear the brunt of the task of explaining price increases to distraught customers. Al Rinkov, president of Manny Industries, a Los Angeles maker of draperies and bedspreads, says, "Salesmen have become official apologists for what's been happening to prices."[31]

The long-term sales contract has little meaning in an inflationary economy. Most contracts allow for higher prices or lower quantities at the time of delivery. Industrial companies that used to issue a price list every year or two are finding that they have to print one each month. Honeywell's Micro Switch Division has inserted price escalator clauses based on the government's wholesale price index into its contracts.[32] Honeywell has also trained its sales force to suggest less expensive products where possible. Harris, a maker of printing equipment, has instructed its sales force to limit price quotations to a maximum of six months.

Shortages and inflation seem to be changing the role of the sales force. More than ever, the salesperson is the company's service agent. He or she must aid the buyer in making an intelligent product selection, explain long delivery times and high prices, and generally act as the buyer's consultant rather than as the seller's salesperson—or as a liaison between the company and the customer.

SUMMARY

The role of the sales manager generally consists of several activities, including establishing sales targets, service goals, and training goals; motivating the sales force; evaluation and control of the sales force; and recruiting salespeople. There is no ideal test that will predict the success of a salesperson.

Selling industrial products requires longer and more extensive training than selling consumer products. Training is designed to build product knowledge, obtain sales experience, and acquaint the salesperson with company policies and objectives.

Motivating the sales force requires special skills and understanding. Expectancy theory suggests that a salesperson's effort depends on the expectation that his or her behavior will produce certain outcomes and the attractiveness to the salesperson of those outcomes. Research has shown that salespeople's performance is dependent on such expectations.

Money is generally thought to be a maintenance factor rather than a motivator. Most salespeople perceive salary as an overall flow of pay in return for a flow of work. Therefore money is not a motivator. However, a commission received within a reasonably short time after a sale can be a strong motivator. If a sales force is paid on a straight salary basis, managerial control is usually enhanced. Yet a straight salary is rarely a successful form of motivation. A straight commission system may be a motivator but does not lend itself to organizational control.

Another important aspect of sales management is the size of the sales force. The workload procedure is often used in determining the number of salespeople needed. A second approach to ascertaining the size of the sales force is marginal analysis. Salespeople are added until the profits generated by the last individual hired equal the cost associated with hiring that person. The marginal approach can also be used to designate sales territories.

About 75 percent of all sales managers set quotas for their salespeople. The basis of most quotas is the sales forecast. When properly established, a quota can be a source of motivation and control. Call record reports are another common sales control device.

The prospect of continued shortages of raw materials and other products has led to new roles for the sales force. The salesperson may now become a goodwill ambassador and an allocator rather than a promoter of merchandise. Often salespeople must explain price increases to customers. In many companies the salesperson is becoming a service agent rather than a sales agent.

KEY TERMS

Transactional analysis (TA)	Product organization
Expectancy theory	Territorial organization
Behavior modification theory	Workload technique
Straight commission plan	Marginal analysis
Straight salary plan	Sales quota
Customer organization	Call record report

QUESTIONS FOR DISCUSSION

1. Explain briefly some of the important sales force goals as outlined in the chapter.
2. What are some of the techniques used by companies in the recruiting of salespeople?
3. Do you agree with the statement that "salespeople are born, not made"? Why or why not?
4. What are some of the objectives of a good sales training program?
5. What is transactional analysis? How is it related to sales management?
6. Discuss some of the factors that can improve the motivation level of a sales force.
7. Briefly outline the advantages and disadvantages of a straight salary plan as compared to a straight commission plan. Can you give examples of cases in which each would be most effective?
8. What are some of the factors that are considered in setting up the sales organization? Is there an ideal organization structure?
9. Explain the workload technique as it relates to sales force size. What are the limitations of this method? Give an example to illustrate your answer.
10. What is a sales quota? Should a salesperson's performance be judged on this basis? Why or why not?
11. Comment on the statement, "The salesperson's role is broadening."

NOTES

1. T. G. Povey, "Spotting the Salesman Who Has What It Takes," *Nation's Business,* 60 (July 1972): 70–71.
2. Thomas R. Wotruba, "An Analysis of the Salesmen Selection Process," *Southern Journal of Business,* 5 (January 1970): 41–51.
3. Ibid.
4. "How Rapistan Ltd. Hired a Salesman," *Sales Management,* 115 (September 8, 1975): 69–70.
5. William L. Shanklin, "Transactional Analysis: A New Technique for Sales Training," in *Proceedings, Southern Marketing Association 1974,* pp. 232–235; see also Thomas A. Harris, *I'm O.K.–You're O.K.* (New York: Avon Books, 1973).
6. "Double Digit Hikes in 1974 Sales Training Costs," *Sales Management,* 114 (January 6, 1975): 54–55.
7. Ibid.
8. Arthur H. Brayfield and Walter H. Crockett, "Employee Attitudes and Employee Performance," *Psychological Bulletin,* 52 (September 1955): 396–424; Frederick Herzberg, B. Mausner, R. Petterson, and D. Capwell, *Job Attitudes: Review of Research and Opinion* (Pittsburgh: Psychological Service of Pittsburgh, 1957).
9. Richard L. Oliver, "Expectancy Theory Predictions of Salesmen's Performance," *Journal of Marketing Research,* 11 (August 1974): 243–253.
10. Gilbert A. Churchill, Jr., Neil M. Ford, and Orville C. Walker, Jr., "Measuring the Job Satisfaction of Industrial Salesmen," *Journal of Marketing Research,* 11 (August 1974): 254–260.
11. Robert W. Sweitzer and Dev S. Paltrak, "The Self-Actualizing Salesman," *Southern Journal of Business,* 7 (November 1972): 1–8.
12. Henry O. Pruden, William H. Cunningham, and Wilke D. English, "Nonfinancial Incentives for Salesmen," *Journal of Marketing,* 36 (October 1972): 55–59; see also Alfred Currie, "Motivating the Young Salesman," *Sales Management,* 113 (August 19, 1974): 44, and "How to Motivate When the Problem Is You," *Sales Management,* 110 (April 30, 1973): 48–54.
13. Derek A. Newton, "Get the Most Out of Your Sales Force," *Harvard Business Review,* September-October 1969, pp. 130–143.
14. Fred Luthans and Robert Kreitner, "The Role of Punishment in Organizational Behavior Modification," *Public Personnel Management,* 7 (May-June 1973): 156–161; see also Fred Luthans and Robert Kreitner, "The Management of Behavioral Contingencies," *Personnel,* 51 (July-August 1974): 7–16.
15. Luthans and Kreitner, p. 159.
16. "It's in the Books," *Sales Management,* 109 (August 21, 1972): 12.
17. René Y. Darmon, "Salesmen's Response to Financial Incentives: An Empirical Study," *Journal of Marketing Research,* 11 (November 1974): 418–426.
18. Much of this section is adapted from Douglas J. Dalrymple and Leonard J. Parsons, *Marketing Management Text and Cases* (New York: Wiley, 1976), pp. 530–531; Walter J. Semlow, "How Many Salesmen Do You Need?" *Harvard Business Review,* May-June 1959, pp. 126–132; and Walter J. Tally, Jr., "How to Design Sales Territories," *Journal of Marketing,* 25 (January 1961): 7–13.

19. See Leonard M. Lodish, "Vaguely Right Approach to Sales Force Allocations," *Harvard Business Review,* January-February 1974, pp. 119–124; see also Henry Lucas, Charles Weinberg, and Kenneth Clowes, "Sales Response as a Function of Territorial Potential and Sales Representative Workload," *Journal of Marketing Research,* 12 (August 1975): 298–305; Michael Heschel, "Effective Sales Territory Development," *Journal of Marketing,* 41 (April 1977): 39–43; and James M. Comer, "The Computer, Personal Selling and Sales Management," *Journal of Marketing,* 39 (July 1975): 27–33.

20. Thomas R. Wotruba and Michael L. Thurlow, "Sales Force Participation in Quota Selling and Sales Forecasting," *Journal of Marketing,* 40 (April 1976): 11–16.

21. Ibid.

22. Ibid.

23. Leon Winer, "The Effect of Product Sales Quotas on Sales Force Productivity," *Journal of Marketing Research,* 10 (May 1973): 180–183.

24. David W. Cravens, Robert B. Woodruff, and Joe C. Stamper, "An Analytical Approach for Evaluating Sales Territory Performance," *Journal of Marketing,* 36 (January 1972): 31–37.

25. See Porter Henry, "Manage Your Sales Force as a System," *Harvard Business Review,* March-April 1975, pp. 85–95.

26. "They Say It'll Take 54 Weeks: That's Like No Delivery at All," *Sales Management,* 112 (January 21, 1974): 27.

27. "Sales Managers: No Beefing on Shortages," *Sales Management,* 111 (September 17, 1973): 20–22.

28. Ibid.

29. "For Selling, There's No Shortage of Challenges," *Sales Management,* 112 (January 21, 1974): 16–17; Paul Blackwell, "Shortages: The Pain We All Feel and What to Do About It," *Sales Management,* 113 (July 22, 1974): 25–28, and "How Can I Keep My Sales Force Running in a Crunch Economy?" *Sales Management,* 112 (January 21, 1974): 8–15.

30. Judith Bauer, "Coping with Inflation, Marketers Cut Costs," *Conference Board Record,* 11 (October 1974): 28.

31. Martin Everett, "The Rewards of Hanging in There," *Sales Management,* 113 (November 25, 1974): 19–24.

32. Ibid.

CASE 22
Iowa American Telephone Company

Four months ago Robert Perkins, a 24-year-old M.B.A. from the University of Michigan, agreed to participate in a rather unique experiment. After spending six months in Iowa Telephone's junior executive training program, Perkins was offered the position of Council Bluffs district sales manager. The junior executive training program rotates young management candidates through the various departments so that they can work and observe company operations. Wayne McKinney, the sales manager, exuded enthusiasm about Perkins' abilities and reassured him that even though no one had ever been promoted to district sales manager in less than fifteen years, he was sure Perkins could do the job.

American Telephone Company supplies 60 percent of all telephone service in Iowa and is one of the largest independent telephone companies in the nation. The state is divided into three districts, each encompassing approximately one-third of the state. District headquarters are Council Bluffs, Des Moines, and Cedar Rapids, respectively. Each district has a sales manager, a business office manager, a plant and production manager, and a traffic manager (who is in charge of long-distance equipment and operators). Each district manager reports to a state manager in Des Moines. State headquarters for American and Des Moines district offices are located in the same building. Each district manager came up through the ranks, has been with the company approximately 20 years, and is 45 or 50 years old.

The district is served by five communications representatives, or salespeople, who call on commercial accounts to sell switchboards, data communication equipment, tie lines, and similar products. Residential and small-business accounts were handled by the business office. Two salespeople with a combined total of 48 years of experience were stationed in Sioux City; Kelso Smith, with 38 years of experience, and Don Brooks, a new salesmen, are headquartered in Des Moines; the remaining salesman, Bill Walker, has 4 years of experience. A bright, aggressive person, he is stationed in Manning.

Perkins realized that he must manage the sales force with tremendous finesse to obtain their respect, since all except Brooks have far more product knowledge than he does. The past four months have been eye opening for Perkins—he has found few correlations between textbooks and reality. There is no formal prospecting; each salesperson watches the papers and construction reports for new business activity and makes a sales call when the time is right. Some salespeople also keep a card file and periodically call on old accounts. Sales training and hiring is done strictly at the state level; new personnel go through a three-week program on company policies, sales techniques, and product knowledge before being assigned to a district.

All salespeople are paid on a straight-salary basis, which seems to suit them fine. New people who are aggressive and competent, like Bill Walker, normally leave the company after a few years. In fact Perkins suspects Walker of using his sales calls as a way of prospecting for a new job.

Sales quotas for the districts are sent down by McKinney each December in the form of percentage increases over the previous year's figure (traditionally 10 percent). While there is no stated policy, the district sales managers usually add the same percentage to each salesperson's sales for the previous year. Perkins has noticed that under this system Smith seems to work fairly hard one or two days a week and do "busy work" the rest of the time. Perkins also suspects that this phenomenon exists to a lesser degree in Sioux City.

Perkins received a short memo in the morning mail from McKinney asking him to outline what steps could be taken to make the sales operation more efficient in his district.

1. Prepare the memo from Robert Perkins to Wayne McKinney.
2. What can Perkins do to motivate and retain Bill Walker?
3. What should Perkins do about Kelso Smith?
4. Are changes necessary in the firm's hiring and training practices?
5. Should sales prospecting procedures be implemented?

23

Sales Promotion and Public Relations

OBJECTIVES

■ To understand the meaning and importance of sales promotion.
■ To note recent trends in sales promotion.
■ To become aware of the role of public relations in improving the total marketing effort.

Our examination of promotion would not be complete without a review of sales promotion and publicity. This chapter analyzes the nature of sales promotion and concludes with a discussion of publicity. Both of these promotion techniques play vital roles in the total promotional mix. As we will see, each function has a unique objective that reinforces advertising and personal selling.

THE IMPORTANCE OF SALES PROMOTION

The stepchild of both advertisers and their agencies, sales promotion is growing at a faster rate than advertising, yet it seems that it is being given less attention. (See Figure 23.1.) It is estimated that $30.5 billion was spent on sales promotion in 1976.[1] Both premiums and point-

445

FIGURE 23.1   Year-to-Year Growth of Advertising and Sales Promotion (in Billions of Dollars)

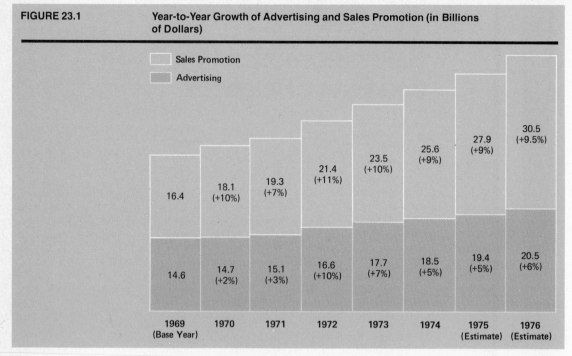

Source: Roger A. Strang, "Sales Promotion, Fast Growth, Faulty Management," *Harvard Business Review*, July-August 1976, 117. Copyright © 1976 by the President and Fellows of Harvard College; all rights reserved.

Note: Advertising doesn't include public relations advertising while sales promotions include direct mail and print media promotion.

of-purchase displays are furnishing the major impetus for growth in this area in the mid-1970s.[2] Premiums and incentives account for the largest slice of the promotional dollar. (See Figure 23.2.)

THE OBJECTIVES OF SALES PROMOTION

Immediate purchase action or attitude modification is usually the goal of sales promotion, regardless of the form it takes. Specifically, the promoter is attempting to increase brand awareness, attract new customers, or increase sales to present customers. (See Table 23.1.) A corollary objective may be to further increase the effectiveness of advertising. Often the two interact "synergistically" to produce higher sales than an equivalent investment in either alone.[3]

In contrast to consumer promotions, which *pull* a product through the channel (by creating demand), trade promotions *push* a product through the channel. Trade discounts may be offered in order to ob-

FIGURE 23.2   Where the Sales Promotion Dollar Goes

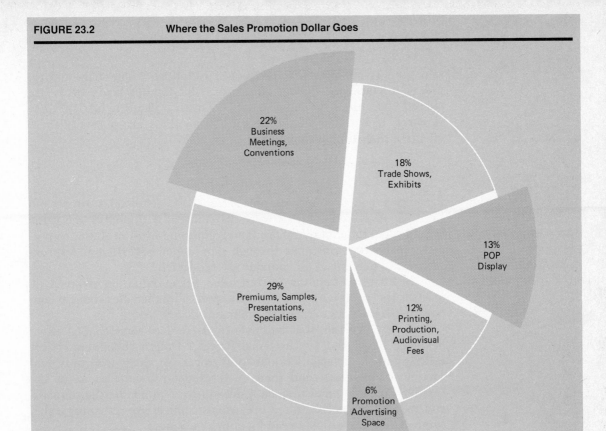

TABLE 23.1   Consumer Promotion Planning Guide

| | Primary Impact | | |
Technique	Brand Awareness	Attract New Customers	Increase Sales to Present Customers
Bonus packs			*
Cash refunds			
Single purchase		*	
Multiple purchase			*
Contests/sweepstakes	*		
Couponing			
Media/mail		*	
In/on pack			*
Multiple			*
Premiums			
Single purchase		*	
Multiple purchase			*
Price-off packages			*
Sampling		*	

tain shelf space for a new product or to induce wholesalers and re-tailers to purchase during off seasons. Sometimes trade deals are offered "because everyone else does." This is difficult to justify, since research has shown that consumer promotions are normally more effective than trade promotions.[4]

TRENDS IN SALES PROMOTION
Samples, Premiums, and Coupons

Premiums, coupons, and samples are at the heart of sales promotion. In 1976, 40 billion coupons were distributed, with an average value of $.14 each, for a total of more than $5 billion.[5] Most of these (56 percent) reach the consumer through newspaper advertising. Approximately 30 percent of all coupons are redeemed.[6]

In effect, couponing is controlled price reduction. Women do most of the redeeming — 63 percent of all adult females redeem coupons while only 35 percent of the males do.[7]

A new program that will eventually replace some coupon offers has been developed by Universal Product Dollars. Shoppers collect coded symbols of various values from grocery products (i.e., universal product codes) and send them in for redemption.[8] This saves the retailer time and money, since it doesn't have to handle the coupons, and redemption is facilitated because consumers are returning coded symbols that are quickly read by optical scanners.

Another trend is tying a premium to a product or service — witness the plethora of Budweiser items, from hot-air balloons to T-shirts. Coca-Cola sold 8 million old-fashioned coke glasses in 1975, capitalizing on both its name and the nostalgia trend.[9] People in places as far away as Tanzania sent $7.95 to Little Olympia Brewery for its logo-bearing backpacks. And 100,000 buyers paid $2.95 for a 4½-foot inflatable Dole banana.[10] Some companies are now publishing catalogs of their premiums. The Budweiser catalog contains over 1000 items! Other firms with less extensive catalogs are Playboy, Coors, Coke, and even U.S. Borax.

Manufacturers are offering more "immediate-reward" pack premiums either on packs, in packs, or as bonus packs. "Free" immediate-reward premiums are also increasing in use as a substitute for straight "cents-off" deals. Pack premiums give consumers greater perceived value than the same amount spent by consumers for "cents-off" promotions.[11] The FTC found that many retailers were not passing the full "10¢ off regular price" rebate on to the consumer. As a result new, strict guidelines have been established for "cents-off" trade deals and the use of such deals has dropped sharply.[12]

Free door-to-door sampling also has dropped considerably owing to the high cost of this technique. Some manufacturers are turning to co-op sampling, in which several different products are delivered in the same container or at the same time. The distribution costs are shared by the various manufacturers.

Another sampling trend is toward "trial-size" containers of salable samples. Minibottles or cartons of a product, such as shampoo or salad dressing, are offered in stores at nominal prices. Retailers like this form of promotion, since it keeps the profit in the store. Consumers also appreciate being able to buy trial-size rather than regular-size containers. It reduces the risk (cost) of trying new products.

Point-of-Purchase Displays

Point-of-purchase (POP) displays consist of display materials and signs placed inside retail stores, usually next to the advertiser's merchandise. The primary value of POP materials is that it places the promotion close to the point of sale. POP materials act as a last-minute inducement to buy the product.

The biggest problem with POP materials is getting retailers to use it. Each year millions of displays, signs, posters, and so forth are discarded without being put up. Limited space and the quantity of materials to choose from have often produced a callous attitude toward POP materials.

Manufacturers are attempting to offset this problem by building better-quality POP materials. Cheap paper signs and crude, ill-conceived displays are vanishing. POP material is often tied in with television or print messages to increase its effectiveness. Recent studies indicate that reinforced POP materials generate more sales dollars than nonreinforced materials.[13]

Business Meetings, Conventions, and Trade Shows

Trade association meetings, conferences, and conventions are an important aspect of sales promotion. It is estimated that 5600 trade shows, conventions, and industrial expositions are held each year.[14] These meetings give manufacturers and wholesalers an opportunity to display their wares to a large audience of potential buyers at relatively low cost. Approximately 80 million people attend trade association conventions each year.[15] The major benefits that promotion managers expect to gain from trade association conventions are shown in Table 23.2.

Recently, however, the Internal Revenue Service has ruled that nonprofit organizations (which includes most trade associations) will have to pay income tax on the trade shows they operate if selling takes place at them. The issue now is, What constitutes selling? Many shows have long banned actual cash transactions, but the new IRS ruling applies to any order written at the show. Probably the greatest impact will be on small exhibitors. John Rousseau, head of the Health

TABLE 23.2   Benefits Expected from Trade Shows

Benefit	Percent
Develop new sales leads	26
Maintain customer contact	25
Introduce new products	15
Meet new customers	15
Sell more to present customers	9
Maintain distributor/dealer contacts	8

Source: "Selling at Trade Shows," *Nation's Business,* August 1976, p. 6.

Care Exhibitors Association, agrees that the rule on selling will hurt smaller members most. "Those people are there to sell," he says. In the dental field, "It is typical for a company to appear in 25 or 30 shows a year, and write 30 percent of its total sales, relying on repeat business for the rest."[16]

Special Forms of Sales Promotion

Many unique and special forms of promotion tend to be highly effective. One example is sponsorship of sporting events. Philip Morris, for instance, sponsors the Marlboro Cup horse race and the Virginia Slims women's tennis tournaments. Both events have provided a high degree of visibility for Philip Morris products. Many of America's large rodeos are sponsored by a competitor of Philip Morris—Winston cigarettes.

Harrah's of Las Vegas engages in a unique form of promotion without ever naming its product. With 3655 slot machines, 544 bingo seats, two sports-betting facilities, four parimutuel wheels, and 159 games of "21," 23 of craps, 11 of roulette, 12 of baccarat, 9 of keno, and 4 of poker, the product becomes rather obvious.[17] But mentioning gambling would violate postal and broadcast regulations. Thus Harrah's relies on quality entertainment as its major form of promotion. In August 1975 the casino offered Frank Sinatra and John Denver in one big show each evening for a week. In addition to the entertainers' fees, Harrah's spent $105,000 advertising the "happening" in various media. (See Figure 23.3.) The response was overwhelming; 586,000 "parties" were turned away during the week because of overflowing crowds.[18]

Another special, albeit less exotic, form of promotion is a newly established network of regional shopping malls that will enable marketers to move their promotions from one center to another. Each mall in the network offers guaranteed weekend traffic of at least 30,000 shoppers. The mall will offer a new display medium that is relatively inexpensive and will reach a fairly homogeneous group of shoppers.[19]

FIGURE 23.3   Harrah's Use of Special Promotion Techniques

Source: John Garbeson, "Selling Without Naming Product—Harrah's is the Expert," *Advertising Age,* May 10, 1976, p. 3. By permission. Copyright 1976 by Crain Communications, Inc.

For example, a travel trailer manufacturer can rotate its trailers through the network and thus expose its wares to many potential buyers.

**PROBLEMS OF SALES PROMOTION MANAGEMENT
Lack of Popularity**

Sales promotion is often considered a stepchild of the total promotional effort. Often responsibility for the function is given to the newest and most inexperienced member of the marketing management team. As a result effective long-range planning for the optimum mix of advertising and promotion seldom occurs.[20] Also, promotion spending is not evaluated in a consistent and objective way.[21] This is probably due to a lack of well-defined sales promotion goals. Jack Worth, vice president–creative director of V&R Enterprises of New York, says, "Promotion is suffering from a 'how-much syndrome.' Too often sales promotion programs emphasize cost rather than marketing objectives."[22]

In more enlightened companies the situation is changing. Better-qualified executives are being hired to supervise the promotion function. New staff positions are being created at the corporate level and established positions, such as supervisor of point-of-purchase materials, are being upgraded to entail broader responsibility.

Some of the problems of sales promotion have stemmed from the use of product managers. Product managers who were interested in rapid promotion found that sales results could be achieved more rapidly through heavy emphasis on sales promotion rather than advertising.[23] While it may be effective in building short-term sales, overemphasis on sales promotion at the expense of advertising can mean the lack of a strong nucleus of brand loyal customers.

Ineffective Management

Without objectives, effective promotion management becomes virtually impossible. Budgeting becomes a question of "How much did we spend last year?" Another common approach is the "leftover approach." Anything that is left over after the advertising budget has been set goes to promotion. It is known that advertising and sales promotion have a positive interactive effect. Yet in many firms the advertising and promotion budgets are prepared independently.

Market research pretesting and posttesting is quite common in advertising but rare in sales promotion.[24] This is rather strange, since premiums can be reliably tested very quickly and at a low cost.[25] Trade allowances are also a problem; many companies fail to check on whether performance requirements are met. In effect, they consider the allowance to be just a way of buying shelf space.

Improving Sales Promotion Management

In addition to improving the caliber of sales promotion personnel, elevating the function to a higher organizational level, and setting specific realistic objectives, several other things can be done to improve promotion management. Robert A. Strang suggests the following steps: analyze spending, select appropriate techniques, pretest, and evaluate in depth.[26]

Strang notes that after specific objectives have been determined, appropriate techniques for achieving them can be selected. Many techniques satisfy more than one objective. (Refer back to Table 23.1.) For example, in a 1975 campaign to attract new users for its "Hefty" trash bags, Mobil Chemical used a sweepstake, premiums, and POP materials, as well as dealer allowances. All techniques should be evaluated in terms of their total costs and sales impact. The possibility of using special packages, the possible loss of sales from complementary items, and the like must not be overlooked.

Pretesting the new promotion is just as important as pretesting a new advertising campaign. Unfortunately, promotion sales effectiveness is just as difficult to measure and predict as advertising effectiveness. For example, redemption rates for a coupon promotion may range from 2 percent to 25 percent, depending on the value of the coupon and the way it is distributed.[27]

The effectiveness of any sales promotion program should be evaluated thoroughly. Sales increases can be due to many factors besides a new promotion campaign. Research at the pretest phase alone will not be adequate. Posttesting to gauge whether or not the promotion objectives have been reached should also be undertaken.

PUBLIC RELATIONS
Goals and Media Alternatives

Public relations, like personal selling, advertising, and sales promotion, is a vital link in a progressive company's marketing communications mix. The following lists enumerate the goals of public relations and the media accomplishing them.

Public-Relations Goals

- *Ultimate Consumers*
  Dissemination of information on the production and distribution of new or existing products.
  Dissemination of information on ways to use new or existing products.
- *Company Employees*
  Training programs to stimulate more effective contact with the public.
  Encouragement of pride in the company and its products.
- *Suppliers*
  Providing research information for use in new products.
  Dissemination of company trends and practices for the purpose of building a continuing team relationship.
- *Stockholders*
  Dissemination of information on: (1) company prospect, (2) past and present profitability, (3) future plans, (4) management changes and capabilities, and (5) company financial needs.
- *The Community at Large*
  Promotion of public causes such as community fund-raising drives.
  Dissemination of information on all aspects of company operations with the purpose of building a sense of unity between company and community.

Media for Internal Public Relations

- *Print*
  Management letters to employees, employee newspapers and magazines, bulletin board announcements, annual and interim financial reports, employee handbooks or manuals, management bulletins for executives and supervisors, pay-envelope inserts, booklets explaining policies and procedures, daily news digests, reading racks, indoctrination kits, posters, and policy statements.
- *Oral*
  Employee and executive meetings, public address systems, open houses, plant tours, family nights, informal talks by key executives on visits to departments, new-employee orientation meetings, employee counseling, panel discussions, grievance and employee–management committees, recordings, and employee social affairs.

- *Audiovisual*
  Motion pictures, color slides and film strips, closed-circuit television, sound slide film, flip charts, easel charts, posters, maps, flannel boards, and product exhibits.

Media for External Public Relations

- *Mass Media*
  Newspapers, magazines, radio, television, annual and interim reports, correspondence, booklets, reprints of executive speeches, program kits and study materials for clubs, educational materials, library reference materials, manuals, and handbooks.
- *Oral*
  Meetings with shareholders, consumers, dealers, suppliers; opinion leaders in plant communities, educators, and legislators; open houses; plant tours; business education days; speeches by employees and executives; visits to community institutions and suppliers; radio and television broadcasts; and community social affairs.
- *Audiovisual*
  Displays and exhibits, motion pictures, sound slide films, charts, maps, posters, slides, television broadcasts, models and construction, and demonstration devices.[28]

Traditionally, public relations has been viewed as little more than image building. As such, it has often been divorced from marketing and other operating units. Although image building is still a basic function of publicity, its role has been expanded and integrated into the total marketing effort.[29] Publicity, for example, is used to establish the credibility of a firm and its products before a sales representative calls on a customer. Public-relations managers help key salespeople and sales managers obtain speaking invitations and then follow through with interesting talks. Public contact by sales managers and representatives helps build company and product familiarity and increases customer receptiveness to an initial sales call.

Building Advertising Credibility

Public relations complements the role of advertising by building product/service credibility. *Public Relations News* states that

> The consumer will increasingly choose products on the basis of corporate preference—especially when choosing new products. This is only human nature; people naturally prefer to deal with companies they know, understand and trust.
>
> Consumers want knowledgeable, straightforward and credible advertising, but they also want credibility reinforcement.[30]

Editorial exposure, such as an endorsement for a specific product or service, is highly valuable, as a promotion manager has noted:

> A message sanctified through acceptance by 'third party' editors, when

perceived by the viewer or reader in the editorial or nonpaid segments of a medium, has more persuasiveness and believability than the advertising, where the sponsor of the message is identified.[31]

An example is the classic introduction of the original Ford Mustang. Everyone first learned about it via editorial exposure. The same is true of the Wankel engine and, by extension, the Mazda. Many years ago an editorial mention of Vicks, and more recently one for Kent cigarettes, created an avalanche of sales.

Aiding in Product Differentiation

Public relations can help an advertiser differentiate its product in a relatively homogeneous market. In the liquor industry, for example, it was a National Mixed Drink Contest for professional bartenders that produced a cocktail that was later named the Pussycat and gave a creative headline writer the opportunity to entitle a story, "How the Pussycat Became a Tiger."[32]

Public relations can play a vital role in any firm's marketing mix. Failure to recognize its potential and integrate it into the communication mix can only reduce the effectiveness of the total marketing effort. Some companies have failed to properly utilize public relations because they claim that the consequences of publicity are difficult to measure. Yet new techniques similar to those used in measuring advertising effectiveness are beginning to overcome the measurement problem.[33]

SUMMARY

Sales promotion has generally been considered a stepchild of advertising and personal selling. Yet sales promotion is growing at a faster rate than advertising, with estimated expenditures of approximately $31 billion. Premiums and point-of-purchase displays are furnishing the major impetus for growth during the 1970s. The objective of sales promotion is usually immediate purchase action or attitude modification rather than long-run behavior modification.

In 1976, 40 billion coupons were distributed with an average value of $.14 each, for a total of more than $5 billion. Many premiums are being tied to a product or service as a form of sales promotion. Coca-Cola, for example, sold 8 million old-fashioned Coke glasses in this fashion.

Door-to-door sampling has decreased owing to its high cost, but trial-size containers of salable samples seem to be taking their place. Retailers prefer this form of promotion because it keeps the profits in the store. Manufacturers also prefer it because they recoup some of their promotional cost.

Other important forms of sales promotion are trade association meetings, conferences, and conventions. It is estimated that 5600 such meetings are held each year. They generally represent an opportunity to display wares and a chance for potential buyers and sellers to come together.

Sales promotion management is generally considered an undesirable position. As a result effective planning and organization are often lacking. However, the situation is changing in more enlightened companies. Better-qualified executives are moving into sales promotion management.

Public relations also plays a unique role in the overall promotional mix. Traditionally, public relations has been viewed as little more than image building. Today, however, the goals of public relations are expanding. Public relations complements advertising by building product and service credibility. Editorial exposure, for example, provides credibility that is not available through advertising. Good public relations can also aid in new-product introduction.

KEY TERMS

Sales promotion
Consumer promotions
Trade promotions
Pack premiums

Co-op sampling
Salable samples
Point-of-purchase (POP) displays
Public relations

QUESTIONS FOR DISCUSSION

1. What is sales promotion? Which of the following activities fall into this category?
   a. A newspaper coupon for Crest toothpaste.
   b. An ad for Winston cigarettes in *Time* magazine.
   c. The annual Playboy sweepstakes.
   d. The marketing manager of a retail chain delivering an address at a local college on "Careers in Retail Management."
2. Explain some of the objectives of sales promotion. Differentiate between consumer promotions and trade promotions.
3. What are some of the problems associated with point-of-purchase displays? How can a marketing manager avoid them?
4. Explain the usefulness of conventions and trade shows to the sales promotion function. Which of the following products could be promoted effectively at such meetings?
   a. A new type of insulation material.
   b. A book on Renaissance art styles.
   c. A new cookbook.
   d. A new brand of liquid detergent.
   e. A health insurance policy for senior citizens.
5. What are some of the difficulties faced by a sales promotion manager? What steps should be taken to rectify them?
6. How could marketing research be used to improve the effectiveness of sales promotion activities? Can you give an example?
7. Explain how public relations could improve a firm's total marketing mix.
8. Comment on the statement, "Public relations enhances advertising credibility."

9. What are some of the public-relations activities that are undertaken to improve employee morale? How does this help the company?
10. What are the different ingredients that make up a company's sales promotion effort? Which one is used most? Why?

NOTES

1. Much of this section is taken from Roger A. Strang, "Sales Promotion, Fast Growth, Faulty Management," *Harvard Business Review,* July-August 1976, pp. 115–124.
2. "Premiums, P.O.P. Showing Big Gains in First Half 1976," *Advertising Age,* July 19, 1976, p. 24.
3. Strang, p. 119.
4. Ibid., p. 121.
5. "Clip, Clip," *Fortune,* 55 (January 1977): 26.
6. Ibid.
7. Ibid.
8. "If Not Coupons, What Can Grocery Manufacturers Use to Promote Products?" *Wall Street Journal,* July 1, 1976; see also "UP Dollars Prepares for Southern California Market Test of Promotional System Based upon Universal Product Code," *Marketing News,* January 30, 1976, p. 3.
9. "Logo Lovers," *Forbes,* 116 (November 15, 1975): 39.
10. Ibid.
11. William Robinson, "Twelve Basic Promotion Techniques," *Advertising Age,* January 10, 1977, pp. 50–55.
12. Eugene Mahany, "Package Goods Clients Agree: Promotion Importance Will Grow," *Advertising Age,* April 14, 1975, pp. 46f.
13. Ibid.
14. Rollie Tillman and C. A. Kirkpatrick, *Promotion: Persuasive Communication in Marketing,* rev. ed. (Homewood, Ill.: Irwin, 1972), p. 312.
15. "News Briefs," *Wall Street Journal,* August 5, 1976; see also Suzette Cavanaugh, "Setting Objectives and Evaluating the Effectiveness of Trade Show Exhibits," *Journal of Marketing,* 40 (October 1976): 100–105.
16. "The IRS Sets Off Trade-Show Tremors," *Business Week,* May 31, 1976, p. 24.
17. John W. Garberson, "Selling Without Naming Product – Harrah's Is the Expert," *Advertising Age,* May 10, 1976, pp. 3f.
18. Ibid.
19. "Marketing Briefs," *Marketing News,* July 2, 1976, p. 2.
20. "Promotions Lack Proper Planning," *Advertising Age,* April 21, 1975, pp. 2f.
21. Ibid.
22. Ibid.
23. Strang, p. 117.
24. Ibid., p. 119.
25. Russell D. Bowman, "Merchandising and Promotion Grow Big in Marketing World," *Advertising Age,* December 30, 1974, p. 21.
26. Strang, pp. 121–122.
27. Ibid., p. 122.
28. James Engel, Hugh Wales, and Martin Warshow, *Promotional Strategy,* 3d ed. (Homewood, Ill.: Irwin, 1975), pp. 489–491.

29. Richard R. Conarroe, "Enter the Salesman as Local PR Man," *Sales Management,* 108 (October 2, 1972): 41–42; Gardner DeWitt, "Winning a Place in the Marketing Mix," *Public Relations Journal,* 30 (August 1974): 20–21; Richard R. Conarroe, "Public Relations Sets the Stage," *Sales Management,* 109 (October 30, 1972): 41–42; Joseph Moran, "Using PR Strategy to Project a New Corporate Image and Help Increase Sales," *Public Relations,* 30 (October 1974): 20–31.
30. Donald G. Softness, "What Product PR Can Do for You in Today's Advertising World," *Advertising Age,* August 2, 1976, p. 19. Copyright 1976 by Crain Communications, Inc.
31. Ibid., p. 20.
32. DeWitt, p. 21.
33. Edward M. Stevens, "Success of Publicity Can Be Tested with Ad Measurement Techniques," *Industrial Marketing,* 60 (February 1975): 55–56.

CASE 23
Northwest Apple Growers

John Turner, manager of the Northwest Apple Growers Association, was disturbed by the fact that a recent market research study commissioned by the Association revealed a decline in per-capita apple consumption from 18.2 pounds in 1958 to 13.4 pounds in 1975. Part of the problem, Turner felt, was inadequate sales promotion.

Previous sales promotional efforts had centered on retailers. The Association offered large cardboard point-of-purchase displays free of charge to any retailer who requested them. Research showed that the merchants used the displays approximately three weeks and that sales normally rose anywhere from 15 to 350 percent, with an average increase of 82 percent.

The market research study suggested that sales promotion be directed more toward the final consumer. The report recommended the following:

1. Establishment of a trade character like the "Pillsbury Doughboy" to maintain continuity and unity in the Association's promotion.
2. A continual stream of recipes, photos, and stories about apples be supplied to food editors throughout the nation.
3. The development of audiovisual aids for schools that point out the nutritional value of apples.
4. Heavy consumer campaigning during the months of October through December, when excessive supplies of fresh apples normally develop.

Mr. Turner must now act on the recommendations of the study.

1. Should Turner follow the advice of the report?
2. What could be done to get more retailers to use the Association's POP display?
3. Do you agree with the policy of giving POP materials only to retailers who ask for them?
4. Is the trade character really necessary? Why or why not?
5. Do you believe that an audiovisual campaign that stresses nutrition will be successful?

VII Marketing Management

24
Strategic Marketing: Planning and Control

OBJECTIVES

■ To understand the concept of strategic marketing planning.
■ To learn the basic steps involved in problem solving.
■ To learn about different ways of organizing the marketing function.
■ To grasp the different techniques used to exercise marketing control.

**DEVELOPING
MARKETING
PLANS**

The goal of planning is to help marketing managers make better decisions. Plans can be divided into two categories: strategic and tactical. Strategic planning establishes the character of the organization and provides long-run direction. It is normally used with reference to fundamental issues, broad perspectives, and long-term periods.[1] Tactical planning, on the other hand, is concerned with efficient use of resources to obtain specific objectives.

The longer the planning time span, the more likely the plan is to be strategic. Polaroid's decision to manufacture and market instant cameras involved a considerable amount of strategic planning. Armour-Dial introduced an "updated version" of its Dial soap in early 1977. This involved tactical planning. The tactical objective

463

was to make sure that retailers had sufficient inventory of the old bars to meet consumer demand through December, but not so much that the company would be hit with returns when the new bars were distributed.[2]

Strategic planning begins with a thorough understanding of both the internal and external environments. Every major factor that can impinge upon the success of the marketing effort should be examined. Richard Abington, director of strategic planning at United Technologies, puts it this way:

> One might visualize the future marketplace as a labyrinth wherein "today" is represented as the starting gate, with all possible industry competitors ready to enter.
>
> If one has a profound understanding, he should be able to diagram the layout of the likely labyrinth and to describe the height and thickness of the walls and the likely movement of choices of the various competitors after each enters the maze.
>
> Aggressive strategy then takes off from this point of profound understanding. It is ideally a committed work plan which allows us to restructure the maze so that we may enter and walk straight through to our market share and profit objectives—while our competitors, with their market predispositions, walk deeply into the maze and are forever trapped behind high and massive walls.[3]

Once the decision-making environments are understood, meaningful and realistic goals can be established. (See Figure 24.1.) Next, courses of action are developed to meet the objectives. A course is then chosen based on careful analysis. The next step in strategic planning is the allocation of the resources necessary to attainment of the stated objectives.[4] This involves budgeting. Typically, budgets are established at the lowest managerial levels and modified or approved by succeeding levels of management.

Budgeting makes it possible to carry out plans. Without funding, planning becomes an empty exercise. Budgeting also serves as a basis for control. Over time, deviations from the budget can be examined. Deviations aren't good or bad per se. Not all events can be anticipated, so some discrepancies should be expected. Budgets may also be used in evaluating managerial performance. If strategic objectives can be reached at a lower cost than the budgeted amount, it is often an indication of effective management.

Budgeting doesn't complete the planning process. The plans must still be put into operation. Authority must be delegated and appropriate activities begun. As the tasks are carried out, necessary control procedures must be implemented and corrective actions taken. The control process will be discussed in more detail later in the chapter.

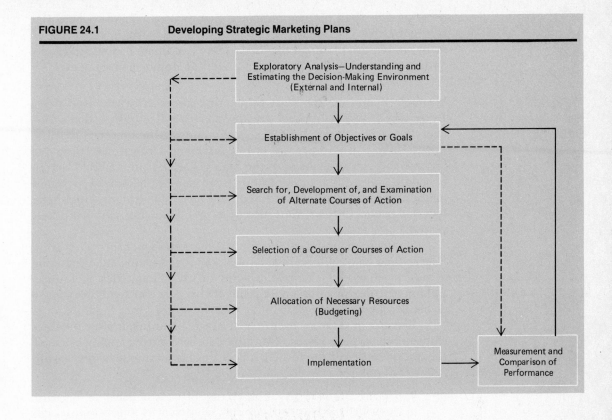

FIGURE 24.1   Developing Strategic Marketing Plans

Exploratory Analysis—Understanding and Estimating the Decision-Making Environment (External and Internal)

Establishment of Objectives or Goals

Search for, Development of, and Examination of Alternate Courses of Action

Selection of a Course or Courses of Action

Allocation of Necessary Resources (Budgeting)

Implementation

Measurement and Comparison of Performance

Advantages of Strategic Marketing Planning

As mentioned earlier, the ultimate aim of strategic planning is better decision making. By forcing managers to assess the marketing environment and forecast future events, it helps them develop a better understanding of various decision alternatives. Management can anticipate changes and have contingency plans (tactical plans) ready in case specific events occur. For example, if competitor X raises prices 10 percent during the next six months, the firm might counter with a 3-percent price increase and a 20-percent increase in promotion stressing its lower price. Having a series of tactical plans derived from a long-run strategic plan helps management react to environmental change calmly and intelligently. Panic and hasty decision making are avoided.

Strategic and tactical planning that is well thought out and is based on inputs from all levels of management typically results in effective plans. Managerial involvement in the process from the bottom up is important because participation leads to better acceptance of the final plan. Lower levels of marketing management do not feel that higher levels are insensitive to their needs. Participation can serve as a form of motivation, since each manager knows where the firm is headed and what the opportunities are. Also, lower levels of management are closer to the "firing line" and may be aware of competitive subtleties that aren't recognized by upper management.

Problems Encountered in Strategic Planning

Strategic planning, like most things that are worthwhile, isn't easy. Even when strategic plans are developed, all too often that's it—everyone gets a warm glow of security and satisfaction now that the uncertainty of the future has been contained.[5] Unfortunately, no one follows through to make sure the plan is carried out. Daniel Carroll, of Gould, says, "Marketing failures can usually be traced to sound marketing plans that were ignored, and not to poor plans which misled the users. Our greatest threat is not believing and using our plans."[6]

Strategic planning can be risky. A marketing manager must often take a stand on a controversial issue without complete data. Producing a new product, for example, always involves some risk of failure. Taking a strong position on an issue of this sort can sometimes make or break a person's career.

Because of the very nature of strategic planning, it often involves extremely complex issues. Planning can be controversial because of the uncertainties of the future. It requires leadership to be successful. As Carroll notes,

> Top management review of marketing plans is optional only in businesses which place a mistakenly low value on marketing or a mistakenly high value on other management concerns. We're really saying that top management has its values out of sync if it is not prepared to participate actively in a review of a marketing plan. Top management is, in effect, saying that the most dynamic of my functions somehow doesn't deserve my time or my attention or both.[7]

Unless strategic planning receives the necessary leadership from top management, it is probably doomed to failure.

Basic company systems often work against effective strategic planning. Good managers, for example, are often promoted before they see the long-run consequences of their actions. Also, incentive compensation is often tied to short-term earnings performance or brand sales. Neither have much to do with long-term strategic marketing success.

Considerations in Strategic Marketing Planning

You can see from the preceding discussion that strategic planning is not without problems. Even so, the planning process is of paramount importance and should not be minimized or ignored. It is management's primary tool for coping with change.

What are some of the factors involved in strategic marketing planning? Generally, three factors serve as determinants for strategic planning: the nature of the market, the product mix, and top management's goals and philosophies.[8]

Development of Successful Strategies

There is, of course, no guarantee of success regardless of the strategy a firm chooses to follow. To cope with this problem a group of over 100 companies and 5 academic institutions has recently developed a program entitled Profit Impact of Market Strategy (PIMS).[9]

The objective of PIMS is to provide a business strategy experience data base. By 1977 the firms had reported 800 experiences covering a five-year period and involving 300 data items. Each experience describes the marketing strategy, the environment, and the results obtained. Computer analysis of the information has revealed a number of interesting findings. For example, if a company's market position is strong, increased research and development expenditures generally lead to higher profits. The following is a summary of major PIMS findings:

- Capital intensity is strongest of the 37 factors. Market position is second.
- High capital intense businesses don't do well because of the high investment in the ROI ratio but mostly because the process of competition works in a particularly vicious way in such industries — that is, because the sheer fact of capital intensity plus high fixed costs injects a note of desperation into competition to keep the expensive plant loaded. This, in turn, produces price weakness, marketing wars, or other rather expensive forms of competition to get the volume needed.
- If you're highly capital intense, then don't spend a lot of marketing dollars to buy volume. The 42 businesses in the data base which did averaged 0.1 percent pretax ROI. Heavy marketing expense with heavy investment expense is simply too much for any one business to bear.
- If you're highly capital intense, try to segment your market to improve your market position. (It also is a disaster to try to combine a high capital intensity with weak market position.) But if you can succeed in segmenting your market sufficiently well so that you can have a strong position in whatever segments you operate, then you can at least project your profitability into a reasonably good neighborhood.
- A high market share business is considerably more profitable than a low market share business.
- There are two ways in which a business can acquire a strong market position — by being big or by being selective in terms of which specific market segments it selects to go after and concentrating its attentions on establishing a dominant position in those selected segments.

- The high quality producer can be considerably more profitable than the low quality producer regardless of his pricing policy—that is, regardless of whether he sells his high quality product for a high price or for a low price. Charging a low price is an inexpensive way to buy market share.
- Businesses with high quality products and strong market positions also are very profitable, averaging 29 percent ROI.
- At the opposite extreme, low quality and weak position, the average is 6 percent ROI.
- Market position and product quality (remember, it's product quality as perceived by the market and includes the service package as well as the characteristics of the gadget itself) can be used as substitutes for each other—that is, if you're weak in one, you can compensate for it by being strong in the other.
- If your market position is weak, premium pricing doesn't pay. It cuts profitability, even if you have superior product quality. If you have superior quality and weak position, then cash in via volume.
- If your market position is weak, don't do R&D, but do introduce new products by "copying," "stealing," imitating, licensing, or buying them. "Imitation is the natural way of competition for the weak. Innovation is the natural way of competition for the strong."
- If your market position is strong, increase your R&D and profitability will go up. (R&D here is R&D performed by ordinary people, not the "strokes-of-genius" kind.)
- If you've got a low quality product, don't advertise it. If you do, you'll have about a 3 percent pretax ROI. Just quietly put a low price on it and find a segment of the market that responds to it.
- Those who introduce new products at the bottom of a recession find it very profitable, partly because it gives the market a little excitement when it could stand a little and partly because it also insulates the business from the occasionally nasty price competition that develops at the bottom of the cycle. It also helps the business pick up additional market share points at a lower cost per point when the market starts growing again.
- It is unfortunately true that it is never a good idea to spend much more than 10 cents of the sales dollar for all marketing functions. In cosmetics and some other lines, you can't help yourself, but still it's a drag on earnings when you exceed this ratio.
- It is generally true that those businesses with a strong market share are underspending on marketing and could afford to spend more, and those with a weak market position are overspending and would be better off if they spent less.[10]

The Relationship Between Strategy Planning and Problem Solving

Strategy development involves the examination of many potential and actual problems. Similarly, tactical planning is complicated by the need to sift through and analyze numerous problems. Kresge's strategic plan in the early 1960s was to get away from the faltering variety

FIGURE 24.2   **A Model for Decision Making**

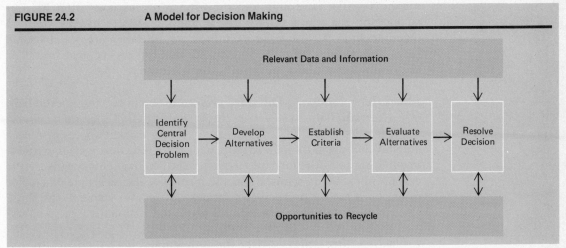

Source: William O'Dell, Andrew Ruppel, and Robert Trent, *Marketing Decision Making: Analytical Framework and Cases* (Cincinnati: Southwestern, 1976), p. 3. By permission.

chain business into the burgeoning field of discounting. This involved dealing with many problems, including the possibility of cannibalizing sales from existing Kresge stores, the need to change merchandise mixes, the different buying patterns of consumers in the discounting field, and the task of finding hundreds of qualified new suppliers.

How should a manager approach strategic problem solving? Figure 24.2 outlines a basic problem-solving model.[11] Problem solving is concerned with developing alternatives to an issue and choosing the "best" means of rectifying the problem. Before alternatives can be developed, the causes of the dilemma must be uncovered. As the marketing model shows, problems can arise from internal sources or from the external environment.

Identifying Problems.   Phenomena are often merely symptomatic of the real difficulty. For example, a decline in sales is not a problem but a symptom. Something either internal (e.g., poor product quality, high prices) or external (e.g., aggressive competitor promotions, better technology) is causing sales to decline. These factors are the real problem. Information gathered through market research or other means that helps marketing managers focus on the true problem is called environmental data (even if it is internal information).

Developing Alternatives.   Once the real problem has been uncovered, alternatives can be developed. Marketing alternatives ultimately result in unique combinations of the marketing mix to solve specific difficulties. Focus groups and brainstorming sessions often help in developing reasonable alternatives. Similar choices can be grouped together and others can be examined for interdependence. In some cases alternatives must be sequenced—before we can test brand A, the product must be approved by the laboratory.

Establishing Criteria.   The third step in problem solving is establishing criteria to help in selecting the best alternative. Common criteria are a target return on investment, a certain market share, or a specific level of promotional exposure over time. The best way of expressing criteria is in the form of "if–then" statements. This means that if certain phenomena occur, a specific form of action will take place. For example, if brand A receives a 20-percent market share in the three test cities, it will be produced and marketed nationally.

Evaluating Alternatives.   After the problem has been defined, alternatives enumerated, and criteria set forth, the alternatives must be evaluated. Many times this requires market research. The data obtained, however, are quite different from environmental data. Now the researcher is gathering data that can be acted upon—data that will be examined in light of specific criteria in order to pick the best alternative.

  A report by the market research department on a new ingredient in a competitor's product is environmental in nature. No action is taken by the firm to alter its product. However, a research project that places the competitor's new formulation in a blind test against our brand to see which is preferred by consumers generates data that serve as a basis for action. Decision criteria would be established such as, "If the tests reveal a 60-percent or higher preference for the competitor's product, we will add the new ingredient to our product."

Making the Decision.   The final step is resolving the problem. If appropriate criteria statements have been established, this is an easy process. Unclear data (borderline situations) or managerial disagreements regarding the alternatives or criteria statements can cause a delay in decision making. If the need to act is not overwhelming, then it may be wise to reexamine the whole problem-solving process. Often, however, management isn't permitted this luxury. Decision making is normally based on less-than-perfect information.

MARKETING ORGANIZATION

Marketing must function within an integrated organizational system in order to achieve its goals in an effective manner. Problem solving and planning occur within one of several forms of organizational structure: product, functional, geographic (market), or matrix. Examples of each form are shown in Figure 24.3.

Product structure is common when a firm markets markedly different types of goods, each serving unique markets. It enables management to develop and focus strategies geared to each product's market. Functional structures concentrate on the development of marketing skills and expertise in specific functional areas (e.g., market research and advertising). Geographic structures enable managers to respond to differing needs of regional customers. Local managers can adapt more readily to unusual market characteristics.

Matrix Organizations

Matrix organization represents a major departure from traditional structures. The role relationships among various managers are quite different from the norm. Rather than being arranged according to a strict vertical authority–responsibility structure, line and staff functions are commingled. Sometimes an individual may act in a staff capacity; at other times he or she may function as a line manager. The basic idea behind the matrix organization is that resource usage is controlled and directed by two opposing sets of managers.

Companies that use the product manager concept often use matrix structures. (See Figure 24.3.) Product managers are held accountable for the sales and profit success of their products, yet they do not always have the authority to, for example, order the advertising manager to develop a certain campaign. Some product managers have relatively little authority while others have complete authority. It depends on the history and nature of the firm.

Marketing's Interaction with Other Departments

Perhaps you may be wondering whether marketing literally dominates the remainder of the organization. The answer is no. No single component should have undue influence over the entire structure. Production requirements, financial and engineering aspects of the company, and many other facets of the operation must be in harmonious balance.

If marketing controlled or dominated the firm, there might be short production runs (to produce great variety—something for everyone); high inventory levels (no stock outages, since this creates dissatisfaction); minimal credit checks (a source of consumer inconvenience and frustration); and short engineering design lead time (in order to react quickly to changing customer desires). (See Table 24.1.)

Marketing's function is to provide information on customer desires and characteristics. It must then work together with the other departments to achieve the firm's overall objectives. This often re-

FIGURE 24.3 Common Forms of Marketing Organizations: (a) Product; (b) Functional;

VP MARKETING
Advertising
Market Research
Manager Toys
Manager Sporting Goods
Sales
Physical Distribution
Sales
Physical Distribution
(a)
VP MARKETING
Advertising
Public Relations
Market Research
Physical Distribution
Sales
New-Product Development
(b)

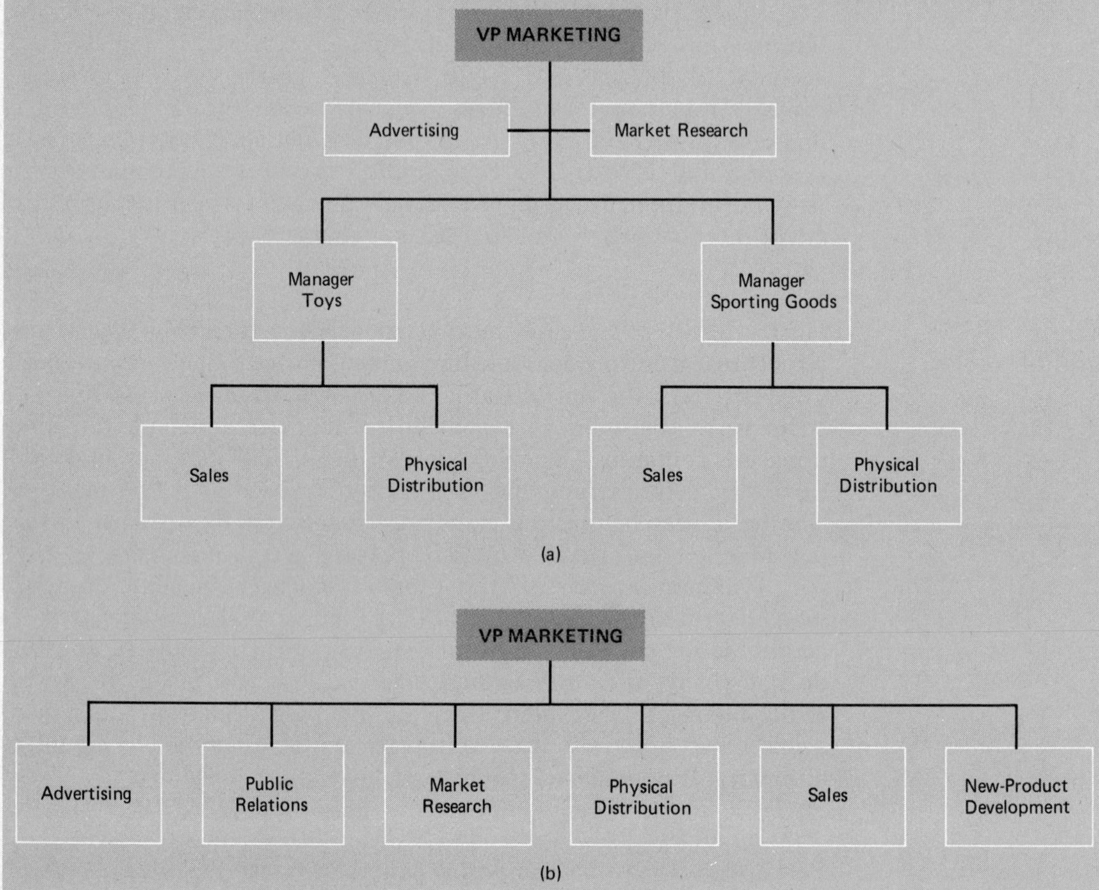

FIGURE 24.3   **(c) Geographic; (d) Matrix**

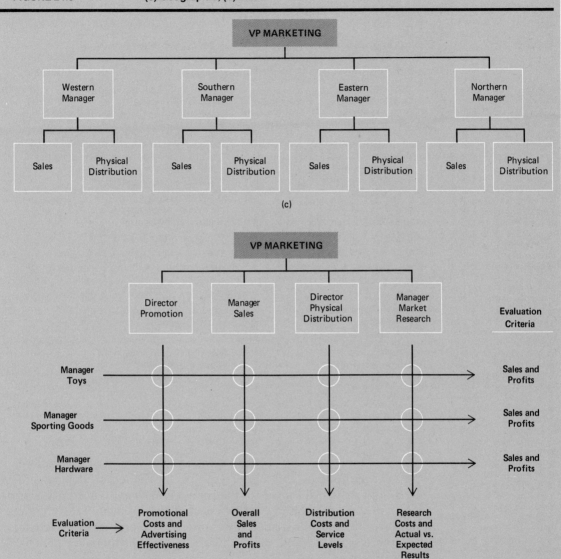

(c)

(d)

TABLE 24.1	Conflicts Between Marketing and Other Departments	
Other Departments	**Their Emphasis**	**Emphasis of Marketing**
Engineering	Long design lead time	Short design lead time
	Functional features	Sales features
	Few models with standard components	Many models with custom components
Purchasing	Standard parts	Nonstandard parts
	Price of material	Quality of material
	Economic lot sizes	Large lot sizes to avoid stockouts
	Purchasing at infrequent intervals	Immediate purchasing for customer needs
Production	Long order lead times and inflexible product schedules	Short order lead times and flexible scheduling to meet emergency orders
	Long runs with few models	Short runs with many models
	No model changes	Frequent model changes
	Standard orders	Custom orders
	Ease of fabrication	Aesthetic appearance
	Average quality control	Tight quality control
Inventory management	Fast-moving items, narrow product line	Broad product line
	Economic levels of stock	Large levels of stock
Finance	Strict rationales for spending	Intuitive arguments for spending
	Hard-and-fast budgets	Flexible budgets to meet changing needs
	Pricing to cover costs	Pricing to further market development
Accounting	Standard transactions	Special terms and discounts
	Few reports	Many reports
Credit	Full financial disclosures by customers	Minimum credit examination of customers
	Low credit risks	Medium credit risks
	Tough credit terms	Easy credit terms
	Tough collection procedures	Easy collection procedures

Source: Philip Kotler, "Diagnosing the Marketing Takeover," *Harvard Business Review,* November-December 1965, p. 72. Copyright © 1965 by the President and Fellows of Harvard College; all rights reserved.

quires compromise and understanding of the other departments' needs and goals. All aspects of the company, however, need to discern the importance of the marketing concept. Every member of the firm must work toward customer satisfaction. Without customer satisfaction there is no market, and if there is no market there are no jobs.[12]

MARKETING CONTROL

The Importance of Control

The management tasks of planning and organizing cannot be effective without control. Control provides the mechanism for correcting actions that are not efficient in aiding the marketing organization reach its objective. Without control, goal achievement becomes a hit-or-miss proposition. Even if a firm is fortunate enough to reach its goals without good controls, the chances are that some resources have been wasted. In summary, a good control system keeps marketing programs on track so that they can reach their goals within budget guidelines.

The Meaning of Control

Essentially, control is making events conform to plans. The process begins with a well-defined set of standards and goals. As you learned in our discussion of advertising, objectives and standards must be clear, concise, meaningful, and measurable.

The process of control consists of (1) setting standards, (2) measuring performance and reporting deviations, (3) doing causal analysis to determine why deviations occurred, and (4) taking corrective action. The process is outlined in Figure 24.4.

Setting Standards. Standards are bases for measuring how well a marketing activity is being performed. If certain standards are met, benefits should accrue to the firm. High inventory turnover, low sales costs, and low advertising costs per thousand exposures will, it is hoped, translate into an increasing sales volume and market share plus higher profitability. A summary of general marketing standards and expected benefits is presented in Table 24.2.

The basis for establishing many standards is a sales and profitability forecast. A sales forecast is an estimate of sales, in dollars or physical units, for a specified future period under a proposed market-

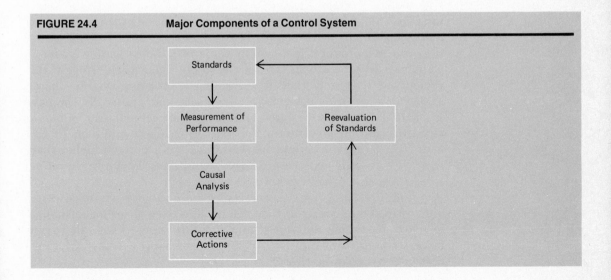

FIGURE 24.4   Major Components of a Control System

TABLE 24.2	General Marketing Standards and Expected Benefits	
Level of Standard	**Expected Benefits**	**Standards**
Internal marketing operations	Sales volume Market share Growth rate Number of sales calls Advertising recall rates	Salesmen's expenses (% of sales) Sales per call Ad cost per thousand exposures On-time delivery percentage Inventory turnover Sales per square foot of space
Customer satisfaction	Purchase amounts Repurchase rate Product quality perception Loyalty to store and brand Organizational image	Product price Number of organizations patronized Time expended per purchase Complaint ratio
Satisfaction of society	Product quality standards Product safety standards Occupational licenses Customer mix Advertising truthfulness	Product life Material requirements Energy consumption

Source: Ben Enis, *Marketing Principles,* 2d ed. (Santa Monica, Calif.: Goodyear, 1977), p. 511. Copyright © 1977 by Goodyear Publishing Co. Reprinted by permission.

ing plan and an assumed set of conditions. It becomes the goal for the marketing department. Sometimes forecasts are made for the entire life cycle of a product, as shown in Table 24.3. This example is a long-term forecast for a product that is already in the maturity stage of the cycle. Note that projections have been made for prices, market share, sales, manufacturing costs, marketing costs, and profits. By comparing actual results with forecast results management can pinpoint strengths and weaknesses in the marketing of the product. In the maturity stage, for example, market share was 1 percent higher than forecast, yet selling costs were lower than projected. On the negative side, the selling price was lower than forecast.

The preceding forecast has its greatest value in strategic planning owing to its long-run time frame. Typically, firms make similar forecasts on yearly, quarterly, and monthly bases. These short-run forecasts help in monitoring week-to-week changes in the effectiveness of the marketing effort.

TABLE 24.3   Long-Run Forecasting for Marketing Control

Product: Tape   **Introduction:** February 1968 to October 1968
Current Period: April 1, 1978   **Latest Revision:** May 10, 1977

	Introductory Period Year 1		Growth Period Years 2–5		Maturity Period Years 6–10		Decline Period Years 11+	
	Forecast	Actual	Forecast	Actual	Forecast	Actual	Forecast	Actual
Average market share	5%	7%	30%	36%	40%	41%	20%	—
Average price per unit	$1.75	$1.65	$1.50	$1.47	$1.40	$1.30	$1.35	—
Sales:								
In units	10,000	14,000	300,000	360,000	400,000	410,000	100,000	—
In dollars	$17,500	$23,100	$450,000	$529,200	$560,000	$533,000	$135,000	—
Manufacturing costs—								
dollars per unit	0.75	0.72	0.68	0.68	0.67	0.67	0.67	—
Selling costs—								
dollars per unit	0.35	0.32	0.18	0.18	0.06	0.05	0.04	—
Distribution costs—								
dollars per unit	0.30	0.30	0.30	0.30	0.30	0.30	0.30	—
Advertising and promotional support:								
Dollars	3,000	5,600	150,000	162,000	80,000	61,500	—	—
Dollars per unit	0.30	0.40	0.40	0.30	0.20	0.15	—	—
Net contribution to profit:								
Dollars	2,000	2,240	—	2,880	320,000	348,500	64,000	—
Dollars per unit	0.20	0.16	—	0.08	0.80	0.85	0.64	—

Source: Information for Marketing Management (New York: National Association of Accountants, 1971), p. 34.

Causal Analysis

MARKETING COST CONTROL. Cost analysis is one of the most important techniques for maintaining marketing control. The marketing mix is a basis for direct costs of many types, such as advertising costs, market test expenses, and sales force expenses. In turn, marketing costs play an important role in determining the profitability of a product or product line.

Unless care is taken in designing an information system, marketing managers will not have the data needed in exercising meaningful control. Here are some examples:

A sporting goods manufacturer designed a promotion pack and display piece for use in department stores, although, for legal reasons, the offer had to be extended to all types of accounts. Post-sales analysis indicated that total sales in one area increased significantly while another region showed only a slight increase. Because the company's information system could not break out data on sales and shipments of the

TABLE 24.4	Returns and Complaints Report					
	Number of Customer Complaints Received					
Summary of Complaints by Source	**1/69**	**2/69**	**3/69**	**4/69**	**5/69**	**6/69**
Miami Plant						
Precooked T-bone						
Overtenderized/mushy	25	22	20	25	30	35
Tough/uncuttable	15	13	14	10	8	3
Wrong size	8	7	7	8	7	6
Other	3	2	2	2	3	4
Subtotal	51	44	43	45	48	48
Chicago Plant						
Precooked T-bone						
Overtenderized/mushy	50	55	48	52	48	47
Tough/uncuttable	28	25	30	29	31	26
Wrong size	11	10	13	12	14	12
Other	7	8	6	6	6	9
Subtotal	96	98	97	99	99	94

display piece by type of account, the marketer decided to forgo a detailed analysis of the promotion pack's effectiveness in department stores and relied instead on field salesmen's weekly reports of market conditions.

A major toilet goods manufacturer prepared a detailed budget of all marketing activities by sales territory and by month. Although the accounting department received information on actual expenditures by area (advertising dollars by market from the advertising agency, promotional shipments from sales invoices, selling costs from the territory sales personnel), the data were not compiled into the territory classifications for comparison with budget. The marketer recognized that he did not, in fact, control the actual expenditures by territory and season.[13]

MARKET SHARE ANALYSIS. A corollary to cost analysis is market share analysis. An increase in market share usually indicates that the firm's marketing mix is more effective than that of its competitors. A declining market share may serve as a basis for investigation of potential areas.

Plant Shipments (Total Cases)	January to June				Cost/Adjustments – January to June	
	Complaints	Percent^a	Adjust- ments	Percent^b	Actual	Per Case Shipped
	4,000	4.0%	3,000	3.0%	$30,000	$0.30
	1,000	1.0	250	0.3	2,500	0.03
	500	0.5	–	–	–	–
	500	0.5	–	–	–	–
100,000	6,000	6.0%	3,250	3.3%	$32,500	$0.33
	5,000	2.0	2,500	1.0	25,000	0.10
	3,500	1.4	1,750	0.7	17,500	0.07
	1,000	0.4	–	–	–	–
	1,000	0.4	–	–	–	–
250,000	10,500	4.2%	4,250	1.7%	$42,500	$0.17

Source: Information for Marketing Management (New York: National Association of Accountants, 1971), p. 34.

^a Number of cases involved in a complaint as a percentage of shipments; includes duplications of reasons.

^b Number of cases actually adjusted as follow-up to complaints as percentage of shipments.

Market share data are generally most meaningful when broken down by sales territory, customer type (e.g., machinery manufacturers, food processors, and mining), and product category. A manager may find, for example, that an overall increase in market share is due to increased sales to a particular type of customer or within a certain territory.

NONFINANCIAL CONTROLS. Not all marketing controls center on financial forecasts and analysis. A typical example of nonfinancial control information is a complaint report. Such data can be used as a basis for quality control and maintenance of customer satisfaction. Table 24.4 is a complaint disposition form for a company selling precooked T-bone steaks. Note that complaints are recorded over a particular period. Also, the complaint disposition is reported along with the cost of making an adjustment. A quick glance at the report tells management that the Miami plant seems to be overtenderizing the meat (4 percent of total shipments). This cost the company $30,000 during a six-month period.

THE MARKETING AUDIT.   Perhaps the broadest control device available to marketing management is the marketing audit. This tool incorporates both financial and nonfinancial reporting. The marketing audit is primarily futuristic in nature. It is designed to aid management in allocating marketing resources efficiently. The following is an outline of the types of information gathered and analyzed in the audit:

Part I
The Marketing Environment Review

A. *Markets*
   1. What are the organization's major markets and publics?
   2. What are the major market segments in each market?
   3. What are the present and expected future size and characteristics of each market or market segment?
B. *Customers*
   4. How do the customers and publics see and feel toward the organization?
   5. How do customers make their purchase or adoption decisions?
   6. What is the present and expected future state of customer needs and satisfaction?
C. *Competitors*
   7. Who are the organization's major competitors?
   8. What trends can be foreseen in competition?
D. *Macroenvironment*
   9. What are the main relevant developments with respect to demography, economy, technology, government, and culture that will affect the organization's situation?

Part II
The Marketing System Review

A. *Objectives*
   10. What are the organization's long-run and short-run overall objectives and marketing objectives?
   11. Are the objectives stated in a clear hierarchical order and in a form that permits planning and measurement of achievement?
   12. Are the marketing objectives reasonable for the organization, given its competitive position, resources, and opportunities?
B. *Program*
   13. What is the organization's core strategy for achieving its objectives and is it likely to succeed?
   14. Is the organization allocating enough resources (or too much resources) to accomplish the marketing tasks?
   15. Are the marketing resources allocated optimally to the various markets, territories, and products of the organization?
   16. Are the marketing resources allocated optimally to the major elements of the marketing mix, i.e., product quality, personal contact, promotion, and distribution?

C. *Implementation*
17. Does the organization develop an annual marketing plan? Is the planning procedure effective?
18. Does the organization implement control procedures (monthly, quarterly, etc.) to ensure that its annual plan objectives are being achieved?
19. Does the organization carry out periodic studies to determine the contribution and effectiveness of various marketing activities?
20. Does the organization have an adequate marketing information system to service the needs of managers for planning and controlling operations in various markets?

D. *Organization*
21. Does the organization have a high-level marketing officer to analyze, plan, and implement the marketing work of the organization?
22. Are the other persons directly involved in marketing activity able people? Is there a need for more training, incentives, supervision, or evaluation?
23. Are the marketing responsibilities optimally structured to serve the needs of different marketing activities, products, markets, and territories?
24. Do the organization's personnel understand and practice the marketing concept?

Part III
Detailed Marketing Activity Review

A. *Products*
25. What are the main products of the organization? What are the generic products?
26. Should any products in the line be phased out?
27. Should any products be added to the line?
28. What is the general state of health of each product and the product mix as a whole?

B. *Prices*
29. To what extent are prices set on cost, demand, and/or competitive criteria?
30. What would the likely response of demand be to higher or lower prices?
31. How do customers psychologically interpret the price level?
32. Does the organization use temporary price promotions and, if so, how effective are they?

C. *Distribution*
33. Are there alternative methods of distributing the product that would result in more service or less cost?
34. Does the organization render adequate service, along with the product, to its customers?

D. *Personal Selling*
35. Is the sales force large enough to accomplish the organization's objectives?

36. Is the sales force organized along the best lines of specialization (territory, market, product)?
37. Does the sales force show high morale, ability, and effectiveness? Are they sufficiently trained and incentivized?
38. Are the procedures adequate for setting quotas and evaluating performance?

E. *Advertising*

39. Does the organization adequately state its advertising objectives?
40. Does the organization spend the right amount on advertising?
41. Are the themes and copy effective?
42. Are the media well chosen?

F. *Publicity*

43. Does the organization have a carefully formulated program of publicity?

G. *Sales Promotion*

44. Are sales promotions used by the organization and, if so, are they well conceived?[14]

Marketing audits are not designed solely for firms that are having difficulty meeting their marketing objectives. All companies utilize the audit system to uncover potential weaknesses and identify cost-cutting opportunities.

A typical marketing audit begins with an examination of the external environment. The major target markets currently being served are scrutinized for growth trends and changing characteristics. Competitive challenges and expected responses to the firm's strategy are forecast. Uncontrollable elements of the marketing environment (see Ch. 2) are analyzed to determine their impact on the marketing mix.

Internally, marketing objectives are reviewed and updated. Marketing plans and programs are studied in order to see how effectively they are reaching objectives. The degree of management participation in planning and implementing new programs is also examined. The final stage of the marketing audit is a thorough review of each element of the marketing mix.

Corrective Action

The marketing audit and market share and cost analysis are useless if corrective action is not taken. Ideally, remedial steps should be taken immediately after the source of the problem has been identified. Rapid action can often help prevent costly mistakes.

Quick reaction time implies that control information is funneled to the proper decision maker. If, for example, the promotional mix needs to be modified, this information should not flow upward through four or five layers of management. Instead, the data should go directly to the person with the authority to take the needed action. Good control mechanisms can lose their effectiveness without timely reporting and action.

SUMMARY

The objective of planning is to help marketing managers make better decisions. Plans can be divided into two categories: strategic and tactical. Strategic planning is long run in nature while tactical planning is concerned with short-run objectives. Planning begins with an exploratory analysis of the total environment. Objectives and goals are then established; from these, planning premises are derived. Alternative courses of action are developed; each alternative is evaluated, and one is selected.

After a course of action has been chosen, derivative plans are established. Resources are then allocated and the plan is implemented. The process continues with evaluation and control. Budgeting makes the entire planning process meaningful. Without budgeting, planning is an empty exercise.

Strategic planning is not always easy. It can be risky for a marketing manager to take a controversial stand. Controversy typically exists because of the complexity of the issues involved. Often managers are promoted before they see the consequences of their plans. These managers are not held accountable for their actions.

Strategic planning involves three factors: the nature of the market, the product mix, and top management's goals and philosophies.

Commensurate with strategic planning is problem solving. Problem solving requires identification of the central problem, development of alternatives, establishment of criteria, evaluation of alternatives, and making the decision.

Planning and problem solving occur within one of several organizational structures: product, functional, geographic, or matrix. The matrix organization represents a departure from traditional structures. Rather than being arranged according to strict vertical authority and responsibility relationships, line and staff functions are commingled. Resource usage is controlled and directed by two opposing sets of managers. Matrix structures are common in product management.

Control provides the means for correcting actions that are not efficient in reaching objectives. Control consists of compelling events to conform to plans. The control process requires developing standards, measuring performance, doing causal analysis to determine why deviations occurred, and then taking corrective action. Causal analysis often takes the form of cost control and cost analysis. Other techniques of causal analysis include market share examination and nonfinancial tools such as complaint reports. The market audit is perhaps the broadest control device available to marketing managers. It is designed to gauge overall marketing effectiveness.

The marketing organization does not dominate the corporation. In fact marketing must interact effectively with production, finance, and other departments. If marketing controlled the organization, many problems might arise. Conversely, domination by any other department may lead to lack of consumer orientation.

KEY TERMS

Strategic planning
Tactical planning
Budgeting
Profit Impact of Market Strategy (PIMS)
Matrix organization

Control system
Cost analysis
Market share analysis
Marketing audit

QUESTIONS FOR DISCUSSION

1. What is strategic planning? Why is it so vital for marketing management?
2. Explain the different steps in the strategic-planning process.
3. What factors influence the strategic-planning process? Discuss the role of top management in preparing strategic plans.
4. Define tactical planning and differentiate it from strategic planning. Give examples to illustrate the difference.
5. Explain the matrix form of organization as used by marketing management. What benefits are derived from this organizational structure?
6. What is a marketing audit? Explain the purpose and scope of such an audit.
7. Outline some of the techniques used for maintaining marketing control.
8. What role does the marketing information system play in strategic planning?
9. What is meant by problem solving? What basic steps should be followed to successfully solve a problem?
10. The average age of Americans is gradually rising. How could this affect the marketing strategy of an insurance company? a health products company?

NOTES

1. George Terry, *Principles of Management*, 6th ed. (Homewood, Ill.: Irwin, 1972), p. 276.
2. "Dial's Clean Sweep," *Sales and Marketing Management*, March 14, 1977, p. 12.
3. "Strategic Planner Needs Profound Knowledge of Market Maze: Abington," *Marketing News*, April 22, 1977, p. 9. Reprinted by permission of the American Marketing Association.
4. This procedure is taken from Robert Trewatha and Gene Newport, *Management—Functions and Behavior* (Dallas: Business Publications, 1976), p. 117.
5. Much of this section is from Louis Gerstner, Jr., "The Practice of Business," *Business Horizons*, 15 (December 1972): 5–16.
6. "Attention to Planning Reveals Extent of Company's Seriousness; Control Assets," *Marketing News*, May 20, 1977, p. 12; see also Michael Etzel and John Ivancevich, "Management by Objectives in Marketing: Philosophy, Process, and Problems," *Journal of Marketing*, 38 (October 1974): 47–55; William King and David Cleland, "Environmental Information Systems for Strategic Marketing Planning," *Journal of Marketing*, 38 (October 1974): 35–40; James Hulbert and Norman Toy, "A Strategic Framework for Marketing Control," *Journal of Marketing*, 41 (April 1977):

12–20; John Hobbs and Donald Heany, "Coupling Strategy to Operating Plans," *Harvard Business Review*, May-June 1977, pp. 119–126; Robert Linneman and John Kennell, "Shirt Sleeve Approach to Long-Range Plans," *Harvard Business Review*, March-April 1977, pp. 141–151; and Peter Lorange and Richard Vancil, "How to Design a Strategic Planning System," *Harvard Business Review*, September-October 1976, pp. 75–81.

7. "Attention to Planning . . . ," p. 12. Reprinted by permission of the American Marketing Association.

8. This section is taken from David Cravens, Gerald Hills, and Robert Woodruff, *Marketing Decision Making: Concepts and Strategy* (Homewood, Ill.: Irwin, 1976), pp. 326–331.

9. "Schoeffler–Cope Team Tells How PIMS Academic–Business Search for Basic Principles Can Get Line Managers into Strategic Planning," *Marketing News*, July 16, 1976, p. 6.

10. Ibid. Reprinted by permission of the American Marketing Association.

11. This section is adapted from William O'Dell, Andrew Ruppel, and Robert Trent, *Marketing Decision Making: Analytical Framework and Cases* (Cincinnati: Southwestern, 1976), pp. 5–145.

12. Some interesting articles on interdepartmental conflict are "Marketing: A Critical Task for the Accountant," *CPA*, April 1975, pp. 72–73; Heinz Jaffe, "Involve Engineers in Marketing Plans: Their Aid Can Boost Profit Potential," *Industrial Marketing*, August 1975, p. 53; and Joseph Meyers, "Placing Engineering Under Marketing's Control," *Management Review*, December 1972, pp. 16–21.

13. *Information for Marketing Management* (New York: National Association of Accountants, 1971), pp. 21–22.

14. Phillip Kotler, *Marketing Management Analysis Planning and Control*, 3d ed. (Englewood Cliffs, N.J.: Prentice-Hall, 1976), pp. 450–451. By permission.

CASE 24
Savin Business Machines

Savin Corporation, headquartered in New York State, has been quite successful in the copying market in recent years. For example, its 1976 sales in this market were $122 million. Savin is a highly marketing-oriented organization. Gabriel Carlin, its marketing chief, says, "We put all of our resources into marketing. We design products that customers need in the future and let others manufacture the product."

Savin has been somewhat of a maverick, using product technology, sales strategies, and pricing policies that depart from the rules of the game in the plain-paper copier field. For years Xerox has set the pace with a powdered-toner technique as the basis for plain-paper copying. Savin, after five years of research, brought to market an innovative machine using a liquid-toner transfer method. This gave it several manufacturing and servicing pluses that the firm is trying to convert into marketing advantages. For example, manufacturing costs are low, thus enabling the firm to sell the Savin 750 model at less than half the price of comparable Xerox equipment. The process also gives the machine a degree of reliability unmatched by competitive units.

Savin is now trying to develop its marketing tactics for the new 750. According to Carlin, the copying market is changing rapidly. The trend is toward buying relatively inexpensive, slow, convenience machines in order to decentralize copying operations. To avoid long queues at a central location, these smaller units are located on different floors for quicker access. Questions that Carlin is facing right now include the following:

1. Should Savin use a direct selling strategy, like Xerox, or a dealer network? Savin wants to move fast, and developing its own major sales force could lead to problems of hiring, staffing, and training. Currently it has twenty-six marketing people directly involved with the dealers; they account for a total of about $7 million worth of business a month. There are also some sales and marketing people in their own branch operations; they average about $3 or $4 million worth of business a month.
2. Should it sell the machines or lease them? If the firm uses a dealer organization, it may have difficulty getting dealers to purchase for resale a machine three to four times as expensive as the coated-paper units they have been handling until now. Few dealers could afford the negative cash flow that can result from renting machines.
3. If Savin uses its own sales force, the company is considering changing the compensation of salespeople from a salary-plus-commission structure to one that is entirely commissions. Carlin realizes that this will in-increase the turnover rate because unproductive salespeople will drop out. Yet if the 770 is as good a machine as Savin hopes it will be, selling should not be difficult.
4. A possible by-product of success that Carlin foresees is a steadily expanding customer base and, as a result, new service problems. Savin is concerned about its service response program and the possibility of de-

veloping improved training curricula. It is also considering installing a computer-based information system that will contain the service record for each machine in the field. However, like everything else, this will be an expensive addition.

5. Savin is engaged in a dispute with its Japanese partner, Ricoh, which manufactures the Savin 770. Under the terms of their agreement Ricoh is to pay Savin a royalty on each machine it sells. In late 1975 Ricoh stopped making payments on the machines it sells in the Far East. One scenario depicts Ricoh terminating production so that it can take over the U.S. market for itself. Savin's president discounts this, however, saying, "They do not intend to stop shipping to us." Savin can cut its Ricoh tie over the next few years. However, industry sources doubt that it can find a match for Ricoh's low cost.

6. If Savin is successful and erodes Xerox's market share, how will the industry leader respond? Savin has considered its target market to be primarily a replacement market. Hence, it has gone after prospects that already had copiers, particularly the Xerox 3100. Savin's advertising consistently boasts that half of its replacements knock out Xerox machines.

You have been hired as a marketing consultant for Savin. Your job is to evaluate the marketing environment and advise management on long-range planning.

1. Advise Gabriel Carlin on a new long-range strategy for the Savin Corporation.
2. Develop a tactical strategy for marketing the Savin 770.

25

Consumerism and Marketing's Social Responsibility

OBJECTIVES

■ To understand the meaning of consumerism.
■ To present a brief overview of the consumerist movement.
■ To examine the response of business to consumerism.
■ To understand the nature of social responsibility.
■ To become aware of different ways in which marketing meets its social responsibilities.

Florence Skelly, vice president of Yankelovich, Skelly and White, one of America's leading social-research organizations, says, "The public's current generalized suspicion of and hostility toward business as an institution is an important element in the consumerist movement."[1] Her company has determined that the public feels that business places too much emphasis on self-interest and on profits. More than half of the American people (including educated and sophisticated consumers) believe that they cannot identify or deal with false or misleading advertising and that they cannot judge by themselves the quality, value, or adequacy of many products.[2]

The mistrust of business in the 1970s generates the support for the consumerism movement. Skelly's research has also revealed widespread public support for protective regulatory action, even when consumers know that they will ultimately pay for it.

WHAT IS CONSUMERISM?

Phillip Kotler views consumerism as a struggle for the balance of power between buyers and sellers. He defines it as a social movement seeking to augment the rights and power of buyers in relation to sellers. The rights and power of both groups are presented in the following list:

- Sellers have the right to introduce any product in any size and style they wish into the marketplace so long as it is not hazardous to personal health or safety; or, if it is, to introduce it with the proper warnings and controls.
- Sellers have the right to price the product at any level they wish provided there is no discrimination among similar classes of buyers.
- Sellers have the right to spend any amount of money they wish to promote the product, so long as it is not defined as unfair competition.
- Sellers have the right to formulate any message they wish about the product provided that it is not misleading or dishonest in content or execution.
- Sellers have the right to introduce any buying incentive schemes they wish.
- Buyers have the right not to buy a product that is offered to them.
- Buyers have the right to expect the product to be safe.
- Buyers have the right to expect the product to turn out to be essentially as represented by the seller.

Additional Rights Consumers Want
- Buyers want the right to have adequate information about the product.
- Buyers want the right to additional protections against questionable products and marketing practices.
- Buyers want the right to influence products and marketing practices in directions that will increase the "quality of life."[3]

Kotler feels that consumers are not getting enough when full product information is lacking and when the public can be highly influenced by Madison Avenue. Thus the balance of power lies with the seller, not the buyer. The balance has been restored in part through restrictive legislation on business activities.

Although consumerism can be viewed as a struggle for power, the specific issues are not always so clear. In fact the relevant consumerist issues vary according to the group that describes them. One study revealed that businesspeople view consumerism as primarily an informational problem.[4] (See Table 25.1.) That is, it's a matter of

TABLE 25.1	What Are the Relevant Consumerist Issues?		
Issues	Students (N = 241)	Nonemployed Women (N = 55)	Businesspeople (N = 71)
Information (such as more informative advertising, clearly written warranties, etc.)	82.2%	89.1%	95.8%
Health and safety (such as testing and evaluation of drugs, stronger auto bumpers, etc.)	80.1	92.7	83.1
Repair and servicing (such as improved servicing of appliances and automobiles)	70.1	85.5	71.8
Pricing issues (such as the high price of food, insurance, hospital care)	59.3	81.8	63.4
Pollution in the environment (such as dirty air, water, excessive billboards)	61.8	47.3	36.6
Market concentration (such as lack of competition in the marketplace)	26.1	45.5	42.3
Product quality (such as frequent obsolescence, product breakdowns)	72.2	89.1	78.9
Consumer representation in government (such as a lack of consumer representation in government agencies)	58.5	69.1	52.1

Source: Norman Kangun, Keith Cox, James Higginbotham, and John Burton, "Consumerism and Marketing Management," *Journal of Marketing,* 39 (April 1975): 5. Reprinted by permission of the American Marketing Association.

getting factual and timely warranties and advertising to the consumer. Nonemployed women believe that health and safety factors are the most important issues. Students tend to agree with businesspeople regarding the importance of good information. However, the student group is almost twice as likely to mention pollution as a consumerist issue.

THE HISTORY OF CONSUMERISM
The Early Years

Contrary to popular opinion, consumerism is not new. The first consumer protection law was passed in 1872; it made it a federal crime to defraud consumers through the mails.[5] Other piecemeal laws passed before 1900 prohibited the sale of unwholesome tea (1883) and barred the importation of adulterated food and drink (1890). Between 1879 and 1905 more than 100 bills were introduced in Congress to regulate interstate production and sale of foods and drugs.[6] A largely apathetic public (and, therefore, Congress) plus strong business opposition resulted in the failure of those bills.

A General Outcry

Perhaps the first general consumerist outcry came in February 1906 with the publication of Upton Sinclair's *The Jungle,* a devastating exposé of the meatpacking industry in the United States. Consider the following paragraph:

> These rats were nuisances, and the packers would put poisoned bread out for them and they would die, and then rats, bread and meat would go into the hoppers together. . . . Men, who worked in the tank rooms full of steam . . . fell into the vats; and when they were fished out, there was never enough of them to be worth exhibiting — sometimes they would be overlooked for days, till all but the bones of them had gone out to the world as Durham's Pure Leaf Lard![7]

The book helped assure the passage of the Pure Food and Drug Act of 1906. Thus consumer outcry over flagrant abuses by business culminated in significant governmental action.

The Modern Consumerist Movement

World Wars I and II slowed the growth of consumerism. Little consumerist activity occurred until the mid-1950s, when the modern consumer movement began. In *The Hidden Persuaders* Vance Packard charged that advertisers were using motivation research and subliminal advertising (appealing to the subconscious) to manipulate consumers. Similarly, Rachel Carson's *The Silent Spring* described the damage to the environment and the food chain caused by the use of pesticides.

The Kennedy Consumerist Message

The growing outcry from both the public and Congress was heard by President Kennedy, who, in March 1962, sent a message to Congress concerning the increasing problem of serving the consumer interest. The President outlined certain rights that all consumers should have:

1. The right to safety — to be protected against the marketing of goods that are hazardous to health or life.
2. The right to be informed — to be protected against fraudulent, deceitful, or grossly misleading information, advertising, labeling, or other practices, and to be given the facts needed in making an informed choice.

3. The right to choose—to be assured, whenever possible, of access to a variety of products and services at competitive prices; in industries in which competition is not workable and governmental regulation is substituted, to be assured of satisfactory quality and service at fair prices.
4. The right to be heard—to be assured that consumer interests will receive full and sympathetic consideration in the formulation of governmental policy and fair and expeditious treatment in its administrative tribunals.

Consumerism Today

Both Congress and the federal regulatory agencies have been quite active in consumer matters in the mid-1970s. The Federal Trade Commission has finally become a major force in the consumer interest after years of criticism for ineffectiveness. The FTC has traditionally been understaffed and lacked the funds to do its job properly.

Twenty-nine major pieces of legislation affecting the consumer were passed between 1958 and 1971. Included in this legislation are the Truth in Packaging Act of 1965, the Truth in Lending Act of 1968, the National Traffic and Motor Vehicle Safety Act of 1966, and other measures dealing with product safety, smoking, environmental quality, child protection, warranties, and restrictions on advertising.

THE FORCES BEHIND THE CONSUMERIST MOVEMENT

There is an overwhelming consensus in the business community that modern consumerism is here to stay.[8] A number of factors gave rise to the growth and permanence of today's consumerism. They include the following:[9]

1. *Structural Conduciveness*
   Advancing incomes and education
   Advancing complexity of technology and marketing
   Advancing exploitation of the environment
   Rising expectations (product performance)
   Psychology of entitlement
2. *Structural Strains*
   Economic discontent (inflation)
   Social discontent (war and race)
   Ecological discontent (pollution)
   Marketing system discontent (shoddy products, gimmickry, dishonesty, poor complaint handling)
   Political discontent (unresponsive politicians and institutions)
   Impersonal nature of the marketplace

3. *Growth of a Generalized Belief*
   Social-critic writings (Galbraith, Packard, Carson)
   Consumer-oriented legislators (Kefauver, Douglas)
   Presidential messages
   Consumer organizations
4. *Precipitating Factors*
   Professional agitation (Nader)
   Spontaneous agitation (homemaker picketing)
5. *Mobilization for Action*
   Mass media coverage
   Vote-seeking politicians
   New consumer interest groups and organizations

The foremost of these factors was the underlying structure of our system. Higher incomes and education levels have resulted in rising expectations with regard to the quality of life. In less developed countries many people are more concerned with the source of their next meal than with the quality of their food. Education has instilled higher-order values in the American public. Americans are more interested in normative values — how things ought to be. The rising complexity of technology further complicates our life and consumption patterns, often in direct contrast with the view of a peaceful "good life."

Americans have also developed a psychology of entitlement.[10] This may be attributed partly to our ever-increasing affluence. A person who once said, "I would like to be sure of a secure job and quality products" now says, "I have a right to a secure job and quality products." In essence, the public has raised its standards and changed its psychology. The slogan of the past, "Let the buyer beware," is now, "Let the seller beware."

Thus a foundation has been laid that nurtures the long-run growth of consumerism. Many structural stresses have developed that demonstrate the system's faults and inequities. Inflation, pollution, racial strife, and the impersonal nature of the marketplace all foster general discontent. Most important is marketing itself. Poor-quality products, unsafe merchandise, misleading advertising, advertising that is in poor taste, price inequities, and planned product obsolescence fuel the fires of consumerism.

Ralph Nader's Center for Study of Responsive Law conducted 2419 interviews with consumers throughout the United States on the subject of purchase problems. Here's a sample of the responses:

Battery operated toys use the batteries up too fast.

The doll's hair fell out four days after Christmas.

I bought a hearing aid for $350. They told me it was new. Then I found out it was second-hand.

They cut the legs off my new sofa when they came to deliver it. They should have measured the front door better.

The turntable cover is too flimsy. It should be stronger, or it should have instructions that you have to handle it very gently.

Radial tires were expensive, and then when they wore out within the 40,000 mile guarantee time, the company didn't honor the promise.

Vacuum cleaner has poor suction, can't fit under appliances, its handle slips.

[Car] seats are uncomfortable, light switch is hard to use, battery wore out after six months, thin paint, springs are starting to poke through the seats.

Bought outside antenna for TV set. The display in the store isn't like the real unit. They installed it sloppily. Might be a fire hazard.

Leather buttons on fur coat fell off, then it split down the back.

Training wheels [on bicycle] broke after four weeks.

Doctor took X-rays in his office and said I was all right. Then he called me up and told me to go to the hospital for more X-rays. I went, but I never found out if anything is wrong.

Brought an iron home after the cord was replaced. When I plugged it in, the lights blew out. The repair shop said that if they looked at it again, they would charge me again.

Painters were sloppy. They spilled paint on the rug.[11]

Many consumers don't bother to complain even when they perceive a problem. It is estimated that only about one-third of the problems are reported.[12] The importance of this statistic can be appreciated when one realizes that the Better Business Bureau alone processed a half-million complaints in 1975.[13] Seventy percent involved service or repair problems.

THE RESPONSE OF BUSINESS TO CONSUMERISM

The response of the business community to consumerism in the early 1970s has not been overwhelming. One study found that 63 percent of the industrial firms polled indicated that they had not been affected by consumerism.[14] Approximately half of the consumer goods companies claimed that consumerism had affected them. A detailed examination of the responses of both groups is presented in Table 25.2. Many companies take an "it's nothing new" approach. They state that they have always been "consumer oriented." Often it seems that this is nothing more than an excuse for lack of action. As Table 25.3 shows, not all firms have been insensitive to consumerism.

TABLE 25.2	The Business Community's Response to Consumerism		
		No. of Companies	Percentage
A. Total Survey Replies			
Industrial products (48)			
Have responded to consumerism		18	11.5
Have not been influenced		30	19.1
Consumer goods (109)			
Have responded to consumerism		57	36.3
Have not been influenced		35	22.3
Are concerned but have not acted		3	1.9
Are not concerned		2	1.3
Other replies (e.g., policy statements)		12	7.6
B. Type of Response			
Improved customer service policies and programs		30	19.2
Created new organization position to deal with consumer affairs		29	18.6
Modified products to make them safer and easier to use and repair		23	14.7
Subjected advertising to more careful review, developed new advertising guidelines, and made advertising more informative		19	12.2
Made labeling and packaging more informative		11	7.1
Have used advertising "to tell our side of the story"		8	5.1
Incorporated ecological appeals in ads or changed them in related ways		5	3.2
Changed packaging to make it recyclable or easier to use		5	3.2
Joined consumer organization		5	3.2

Source: Frederick Webster, Jr., "Does Business Misunderstand Consumerism?" *Harvard Business Review,* September-October 1973, p. 91. Copyright © 1973 by the President and Fellows of Harvard College; all rights reserved.

SOCIAL RESPONSIBILITY
The Nature of Social Responsibility

So far our discussion has centered on the nature of consumerism. From the corporate viewpoint consumerism is simply one dimension of social responsibility. Social responsibility, like love, means different things to different people. Generally, it refers to corporate concern for social welfare. The problem comes in establishing the parameters of social welfare.

Ernst and Ernst, the large national accounting firm, reports that 346 of *Fortune*'s top 500 corporations made social-measurement disclosures in 1974. This represented a 45-percent increase since 1971. The most frequent area of disclosure was environmental control, with 447 references.[15] (See Table 25.3.) In some cases multiple references

TABLE 25.3	Dimensions of Social Responsibility Based on Frequency of Corporate Reporting–*Fortune* 500	
Topic		**Frequency**
Environmental control		447
Equal opportunity		421
Community involvement		321
Personnel (health and safety)		206
Products		70
Miscellaneous		46

Source: William Shanklin, "Corporate Social Responsibility: Another View," *Journal of Business Research,* 4 (February 1976): 76.

were made. Marketing is simply one facet of a corporation's social responsibility.

The question may arise, Is social responsibility an ethical issue for the individual businessperson or is it an issue that concerns the role the corporation should play in society? A *Harvard Business Review* study of 1227 business executives found that they think it is both.[16] Responsibility for both the individual and the corporation tends to be defined in terms of the social arrangements and obligations that make up the structure of our society (for example, a pledge to hire the hard-core unemployed). Ethics concerns the rules by which those responsibilities are carried out. Hiring hard-core unemployed for jobs that management plans to abolish in the near future would be poor ethics. Thus it is extremely hard to separate the rules of the game from the game itself.

Social Responsibility and Power

Keith Davis, a well-known management scholar, claims that social responsibility arises from social power.[17] He feels that the business community has immense social power. Business' social responsibility therefore arises from concern about how its actions will affect society. Davis feels that business is obligated to take actions that protect and enhance society's interests.

If, in the long run, business does not use social power in a manner that society considers responsible, it will lose that power. In other words, governmental regulation will supplant private enterprise. For example, the charging of excessive interest rates led to truth-in-lending legislation.

The Role of Government

The multitude of laws and regulations issued by various levels of government have reduced the degree of voluntary social responsibility on the part of business. For example, laws on nonreturnable containers have eliminated such containers in some states. The issue is

TABLE 25.4	Business, Government, and Consumer Responsibilities for Consumer Protection		
Consumer Protection Area	Group Assigned Primary Responsibility for Each Consumer Protection Area[a]		
	Business	Government	Consumers
Providing adequate information to assist consumers in making purchase decisions	90%	6%	6%
Protecting consumers from abuses (e.g., fraud and deceit)	32	58	13
Protecting consumers from their own buying mistakes (e.g., a cooling-off period on door-to-door sales)	27	33	43
Protecting consumers from their own views of appropriate buying priorities	11	7	83

Source: Stephen Greyser and Steven Diamond, "Business Is Adapting to Consumerism," *Harvard Business Review,* September-October 1974, p. 54. Copyright © 1974 by the President and Fellows of Harvard College; all rights reserved.

[a] Data sum to more than 100% across because of tie first-place votes.

no longer subject to decisions by the bottlers. The growth of institutionalization via government decree is a major reason why executive interest in the issue may be waning.[18] Efforts to demonstrate or "showcase" social accountability have abated since the early 1970s. Instead, the prevalent attitude is, "Let's get on with it" in a no-nonsense fashion.

What should be the government's role in the consumerism phase of social responsibility? The *Harvard Business Review* survey discussed earlier suggests that the main function of government is to protect consumers against fraud, deceit, and the like.[19] (See Table 25.4.) The consumer's responsibility is to be informed and to develop buying priorities. Business' major task, in turn, is to provide accurate decision-making information.

Government protects consumers through a variety of laws and agencies. You will recall, for example, our discussion of the legislation that deals with pricing—and that's only a single variable in the marketing mix! The major governmental bodies that handle consumer complaints are the following:

- States' attorney general's office.
- The Federal Office of Consumer Affairs.
  A catchall agency for complaint referrals.
- The Consumer Product Safety Commission.
  It gives and receives much information on unsafe products.
- The Food & Drug Administration.
  Similar to the CPSC, but for ingestibles.

- The Interstate Commerce Commission.
  It handles household moving and shipping claims.
- While the Civil Aeronautics Board is supposed to handle air travel complaints, it simply refers them to the offending airline.[20]

As you can see, there is no shortage of sympathetic ears. Of course the costs of protection are eventually passed on to the consumer in the forms of higher prices and taxes.[21] Also, not all regulations and decrees seem to be based on intelligent decision making.[22] Witness the public reaction to the proposed ban of saccharin. A person must consume approximately 800 diet soft drinks a day to take in an amount of saccharin equivalent to the dose at which some rats develop bladder cancer. (See Figure 25.1.)

| FIGURE 25.1 | An Example of Over-Zealous Consumer Protection: A Person Would Have To Drink 1250 Cans of Diet Pepsi a Day To Ingest the Dose of Saccharin That Is Considered Carcinogenic *in Rats* |

Source: Marketing News, April 8, 1977, p. 2. By permission of the American Marketing Association and PepsiCo, Inc.

TABLE 25.5	Companies Responding Effectively to Consumer Pressures	
Company		**Percent of Respondents Mentioning Company**
American Motors		21.5%
Sears, Roebuck		13.0
Ford		12.9
General Motors		7.6
AT&T		6.4
General Electric		5.2
Whirlpool		4.1
IBM		2.4
Procter & Gamble		2.4
J. C. Penney		2.2
Zenith		1.9
Volkswagen		1.8
Xerox		1.8
Exxon		1.7
Maytag		1.7

Source: Stephen Greyser and Steven Diamond, "Business Is Adapting to Consumerism," *Harvard Business Review*, September-October 1974, p. 56. Copyright © 1974 by the President and Fellows of Harvard College; all rights reserved.

Socially Responsible Businesses

Many companies are taking the initiative in marketing social responsibility rather than waiting for governmental actions. Referring once more to the *Harvard Business Review* study, Table 25.5 indicates which firms are perceived to be doing the best job in responding to consumerism. These examples only scratch the surface, however. Many other firms provide a variety of social-marketing services, often with little fanfare.

ORGANIZING FOR SOCIAL RESPONSIBILITY

An effective long-range response to society's demand for social responsibility on the part of large corporations requires both planning and organization. One of the first steps to be taken is the development of social-responsibility policies. The following are a few examples:

Change corporate practices that are perceived as deceptive. The consumer affairs division should identify corporate practices that are perceived as deceptive and/or antagonistic by consumers. These practices should be reviewed and a viable resolution of the problem developed. Examples of such corporate practices include packaging, credit, advertising, warranties, and the like.

Educate channel members to the need for a consumerism effort throughout the channel system. Recognition of the need for a consumerism effort by all members of the channel will aid in the development of an industry consumerism program which will enhance performance of the channel system and provide better customer satisfaction. Moreover, a firm must be willing to eliminate an organization from its overall channel system if that organization is unwilling or unable to work within the constraints of corporate policy.

Incorporate the increased costs of consumerism efforts into the corporate operating budget. Unless the consumer affairs division is budgeted sufficient money to carry out its mission, it will be little more than a facade and its effectiveness will be hampered. These costs will be reflected either in higher prices or lower margins unless the consumer program affects sales sufficiently to lower costs commensurately. To date little or no research exists to document the market responses to such programs. However, it does seem apparent that substantial costs will be incurred by firms not meeting their responsibilities to the consumer because of both governmental and legal actions.[23]

Perhaps these guidelines may seem too ambitious for many firms. Yet consumerism is here to stay. In order to avoid further governmental regulation and legislation, companies must effectively respond to ever-increasing societal demands. The proper response necessitates strong, imaginative policies and planning.

SUMMARY

Consumerism is essentially a struggle for power between buyers and sellers. However, the specific issues involved are not always clear.

Consumerism is not new. The first consumer laws were passed in 1872. Modern consumerism is generally considered to have begun after World War II. President Kennedy's message on the rights of consumers (the right to safety, the right to be informed, the right to choose, and the right to be heard) provide the foundation for today's consumerism. The Federal Trade Commission is a major force overseeing the interests of all consumers.

The business community's response to consumerism has not been overwhelming. Most industrial-goods firms, in fact, claim that they have not been affected at all by consumerism. Only half of the consumer goods companies claim that consumerism affected their organization.

Part of the lack of response to consumerism is due to failure to understand the nature and scope of social responsibility. Although social responsibility seems to be the norm in most of America's largest corporations today, it still lacks acceptance by intermediate-sized and smaller firms. As with consumerism, the issues involved in social responsibility are somewhat clouded. Philosophically, social responsibility arises from social power. The business community has extensive social power and must therefore exercise it in a responsible fashion or be subject to further governmental regulation.

Meeting social responsibilities requires both planning and organization. Firms must change practices that are perceived as deceptive, help educate channel members in the importance of social responsibility, and incorporate the cost of such efforts into the firm's operating budget.

KEY TERMS

Consumerism   Social responsibility
Informational problem   Social power
Psychology of entitlement

**QUESTIONS
FOR DISCUSSION**

1. Do you agree with Kolter's view of consumerism? Why or why not?
2. What are your views on the statement, "Businesspeople view consumerism as primarily an informational problem."
3. Do you agree with the consumer rights advocated by President Kennedy? Do you feel that they should be extended?
4. Advertising and marketing research are coming under increasing attack from consumer advocates. What steps should marketing managers take with regard to this problem?
5. Do you think corporations have the right or the responsibility to get involved in social-welfare activities? Why?
6. A number of social-responsibility policies were put forward in this chapter. Can you think of others that could help marketing management become more socially responsible?
7. The Lockheed scandal brought out a different type of ethical problem. According to the company, payoffs to agents are acceptable in international sales transactions. If you were the international marketing manager, would you still pursue the sale? Why or why not?

NOTES

1. Florence Skelly, "Measuring Public Policy Pressures on Marketers," speech before the San Francisco Chapter of the American Marketing Association, March 11, 1976.
2. Ibid.
3. Phillip Kotler, "What Consumerism Means for Marketers," *Harvard Business Review*, May-June 1972, pp. 48–49. Copyright © 1972 by the President and Fellows of Harvard College; all rights reserved.
4. Norman Kangun, Keith Cox, James Higginbothom, and John Burton, "Consumerism and Marketing Management," *Journal of Marketing*, 39 (April 1975): 3–10.
5. Ralph Gaedeke, "The Muckraking Era," in Ralph Gaedeke and Warren Etcheson, eds., *Consumerism: Viewpoints from Business, Government, and the Public Interest*, [San Francisco: Harper & Row (Canfield Press), 1972], pp. 57–59.
6. Ibid.
7. Robert Herrmann, "The Consumer Movement in Historical Perspective," in David Aaker and George Day, eds., *Consumerism: Search for the Consumer Interest*, 2d ed. (New York: Free Press, 1974), pp. 10–18; the original passage is from Upton Sinclair, *The Jungle* (Garden City, N.Y.: Doubleday, 1906).

8. Stephen Greyser and Steven Diamond, "Business Is Adapting to Consumerism," *Harvard Business Review,* September-October 1974, pp. 38–58.
9. Adapted from Kotler, p. 51.
10. Arthur White, "Changing Rules of the Game in the American Marketplace," *Public Relations,* October 1972, pp. 6–8.
11. Arthur Best and Alan Andreasen, *Talking Back to Business: Voiced and Unvoiced Consumer Complaints* (New York: Center for the Study of Responsive Law, 1976), p. 19.
12. Ibid., p. 39.
13. "Marketing Briefs," *Marketing News,* March 26, 1976, p. 3.
14. Frederick Webster, Jr., "Does Business Misunderstand Consumerism?" *Harvard Business Review,* September-October 1973, pp. 89–97.
15. William Shanklin, "Corporate Social Responsibility: Another View," *Journal of Business Research,* 4 (February 1976): 76.
16. Steven Brenner and Earl Molandes, "Is the Ethics of Business Changing?" *Harvard Business Review,* January-February 1977, pp. 57–71; see also Kenneth Roering, Robert Schooler, and Fred Morgan, "An Evaluation of Marketing Practices: Businessmen, Housewives and Students," *Journal of Business Research,* 4 (May 1976): 131–144, and James Patterson, "What Are the Social and Ethical Responsibilities of Marketing Executives?" *Journal of Marketing,* 30 (July 1966): 12–15.
17. Keith Davis, "Five Propositions for Social Responsibility," *Business Horizons,* June 1975, pp. 19–24.
18. Shanklin, p. 75.
19. Greyser and Diamond, p. 54.
20. "No Shortage of Sympathetic Ears," *Business Week,* October 11, 1976, p. 114. Reprinted by special permission. All rights reserved.
21. See Paul Busch, "A Review and Critical Evaluation of the Consumer Product Safety Commission: Marketing Management Implications," *Journal of Marketing,* 40 (October 1976): 41–49; William Cunningham and Isabella Cunningham, "Consumer Protection: More Information or More Regulation?" *Journal of Marketing,* 40 (April 1976): 63–68; Gilbert Burck, "High-Pressure Consumerism at the Salesman's Door," *Fortune,* July 1972, pp. 70f.; "A New FTC Rule Irks the Banks," *Business Week,* May 24, 1976, p. 35; Thomas Shepard, Jr., "We're Going Too Far on Consumerism," *Readers Digest,* February 1971, pp. 147–150.
22. Orville Waler, Jr., Richard Sauter, and Neil Ford, "The Potential Secondary Effects of Consumer Legislation," *Journal of Consumer Affairs,* 8 (Winter 1974): 144–155.
23. Richard Buskirk and James Rothe, "Consumerism—An Interpretation," in Gaedeke and Etcheson, p. 88. Reprinted by permission of the American Marketing Association.

CASE 25
East–West Manufacturing

East–West Manufacturing, one of the largest corporations in the United States, is a major manufacturer of consumer appliances as well as electrical engines, power plants, aircraft engines, and virtually any other product that makes or uses electricity. Hoping to capitalize on the ecology movement, it has come up with a new line called "homecology products." These items include an electric can opener for cleaner food (according to its ad) and an electric water conditioner for cleaner water. One new product that East–West touts is a small new electric washer/dryer combination that cleans clothes using less detergent.

Environmentalists have jumped on East–West with both feet. They say that its advertising comes suspiciously close to making the same old sales pitches in an ecologically fashionable vocabulary. The critics feel that such advertising is especially ironic when it comes from companies whose products or manufacturing facilities increase the demand for electric power (the production of which is a major, if indirect, source of pollution) or whose products wind up as substantial quantities of solid waste.

A few of the critics say that such promotion is blatantly false; others just say it is subtly deceptive. The cost of such advertising, they say, in some cases may far exceed the amount of money the companies are spending to directly reduce pollution or other environmental damage caused by their products and production facilities.

East–West defends its brand-new advertising campaign on the ground that the products advertised "create a better home environment." Also, the company says that its new washer unit uses 150 watts of electricity—less than a conventional washer. In response to the observation that the three new electrical products in the campaign use a total of 185 watts, or 35 watts more than the washer saves, an East–West spokesman says, "That's nitpicking."

Ann Boswell, vice president for consumer affairs at East–West, is concerned about the adverse publicity that the new advertising campaign has generated. The president of East–West shares her concern. Yesterday he sent a memo to Boswell asking for a new policy whose goal is to make certain that this does not happen again. He also asked for a general procedure that would enable the company to take the initiative in matters related to consumerism rather than simply reacting to critics. He has asked Boswell to prepare a strategy that aggressively promotes East–West's good deeds and avoids mention of any negative actions by the company.

1. Prepare Ann Boswell's memo to the president.
2. How would you respond to the critics of East–West's new campaign? Is it reasonable for East–West to assume that there is a market for ecology-related products? If so, how should that market be approached? Part of Boswell's plan is to develop a consumer affairs audit for the company. What should be included in a consumer affairs audit?

26

International Marketing

OBJECTIVES

■ To understand the worldwide importance of international marketing.
■ To become aware of the impact of multinationals on the world economy.
■ To learn about different ways of entering the international market.
■ To gain insight into the cultural–political environment of international marketing.
■ To understand the basic elements underlying the development of an international marketing mix.
■ To learn about the forms of organization used in international marketing.

In this chapter we will examine the role of marketing in economic development and, perhaps, world peace and understanding. We begin with the nature of economic growth and the maturity of world economies. We then move from the macro view to a micro perspective. The nature and functions of the huge multinational corporations are presented. Techniques for "getting involved" in international marketing are discussed, along with the many considerations that a marketing manager must understand in order to be effective in international marketing. The chapter concludes with an explanation of how a firm can organize for international marketing.

WHY GET INVOLVED? A MACRO PERSPECTIVE

In the broadest sense, international marketing has a lot to offer. Economic advantages can accrue from foreign trade. As people engage in international commerce, it can lead to greater mutual understanding. It can be hoped that this will translate into a modicum of world peace. Perhaps just as important is the role marketing can play in developing nations. Starvation is a strange and distant concept to most of us. Yet it is very real in the world today. If marketing can deliver more food by reducing spoilage, humanity will be better off.

Exchange between countries like Russia and the United States also builds stronger ties between those countries. Interdependence among nations means that they have a stake in each other's future. J. Paul Austin, president of Coca-Cola, says,

> Greater opportunities for free trade mean greater assurance of worldwide freedom. The commitment of international business, or world traders headquartered on all the continents, calls for an open interchange of goods, services, communications, and ideas. Increasingly, this will mean a dynamic force toward world peace.[1]

International marketing is by no means a panacea for the world's problems. Yet if it generates closer cooperation and better understanding among people everywhere it will have performed an invaluable service for all of us.

THE IMPORTANCE OF TRADE TO THE UNITED STATES

U.S. imports, exports, and direct investment in foreign lands are shown in Table 26.1. America is truly a full participant in world trade. Our direct investment abroad, for example, has grown from slightly under $4 billion a year in 1960 to over $30.5 billion in 1974.

Table 26.2 shows where American firms are making their international investments. Note that almost three-quarters of the total invested is going to developed nations.

During the same period U.S. exports grew from $27.4 billion to $142 billion. Even though our exports have exceeded our imports each year, our balance of payments typically reveals a deficit. This is due to military and other expenditures abroad by the federal government.

American exports consist primarily of agricultural products and manufactured goods. The latter include many manufactured goods ready for sale in foreign markets as well as component parts and intermediate products used in manufacturing. Rolls-Royce, for example, admits that the drive train that propels the wheels of the world-famous Rolls is made by Oldsmobile and that its automatic transmission is by Borg-Warner.[2]

TABLE 26.1

U.S. International Transactions, 1960–1974 (In Millions of Dollars)

Type of Transaction	1960	1965	1970	1971	1972	1973	1974	1975
Exports of goods and services	27,595	39,548	62,483	65,614	72,664	102,154	144,773	148,410
Imports of goods and services	23,555	32,443	59,545	65,870	78,618	98,249	141,187	132,141
U.S. private capital flows, net	3,878	3,793	6,920	10,060	8,708	13,998	32,323	27,061

Source: U.S. Department of Commerce, Statistical Abstract of the United States, 1976 (Washington, D.C., 1977), p. 825.

TABLE 26.2   Direct Investments Abroad—Value and Income Receipts, by Country

Country	Private Long-Term Direct Investments (Value at Yearend)				
	1960	1965	1970	1972	Total
All areas	31,865	49,474	78,178	94,337	107,268
Developed countries	19,319	32,313	53,145	64,359	74,084
Canada	11,179	15,319	22,790	25,771	28,055
Europe	6,691	13,985	24,516	30,817	37,218
United Kingdom	3,234	5,123	7,996	9,582	
European Economic Community (EEC)	2,645	6,304	11,774	15,720	31,257
Belgium and Luxembourg	231	596	1,529	2,143	2,514
Denmark and Ireland					847
France	741	1,609	2,590	3,443	4,259
Germany	1,006	2,431	4,597	6,260	7,954
Italy	384	982	1,550	1,989	2,301
Netherlands	283	686	1,508	1,885	2,266
United Kingdom					11,115
Other Western Europe	812	2,557	4,746	5,515	5,962
Japan	254	675	1,483	2,375	2,733
Australia, New Zealand, and South Africa	1,195	2,334	4,356	5,395	6,079
Less-developed countries	11,129	15,177	21,448	25,235	27,867
Latin American Republics	7,481	9,440	12,252	13,667	14,797
Mexico, Panama, and Other Central America	1,542	2,358	3,661	638	653
Argentina	473	992	1,281	1,403	1,407
Brazil	953	1,074	1,847	2,505	3,199
Chile	738	829	748	620	619
Colombia	424	526	698	737	727
Peru	496	565	688	712	793
Venezuela	2,569	2,705	2,704	2,700	2,591
Other	287	391	626	868	893
Other Western Hemisphere	884	1,445	2,508	3,130	3,655
Other Africa	639	1,390	2,614	3,091	2,830
Middle East	1,139	1,536	1,617	1,992	2,682
Other Asia and Pacific	984	1,366	2,457	3,354	3,903
International and unallocated	1,417	1,985	3,586	4,743	5,317

Source: U.S. Department of Commerce, Statistical Abstract of the United States, 1975 (Washington, D.C., 1976), p. 801.

TABLE 26.3   The Fifty Largest Multinationals

Rank	Company	Headquarters	Sales ($000)	Net Income ($000)
1	Exxon	New York	48,630,817	2,640,964
2	General Motors	Detroit	47,181,000	2,902,800
3	Royal Dutch/Shell Group	London/The Hague	36,087,130	2,347,766
4	Ford Motor	Dearborn, Mich.	28,839,600	983,100
5	Texaco	New York	26,451,851	869,731
6	Mobil	New York	26,062,570	942,523
7	National Iranian Oil	Tehran	19,671,064	17,175,182
8	Standard Oil of California	San Francisco	19,434,133	880,127
9	British Petroleum	London	19,103,330	324,615
10	Gulf Oil	Pittsburgh	16,451,000	816,000
11	International Business Machines	Armonk, N. Y.	16,304,333	2,398,093
12	Unilever	London/Rotterdam	15,762,219	517,614
13	General Electric	Fairfield, Conn.	15,697,300	930,600
14	Chrysler	Highland Park, Mich.	15,537,788	422,631
15	International Tel. & Tel.	New York	11,764,106	494,467
16	Standard Oil (Ind.)	Chicago	11,532,048	892,968
17	Philips' Gloeilampenfabrieken	Eindhoven (Netherlands)	11,521,549	212,940
18	ENI	Rome	9,983,105	(37,026)
19	Française des Pétroles	Paris	9,927,775	34,731
20	Renault	Paris	9,352,884	N.A.
21	Hoechst	Frankfurt	9,332,979	188,010
22	Shell Oil	Houston	9,229,950	705,838
23	BASF	Ludwigshafen on Rhine	9,202,592	241,176
24	Petróleos de Venezuela	Caracas	9,083,587	876,153
25	Daimler-Benz	Stuttgart	8,938,321	164,182

THE IMPACT OF MULTINATIONALS

American firms that do a lot of exporting are referred to as multinationals. A multinational corporation is a firm that moves resources, goods, services, and skills across national boundaries. Yet a multinational is more than a business entity. As Neil Jacoby puts it,

> The multinational corporation is, among other things, a private "government," often richer in assets and more populous in stockholders and employees than are some of the nation-states in which it carries on its business. It is simultaneously a "citizen" of several nation-states, owing obedience to their laws and paying them taxes, yet having its own objectives and being responsive to a management located in a foreign nation. Small wonder that some critics see in it an irresponsible instrument of private economic power or of economic "imperialism" by its home

Rank	Company	Headquarters	Sales ($000)	Net Income ($000)
26	U.S. Steel	Pittsburgh	8,604,200	410,300
27	Volkswagenwerk	Wolfsburg (Germany)	8,513,304	399,164
28	Atlantic Richfield	Los Angeles	8,462,524	575,178
29	E.I. du Pont de Nemours	Wilmington, Del.	8,361,000	459,300
30	Bayer	Leverkusen (Germany)	8,297,808	181,364
31	Nippon Steel	Tokyo	8,089,530	38,572
32	Siemens	Munich	8,060,411	221,969
33	Continental Oil	Stamford, Conn.	7,957,620	459,994
34	Thyssen	Duisburg (Germany)	7,947,640	105,499
35	Toyota Motor	Toyota City (Japan)	7,695,997	345,433
36	Nestlé	Vevey (Switzerland)	7,627,869	348,922
37	ELF-Aquitaine	Paris	7,536,225	340,108
38	Imperial Chemical Industries	London	7,465,412	442,328
39	Peugeot-Citroën	Paris	7,346,998	287,426
40	Petrobrás (Petróleo Brasileiro)	Rio de Janeiro	7,252,110	934,579
41	Western Electric	New York	6,930,942	217,383
42	Hitachi	Tokyo	6,680,423	200,337
43	BAT Industries	London	6,668,743	323,541
44	Nissan Motor	Yokohama (Japan)	6,583,517	273,005
45	Procter & Gamble	Cincinnati	6,512,728	401,098
46	Tenneco	Houston	6,389,236	383,500
47	Union Carbide	New York	6,345,700	441,200
48	Westinghouse Electric	Pittsburgh	6,145,152	223,217
49	Mitsubishi Heavy Industries	Tokyo	6,137,230	47,711
50	Saint-Gobain-Pont-à-Mousson	Paris	5,979,469	98,775
	Totals		644,674,819	46,085,128

Source: "The Fifty Largest Industrial Companies in the World," Fortune, August 1977, p. 240.

country. Others view it as an international carrier of advanced management science and technology, an agent for the global transmission of cultures bringing closer the day when a common set of ideals will unite mankind.[3]

The size of the multinationals is mind boggling. Table 26.3 indicates the sales and income of the fifty largest multinationals. To put it in perspective, the sales of Exxon, Royal Dutch/Shell Group, and General Motors were larger than the GNP of all but fourteen nations in the world.[4] Today more than half of the earnings of such well-known American companies as Colgate-Palmolive, Heinz, Hoover, Mobil, National Cash Register, and Exxon come from abroad.[5]

WAYS OF ENTERING THE INTERNATIONAL MARKET

A company does not have to be a huge multinational organization to enter international marketing. There are a wide variety of techniques for penetrating global markets, and a variety of risk levels as well. (See Figure 26.1.) Actually, internationals can be relatively risk free and uncomplicated, yet 95 percent of America's firms do not make an effort to sell their products overseas.[6]

Reluctance to enter the international scene may stem from several factors. First, international operations are usually characterized by greater uncertainty than domestic operations. A second problem is that of obtaining good information in foreign markets. This will be discussed in more detail later in the chapter. Lack of good information, of course, increases the difficulty of decision making.[7] A third factor was initiated by the 1974 price increase in many petroleum-based products. Oil-importing nations were forced to adopt policies

FIGURE 26.1   Methods of Entry and Risk Levels for International Marketing

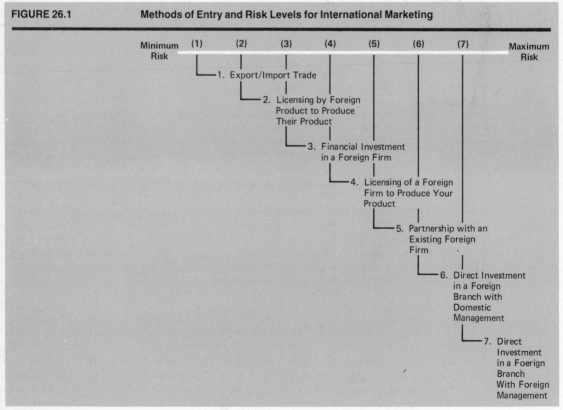

Source: David Kollat, Roger Blackwell, and James Robeson, *Strategic Marketing* (New York: Holt, Rinehart and Winston, 1972), p. 173. Copyright © 1972 by Holt, Rinehart, and Winston, Inc.

aimed at conserving hard currencies. This tended to discourage importation of nonessential consumer products. In Europe, America's biggest customer, lingering uncertainties over unemployment and inflation caused consumers to cut back drastically on unnecessary spending.[8]

Exporting

If, despite such difficulties, a company decides to pursue international opportunities, exporting is usually the least complicated of those opportunities. Sales can be made through individuals or firms located in America that are known as buyers for export. A buyer for export is usually treated as a domestic customer and is served by the domestic sales force. The buyer for export is essentially a middleman who assumes all of the risks and sells internationally for its own account. In essence, the American firm is involved only to the extent that its products are ultimately purchased in foreign markets.

A second form of exporting involves delegating international marketing responsibility to an export representative such as a combination export manager (CEM) located in the United States. The combination export manager identifies market opportunities, handles the international paper work, makes product modification recommendations, and sells the product abroad. Often a CEM serves as an export representative for a number of different companies producing noncompeting goods. It becomes the export department for a manufacturer and works on a commission basis.

Direct exporting is the preferred alternative for the producer that wants to maintain complete control over its export activities and also avoid middleman fees. The producer deals directly with foreign customers by using traveling salespeople or appointing foreign firms as representatives. Sometimes foreign sales offices are established where there is sufficient demand to justify the expenditure. Sometimes a company decides that a foreign sales agent/distributor is the most economical means of obtaining direct international sales. The Department of Commerce has an agent-distributor service that each year helps about 5000 American companies find an agent or distributor in virtually every country in the world.[9]

Licensing

A more aggressive move into the international market without direct manufacturing is licensing. The licensor agrees to let another firm use its manufacturing process, trademark, patents, trade secrets, or other knowledge of a proprietary nature. The licensee agrees, in turn, to pay the licensor a royalty or fee agreed upon by both parties.

Care must be taken by the licensor to make certain that it can exercise the control over the licensee's activities necessary to ensure proper quality levels, pricing structure, adequacy of distribution, and so forth. Licensing may create a new competitor in the long run if the licensee decides to void the license agreement. International law is often ineffective in prohibiting such actions.

One common way of maintaining effective control is to ship one or more critical components from the United States. If the licensee doesn't possess the technology or facilities to produce the parts, control will be maintained. A second control technique is local registration of patents and trademarks by the U.S. firm, not by the licensee. Some companies add a provision in the licensing agreement for renegotiating contracts to cover new products and improvements in technology. International franchising has approximately the same advantages and pitfalls as licensing.

Contract Manufacturing

Firms that do not want to become involved in licensing arrangements may engage in contract manufacturing. This is simply private-label manufacturing by a foreign company. The foreign company produces a certain volume of products to specifications, with the domestic firm's brand name affixed to the goods. Marketing is usually handled by the domestic company.

Contract manufacturing enables the domestic firm to broaden its international market base without direct investment in new plant and equipment. Often foreign manufacturing, particularly in labor-intensive industries, results in significant cost savings. These savings enable the domestic company to compete internationally on a price basis, something that would otherwise be impossible. Using cheap labor enables the firm to sell the product at a lower price. Contract manufacturing may enable a company to build a market position and develop brand loyalty. After a solid base has been established, the domestic firm may switch to direct investment or a joint venture.

Joint Ventures

Joint ventures are quite similar to licensing agreements except that the domestic firm assumes an equity position in a foreign company. Naturally, this is more risky than the other options just discussed. It does, however, give management a voice in company affairs that it might not have under licensing.

The key to a successful joint venture is selecting the right foreign company and then maintaining effective communications. Attitudes toward marketing, production, financial, and growth policies must be clearly delineated. Also, governmental restrictions should be fully explored before the joint venture agreement is made final. A number of countries require that the local firm maintain at least 51-percent ownership in any joint ownership arrangement.

Direct Investment

Direct investment in wholly owned manufacturing and marketing subsidiaries offers the greatest potential rewards. Naturally, the possibility of substantial rewards means greater risk. Firms may make direct investments because no suitable local partner can be found. Others form wholly owned operations in order to maintain complete control.

Countries that lack strong nationalistic policies may offer foreign companies substantial tax concessions and/or make long-term loans at favorable interest rates. Puerto Rico, for example, not only makes significant tax concessions but will also construct the plant when necessary. It then leases the plant to the investor and assists in recruiting local managerial personnel as well as a work force.

On the other hand, direct investment may be discouraged or prohibited in countries like Japan or Chile. Currency devaluations can cost firms millions of dollars. Moreover, the firm may have difficulty repatriating profits. Argentina and Brazil allow a maximum of 12 percent of profits to be remitted to the home country.[10] Multinationals sometimes develop ingenious schemes to extract a much greater level of profits from their foreign operations. Volkswagen sent $100 million back to Germany as payments for its parent's technical advice and expertise over a ten-year period.[11]

The biggest threat to direct investment is expropriation of assets. As nationalistic feelings rise throughout the world, the possibility of expropriation increases. Cartels such as OPEC continue to develop in terms of basic commodities and raw materials. As they grow, these organizations often expropriate assets of the multinationals.

THE CULTURAL–POLITICAL ENVIRONMENT OF INTERNATIONAL MARKETING
Political Considerations

A major reason why firms have their assets expropriated is lack of understanding of the cultural and political environment in which they are operating. Failure to appreciate emerging nationalist feelings can ultimately result in expropriation. Such problems can be avoided by allowing citizens of the host country equity participation in the operation.

Government policies run the gamut from no private ownership or individual freedom to little central government and maximum personal freedom. As the rights of private property increase, government-owned industries and centralized planning tend to decrease. Rarely will a political environment be at one extreme or the other. India, for instance, is a republic, but it has shades of socialism, monopoly capitalism, and competitive capitalism in its political ideology.[12] In countries such as Greece and Spain, individual freedoms are highly restricted but private enterprise is allowed to flourish almost unhindered.

Failure to understand foreign governments and their modes of operation can each lead to marketing failures like this one:

A major pharmaceutical manufacturer a number of years ago developed a process for coating rice with Vitamin A that could withstand cooking. The company believed, with considerable justification, that a serious public health problem endemic to the Far East could be alleviated through this process.

The Philippine government welcomed the process, promising total cooperation, and went to the extent of enacting legislation to compel all rice millers to incorporate the process.

When the rice millers refused en masse to go along with the new government regulation, it was learned that the Philippine authorities had really intended that the Vitamin A program provide a means of determining quantities of rice that were milled, thereby enabling the government to collect its taxes which the millers had evaded successfully for years.[13]

Cultural Considerations

Often more subtle than political considerations in international marketing are cultural factors. Consider the following examples:

In England, Germany and Scandinavia, beer is generally perceived as an alcoholic beverage. In Mediterranean lands, however, beer is considered akin to soft drinks. Therefore, a study of the competitive status of beer in Northern Europe would have to build in questions on wine and liquor. In Italy, Spain or Greece the comparison would have to be with soft drinks.

In Italy, it's common for children to have a bar of chocolate between two slices of bread as a snack. In France, bar chocolate is often used in cooking. But a West German housewife would be revolted by either practice.

A third of all German and Dutch businessmen take their wives with them on business trips, as opposed to only 15% of their English and French counterparts. As a study for one hotel delicately put it, the criteria each group uses in judging hotels and the services they offer are clearly different.

A *Reader's Digest* study of consumer behavior in Western Europe once astonished everyone by reporting that France and West Germany consumed more spachetti than Italy. The reason for this curious finding was that the question dealt with packaged and branded spaghetti. Many Italians buy their spaghetti loose.

Palacio Mateos, who is in charge of Spain's food education campaign, has called upon housewives to drop traditional superstitions so that their families may eat better and live healthier. His report indicates that many Spaniards are so superstitious that they refuse even to taste such products as butter, cheese, fish and even pasteurized milk. On the other hand, citizens in Cuenca Province spend half their food money on chocolate.[14]

TABLE 26.4	Important Cultural Considerations in International Marketing	
Differences in These Cultural Factors	**Affect a People's Values and Habits Relating To:**
1. Assumptions and attitudes	Time One's proper purpose in life The future This life versus the hereafter Duty, responsibility
2. Personal beliefs and aspirations	Right and wrong Sources of pride Sources of fear and concern Extent of one's hopes The individual versus society
3. Interpersonal relationships	The source of authority Care or empathy for others Importance of family obligations Objects of loyalty Tolerance for personal differences
4. Social structure	Interclass mobility Class or caste systems Urban–village–farm origins Determinants of status

Source: Avind Phatak, *Managing Multinational Corporations* (New York: Praeger, 1974), p. 139. Reprinted by permission.

As these examples show, the probability of failure is high without a thorough knowledge of a country's culture. Some of the important cultural considerations are listed in Table 26.4. A number of additional examples will be discussed in the next section.

DEVELOPING AN INTERNATIONAL MARKETING MIX
International Market Research

Before developing an international marketing mix, a company must obtain market information. As already mentioned, cultural traits can strongly influence all the elements of the basic marketing mix. There are two basic ways of examining an international market: (1) analysis of secondary data and (2) marketing research.

Secondary data have the same advantages in the international market as they do at home. They are relatively inexpensive and can usually be obtained more rapidly than primary data. National economic statistics and industry analyses published by the U.S. Department of Commerce are excellent sources of secondary information.

International marketing research utilizes the same tools, techniques, and theory as domestic research. Yet it is done in vastly different environments. In some countries a woman would never consider being interviewed by a male interviewer. Drawing samples based on known population parameters is often difficult owing to a lack of secondary data. In some cities in South America, Mexico, and Asia, street maps are unavailable; in some large metropolitan areas of the Near East and Asia, streets aren't identified and houses aren't numbered.

Product Considerations

Despite the difficulties often faced in conducting international research, some information is always better than none. After research information has been obtained, the marketing mix can be developed. Marketing managers can select from several product–communications alternatives:[15]

- One product–one message
- Product invention
- Product extension–communication adaptation
- Product adaptation–communication extension

One Product, One Message. The simplest strategy is to offer the same product and the same message throughout the world. For example, PepsiCo offers the same product and uses the same promotional theme everywhere. Wrigley's chewing gum and Levi's follow the same philosophy. The advantages of using this strategy include economies of scale in production; marketing economies (e.g., uniform sales training and promotion); and universal availability for mobile consumers.[16]

Product Invention. Often, however, a single product isn't feasible. Incomes will not justify a mass market. Moreover, consumers use products differently. For example, in many countries clothing is worn much longer between washings than in America. Thus the fabric must be more durable. Goodyear developed a tire to handle the tough driving conditions on Peru's roads. It contained a higher percentage of natural rubber than tires manufactured everywhere, and had better treads. As a result Peruvians preferred it to other tires. National Cash Register developed the NCR80, a crank-operated cash register. It is selling thousands of NCR80s in the Philippines, the Orient, Latin America, and Spain. With about half the parts of more advanced registers, the machine sells for about half the price of the cheapest models available in America.[17] Some typical product modifications and the factors causing the change are shown in Table 26.5.

Product Extension–Communication Adaptation. It may be possible to maintain the same basic product but alter the communication strategy. Bicycles and motorcycles are primarily pleasure vehicles in America. In many parts of the world, however, they are a family's major mode of transportation. Promotion in these countries can stress durability and efficiency. American advertising, in contrast, may emphasize escaping and having fun.

TABLE 26.5	Product Characteristics	
Key Factor	**Design Change**	
Level of technical skill	Product simplification	
Level of labor costs	Automation or manualization of product	
Level of literacy	Remaking and simplification of product	
Level of income	Quality and price change	
Level of interest rates	Quality and price change (investment in high quality might not be financially desirable)	
Level of maintenance	Change in tolerances	
Climatic differences	Product adaptation	
Isolation (heavy repair, difficult and expensive)	Product simplification and reliability improvement	
Differences in standards	Recalibration of product and resizing	
Availability of other products	Greater or lesser product integration	
Availability of materials	Change in product structure and fuel	
Power availability	Resizing of product	
Special conditions	Product redesign or invention	

Source: S. B. Prasad and Y. Krishna Shetty, *An Introduction to Multinational Management* (Englewood Cliffs, N.J.: Prentice-Hall, 1976), p. 154. © 1976. Reprinted by permission.

Product Adaptation–Communication Extension. A fourth strategy is to utilize the same promotional theme throughout the world and alter the product to meet local conditions. Campbell Soup learned this lesson the hard way. The familiar red-and-white label was sacrosanct and the company's communications mix and product remained the same. In England the company failed to explain how to prepare its condensed soups. No one told people to add water to the small can of condensed soup. Since the can looked relatively more expensive next to larger cans of ready-to-eat soup, sales suffered. In this case the product change was an entirely new label explaining how to prepare condensed soup. Campbell lost an estimated $30 million in sales before the problem was corrected.[18] On the other hand, one of the world's largest multinational firms, Exxon, has used the "Put a Tiger in Your Tank" theme successfully throughout the world. The gasolines, of course, are blended for local conditions and engine specifications.

Pricing

Once an international product strategy has been determined, the remainder of the marketing mix can be selected. Pricing presents some unique problems in the international sphere—in fact the technicalities of export–import pricing are far beyond the scope of this book.

Selling to developing nations often poses special pricing problems owing to a lack of mass purchasing power. Sometimes products can be simplified, as in the NCR example, to enable the firm to lower prices substantially. However, the firm must not assume that low-income countries are willing to accept lower quality. The nomads of the Sahara, although they are extremely poor, purchase expensive cloth to make their clothing. Their very survival in harsh conditions and extreme temperatures requires this expense.

Also, pockets of wealth exist in virtually every country. At least a small number of expensive luxury items can be sold almost anywhere. The Lamborghini car sells for over $30,000. The country with the lowest per-capita income in Europe is Portugal. Yet the largest single market for Lamborghinis is Portugal. Portuguese are very status conscious, and the wealth of the country is highly stratified.[19]

Some companies overproduce certain items and end up dumping them in the international market. Government tariffs and pricing decrees further confuse the pricing problem. In addition, fluctuation in international monetary exchange rates can make a product relatively "cheap" overnight. Conversely, it can price a product that was at a competitive level almost out of the market. Such was the case with Japanese and German automobiles in the United States during the early 1970s. Some companies are avoiding the pricing issue by returning to direct bartering.[20]

Promotion

The international advertising and promotion function tends to be highly standardized among multinational firms, according to a 1975 study.[21] Headquarters develops a prototype campaign and then lets the various subsidiary operations adapt it to local conditions. Goodyear has used this method successfully in developing localized ads based on a worldwide theme, approach, and format. In contrast, probably the least standardized of all marketing decisions is the media strategy.[22] Commercial television time, for example, is readily available in Canada, severely restricted in Germany, and totally unavailable in Sweden.

Some cultures view a product as having less value "if it has to be advertised." The hard-sell tactics and sexual themes so common in America are taboo in many countries. Sometimes media are controlled by the government, which restricts or eliminates advertising. In India, for instance, television commercials are limited to twenty seconds and can be only visual.[23]

Language barriers and translation problems have generated numerous headaches for international marketing managers. Witness the following examples:

> Chrysler Corp. was nearly laughed out of Spain when it copied the U.S. theme advertising, "Dart is Power." To the Spanish, the phrase implied that buyers lack but are seeking sexual vigor. Ford goofed when it named its low-cost "third world" truck "Tiera," which means "ugly

old woman" in Spanish. American Motors has had its problems too. Market research showed that AMC's "Matador" name meant virility and excitement, but when the car was introduced in Puerto Rico it was discovered that the word meant "killer"—"an unfortunate choice for Puerto Rico, which has an unusually high traffic fatality rate."[24]

Distribution

Solving promotion, price, and product problems doesn't guarantee international marketing success. The firm still has to obtain adequate distribution. The Japanese system is considered the most complicated in the world. Imported goods wind their way through layers of agents, wholesalers, and retailers. "Our trade distribution channels are historical, traditional ones," a trade ministry official says, "and it will be extremely difficult for the Japanese government to change such traditional channels."[25]

Kentucky Fried Chicken Japan observes that "everything in Japan starts in Tokyo." Its three initial stores in Osaka were a mistake. Fay Weston, chairperson of KFC Japan, notes, "We goofed—you can't start in Osaka and expect to creep into Tokyo. All three stores were a total disaster."[26]

The hotel-catering industry has encountered the following intricacies in international distribution:

A Bermuda foodservice dealer publishes a map to remind suppliers that he's closer to the port of New York than to Miami.

Trucking across the Sahara Desert proves to be the fastest route to ship goods to coastal Nigeria, whose port at Lagos is glutted.

Lack of freezer capacity stymies expanded use of frozen convenience foods in some less developed countries.

Cairo, Amman and Kuwait are vying to replace Beirut as the center of Middle East distribution.

Cash-and-carry wholesalers are growing and becoming more important in Europe.[27]

For a variety of reasons American-type retail outlets aren't practical in developing countries. For example, supermarkets encounter many cultural taboos. Many foods are highly perishable, since the use of preservatives is uncommon. Thus shoppers don't welcome packaged goods because they believe that food in a package would be spoiled. Also, most consumers don't have the storage space to keep food for several days. Refrigerators, when available, are usually small and don't allow for bulk storage.[28]

Sometimes channels simply don't exist. This is true not only in developing nations but in industrialized countries as well. Procter and Gamble sells soap and its other products from door to door in the Philippines, Iran, and a number of developing countries. Lack of storage facilities and adequate highway and road systems also complicate international distribution.

Political and governmental actions can also hinder distribution. In Central America, cargo moving by truck must be unloaded at the border of each country. It is then placed on a truck registered in the country being entered.

Cartels can also block distribution channels. General Tire was forced out of Europe because the tire cartel would not tolerate its presence and made its channels ineffective.[29] Israel's huge wholesaler, Hamashber Hamerkazi, handles about one-fifth of the country's wholesale trade and maintains partial ownership of twelve major industrial firms.[30] The company has tremendous political and economic clout in Israel's distribution system.

In general, adequacy of distribution can be tied to level of economic development. The following list summarizes the results of several studies that reveal a correlation between increasing complexity of distribution and economic growth.

Wholesaling
1. The influence of the foreign import agent declines with economic development. Local production requires a different kind of wholesale operation.
2. Manufacturer–wholesaler–retailer functions become more distinct and separate with economic development. In Turkey, for example, the wholesaler plays a strong role in organizing production as well as distribution.
3. Wholesaler functions approximate those in North America with increasing economic development.
4. The financing function of the wholesaler declines, but wholesale markups increase with increasing development.

Retailing
1. The more developed countries have more specialty stores and supermarkets, more department stores and more stores in rural areas.
2. The number of small stores declines and the size of the average store increases with increasing development.
3. The role of the peddler and itinerant trader and the importance of the open-air market decline with rising development.
4. Retail margins get larger with economic development.[31]

ORGANIZING FOR INTERNATIONAL MARKETING
Centralization Versus Decentralization

Effective marketing in an international setting requires good organizational planning. A key issue that arises early in the decision process is degree of centralization. Some companies centralize marketing decision making at company headquarters, while others favor a decentralized structure. The tremendous dissimilarities among nations mentioned in this chapter speak strongly for at least some degree of local autonomy. Yet integration of talent and resources, as well as overall control, requires a certain amount of centralization.

The trend among large multinationals in the 1970s is back to centralization.[32] As one executive says,

> The whole idea of setting up the regional office was to exercise control and coordination. We think it's more efficient to have some highly qualified senior guys here at headquarters who get more involved in subsidiary operations than to duplicate management skills at the country level. It's a way of life for us now and the subsidiaries are accepting it more and more.[33]

Companies selling "culture-free" products can usually centralize more readily than those that offer "culture-bound" products (e.g., food) that require significant adaptation to local conditions.

SUMMARY

America is a full participant in world trade. Our direct investment abroad is over $30 billion a year. Most of this money goes to developed nations. Our exports amount to over $140 billion a year and consist primarily of agricultural commodities and manufactured goods.

The firms that are responsible for most of the activity in international trade are referred to as multinationals. A multinational corporation is one that moves resources, goods, services, and skills across national boundaries. Many multinationals are huge organizations.

There are a variety of techniques for pursuing international trade. They range from simple exporting or importing to direct investment abroad with a foreign branch and foreign management.

In order to be effective in international trade, it is necessary to understand the cultural and political environments within which the firm is operating. A second prerequisite for success in international marketing is to obtain market data. This can take the form of secondary data or direct market research. International market research uses the same tools, techniques, and theory as domestic research, but it is conducted in vastly different environments.

The marketing mix typically begins with product considerations. Basic product strategies are: (1) one product–one communication message; product invention; product extension–communication adaptation; or product adaptation–communication extension.

Pricing presents some unique problems in international marketing. Expensive products are sometimes bought by poor people who do without other goods and services in order to make certain purchases. Also, in very poor countries there are pockets of wealth that allow for limited purchasing of expensive luxury items. Credit and inflation further complicate international pricing.

Promotion is the most highly standardized marketing function in multinational firms. Typically, headquarters develops a prototype campaign and lets the various subsidiary operations adapt it to local situations. Media strategy varies markedly from one country to another because of great differences in the availability and coverage of media.

In many countries distribution is extremely primitive. In others, it is tradition bound. It is often difficult to obtain adequate dealers. Sometimes channels simply don't exist. In other situations political and governmental actions can hinder distribution through tariffs, embargoes, and transshipment regulations.

Putting the international marketing mix into operation requires good planning. Some companies centralize marketing decision making; others use a decentralized structure. The great socioeconomic and cultural differences among various nations suggests the need for some degree of decentralization. However, the resultant lack of control has caused many of the large multinationals to recentralize some of their marketing operations.

KEY TERMS

Multinational corporation
Exporting
Licensing
International franchising
Contract manufacturing

Joint venture
Direct investment
Product–communications alternatives
Dumping

QUESTIONS FOR DISCUSSION

1. What is international marketing? Discuss it in a macro context.
2. List the different types of international operations and identify the level of risk associated with each.
3. Differentiate between contract manufacturing and joint ventures. What advantages does each offer to the parent company?
4. What are some of the factors that should be considered before adopting a program of direct investment in Canada? in Thailand? Are there any significant differences?
5. Explain some of the cultural factors that affect international marketing. Can you think of some examples?
6. What are some of the problems encountered in international marketing research?
7. Assume that Pizza Hut wants to expand to Kuwait. What element of the marketing mix would it have to alter?
8. Small Chemical manufactures a chemical that could have limited usefulness in several Asian countries. Assume that you are the firm's marketing manager. How would you go about trying to exploit this market? Give reasons for your answer.
9. Briefly outline the different product–communications alternatives available to international marketers.
10. What are some of the problems encountered in international distribution activities? Give a few examples.
11. Outline the advantages to be gained through centralized international marketing as compared to a decentralized structure. Which of the or-

ganization forms would be more suitable for marketing the following products?

a. calculators
b. special steel tubing
c. soft drinks
d. sporting equipment

NOTES

1. J. Paul Austin, "World Marketing as a New Force for Peace," *Journal of Marketing,* 30 (January 1966): 1–3.
2. "Made in USA," *Sales and Marketing Management,* April 11, 1977, p. 63.
3. Neil Jacoby, "The Multinational Corporation," *Center Magazine,* 3 (May 1975): 37. Reprinted by permission from *The Center Magazine,* a publication of the Center for the Study of Democratic Institutions, Santa Barbara, California.
4. Robert Stauffer, *Nation Building in a Global Economy: The Role of the Multinational Corporation* (Beverly Hills: Sage Publications, 1973), p. 13.
5. Robert Warren Stevens, "Scanning the Multinational Firm," *Business Horizons,* 14 (June 1971): 48.
6. F. R. Lineaweaver, "Key to Company Growth: Effective Export Distribution," *Distribution Worldwide,* October 1970, p. 55.
7. Richard Holton, "Marketing Policies in Multinational Corporations," *California Management Review,* 13 (Summer 1971): 57–67.
8. David McIntyre, "Your Overseas Distributor Action Plan," *Journal of Marketing,* 41 (April 1977): 88–90.
9. "Agent–Distributor Service Now Going Worldwide," *Commerce Today,* March 5, 1973, pp. 12–13; see also J. Don Weinrauch and C. P. Rao, "The Export Marketing Mix: An Examination of Company Experiences and Perceptions," *Journal of Business Research,* 2 (October 1974): 447–452; C. P. Rao, "Industrial Marketing in the International Setting," *Arizona Business* (Arizona State University, Bureau of Business and Economic Research, Tempe, Ariz., March 1974), pp. 12–18; and *The Financing of Exports and Imports: A Guide to Procedures* (New York: Morgan Guaranty Trust Company, 1973); an excellent overall review is *Export Marketing for Smaller Firms* (Washington, D.C.: Small Business Administration, 1973).
10. "The Ticklish Task of Repatriating Profits," *Business Week,* September 6, 1976, p. 77.
11. Ibid.
12. Arvind Phatak, *Managing Multinational Corporations* (New York: Praeger, 1975), pp. 16–17.
13. John Liebman, "Planning for Foreign Marketing Takes Both Learning, Unlearning," *Industrial Marketing,* May 1974, p. 52.
14. The first four examples are taken from Lee Adler, "Special Wrinkles in International Marketing Research," *Sales and Marketing Management,* July 12, 1976, pp. 62–63 (By permission; copyright 1976); the final example is from Philip Cateora and John Hess, *International Marketing,* 3d ed. (Homewood, Ill.: Irwin, 1975), p. 88; for other examples see William Cunningham, Russell More, and Isabella Cunningham, "Urban Markets in Industrializing Countries: The São Paulo Experience," *Journal of Marketing,* 38 (April 1974): 2–12; Donald Hempel, "Family Buying Decisions:

A Cross-Cultural Perspective," *Journal of Marketing Research,* 11 (August 1974): 295–302; and Robert Green and Eric Langeard, "A Cross-National Comparison of Consumer Habits and Innovator Characteristics," *Journal of Marketing,* 39 (July 1975): 34–41.

15. See Warren Keegan, "Multinational Product Planning: Strategic Alternatives," *Journal of Marketing,* 33 (January 1969): 58–62; a number of other good articles on international product strategies include David McIntyre, "Multinational Positioning Strategy," *Columbia Journal of World Business,* Fall 1975, pp. 106–110; William Rapp, "Strategy Formulation and International Competition," *Columbia Journal of World Business,* Summer 1973, pp. 98–112; Ralph Sorenson and Ulrich Wiechmann, "How Multinationals View Marketing Standardization," *Harvard Business Review,* May-June 1975, pp. 38–51; and Richard Holton, "Marketing Policies in Multinational Corporations," *California Management Review,* 13 (Summer 1971): 57–67.

16. Vern Terpstra, *International Marketing* (Hinsdale, Ill.: Dryden Press, 1972), p. 212.

17. Both the Goodyear and National Cash Register examples are taken from Terpstra, pp. 248–249.

18. Cateora and Hess, p. 342.

19. F. T. Haner, *Multinational Management* (Columbus, Ohio: Merrill, 1973), p. 202.

20. See Jack Kaikati, "The Reincarnation of Barter Trade as a Marketing Tool," *Journal of Marketing,* 40 (April 1976): 17–24.

21. Ralph Sorenson and Ulrich Wiechmann, "To What Extent Should a Consumer Goods Multinational Corporation Vary Its Marketing from Country to Country?" *Harvard Business Review,* (May-June 1975), p. 42.

22. Ibid.

23. Prasad and Shetty, p. 159.

24. Cateora and Hess, pp. 402–403.

25. Mike Tharp, "Marketing in Japan Takes Twisty Turns, Foreign Firms Find," *The Wall Street Journal,* March 9, 1977, pp. 1, 33.

26. Ibid.

27. "World Roundup," *Marketing News,* April 23, 1976, p. 111. Reprinted by permission of the American Marketing Association.

28. Arieh Goldman, "Outreach of Consumers and the Modernization of Urban Food Retailing in Developing Countries," *Journal of Marketing,* 38 (October 1974): 8–16; see also Johan Arndt, "Temporal Lags in Comparative Retailing," *Journal of Marketing,* 36 (October 1972): 40–45.

29. Cateora and Hess, p. 526.

30. Ibid., p. 515.

31. Vern Terpstra, *International Marketing* (Hinsdale, Ill.: Dryden, 1972), pp. 311, 316.

32. Ulrich Wiechmann, "Integrating Multinational Marketing Activities," *Columbia Journal of World Business,* Winter 1974, p. 10; see also C. K. Prahalad, "Strategic Choices in Diversified MNCs," *Harvard Business Review,* July-August 1976, pp. 67–78, and H. A. C. van Riemsdijk, "Optimizing Overseas Marketing: Rely on the Team Approach," *Industrial Marketing,* July 1976, pp. 82–84.

33. Wiechmann, p. 10.

CASE 26
The Phelps Company

The Phelps Company, a manufacturer of drying equipment for grain elevators, was founded in 1951. Grain elevators utilize a drying and blowing system to speed the process of removing moisture from crops; they require specialized blowing equipment. Phelps has been very successful in capturing a large share of the market throughout the Midwest. In fact it now feels that it has achieved its market potential in the United States.

John Cain, president of the company, is contemplating entering the international market. He has no experience whatsoever in the field and doesn't know where to turn. First, he wonders how to gather information on where the greatest sales opportunities exist. Second, he is concerned about different customs, governmental regulations, and specifications that might present formidable barriers to international marketing, and would like to know how these might be overcome. Third, he has no idea how the firm could enter the international sphere. In short, he feels like a babe in the woods.

1. As an international consultant hired by the Phelps Company, provide a consulting report that answers the questions John Cain is asking.
2. Which method of entering the international market would you recommend? Why?

Author Index

Abbott, L., 297, 301
Ackerman, K., 279, 282
Adkinson, J. E., 406
Adler, L., 107, 117, 212, 221, 313, 516, 525
Allport, G., 87, 95
Alpert, M. I., 53, 297, 301
Ames, B. C., 5, 18, 127, 140
Anderson, B. B., 349, 363
Anderson, E. E., 316
Anderson, W. T., Jr., 53
Andreasen, A., 497, 505
Appel, D., 53
Armstrong, G. M., 179
Armstrong, S., 107, 117
Arndt, J., 526
Assael, H., 43, 44, 53
Austin, J. P., 508, 525
Axelrod, M., 106, 117

Bailey, E. L., 310, 316
Balachandran, V., 34
Ballachey, E. L., 11, 19, 367, 383
Barksdale, H. C., 176, 178
Barry, T., 62-65, 73
Bartels, R., 18
Bates, A., 257, 262
Bauer, J., 336, 342, 438, 442
Bauer, R. S., 74, 349, 363, 370, 384
Baumal, W. J., 34
Bedeian, A. G., 316
Beier, F. J., 221
Bellenger, D. N., 104, 106, 117
Benne, K. D., 11, 19
Bennett, P. D., 74
Bennett, S., 298, 301
Bennigson, A. A., 190, 192, 197
Berenson, C., 107, 117
Berkus, D., 238, 241
Berry, L. L., 246, 260
Bessom, R. M., 22
Best, A., 497, 505
Bever, T. G., 349, 363
Bigaux, B., 94
Blackwell, P., 338, 342, 436, 442
Blackwell, R., 83, 95, 512
Blankenship, A. B., 34
Blattberg, R., 53
Blumberg, H., 107, 117
Boewadt, R., 316
Bogart, L., 34, 350, 358, 363, 364
Boone, L. E., 213, 222
Booz, A., 127, 128, 130, 138, 141
Booz, H., 127, 128, 130, 138, 141
Borchard, W. M., 182, 183, 196
Boring, R. A., 301, 316
Bowersox, D., 228, 240, 264, 269, 278, 281, 282

Bowman, R. D., 452, 457
Boyd, H. W., 103, 105, 106, 107, 116, 117
Bramel, D., 350-351, 363
Brayfield, A. H., 430, 441
Brenner, S., 499, 505
Britt, S. H., 349, 363
Brooks, D. G., 316
Brown, H. L., 317
Brown, R. G., 356, 364
Brubaker, D., 193, 198
Bruno, A. V., 133, 138, 141
Bucklin, L. P., 221, 261
Buel, V. P., 127, 140
Burck, G., 505
Burger, P., 100, 116
Burton, J., 492, 493, 504
Busch, P., 505
Buskirk, R., 502-503, 505
Buson, P., 421, 424
Buzzell, R. D., 291, 301

Calder, B. J., 106, 117
Capwell, D., 430, 441
Carmone, F. J., 53
Cash, W., 74
Cateora, P., 516, 519, 520-521, 522, 525, 526
Cavanaugh, S., 457
Cayley, M. A., 74
Chandran, R., 192, 197
Chentnik, C. G., 273, 282
Chin, R., 11, 19
Choffray, J.-M., 384
Chung, L., 107, 117
Churchill, G. A., Jr., 107, 110, 111, 117, 118, 432, 441
Clarke, D. G., 372, 384
Claxton, J. D., 178
Claycamp, H. J., 179
Clayton, H. L., 174, 179
Cleland, D., 484
Clewett, R. M., 127, 140
Clowes, K., 442
Coen, R. J., 252, 261, 370
Cohen, D., 401, 406
Cohen, M., 334, 342
Colby, S., 100, 116
Colley, R. H., 353, 364
Comanor, W. S., 384
Combs, L. D., 189, 197
Comer, J. M., 442
Conarroe, R. R., 454, 458
Cook, G., 107, 117
Cooper, P., 333, 341
Copeland, M. T., 160
Corr, A. W., 342
Cox, E. P., 53, 95

Cox, K., 65, 66, 73, 99, 106, 107, 108, 116, 117, 492, 493, 504
Cox, R., 15, 19
Cravens, D. W., 34, 437, 442, 467, 485
Crissy, W., 246, 260, 316
Crockett, W. H., 430, 441
Crutchfield, R. S., 11, 19, 367, 383
Culea, J. P., 349, 363
Cunningham, I., 505, 525
Cunningham, I. C. M., 95
Cunningham, S. M., 74
Cunningham, W. H., 432, 441, 505, 525
Currie, A., 441

Dalrymple, D. J., 435, 441
Danielenko, R., 385
Darmon, R. Y., 433, 441
Davenport, J. W., Jr., 424
Davis, H., 94
Davis, K., 499, 505
Dawson, L., 10, 11, 18, 19
Day, G., 84, 95
DeHayes, D., Jr., 266, 281
De Vos, R., 15
DeWitt, G., 454, 455, 458
DeWolf, J. W., 390-391, 405
Dhalla, N. K., 54, 167, 169, 178
Diamond, S., 495, 500, 502, 505
Dixon, J., 282
Donnelly, J. H., Jr., 178, 221, 351, 364
Doyle, P., 95, 384, 394, 405

Eastlack, J. O., Jr., 132, 141
Edwards, J. D., 275, 282
Ehrlich, D., 351, 364
El-Ansary, A. I., 213, 221
Elsner, D. M., 255-256, 261, 398, 399, 406
Engel, J. F., 74, 83, 95, 362, 364, 391, 405, 454, 457
English, W. D., 432, 441
Enis, B. M., 19, 99, 106, 107, 108, 109, 116, 117, 118, 316, 476
Erickson, L., 7, 8
Etgar, M., 211, 221
Etzel, M. J., 178, 484
Evans, R. B., 424
Evans, W. W., 421-422, 424
Everett, M., 376, 385, 439, 442

Faltermayers, E., 336, 342
Farris, P. W., 375, 384
Feldman, L. P., 8-9, 18
Fenwich, L., 384
Fenwick, I., 394, 405

Ferber, R., 94
Festinger, L., 350–351, 363
Fish, G., 192, 197
Ford, N. M., 432, 441, 501, 505
Foust, J., 57, 73
Frank, R. E., 53, 74
Freedman, J. L., 351, 364
Frey, T. D., 316
Friedman, L., 333, 341
Friedman, R., 31, 34
Friedman, W., 279, 282
Fulcher, D., 53
Fuller, C., 107, 117

Gabor, A., 333, 341
Gaedeke, R., 493, 494, 504
Gale, B. T., 291, 301
Gallagher, V., 272, 282
Garberson, J., 450, 451, 457
Gardner, D. M., 316
Gensch, D. H., 74
Geoffrion, A. M., 282
George, W. R., 176, 178
Gerster, L., Jr., 366, 484
Gill, L., 213, 221
Goldman, A., 521, 526
Gonsior, M. H., 301, 316
Good, R. E., 99, 116
Goodin, O., 273, 282
Goodstadt, M. S., 107, 117
Gordon, T. J., 127, 141
Granger, O., 333, 341
Granick, D., 342
Grashof, J., 276
Gray, D. A., 431
Green, P. E., 46, 47, 53, 110, 113, 116, 118
Green, R. T., 95, 178
Greenberg, B. A., 104, 106, 117
Greer, T., 18
Greyser, S. A., 246, 260, 349, 363, 370, 384, 495, 500, 502, 505
Gronhaug, K., 88, 89, 95
Gross, A., 332, 341
Gubar, G., 70–71
Guiltinan, J. P., 335, 342

Haddock, R., 333, 342
Haley, R. I., 46, 53, 141
Hamelman, P. W., 179
Hanan, M., 130, 141, 415, 423
Hanna, N., 19, 338, 342
Hansen, R. W., 94
Harberger, A. C., 298, 301
Harding, M., 394
Hare, A. P., 107, 117
Hargreaves, G., 178
Harness, E., 126, 140
Harris, K., 375, 384
Harvey, M., 62–65, 73, 192, 197
Harwood, D. L., 390, 405
Hauer, F. T., 520, 526
Haugh, L. J., 30, 34, 312, 316
Hawkins, D. I., 103, 104, 107, 108, 109, 110, 116, 117, 118

Heany, D., 485
Hempel, D., 525
Henry, P., 438, 442
Herrmann, R., 494, 504
Herzberg, F., 430, 441
Heschel, M., 442
Heskett, J. L., 221, 222
Hess, J., 516, 519, 520–521, 522, 525, 526
Higginbotham, J., 65, 66, 73, 492, 493, 504
Hill, R. M., 131
Hills, G., 467, 485
Hise, R. T., 179
Hlavacek, J. D., 131, 313
Hobbs, J., 485
Holmes, J. H., 34, 54
Holton, R., 512, 525, 526
Honomichl, J. J., 98, 100, 101, 116
Hony, A., 60
House, R., 254, 261
Houston, M. J., 261
Hughes, G. D., 141
Hulbert, J., 484
Hunt, S. D., 12, 13, 19, 221, 364
Hutchinson, P., 95
Hutt, M. D., 74
Hynes, D., 197

Ivancevich, J. M., 351, 364, 484
Ivy, C., 28–29

Jackson, R. A., 314, 317
Jacoby, J., 197, 333, 342
Jacoby, N., 28, 34, 510–511, 575
Jaffe, H., 485
Jaffe, L. J., 94
Jenkins, J. J., 350, 363
Johnson, J. C., 213, 222
Johnson, R., 54
Jolson, M. A., 130, 141, 415, 423, 441
Joselyn, R. W., 103, 116

Kahplas, H., 431
Kaikati, J., 526
Kamen, J., 333, 342
Kameschen, D. R., 309, 316
Kangun, N., 492, 493, 504
Kanuk, L., 107, 117
Keegan, W., 526
Kegerreis, R. J., 74
Keiser, S. K., 406
Kelly, R. F., 246, 260
Kendall, C. L., 189, 197
Kenderdine, J., 257–258, 262
Kennell, J., 485
Kerby, J. K., 80–81, 85, 94, 95
Kerin, R. A., 192, 197, 198
Kershaw, A. G., 275, 284
Kilbourne, W. E., 334, 342
King, A. L., 314, 317
King, W., 484
Kinnear, T., 74
Kirkpatrick, C. A., 424, 449, 457

Kizilbach, A. H., 19, 338, 342
Klahr, D., 53
Klompmaker, J. E., 141
Kollat, D., 83, 95, 512
Kotler, P., 3–4, 7, 8–9, 10, 11–12, 18, 19, 34, 78, 405, 480–482, 485, 492, 496, 504, 505
Krampf, R., 54
Krech, D., 11, 19, 367, 383
Kreitner, R., 432, 441
Kronitz, R., 107, 117
Krum, J. R., 406
Kushner, L., 191–192, 197

LaLonde, B., 276, 279, 282
Lambert, D., 279, 282
Lambin, J.-J., 369, 371, 372, 373, 384
Lamon, L. M., 334, 342
Langeard, E., 178
Lanzillotti, R. F., 34, 290, 291, 301
Larson, C., 256, 261
Lathrope, R., 74
Lazer, W., 8, 18
Lazerfield, P. F., 367, 383
Leavitt, H. J., 316, 424
Lee, L. C., 94
Lehmann, D., 161
Leininger, W. E., 431
Leslie, L., 107, 117
Lessig, V. P., 53, 246, 260
Levine, P., 48, 54
Levitt, T., 167, 361, 364
Levy, S. L., 9, 11–12, 18, 19
Lewis, R., 7, 8, 18
Liebman, J., 516, 525
Lilien, G. L., 373, 384
Lincoln, A., 240
Linder, B. J., 301
Lineaweaver, F. R., 512, 525
Linneman, R., 485
Lipson, H., 6
Little, R. W., 221
Lodish, L. M., 442
Lopata, R. S., 227, 230, 238, 240, 241
Lorange, P., 485
LoScuito, L. A., 351, 364
Lucas, H., 442
Luck, D. J., 18, 19, 126–127, 129, 140, 141
Luthans, F., 432, 441
Lynagh, P., 281

McCammon, B. C., 210, 211, 221, 257–258, 262
McCann, J., 41, 53
McCarthy, E. J., 186, 188, 196, 197
McClure, P. J., 246, 260
McConnell, J. D., 301, 316
McCullough, T. D., 334, 342
McDaniel, C. M., 189, 197, 247, 260
McDonald, P. R., 132, 141
McGinnis, M. A., 179

McGuire, E. P., 192, 197, 342
McGuire, W. J., 350, 363
McIntyre, D., 513, 525, 526
McKeon, J. C., 240
McNamara, C., 7, 16, 18
Maggard, J. P., 54
Mahamy, E., 448, 449, 457
Mahatoo, W., 54
Majgard, J. P., 74
Makens, J., 255, 261
Malcolm, J., 18
Manouso, J. R., 178
Markin, R. J., Jr., 69, 74, 81, 83, 85,
     95, 351, 363
Marquardt, R., 255, 261
Marshall, C., 9
Martineau, P., 246, 260
Masini, A., 276, 385
Maslow, A. H., 85–86
Mason, J. B., 221, 251, 261
Massy, W. F., 53, 74
Mausner, B., 430, 441
Maxwell, J. C., 298, 301
May, E. G., 246, 260
Mayer, G., 379, 385
Mayer, M., 251, 261
Mazis, M. B., 406
Mazze, E. M., 179
Melnick, E. L., 332, 341
Merriwether, J., 273, 282
Merton, R. K., 367, 383
Meyers, J., 485
Miller, J., 351, 364
Mitchell, D., 271, 282
Molandes, E., 499, 505
Monroe, K. B., 333, 341
Moore, R., 525
Moore, R. L., 317
Moran, J., 454, 458
Morgan, F., 505
Morgan, J., 98, 116
Moritz, D. B., 275, 282
Morrill, J. E., 361, 364
Morrison, D. G., 53
Mott, P., 94
Moyer, M. S., 262
Mulle, S. C., 217, 222
Munsinger, G. M., 94
Muse, W. V., 74
Myers, J. H., 53
Myers, R. H., 246, 260

Nask, J. F., 301
Nelson, P., 371–372, 384
Neppl, W., 257, 262
Neptrom, H., 316
Nerlove, S. B., 53
Nevin, J. R., 221
Newport, G., 464, 484
Newton, D. A., 432, 441
Nickels, W., 262

Nuckols, R. C., 108, 117
Nylen, D. W., 400, 406

O'Brien, T., 354, 364
O'Dell, W. F., 108, 117, 469, 485
O'Gara, J., 400
Oladipupo, R., 62, 73
Oliver, L., 74
Oliver, R., 432, 441
Olson, P., 333, 341
Osborn, A., 141
O'Shaughnessy, J., 161
Osmarski, F., 18
Ostlun, L. E., 178
Ostlund, H., 82, 95
Overton, T. S., 107, 117
Oxenfeldt, A. R., 316, 342

Packard, V., 80, 94, 367, 383
Padberg, D. L., 334, 342
Palda, K. S., 354, 364
Parkinson, T. L., 194, 198
Parsons, L. J., 316, 435, 441
Pathak, D. S., 246, 266, 432, 441
Patterson, J., 505
Pearson, A. E., 413, 423
Perloff, R., 351, 364
Perreault, W., 267–268, 282
Person, M., 271, 282
Pessemier, E. A., 298, 301
Peters, M. P., 178
Peters, W. H., 74
Peterson, R., 74, 430, 441
Peterson, R. A., 171, 178
Phatak, A., 515, 517, 525
Plummer, J., 67, 68, 74
Poprelary, D. T., 178
Portis, B. D., 246, 260
Posner, R. S., 418, 419, 423
Povey, T. G., 427, 441
Prahalad, C. K., 526
Prasad, S. B., 519, 520, 526
Prasad, V. K., 247, 261, 375, 384
Price, W. B., 316
Pruden, H. O., 432, 441

Rao, C. P., 525
Rao, M., 384
Rao, V. R., 53
Rapp, W., 526
Rathmell, J., 18
Rawl, L. G., 29, 34
Read, D., 405
Reed, J., 441
Reynolds, A., 341
Reynolds, F., 6
Rich, S., 246, 260
Richard, L., 213, 221
Riemshijk, H. A. C., van, 526
Ries, A., 376, 384
Ripley, G. B., 107, 117

Ritchie, R. T., 108, 117
Robertson, T. G., 84, 95, 178
Robeson, J., 512
Robicheaux, R. A., 213, 221, 288,
     289, 301
Robinson, W., 448, 457
Roe, R., 255, 261
Roemunich, R., 275, 282
Roering, K., 221, 505
Rogers, E. M., 168, 171, 178
Rogers, T., 107, 117
Romney, A. K., 53
Roscoe, A. M., Jr., 43, 44, 53
Ross, M. H., 313, 317
Rothe, J. T., 179, 334, 342, 502–
     503, 505
Rozen, L., 262
Rucks, C., 221
Ruppel, A., 469, 485
Russ, F. A., 189, 197, 267–268,
     282, 424
Ryan, J. K., 246, 260
Ryan, M. R., 314, 317

Samlow, W. J., 435, 441
Samuelson, G., 94
Sapir, E., 348, 363
Sauter, R., 501, 505
Savage, A. H., 301
Saxton, L. F., 409, 423
Schiff, L. S., 29–30, 34
Schmalensee, R., 369, 384
Schonbach, P., 351, 364
Schoner, B., 99, 116
Schooler, R., 505
Schultz, A. W., 396, 405
Scott, C., 107, 117
Scott, R. A., 94
Semon, T., 161
Sen, S., 53
Senft, H., 94
Sexton, D. E., Jr., 53, 73
Shanklin, W. L., 430, 498, 499,
     500, 505
Shapiro, B. P., 18, 311, 316, 418,
     419, 423
Sharp, H., 94
Sharpe, L., 74
Sheldon, E. B., 94
Shepard, R. N., 53
Shepard, T., Jr., 505
Sherer, F. M., 294, 301, 328, 329,
     341
Sheth, J. N., 94
Shetty, Y. K., 519, 520, 526
Shoaf, F. R., 178, 332, 341
Shoemaker, R. W., 178
Shuptrine, F. K., 18, 94, 189, 190,
     197
Silk, A. J., 384
Siller, F. R., 178

Sims, J. T., 301
Sinclair, U., 494, 504
Skelly, F., 491, 504
Sletmo, G., 273, 282
Smart, A., 19, 338, 342
Snyder, R. E., 267, 281
Softness, D. G., 454, 458
Soldner, H., 261
Sorenson, R., 520, 526
Southwood, A., 57, 73
Staelin, R., 74
Stafford, J. E., 65, 66, 73, 316
Stamper, J. C., 437, 442
Stanton, W. J., 103, 116, 178
Stapel, J., 333, 341
Stasch, S. F., 103, 105, 106, 107,
   116, 117, 127, 140
Staudt, T. A., 141
Stauffer, R., 511, 525
Stephens, L. F., 317
Stephenson, R., 246, 254, 260, 261,
   268
Stern, L. W., 213, 221, 222
Stevens, E. M., 455, 458
Stevens, R., 256, 262, 511, 525
Stewart, W., 267, 269, 282
Stiles, D., 313, 317
Strang, R. A., 445, 446, 447, 448,
   451–452, 457
Sudman, S., 110, 111, 118
Sultan, R. G. M., 291, 301
Swan, J. E., 189, 197, 312, 316
Sweitzer, R. W., 246, 260, 432, 441
Swenson, H. C., 192, 197

Takas, A., 10, 18
Tamsons, H., 316
Tannenbaum, S. I., 375, 384
Tarpey, L. X., Sr., 197
Tauber, E. M., 141
Taylor, D. A., 116
Taylor, J. W., 74, 174, 175, 178,
   179
Taylor, R., 266, 281
Taylor, W. C., 124, 140

Terpstra, V., 518, 522, 526
Terry, G., 463, 484
Thams, R., 316
Tharp, M., 521, 526
Thompson, D. L., 412, 423
Thompson, J. W., 421–422, 424
Thrasher, C. L., 341
Thurlow, M. L., 435, 442
Tigert, D. J., 74
Tillman, R., 449, 457
Tollefson, J. O., 53
Toman, R., 333, 342
Tosi, H. L., 212–213, 221
Toy, M., 484
Treas, C. E., 314, 317
Trent, R., 469, 485
Trewath, R., 464, 484
Trytten, J. M., 390, 405
Tull, D. S., 103, 104, 107, 108,
   109, 110, 113, 116, 117, 118, 301
Tully, J., Jr., 435, 441
Twedt, D. W., 102, 116, 134, 141

Udell, J. G., 301, 316, 357, 364
Uhl, J. N., 317
Uhl, K., 99, 116
Unberger, N., 255, 261
Underwood, B. J., 350, 363

Vancil, R., 485
Van Tassel, C., 73
Venkatesan, M., 178
Venkatesh, A., 127, 140

Waldo, C., 42, 53
Wales, H. G., 116, 454, 457
Walker, O. C., Jr., 432, 441, 501,
   505
Wall, K. A., 74
Walters, G., 77, 79, 94
Warshaw, M. R., 362, 364, 391,
   405, 454, 457
Wasem, G., 34
Weale, B. J., 246, 260
Weale, W. B., 246, 260

Weaver, P., 191
Weber, J. E., 94
Webster, F., Jr., 231–232, 240, 497,
   498, 505
Weigard, R., 256, 261
Weigast, E. H., 94
Weil, A., 89, 95
Weinberg, C., 442
Weinrauch, J. D., 525
Weiss, E. B., 19, 186, 187, 196
Wells, H. G., 362, 364, 391, 405
Wells, W., 66, 67, 68–69, 70–71, 74
Wentz, W. B., 99, 100, 116
Westfall, R., 103, 105, 106, 107,
   116, 117
White, A., 496, 505
White, I., 178
Wiechmann, U., 520, 523, 526
Wilemon, D., 127, 140
Wilkes, R. E., 94
Wilkie, W. I., 375, 384, 402, 406
Wilkinson, J. B., 298, 301
Willett, R., 268
Williams, J. D., 54
Wilson, D. T., 421, 424
Wilson, T. A., 384
Wind, Y., 53, 74, 179
Winer, L., 29–30, 34, 436, 442
Wise, G. L., 314, 317
Wiseman, F., 74
Woodruff, R. B., 437, 442, 467, 485
Woodside, A. G., 94, 301, 405, 424
Wortzel, L. H., 74
Wotruba, T. R., 427, 428, 436, 441,
   442
Wright, J., 256, 261

Yaeger, D. S., 257, 262
Yuspeh, S., 167, 169, 178

Zaltman, G., 8–9, 18, 100, 116
Zarecor, W. D., 141
Zeltner, H., 187, 196, 256, 262
Ziff, R., 74
Zimmerman, E., 385

Subject Index

A&P, horizontal marketing system with Southland, 212
Aamco Transmissions, 43
Aaron Brothers, 257
Abington, Richard, on strategic planning, 464
Accessibility, and segmentation, 41, 42
Accessories, industrial goods, 154–155
Actual demand curves, 297–298
Adler, Lee, 212
Administrative distribution systems, 211–212
AdTel, 398
Advertising, 354, 355. *See also* Promotion; Public relations; Sales promotion
  audience measurement, 398–399
  bait-and-switch, 332–333, 403
  communication effectiveness tests, 396–398
  communication goals, 388
  company budgets, 367, 368–369
  comparative, 374–375
  controversy, 371
  cooperative, 376–377
  corrective, 402
  credibility, public relations in building, 454–455
  deceptive, 401–402
  effectiveness measurement, and media audiences, 396–399
  goals, 387–388
  institutional, 374
  macro impact, 367–372
  media, 377–381
  micro effects, 372–377
  product, 374
  regulation, 401–403
  and sales, 372, 388, 392–393
  selective/competitive, 374
  self-regulation, 402–403
  shortage, 375–376
  total expenditures, 366–367
  types, 373–374
  unfair, 402
  volume, 370
Advertising agencies, 399
  compensation, 401
  functions, 400–401
  switching, 401
Advertising budget
  arbitrary allocation, 389
  market share approach, 390–391
  objective-and-task approach, 391
  percent of sales, 390

Advertising campaign
  media scheduling, 394–395
  message, 394
  nature of, 391, 394
Affiliative groups, 82
Age mix, population, 57
Agents
  in distribution channels, 209
  wholesalers, 235–236
Agricultural assemblers, 236
AIDA concept
  and hierarchy of effects, 353–354
  and selling, 417
Alberto-Culver Co., new product pricing, 321–322
Alcoa, institutional advertising, 374
Allegheny Ludlum Industries
  product mix, 172
  shortage advertising, 376
Allied stores, 252
Allocation, arbitrary, advertising budget, 389
Allport, Gordon, 87
Almart-T. B. Hunter, 252
Alternatives, in problem solving, 469–470
American Association of Retired Persons, 59
American Cola Co., case study, 75
American Marketing Association, 102
American Photo Art, case study, 283
American Research Bureau (ARB), 100, 101
Amway, 253
Anaconda Cooper Corp., 154
Analysis, preliminary, in designing marketing research project, 103–104
Anderson-Clayton Foods, marketing research, 102
Antitrust, Heinz suit against Campbell, 30
Arbitron, 398
Area samples, 111
Arlen Realty and Development, 256
Arm and Hammer, product repositioning, 165
Armour Dial, 50
  tactical plans, 463–464
Aspiratory reference groups, 82
Assael, Henry, 44n
Assortment, middlemen in eliminating discrepancies of, 204–207

Attitudes
  and advertising, 367–368
  measures, 397
  and social marketing, 11
Auction companies, 236–237
Audience
  and advertising effectiveness measurement, 396–399
  duplication, 395–396
  and media selection, 377
Audit, marketing, 480–482
Audit Bureau of Circulation (ABC), 398
Austin, J. Paul, on international marketing, 508
Automobile industry, perceptual mapping, 46–47
Avon Products, 253
Awareness stage, in product adoption, 168, 170
Ayer (N. W.) & Son, 98

Background investigation, in preliminary analysis, 103
Bait-and-switch advertising, 332–333, 403
Bait pricing, 332–333
Baraba, Vincent, 57
Basing-point pricing, 328–329
Beatrice Foods, advertising budget, 390
Bechtel, 336
Beer industry, market segmentation, 44–46
Behavior. *See also* Buyer behavior
  and experience, 84–85
  information, 109
  and needs, 85–86
  and perception, 83–84
  and personality, 87
  and self-concept, 86–87
Behavioral dimensions, distribution channels, 212–214
Behavioral sciences, and selling, 421–422
Behavior modification, and promotion, 351–352
Beldon Associates, 398
Bell Telephone System, 43, 44
  shortage advertising, 376
Benefit segmentation, 40
  and perceptual mapping, 46–47
Bennett, Peter, 65
Benson & Benson, 101
Bergen Brunswig, 256
Bernstein, Joan, 375
Bessom, Richard M., 22n
Best Products, 258

Bidding, competitive, 335
Bid pricing, 335
Bissell, 134
Boeing Co., sales approach, 418–419
Bon Vivant, 192
Bonwit Teller, 251
Borden, Inc.
  advertising budget, 391
  television advertising, 380
Brand(s), 182–183
  battle of, 187–188
  family, 184
  loyalty, 189
  manufacturers or dealers, 184–186
  preference, 188–189
Branding, advantages of, 184
Brand ownership, and channel power, 213–214
Braniff Airlines, 102
Breakeven, concept of, 305–309
Breaking bulk, as wholesaler function, 228
Bricklin, Malcolm, 128
Bristol-Myers, Co., 310
Brokers, 235
  in distribution channels, 209
BSR, penetration pricing, 323
Budget. See also Advertising budget
  and marketing plans, 464
  promotional plan, 360
Budweiser, sales promotion, 448
Bulova Watch Co., 190
Burger King, 100
Burton, John, 493n
Busch, Paul, 421
Business. See also Industry
  advertising budgets, 367, 368–369
  distribution systems, 211
  marketing research departments, 102–103
  response to consumerism, 497–498
  socially responsible, 502
Business meetings, and sales promotion, 449
Business service, 174
Butler Brothers, 238
Butler Buildings, 154
Buyer(s)
  distribution channel's role in locating, 207–208
  for export, 513
  government, in distribution system, 210
Buyer behavior
  complexity of, 77–78
  and culture, 83
  defined, 77
  governmental, 89–92
  and holistic psychology, 80–81
  industrial, 88–89

and learning theory, 78–79
  model, 83, 87–88
  and psychoanalytic theory, 79–80
  and social-anthropological theory, 81–82
Buzell, Robert, D., 291n

Cable television, 380
  panel tests, 398
Call record reports, sales force, 438
Campbell Soup Co.
  Heinz suit against, 30
  product for foreign markets, 519
Capital goods, 153–155
Career
  in marketing, 16
  selling as, 412–413
Carriers
  legal, 278
  private, 278
  small-shipment, 277
Carroll, Daniel, on strategic planning, 466
Carrying cost, 275
Carson, Rachel, 494
Cartels, and distribution in international markets, 522
Cases
  American Cola Co., 75
  American Photo Art, 283
  Cessna Aircraft, 119
  Condor Kite Co., 162
  Creamoline Corp., 96
  East-West Manufacturing, 506
  Farmer Co., 242–243
  first sales job, 425
  General Pet Products, Inc., 142–143
  Gray Trail Bus Line, 263
  Great Northwest Amusement Park, 180
  Iowa American Telephone Co., 443–444
  Mayfield Chemical Corp., 343
  Midcontinent Perfume Co., 319
  Mumford toasters, 20
  New Mexico Trailmaker Bus Line, 302
  Northeast National Bank, 407–408
  North Star Service, 55
  Northwest Apple Growers Association, 459
  Phelps Co., 527
  RSVP Restaurants, 386
  Savin Business Machines, 486–487
  Shiner Brewery, 35
  Southern Lubricants, 365
  Welch grape soda, 223–224
Cash-and-carry wholesalers, 232–233
Cash discounts, 325
  reducing, 337

Catalogs, characteristics, 381
Causal analysis, in marketing control, 477–482
Census of Population, 103
Center for Study of Responsive Law, 496–497
Centralization vs. decentralization, in international marketing, 522–523
Central-location telephone interviewing, 107
Cents-off promotion, 332, 448
Certification and labeling, 194
Cessna Aircraft Co., case study, 119
Chains
  department stores, 250
  mass merchandising shopping stores, 251
Channels. See Distribution channels
Chrysler Corp., promotion in international markets, 520
Clairol, 50
Classification system
  industrial goods, 153–158
  retailing, 248–249
Clayton Act (1914), 296
Closing techniques, selling, 420
Cluster samples, 111
Coca-Cola Co., 175
  horizontal marketing system with Dr. Pepper, 212
  sales promotion, 448
Cognitive dissonance, and communication, 350–351
Colby, Irene, 386
Colgate-Palmolive Co., 126
Colley, Russel, on promotion objectives, 353
Combination export manager, 513
Commerce Business Daily, 89
Commission merchants, 236
Commission system, 432–433
Committees, selling to, 414
Common carriers, 278
Communicability, and product adoption, 170
Communication
  adaptation, and product extension, 518
  advertising, tests of effectiveness, 396–398
  as advertising goal, 388
  and cognitive dissonance, 350–351
  defined, 348
  distribution channel's role in, 207
  extension, and product adaptation, 519
  flow, 348–349
  and learning, 349–350
  of marketing research study results to management, 114

in new product development,
135
and perception, 349
and persuasion, 350
selling as, 410–411
Company-related distribution factors, 217–218
Comparative advertising, 374–375
Compensation, advertising agencies, 401
Competition
domestic, 30
foreign, 30
models of, 294
and price, 310–311
and pricing objectives, 291
Competitive bidding, 335
Complexity, and product adoption, 170
Component parts and materials, 156–158
Computer, in retailing, 256–257
Computer interviews, 108
Concentrated marketing, 43
Concentration
industry, 150
population, 59
Condor Kite Co., case study, 162
Conference Board, 192
Conflict, channel, 214
Conrail, 279
Conservatism, in new-product development, 132
Consistency, product line, 172–173
Constantino Brokerage, 238
Consumer. *See also* Consumerism
advantages of branding to, 184
behavior. *See* Buyer behavior
in marketing mix, 26–27
product adoption process, 168, 170
selling to, 414–415
Consumer goods, 144–145
convenience, 145–147
shopping, 147–148
specialty, 148
unsought, 148
Consumerism
business response to, 497–498
defined, 492–493
forces behind movement, 495–497
history, 493–495
issues, 493
and physical distribution, 279–280
Consumer Product Safety Act (1972), 191–192
Consumer Product Safety Commission, 192

Consumer protection
overzealous, 501
responsibility for, 500
Consumer spending patterns, 64
Contract carriers, 278
Contract manufacturing, and international market, 514
Contractual distribution systems, 212
Contractual power, channel, 214
Control
channel, 213–214
and evaluation of sales force, 436–438
marketing, 474–482
and salary, 433
Convenience goods, 145–147
Convenience sample, 111
Convenience stores, 248
Conventions, and sales promotion, 449
Cooperative advertising, 376–377
Cooperatives, producers', 233–234
Copyrights, 182
Corporate distribution systems, 211
Corrective action, and marketing control, 482
Corrective advertising, 402
Cost
and breakeven concept, 305–309
of carrying inventory, 275
distribution, and number of warehouses, 245
economic, 317–318
joint, product line pricing, 334–335
of marketing, 15–16
market introduction, 138
and markup pricing, 304–305
media, 395
and media selection, 377
ordering, 274–275
physical distribution, 266–267, 269–270
sales training, 430
stock turnover, profits, and, 305
test marketing, 138
types, 303
Cost control, marketing, 477–478
Cost curves, 318
Cost-oriented strategies, pricing, 335–336
Cost schedules, 317
Coupons, in sales promotion, 448–449
Cox, Keith, 65, 109n, 493n
Cravens, David W., 437n
Creamoline Corp., case study, 96
Creative boutiques, 401

Creative marketing, 11–12
Credibility
advertising, public relations in building, 454–455
media, 378
Criteria, in problem solving, 470
Crosstabulations, 113
Cultural considerations, international marketing, 516–517
Culture, and buyer behavior, 83
Customer, wholesaler in anticipating needs of, 226–227
Customer groups and organizations, 10
Customer interaction, selling, 421–422
Customer organization, sales department, 434
Custom Research, 101

DAGMAR, 353
Data
analysis, in marketing research study, 112–114
needs and sources, 104–109
processing, 112
Data Development, 101
Data-gathering forms, designing, 109–110
Davis, Keith, 499
Dayton-Hudson Corp., 252
Dayton Malleable Iron, 311
Deal, secret, and price discrimination, 297
Dealer, and manufacturer's brands, 186
Dealer brand, 184–186
advantages and disadvantages, 187
growth of, 187–188
Dealey, I. K. Jr., on selling, 409
Decentralization vs. centralization, in international marketing, 522–523
Deceptive advertising, 401–402
Decision making and problem solving, 470
Decision roles and organizational position, in industrial purchasing, 88–89
Decisions Center, 101
Decline, in product life cycle, 166–168
Decoding, communication, 349
Defense mechanisms, 87–88
Defensive behavior, 88
DeHayes, Daniel Jr., 266n
deKadt (Peter) Research, 101
Delayed-quotation pricing, 336
Deletion, product, 174

Demand
defined, 291
elasticity, 292–294
estimating, 297–298
fluctuations, industrial goods,
152–153
insensitivity to price, 152
and segmentation, 41–42
statistical estimation of, 298–
299
Demand curve, 293
actual, 298–299
Demand-oriented strategies, pric-
ing, 336–337
Demand schedule, 293
Demographic factors, and market-
ing, 32
Demographic segmentation, 40
Demonstration and presentation,
sales, 419–420
Department stores, 249–250
Dependence and financial strength,
channel member, 213
Depth and width, product, 172
Derived demand, industrial goods,
152
De Vos, Richard, 15n
Dhalla, Nariman K., 169n
Diamond, Steven, 500n, 502n
Diamond Shamrock Corp., 438
Differentiated marketing, 43–46
Diffusion, defined, 168
Direct investment in international
market, 514–515
Direct mail, 380–381
Direct retailing, 252–253
Discount stores, 252
Discounts and allowances, 324–
325
Distribution. See also Distribution
channels; Physical distribution
costs, and warehouses, 245
in international marketing mix,
521–522
and price, 311
Distribution center vs. warehouse,
271–272
Distribution channels. See also
Physical distribution
basic systems, 209–210
behavioral dimensions, 212–214
company-related selection factors, 217–218
in creating satisfaction, 208–209
and intensity of market coverage, 218–219
market-related selection factors,
216–217
middlemen in, 204–208
selection, 214–216
service, 210
vertical, 210–212
Distributors, industrial, 209, 231–
232
Door-to-door interview, 106

Door-to-door retailing, 253, 414–
415
Drop shippers, 233
Dr. Pepper, horizontal marketing
system with Coca-Cola, 212
Ducommun, 335, 336
Duplication, media, 395–396
Du Pont de Nemours (E. I.) & Co.,
130
and Corfam, 128

Early adopters, new product, 171
Early majority, in product adop-
tion, 171–172
Eastman Kodak Co., 265
East-West Manufacturing, case
study, 506
Economic consequences of adver-
tising, 368–369
Economic costs, 317–318
Economic factors, and marketing,
28
Economic order quantity (EOQ),
274
Economy
mixed, 287
and selling, 438–439
Ego, 79
Elasticity of demand, 292– 294
and advertising, 370–372
Elderly market, 59
Electronic funds transfer systems
(EFTS), 256–257
Ellis, Willard, 190
Emergency items, convenience
goods, 145–146
Employees, advertising, 366–367
Employment, retailing, 245
Encoding, communication, 348
Energy costs, and marketing, 29–
30
Energy crisis
and physical distribution, 279
and shortage advertising, 376
Enis, Ben, 109n
Environment
external, 26–27
industrial goods purchasing, 153
and international marketing,
515–517
marketing, 22
Erickson, Leo, 8n
Ernst and Ernst, 498
Escalator clauses, pricing, 336
Esteem need, 86
Ethics, and social responsibility,
499
Evaluation
and control of sales force, 436–
438
in product adoption, 168, 170
Exclusive distribution, 219
Executive interview, 107
Exempt carriers, 278

Expectancy theory, motivation,
431
Expenditures, adversiting, 366–367
Experience
and behavior, 84–85
and sales training, 429
Experiments, in marketing research study, 108–109
Exporting, and international market, 513
External factors affecting marketing, 28–32
Extinction pricing, 323–324
Exxon, product for foreign markets, 519

Fairchild Industries, 336
Fair Packaging and Labeling Act
(1967), 194
Falcon Hang Gliders, and choosing
distribution channel, 215–217
Family
and income, 63
as reference group, 82
Family brands, 184
Farmer Co., case study, 242–243
Farm products, 156
Featherlite, 43
Federal Express, 277
Federal Trade Commission (FTC),
254, 295–296, 299
and comparative advertising, 375
and consumerism, 495
growing powers, 31
Federal Trade Commission Act
(1914), 297, 401
Wheeler-Lea Amendment, 332,
401
Federal Trade Commission v.
Sperry & Hutchinson Co., 401
Federated Department Stores, 250,
252
Feedback
in behavior model, 88
communication, 349
Feldman, Lawrence, 8
Field service firms, 100–101
Financial incentives, 432–433
Financial strength, and depen-
dence, channel member, 213
Financing
distribution channel's role in,
207
as wholesaler function, 228
Firm, advantages of branding to,
184
Fisher Price, 190
Flexible pricing, 330
FOB origin, 326
FOB pricing, 326–327
Focus group interview, 106–107
Follow-up
promotional plan, 361
in selling process, 420–421

Food and Drug Act (1906), 193–194
Ford, Henry, 40
Ford Motor Co.
  and Edsel, 128
  promotion in international markets, 520–521
Forecasting
  long-run, for marketing control, 477
  and physical distribution, 265
Foreign governments, and marketing, 32
Forest Service, U.S., 59
Form, data-gathering, 109–110
Form utility, and distribution channel, 208
Franchising, 253–255
Frank, Newton, 48
Franklin Mint, direct mail, 381
Free enterprise, defined, 287
Freight absorption pricing, 329–330
Freight forwarders, 277–278
Freud, Sigmund, 79, 80
From-home telephone interviewing, 107
Fuller Brush Co., 253
Functional discounts, 324–325
Funds, available, and promotion, 358–359
Full-service wholesalers, 321

Galbraith, John Kenneth, 368
Gale, Bradley T., 291n
Gallup and Robinson, 375
The Gap, 251
General Electric Co.
  goal, 24
  shortage advertising, 376
General Foods Corp., 28, 43, 100
  and cereal industry oligopoly, 296
  marketing research, 102
  packaging management, 193
  product mix and product line, 173
General-line wholesalers, 230–231
General Mills, Inc., 100, 130
  and cereal industry oligopoly, 296
General Motors Corp., 43, 190, 253
  last Cadillac convertibles, 148
  product recall, 192
  television advertising, 380
General Pet Products, Inc., case study, 142–143
General Tire & Rubber Co., and European tire cartel, 522
Geographic pricing policies, 325–330
Geographic segmentation, 40

Georgia-Pacific Corp., 438
Gerber Products Co., 32, 175
Gestalt psychology and buyer behavior, 80–81
Gillette Co., 43, 50
Glaskowsky, Nicholas A. Jr., 277n
Goals
  advertising, 387–388
  importance of, 23–24
  for nonprofit organization, 24
  for profit-oriented organization, 24
  public relations, 453
Gold Circle stores, 252
Goodell, Phillip W., 310
Good Housekeeping seal, 182, 194
Goods
  consumer, 144–148
  middleman in facilitating flow of, 204–208
Goodyear Tire & Rubber Co., 190
  product for foreign markets, 518
Government
  buyer behavior, 89–92
  buyers, in distribution system, 210
  and social responsibility, 499–501
Grant (W. T.) Co., bankruptcy, 252
Grashof, John, 276n
Gray, David A., 431n
Gray Trail Bus Line, case study, 263
Great Northwest Amusement Park, case study, 180
Green, Paul, 47n
Greyser, Stephen, 500n, 502n
Grocery Warehouse, 258
Gronhaug, Kjell, 89n
Groups, and buyer behavior, 81–82
Growth, in product life cycle, 165–166

Hallmark Cards and Gifts, 252
Halo effect, and store image, 247
Hamashber, Hamerkazi, 522
Hanan, Mack, on venture group, 130
Harrah's, sales promotion, 450–451
Hart, Schaffner & Marx, distribution system, 211
Head-on positioning, 50
Heinz (H. J.) Co., suit against Campbell Soup Co., 30
Heskett, J. L., 277n
Heterogeneous merchandise, shopping goods, 147–148
Hickory Farms, 252, 257
The Hidden Persuaders (Packard), 494

Hierarchy
  of effects, and AIDA concept, 353–354
  of needs, 85–86
Higginbotham, James, 65n, 493n
Hill, Richard M., 131n
Hlavacek, James, 131n
Holistic psychology, and buyer behavior, 80–81
Holtcamp, Robert J., 323
Holt, Rinehart and Winston, commission system, 432–433
Homogeneous merchandise, shopping goods, 147
Honeywell Inc., 439
Hooper-Starch, 397, 398
Hopkins, George, 55
Horizontal marketing systems, 212
Hovland, Carl, 350
Hunt, Shelby, 13n

IBM Corp., 154
Id, 79
Identification, as defense mechanism, 88
Image store, 246–247
Immediate-reward packs, 448
Impulse items, convenience goods, 146
IMS International, 101
Income, and families, 63
Independent Grocers' Association, 186
Industrial distributors, 231–232
  in channel system, 209
Industrial goods
  classification system, 153–158
  defined, 149
  market characteristics, 149–153
Industrial users, in distribution channel, 209
Industry. See also Business
  buyer behavior, 88–89
  concentration, 150
  large firms, 149
  relocation trends, 149–150
Ineffectiveness of sales promotion management, 452
Inflation
  long-term, and pricing, 335
  and marketing, 28
  and selling, 438–439
Informal investigation, in preliminary analysis, 103–104
Information
  and promotion, 352
  types solicited by marketing researchers, 109–110
Innovation, 168
Innovators, 168, 171

Input from other departments, 24–25

Insistence, brand, 188–189

Installations, industrial goods, 154

Institutional advertising, 374

Intelligence system, 27–28

Intensive distribution, 218

Intentions information, 109

Interest stage in product adoption, 168, 170

Internal Revenue Service, ruling on trade shows, 449

Internal structure, 23–25

International market. *See also* International marketing; International marketing mix; Marketing
and contract manufacturing, 514
direct investment, 514–515
entry methods, 512–515
and exporting, 513
and joint venture, 514
licensing, 513–514

International marketing. *See also* International marketing mix; Marketing
centralization vs. decentralization in, 522–523
cultural considerations, 516–517
importance of, 508–509
macro perspective, 508
and multinationals, 510–511
organization for, 522–523
political considerations, 515–516

International marketing mix. *See also* Marketing mix
developing, 517–522
distribution in, 521–522
pricing, 519–520
product considerations, 518–519
promotion in, 520–521

Interviews
computer, 108
personal, 106–107
in recruiting and screening salespeople, 427–428
telephone, 107

Introduction, in product life cycle, 165

Inventory control
and computer in retailing, 256
and physical distribution, 273–276

Inventory turnover, costs, and profits, 305

Invisible hand, principle of, 10–11

Iowa American Telephone Co., case study, 443–444

ITT Continental, corrective advertising, 402

Irion, Randy, 322

Ivie, Robert M., 277n

Ivy, Conway, on economic factors, 28–29

Jacoby, Neil, on multinationals, 510–511

Jay Manufacturing, 154

Jobbers
rack, 232
truck, 233

Joe Namath's Girls, 255

Johnson & Johnson, 50, 310

Joint costs, product line pricing, 334–335

Joint venture, and international market, 514

Jungle, The (Sinclair), 494

Kangun, Norman, 493n

Kassarjian, Harold, 65

Kellogg Co., and cereal industry oligopoly, 296

Kellwood Co., 213

Kennedy, John F., consumerist message, 494–495

Kentucky Fried Chicken, 255

Kentucky Fried Chicken Japan, distribution, 521

Kershaw, Andrew G., on comparative advertising, 375

Kimberly Clark Corp., 126

Kinney Shoes, 252

K-Mart stores, 100, 252

Kotler, Philip, 3, 8, 9, 10n, 11, 78n, 474n
on consumerism, 492

Kresge stores, 252
strategic planning and problem solving, 468–469

Kroehler Manufacturing Co., 190

Labeling
legislation, 193–194
metric conversion, 194
seals and certifications, 194

Laggards, 168, 172

LaLonde, Bernard, 276n

Lambin, Jean-Jacques, 369, 371n

Language, and promotion in international markets, 520–521

Lanham Act (1946), 183

Lanzillotti, John, 290

Late majority, product adoption, 172

Lazer, William, 8

Leader pricing, 332

Leadership, channel, 213–214

Leadership pricing, theory of, 294–295

Learning and communication, 349–350

Learning theory and buyer behavior, 78–79

Legal carriers, 278

Legal factors in marketing, 30–31

Legislation
labeling, 193–194
and marketing, 30–31

pricing, related to market structure, 295–296
warranty, 189–190

Leininger, Wayne E., 431n

Levi Straus, 190

Levitt, Theodore, 167n

Levitz Furniture Corp., 258, 402

Levy, Sidney, 9, 11

Lewis, Richard, 8n

Liability, product, 192

Licensing, and international market, 513–514

Life style
dimensions of, 66
and life cycle, 69–71
segmentation, 66–68
and social class, 68–69

Liggett & Myers Inc., penetration pricing, 323

The Limited, 257

Limited-function merchant wholesalers, 232

Lipson, Harry, 6n

Little Olympia Brewery, sales promotion, 448

Living standards, and marketing, 14–15

Logistical coordination, in physical distribution, 265

Logotypes, 182

Love need, 86

Low-margin products, elimination of, 335–336

Loyalty, brand, 189

Macro impact, advertising, 367–372

Macro perspective on international marketing, 508

Magazines. *See also* Media
audience measurement, 398
characteristics, 378–379

Magnavox Co., horizontal marketing system with Xerox, 212

Magnuson-Moss Warranty-Federal Trade Commission Improvement Act (1975), 190

Mail order retailing, 252–253

Mail order wholesalers, 234

Mail surveys, 107–108

Mall, 255

Mall intercept interview, 106

Management
communicating marketing research study results to, 114
of new-product development, 128–132
packaging responsibility, 193
physical distribution, 264–266
product life cycle as tool of, 165
sales promotion, 451–453

Manufacturer
product liability defenses, 192
sales branches, 234–235

Manufacturer's brands, 184–186

advantages and disadvantages, 186

future of, 188

Manufacturers' representatives, 235–236

Marginal analysis and sales territory, 435

Market
characteristics, and promotion, 358

and distribution factors, 216–217

intensity of coverage, and choice of distribution channels, 218–219

introduction, in new-product development, 138

Market Facts, 108

Marketing. See also International marketing; Marketing mix; Marketing organization; Marketing research; Market segmentation; Market share; Selling
audit, 480–482

control, 474–482

cost control, 477–478

costs of, 15–16

defined, 3–4

horizontal systems, 212

model and definition of, 23

nature of, 39–40

ranking of activities, 288–289

scope of, 12–13

work functions, 7–8

Marketing concept
broadened, 8–10

defined, 4

implementing, 4–5

in service organizations, 176

Marketing information systems (MIS), 99

Marketing mix. See also International marketing mix; Marketing research
defined, 6–7

physical distribution in, 271

and price, 288

role of, 25–26

Marketing organization, 470–471
forms of, 472–473

matrix, 471

and other departments, 471, 474

Marketing planning. See Strategic marketing planning

Marketing research. See also Marketing
communicating results to management, 114

corporate departments, 102–103

data collection and analysis, 112–114

defined, 98

designing data-gathering forms, 109–110

designing project, 103–104

development of, 98–99

firms, 100–101

international, 517–518

preliminary analysis, 103–104

processing of data, 112

and sales promotion, 452

selecting sampling procedures for, 110–112

Marketing system
integrated, 21–25

monitoring change in, 27–28

Market segment, and promotional plan, 360

Market segmentation
benefit, and perceptual mapping, 46–47

criteria for, 41–42

forms of, 40–41

patterns of, 42–46

problems, 47–48

product differentiation, product positioning, and, 48–51

Market selectivity, media, 378

Market share. See also Advertising; Marketing; Promotion; Selling
and advertising, 373

and advertising budget, 390–391

analysis, 478–479

as pricing objective, 290–291

Markets In Focus, 398

Market structure, and pricing legislation, 295–296

Markin, Ron Jr., 81n

Markup pricing, 304–305

Marshall, Christy, 9n

Maslow, A. H., hierarchy of needs, 85–86

Mass merchandising, shopping chain, 251

Materials handling, 272–273

Materials management, and physical distribution, 265

Matrix organization, 471

Matsushita Electric Corp., product recall, 192

Maturity, in product life cycle, 166

May department stores, 252

Mayfield Chemical Corp., case study, 343

McDonald's, 100, 252, 253, 255

McNutt, Carl, 55

Media
advertising, 377–379

audience measurement, 398–399

characteristics and trends, 379–381

costs, 395

duplication, 395–396

key characteristics, 377

and public relations, 453–454

qualitative aspect, 395

scheduling, 394–395

selecting, 377–379

Media mix, promotional plan, 361

Memory, and learning, 350

Merchandise marts, 237

Merchandisers, rack, 232

Merchant wholesalers, 229–234

Merrill, John, 361

Mervyn's, 257

Message
advertising campaign, 394

promotional plan, 360

Metric conversion, and labeling, 194

Micro effects, advertising, 372–373

Midcontinent Perfume Co., case study, 319

Middlemen, in facilitating flow of goods, 204–207

Miller, Byron H., 419

Minerals, production, 155

Minnie Pearl's Fried Chicken, 255

Missionary salespeople, 416

Missouri Valley Petroleum, advertising budget, 391

Mixed economy, 287

Mobil Chemical Corp., sales promotion, 452

Mockler, Colman M. Jr., on new-product development, 132

Model
of competition, 294

marketing, 22–23

Modification
product, 173–174

promotional plan, 361

Monetary rewards, selling, 413

Money
and population, 62

and sales force motivation, 432

Monsanto Co., 130

Montesano, Joseph L., 135

Montgomery Ward, 186, 251

Morton-Norwich Products, Inc., 272

Morton Salt Co., logo change, 174

Motivation
expectancy theory, 431

financial incentives, 432–433

nonfinancial, 432

of sales force, 430

MPI Marketing Research, 101

Multinationals, 510–511

Multiple basing point pricing, 329

Multiple distribution channels, 217

Multiple-unit package pricing, 331
Mumford Toaster Products, case
    study, 20

Nader, Ralph, 496
National Advertising Division,
    Council of Better Business
    Bureaus, 402, 403
National Advertising Review
    Board, 402-403
National Biscuit Co., packaging
    management, 193
National brand, 184-185
National Cash Register, product
    for foreign markets, 518
National Commission on Product
    Safety, 191
National Family Opinion Re-
    search, 108
National Retail Tracking Index,
    353
National Traffic and Motor Vehi-
    cle Safety Act (1966), 495
Natural resources, shortages, and
    marketing, 29-30
Needs
    and behavior, 85-86
    and social marketing, 10-11
Newman-Stein, 101
New Mexico Trailmaker Bus Line,
    case study, 302
New product. See also New-
    product development; Product;
    Product life cycle
    importance. 127-128
    macro view of, 126
    mortality of ideas, 138
    pricing, 321-324
    venture management, 130-132
New-product committees, 129
New-product department, 129
New-product development. See
    also New product; Product;
    Product life cycle
    conservatism in, 132
    idealized view, 136-137
    management of, 128-132
    organization, 132
    risk, 128
    stages, 132-139
Newspapers. See also Media
    audience measurement, 398
    characteristics, 378, 379
Nielsen (A. C.) Co., 100, 101, 108,
    398
    television ratings, 398-399
Noise level, media, 378
Nonfinancial controls, marketing,
    479
Nonfinancial motivation, 432
Nonprobability samples, 111-112
Nonprofit organization
    goals for, 24
    marketing scope, 8-10, 12-13
Nonrecognition of brand, 188

Norms, 82
Northeast National Bank, case
    study, 407-408
North Star Service, case study, 55
North State Bank, 55
Northwest Apple Growers Associ-
    ation, case study, 459
Norwich Pharmacal Co., computer
    and distribution center net-
    work, 272
NPD Research, 108

Objections, handling, in selling,
    420
Objective-and-task approach, ad-
    vertising budget, 391
Objectives
    marketing, 25
    physical distribution, 267-268
    promotion, 352, 353
    promotional plan, 359-360
    sales management, 426-427
    sales promotion, 446-448
    sales training, 428
Observation, in marketing research
    study, 108
Ocean Spray, corrective advertis-
    ing, 402
Odd-even pricing, 333
O'Dell, William, 469n
O'Gara, James, 400n
Oligopoly, cereal industry, 296
Olympia Brewing, distribution
    costs, 266-267
One Hour Martinizing, 255
One-way frequency count, 113
Opinion Research (ORC), 101
Opportunity exploration, in new-
    product development, 134
Order cycle time, 268
Ordering cost, 274-275
Order processing, 275-276
Organization
    and customer groups, 10
    for international marketing,
        522-523
    new-product development, 132
    position, and decision role, in in-
        dustrial purchasing, 88-89
    sales department, 434
    for social responsibility, 502-503
Organization of Petroleum Export-
    ing Countries (OPEC), 32
Outdoor advertising, 381
Oxtoby-Smith, 101

Packaging, 193
Packard, Vance, 494
    on advertising, 367
Parents Magazine seal, 194
Parkinson, Thomas, 194
Particularized marketing, 42-43
Pass-along rate, magazines, 378-
    379
Patent, 182

Patent Office, U.S., 183
Pathak, Dev, 432
Patronage, store, 246-248
Penetration pricing, 322-324
Penn Central Railroad, 279
Penney (J. C.), 186, 187, 251, 252
Pepsico, Inc., 59
Perceived quality, and price, 311-
    313
Perception
    and behavior, 83-84
    and communication, 349
Perceptual mapping, and benefit
    segmentation, 46-47
Personal freedom, in selling, 412
Personal interviews, 106-107
Personality, and behavior, 87
Personal selling, 355, 356
Personal service, 174
Personnel
    department stores, 250
    selling, 412
Persuasion
    and communication, 350
    and promotion, 352
Petroleum bulk plants, as as-
    semblers, 236
Phatak, Avind, 517n
Phelps Co., case study, 527
Philip Morris
    advertising for Merit cigarettes,
        30
    and differentiated market seg-
        mentation in beer industry,
        44-46
    packaging, 193
    sponsorship of sporting events,
        450
Physical distribution, 272-273. See
    also Distribution channels
    activities, 265-266
    costs, 266-267, 269-270
    freight forwarders, 277-278
    functions, 270-276
    inventory control, 273-276
    legal carriers, 278
    in marketing mix, 271
    objectives, 267-268
    small-shipment carriers, 277
    transportation modes, 276-277
    trends, 279-280
    warehouse locations, 270-272
Physiological needs, 86
Physiological tests of advertising
    effectiveness, 397-398
Pier One, 252, 257
Piper Aircraft, 154
Planning. See Strategic marketing
    planning
Plummer, Joseph, 67n
Point-of-purchase display, 449
Polaroid Corp., 265
    product mix, 172
Political considerations in interna-
    tional marketing, 515-516

Political factors in marketing, 30–31
Popularity, sales promotion management, 451–452
Population
  age mix, 57
  concentrations, 59
  elderly market, 59
  maturing, 57–59
  mobility, 61–62
  and money, 62
  segmentation by race, 62–66
  total, 57
Positioning, in retailing, 257
Position power, channel, 214
Possession utility, and distribution channels, 208
Pottery Plus, 257
Power
  channel, 213–214
  and social responsibility, 499
Prasad, S. B., 519n
Prasad, V. Kanti, 247n
  study of comparative advertising, 375
Preferences
  and advertising, 372
  brand, 188–189
Preliminary analysis, in designing marketing research project, 103–104
Premiums, in sales promotion, 448–449
Presentation, and demonstration, sales, 419–420
Prestige pricing, 313
Preston, Charles K., 335
Price. *See also* Pricing
  and competition, 310–311
  competition, service firms, 175
  consciousness, 313–314
  discrimination, 297
  and distribution, 311
  and elasticity of demand, 292
  fixing, and price leadership, 295–296
  industrial goods, demand's insensitivity to, 152
  leadership, 294–297
  lining, 331–332
  and marketing mix, 288
  and perceived quality, 311–313
  and product life cycle, 310
  and promotion, 311
  shading, 336–337
  single, 330–331
  skimming, 321–322
  variability, 330
Pricing. *See also* Price
  bait, 332–333
  basing-point, 328–329

cents-off promotion, 332
cost-oriented strategies, 335–336
demand-oriented strategies, 336–337
discounts and allowances, 324–325
extinction, 323–324
flexible, 330
FOB, 326–327
freight absorption, 329–330
geographic policies, 325–330
and governmental purchasing behavior, 92
importance, 289
in international marketing mix, 519–520
leader, 332
legislation related to market structure, 295–296
and long-term inflation, 335
and market share, 290–291
markup, 304–305
in meeting competition, 291
multiple-unit package, 331
new product, 321–324
odd-even, 333
penetration, 322–325
product line, 334–335
psychological, 333
realistic, 289–290
shortage, 337–338
special policies, 330–334
target return, 290, 309
uniform delivered, 327
unit, 333–334
zone, 327–328
Primary data, needs and sources, 104–106
Private brand, 185
Private carriers, 278
Probability sample, 110–111
Problem solving, and strategic planning, 468–470
Procter & Gamble Co., 50, 100, 126
  advertising budget, 367, 390
  distribution in international markets, 521
Producers' cooperatives, 233–234
Product. *See also* New product; New-product development; Product life cycle
  adoption, 168–172
  advertising, 374
  classification system, 148–149
  considerations, international marketing mix, 518–519
  defined, 124–126
  labeling, 193–194
  liability suits, 192
  packaging, 193

and promotion, 357–358
  recall, 192–193
  repositioning, 164–165
  safety record, 191
  warranty, 189–190
Product differentiation
  market segmentation, product positioning, and, 48–51
  public relations in aiding, 455
Production, and marketing, 24–25
Product knowledge and sales training, 429
Product life cycle
  characteristics, 164–165
  decline, 166–168
  growth, 165–166
  introduction, 165
  maturity, 166
  and price, 310
  and promotion, 358–359
  stages, 165–168
  strategic considerations, 169
  use of, 168
Product line
  consistency, 172–173
  and distribution, 216
  pricing, 334–335
Product manager concept, 126–127
  and matrix organization, 471
Product mix, 172–173
Product organization, sales department, 434
Product positioning, market segmentation, and product differentiation, 48–51
Product-related distribution factors, 216
Product strategy
  deletion, 174
  mix, 172–173
  modification, 173–174
Professionals, selling to, 414
Professional sales representative, 415–416
Profit, costs, and stock turnover, 305
Profit Impact of Market Strategy (PIMS), 467–468
Profit-making organizations
  marketing scope, 12–13
  goals for, 24
Profit plan, preliminary, in new-product development, 134–135
Promotion. *See also* Advertising; Public relations; Sales promotion
  AIDA concept and hierarchy of effects, 353–354
  and behavior modification, 351–352
  cents-off, 332

Promotion *(Continued)*
forms, 354–355
and funds available, 358–359
and information, 352
in international marketing mix, 520–521
and market characteristics, 358
objectives, 352, 353
personal selling, 355, 356
and persuasion, 352
and possession utility, 208
and price, 311
and product, 357–358
and product life cycle, 358–359
publicity 355, 356–357
reminder, 352–353
sales, 355, 356
as wholesaler function, 227–228
Promotional allowances, 325
Promotional mix, 361
Promotional plan
following up and modifying, 361
implementation, 359–361
measuring effectiveness of, 361
Prospecting, in selling, 417–418
Psychographic segmentation, 40, 66–71
Psychological pricing, 333
Publicity, 355, 356–357
Public relations. *See also* Advertising; Promotion
and aiding product differentiation, 455
and building advertising credibility, 454–455
goals and media alternatives, 453–454
Public Relation News, 454
Publics, in marketing mix, 26–27
Purchasing, industrial goods, 152, 153
Purchasing agents, selling to, 413
Purchasing behavior. *See* Buyer behavior
Pure Food and Drug Act (1906), 494

Quaker Oats Co., 126
Quality
and advertising, 369–370
perceived, and price, 311–313
Quantity, middlemen in eliminating discrepancies in, 204
Quantity discounts, 324, 337
Quota, sales, 436
Quota attainment, sales force, 436–437
Quota sample, 111–112

Race, population segmentation by, 62–66
Rack merchandisers, 232
Radio. *See also* Media
audience measurement, 398
characteristics, 378, 379
Ralston Purina Co., 43, 126

Randall Park Mall, 255
Random sample, 110–111
Rapiston, 427
Rationalization, as defense mechanism, 88
Raw materials, 155–156
Recall
advertising effectiveness test, 396–397
product, 192–193
Reception, communication, 348–349
Recognition
advertising effectiveness test, 397
brand, 188
Recruiting of salespeople, 427–428
Reference group, 81–82
Reference group self, 86
Regional malls, 255
Regulation
advertising, 401–403
and marketing, 30–31
Relative advantage, and product adoption, 170
Relocation trends, industry, 149–150
Reminder promotion, 352–353
Replacement markets, 157
Repositioning
product, 164–165
and product life cycle, 167–168
Repression, as defense machanism, 88
Reproduction capability, media, 378
Research 100, 101
Research in Perspective, 101
Resident buyers, 237
Resources
requirements, 27
scarce, and social marketing, 11–12
Response rates, and segmentation, 41, 42
Retailers
giant, 245–246
selling to, 413
Retailing, 414–415. *See also* Sales; Selling; Wholesaling
classification system, 248–249
direct, 252–253
franchising, 253–255
importance, 245–246
largest companies, 246
nonservice sales, 269
operation methods, 249–253
shopping centers, 255–256
site selection, 256
store patronage determinants, 246–248
trends, 256–258
warehouse, 257–258
Return on investment (ROI), target, as pricing objective, 290

Rexall stores, 253
Reynolds, Fred, 6n
Rinkov, Al, on selling and inflation, 439
Risk
and brand loyalty, 189
new-product development, 128
and store patronage, 247–248
Risk taking, as wholesaler function, 229
Robicheaux, Robert A., 288n, 289n
Robins, Roger R., on new-product development, 132
Robinson-Patman Act (1936), 297, 325
Rogers, Everett, 171
Rousseau, John, 449–450
Roy Rogers Roast Beef, 255
RSVP Restaurants, case study, 386

Safety, product, 191–192
Safety needs, 86
Safety stocks, 274
Safeway stores, sales volume, 246
St. Joe Minerals, shortage advertising, 376
Salary, and control, 433
Sales. *See also* Selling
and advertising, 372, 388, 392–393
compensation and incentive plans, 433
management objectives, 426–427
and new products, 128
nonservice retailing, 269
percentage, advertising budget, 390
retail, 245
Sales branches, manufacturers, 234–235
Sales department
developing territories, 435–436
devising quotas, 436
organization structure, 434
size of force, 435
Sales force
call record reports, 438
evaluation and control of, 436–438
motivation of, 430
quota attainment, 436–437
size of, 435
Salespeople. *See also* sales; Selling
candidate sources, 428
missionary, 416
professional, 415–416
recruiting and screening, 427–428
technical specialists, 416
Sales promotion, 355, 356. *See also* Promotion; Sales; Selling
business meetings, conventions, and trade shows, 449–450
importance, 445–446
management, 451–453
objectives, 446–448

point-of-purchase display, 449
samples, premiums, and cou-
    pons, 448–449
special forms of, 450–451
Sales quotas, devising, 436
Sales territories, developing, 435–
    436
Sales training, 428–429
    costs, 430
Samples, in sales promotions, 448–
    449
Sampling procedures for marketing
    research study, 110–112
Satisfaction, distribution channels
    in creating, 208–209
Savin Business Machines, case
    study, 486–487
Scheduling, media, 394–395
Schultz, Arthur W., on advertising,
    396
Screening, in new-product develop-
    ment, 134
Seals, and labeling, 194
Searle (G. D.) & Co., 175
Sears, Roebuck & Co., 100, 186,
    187, 213, 251
    charged with bait-and-switch ad-
        vertising, 332–333
    distribution system, 211
    sales volume, 246
Seasonal discounts, 325
Secondary data, 104, 105
Secret deals, and price discrimi-
    nation, 297
Selective/competitive advertising,
    374
Selective distribution, 218–219
Self-actualization need, 86
Self-concept, and behavior, 86–87
Self-regulation, advertising, 402–
    403
Selling. See also Retailing; Sales;
    Wholesaling
    agents, 237
    and AIDA concept, 417
    behavioral science contributions
        to, 421–422
    as career, 412–413
    closing techniques, 420
    to committees, 414
    as communication, 410–411
    to consumers, 414–415
    customer interaction, 421–422
    and economy, 438–439
    follow-up, 420–421
    functions, 411
    handling objections, 420
    importance, 411
    and inflation, 438–439
    monetary rewards, 413
    nature of, 410–411
    personal freedom, 412–413

personnel, 412
presentation and demonstration,
    419–420
to professionals, 414
prospecting, 417–418
to purchasing agents, 413
sales approach, 418–419
as wholesaler function, 227–228
to wholesalers and retailers, 413
Selling Areas-Marketing, Inc.
    (SAMI), 100, 101
Service distribution channels, 210
Service positioning, 50
Services, 158
    shared, physical distribution,
        279
    strategy, 174–176
    unbundling of, 337
Sewell, Phyllis, 58
Shanklin, William, 499n
Sherman Act (1890), 296
Sherwin-Williams Co., distribution
    system, 211
Shetty, Y. Krishna, 519n
Shiner Brewery, case study, 35
Shipment pricing without notifica-
    tion, 337
Shippers, drop, 233
Shopping centers, 255–256
Shopping goods, 147–148
Shopping malls, sales promotion
    in, 450–451
Shopping stores, 249
    mass merchandising chains, 251
Shortage advertising, 375–376
Shortage pricing, 337–338
Shortages, and selling, 438
Shuptrine, Kelly, 189, 190
SI (Système International d'Un-
    ités), 194
The Silent Spring (Carson), 494
Simmons, 398
Sinclair, Upton, 494
Singer Co., 175
Singer Sewing Outlets, 252, 253
Single-line wholesalers, 230–231
Single-price policy, 330–331
Site selection, retailing, 256
Situation analysis, 103
Skelly, Florence, 491
Small-shipment carriers, 277
Smith, Adam, 10
Social-anthropological theory, and
    buyer behavior, 81–82
Social class, and life style, 68–69
Social factors affecting marketing,
    28
Social marketing, 10–12
Social power, and selling, 421
Social responsibility
    and government, 499–501
    nature of, 498–499

organizing for, 502–503
and power, 499
Society
    implications of product for, 124–
        126
    and marketing mix, 26–27
Source, communication, 348
Southern Lubricants, case study,
    365
Southland stores, 100
    horizontal marketing system
        with A&P, 212
Specialty goods, 148
Specialty retailing, growth, 257
Specialty stores, 249
    as retail operation method, 251–
        252
Specialty wholesalers, 231
Sporting events, sponsorship of,
    450
Stafford, James, 65
Stamper, Joe C., 437n
Standard metropolitan statistical
    areas (SMSAs), 59–60
Standards, in marketing control,
    475–476
Staple items, convenience goods,
    145, 146–147
State-of-being information, 109
State-of-mind information, 109
Statistical estimation of demand,
    298–299
Steak & Ale, 100
Stephenson, Ronald, 268n
Stewart, Wendell, 265n, 269n
Stimulus, and perception, 349
Stock turnover, costs, and profits,
    305
Storage
    distribution channel's role in,
        208
    as wholesaler function, 228
Store
    image, 246–247
    patronage determinants, 246–248
Strang, Roger A., 446n, 447n
Strang, Robert A., 452
Strategic marketing planning, 463–
    464
    advantages, 465–466
    considerations in, 466–467
    developing successful strategies,
        467–468
    problems, 466
    and problem solving, 468–470
Strategy
    product, 172–174
    in new-product development,
        135
    service, 174–176
Stratified sample, 111
Strong, E. K., 353

Structure, marketing, 23–25
Substantiality, and segmentation, 41
Sultan, Ralph G. M., 291n
Sunrise Hospital, 9
Superego, 80
Super Value Stores, 238
Supplies, 158
Surveys, in marketing research study, 106–108
Sweitzer, Robert, 432
Switching, advertising agencies, 401
Syndicated-service research firms, 100

Tactical planning vs. strategic, 463–464
Target Group index (TGI), 100
Target market, 25
  promotional plan, 360
Target stores, 252
Target return on investment, as pricing objective, 290
Target return pricing, 309
Taylor, Robert, 266n
Technical specialists, 416
Technology
  and marketing, 32
  and physical distribution, 279
Telehone industry, market segmentation, 43, 44
Telephone interviews, 107
Telephone selling, 253, 415
Television. See also Media
  audience measurement, 398–399
  characteristics, 380
Territorial organization, sales department, 434
Test marketing, in new-product development, 135, 138
Texas Instruments, penetration pricing, 323
Textron, Inc., shortage advertising, 376
TGI, 398
3M Co., 130
Time, order cycle, 268
Time utility, and distribution channels, 208
Timex, 32
Tonka Industries, 51
Tosi, Henry, on distribution channel members, 212–213
Total costs, physical distribution, 269–270
Total-product concept, 125
Trade, International, 508
Trademarks, 182
  infringement remedies, 183–184
  lifespan, 183
  registration, 183
Trade-offs, in marketing mix, 25–26

Trade shows, and sales promotion, 449–450
Traffic Audit Bureau (TAB), 381
Transactional analysis, in sales training, 429, 430
Transactions, middlemen in reducing number of, 204
Tramsmission channel, communication, 348
Transportation
  and physical distribution, 276–277
  as wholesaler function, 228–230
Trial-size containers, 449
Trial stage in product adoption, 168, 170
Truck jobbers, 233
Truth in Lending Act (1968), 495
Truth in Packaging Act (1965), 495
Turnover, inventory, calculating, 305
Twedt, Dik, 102n

Udell, Jon, 357
Unbundling, of services, 337
Underwriters Laboratory, 182, 194
Undifferentiated marketing, 42
Unfair advertising, 402
Uniform Commercial Code, 189
Uniform delivered pricing, 327
Union Carbide Corp., 130
United Rent Alls, 255
Unit pricing, 333–334
Universal Product Dollars, 448
Unsought goods, 148
Upjohn Co., 175
Users, industrial, in distribution channel, 209

Values
  and advertising, 367–368
  and social marketing, 11
Variability, price, 330
Varoom, Victor, 431
Venture management, new-product, 130–132
Venture stores, 252
Venture team concept, 131
Vertical distribution channels, 210–212
Volume segmentation, 40

Walters, Glenn, on learning theory of buyer behavior, 79
Walzer, Edgar B., 314
Want satisfaction, interpretation of, 124–126
Warehouses
  and distribution costs, 245
  location, 270–272
  retailing, 257–258
Warner-Lambert Co., and Listerol, 128
Warranty
  defined, 189

legislation on, 190
  complexity, 189–190
Weaver, Paul, 191n
Webster, Frederick Jr., 498
Weinberg, R. S., 372, 384
Weissman, George, on packaging, 193
Welch's Foods, case study of grape soda, 223–224
Wella Corp., new-product pricing, 321–322
Wells, William, 67n, 68
Western Auto stores, 238
Westinghouse Electric Corp., and choosing distribution channels, 215–217
Wheeler-Lea Amendment to FTC Act, 332, 401
Wholesalers
  functions, 226–229
  merchant, 229–234
  selling to, 413
Wholesaling. See also Retailing; Sales; Selling
  agricultural assemblers, 236
  auction companies, 236–237
  brokers, 235
  commission merchants, 236
  defined, 226
  manufacturers' agents, 235–236
  manufacturers' sales branches, 234–235
  merchandise marts, 237
  resident buyers, 237
  selling agents, 237
  trends, 238
Wide Area Telephone Service (WATS), 107
Willett, Ronald, 268n
Wilson, David, 421
Woodruff, Robert B., 437n
Woolco stores, 252
Woolworth's, 252
Work functions of marketing, 7–8
Workload
  and sales territory, 435–436
  and size of sales force, 435
World Book Encyclopedia, 253
Worth, Jack, on sales promotion, 451
Wright and McGill, 190

Xerox Corp., 32
  horizontal marketing system with Magnavox, 212
  product differentiation, 48
  product mix, 172

Yuspeh, Soma, 169n

Zale Jewelers, 252
Zaltman, Gerald, 8
Zenith Radio Corp., 190
Zero population growth (ZPG), 57
Zone pricing, 327–328

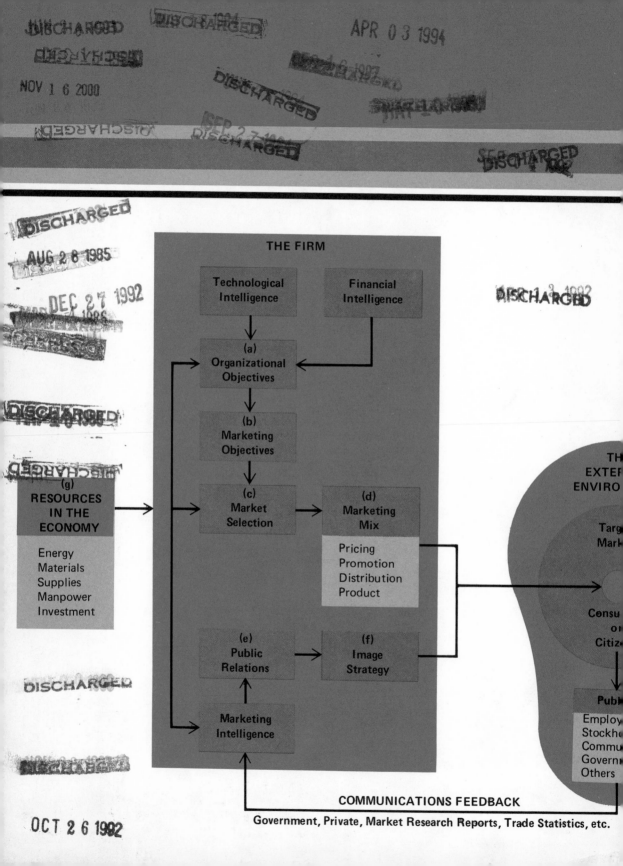

THE FIRM

Technological Intelligence

Financial Intelligence

(a) Organizational Objectives

(b) Marketing Objectives

(c) Market Selection

(d) Marketing Mix

Pricing
Promotion
Distribution
Product

(e) Public Relations

(f) Image Strategy

Marketing Intelligence

(g) **RESOURCES IN THE ECONOMY**

Energy
Materials
Supplies
Manpower
Investment

TH EXTER ENVIRO

Targ Mark

Consu or Citize

Publ

Employ
Stockh
Commu
Govern
Others

COMMUNICATIONS FEEDBACK

Government, Private, Market Research Reports, Trade Statistics, etc.